Representing the New World

Representing the New World:
The English and French Uses
of the Example of Spain

Jonathan Hart

palgrave

REPRESENTING THE NEW WORLD
© Jonathan Hart, 2001

First published 2000 by
PALGRAVE
175 Fifth Avenue, New York, N.Y.10010 and
Houndmills, Basingstoke, Hampshire RG21 6XS.
Companies and representatives throughout the world

PALGRAVE is the new global publishing imprint of St. Martin's Press LLC
Scholarly and Reference Division and Palgrave Publishers Ltd (formerly
Macmillan Press Ltd).

ISBN 0-312-23070-2 hardback

Library of Congress Cataloging-in-Publication Data

Hart, Jonathan Locke, 1956-
    Representing the New World : the English and French uses of the example
of Spain / by Jonathan Hart.
        p. cm.
    Includes bibliographical references and index.
    ISBN 0-312-23070-2
    1. America—Colonization—Historiography. 2. America—Colonization—
History—Sources. 3. America—Early accounts to 1600—History and criticism.
4. Spain—Colonies—America—Historiography. 5. Spain—Foreign public
 opinion—History—Sources. 6. Spain—Territorial expansion—Historiography.
7. Imperialism—Historiography. 8. Spaniards—America—Histography.
9. Travelers' writings, English. 10. Travelers' writings, French. I. Title.
E141 .H37 2001
325'.346'097—dc21   2001021804

A catalogue record for this book is available
from the British Library.

Design by Westchester Book Composition

First edition: September, 2001
10 9 8 7 6 5 4 3 2 1

Printed in the United States of America.

For Anthony Pagden

CONTENTS

PREFACE AND
ACKNOWLEDGMENTS

The subject of this book is the contradictory and ambivalent uses that French and English writers had in representing the example of Spain in the New World, particularly from 1492 to 1713. This study, which has seen its share of delays, involves a close examination of the texts, something integral to my method and aims. My book asks the reader to experience the primary texts close-up and in terms of their rhetorical methods and linguistic complexity. The important thing is that readers engage with the primary texts as well as with my interpretations of them. If this study, partly through its uses of the close examination of texts, sends readers back to the primary documents to see them whole, so much the better. Here I am attempting to present the ambivalence, intricacy, and contradiction in the texts to readers across the disciplines and to trace systematically and comparatively English and French responses to Spain's colonial enterprise in the Americas and studies the fictions of imperial expansion. More specifically, I am maintaining that the construction of Spain within the political and literary mythographies of France and England is a great deal more complicated and paradoxical than has hitherto been acknowledged. The French and English imitated the model of Spain in the colonization of the New World, as the Spanish were the pioneers, in ambivalent and intricate ways that did not simply involve enmity or reflect the Black Legend of Spain.

Before proceeding to the Introduction, which says much more about this topic, I would like to set out principles regarding the primary texts and translation, to express my thanks, and to record acknowledgments. Whenever I could, I have transcribed primary works as they appear in order to approximate them as closely as possible. In Richard Hakluyt's "Discourse on Western Planting," I have followed the practice of David and Alison Quinn of italicizing a letter represented in the text by an abbreviation. Originally the volume was to contain the original languages, but editorial decisions led to a change and so I set out unexpectedly on a journey into translation. When no translation of primary texts in French and other languages was available, or a translation departed too much from the literal sense of the original, or when there were several editions containing significant differences, I provided a translation. In the notes I have indicated my translations. My thanks for permission to reprint on the book cover the image from the 1493 Basel edition of Columbus's Letter in the Grenville Kane Collection, Department of Rare Books and Special Collections, Princeton University Library. Whereas I wrote the book long before I was at Princeton, I am grateful for the hospitality, advice, and support I have received from the university, library, Department of History, and Committee for Canadian Studies in the final technical stages of the volume (the work I am completing at Princeton will express more specific debts to colleagues there). I had the pleasure of writing and researching this book mainly in the two Cambridges. At Cambridge, I was fortunate to gain a new perspective on the history of the colonization of the New World. My greatest debt is to Anthony Pagden, who led by example. It is an honor to dedicate the book to him. In the Faculty of History, I wish to thank Peter Burke and Mark Kaplanoff especially, and at Clare Hall the president, fellows, students, and staff, most particularly Anthony Low, John Garrod, Marjorie Chibnall, and Philip Charrier. At Harvard, I want to thank the Department of Comparative Literature and its chair, Jan Ziolkowski, for having me as a Fulbright Faculty Fellow; Marjorie Garber, Barbara Johnson, and other members of the Department of English for their support when I returned to research in this field so long ago now; and Donald and Cathleen Pfister, co-masters of Kirkland House, and the members of that house for the kindness and hospitality they showed me once more as I completed the book. The Social Sciences and Humanities Council of Canada, the Fulbright Commission, the British Council, and the University of Alberta all provided crucial support for this and associated research. My thanks also to my hosts at the following universities--Wales, Warwick, Montpellier III, Melbourne, Deakin, Stirling, Harvard, and Cambridge--for inviting me to talk about this and related topics and to the librarians who have helped, especially at the Manuscript Room, University Library, Cambridge; the British Library; the Bodleian; la Bibliothèque Nationale; Houghton Library, Harvard; the Boston Public Library; John Carter Brown Library; the Bermuda Archives; the Bermuda Public Library; the National Library of Canada; Thomas Fisher Rare Books Library, University of Toronto; the Baldwin Room, Metropolitan Toronto Library; and the Bruce Peel Special Collections, Rutherford and Cameron Libraries, University of Alberta. I have also learned from the lectures of others, such as those by John Elliott, whom I had the good fortune to hear at University of Warwick and Brown University. Nicholas Canny, Nicole Mallet (who was kind enough to review my French translations), the anonymous readers, my editor, Kristi Long, and others have helped to improve the book, although whatever faults remain are my own. Owing to the perceptiveness, knowledge, and skill of these close readers, I have taken the liberty to take their suggestions whole at many points. Kristi Long and her colleagues, Donna Cherry and Matthew Ritter, at Palgrave were admirable in moving the project along. Thanks also to others for their support and encouragement: Alfred and Sally Alcorn, Ross Chambers, Natalie Zemon Davis, Patricia Demers, Olive Dickason, Milan Dimić, G. Blakemore Evans, Philip Ford, Sophie Goldsworthy, Peter Hulme, Ric Kitowski, Elena Levin, Paul Morrison, Glenn Rollans, Ray Ryan, and Robert Rawdon Wilson. Thank you to the editors of the official proceedings for 1994 and 1997 of the International Comparative Literature Association, to Jean Bessière, to Theo D'haen and to the editors of the *Canadian Review of Comparative Literature/Revue Canadienne de Littérature Comparée* for earlier and different versions of brief sections from this book, which are listed in the notes. More generally, I owe a debt to those scholars who went before. My final thanks are to my friends and family, most especially to my wife, Mary, and our twins, Julia and James.

CHAPTER 1

Introduction

This study is an essay in the historiography of expansion. It will focus on the interpretation of texts and will provide contextual discussions only as they illuminate these key works concerning expansion. The texts discussed in the chapters ahead warrant the attention of close reading, and some of them are not well known and deserve more of an audience. What this book brings to the field is an up-close and detailed analysis of works. It draws its method from rhetorical analysis, which connects literary analysis with intellectual history. The variegated texts of European expansion, while traditionally not considered to be high literature or elegant works of historiography or philosophy, deserve close attention to their language. This book owes much to the editors who have provided notes and commentary on some of the primary texts I have examined. What this study attempts is to provide close attention to the texts themselves and to them as intertexts, or a group of interconnecting works, on the New World.

Owing to the uneven development of the field of New World studies and the almost nascent studies of the Atlantic world, the ways Africa, Europe, and the Americas relate culturally and historically, and the different audiences for such a study—readers with interests in travel literature, European history, ethnography, Native American culture, and other subjects—I have chosen to summarize some texts more than I might have otherwise as well as providing close readings for others. Close attention, then, can mean close reading but is not synonymous with it, for summary, context, and hybrids of these and other forms of analysis combine to emphasize the importance of these texts.

In classical antiquity and until the rise of scientific history, history and literature were considered to be close rhetorical arts. Today there are still many historians who recognize the importance of narrative in their work. Literary studies and history both involve interpretations of texts and both try to distinguish between the factual and the fictional in the documents at hand. Each study, not to mention related fields in ethnology and philosophy, gains from the other's perspective. The literary focus on how texts are made and express themselves and the historical concentration on interpreting events or ideas about events bring something important to the documents related to the New World that this study considers. Both points of view, the literary and the historical, will work together. This doubleness is an aspect of rhetoric, the art of persuasion or how the formal properties of a text affect its readers.

The rhetoric of texts suggests, through a making of texts, or a linguistic rendering, a seeking and questioning of truth claims through past events, fictions, and reason. Ambivalence, ambiguity, and the indeterminacy of meaning are crucial in an awareness of the language of any texts and certainly of the ones that this book examines. In this study I shall assume that discourse is related to and can express the world but does not subsume reality itself. That expression is refractory but is something historians and others who seek to describe reality, or an aspect of reality, attempt and revise in their interpretations. The historical is more than epistemic shifts founded on a rhetorical figure reflective of its own time. A notion of an event that is beyond the text or that the representation approaches but never reaches—what might be called the asymptotal nature of textuality—enriches literary notions of the text because it calls attention to the deficiencies of language and the shortcomings of history as word in relation to history as event. The event humbles the language that tries to describe and interpret it, but the language is the tool for the historian to represent it. While this crux is something historians have long been aware of, it is a temptation for literary scholars to elide history as word and as event rather than recognizing its double nature. The historian's words gesture beyond the historical text and the limitations of the archive while leaving space for new evidence and interpretation. The history of textuality here allows for the assumption that some agency is possible in the apparently determined framework of history. The vexed mutuality and interdependence of history as event and history as text is one of the key assumptions of this study.

Techniques of close reading also open up new ways of discussing texts that have often not been deemed worthy of detailed literary and rhetorical analysis or of placing others by more literary authors in a wider context. The interdisciplinarity and the comparative basis of the project should provide such contextual matter. Comparisons among cultures should open up new perspectives on the individual nations as well as the relation among them and with other peoples.

A productive but vexed tension exists between an ethical or philosophical view of history that cuts across periods and the very historical difference that resists such transhistorical generalizations. History needs a method to make sense but must take into account changing distinctions and conditions. The shape of meaning rubs against specific examples. The past has an uncertain strangeness.

It is precisely this close attention to important individual texts of the historiography of expansion, framed first in the political and legal documents of the first few decades after the "discovery" of the New World, that will allow for a more general understanding of that historiography. These texts, which include eyewitness accounts, histories, cosmographies, confessional journeys, patriotic poems, and a kind of historical romantic drama that Polonius might have recognized, reveal a more complex view of the relations among Spain, England, and France in their expansion into the New World. The individual chapters will be structured chronologically but also, each in its own manner, according to topics that are central to these expanding empires and often based on the various genres of writing about the past. The shape of the book is, then, interpretative in that it is based on types of texts that yield certain kinds of interpretations of imperial expansion. Without a close examination of the rhetorical workings of these texts, it would be tempting to fall back into the received general notions of this European expansion into America.

The texts are full of surprises and complications, so that their rhetoric and representations qualify generalizations about the rhetorical and reflective aspects of the historiography of expansion. The assumption in this study is that tracts and propaganda need to be read as closely and as carefully as poetry in order to give historiography its due, and this method is particularly important in a field, the colonization of the New World, in which primary texts, like those of Columbus, Cartier, and John Smith, are not assumed generally to have the intellectual content of texts in philosophy and political theory, although there are exceptions like works by Montaigne and Ralegh. It is one of the aims of this book to show the rhetorical complexity of some of these less esteemed and more instrumental texts as well as the importance of their portraits of Spain to England and France. Moreover, the rhetorical motifs or "ideas" themselves possess a movement bigger than any one text, including the well known works of the more literary and philosophical writers.

The importance of the study is that it is the first extensive attempt to explore the ambivalent and contradictory ways the English and French manipulated the example of Spain in their own accounts of the "discovery" and settlement of the New World from 1492 to 1713. The ambivalence and contradiction arose from a double and often simultaneous movement in English and French writing about Spain and the New World—emulation and condemnation. In attempting to claim part of the Americas, England and France sought many strategies in their relation with Spain from Columbus's landfall to the Treaty of Utrecht, which ended the War of the Spanish Succession (1702–1713)—coexistence, circumvention, rivalry, and displacement. This specific comparative problem of the European colonization of the New World has yet to be examined in a systematic manner. While not being able to follow all the implications this problem raises, this study should help to fill an important gap while assuming, as do studies in other comparative disciplines such as comparative literature, that comparisons teach us about the national interests at hand. While John Elliott, Anthony Pagden, and others have produced significant work in the area of comparative history in the Atlantic world, their principal interests have been in other aspects of politics and ideology.[1] Whereas Elliott's and Pagden's important studies have begun from a Spanish perspective, my book discusses how Spain's European neighbors, chiefly France and England, view Spain in their own imperial efforts and in the expansion into the western Atlantic.

Although concerned with the political and ideological, my study centers on the textual and rhetorical nature of representing Spain in English and French texts about the New World. These texts, which range from pamphlets through histories to plays and poems, served the ends of polemics and propaganda. I am using "rhetoric" in Aristotle's sense as the art of persuasion, which is an especially appropriate definition in polemics and propaganda and in the pleading and proofs of prefatory matter, which is a central focus of this study. Many of the writers would have had rhetoric as a focus of their education in school and one of the important parts of their university training (for those who were so trained). Aristotle emphasized belief or *pistis,* what people recognized as probable, as the essence of this persuasion. He also argued for three modes of rhetorical proof: *logos,* or the appeal to reason; *pathos,* or the appeal to emotion; and *ethos,* or the appeal to ethics. In much of the work examined in this study, *pathos* is the chief means of persuading the audience.[2] Much of medieval and Renaissance rhetoric had an Aristotelian foundation even if it was mediated through Cicero, Quintilian, Seneca, and others.[3] The aspect of rhetoric that informs this study is the general relation between speaker and audience, writer and reader, especially in terms of persuasion and not an analysis of the schemes and tropes as a specific handbook of the technical means of that persuasion. My method is in keeping with some recent philosophical discussions of rhetoric that consider rhetoric generally rather than concentrating on the nomenclature of its techniques, which is something literary criticism has done in great detail.[4] Much of the prefatory matter combines forensic, deliberative, and epideictic rhetoric. Forensic rhetoric is legal but in terms of this study includes legal arguments and not arguments before literal judges. Deliberative rhetoric is directed to those who must decide how to act; what is useful and harmful in defense, trade, and legislation, war and peace; and, more specifically, what are the benefits and drawbacks of taking action in colonization. My interest is in the ambivalence of assessing and making decisions and of considering past decisions as examples for future action or discourse. Epideictic rhetoric is ceremonial and involves praising honor and virtue and censuring weakness and vice, but my concern is with the ambivalence of considering past decisions as examples for future action or discourse.[5]

This study concentrates this emphasis on representation and rhetoric often but not exclusively in the preliminary material of the primary texts because they are especially revealing. In order to emphasize the rationale and rationalization of the writers, this analysis will focus most on the prefatory matter of non-fictional texts. The primary texts with which my study will be mainly concerned include eyewitness accounts, which insist on their plainness and truth, and highly self-conscious rhetorical performances. In promotional literature about the New World, the writer had to convince the patron, king, or nation to support colonization or the brand of colonization the writer was promulgating. From the seemingly basic text of Cartier to the sophisticated representations of Montaigne and Ralegh, some similar contradictions and ambivalences toward Spain were played out. The themes that recurred about Spain in these texts were envy and emulation; rivalry and displacement; gold and God; cruelty to Natives or other Europeans; coexistence and redemption.

In arguing for ambivalence and contradiction in the English and French representations of the example of Spain, this study attempts to demonstrate a mixed response to Spain in the New World. It will choose neither the Black Legend of Spain nor, in Charles Gibson's phrase, the "White Legend" of Spain.[6] Instead, it seeks to delineate the complexity and ambiguity of the French and English representations. The Black Legend or *La Leyenda Negra,* which may have grown out of the encounter with the New World and the Wars of Religion in the sixteenth century, may have begun with William of Orange's *Apologia* (1580) in response to Philip II's ban or proscription of the leader of the revolt in the Netherlands. Others, however, have seen earlier origins for this legend in the reaction of Italy to Spanish hegemony or in Reformation Germany, but it was a Spaniard, Julián Juderías, who in 1914 first gave this anti-Spanish reaction a name.[7] The charges against Philip in the Netherlands came to be applied to Spain as a nation in its policy there but also in relation to its role in the Inquisition and in the conquest of America.[8] In the Spanish-speaking world the Black Legend is still an issue.[9] Recent discussions of the Black Legend also occur in French and English.[10] Bartolomé de Las Casas, who plays a central role in this study as the French and English translated his work at times of crisis from 1579 onward, is controversial because he is often praised for his representation, or is blamed for his misrepresentation, of Spanish colonization in the New World. Other countries translated Las Casas and used his work to build anti-Spanish propaganda. At first, the French and English sought to imitate Spain but then, along with the Dutch, they drew on writers like Las Casas to develop the Black Legend of Spain.[11] Lewis Hanke and others inside the Spanish-speaking world and without, often in defense of Las Casas or Spain, have tried to stress this penchant of the Spanish for self-criticism. Hanke reports the popular Spanish saying that if one speaks well of England, he is English; if one speaks ill of Germany, he is French; if one speaks ill of Spain, he is Spanish. Even after Ferdinand VII had lost most of his dominions from 1810 onward, he ordered a thorough investigation of Spanish archives for evidence to show the justice of Spain's policies in the New World.[12] The text, its legal status and its language or rhetoric, was part of the debate within Spain over the New World as well as part of the Black Legend, in which the French and English texts display or fashion dramatically a rhetoric of blame. In seeking truth amid praise and blame, these Europeans used study, research, and discourse to establish and maintain, justify and criticize their own nations and empires and those of their rivals. Empire, as we shall observe here and throughout this book, was translated in many ways, and the term "translation" bore various meanings.

The study should break new ground by treating French and English texts concerning colonial enterprise as parts of a propaganda campaign to emulate and supersede Spain's accomplishments in the New World. In such a campaign it is to be expected that English Protestants were engaged with French Huguenots against a common foe, but more surprisingly, national self-interest cut across the lines of religion, so that, for instance, French Jesuits and English Protestants often pursued common arguments about the theory and practice of Spanish colonization during the period under study. This finding in turn sustains my other argument that foreign authors admired the success of the Spaniards in establishing an overseas empire while simultaneously deploring the human suffering that they had brought upon the Native Americans they encountered. While this book concentrates on texts concerning colonization that had been translated into French and English because these texts reveal how, and the degree to which, the opinions under discussion traveled across national boundaries, the study also examines works that address or "translate"—that is, carry across, adapt, or transmogrify—the trope of Spain or Spanish influence in the colonization of the New World.

Whereas the body of this book begins by showing that the foundations of French and English responses to Iberian activity in the Atlantic and to the donation of Pope Alexander VI in the 1490s had been mostly laid before the issues became complicated by the divisions and rivalries that resulted from the Reformation, the study itself can, owing to limits of space, only suggest, but cannot explore, those tensions in terms of Europe itself. For better or for worse, the primary focus of this volume is the Atlantic world, and while I would like to concentrate more on the origins of the animosities in European rivalries, my development of that point of view will have to wait for another study. It is true, for example, that some important aspects of the Franco-Hispanic hostilities had their beginnings in the Italian wars. The rivalries in the Americas did, however, transform and complicate the European tensions and conflicts. The Netherlands, which I focus more on here, was crucial for Spain, France, and England, Catholics and Protestants, and occupied a central place in the period under discussion. Origins, as fascinating and significant as they are, can involve such a prologue that they become the theme and it is difficult to get to the later topic in question.

The method of selection of texts centers on those espousing propaganda or those set out to persuade or convince others, often a monarch, prospective settlers, or like-minded people, of ways of improving the imperial expansion or the interests of England and France in the New World. The selected texts are not exclusively persuasive or rhetorical texts or ones that function as propaganda: even texts that veer toward propaganda can be intricate, especially in their ambivalent and contradictory meanings. Rhetoric, then, or the art of persuasion as Aristotle termed it, is what might also be called the relation between speaker and audience, writer and reader, a more general definition of rhetoric that provides a focus of my method in the selection of texts. This book uses both senses of the term "rhetoric," which are related but not identical as writers and speakers can try to affect the audience in other ways than persuasion. Persuasion, defined broadly, can mean the approval or agreement that the writer has gained from the readers, or toward which the author has moved them. As much as possible, I have included a wide array of works that seek to persuade an audience about the example of Spain, whether the representation is part of literature, commerce, government policy, or any other key area. How the writers have sought to affect readers is the domain of rhetoric, a key verbal art of the period and one that has come to be significant in our times. Rhetoric, which can be limited to a narrow notion of persuasion or can represent the entire scope of the relation between writer and reader, should provide a means of exploring these early representations of the New World, especially emphasizing the Aristotelian notion of rhetoric as the art of persuasion in texts that have a strong element of propaganda. It is inevitable that I will have left out a text that one of my readers will think important, and there are no excuses for this, except perhaps to say that the archive is vast and my method of close attention involves a near and detailed analysis rather than a katascopic or horizontal comment or allusion in a larger narrative. Close attention takes space, but that is one of the main points of this study: these texts deserve more detailed attention. High cultural texts, which I have discussed closely elsewhere, are not the only works deserving of such analysis.

All books, no matter how accomplished, have a shadow book filled with wishes for topics born of more time and space. It would also be wonderful to try to find out the extent of knowledge of those who read Spanish in France and England from 1492 and 1713, but this itself is worthy of a separate study of the universities and the reading public. If there were more scope here, I would also focus more on natural history, catechisms, translations of spiritual works, word lists, and dictionaries of Indian speech, particularly after the French Jesuits undertook to emulate the Spaniards in the work of conversion, as well as the pictorial representation of America in maps and architectural models for towns, in the work of artists like Jacques Le Moyne de Morgues, and in the White-Harriot illustrations and perhaps any Spanish antecedents, if any existed, for these two collections of visual art. These works are materials for another study: the texts of persuasion, promotion, and propaganda, which form the core of my book, are good test cases because if there is ambivalence and contradiction in such works then the English and French representations of the example of Spain from the late fifteenth century into the early eighteenth century are not simply supports for the Black Legend of Spain. That is one of the principal arguments of this volume. The selection of texts should throw into relief the positive and not simply the negative uses of Spain in England and France as these countries were attempting and then achieving permanent colonies in the New World.

In this study I set out to illuminate three main areas: to show the rhetorical complexity of the texts of travel as well as the importance of their depictions for Spain, France, and England; to present the ambivalent and contradictory responses of France and England to Spain from Columbus's landfall to the end of the War of Spanish Succession, when it became apparent just how much Spain had lost influence in Europe; to demonstrate the significance of translations in both disseminating and shaping knowledge surrounding the colonizing of the New World. By combining three major cultural traditions—those of France, England, and Spain—I attempt to reveal interactions about the way the New World was represented in writings and to contribute to the political and social contexts of these writings. This book reassesses perceptions in the early modern Atlantic world of the Americas, both collectively and according to the different dynamics of each country. As this is the first extensive consideration of how English and French sources manipulated the example of Spain in their interpretations of the "discovery" and settlement of the New World, this study takes a large geographical and temporal sweep in the hopes that it will stimulate new and more specialized work in selected periods between 1492 and 1713. In order to make such a wide geographic and historical scope coherent while avoiding the concentration of the material into a few reductive perspectives or becoming lost in the complexity of the material, I have concentrated on the textual and rhetorical nature of the representation of Spain in English and French texts about the New World, organizing the material chronologically and thematically in the chapters and have focusing my attention mainly on the prefatory material to New World texts, including eyewitness accounts and promotional literature as they relate to the American colonies. The prefatory material often reveals the rhetorical or textual strategies of the authors, especially in their relations with their readers, a central focus for this book.

The combination of English and French sources is designed to help alert the reader to the comparative complexities of how Spain's imperialistic activities were interpreted by rival nations, England and France, the one becoming primarily a Protestant power and the other primarily a Catholic one. This study treats, in varying degrees of detail, many well-known figures, such as Richard Eden, Nicolas Le Challeux, Richard Hakluyt the Younger, Walter Ralegh, Samuel de Champlain, Robert Johnson, and Samuel Purchas, as well as less-known tracts. Given the wealth of materials, I have had to be highly selective but have tried to make sensible choices in terms of keeping the overall progression of the book and its clarity of expression. For instance, in chapter 4, I concentrate on Hakluyt's "Discourse" rather than on the *Divers Voyages* because the latter is better known and has received more commentary and the former deserves much more attention.

Whenever possible I have tried to focus beyond the New World itself, taking into account wider perspectives about the political and social interactions of the countries I am discussing. French and English representations of the Spanish, for instance, have much to do with the Dutch revolt against Spain in the Netherlands. More generally, Europeans tended to be much more interested in the Americas when they could be seen reflecting on distinctly European issues. It is also important to put the interest in the American enterprise in perspective: for all the sixteenth-century French travel texts I cite, on the numerical evidence of literature alone, France was far more interested in Turkey than in the New World. In attempting to analyze the materials in a careful and discriminating manner, I have tried to guard from falling into the teleological trap of attributing to early European travelers or settlers nineteenth- or twentieth-century attitudes. Rather, I am crucially concerned to point out the difference in perspectives.

This book, the only detailed and extensive discussion of the English and French uses of the example of Spain, will set out the legal and political grounds of precedent and possession in the New World and will trace the ways France and England emulate and distinguish themselves from Spain's role as the first colonizer of the Americas, how they praise and blame the Spanish conquest, and then slowly, as they establish permanent colonies and as the power of Spain declines in Europe, how they distance themselves from that model. That example of Spain, it will be discovered, had unexpected staying power even beyond the period in question.

Early on in the historiography of the New World, historians sometimes observed this early use of the example of Spain. In *The History of the American Revolution* (1789), for instance, David Ramsey said that Henry VII's letters patent to John Cabot (1496) and Elizabeth I's to Ralegh (1584) had echoed Alexander VI's Bulls of Donation by granting rights to "conquer and possess."[13] Even after most of the British North American colonies gained their independence, a writer like Ramsey could return to the papal donations with some sarcasm, which he did on the opening page of his history of the American Revolution: "Pope Alexander the sixth, with a munificence that cost him nothing, gave the whole Continent to Ferdinand and Isabella of Spain. This grant was not because the country was uninhabited, but because the nations existing there were infidels; and therefore in the opinion of the infallible donor not entitled to the possession of the territory in which their Creator had placed them."[14] Although the English had dispossessed the Natives as well, Ramsey continued in the same vein: "This extravagant claim of a right to dispose of the countries of heathen nations, was too absurd to be universally regarded, even in that superstitious age. And in defiance of it, several European sovereigns though devoted to the See of Rome understood and successfully prosecuted further discoveries in the Western hemisphere."[15] Ramsey did not deny the discoveries of Columbus and Vespucci, and more interestingly he observed the English imitation of the Spanish title to the New World: "Henry the seventh of England, by exertion of an authority similar to that of Pope Alexander, granted to John Cabot and his three sons a commission" and took possession of a large part of North America.[16] The contradiction was evident even this late: if the pope's claim was absurd, so too was Henry VII's. While this exemplarity had surprising tenacity, my reading of the primary texts, which I set out in the next few chapters, will reveal the mixed nature of the uses to which France and England put the model of Spanish colonization in their own expansion into the Americas.

The French and the English gradually came to abandon the example of Spain as Spanish hegemony declined and it became clear that precious metals held little future, largely but not completely because there appeared to be none in North America and the kind of political cultures France and England—England in particular—were becoming made the Spanish model of conquest and settlement untenable. Increasingly, the English came to regard conquest as something undesirable, so that for some, imperialism and expansion became proud and self-destructive enterprises.[17] The French—Jacques Cartier for instance—set out for gold as Columbus had, but later settled for farming, fishery and the fur-trade—something, as Anthony Pagden has pointed out, the hidalgo would not consider.[18] The motives behind the three French colonial enterprises of the sixteenth century—Cartier and Roberval in Canada, Villegagnon in Brazil, Ribault and Laudonnière in Florida—were, according to Philip Boucher, to look back to the Spanish conquest rather than ahead to New France.[19] All the while, French and English writers advocated attacks on Spain and its displacement, a good example of which was Philippe Duplessis-Mornay's "Discours . . . sur les moyens de diminuer l'Espagnol" (1584).[20] Such plans for attack motivated the

English in the Western Design of 1654–55 and the War of Jenkins's Ear of 1739–48, even as the Dutch were their chief commercial rival until the late 1690s when France, already by then a great political power, assumed that role. A complex of ideas, some having their origins in the first decades after the "discovery," persisted even as the French and British shifted their interests from being lords and converting the Natives to commerce and commodities. The combination of these attitudes was best exemplified in Richard Hakluyt the Younger's "Discourse of Western Planting" (1584), a text that borrowed heavily from Huguenot sources in France, where he was posted, and one to which I pay particular attention in a detailed textual interpretation in chapter 4, at the heart of this study.[21]

At least rhetorically, early modern Spain, England, and France inherited and used the trope, current from the ancients onward, of *translatio imperii* or the translation of empire.[22] Although my study is not concerned with the application of this idea in European expansion into the New World, it does relate directly to the ambivalence in the English and French representations of the relation between Spain and the Natives and their own countries and the Amerindians.[23] This representation of the Natives is a recurrent theme of how England and France used the example of Spain in the Americas. Often this translation involved an overcoming of other "barbarous" cultures as well as an inheritance from a previous empire.[24] Much of the representation of America generally— and Spain's presence there specifically—depended on translation. The translating of works related to the trope of the translation of empire; the English and the French translated Spanish works about the New World as well as their own representations, so that the translation of faith or of empire, as figurative as those ideas could at times become, relied literally on translators.

The translation of study was part of the translation of empire. This relation, even as it related to texts in France and England borrowing or transmuting Spanish works, was intricate and often involved French and English cultural connections. One such example of the importance and challenges of translation in texts about the New World is the relation among Montaigne, John Florio, and Montaigne's Spanish sources. In 1603, Michel de Montaigne's English translator, John Florio, asked whether he should apologize for translation, which gave birth to all science, while still upholding the name of the Greeks: "and the Greekes drew their baptizing water from the conduit-pipes of the Egyptians, and they from the well-springs of the Hebrews or Chaldees."[25] Florio fluctuated between questions and rhetorical questions in establishing an implicit connection between translation of knowledge and translation of empire: "And were their Countries so ennobled, advantaged, and embellished by such deriving; and doth it drive our noblest Colonies upon the rockes of ruine?"[26] The translation of influence from the Spanish to the French and English can be seen in Montaigne's relation to the Spanish and in Florio's translation of Montaigne into English. Peter Burke and others note Montaigne's debt to Spaniards. Just as in their ethnographical writing Bartolomé de Las Casas, André Thevet, Jean de Léry, Michel de Montaigne, and others used different cultures to criticize European culture, following classical works like Tacitus's *Germania* which employed the manly German barbarians to reproach the effeminate Romans, so too does the otherness of the past provide a critique of stereotyping or over simplifications of the past. The "Germania syndrome," to borrow Peter Burke's phrase, was a means of criticizing European culture through the cultures of others.[27] For Florio, translation moved knowledge from the universities into the commons, which was a good process: "Learning cannot be too common, and the commoner the better."[28] Translation, like translation to the New World, often meant a new kind of mobility, a way of using knowledge to build a new life for the individual or a new empire for the European power.

Translation is an important part of textuality, a kind of re-presentation of other texts that also builds on other works that in part purport to represent the world or reality, in this case the reality of the New World. Texts imitate other texts as well as the world, something each student would know in the schools and universities in practice if not in theory. Such imitation differs from empirical *mimesis,* or the observation of nature, a representation of reality that Copenicus, Francis Bacon, and Galileo were attempting. This textual imitation reproduces other texts, the way the genres of literature rework and transmute the conventions and rules of earlier works. Text begetting text can occur at the lexical, grammatical, and stylistic levels, as the students who read chapter 33 of Erasmus's *De duplici copia verborum ac rerum* learned from the example of a sentence that he reshaped in 150 ways, a practice they were invited to imitate, perhaps not with the expectation of such virtuosity. While I could concentrate on a very few texts in such detail, I have decided to interpret "representation" more widely and to discuss these linguistic matters only when they relate to the rhetoric involved in the ambivalent and contradictory ways in which the French and English texts represent the Spanish in the New World. This representation happens in textual echoes, allusions, and claims of reflecting the Spanish colonies in the Americas.

Mimesis or imitation are equivalents to what my study terms "representation," a vexed term that has a complex history from Plato onward. As I am using working definitions, which I state and then make apparent through their application (as opposed to theoretical discussions), here I wish to call attention to a particular aspect of representation—the Renaissance notion of imitation at the heart of its translation theory. Imitation of the classics involved borrowing what was best from them.[29] Translation, as my study demonstrates, also included a challenge to, as well as an imitation of, the Spanish, French, and English texts about the New World that were being rendered and interpreted.[30] The English and French looked to works by Spaniards and to those of each other as well as to classical views found in Aristotle, Pliny, Cicero, and others. The Spanish had written most about the New World until the 1580s, so that the English and French had to come to terms with their writings as something to emulate and challenge, to use negatively and positively in a competition for a place in the New World.[31]

Just as "representation" and its cognates are problematic terms, so too are "New World," as well as "Americas" and "America." The world of the western Atlantic was new to Europeans, as Shakespeare's Prospero reminded his daughter, Miranda, who had seen a "brave new world" in the island she inhabited, that it was new to her. The Natives of these lands used neither "New World" nor the other terms I sometimes substitute for it as a means of destabilizing it and showing its limitations. While I have opted to use the title *Representing the New World,* I recognize that both its key terms are wanting but the best available.

The chapters, following this introductory chapter, are arranged chronologically to emphasize the particulars and change in the example of Spain. As the study is largely about the French and English representations of this example, the dates that define the shape of the chapters most often reflect something important to them or in their countries. The second chapter ranges from Columbus's landfall to the deaths of François I and Henry VIII. It sets out a wider context in the study as a whole. While addressing the legal and textual anxieties among the French and English over Columbus and Spain being the first Europeans to "discover" the "New World" and over the pope's division of that new-found land between Portugal and Spain, it discusses how France and England attempted to learn from Spain and to challenge it in the Americas. The third chapter explores the time of their deaths to Nicolas Le Challeux's account of the Spanish massacre in Florida (a turning point in representations of the Spanish in Europe). It analyzes the praise for Spain in England during the reign of Mary and the first important French description of Spanish cruelty in the New World. The fourth chapter, which examines the period from the aftermath of this publication to the defeat of the Spanish Armada, includes a discussion of the anti-Spanish tracts of the 1560s and 1570s to the narratives leading up to the Armada (1567–88) and the intensification of rivalry with Spain as both France and England were trying to expand and establish colonies. The fifth chapter ranges from the ascension to the throne of Henri IV in France and the appearance of Richard Hakluyt's *The Principall Navigations* in England to the beginning of the English Civil War. It demonstrates that the ambivalent and contradictory representation of Spain in the New World was not—as can be seen, for instance, in Marc Lescarbot's *L'Histoire de la Nouvelle France* (1609)— simply a matter of religion. In this chapter I observe that once France and England established permanent colonies in the New World and Spain began to decline in this period, the sustained intensity of anti-Spanish sentiment abated into periodic eruptions of the Black Legend of Spain. The sixth chapter, which examines the time from the ascension of Louis XIV to the French throne to the Treaty of Utrecht that ended the War of the Spanish Succession (1643–1713), shows a shift in rivalry among the European powers. While Spain was still a force to be reckoned with, it was no longer the greatest power. Increasingly, France and England were rivals in America and also contended with the Dutch and, by the end of the period, France and Spain, both ruled by the Bourbons, were allies. The Conclusion highlights a few of the findings of the study and suggests a few implications beyond 1713.

The time periods covered in the chapters are of different lengths, as in part, the years 1554 to 1608 but especially up to 1588, the defeat of the Armada, were crucial because after the French and English established permanent colonies and Spain began to decline and collapse, the representations of Spain were not as concentrated and as extensive. The French and English in the 1550s through to the early years of the seventeenth century were obsessed with Spain because they were trying to emulate its power to create American colonies while also finding it to be a block to their ambitions. Once they had a foothold in North America and established spheres of influence, the problems of origins, legitimacy and rivalry continued but they were less pressing. Although each chapter shares the themes outlined at the beginning of the Introduction, the emphasis on these various themes changes over time.

Even if origins and legitimacy appeared less pressing toward the end of the seventeenth century and beginning of the eighteenth century than they did in the wake of Columbus, they were more apparent than might be expected. During the first 60 years of representing the New World, these concerns over the beginnings and legality of European conquest in the Americas were central to the way the English and the French thought about their own designs in relation to those of Spain in the western Atlantic.

It is to the written evidence concerning the example of Spain from 1492 to 1547 that we now turn in the next chapter. The matter of origins and contact for Europeans in the New World demonstrates that a tension existed between national interest and the common inheritance of Christendom, which manifested itself from the fall of the Roman Empire. In the next chapter I will explore this theme and will take up the background in a way that amplifies this friction among and beyond the three nations: Spain, France, and England. Chapter 2 will examine the religious, legal, and political ideas for and against expansion into the New World that occurred in roughly the first six decades after Columbus's landfall in the western Atlantic. The English, while quick to "discover" (or "re-discover" what the Vikings had explored and settled) the North American continent, soon lost momentum, and for the period in question and beyond, the French made this northern part of America a priority. England and France, while having accomplished a great deal in the exploration of North America, had no success in settling it, so that this inability to establish permanent settlements gave Spain more momentum in the New World and placed these countries in the shadow of Spain. Before and after Columbus, whether in Spain, France, England, and other Western European countries, the merits and demerits of expansion played an important role in legal, religious, political, and economic debates. For instance, Portugal had rejected Toscanelli's plan for western exploration well before it had Columbus's. While new empires were being established, they were also being questioned.

CHAPTER 2

Establishing and Questioning Empire, 1492–1547

During the first decade of the sixteenth century, the French began to be engaged in exploration just as the Spanish and the English crowns had done since the 1490s, but the French crown did not become actively involved until the 1520s. For sixty years after the deaths of François I and Henry VIII, neither France nor England was able to establish a permanent colony in the New World as the Spanish and Portuguese had done. The English and the French followed the example of Spain and became worried about the Spanish claim to—and power in—the New World. Pre-Columbian exploration suggests a complicated situation among European powers and their desires and plans for expansion: it was not always clear that in the late fourteenth and into the seventeenth century Spain would set the example for western expansion for other European countries.

The classical and medieval past, the European context, as well as an awareness of the cosmopolitan intellectual, commercial and seafaring climate surrounding the expansion into the Western Atlantic, all modify the overestimation of the originality, independence, and greatness of each of the empires. During the late Middle Ages, Europeans shared their knowledge of geography, exploration, and history. This was as true of the French and English as it was of the Spanish, Portuguese, Italians, Dutch, and other nationalities. Some of this knowledge was fanciful, some not. One central aspect was geography, what we might now think about as a topos, an imaginary geography.[1] The Italian influence on all the Atlantic empires began in the Middle Ages. Years later Henry the Navigator and Columbus read Marco Polo's account with interest.[2] Although England and France could draw on the classical and their national pasts, they could not discount the experience of Spain and Portugal in the matter of colonization. France and Castile, as well as Italy and Portugal, played significant roles in the pre-Columbian expansion of Europe.

In the fourteenth and fifteenth centuries Portugal and Spain were rivals in exploration. The rediscovery of the Canary Islands created a conflict between Portugal and Castile in the late thirteenth century. In 1344, Don Luis de la

Cerda, admiral of France and great-grandson of Alfonso the Wise, obtained a bull from Clement VI to Christianize the islands, believed to be the Fortunatae Insulae of the ancients, and was crowned prince of this domain in Avignon. Castile and Portugal put aside their differences and supported Luis, but after he failed to take possession, they continued their struggle. Subsequent papal bulls favored one side, then the other, and the question of ownership was not settled until 1479, when, by the Treaty of Alcaçovas, Portugal ceded the Canaries to Castile.[3] The second controversy between Portugal and Castile was over Africa. After the conquest of Ceuta in 1415 with military expeditions in Morocco and with voyages to Guinea, Portugal made its claim in Africa, where in the 1440s and 1450s slaves and gold made for a lucrative trade. As they had in the case of the Canaries, the kings of Castile based their claim to conquest in Africa on its possession by their ancestors, the Visigoths. By 1454, the two countries were embroiled in this African controversy. On January 8, 1455, Nicholas V issued the bull *Romanus pontifex* that gave exclusive rights to King Alfonso of Portugal in this African exploration and trade. This ruling extended the bull *Dum diversas* (June 18, 1452), in which Nicholas had given Alfonso the right to conquer pagans, enslave them, and take their lands and goods. Nicholas's predecessor, Eugenius IV, had in the bull *Rex regum* (January 5, 1443) taken a neutral stance between Castile and Portugal regarding Africa. The Castilians would not accept the authority of the papal letters and continued to claim Guinea until 1479, when, after the War of Succession (in which Alfonso invaded Castile in an attempt to annex it), Portugal ceded the Canaries and Castile acknowledged Portugal's claim to Guinea, the Azores, Madeira, and the Cape Verde Islands.[4]

Papal bulls, then, were not permanent laws and were not always accepted as remedies by the parties involved in the disputes. From the late fifteenth century onward, Portugal and Spain would, however, insist that other nations, like France and England, abide by the papal bulls dividing the "undiscovered" world between the Iberian powers. After 1492, however, Spain dominated the discourse about the New World.

Both the late Middle Ages and the early modern period presented rivalries in trade and territorial expansion. Rivalry between the French and the Castilians began early. The French, having played a central role in the crusades, tried to recreate their glory. In 1390, the duke of Bourbon, seeking to rekindle the spirit of Saint Louis, prepared for an expedition to Barbary, which the Genoese proponents of this undertaking probably wanted to use as a means of eradicating corsairs. Holiness and gold—the spirit of crusade and the hope of commerce—beckoned in Barbary. Two of the men who were contracted to serve with Bourbon in Barbary were Jean de Béthencourt and Gadifer de la Salle. On May 1, 1402, they set out to conquer the Canary Islands for France, but relying on Castilian supplies and facing the jealousy of Castile and the indifference of France, these explorers yielded the islands to Castile. Castile gained much as the Canaries—whose winds, it would turn out, allowed relatively easy passage to the New World—became strategic for supplying ships making the voyage. *Le Canarien,* written by a cleric and extant in two versions, each favoring one of the conquerors against the other, proclaimed the motives de Béthencourt and de la Salle had in conquering the Canaries: God and gold. They were to honor God, increase the Christian faith, and seek the River of Gold.[5]

Other nations also sought to find lands that circulated in traditions, folklore, mythology, and legend. During the 1480s and 1490s, in the Atlantic the Bristolians sought "Brasil," and the Portuguese and Flemings in the Azores searched out "Antilia."[6] The desire to seek new and mythical lands was well entrenched among various European states before Columbus's proposals and the enterprise of the Indies.

Although Spain set the example in the New World, it relied on classical and medieval antecedents that constituted a shared European cultural inheritance. The influence of classical and medieval myths, geography, history, and religion is undeniable. While the origins in Herodotus, Aristotle, Thucydides, Ptolemy, Cicero, and others have been well documented, the medieval background deserves to be better known.[7] It is surprising how much Cartier's and Frobisher's search for gold owed to Columbus's, but it is even more astonishing how much this desire was constructed in terms of medieval romance and later refractions of that genre. This romance tradition owes something to epic, although Homer and Virgil made honor, not wealth, the code by which their heroes live, and to Greek romance. The quest left the conquerors to follow Arthur as much as Pliny, and sometimes the romantic aspect became as triangulated as anything experienced at Camelot. Rustichello, a writer of Arthurian romance, had told Polo's story in terms of that genre and in French. Bernal Díaz relied on romance, and *El Cid* provided an example of the *reconquista* for the *conquistadores*. The fictions of journey and the poetics of quest, through the mobility, transmutation, and persistence of myths and literature, comprised part of the intellectual inheritance of the Spanish, French, and English as they forged their national identities and empires simultaneously. The encounter of Spain with the New World challenged the preponderant power of the time, France, to catch up.

The emphasis of this study is more on the effect of the Spanish encounter on the English and French and how, purposefully and inadvertently, even in this rivalry, they shared knowledge that led to and fostered colonies in the New World. For much of the period from Columbus's landfall to the end of the War of the Spanish Succession, Spain developed, through its early colonization in the Americas, a predominant place in Western Europe. From the 1490s into the 1520s, France was fighting to keep its Italian possessions.[8] England, which had lost most of its French possessions under Henry VI, got off to a good start in the exploration of the New World but began to lag behind Spain and, except for the piracy of Drake, would only begin to goad the Spanish in the Netherlands and with the defeat of the Armada under Elizabeth I. Even though the emphasis in this study is on Spain, England, and France from 1492 until 1713, other nations and other periods are necessarily part of the narrative. Ideas about empire and exploration crossed temporal and national boundaries by way of Latin and vernacular translations, travelers, ambassadors, merchants, armies.[9] Like Columbus, the English and French explorers had to measure received geographical knowledge against the experience of the New World. Intellectual and material motives guided Columbus and the expansion of Spain and other European powers. For example, Columbus seems to have found encouragement in Pierre d'Ailly's *Imago Mundi*, which stressed the shortness of distance across the Atlantic from Europe to India.[10] A transmission of knowledge through texts moved across borders.

The discussion that follows will include the reluctance of Europeans to expand westward; the legal and political differences over the origins and claims of the Spanish discovery of the New World; the English and French attempts at exploration as a means of challenging this legal and political priority; the anxiety that Spain felt over the challenge of its anxious rivals for the New World—England and France—particularly in the Cabot voyages; the growth of the fisheries off Newfoundland; and the scarcity of writing about the New World, at least relative to that by the Spanish, in France, but especially in England, until the second half of the sixteenth century. The extensive writing about the New World in Spain reflected its leadership and material means of colonizing these new lands, whereas the relative scarcity of such texts in France and England suggested in part more interest in internal and European matters than in expansion to the New World. It remains, however, an enigma why John Cabot did not write an account as Columbus, Verrazzano, and Cartier did.[11] These explorers often faced some strong opposition and needed powerful friends at court. Before Columbus especially, but to some extent after him, there was ample resistance to expansion overseas.

This ambivalent response in European nations is the questioning that is too often forgotten, especially when reading the present back on the past, the sort of prophecies that Shakespeare, knowing the earlier history, was able to place in his characters' prophecies of the future.[12] This retrospective teleology, while understandable enough in any subject but common in historical writing, needs to be addressed with some skepticism. Our ambivalence may be to understand retrospective teleology as it relates to representing the New World but to be skeptical of this backward projection of a forward telos. The ambivalence and contradictions that haunted Europeans then, while having taken a different but related form in recent years, depends in part on the ghost of future past. It is to the ambivalent, oppositional, and alternative views in the late fifteenth century and early sixteenth century, and to the voyages that they opposed but could not halt, that we now turn.

II

Part of the ambivalence and contradiction in European attitudes toward the New World derived from a division from within.[13] An undertow of reluctance comprised an aspect of the attitudes of each of the European powers to overseas voyages. In the fifteenth century Portugal was cautious about expansion, looking after national self-interest and control. The Portuguese court had turned down Toscanelli's proposal for a westward voyage in 1474 and dismissed Columbus ten years later. A royal council in Spain rejected Columbus's petition, so he sought an audience with Ferdinand and Isabella, to whom he was connected through his Portuguese wife. During their meetings in December 1486 and January 1487, the Columbus commission, composed of *letrados* (mainly university-educated lawyers at court) and *sabios* (men learned in cartography and astronomy), rejected Columbus's arguments and passed their findings along to the Spanish sovereigns.[14] This kind of opposition was not enough to stop Columbus's project, but it qualifies any notion of Spain or Europe as embracing western expansion and empire without reserve and caution.

Another kind of opposition from within occurred in the ambivalence in European representations of the lands and peoples of the New World: they were fierce and paradisal. Columbus and Verrazzano (at least as we have his account in Italian) could display that ambivalent attitude in the same sentence. The idealization of the land and its peoples as comprising paradise, even as they were sometimes made into barbarians in rough places, was a promotional tactic that was meant to appeal to religious dreams of the Ten Lost Tribes of Israel and to conjure the riches of Asia. Beyond this trope of God and gold, even in its implicit form, was the possibility for the ideal aspect of the representation of the Natives and the new lands to provide a standard against which to judge the corruption of Europeans.[15]

The opposition to expansion came from within the church and court establishments themselves. Their opposing voices could be ambivalent, owing in part to their stake in political and religious institutions. Once the expansion occurred, however, these opponents in Spain and Portugal of the New World could only slow or criticize its development, whereas in England and France, owing to internal and European policies, the opposition could contribute to the neglect, fits, starts, and failures of English and French colonization.

This opposition could delay and make difficult expansion, but exploration and settlement went forward nonetheless. Spain did expand westward: it drew on an intellectual legacy from the ancients and from medieval Europe and soon became the leader in the New World. In expansion, Spain, along with Portugal, sought a legal justification for its claim to new territories. A legal foundation developed in support of exploration before and after 1492. The English and the French would challenge this legality and then imitate aspects of it to justify their own rule over Native Americans.

The legal justification for the exploration and settlement of the New World was based on papal rulings. The bull *Romanus pontifex* had given the Portuguese the right to reduce the infidels to slavery, so that the inhabitants of these new lands—"so unknown to us westerners that we had no certain knowledge of the peoples of those parts"—had no rights because they were not Christian.[16] In the New World, the Natives were deemed barbarous and not infidels, so that their potential for conversion saved them, at least theoretically, from slavery. The papacy continued to play a role in legitimizing exploration after Columbus's landfall in the New World.

The French and the English, who had not taken up Columbus's enterprise of the Indies as Spain had, now had to try to catch up to the Spanish. In this they had to contravene the wishes and the gift of the pope, set out in the bull of May 4, 1493, which, in response to Columbus's first voyage to the New World, divided the parts of the world yet unknown to Christians into two spheres, one for Spain and the other for Portugal. The pope, who had Iberian connections, issued a direct threat to those who might not accept his donation:

> under the penalty of excommunication *late sententiae* to be incurred *ipso facto,* should anyone thus contravene, we strictly forbid all persons of whatsoever rank, even imperial or royal, or of whatsoever estate, degree, order, or condition, to dare, without your special permit or that of your aforesaid heirs and successors, to go for the purpose of trade or any other reason to islands or mainlands, found and to be found, discovered and to be discovered towards the west and south, by drawing and establishing a line from the Arctic pole to the Antarctic pole, no matter whether the mainlands and islands, found and to be found, lie in the direction of India or toward any other quarter whatsoever, the said line to be distant one hundred leagues towards the west and south, as is aforesaid, from any of the islands commonly known as the Azores and Cape Verde; apostolic constitutions and ordinances and other decrees whatsoever to the contrary notwithstanding. . . . Let no one, therefore, infringe, or with rash boldness contravene, this our recommendation, exhortation, requisition, gift, grant, assignment, constitution, deputation, degree, mandate, prohibition, and will. Should anyone presume to attempt this, be it known to him that he will incur the wrath of Almighty God and of the blessed apostles Peter and Paul.[17]

This kind of threat against other Christian princes breaking the exclusive rights of the parties named in the donations occurred in earlier bulls, like *Romanus pontifex*. The Spanish and the Portuguese accepted the terms of this bull, except they shifted the line of demarcation from 100 leagues to 370 leagues west of the Cape Verde Islands in the Treaty of Tordesillas in 1494, and although claiming the spheres of ownership that the pope had set out, they gave each other rights of passage across each other's territory. Spain and Portugal confirmed these terms, including the changes to the bull *Inter caetera* in the Treaty of Madrid in 1495. The bull *Ea quae* of 1506, issued after Vasco da Gama had rounded the Cape of Good Hope, also made this confirmation. While the Reformation changed the attitude of other countries, like England and the Netherlands, to the authority of the papal disposition and while Catholic France resisted this donation, monarchs, when issuing commissions to their own explorers, instructed them not to seize land already claimed by another Christian prince. To claim title, the explorers supplemented the bulls by planting crosses with the royal coats of arms on the "new-found" lands.[18]

If there was disagreement within European nations over expansion to the New World, Europe itself was divided. This division possessed its own form of opposition. The English and French opposed the papal donation to Spain and Portugal even while they imitated these leading colonial powers. That the English and French monarchs sent out their own expeditions to the New World showed a practical disregard for the papal bulls.

England preceded France in voyages that successfully reached the New

World. The Bristol merchants had been attempting westward exploration before Columbus: John Lloyd is said to have sought the Island of Brasil in 1480.[19] On March 5, 1496, at Westminster, the Lord Chancellor of England considered a bill of John Cabot and his sons.[20] In the first letters patent granted to Cabot, citizen of Venice, and his sons, on March 5, 1496, Henry VII granted to them and their heirs and deputies the right to sail to any foreign parts in the eastern, western, and northern sea at their own expense:

> to find, discover and investigate whatsoever islands, countries, regions or provinces of heathens and infidels, in whatsoever part of the world placed, which before this time were unknown to all Christians. . . . and [we] have given license to set up our aforesaid banners and ensigns in any town, city, castle, island or mainland whatsoever, newly found by them. And that the before-mentioned John and his sons or their heirs and deputies may conquer, occupy and possess whatsoever such towns, castles, cities, and islands by them thus discovered that they may be able to conquer, occupy and possess, as our vassals and governors lieutenants and deputies therein, acquiring for us the dominion, title and jurisdiction of the same towns, castles, cities, islands and mainlands so discovered.[21]

The patent then stated that Henry would allow Cabot and his sons and heirs to have all the profits and goods, free of customs, except for the fifth that must be paid to the crown. During the last half of the sixteenth century, the English anxiety over Spanish claims to the New World and their own desire for legitimization there would make Cabot part of a search for a claim to the Americas that was stronger than Spain's. In *Divers Voyages* (1582) Hakluyt printed this patent for the first time as part of the general promotion of English colonies in North America during the Elizabethan and Jacobean reigns. The second patent from Henry VII to Cabot, which confirmed the first, appeared in Hakluyt's *Principall Navigations* in 1589.[22] The English claim to North America, which contravened and ignored the papal bulls giving Spain and Portugal all unknown lands at one level but which later showed some anxiety over the pope's donations at another level, was replayed in the sixteenth century and beyond. The anxious responses occurred on different sides of the divide as Spain itself paid close attention to what Cabot was undertaking for England.

Spain opposed the expansion of England and France to the New World. Spanish intelligence must have been sensitive to English and French rivalry, for in Tortosa on March 28 of that same year, the Spanish sovereigns wrote to Gonzales de Puebla:

> In regard to what you say of the arrival there of one like Columbus for the purpose of inducing the King of England to enter upon another undertaking like that of the Indies, without prejudice to Spain or to Portugal, if he [the king] aids him as he has us, the Indies will be well rid of the man. We are of opinion that this is a scheme of the French king's to persuade

the king of England to undertake this so that he will give up other affairs. Take care that you prevent the king of England from being deceived in this or in anything else of the kind, since wherever they can, the French will endeavour to bring this about. And things of this sort are very uncertain, and of such a nature that for the present it is not seemly to conclude an agreement therein; and it is also clear that no arrangement can be concluded in this matter in that country [England] without harm to us or to the King of Portugal.[23]

The Spanish king and queen, showing some anxiety and self-interest of their own, obviously took seriously the English threat to the monopoly Spain had with Portugal in the New World, which the pope and the two countries had worked out in the previous three years. This anxiety extended to a rivalry with the French in Europe generally and in Italy specifically, which could not be suppressed even in the Spanish monarchs' interpretation of English preparations to stake a claim in the New World. It was not until the reign of Philip II (1556–98) that American silver affected the European economy and balance of power in ways obvious to Europeans, so that the anxiety of the Spanish monarchs was not surprising under the circumstances.[24] France especially was a great power and was suspected of enlisting England to thwart Spain. Cabot's voyage in 1497 demonstrated Henry VII's determination to continue that interest in westward exploration: his regard appears to have been more for English national self-interest rather than for relations with France or Spain.

Henry VII did not seem to have attempted to keep the voyage and his ambitions in the New World a secret. Venetians, Milanese, Spaniards, and others knew about Cabot and sent letters home from England that discussed his voyage. On August 23, 1497, from London, Lorenzo Pasqualigo wrote his brothers in Venice: "That Venetian of ours who went with a small ship from Bristol to find new islands has come back and says he has discovered mainland 700 leagues away, which is the country of the Grand Khan, and that he coasted it for 300 leagues and landed and did not see any person"[25] The letter reported that although Cabot did not see people on the lands in the New World, he noticed notched trees and returned with snares and a needle for making the nets he found there, so that Cabot assumed that there were inhabitants. It also noted that his provisions were low and forced him to rush back, that his voyage took three months, and that Henry VII thought the voyage a success. On August 24, 1497 the duke of Milan received a dispatch that a Venetian mariner had discovered new islands, including the Seven Cities, and had arrived in England safely and that the English king planned to send him out on a voyage with 15 or 20 ships the following spring.[26] The Milanese ambassador then provided more information for the duke on December 18, 1497: "Zoane Caboto," a Venetian of humble origins and an expert in navigation with a fine mind, had helped the king of England gain a part of Asia without a stroke of the sword—Cabot is a man "who, seeing that the most serene kings, first of Portugal, then of Spain have occupied unknown islands, meditated the achievement of a similar acquisition for his majesty aforesaid."[27] In this third-party account, the lands that Portugal then

Spain occupied drew Cabot and, therefore, the English monarch, to exploration. The example of Spain in the New World was not, then, something that Spanish national pride had manufactured but a phenomenon that Italian diplomats, whose states were so vital in providing pilots, finance, and ideas to other European nations, observed in the 1490s.

John Cabot seems to have written nothing about his "discovery" of North America, so that we have to rely on the charter given him and the diplomatic dispatches from England to Italy to garner some sense of his voyage, which was an important challenge to Spain. Even the Italians displayed ambivalence over their own role in the discovery in the New World. The Milanese ambassador said that he had heard Cabot describe the itinerary of his westward journey, the hoisting of the royal standard to take possession for Henry VII, the taking of tokens, Cabot's reliance on English companions to swear to the truth that a poor foreigner spoke, his description of the world in a map, his solid sphere that set out the voyage, the temperateness of the climate (the belief that silk and Brazil wood were native in the new-found lands), and the ocean teeming with fish. The ambassadorial report attested to Cabot's greater ambitions of sailing from the islands he claimed to be Cipango (Japan), where the Venetian mariner believed all spices and jewels of the world had their origin, a conclusion he deduced from his earlier trip to Mecca, where he had spoken with traders and where he had extrapolated that this desired land must be in the north toward the west. All this Cabot spoke plainly, and the English king, whom the ambassador called wise and not prodigal, believed and provided for him, including a pledge of prisoners to form a colony: "and they will proceed to that country to form a colony, by means of which they hope to establish a greater dépôt for spices in London than there is at Alexandria."[28] After giving some credence to the words he had heard Cabot utter, including an assessment that the Bristol merchants backed the Venetian, and having stated the voyage should take no more than a fortnight from Ireland, the Milanese ambassador showed his satirical bent, telling the duke that a Burgundian companion of the mariner said that Cabot, who was called the admiral and thought of himself as a prince, had promised him an island and his Genoese barber another. The ambassador reported that Cabot had pledged bishoprics to poor Italian friars who were to go on the voyage, and that as he had made friends with Cabot, he himself might be given an archbishopric. Despite Cabot's princely generosity, the ambassador asked the duke of Milan to maintain for him the safer benefices he had provided and to keep for him any new ones that became available in his absence. The modulation here was between admiration for the admiral, who had clearly followed Columbus in his title and ambition to find Cipango, and a social satire on the pretensions of men of humble birth, like Cabot, who would arrogate to themselves titles, authority, and riches as they gained the favor of a powerful monarch. Almost unobtrusively in the dispatch, the word "colonia" (colony) was mentioned. The ambassador of Milan in London implied that as wise as Henry was, he had imperial longings. Behind the rivalry between Spain and England there were Italian mariners like Columbus and Cabot. Verrazzano, a Florentine, would make the first official French voyage across the North Atlantic in 1524. In addition to the practical knowledge of Italian mariners, the theorists and scientists of the Italian Renaissance also gave the Spanish, English, and French some of their cultural tools in colonizing the New World.[29] As Jacob Burckhardt says, "At the time when Spain gave Alexander VI to the Italians, Italy gave Columbus to the Spaniards."[30]

In this context, when Henry VII allowed Cabot to operate openly and to speak his mind even to the Milanese ambassador, it is not astonishing to discover that the Spanish, too, had heard about Cabot and the plans for English expansion in the New World. Henry himself spoke with the Spanish ambassador, Pedro Ayala, about the plans behind Cabot's voyages. Ayala began his dispatch of July 25, 1498, which was partly written in cipher, saying that he thought that Ferdinand and Isabella would already have heard about the English fleet setting out as a result of last year's discovery. He then appealed to his status as an eyewitness: "I have seen the map made by the discoverer, who is another Genoese like Columbus, who has been in Seville and at Lisbon seeking to obtain persons to aid him in this discovery."[31] This opinion may confirm John Stow's later view that Cabot was originally from Genoa, but more importantly, it linked Cabot with Columbus. Both had hawked their ideas of sailing west to Asia. Spain had sent Columbus to the New World before England could even if Columbus had negotiated with the English: now England backed Cabot when Spain would not. Portugal had spurned both Columbus and Cabot. Ayala admitted that over the past seven years the Bristolians had equipped caravels to seek "the island of Brazil and the Seven Cities according to the fancy of this Genoese."[32] Some priests seem to have accompanied John Cabot on his last voyage. In French and English America, Natives came directly under the spiritual jurisdiction of the pope, whereas in Iberian America they were under royal patronage (the *patronato real* in the Spanish colonies by 1508 and the *padroado* in Portuguese colonies by 1514).[33] The ambassador said that the success of Cabot's first voyage had made Henry outfit five vessels with a year's provisions for the second voyage: "Having seen the course they are steering and the length of the voyage, I find that what they have discovered or are in search of is possessed by Your Highnesses because it is at the cape which fell to Your Highnesses by the convention with Portugal'.[34] Cabot was expected back in September, and Ayala would inform the king and queen what had happened. If the ambassador acknowledged the discovery, then he would not allow for its legitimacy—in this account Henry VII would have none of this: "The king has spoken to me several times on the subject. He hopes the affair may turn out profitable. I believe the distance is not 400 leagues. I told him that I believed the islands were those found by Your Highnesses, and although I gave him the main reason, he would not have it."[35] The dispute was twofold. First, did England accept the papal bull dividing the "undiscovered" lands in the Atlantic between Portugal and Spain? Second, had England "discovered" lands that Spain had already claimed?

The two issues slipped into each other in this cat-and-mouse game between England and Spain. The symbolic realm of a map became the "world" in which the Spanish ambassador and English king disputed territory: "Since I believe Your Highnesses will already have notice of all this and also of the chart or mappemonde which this man [Cabot] has made, I do not send it now, although it is here, and so far as I can see exceedingly false, in order to make believe that these are not part of the said islands."[36] In this dispatch Ayala made his monarchs, and not Columbus, the discoverers of the New World. The inaccurate world of late-fourteenth-century maps allowed evasion to Henry VII and indignation to the Spanish ambassador. Medieval monarchs, such as King John in England, did not always accept the authority of the pope, especially when it circumscribed the ambitions of rulers and their states, and it is not certain how much Henry VII was working in this political tradition. For England and Spain both, these "new-found lands" were both Asia and the New World. If they were Cipango or Cathay, how could Spain and England claim them unless they were unoccupied? If they were new lands, then how could Columbus and Cabot pretend they were Asia?

The Portuguese thought that the land Cabot encountered was quite possibly in their sphere as set out in the Treaty of Tordesillas (370 leagues west of the Cape Verde Islands). It was possible that after Vasco da Gama lost two-thirds of his crew on his eastern voyage (he returned in September 1499), the Portuguese considered a westward route to be shorter, cheaper, and less punishing. Having watched Columbus's success and heard about Cabot's news of fish, timber, and a possible northwest route to Asia, the first great exploring nation of the fifteenth century now followed the English lead. On October 28, 1499, King Manuel of Portugal issued letters patent to João Fernandez to make a voyage to discover new islands in the North Atlantic.[37] The Portuguese king issued similar patents to Gaspar Corte Real on May 12, 1500, and for a second voyage in 1501; to Miguel Corte Real in January 1502; for a fourth voyage in 1503. When the Corte Real brothers were lost and the hope for a northwest passage grew dim, the Portuguese gave up on Newfoundland for some time to come, except for the fisheries. Fernandez took his ideas to Henry VII just as Sebastian Cabot would leave England for Spain in order to find backing for his expeditions. In 1501, from Bristol, merchants from the Azores and England joined together to petition for a patent to seek out the new lands in the northwestern Atlantic.[38] The Company of Adventurers to the New Found Lands was to serve as a model for later companies that helped to extend English trade and settlement to new lands.

The Cabots, even more than Fernandez, illustrated the international nature of the exploration of the New World and the national rivalries among the European nations. These countries had not defined themselves or their self-interest in definitive terms, something we can observe in this section and chapter but also throughout the book. The story of the Cabotos or Cabots is one of Italy, England, and Spain and does not, in the case of Sebastian Cabot, represent a simple succession or linear narrative.

On April 3, 1505, Henry VII issued two Privy Seal warrants, one to the customers of Bristol and the other to the Exchequer, to pay Sebastian Cabot an annuity of ten pounds.[39] In 1508–09 Sebastian sailed to Newfoundland. By the autumn of 1512, Cabot, having received permission from Lord Willoughby, his immediate commander when he served with the marquis of Dorset's army for the invasion of Guienne, began duty as a naval captain in the service of Spain. Henry VIII, preoccupied with the wars in Europe, did nothing to stop Cabot, who returned to England to fetch his family. In 1520–21 Cabot may have sought English employment and in 1522–23 was trying to convince Venice to support his voyages. By 1538, Cabot, long in the service of Spain, had asked Thomas Wyatt, the English ambassador to Spain, to recommend him to Henry VIII, but to no avail. Probably in about 1548, Cabot left Spain and spent his last decade with a pension under Edward VI and Mary. His itinerant career as a captain and mapmaker for hire demonstrates the fluidity of borders and the business and government practices of the late fifteenth and early sixteenth centuries.

Sebastian Cabot serves as a reminder of how national rivalries and religious contention, brought on by wars and the Reformation, did not stop this multinational and cosmopolitan world of exploration. The English and French uses of the example of Spain incorporated this transgression of boundaries, this pan-Europeanism, and represented one factor in the ambivalence that these nations displayed in their rivalry with Spain. The Spanish crown itself, so put out by John Cabot, was happy, nearly fifteen years later, to hire his son. The younger Cabot, like his father, later became a symbol, trope, and exemplum in the English bid to find origins to legitimize their interests to colonize the Americas. Some of the writers in England and on the continent confused John and Sebastian Cabot.

From the 1490s to the 1590s, the Cabots made appearances in a wide variety of Western European texts about the New World.[40] These references and representations showed that the Cabots became part of English national self-interest in the promotion of empire, an aspect of the telling of the narrative of the New World and the making of maps and part of the building of European trade in the Americas. Mariners, historians, and mapmakers wanted to compile as much information as possible for the sake of knowledge but also for the practical interests of business and state. This transmutation and the literal and figurative translation of the Cabots, especially of Sebastian, represented a two-way ambivalence. England and Spain were ambivalent about Sebastian, as he was about them. He sought a living, and they permitted him passage to a rival country. The Italians, French, and Portuguese also interpreted him in that doubling realm of Europe and of the nation state. Sebastian was Venetian but served the two chief contenders of the first two decades of exploration to the New World: Spain and England. Neither country seemed to mind allowing its rival to use his services: their competition had a component that was strangely cooperative. It might be said also that the whole business Cabot was engaged in was of little interest at that given time or that the machinery for controlling these kinds of migrations was not yet in place. The competitive and monopolistic model coexisted with the medieval ideal of Christian cooperation. The mobility of Italian mariners and capital seemed to reflect a paradigm shift and complicated the rivalry among the Spanish, English, and French. How England and Spain used Sebastian Cabot indicated the uneven development of the ways of conceiving of, mapping and possessing the New World.

John Cabot's voyage had alerted other nations to the great stocks of fish in the banks off the northeast coast of North America, and the fishermen of Western Europe soon sought this fishery, sometimes despite the official policies of their respective countries.[41] Cabot and his crew claimed that England would no longer need the Iceland fishery and described the role of Corte Real in the establishment of a Portuguese fishery in Newfoundland that flourished until the end of the sixteenth century. The Newfoundland fishery would be a place of conflict. In 1506 the Portuguese imposed a tax on Newfoundland cod brought to Portugal.[42] In 1585, Bernard Drake captured 600 Spanish prisoners there.[43] Newfoundland itself became a figure for the rivalry, cooperation, claims, and counterclaims of the European powers.

Perhaps the most tenacious heirs to the elder Cabot were the French fishermen, later the men of the French shore in Newfoundland and of St. Pierre and Miquelon. Two decades before official French voyages to North America, French fishermen were involved in the fisheries near Newfoundland. This commercial fishing as a response to Spain and England was something France maintained by keeping St. Pierre and Miquelon at the end of the Seven Years War (1756–63). In some ways the fishermen kept up contact with and interest in North America for the French between Cartier and Champlain.[44] According to Ramusio, by 1504 Breton fishing vessels went as far as Newfoundland, and in 1508 the *Pensée* sailed from Dieppe to Cape Bonavista. The ship, which belonged to Jean Ango, later viscount of Dieppe, brought back seven Natives and their arms, canoes, and belongings. This followed the Columbian tradition of kidnapping Natives in the New World, something Paulmier de Gonneville had done on his return from Brazil to Honfleur, when he took Essomericq back with him.[45]

King Ferdinand of Spain also continued his interest in the lands the Cabots had visited. In October 1511 he concluded a compact with Juan de Agramonte, a Catalan, for a voyage to Newfoundland, which Queen Joanna ratified, but no record exists to show whether Agramonte and his Breton pilots ever made the journey.[46] The documents mention that Agramonte was to set out to find "the secret of Newfoundland" with a crew of Spaniards (except two of the pilots might have been Bretons or from another nation with experience there), but owing to the agreement between Spain and Portugal (the Treaty of Tordesillas), he was not to venture on to the lands of Manuel, king of Portugal, who had married Ferdinand's daughters, Isabella and Maria.[47] Even Spain, which took the lead in voyages to the New World, found itself in an ambivalent and contradictory situation. Ferdinand would not recognize any discovery of Newfoundland outside his Iberian family, whose bonds had been cemented by treaties and marriages, but he needed the help of Portuguese, French, or English pilots.

The Breton pilots seemed acceptable to the king of Spain, who gave Agramonte permission to buy provisions in Brittany. The king, who hoped that Agramonte would find gold and other useful things in Newfoundland, also obliged himself to free Agramonte from prison should anyone detain him at the instance of any Christian king, thereby admitting the existence of nations "hostile" to Spain's claim to the New World.[48] Ferdinand did not mention the English but appeared to allow the French some part in the expedition. That implied distinction might have had to do with the official and originary nature of John Cabot's voyage to Newfoundland as opposed to French fishing expeditions there.

Sebastian Cabot had become useful to Ferdinand, who wrote to him on September 13, 1512, and whose chief chaplain and whose secretary, on behalf of their monarch, spoke with Cabot in Burgos about "the navigation to the Indies and the island of the Codfish," that is to the West Indies and Newfoundland.[49] By this time, the Breton, Portuguese, English, and French fishermen seemed to have been making annual trips to the fishing banks off the coast of Newfoundland. Records suggest that Newfoundland cod was having an economic impact on the western coast of France.[50] The records also show the English fishing fleet active in the Newfoundland fishery.[51]

The "race" for Newfoundland continued during the 1520s: the Portuguese, Spaniards, French, and English all sent out voyages. During the spring of 1521, Cardinal Wolsey wanted to send five ships to Newfoundland, but the companies in the city would not provide adequate support. In an answer made to certain of the king's council about the projected expedition to Newfoundland, the Wardens of the Drapers of London questioned the risk, especially of relying on the word of Sebastian (in all likelihood, Sebastian Cabot), who they alleged had never been there himself but had relied on his father's word.[52] The English had to wait until 1527 to send out a voyage. On March 13 and May 22, 1521, Alvares Fagundes, from Vianna, a fishing town with links to Newfoundland, received a grant of land from King Manuel of Portugal should he discover it in the Portuguese sphere. He explored the coast from Newfoundland to Nova Scotia.[53] On March 27, 1523, Charles V, issued an agreement with Stephen Gomez, a Portuguese, to command a voyage in search of a northwest passage on behalf of Spain. Charles stipulated that Gomez not approach any of the possessions of his cousin and brother, the king of Portugal (John III was the son of Charles V's aunt Maria and married his sister Catalina).[54] During the winter of 1524–25, Gomez made the voyage.

Binot Paulmier de Gonneville, a Norman, sailed to Brazil on the aptly named ship *L'Espoir* (1503–05), and the French took another major step in claiming new lands with Verrazzano's voyage to North America in 1523–24. The opening of Gonneville's account explained how two Portuguese, "Bastiam Moura" and "Diègue Cohinto," helped the Normans find the route to the Indes, something illegal under Portuguese law at the time.[55] The French were beginning to challenge the Portuguese in Brazil and the Spanish in North America.

III

France was more active than England was in exploring the northern reaches of North America from the 1520s to the 1570s. Even still, during the sixteenth century the French produced a small number of narratives compared to the Spanish and Portuguese.[56] The French made claims not too dissimilar to those of the English, that they in fact had discovered America, so that the need to precede the Spanish and Portuguese was a challenge to France and England both.

In 1647, E. Cleirac claimed that the Basque whalers had preceded Columbus to the New World by a hundred years when they allegedly discovered Newfoundland and New France. As late as 1785, Charles Desmarquets asserted that in 1488 Captain Jean Cousin from Dieppe had discovered the New World and the route to India via the Cape of Good Hope, something that Charles-André Julien, considering the contradictory evidence, refuted in 1946. Such nationalistic hopes never seem to go away, but they are far less widespread than they once were in Britain and France.[57] France sent expeditions to North America after those to the West Indies and South America. Having discussed the impact of the Cabots, here we shall examine two key voyages from France: those of Paulmier de Gonneville and Giovanni da Verrazzano.

Complexity and ambiguity occur at a key moment in Gonneville's text, so that regional, cultural, religious, and international interests qualify those of France as a nation and its monarch. Gonneville's relation of the voyage to Brazil in 1504 is the oldest account in French concerning an eyewitness report of the New World.[58] Although Gonneville was in the Portuguese sphere and did not attend to Spain, some of his observations were similar to Columbus's. Whereas the Natives in Columbus's account of his first voyage thought the Spanish gods, those Gonneville encountered considered the French to be angels.[59] Like the aboriginals that Bernal Díaz described in his account of Cortés's conquest, those Gonneville meets were much taken by the power of writing.[60] Jacques Cartier also maintained that the Natives thought the French to be gods and, like Gonneville, planted a cross as a sign of possession. Gonneville used the French pattern of taking possession, which involved Natives symbolically or literally as part of the audience during the ceremony of planting the cross. Apparently, René Laudonnière supposed that Verrazzano had planted a cross that had convinced the Spanish that the territory was French.[61]

Two details complicated Gonneville's act of possession. First, despite all the talk of an opposition between Rome and France over the bull of 1493, Gonneville described the inscription on the cross in a way that accounted for both parties.[62] Pope Alexander VI, King Louis XII of France, and the French admiral Mallet de Graville appeared in apparently descending order as a sign that Christians had arrived in that country, hardly a defiant nationalist gesture against the author of the donation that was supposed to divide the undiscovered world between Spain and Portugal. Second, another part of the Latin inscription suggested how the regional or provincial aspect of this voyage and ceremony also complicated national sentiment: "Here Paulmier de Gonneville raised this sacred monument while associating intimately the tribe and the Norman lineage [descendants]."[63] Gonneville saw bringing Christianity to the Natives as the custom of all those who came to the Indies and said that the Native chief, Arosca, wanted his son, Essomericq, to return to France to live in Christiandom. The French promised the father and the son that Essomericq would be returned home after twenty moons at the latest. Arosca, according to Gonneville, was interested in the French tools and weapons, which to them was as gold, silver, and gems were to Christians. After Arosca had asked the captain to swear to return at the promised time and the ship was departing, the Native people gave a great cry and pledged to care for the cross.[64]

Like Columbus, Gonneville read the signs, but their meaning was not always as simple and clear as these European captains thought.[65] These early voyages involved death. The kidnapping of Natives occurred on Gonneville's voyage as it had on Columbus's. On the way home, the French were stricken with sickness. A debate began on whether Namoa, the 35– to 40–year old companion of Essomericq who developed a terrible fever, should be baptized. The learned Monsieur Nicole said that it would be profane to baptize Namoa because he did not know the beliefs of the church as should someone who had reached the age of reason. For some reason, however, Nicole administered the sacrament to Essomericq, who was sick, and baptized him Binot, after one of Essomericq's godfathers, Gonneville. The baptism seemed to serve as medicine to body and soul because "the said Indian" recovered and was now in France. Near Porto-Seguro, when the French went ashore unarmed, looking for water, the Natives attacked them and killed a page and took a French soldier and mariner prisoner, while another Frenchman, Le Febvre, whose curiosity led him ashore, died before he could get into the ship. In the account, Gonneville, like Columbus, represented good Natives and bad Natives, thereby revealing, through his relations with the Natives, a division of and ambivalence toward the New World. At the second landfall, the Natives, who looked like those who had attacked the French on the first landing, were peaceful. During this incident, the French trapped two Natives, but they jumped overboard three leagues from the shore and, in Gonneville's view, being such good swimmers, would survive.[66]

For Gonneville, as for Columbus, conflicts occurred among countrymen and not simply with the Natives. Gonneville's journey home illustrates this point as France was subject to regional rivalries and piracy. After sailing by way of the Azores and Ireland, they came to Jersey and Guernsey, where an English and a Breton pirate attacked them. The Norman expedition could not count on a peaceful passage near Brittany: Gonneville lost 14 people as a result of the fight and gave their names. After two years, he arrived in Harfleur with 28 of 58 men.[67] Gonneville, Andrieu de La Mare, and Anthoyne Thiéry lost their journal with the ship, which Gonneville preferred to lose rather than yield to the Breton pirates (May 7, 1505), and so presented their report in the form as set out by law.[68] Differences within "nation states" also complicated the national identities and made difficult the expansion of these European "empires."

The story did not end there. After *l'Espoir* was shipwrecked, Essomericq settled in Honfleur and married one of the close relatives of his godfather Gonneville, whose name and some of whose goods he inherited. In 1658, Essomericq's descendants contested paying taxes because they were foreigners and because their ancestor had wanted to return home as Gonneville had promised him. Essomericq's descendants in France requested a reduction in taxes and appealed to Gonneville's text as evidence that their ancestor had intended to return home after a short while but could not owing to his forced journey.[69] The mixing of cultures as well as the differences within a culture make generalizations about Europeans and Natives, however necessary for the shape of any interpretation or argument, refractory. From the case of Essomericq, French culture, for instance, was changing, and in France and in the New World had begun to incorporate or consider aspects of the Amerindian. This *métissage* increased after Gonneville's account in the first decade of the sixteenth century.

The French seemed to have made a more concerted effort than the English did in the exploration of the New World from about 1520 to 1542. In a well-known instance, François I (1515–47) asked to be shown Adam's will as evidence of France giving up the right to territory in the New World.[70] He would not accept this "divine" law that underpinned the agreement between Portugal and Spain but instead adopted the principle of first possession by Europeans.[71] The Natives were to have no rights of possession of their lands because they did not occupy them as Europeans did—that is, in a permanent civil society or a Christian society. The French and English designs in Europe and overseas were not as successful as their monarchs may have wished: in contrast, the Spanish king grew more and more influential. François and Henry VIII had both aspired to being the Holy Roman emperor, but the election of the young Charles I of Spain as Emperor Charles V maintained the Habsburg succession and meant that the French king felt that Spain hemmed in France from Flanders through Burgundy and Italy to Spain itself. France claimed Milan and other parts of Italy, and a war with Spain began in 1521. The rivalry between France and Spain meant setbacks for each crown even as Spanish power was on the rise in the sixteenth century.

Although the French king was concerned with the interests of France in Europe, which often involved opposing Spain, he did turn to the Americas as a means of supporting those same goals. French pirates harassed Spanish vessels. In 1522, Magellan, a Portuguese in the service of Spain, rounded the tip of South America, and after he perished, Sebastían del Cano completed the first circumnavigation of the globe with a rich cargo of spices from Asia. That same year, the corsair Jean Fleury, one of Ango's captains, carried back to France the plunder Cortés had taken from Montezuma. The gold of Mexico and Peru would send the French in search of riches in North America, just as Magellan's voyage was another reminder of the passage to—and trade with—Asia.

As surviving members of Magellan's crew could attest, the southern extremity of the Americas made for difficult passage. The Spanish knew the coast north to Florida but not to the cod fisheries, so that hope for a short northwest passage to Asia remained. The French joined the English and Spanish in the search for such a passage. Verrazzano was a Florentine living in Rouen and a member of a network of Italian merchants, principally from Florence, who lived in Lyon, Paris, and Rouen and traded under the French flag. Three of the Florentines who backed Verrazzano were bankers who a few years before had given François I substantial financial help. Foreign merchants sometimes lived and traded under the protection of the government where they lived: the merchants of the Hanseatic League in the Steelyard in London, the English wool merchants in Bruges, the English in Andalusia and the Florentine community in Lyon, one of whose syndicates financed Verrazzano.[72] Verrazzano's expedition of 1523–24 raided the Spanish coast and then, reduced to one ship, proceeded to North America at 34 degrees of latitude, then sailed north to avoid Spanish ships.

Like Gonneville, Verrazzano displayed some goals and attitudes similar to those of Columbus: his seeking of a passage to Asia and his description of the Natives are two cases in point. After meeting Natives, Verrazzano claimed the land near North Carolina and called it Francesca. After sailing from the Carolinas to Nova Scotia, which included taking detailed notes on Natives, vegetation, and rivers, Verrazzano returned home without having discovered a northwest passage. He seemed, however, to have thought that the Hatteras banks were a long, thin finger of land that separated the Ocean Sea from the Indian Ocean.

Verrazzano's narrative, though so long neglected in France, deserves close attention. The neglect or unfortunate fate of the relation of Cartier's second voyage and Jean Ribault's narrative are other instances of French originals or versions being lost, perhaps owing to the destruction of the civil war or Wars of Religion in France. Unfortunately, we do not have Verrazzano's original report in French for the king, but four Italian versions have been preserved, Ramusio's version of 1556 being the only one known for years, and an English translation of the Italian text in Ramusio appeared in *Divers Voyages* (1582) and *The Principall Navigations* (1589) by Richard Hakluyt the Younger, a key figure later in my study.[73] Like Columbus's texts, Verrazzano's work displays textual uncertainty. There are four versions of Verrazzano's narrative of the voyage, three of which are full accounts in the form of a letter the leader of the expedition, Verrazzano, to François I, who authorized the voyage. René Herval's French translation from the Italian appeared in 1933.

In this important text, Verrazzano addressed François I and described how they sailed along the coast of Spain ready for war. His account of the kindness the Natives showed in rescuing one of the young French sailors in rough seas is touching.[74] He extolled the beauty of the men and women of one of the aboriginal peoples whom they met.[75] Some of his statements about ideal and Arcadian Natives and land were reminiscent of Columbus and foreshadowed Montaigne. For the most part, however, Verrazzano's representation appeared to derive from experience—he described the Natives as wise, generous, and courteous. Sometimes a sentence or two suggested sincerity by the simplicity of the tone, which is still conveyed in translation: "They are very generous and give away all they have. We made great friends with them."[76] For 15 days, Verrazzano and his crew stayed among them as guests: the Natives, who did not value gold because of its color, examined the French weapons out of curiosity but did not desire them and laughed at the mirrors, refusing them after a brief glance. Like Columbus and Gonneville, Verrazzano met friendly Natives and unfriendly Natives, although he appeared to have been more fortunate because those to the north whom he described as barbarous seemed only to lack courtesy. After the trading was over, they mocked the French by showing their buttocks and laughing, but they offered Verrazzano and his crew no violence.[77] The trope of or belief in good Natives, bad Natives, was carried on. Sailing further to the north, Verrazzano made a surprising generalization that qualified any assessment of his judgment: "We made no contact with the people and we think they were, like the others, devoid of manner and humanity."[78]

In the Natives whom Verrazzano encountered Thomas More could not have hoped for a better example of a people who, like the Utopians, did not admire

gold. It is possible that Verrazzano had read *Utopia,* which would then complicate the relation between his experience in the New World and the fictional and
utopian elements that he might have brought to his narrative.[79] The themes of
God and gold, which occurred in Vespucci, who sailed under the Spanish flag,
were central to Thomas More's fiction of the New World. Vespucci told of the
baptism of many Natives, a topic More represented in the coming of Christianity to Utopia. The Indians did not value gold or gems and almost despised them,
Vespucci said, while educated Europeans would have read Peter Martyr's
account of the Spanish lust for gold in *De orbe nouo,* Decades 1, 3. More's satire
played on this difference between the worldly greed for gold of Christians and
the spiritual indifference to it of the Utopians. In Utopia there are gold and silver chamber pots, fetters for slaves, ornaments, and crowns for criminals. The
children there play with gems as toys. The Anemolian ambassadors to Utopia
cause disgrace and amusement by decking themselves out in precious metals and
gems. Although probably alluding to Lycurgus's reforms in Sparta, where iron
became legal tender in place of gold and silver, More's Lucianic allegory also
amplified the contrast between the Native indifference and contempt for gold
and the Spanish greed for it.[80] Tzvetan Todorov maintains that Vasco de Quiroga,
a member of the administration in Mexico and later bishop of Michoacán, made
the Natives part of his own utopian project, which Lucian and More influenced.[81] Vespucci influenced More. Here is an example of someone in the Spanish service affecting an English writer, who affected a Spanish writer, who later
became a model in Pierre d'Avity's work, which was translated from French
into English by Edward Grimstone, and will be examined later.[82] It is possible,
then, that directly or indirectly Verrazzano was part of this circulation of ideas or
intertextuality.

Verrazzano, like Vespucci before him and unlike More and the humanists, was
both explorer and recorder. Both those Europeans who were eyewitnesses and
those who were not could see the Natives in utopian and dystopian terms, as we
shall observe in chapter 3 in such encounters as the debate between Bartolomé
de Las Casas and Ginés de Sepúlveda. Verrazzano would have other European
precedents derived from texts by those who had been to the New World and
those who had not. Like Cabot before him and Cartier after him, Verrazzano
tried to keep clear of the Spanish colonies while finding territory for France and
a passage to Asia. Having avoided the Spanish in Florida, Verrazzano was
reminded that he had reached the lands the English had discovered. Verrazzano
wrote: "After sailing CL leagues in a northeasterly direction we approached the
land which the Britons once found, which lies in 50 degrees."[83] Having run out
of provisions, the French set off for home. To conclude, Verrazzano said that the
French supposed that the Natives had no religion, a conclusion Columbus
reached on his first voyage; he then gave cosmographical readings of the voyage
and made geographical interpretations that contradicted his earlier view that
America was near Asia and that were closer to actuality.[84] He probably did not
know that Magellan and his crew (without their captain after his death in the
Philippines) had circumvented the globe (1519–22), so his speculations were out
of date. Verrazzano seemed to have known Magellan in Lisbon in 1517 and had

accompanied or followed him in his departure for Spain.[85] Here is another debt the French owed to the Portuguese and Spanish.

While Verrazzano sailed the waters of the New World, the French fought battles in Europe. Nor did the explorer know the fate of the king to whom he addressed his letter. François, who had aligned himself with Turkey and the German Protestant states, was defeated and captured at the battle of Pavia in 1525.[86] When Erasmus's friend, Andrea Ammonio, an Italian and secretary to Henry VIII, informed Erasmus of this league against France, Erasmus responded: " Suppose the French are expelled from Italy. Would you rather have the Spaniards as lords"?[87] Erasmus's question would become even more pressing when Spain sacked Rome in 1527. The Black Legend of Spain was foreshadowed or had early origins in Italy and elsewhere. When Verrazzano's ship, the *Dauphine,* returned to France, the French king was a prisoner of his chief rival, the emperor. This situation possessed some drama: François was in the hands of Charles V as Henry VIII looked on.[88]

IV

After discussing explorers such as John and Sebastian Cabot, Gonneville, and Verrazzano, I will now turn to English books as well as French and other Continental accounts of the New World by those who had not been there. Writings that were not eyewitness reports played an important role in the exploration and settlement of the Americas. Some of the French and English writing about the New World involved writers who had not seen America but who wished to promote it or to translate work by others in the service of Spain. Whereas Gonneville's voyage produced a written account, the English voyages did not yield any written narratives, and no book appeared in English about voyages until about 1511 when Jan van Doesborch printed *Of the newe landes . . .* in Antwerp. This book contained three sections and presented a description of "Armenica" or America, including accounts from Vespucci: descriptions of Africa, by Balthasar Springer, an agent of Anton Welser, the German financier; accounts of Eastern Christians; and a version of Prester John's *Letter.* By 1511, on the Continent, there were already versions of Columbus's *Letter* in six countries; Italian, Latin, and German editions of Vespucci; and newsletters about the Portuguese in India from German and Italian presses, while nothing had appeared in English. Only one edition of Doesborch was published, and no printer in England, despite having the capacity, decided to follow this lead. Apparently there was little market for the printing of travel narratives in English.[89] Even though the English had begun well with the practical knowledge of the voyages of the Cabots, the nation, even more than France, showed an apathy toward, and ignorance of cosmography and mathematics, producing its first printed text on basic arithmetic in English or by an Englishman in 1543.[90] Although England and France were challenging Spain, they were doing so in fits and starts, and in both countries overseas expansion often met with opposition.

One example of such opponent is Thomas More, but he was more interested in social values than with expansion.[91] More represented criticisms of England, France, and Spain. Even though More's character, Raphael, exalts Cardinal Morton (ca. 1420–1500), in whose household More once served, More allowed for a critique of England. Nor did France escape criticism. Although not entirely spared in More's satire, Spain made few explicit appearances in *Utopia*.[92] More's Peter Giles was drawing on Vespucci's accounts, such as *Cosmographiae Introductio* (1507) from about ten years before. Raphael travels to Cape Frio in Brazil to Calcutta and back home, a member of the Spanish expedition but saved by his own countrymen and perhaps his philosophy, which, if the sayings are a guide, derives as much from his reading of Lucian, Augustine, and Cicero as of Plato. The English More and the Flemish Giles are left to the defining example of a Spanish voyage in a new world divided between Portugal and Spain.[93] More wrote in Latin, but there were also texts in English that alluded to and addressed the New World.

The first book in English about the New World printed in England was an interlude by John Rastell, Thomas More's brother-in-law, which he published after his planned voyage to America failed. His two ships got no further than Waterford as his purser and master wanted to pursue piracy instead of Newfoundland. After Rastell's refusal to go along with their plan, they left him and sold the provisions. Rastell's *A new interlude of the four elements,* has a character, Experience, describe the New World and successful voyages to its northern parts. The play called for more English exploration and for an overseas empire. The question of origins resurfaced as it would throughout the period between 1492 and 1713: "O what a thynge had be than/ Yf that they that be englyshe men/ Myght have ben the first of all/ That there shulde have take possessyon/And made furst buylding & habytacion,/ A memory perpetuall!"[94] Rastell had chosen the English language consciously to debate the issues of the New World, whereas the year before More had decided on Latin. At first glance, it is possible that Rastell used English in order to reach a wider mercantile population and to promote the colony commercially as the most powerful merchants appeared less eager to invest in ventures to the New World than the king was. For instance, in 1521, More was a member of the King's Council, while Henry VIII offered one of his ships if the merchants of London would provide five ships for a voyage to America, but the merchants appear to have worried about losing their Spanish and Continental trade if they tried to trade in the New World. In 1521, war broke out with France: no voyage took place.[95]

In England of this time, the texts of promotion were more often letters or government documents rather than books. The Bristolian merchants, for example, continued to look westward. In 1527, Robert Thorne, a native of Bristol resident in Spain, addressed Henry VIII and Dr. Lee, English ambassador in Spain, to ask them to support a venture to seek a northeast passage to the East Indies, but these two letters were not printed until 1589, when Hakluyt included them in *Principall Navigations.* Nor did any printer publish a narrative concerning John Rut's voyage to Newfoundland in June and July of 1527, and it was for Oviedo, a Spanish historian, to mention that Rut went as far south as the West Indies in search of a passage through America.[96]

Translation also began to provide information about Spain and the New World. Despite the disruptions in religion and politics in Europe, French and English translators did produce some books about strange new lands. In 1516, the same year as the publication of More's *Utopia, De orbe nouo decades* of Pietro Martire d'Anghiera (Peter Martyr) appeared separately.[97] The French translation of 1532 abridged the three decades of the 1516 edition as well as presenting similar versions to Cortés's second and third letters published in Nuremburg in the same volume as Martyr's *De rebus, et insulis noviter repertis* (1524).[98] In this translation Spain could provide a positive example for the French. This translator aimed the book at the court as he dedicated it to "Charles duc Dangolesme," the third son of François I.[99] The tone was serene, explanatory, and laudatory.

The untitled prefatory matter explained that these three decades, or three books of ten about "the New World, of the Ocean Sea, and of Cuba, which was considered a continent and continuous to the Indies, was composed in Latin by the noble historiographer, Peter Martyr of Milan, councillor of the kings of Spain."[100] Here the praise was more generous and factual than in the prefaces and dedications of translations of works concerning the Spanish colonies from the mid-century onward, some of which began to blacken the name of Spain. The geographical description in the translator's explanation showed that the Europeans were still hungry for information—particularly cartographical knowledge—about the New World, something the Spanish possessed more than any other European nation. In a kind of metatranslational strategy, perhaps an example of a metadedication, the unnamed translator referred to Martyr's original dedications, so that these dedicatory decisions in Spain became part of the French dedication. Like an epic list, the names of noble or eminent dedicatees, such as cardinals, counts, and popes, served as a prologue to the dedication of the French translation to the duke himself. The French translator praised Martyr's concern for historical truth and use of firsthand sources.[101] This list of the great should have flattered the duke. Nowhere was there a hint that their Spanish or Italian nationality was a matter for scorn or critique. Not even the name of Alexander VI, who divided the New World between Spain and Portugal, engendered criticism when he was mentioned. The dedication also emphasized knowledge of the unknown and stressed that Martyr, the Spanish councilor, drew on the best that was known and written by those who had navigated to and were conversant with those new lands. In the vulgar tongue the translation would present these new and pleasant things, unknown to the French, to the historians and cosmographers among the Jews, Greeks, and Romans. The duke to whom this book was dedicated (the dedication was reiterated) liked to read "new things." [102] It would be very pleasant, the translator continued, for God to give Christians the grace to encompass the earth, more than Ptolemy and the historiographers knew, something that was done in a voyage of 1520–21. He repeated the profession of great joy that all over the world the name of Jesus Christ was heard and that many obeyed it. The dedication ended in prayer: "All-powerful God, may you turn this discovery of all the world to his honor and to his glory."[103] This vision of unity harkened to a time before the Reformation had challenged papal authority. The idea of world dominion for Christianity recalled the background of the crusades and the search for Prester John. In time the anti-Spanish rhetoric of French Protestants and of those jealous of Spain at court would counter and coexist with this celebration of a unified Christian mission, the reign of Christ as universal monarch.

The opening of this French translation of Peter Martyr, which followed a brief dedication, echoed this view of a universal evangelization and placed Columbus and Spain at the origin of the exploration of the New World, which Martyr emphasized with his title: "In the year 1492 a Genoese named Christopher Columbus obtained ships from the king of Spain, Ferdinand, and the queen, Isabella, his wife, to search towards the west for . . . new islands and lands, from which the Christian regions could be enriched with precious stones, scented things, gold, silver and many other noble and profitable things. . . . [let us] seek them more amply to make them know the scriptures, and the treasure of life that is our Lord Jesus Christ."[104] Christ would come to the New World, which would in turn give Christians great riches. Within three pages, Columbus and his crew reacted joyously to the discovery of six islands, the first called Hispaniola ("Espaignole"). In the middle of his text, the French translator also included an excerpt from Martyr's "sixth book of the third decade," which was partly comprised of a description of the Cabot journey, from England to Newfoundland as related by Sebastian Cabot.[105] The English priority in the North Atlantic was also something the French later contested.

It is, then, too simple to see an unambivalent and uncontradictory relation between France and Spain, France and the papacy, or to discuss those connections without some discussion of England or the Western European context. Tensions existed at official and unofficial levels. Besides the court, the fishermen, merchants, and pirates all had their own relations with the New World. The French view of the example of Spain was positive and negative: refractory. Even in the background of the voyages of Jacques Cartier to what is now called Canada occurred in a framework that had to take into account and modify the rights of the Spanish and Portuguese as defined by the pope during the 1490s. How France approached Spain depended in part on its relations with Rome.

V

There could be a double movement in France's relations with Rome pertaining to the monopoly it had given to Spain and Portugal in the exploration of the New World. The personal and political connections of the various popes may have made some difference to their positions concerning the Americas. As observed earlier, during the 1490s, the pope had Iberian connections, whereas, as we shall see here, his successor in the early 1530s had a family member in a key post in France. On one occasion, as much as François I seemed to ignore the papal donation dividing the "unknown" world between the Iberian powers, he sought to avoid the condemnation of Rome. On his behalf, through his relations with Cardinal Hippolyte de Médicis, archbishop of Montréal and nephew to the pope, Jean Le Veneur, bishop of Lisieux, approached Clement VII, who declared in 1533 that the bulls of 1493 applied to lands known to the Spanish and Portuguese before that date. The year before, when the French king had come on a pilgrimage to Mont-Saint-Michel, where Le Veneur was also the abbot, Le Veneur had proposed to the king that he back a voyage of discovery and presented Jacques Cartier, whose relative was a manager of the finances of the abbey, as his choice to lead it. Apparently, the success of that mission helped to make Le Veneur a cardinal. Similarly, Paul III (1534–49), Clement's successor, did not intervene in the French colonization of America, a policy that troubled Charles V.[106] As I have stressed, Spain's great power did have limitations, and it was not able to prevent the English and the French from exploring the northern parts of the New World. Even Spain, which set such an example in its colonization of the Americas, was not immune to disappointment and uncertainty: France was mounting a considerable challenge.

One of the most important aspects of the Cartier voyages was that they were official and financed by the crown. The goals set for Cartier were to find new lands full of riches, particularly gold, and to discover a passage to Cathay by the west.[107] Cartier's first voyage in 1534 accomplished neither of these aims. On July 24, 1534, he planted a great cross in the Gaspé and took possession of Canada for his king.[108] Cartier brought back two Natives as proof of the discovery and as potential interpreters, a common custom from Columbus onward. These Natives, who learned French in Brittany and, perhaps hoping to find a way home, boasted of the riches of Saguenay, a kingdom to the west, which Cartier seemed to have confused with the Cathay of Marco Polo.[109] The desire for rich mines, especially of gold, based on the Spanish experience in Mexico and Peru, prompted François I to support Cartier in a second voyage. On this voyage of 1535, Cartier brought some gentlemen and the two Native interpreters. Cartier mistakenly sought the kingdom of the Saguenay and was trapped for the winter at Hochelaga, where Montréal now stands. Scurvy killed 25 of his men in a few weeks, and a plant that the Natives offered the French cured the remainder. Cartier's gratitude was expressed when he took the two interpreters, two important Natives, and their leader Donnacona back to France. For the king, the lack of gold from these voyages was probably a grave disappointment.

Although François I had approached Rome with some care in order to legitimize Cartier's voyages specifically and the French ambitions of exploration more generally, he and his government, whatever the disappointment over the lack of Canadian gold, were able to keep their plans quiet. Apparently, according to Charles-André Julien, the diplomatic correspondence and espionage in London, Lisbon, and Valladolid on the eve of the third voyage suggest that Cartier's discoveries were unknown to France's rival European powers.[110] As for the French king, he turned his attention to war with Spain, which proceeded until the truce at Nice on June 18, 1538. From 1538 to 1541, the king of France waited to see how the pope would rule in answer to Charles V's desire for a condemnation of those who would contravene the bull of Alexander VI. The French goal was now said to be conversion of the Natives, which made it difficult for the pope to condemn. Donnacona's description of gold, according to Marcel Trudel, was the true motivation for French exploration, and this religious motive was a necessary façade to circumvent Portugal and Spain without offending the pope.[111]

In the course of discussions with the ambassadors of Charles V and John III of Portugal, François elaborated a new policy toward colonization. The doctrine was as elegant as it was simple: permanent occupation rather than discovery created possession.[112] He turned the Portuguese doctrine of *terra nullius*, begun in their exploration of Africa in the fifteenth century, against Portugal and Spain. In the fifteenth century the Portuguese had posts, instead of colonies in Africa, so that the exact nature of this claim to possession there is not entirely clear, but for an argument for the Portuguese precedence in the use of *terra nullius* in Africa.[113] This legal doctrine of *terra nullius* came to affect the English colonies as much as those of the French: for instance, as late as 1971 Justice Richard Blackburn had confirmed *terra nullius* in Australia, and it took until 1992 for the High Court of Australia to reject it.[114] The French king issued formal orders to French seamen not to go to places in the New World occupied by the Portuguese and Spanish. On December 27, 1540, the Spanish ambassador in France wrote the emperor Charles V and outlined the issue between Spain and France regarding the New World:

> Sire,
> I again spoke with the King of France concerning the navigation of his subjects to the Indies, not neglecting any of the points contained in your letters, not any of which I thought might have the desired effect, to which he replied as before, that he could not desist from giving the said licence to his subjects for any place whatever, but at least they will not touch at places belonging to your Majesty, nor go to the parts not discovered by his predecessors, and belonging to his crown more than thirty years before the ships of Spain or Portugal sailed to the new Indies; and as to what I told him that permission to navigate these parts was conceded to your Majesty's predecessors by the Pope, and applied to them, he answered that the Popes hold spiritual jurisdiction, but that it does not lie with them to distribute lands among kings, and that the Kings of France, and other Christians, were not summoned when the partition took place; and in conclusion, Sire, I have not been able to settle anything but that his subjects shall not go to your lands or ports. In truth, I think he has in mind the populated and defended places, because he said that passing by and discovering with the eye was not taking possession. Your Majesty will understand what this means, and will know how to provide accordingly, as in truth is necessary.[115]

The French king would stay away from areas that Spain possessed but not those in its sphere that were yet to be possessed.

The primary aim of France in Canada, besides the demonstrative one of religion and the underlying one of riches, shifted to settlement. Roberval's commission of January 15, 1541 showed settlement as part of the French policy for the New World, for in it François said that his deputy should not encroach on the property of any other prince, including those of Spain and Portugal.[116] As of January 1541, Roberval would be the captain general and master pilot because he had the background to be a governor and could finance the voyage and Cartier would play a supporting role. This shift in French colonization policy continued to interest Charles V, who wanted to squash any French attempt to encroach on his rights to the New World. He had his ambassador and spies in France watching what they still considered to be the Cartier expeditions.[117] The emperor and his government kept guessing where the French might land and what might be done to build up defenses against them. This uncertainty was present in the letter of the emperor to the cardinal of Toledo on May 7, 1541. Charles V approved of the idea of sending arms to the Spanish colonies and hiding their gold and silver in a safe place. He was also glad that the bishop approved that he would wait to ask the king of Portugal to refuse the French ships in his ports until the response of the king of France and the pope to Spanish representations:

> until further representations had been made to the King of France, and to our most Holy Father, that he might see what little right the said King had to do what he is doing, it being in direct contravention of the treaty agreed upon with the intervention of his Holiness; as also because we hold the right to these Indies by concession and permission of the Apostolic See. In regard to this you think that stress should be laid chiefly upon the fact that they were discovered, conquered and peopled by ourselves and our predecessors at great cost, and that we have continued in the peaceful possession and ownership of these lands, and not to insist much upon the concession of the Apostolic See, as the said King of France attaches but little importance to this; you have therein spoken well, and thus it was agreed here, and although we have learnt that his Holiness has approached the said King through the medium of his nuncio in France, we have no news of the decision come to; when we do hear, I will cause you to be advised thereof.[118]

The emperor did take the pope's role seriously and was trying to develop a policy that would counter or balance the position that François I was developing in regard to the New World. Just as Henry VII had ignored the claims of Spain and Portugal to the New World, so did the French king. Under Elizabeth I, the English would take up a similar policy for the Americas to the one that François developed more explicitly and extensively than any other rival to the monarchs of Spain.

Two days after writing the note to the cardinal, the emperor, having received news from his ambassador in France that the expedition would soon be underway, added to his letter. Even though Charles V agreed with the cardinal that should the French settle in the Northern Sea necessity would compel them to leave it, he thought that it would be good to explore whether these lands lay within the Spanish sphere. In emphasizing French and English anxiety over the

Spanish success in the New World, it is easy to forget how anxious Spain was over the prospect of rivals in the Americas. Although the anxiety of Spain is not the primary focus of this study, its existence needs to be stated in order to complicate the fears France and England had of the Spanish empire. French and English representations of Spain, particularly from the 1570s onward, tended to describe Spain as haughty and disdainful, a threat to its neighbors, whereas Charles V's correspondence revealed a sense of vulnerability and anxiety over France:

> and I must not neglect to warn you that even if this land, where the said French are going to settle, does not lie within our limits, and is of little value, they may from thence go farther afield and reach our lands within our limits, which would be a great anxiety and bring destruction upon our colonies; and by building fortresses and settling in that land, they may take root and fortify themselves, and it will be difficult to drive them out, unless it be done speedily.[119]

Charles V hoped that his brother-in-law, John III of Portugal, would join him in taking action against the French, but it seems that the Portuguese did not want a breach with France. This defensive but aggressive attitude on the part of Spain foreshadowed the position Charles's son, Philip II, would take against the French in Florida.

In June 1542, the Councils of State and of the Indies recorded that through a spy they had learned that the French had entered by way of the coast of the Bacallaos, "a land which the Bretons claim to have discovered long ago."[120] A marginal note at this place in the memorandum showed how important origins and first discovery were to the Spanish as well as to the French and English: "In old maps they say, in some, lands of the Bretons; in others, Portuguese land; in others, that the French discovered it. In another in Latin: "This land is called the Codfish land which a certain chief Pilot of the King of England discovered. There is a great store of fish called Codfish."[121] These maps, as the Spanish would know, encapsulated the conflict over these lands. In Newfoundland the Spanish were not there first, and they had conceded the land to the Portuguese. Nonetheless, the councils extrapolated that the further 700 leagues that the French said they had to travel from Newfoundland placed the territory Cartier was exploring within the Spanish sphere as defined by the pope and the two Iberian powers in the 1490s. Mistakenly, the councils thought that the addition of 700 leagues would take the French to the Bahama Channel,

> which is the best position that they could take, when war breaks out with France, to inflict injury upon the vessels from the Indies, since most of them come through the said Bahama Channel, and not one could pass without being taken. This must be their chief object in making settlements on this coast, since, although the land is unproductive, this route is of the greatest importance for their purpose. If this is the case, it is clear that they are going for the purpose of colonizing within your Majesty's line of demarcation.[122]

The Spanish were responding to their fear rather than concentrating on the location of New France and the kingdom of the Saguenay, and, understanding this problem, the councils suggested that they should track the French fleet with two caravels (one more than the emperor had suggested). They seemed to think war with France was inevitable and that America was now an integral part of the theater of war for European powers. Their recommendation was to prepare these ships for battle with the French, a preparation that included the outfitting of 500 soldiers, all of which should be done with dissimulation, so that the French could not say that Spain had broken the truce and provoked the war. A captain-general should be appointed to discover and conquer this new land: the only money left to finance it was gold and silver from Peru waiting in Panama and that could be shipped if that were the wish of the emperor.[123]

On occasion, the Spanish themselves saw the French as imitating them and were anxious about that mimesis even if they considered the French to be misguided in the basis of imitation. For instance, the cardinal of Seville saw this aspect of the colonial policy of France. Replying to the memorandum of the council that same month, he gave his opinion about the French fleet. With diplomacy, the cardinal agreed with the councils but suggested that the caravel or caravels be given a clear title to sail, so that when they made their way into the French fleet, they would not be regarded as spies and enemies. Nor did the cardinal concur with the councils that the French were considering the Rio de la Plata or the Bahamas or that they were thinking of establishing colonies to prey on Spanish ships and thereby break the truce with Spain. He thought that men feared that the truce would be broken and should hope for peace to prepare the finances necessary for a great war. Putting his diplomacy aside, the cardinal called the theory of the French preparing colonies for piracy nonsense ("locura"). Instead, the French were following the example of Spain:

> Their motive is that they think, from what they learn, that these provinces are rich in gold and silver, and they hope to do as we have done; but, in my judgment, they are making a mistake; for if there are no fisheries, this whole coast as far as Florida is utterly unproductive. In consequence of which they would be lost, or at best would make a short excursion, after losing a few men and the greater part of all they took from France.[124]

The French sought gold and silver as the Spanish had done, but in the cardinal's view, they were doing so in the wrong place, and, he implied, with such faulty intention that the French would be lost or suffer losses.

The Spanish decided to seek out Cartier: they sent out two caravels in the summer of 1541, one to the West Indies and the other to Newfoundland. The first returned to Spain in January 1542 without a report of Cartier, and the second came back on July 25, 1542 and described Cartier's mission in the St. Lawrence. On November 3, 1541, just over a week before Cartier's will was registered, the Spanish ambassador to France wrote to the emperor saying that Spain should block the design of Roberval, who, having encountered difficulties with outfitting vessels with crew and provisions, decided the enterprise would be abandoned. The ambassador added that Cartier, already in Newfoundland, part of the Portuguese sphere, would face the measures Portugal considered necessary to secure its own trade and navigation.[125] Roberval eluded the Spanish. How much danger Cartier and Roberval were in is unknown, but the Portuguese and Spanish did not or could not attack them in the North Atlantic. In about twenty years in Brazil, the Portuguese would take military action against the French while the Spanish would do the same in Florida during the 1560s. Together Portugal and Spain policed their areas according to the line on which they and the pope had come to agree as the demarcation of empire.

So with five ships containing enough supplies for two years, Cartier set out on May 23, 1541 while Roberval, after requisitioning prisoners for colonists and practicing piracy to recoup the costs of the voyage, sailed with three ships on April 16, 1542.[126] Roberval, who had joined with Pierre de Bidoux, one of the most notorious French pirates of the day, had to lay off St. Malo because he was not prepared to go to Canada and he dared not land in France owing to the piracy he had committed against French, English, and other ships.[127] One of the ironies of this raid can be observed in the diplomatic correspondence addressing Roberval's piracy before his departure for North America. When some English merchants complained to Henry VIII that Roberval had robbed them on the pretext that as the pirated goods were laden in Spain, they belonged to the Spanish, Henry instructed his ambassador in France, Paget, to seek an audience with the French king, where he delivered to François a letter from the French ambassador in England, Marillac. This letter, dated February 22, 1542, made the charge against Roberval, who after all was himself trying to elude Spain on behalf of a French king who was shaping a policy for the New World that circumvented Spanish claims there, for seizing the 600 quintals of iron and the 400 morocco skins. The seizure was made "under the pretext that he said the merchandise in question was loaded in Spain and belonged to Spain."[128] Roberval used the example of Spain to rob the English in the name of France. In a letter to Henry VIII of March 13, 1542, Paget reported François's reaction to the English request and to the French ambassador's letter, which the English ambassador had just received and delivered. The French king promised to apprehend Roberval, "for he had deceived him, he saide, like a false traitour thefe; ffor Vale [Roberval] promised him to conquerre the land of Canados to him," but now, the king said, he lay off the coast of Britanny and robbed French and English ships and "he shalbe hanged by the neck if I catch him," a threat François wanted Paget to report to Henry VIII when he wrote him.[129] When asked about restitution, the French king replied that he had merchants in England with like causes, so that if Henry VIII would consider their wrongs, he would do the same for these English merchants. Apparently much of the English and French concern surrounding the third Cartier expedition was over piracy. François's talk of conquering echoed the language of Spanish expansion in the New World. How theatrical or sincere the French king was in this instance is an open question, but he wanted to impress Henry VIII, who was about to the join him in a war against Charles V, although François never punished Roberval.[130]

This was by far the most ambitious French expedition to date. After their rendez-vous in Newfoundland, Cartier, thinking he had found gold and diamonds, disobeyed Roberval's orders and returned to France. Roberval, a Protestant, could not find the kingdom of the Saguenay.[131] Perhaps François was showing religious tolerance in his choice of leader, but he might also have relied on the expertise and money of the Protestant nobility in Normandy and Britanny just as he had depended on the Florentine merchants in Lyon. The king's purse was often empty owing to the wars. It is possible that Roberval had some designs to create a Protestant colony in Canada like those the French later attempted in Brazil and Florida. On January 26, 1541, a Mr. Wallop reported to Henry VIII on the French expedition, whose pilot, he said, was Cartier, and whose captain of the footmen was Clement Marot, "who heretofore fledde owte of this Realme for the lutheryan secte" and who, in 1535, along with Roberval, had been condemned as a heretic but had escaped.[132] Like Jean Ribault, who will be a central figure in this study, Roberval also had riches and piracy on his mind.

Although the French came to criticize the Spanish empire in the Americas, their own intentions, discourse, and actions were as intricate and contradictory as those they censored. Cartier received no formal recognition from the king and seemed to be have lived thereafter in St. Malo. His only literal appearance in Rabelais occurs among the credulous geographers and historians who listened to the fabulous stories of the ancient Ouyr-Dire (Hearsay). Apparently, if the number of books about Turkey and the few on America is any indication, in the first half of the sixteenth century, the French were more interested in the Turks than in Native Americans.[133]

Even still, America was of enough interest to France that the king supported voyages there. A few examples from the Cartier narratives will demonstrate that Spain was a consideration for the French as they explored North America. Whether Cartier, Belleforest, or Jehan Poullet wrote the dedication or relation of the second voyage is still a matter of debate.[134] The account of Cartier's first voyage was known, until 1867, through the Italian of Ramusio that was translated back into the French from the Italian translation in 1598. The narrative of the second voyage existed in several copies, but only in 1863 was an exemplary copy discovered in the British Museum (Paris edition of 1545). The narrative of the third (the voyage of Cartier and Roberval), which was not as precise as Cartier's earlier accounts and may have been a summary or redaction, was available in an English version, possibly based on originals Hakluyt found in 1583 in Paris, where he lived for five years.[135] Perhaps the most notable characteristic of Cartier narratives was their precise and effective descriptions of the physical world. It is easy to forget other more overtly ideological aspects.

Considering how important French Protestants were to the exploration of the New World and that Cartier had to work with Roberval, a Huguenot, on his third voyage, his orthodox Catholic and anti-Protestant stance, or that of the person chosen to represent the second voyage to the king, comes as a surprise. The spreading of the Catholic faith was a prime rhetorical concern in the narrative of the second voyage. Cartier spoke of "wicked Lutherans" as clouding the shining light of their very holy faith and of the Christian princes, as pillars of the Catholic Church, as enforcing the increase "just as the Catholic King of

Spain has lands that, by his commandment, were discovered to the west of his countries and kingdoms, which, beforehand, were unknown to us, strange and outside our faith, like New Spain, Isabella, Mainland, and other islands, where there are found innumerable people who were baptized and reduced to our very holy faith."[136] The example of Spanish Catholic evangelization was held up to the French king even as he was attempting to circumvent Spain. Although Cartier's expedition was looking for gold, diamonds, and other riches and had set out to take possession of Canada for France, the crusade of conversion was held out as the motivating force for French colonization. That goal of evangelization did not prevent Cartier in 1541 and Roberval in 1542–43 from going on expeditions to find the precious metals of the kingdom of the Saguenay.[137]

The theme of failure haunted French colonization in the New World as it did that of their English counterparts. Although between 1555 and 1565 the French colony in Brazil under Villegagnon and then the one in Florida under Jean Ribault and René de Laudonnière during the 1560s failed, according to Frank Lestringant, they fascinated the French more than did Cartier's voyages because the tropics caught the imagination of France whereas the cold winters of Canada did not.[138] The riches Spain had discovered in the New World also remained as an example for the French.

VIII

During the 1530s and 1540s, the English did little to maintain their claim to North America, which seemed to becoming a French sphere of influence. The English also left fewer textual traces of their early exploration than did the French. Even though under Henry VII the Bristol merchants had explored America, no exploration literature appeared during his reign. Henry VIII took an interest in trade and navigation, but he did not, as François I did, make a concerted effort to explore or settle the New World. London participated in the Iberian trade through Antwerp, and Henry became preoccupied with the Reformation and his conflicts with the pope and Continental monarchs. In 1533 the only book published about European discoveries in the last two decades of Henry VIII's reign appeared. William Rastell, son of John, the author of *Interlude of the Four Elements,* printed *The Legacy or Embassate of Prester John unto Emanuell, Kynge of Portyngale,* the only translation from Portuguese travel narratives to the middle of the century.[139] John More, the son of Thomas, was the translator, and the book may have had something to do with the interest in the "Prester John" embassies from Ethiopia to Portugal in 1513 and 1531.[140] The More-Rastell circle seem to have oscillated between utopian ideals and practical exploration. During the 1540s, the English voyages to Brazil, which William Hawkins probably began in the 1520s through his contacts in La Rochelle and Rouen, appear to have been discontinued because large vessels were needed in the war with France.[141] Roger Barlow, a Bristol merchant who had been a resident in Seville and had known Robert Thorne there, had gone on a voyage on a Spanish ship en route to the East Indies in 1526 but had reached South America only.[142] With Thorne, he had hoped to present a plan to

Henry VIII to send an expedition through a northeast passage to the East Indies, but Thorne died in 1532.[143] Failure was long part of early English colonization in the New World as it was for the French. The Europeans relied on Natives and were not able to assert assimilationist policies in the early years.[144] This presentation was delayed until 1540, when Barlow accompanied his proposal with a manuscript translation of Martin Fernández de Enciso's *Suma de geographia,* in which Barlow interpolated his own experience, especially his voyage to South America. Henry, however, did not answer Barlow's wish to give authority so the manuscript could be printed.[145] Although the Spanish ambassador wrote from England in May 1541 saying that an expedition for a northwest passage was about to set off, no record for such a voyage is extant. From 1535 to 1547, no travel literature appeared in England.[146] Concerning the exploration of the New World, France had left England behind for the time being.[147]

Despite the English discovery of Newfoundland, Spain and Portugal agreed that it was in the Portuguese sphere, and they fought with the French in the fisheries there. Cartier himself seems to have been involved in the Portuguese trade as he acted as an interpreter in 1543–44. Cartier's voyages were punctuated with wars between Spain and France. Spain's conquests of Mexico and Peru appear to have motivated François I, whose ambitions for riches and conquest in the New World caused strains with Spain. In 1536, François I and Charles V were at war, a month before Cartier returned home from his first voyage. On June 18, 1538, Paul III had the two rival rulers agree to a ten-year peace. Still, the kingdom of the Saguenay, promising riches like Mexico and Peru, haunted the French king, who employed a Portuguese pilot and Cartier in the quest for this realm. According to Charles in 1540, François broke the conditions of the truce the pope had brokered. In July 1542, Spain and France were at war and on September 18, 1544 the two rulers made peace. The kingdom of Saguenay receded from the mind of the French king, who, unlike Henry VIII, had made a concerted effort in exploration and colonization. From 1542 to 1547, when François and Henry both died, France took much less interest in the New World.[148] For the next 20 years, however, the French were more involved in the Americas than were the English, who began to look to the French model of circumventing Spain and to French Protestant martyrs in the New World as weapons against the great Spanish empire.

Another change, then, which by the 1520s could not be ignored as a temporary heresy, was Martin Luther's challenge to Rome. The princes of Europe had a new dimension to consider in the expansion to the New World—religious division. The relations between England and Spain that broke down with Henry's first "divorce," are well known and serve as a reminder why Spain might feel some hostility for England. England and Spain were close in the early decades of the sixteenth century. Henry VIII wanted a male heir and to maintain the Spanish alliance and dowry, which Henry VII had forged. In 1527, Henry VIII applied to Pope Clement VII for a dispensation to dissolve the marriage to Catherine of Aragon. The pope was mindful of the power of Emperor Charles V (Charles I of Spain), Catherine's uncle, and, subject to the emperor's control, delayed his response. Beginning in the 1520s and 1530s, the spread of

Protestantism complicated the English and French uses of the example of Spain with religious division, difference, and rivalry.

The race for possession of the New World in the last decade of the fifteenth century and the first decade of the sixteenth involved political and economic contention, but increasingly, religious competition and strife helped to define, though never exclusively, the attitude toward Spain in Western Europe. French and English Calvinists were instrumental in exploring and settling the New World.[149] Catholic and Protestant majorities and minorities in various countries tempered the view of Spain. The interest of each country or dynasty balanced religious positions for and against the Spanish holy war contra Protestants. Both Protestants and Catholics could be intolerant of, and violent against, the other faith. Just as the papal bulls and their reception were political in the fifteenth century, the Reformation and Counter-Reformation did not separate religion and politics. The politics of the exploration and the settlement of the New World were also expressions of the political ambiance in Europe. Those politics were treacherous and unstable and involved atrocities on both sides.

During the sixteenth century, Protestantism was becoming dominant in England, Germany, and the northern Netherlands and was strong in France. Spain, the champion of Catholicism, now faced a war of propaganda based on religious division. Evidence of this division can also be found in subsequent chapters of my study. The French came to ban Protestants from New France a few years after its inception and the founders of Virginia, Plymouth, and the Massachusetts Bay colonies (and even some in Catholic Maryland) argued against Catholics in English America. The dissension in Maryland is one of the strands in chapter 6. One of the periods of anti-Spanish and anti-Catholic sentiment in sixteenth-century England was the time of the Armada.[150] For instance, in writing to Elizabeth I, Lord Grey justified the massacre of the garrison at Smerwick after their surrender by saying they were brigands, as opposed to soldiers, who were invading a foreign country under the authority of the pope, "a detestable shaveling, the right Antichriste and general ambitious tyrant over all right principalities," and not a recognized Prince like Philip II.[151] This kind of rationalization to enact violence against enemies because of religious difference is something we shall observe in the Spanish massacre of the Huguenots in Florida under the pretext that they were heretics who were not conducting the official business of the king of France. Protestants and Catholics used this kind of diplomatic duplicity to enact atrocities.

In English and French, Protestant propaganda against Catholicism began to gather strength from the 1530s onward but it was not really until the 1560s that religious strife spread to the New World. The creation of the Anglican church in 1533; the founding of the Society of Jesus by the Spaniard, Ignatius Loyola, in 1534 (taking its name in 1537); the publication of Calvin's *Institutes* in 1535; the Council of Trent (1545–63), first session to reform the clergy (1545–47), second session on the sacraments and Eucharist (1551–52), and the third session on pontifical supremacy (1562–63); and the first national synod of French Protestants in Paris in 1559 all demonstrated the increasing differences between Christians in this period, something that spilled over into the New World. The

Black Legend began to take shape in a new spiritual race for the New World, Spain championing the spirit of the papal bull of 1493 and England opposing it. In terms of religion, France in the sixteenth century was caught between Protestant and Catholic. But for England and France, part of the ambiguity was that France was not securely Catholic until 1685 and England firmly Protestant until 1688. Mary Tudor of England and Henri IV of France were just two examples of the swings in religion. Ambivalence and instability in religion in this period caution against our assuming a narrative that focuses solely on religious opposition to Spain in northern Europe.

The geography of the soul was, like Europe exploring the New World, sundered between nation and Christendom. For the first time, religious difference among Christians now divided European nations against themselves. The empires, full of uncertainty and strife, were not ready to give a consensual civilization to the Natives. Although Europeans—Spanish, French, English—all shared a common heritage and continued to recognize this history, they now came to fight each other as infidels within the faith. The critique of Spain became more fierce and virulent in proportion to its power, the dreaded universal monarchy, and, among Protestants, its insistence on the church of Rome as the only true religion. Yet, during the 1550s, some, like Richard Eden, could celebrate the marriage of Philip and Mary Tudor, both Catholics, as a union between Spain and England that might present great imperial prospects. These events and the intensification of anti-Spanish sentiment in France, England, and elsewhere in Western Europe complicated further the example of Spain. By the 1560s the conflicts in Europe began to intensify in the Americas with dire results.

CHAPTER 3

Uncertainty and Strife, 1548–1566

With the deaths of Henry VIII and François I in 1547, England and France faced with uncertainty the greatness of Spanish power. Spain was indisputably the world power, its empire in the New World being unrivaled, and the riches from those colonies, especially silver, were transforming the Western European economy. In Charles V's instructions to his heir in 1548, the emperor recommended that in regard to the Indies Philip keep his eye on the French to ensure that they not send a fleet there, but added that in their previous attempts, the French had not proved tenacious, so that if the Spanish provided strong opposition, France would yield and withdraw.[1] By the time Philip II ascended the Spanish throne in 1556, the revenues from silver were reaching levels that France and England could only envy and could not ignore. Nonetheless, even at such a crucial time, it is too simple to think of England and France as unreserved enemies of Spain. Neither Henry nor François, each ruling for over 30 years, would shy away from working with Spain when he thought he needed to do so. For a time, Henry VIII had been the son-in-law of Ferdinand of Aragon, who also served as the regent in Castile and who had the English king support him against France with the result that Spain alone gained from the war. In 1554 Henry's daughter, Mary Tudor, was married to Philip of Spain, and remained so until her death in 1558.

Even France and Spain, rival superpowers of the sixteenth century, could reconcile amid their many wars with each other. The French attacks on Spanish treasure ships and colonies in the West Indies and Jacques Cartier's third voyage in 1541 disturbed Spain, and in the year after the peace of 1544, in compliance with the emperor's demand, François I forbade his subjects to go to the Spanish overseas possessions.[2] The French king may have been disappointed in Cartier's failure to find gold and diamonds in New France.[3] The rivalry with Spain involved doublethink on both sides. England and France wanted a share in the rich Spanish trade, whether lawfully or unlawfully, but sometimes settled, on paper at least, on giving up that trade. Spain thought that if it did not acknowledge the existence of the English and French in the New World, they would not have a right to be where they were. The legal fictions masked French, and later English, piracy and the inability of Spain and Portugal to keep English, French, and Dutch interlopers out of the western Atlantic. Such diplomatic ambivalence continued in the generation after Henry and François.

In examining French and English exploration of and designs on the New World and writing about it, I will more specifically discuss Richard Eden and his use of translation to advocate English colonization and then the imperial union of Spain and England and analyze eyewitness accounts of the conflict between the French and Spanish in Florida—Thomas Hacket's translation of Jean Ribault (the original was lost) and Nicolas Le Challeux's narrative.[4] These are key texts with apparently different aims: Eden's work appears to be that of a champion of the potential alliance of England with Spain, whereas the Ribault and Le Challeux texts are French Protestant works that help to produce, in France and England, the Black Legend of Spain. The analysis of these important texts will demonstrate a shift in the representation of Spain in the 1560s, when the French and then the English, mainly because of the events in Florida and in the Netherlands, began to develop an intricate anti-Spanish rhetoric. The complaints against Spain heard before paled beside this propaganda that arose in the French and English languages from London through Amsterdam and Paris to Geneva.

I

Although the French were more active in the New World than were the English, England drew closer to Spain in the 1550s in a way that might have changed the course of European history and the relations between the two countries. After a brief discussion of a couple of instances of French texts in this decade, I will focus on a text that concerns the marriage of Philip and Mary, a turning point in the example of Spain. After the death of Mary, a Catholic, which dissolved this fragile but potentially strong political alliance, Elizabeth I came to power, and the fortunes of Protestants in England improved steadily. In the 1580s and beyond, some English advisors, like Richard Hakluyt the Younger, were close to the French Protestants, whose destruction in Florida and whose experiences in the civil wars in France left English Protestants to take up colonization. Those Protestants who could most oppose or encroach on the great power of Catholic Spain in the colonization of the New World were now English.

Nonetheless, from the 1530s to the 1570s, the French had the upper hand over the English in the exploration of North America. French pirates terrorized Spanish America and disrupted the trade between the colonies and Spain well before Drake and the other Elizabethan seadogs harassed the great power. During the sixteenth century everyone but the French fishermen avoided sailing the North Atlantic in winter.[5] Through hunting, the Basque fishermen from northern Spain and southwestern France developed an interest in the fur trade. They blurred the boundaries between the rival states of Spain and France. The

Basques qualify my generalization about French dominance of the western North Atlantic in the sixteenth century.[6] The Bretons and Normans primarily were developing a fur trade along the Saint Lawrence River and had established a post at Tadoussac.

Although developing close connections with the Americas, the French court was sometimes preoccupied with other types of new worlds. Despite its title, Guillaume Postel's *Les Tres-merveilleuses victoires des femmes du Nouveau Monde, et comment elles doibvent à tout le monde par raison commander, & même à ceulx qui auront la Monarchie du Monde vieil. . .* (1553), dedicated to Marguerite de France, began by begging the question of the topic it advertised and by contributing to "la querelle des femmes." America continued the myth of the Amazons, which was a central trope in the early modern battle of the sexes. The book's second part, *La Doctrine du siecle doré, ou de l'evangelike regne de Jesus Roy des Roys,* was a typological, prophetic, and apocalyptic look at history, including an allegory of the sexes. The New World was a state of the soul in the redemption of Christ, the true king, as opposed to the false tyrants. In *Les Tres-merveilleuses victoires des femmes du Nouveau Monde,* Postel presented a different use of Amazons and the feminine from that in Columbus's account of the New World. The relation between gender and empire, of America as a woman, is something that has received increasing attention.[7] The imitation of various precedents from Spanish texts about the New World and the role of religion in the rivalry between Spain and other European nations is intricate. As we shall soon observe, the case of Sebastian Cabot, who worked for England then Spain then England, and his meeting with André Thevet, the French cosmographer, complicates the easy division of the world into Catholic and Protestant, or French and English, in the relations with Spain.

Not until about 1580s, when Drake, Walsingham, Ralegh, Hakluyt, and others made a concerted intellectual and material effort, did the English become serious contenders with the French for the lands north of the Spanish colonies. Even though the English and the French continued to seek the riches of the New World and rivaled Spain and Portugal in searching for a northwest passage, they began, from the deaths of Henry VIII and François I to the Spanish Armada, to intensify their attacks on Spain. The rise of Protestantism and the jealousy over the riches and political power of Catholic Spain were largely responsible for this onslaught from Germany, the Netherlands, France, and England. If the beginnings of the Black Legend were in the anti-Spanish feeling in Italy of the 1490s to 1530s and in Reformation Germany from 1517 onward, the climax primarily occurred as the result of the following factors: the rapid increase in Spain's economic and political power, Spanish insistence on its "shared monopoly" with Portugal in colonizing lands unknown to Europeans, the Inquisition, the massacre of the Huguenots in Florida, the war in the Netherlands, and the Spanish Armada.

Here, I will call attention, especially to those beyond the French-speaking world, to other significant sources of the Black Legend of Spain, especially to Ribault and Le Challeux. The well-known texts of the Black Legend should not, however, be neglected because this study will place them in some contexts that are suggestive and less familiar. One of the chief means in spreading this anti-Spanish sentiment among other nations was the use against Spain of the oeuvre of Las Casas, a critic of Spanish colonization but a supporter of the Spanish emperor and empire, a devout Spaniard who would never have approved of the end to which these heretics put his work. The very ability the Spanish had in criticizing themselves became a weapon of intolerance and a tool against an increasingly intolerant Spain.[8] The French and English use of Spain's self-criticism through vernacular translations, particularly that of Las Casas, is something I will explore in subsequent chapters because Las Casas was used as a weapon against Spain in France beginning in 1579 and in England in 1583 and continuing well beyond 1713. In fact, Las Casas appeared in English-speaking countries as a weapon of propaganda late in the day. For instance, his account of the destruction of the Indies was printed four times in the period of the Spanish-American War of 1898.[9] Although ambivalence continued in the relation of France and England to Spain, as religion could never drive away economic desire and greed, the period of Elizabeth's reign, 1558 to 1603, coincided with the greatest depth of anti-Spanish feeling in England and France. This feeling never quite disappeared and became an archive in later conflicts with Spain. Throughout, the French and English desire to have the wealth of Spain conflicted with religious ideals in their attempts to colonize the New World.

The English began to renew their interest in the New World about the time Sebastian Cabot returned to England from Spain in 1547. For the next six years, Cabot tried to win support for several projects: the search for a northwest or northeast or polar passage, an expedition to Peru and a commercial enterprise to Guinea. In about 1550–51, André Thevet reported that he met Cabot, who was then trying to coordinate French and English exploration and settlement in the New World. Thevet claimed to have met Cabot at Cartier's house in St. Malo and to have heard him speak about the coast of North America from Canada to Florida and about his plans to create a New England in Peru.[10] This coordination of French and English efforts in the New World, even if only a wish or an observation in the controversial Thevet's text, suggests, like the alliance of Mary and Philip, only less actual, potential ways colonization could have gone. These potentialities cut across national, religious, and linguistic lines. In the example of Spain, despite these roads not taken, we shall come across important instances that complicate the expected.

Even though England had not developed an advantage in the generations after John Cabot landed in the northeastern coast of North America, it did, as we have seen and will see, make some efforts in exploration. Even under the minority rule of Edward VI, the English had some plans for exploring the New World. From London, Jehan Sheyfue wrote to the Queen Dowager in Vienna on June 24, 1550 about the rumors circulating for six months that England was outfitting two ships to travel to the East or to take some action against the Scots or French or to find gold in an island to the north and that to this end, they still held Cabot and until recently had detained Jean Ribault, a young Frenchman in the king of England's service and a good navigator and an expert pilot.[11] Early the next year Sheyfue reported from London that Ribault was confined to the Tower and, with Cabot, had a commission to discover some islands or find an Arctic polar route to the Indies.[12] In the year of Edward's death and the crowning of Mary, Sheyfue continued to report on English vessels for voyages, in March on a voyage toward Iceland led by Villevi (Willoughby), in April on how Sebastian Cabot told him more about the voyage, and in May about a northeast or a northwest route to the East for the voyage and the various debates on whether such a path was practicable.[13] The report of April 10 was illuminating as Cabot had been in the service of the English crown, then the Spanish, and again the English. He appeared to be letting Charles V know about English plans, but in the same dispatch, he responded to the remark that the English destination of Chamchina comprised part of the emperor's conquest by saying that such a view interested the king of Portugal and the emperor only where others would likely claim that the land belonged to the first to occupy it.

Three years before Charles V gave Spain to his son, Philip, he was obviously interested in English designs on the New World and the transition between Edward and Mary, which would involve negotiations over a dynastic marriage between Mary and Philip.[14] Besides Sheyfue, three other ambassadors also served Charles in London: the four, whose names were evidence of the polyglot nature of the Habsburg empire, sent a joint dispatch about Sebastian Cabot's popularity with the people of London, who believed him to be steeped in the secrets of English navigation.[15] The roles of Spain, England, and France in the exploration and settlement of the New World were bound up here, both at the level of personnel on the voyages and of dynastic rivalries and marriages. Even in their moments of greatest political, economic, and religious contention, the royal houses never closed their doors to one another. Each was a great prize to be eyed and envied and, if possible, taken. The kings did not write the pamphlets and histories that made up so much of the historiography of expansion to the New World. That is one reason for balancing the treaties and diplomatic dispatches, whenever possible, with the court and popular discourse of the time. Power and wealth provided antidotes to anti-Spanish ideology for the kings and queens of England and France.

The English continued to be slow to develop their interests in America. Few English books focused on that topic. During the reign of Edward VI (1547–53), Ralph Robinson's English translation of More's *Utopia* (1551) and Anthony Ascham's *A Lytel Treatyse of Astronomy* (1552), which spoke of giants and cannibals in the New World, appeared.[16] A crisis in the English succession brought a new shift in the relations among England, France, and Spain. The English would soon have to think of their interest in the New World in conjunction with that of Spain.

After the death of Edward in July 1553 and the failed attempt of Northumberland, the lord protector, to make Lady Jane Grey queen, Mary fulfilled her father's will and an act of parliament and succeeded her dead brother. She annulled her mother's divorce and established her own legitimacy. The Valois and Habsburg tried to influence Mary in her decision to marry; Mary's first parliament counseled her against marriage to Prince Philip of Spain; the French backed Edward Courtenay, earl of Devon, but to no avail. France did not want the Habsburg lands to surround it completely: Spain, Italy, Germany, the Netherlands, and now England. The ascension of Mary and the marriage proposals to her reveal another dimension of the relations among Spain, England, and France. Those who would argue too unambiguously for the Black Legend of Spain would occlude the other strands in the positive alliances, and rivalries among these three nations. It is part of these ambivalent relations that allies can also be rivals: contradictions are not necessarily counterlogical. In this case being a rival that would be an ally or an ally with tendencies toward rivalry makes sense in these complex connections among the three countries. Xenophobia against the French, opponents in war, and the Italians, Germans, and Netherlanders, as rivals in business had occurred in England during Henry VIII's reign. Anti-Spanish sentiment, though present, was not as strong as other English alienations.[17]

The Tudors and Habsburgs had long been allies, and the key to their alliance was the common economic interests of England and of Burgundy and Spain in the Netherlands. With the proposed marriage of Philip and Mary, the Tudors and Habsburgs were attempting to shore up an old alliance, which was experiencing stress with the collapse of the Antwerp market in 1553 and the growth of the Spanish and Portuguese monopoly in the New World. England was seeking new markets and looked on the monopoly in the Americas as something it had to challenge. Charles V had given Philip experience in the Netherlands, and it was to advance the security of the Netherlands, and not Spain, that led the emperor to propose this so-called Spanish marriage. The marriage would be popular with the Burgundian and Flemish nobles and would safeguard trading routes in the seas between Spain and the Netherlands and would check French interests in England and the Low Countries. The Spanish treasury, which helped to fund Charles's campaigns in the Netherlands, was almost exhausted and he sought a dynastic marriage first with the affluent royal house of Portugal by exploring a marriage of Philip to the Infanta Maria and then, when it seemed that John III was slow in deciding on the dowry, with Mary, a relative.

After Edward VI's death, Charles shifted his dynastic sights on the new English queen. Charles also feared that besides the French influence at Mary's court, his own brother intended to send envoys to discuss a possible marriage between the Archduke Ferdinand and Mary. Antoine de Noailles, the French ambassador, attempted to stir up xenophobic sentiment in England in order to promote Courtenay, the English suitor the French supported. Court, parliament, and commons expressed fears about "Spaniards" taking their coveted patronage appointments and "invading" their kingdom. The French and Venetian ambassadors, Flemish merchants, and Spanish exiles spread rumors about the foul and cruel behavior of Spanish lords and soldiers.[18] In her diplomatic history, which recognizes the shortcomings of ambassadorial dispatches when it comes to discerning cause and motivation, Joan Marie Thomas attempts to analyze the negotiations leading up to the marriage of Philip and Mary and their reign rather than follow earlier historiography, especially from 1688 onward, too much of which cites the Spanish marriage as evidence of engrained English dislike and distrust of Spain.[19]

Even if England and Spain were drawing closer together, much to the dismay of the French court, the relations between these two countries were uneasy. This was to be an alliance that was and was not. Simon Renard, who replaced Sheyfue as resident ambassador in England in September 1553, asked Charles to protect Philip in the middle of this barbarous and inconstant nation.[20] The French propaganda against the match seemed to be in concert with the feelings of a significant part of England, and Renard blamed it for stirring up anti-Spanish attitudes, even as France was losing the struggle to prevent the match with Philip. Much of the fear in England was over the possibility of having any foreign prince as king, which would threaten the integrity and independence of England, and this fear of foreign power explained in part some of the sentiment against Philip. The Flemish council of state and the privy council of England negotiated the marriage contract. To speak about Spain without the European empire of the Habsburgs, as we shall see repeatedly throughout this study, would be to simplify the context. In the example of Spain, the Netherlands played a central role.

In drafting the treaty, Charles V tried to take into account the objections of the English, his Flemings, and Philip's Spaniards and used as models the marriage of Charles the Bold and Margaret Plantagenet in 1467 and the treaties of mutual defense between the Netherlands and England in 1542 and 1546. Charles explained the treaty to the estates of the Netherlands before sending it to London. Philip was in his father's hands, and the marriage treaty was unpopular at the court in Valladolid, especially the assignment of the Low Countries to the first-born of Philip and Mary, which would disinherit Philip's son, Don Carlos, the Spanish heir. Philip was displeased with the provisions that required him to keep England out of his war with France and to honor the treaty of friendship between France and England. Philip was not allowed to make appointments in church and state. If Mary died childless, then Philip would no longer be king of England. If they had an heir, the child would inherit Philip's title in the Netherlands and Burgundy and Mary's in England. Although Philip swore publicly to uphold the articles of the treaty, he did not consider himself or his successors bound to them because he had not negotiated the marriage himself. A month after the failure of Sir Thomas Wyatt's rebellion against the queen and the proposed marriage, Mary was wedded to Philip by proxy. In July 1554 they were married in person in Winchester Cathedral.[21] During the reign of Mary, English interest in Spain and the New World increased and, with Richard Eden, reached a critical mass that in retrospect can be seen to have allowed for serious plans for permanent colonies in America.[22]

II

Richard Eden's work, which is indicative of the complexity of the English response to the alliance with Spain and plans for exploration, came out at a time when England was showing a revived concern with voyages, trade and the New World. Despite the disturbance and unsureness of the reigns of Edward VI and Mary Tudor, the English, who lagged behind the Spanish, Portuguese, and

French in voyages, took a renewed interest in expansion, though much of this voyaging derived from the necessity of finding new trading partners. Between 1546 and 1552 trade with Barbary seemed to have been established. In 1553 Hugh Willoughby led an expedition in search of a northeast passage to Asia and discovered access to Russia by sea; Thomas Wyndham sailed to Guinea on a trading mission; Richard Eden brought out *A Treatyse of the newe India,* his translation of a section of the fifth book of Sebastian Münster's cosmography.

In the dedication to this last work to John Dudley, earl of Warwick and duke of Northumberland, Eden invoked Alexander the Great and celebrated writing as much as "marcial affayres," Homer as much as the Achilles he represented, in the honoring of the fame of valor and courage.[23] Here, he also expressed his dismay at the chasm between English knowledge of the New World and that of other Europeans, most notably the Spanish. In Eden's account the English had produced one imperfect and erroneous work on the Americas (and here he was probably referring to the slight work, *Of the newe landes,* which Jan van Doesborch printed in Antwerp in 1511), something that could not compare favorably to Peter Martyr's *Decades.* The gap between what the title of the book on the New World in English promised and what it delivered was like a man professing to write of England and treating "onelye of Trumpington a vyllage wythin a myle of Cambrydge."[24] Eden outlined his motives for translating Münster as wishing to encourage more English voyages through a better knowledge of cosmography and to celebrate the recent expeditions that England had recently undertaken and to help those who would take further voyages to the New World. To those who would go on such a journey, his book would be a small glass in which to see some light.[25] The Spanish and Portuguese had proved with their circumnavigations that the earth was round. As polite as Eden was about the errors of inherited opinions from great books, he saw the experience of Portugal and Spain in their voyages as improving knowledge. After many biblical allusions to bolster his view that God gives knowledge and that experience is the greatest teacher, Eden quoted Saint. Paul, "That GOD made of one bloudde, all nacions of menne, to dwell vpon the hole face of the earth."[26] Eden said he had intended to talk about strange things and monsters, which appeared in the book, but time had hindered him from giving sensible reasons, so that he left off with the view that whatever God pleases to do in heaven and earth is done.[27] Besides using the Bible to support the importance of experience, Eden implied that through imitation the English could take up their place beside the Spanish and Portuguese in their passage to Asia.

Northumberland, one of the people to whom Eden had dedicated this earlier work, supported Lady Jane Grey, so that once Mary had overcome the challenge to her succession, Eden had to motivate his rhetoric in a new direction: the new queen. The title of the next work that Eden translated showed that the ascent of Mary months after his last work appeared had shifted the implicit call to compete with the Spanish to a vision of a joint imperial destiny brought about by the marriage of Philip and Mary:

The Decades of the newe worlde of west India, Conteynyng the nauigations and conquestes of the Spanyardes, with the particular descripcion of the moste ryche and

large landes and Ilandes lately founde in the west Ocean perteynyng to the inher-
itaunce of the kinges of Spayne. In the which the diligent reader may not only con-
syder what commoditie may hereby chaunce to the hole christian world in tyme to
come, but also learne many secreates touchynge the lande, the sea, and the starres,
very necessarie to be knowen to al such as shal attempte any nauigations, or other-
wise haue delite to beholde the strange and woonderfull woorkes of God and nature.
Wrytten in the Latine tounge by Peter Martyr of Angleria, and translated into
Englysshe by Richarde Eden.[28]

The titular announcement emphasized Spain as an example and a champion of a united Christendom and did so in English. According to "The Epistle," Philip wooed Mary in English.[29] Perhaps out of respect for Philip's English or as an allusion to Latin as the language of humanism and of Catholicism, Eden used Latin to preface his English translation.[30] He addressed the monarchs, joining their titles in one imperial theme: "Most Potent and Serene Philip, and most Serene and Potent Mary, by the grace of God King and Queen of England, France, Naples, Jerusalem and Ireland: Defenders of the Faith, Princes of Spain and Sicily, Archduke of Austria . . . Richard Eden wishes you perpetual happiness."[31] This honorific address or salutation on the first page used the typography of an inverted pyramid or triangle, which had the unfortunate effect of literally enlarging Philip and diminishing Mary, although Eden listed Mary's possessions first and wished for their perpetual happiness. He then welcomed the royal couple to London, making their entry an imperial triumph applauded by the English.[32] Eden said he was in the crowd on August 18, 1554 to watch the procession of Philip and Mary and was so excited that he wanted to give an extemporaneous oration. Only the presence of the royal couple restrained him from doing so: his thoughts then turned to writing. As he doubted his own creative powers, he decided on translations that would celebrate the glory of Philip's ancestors in the New World, which in turn would glorify Philip.

"The Epistle" created a theatrical scene in which the humble Eden represented the glory of this royal couple in procession in a street pageant, as in a theater of the world, a perpetual spectacle, something of eternal memory, like the great mythological feats the author represented and the glory of the spread of Christianity in the West Indies.[33] In contemplating such events of fame and splendor, Eden remembered that in his youth he had read Peter Martyr's *Decades . . .* , which was dedicated to the illustrious Ferdinand, Philip's grandfather. Eden who had left Mary out of his triumphant tableau for the moment, praised Martyr as a historian and natural philosopher who investigated the works of nature, "of which your India is full," making no mistake as to who was in possession of the New World.[34] In order to tell of the treasure of gold, gems, spices, and merchandise in the West Indies and how much was taken to Spain annually, Eden said he had added Oviedo's *Summario de la natural y general historia de las Indias* (1526), which was dedicated to Philip's father, Charles V. To complete his genealogical movement of history as memory, Eden mentioned the recent works he had included. The past moved the present; all Spanish glory led to Philip; this would be an empire for all the Christian world. In this translation of empire Eden cited what Seneca said to Nero: that virtue not exercised merits small praise.[35] In his courtly Latin, Eden expected great deeds from a crown under which Spain and England were united: he also wished that their glory would be remembered perpetually, which would soon lead him to Cicero, but for now brought him to invoke God.[36] It becomes increasingly apparent, however, that this rhetoric of praise is part of a more complex framework of language than it first seems.

"The preface to the reader" reveals the ambivalence and contradictions in Eden's representation of a united Spain and England. Whereas in 1553 Eden appealed to Aristotle as an authority for the view that sense is the basis of experience, which is the ground of knowledge insofar as it confirms speculation and reason, he now turned to Cicero as the source of the idea that men excel beasts, who are ruled by sense alone. Cicero provided Eden with an example of the historical and trans-temporal, the human quest for the memory of immortality and renown, of nurturing knowledge through eye and ear "such thinges as are commendable in theyr predicessours."[37] Memory implied a moral judgment. Eden invoked Cicero's idea of the historian as the light of truth and the life of memory.[38] Not veering too far from Cicero, Eden saw the subject of history as representing "eyther the famous factes of woorthy men, or ingenious inuentions of experte artificers."[39] It is possible that Virgil's Fama in book four of the *Aeneid* was in the background here and related to the debate over the separation of manly deeds and effeminate words, something that informed Eden's prefatory matter and was an anxiety expressed in Shakespeare and other Renaissance writers.[40] The "most permanent and trewe glory," Eden suggested through his act of writing, was in the written record.[41] The notion of "glory" was akin to the French emphasis on "gloire" that, in chapter 5, we will encounter in Marc Lescarbot's work. Books were part of the memory of the translation of empire and the glory of civilization. This true glory, which differed from the inertness of fame, enhanced life and did not consist of lifeless heaps of stones like pyramids. The building of ships, bridges, buildings, and towns constituted a constructive magnificence that benefited all people. There was, then, a moral duty to the *civitas,* which Eden never mentioned explicitly but instead set up in an implicit contrast with "the fonde and barbarous ostentation of superfluous riches."[42] Once again, Eden called on Cicero, saying that deeds involving riches and craftsmanship were glorious if they benefited one's country or citizens or all humankind. Notions of civility in opposition to barbarism were never far from the surface in discussions of the New World.

The example of Spain as the translator and upholder of historical destiny, civility, and empire is something Eden pursued in a rhetoric that alluded to Virgil's seminal founder, Aeneas, with a Latin quotation. In this context Spain was part of a heroic history of memorable deeds. If the poets spoke of this instance of true glory as ambrosia and nectar and transformed men into immortal and happy souls—gods—then Eden thought he had licence to praise the kings of

Spain as heroes among men. If a man can be a god to men as the Scriptures make of Moses and others, then, Eden said,

> the kynges of Spayne of late dayes (if I may speake it without offence of other) may so much the more for theyr iust desertes and good fortune be compared to those goddes made of men (whom the antiquitie cauled Heroes and for theyr manyfolde benefites to man kynde honoured theym with diuine honoure) as theyr famous factes so farre excell al other, as I dare not speake to such as haue not yet harde or redde of the same, least the greatnesse therof shulde at the first brunte so much astonyshe the reader that he myghte geue the lesse credite to the autoure of this booke, who neuerthelesse hath moste faythfully wrytten this hystorye of suche thynges whereof he hath seene a greate parte him selfe (as being by the most holy catholyke and puissaunt kynge Ferdinando appoynted a commissionarie in thaffayres of India) and gathered the residewe partly by information and partly out of the wrytinges of such as haue byn (as Vyrgyll wryteth of Eneas, *Et quorum pars magna fui*) that is, doers and parte of such thynges as are conteyned in the hystorie.[43]

Despite Eden's apparently inadvertent slip from "glory" to "fame" in describing the accomplishment of the heroic Spanish kings, the translator continued his rhetorically deferent position toward Martyr, whom he lauds, magnifies, and supplements, thereby ignoring his own topos of inexpressibility. Eden followed Martyr in a tradition of Spanish historiography in which the historians also participated in history and, in doing so, followed the impeccable imperial precedent of Aeneas. These governors, admirals, pilots, and others, having subdued the lands and seas, wrote the truth in books that are monuments to their actions.

In the fashion of a Christian humanist, Eden joined scriptural and classical authority. Like English and French writers about the New World before and after him, Eden returned to papal authority on which Spain's claim to the New World rests. The role of the pope in the donation of territory is something that is repeated over and over in texts about the Americas, but there was sometimes a gap between discourse and what happened in the world. For instance, as much as the French had looked at the riches of Spain as an example to be emulated and envied, France made early inroads into the authority of Portugal and Spain in the New World. When François I died in 1547, his colonial policy of discovery, conquest, and settlement had influenced the European powers. I am not sure, however, that the papal bulls had been superseded as much as W. J. Eccles claims.[44] In other words, the legacy of these bulls was still influential in France and England with writers, like Eden, who concerned themselves with the New World, but these countries had disputed and would continue to challenge the grounds of papal authority in these matters. There were, however, variations on this theme: the bulls were important to Eden for a reason quite different from those of the other English writers about the New World before and after the reign of Mary I.

Eden still considered that the bulls were central to the forging of a mythology of union between Spain and England and in creating a joint imperial effort. In the papal bull of 1493, which Eden placed in Latin and then English at the end of the third decade or the end of his selection from Martyr, Alexander VI had at the opening provided the donation because of the work of conversion of the monarchs of Spain and had at the close praised empire as one of the good things emanating from God. Eden said "that the Catholyke fayth and Christian religion, specially in this owre tyme may in all places bee exalted, amplified, and enlarged, wherby the health of soules may be procured, and the Barbarous nations subdued and brought to the fayth. . . . In him from whom Empyres, dominions, and all good thynges doo procede: Trustynge that almyghtie god directynge yowre enterprises, yf yowe folowe yowre godly and laudable attemptes, yowre laboures and trauayles herein, shall in shorte tyme obteyne a happy ende with felicitie and glorie of all Christian people."[45] I have quoted from Eden's translation of the bull into English, which appears to be the first extant, because this would have been the first time that members of the English reading public would have been able to read this donation in their mother tongue. Eden called upon sacred and poetic sources to celebrate the heroic history of Spain in the Indies, so that classical and Christian Rome sanction the translation of empire to Philip. To emphasize the power and glory of Spain, Eden did not include in his book the papal donation to Portugal.[46] Like Alexander VI, Eden developed the theme of Spain as a propagator of the true faith.

In "The preface" Eden continued to focus on Spain and the West Indies, stressing the house of contracts in Seville that dealt with contractual arrangements for the New World, the council of the Indies, and the heroism of the Spaniards in the text and in marginal titles. Eden became a defender of the justice of the Spanish empire, a position opposite to that taken by proponents of the Black Legend, like Hakluyt in "Discourse" (1584), whose views took hold in the 1560s and never quite went away. The comparison to Hakluyt, whose work will receive close attention in the next chapter, is appropriate because Eden's was the great collection of travel narratives before *Diuers Voyages* (1582) and its successors, but even Hakluyt was more temperate in his published work than he was in "Discourse," his extended memorandum to Walsingham and Elizabeth I. Just as Las Casas would be used by propagators of the Black Legend to attack Spain from within, so too was Martyr called on as an Italian whose objectivity supported the Spanish as an exemplar of empire:

It is therefore apparent that the heroical factes of the Spaniardes of these days, deserue so greate prayse that thautour of this book (beinge no Spanyarde) doth woorthely extolle theyr doynge aboue the famous actes of Hercules and Saturnus and such other which for theyr glorious and vertuous enterpryses were accoumpted as goddes amonge men. And surely if great Alexander and the Romans which haue rather obteyned then deserued immortall fame among men for theyr bluddye victories onely for theyr owne glory and amplifyinge theyr empire obteyned by slawghter of innocentes and kepte by violence, haue byn magnified for theyr owne glory and amplifyinge theyr empire obteyned by slawghter of innocentes and kepte by violence, haue byn magnified for theyr doinges, howe much more then shal we thynke these men woorthy iust commendations which in theyr mercyfull warres ageynst these naked people haue so vsed them selues towarde them in exchaungynge of benefites for victorie, that greater commoditie hath therof ensewed to the vanquisshed then the victourers.[47]

Eden was employing a typology of empire. Even though a translation of empire occurred between the Greeks and Romans to the Christian empire of pope, Holy Roman emperor, and king of Spain, the new imperial order was not exactly the same as the old. Christ redeemed Adam just as the New Testament was the redemption of the Old. The Christian telos of the Spanish empire in the New World replaced with grace and salvation the violent ends of pagan empires. Thus, as the allusion to the slaughter of the innocents suggests, the justice of Christ superseded the tyranny of Herod: the imperium of Spain had a mission.

The Natives, who in the Black Legend would become the unwilling victims of demonic impostures of true Christians in the Spanish colonies, were represented here as fortunate to have the Spaniards redeem them. Eden said that they considered gold, pearls, and precious stones as superfluous and received in return unnamed commodities that he avowed they esteemed much more than what they yielded to the Spanish. Well-trained in rhetoric and debate, he raised objections only to answer them:

But sum wyll say, they possesse and inhabyte theyr regions and vse theym as bondemen and tributaries, where before they were free. They inhabite theyr regions indeede: yet so, that by theyr diligence and better manurynge the same, they maye nowe better susteyne both, then one before. Theyr bondage is suche as is much rather to be desired then theyr former libertie which was to the cruell Canibales rather a horrible licenciousnesse then a libertie, and to the innocent so terrible a bondage, that in the myddest of theyr ferefull idlenesse, they were euer in daunger to be a pray to those manhuntynge wooulues. But nowe thanked be God, by the manhodde and pollicie of the Spanyardes, this deuelysshe generation is so consumed, partely by the slaughter of suche as coulde by no meanes be brought to ciuilitie, and partly by reseruynge such as were ouercome in the warres, and conuertynge them to a better mynde.[48]

Having incorporated into the Spanish conquest of the New World the qualities of civility and *virtú,* Eden also followed Columbus in dividing the Natives into good Natives as those who help and acquiesce, and bad Natives, those who oppose them: the Spanish liberated the Natives through religion and civility. The "bad Natives" Columbus had represented as cannibals and Amazons. The distinction between liberty and licence, one that John Milton would later take up, is part of an imperial discourse in which the forces of empire liberate the indigenes from their primitiveness, barbarity, strife with treacherous neighbors, pagan beliefs, and laziness. Spain liberated these men who were said to be free.

The imperial discourse of France and England would replicate this language of liberty for their own ends well into the twentieth century. Sometimes they would cast the Spaniards as the treacherous party, the cannibals devouring the innocent Natives, but the paternalism, Christian and secular, differed little from Eden's rendition on behalf of Spain here.[49]

Eden's work looks back to earlier Spanish works and its "translation" was something Hakluyt the Younger and Samuel Purchas later assumed but only with more anti-Spanish elements. During the 1580s and 1590s, as we shall observe in the next two chapters, Hakluyt, Ralegh, and others would, however, tell their queen and their nation that the Natives waited for the English to liberate them from their Spanish oppressors. Behind many travel narratives in the English Renaissance, such as Hakluyt's "Prose Epic of the modern English nation" (including Purchas's continuation of it), which we shall discuss in chapter 5, lay a whole network of Spanish, French, and English sources about mediation and the relation between Europeans and Natives.[50] The various European representations of the Native did so in terms of the needs, wants, and requirements of those countries.

By the time Eden was writing this preface in English to celebrate Spain and Philip to England and Mary, the Spanish had already initiated this debate over the benefits and detriments of their American empire. Part of the example of Spain, as Eden's collection shows, even with its misleading title that overstresses the selection from Martyr, was an intellectual climate where debate over empire could occur. In this regard, Spain was reminiscent of Rome as it moved from republic to empire while it also looked ahead to similar controversies in France and England. These debates, as to be expected, were framed in European terms, although in certain cases some attention was given, and respect paid, to the otherness of the aboriginal peoples.

In his defense of Spain in the New World, Eden called upon biblical precedents. God commanded Moses in his wars to save neither man nor woman nor child and did not, Eden implies, bring any commodities to the lands he overcame and possessed. Echoing Isaiah, this prophet newly inspired with a name appropriate to the task praised the work of the Spanish in America in terms of the promised land and the triumph of Christ.

> But the Spaniardes as the mynisters of grace and libertie, browght vnto these newe gentyles the victorie of Chrystes death wherby they beinge subdued with the worldely sworde, are nowe made free from the bondage of Sathans tyrannie, by the myghty poure of this triumphante victourer, whom (as sayth the prophet) god hath ordeyned to be a lyght to the gentyles, to open the eyes of the blynde, and to delyuer the bounde owt of pryson and captiuitie.[51]

Eden was not certain what other men fantasized about this question, but he implied that a contrary view involved a slender capacity, an effeminate heart, and a bestial regard for one's own dunghill instead of a looking upward in contemplation of God's work and the spreading of the Christian faith across the world.

This enlargement of Christendom should cause rejoicing among the good and honest and add "to the confusion of the deuyll and the Turkysshe Antichryste."[52] Just as in his history Oviedo had written to the emperor saying that each true Spaniard should rejoice that his kings had brought a new part of the world into Christ's congregation, so too did Eden, likening himself to Oviedo, think that all true Christians should celebrate for the delivery of their own brethren from the serpent. In 1492, Columbus helped to defeat "the greate serpente of the sea Leviathan" who misted the eyes of men and kept them from these new lands; not until 1433 had the church any knowledge of Prester John, "the Christian Emperour of Ethiope."[53] Such wonderful things came to light after being hidden by "vnsearcheable providence," which Eden had been interpreting and continued to read, including the glorious reign of "the ryght noble, prudent, and Catholike kinge of Aragon Don Ferdinando grandfather to Themperours maiestie by his eldest dowghter, & to the queenes hyghnesse by his seconde dowghter the most vertuous lady queene Catherine her graces moother," which knew more famous deeds than those the Greeks and Romans had glorified.[54] Eden supplemented biblical authority and providential history with dynastic genealogy: Philip and Mary shared a glorious Spanish past. The allusion to Catherine of Aragon reminded English readers that this was not the first Spanish match.

The biblical patriarchs and prophets did not often measure up to the Spanish monarchs. Eden claimed that the favor of God was known through the benefits he gave to men and that he showed greater grace to Ferdinand than to Noah, for by and through this king of Spain "he saued not onely the bodies but also the soules of innumerable millions of men inhabytynge a great part of the worlde heretofore vnknowen and drown in the deluge of erroure."[55] Ferdinand also outdid Abraham and Israel by becoming, through the increase of Christians in these lands, the "Second Abraham" to the "Second Israel."[56] In this typological and allegorical reading of history through the Bible, Eden continued his hyperbolic hermeneutics, this time making Ferdinand's miraculous opening up of the Ocean Sea greater than the miracle of Moses parting the Red Sea. Spain had "planted a newe Israell" in this new land.[57] David and Solomon paled in comparison with Ferdinand (and Isabella seems to have been lost in Eden's manly historical cosmos). For all his wisdom and riches, Solomon never sailed the antipodes, and his empire was small and his gold meagre compared with the empire of Ferdinand in the West Indies. Jason and the Argonauts were no match for the king of Spain and his navigators. This Ferdinand drove from Spain the Moors, or Saracens, and Jews who threatened all the "Christian Empire."[58] Eden's Ferdinand was the champion of the Christian faith and a great leader who also took Naples back from the French, and he left a legacy to his successors, Charles V and Philip. As Eden's religious affiliation was something that apparently caused suspicion at court, this rhetoric of Christian solidarity, while seeking preferment, is not obviously a product of the Counter-Reformation.

This paean to Spain led to an apostrophe to England (as the title in the margin underscores): "Stoope Englande stoope, and learne to knowe thy lorde and master, as horses and other brute beastes are taught to doo."[59] In a series of questions, Eden depicted England as unthankful, a painted whore with Christ in her mouth and a devil in her heart, licentious and self-destructive, a serpent devouring her own mother, an outrageous creature fallen into infirmity and deformity. Eden asked England to look into a "pure glass" and see all the monstrous shapes and deformities "vnder the shape of man."[60] More monstrous than these monstrous births were the diverse interpretations men make of them. Eden exempted his own interpretation from these monstrosities as he glossed why people deform their minds with monstrous talk of rebellion, strife, malice, "and suche other deuilysshe imaginations." This apostrophe to England was a series of addresses: "O Englande whyle tyme is giuen thee, circumcise thy harte."[61] The French would also come to lament internal strife in the Wars of Religion over the following three decades. Marc Lescarbot would take a whole preface in his *Histoire de la Nouvelle France* (1609) to address France in a call for earthly and heavenly glory in colonization. Here, Eden asked England to recover her ancient beauty and, now that she had a king and queen who desire her, to remember her duty, for they would embrace her if she would draw near to them. Otherwise, if she were to remain stubborn, they would use a whip to demand her obedience. God had sent these peaceful princes to lead England from its Babylon, its captivity, and other biblical and mythological imbroglios Eden represented. He warned England of the fantasies that dance in the heads of people who are ignorant of what they talk about and the faults they find in others. In an abstract allegory and typology, Eden raised objections against phantom objections, never being precise in the criticism against Philip and Spain that he was addressing and implying that some of the causes of that anti-Hispanic sentiment were self-loathing and effeminacy.

Although Eden was advocating that England join with the glory and fame of Spain, he tried to provide a sense of his own balance. He gave some specific English grievances against Spain, even though he did so only to satirize them. He was attacking rumor. By listing these rumors he was expressing what should not be expressed, so that even as he refuted these rumors, he gave them some life. During the English Renaissance, Rumor was a figure closely allied with Fame, Supposition, and Report in pageants. Stephen Hawes, Raphael Holinshed, and Shakespeare all showed the monstrous tongues of these allegorical figures, who are often represented as a female or figure of ambiguous gender.[62] Eden imagined the seditious and iniquitous lies, ones akin to the staple impugnings that constitute the Black Legend, circulating in England: "Spayne is a beggerly countrey sayth one: Themperour is but poore sayth an other: He is deade sayth an other: The Indies haue rebelled sayth an other, and eyther there commeth no more golde from thense, or there is no more founde nowe."[63] The hopes and prejudices of England against Spain that Eden imagined in a kind of rhetoric of the putative prompted him to provide an answer.

In defense of Spain, Eden called on classical authorities like Pliny, who praised its civil government, and Diodorus Siculus, who told of the rich silver mines in Spain that supplied Greece, Asia and other places. Julius Solinus, Strabo, Stratius, and Claudius all praised Spain, and Eden dared to say that Spanish wool was barely inferior to that of England and that its apples were better than those in

England. The commodities of Spain, in classical sources and in Eden, resembled those in the New World so praised by Spanish writers and, later, by others from France and England.[64] Praising the example of Spain, Eden supposed, ran certain risks at home: "But if I shuld here particularly and at large declare howe Englande is in fewe yeares decayed and impouerysshed, and howe on the contrary parte Spayne is inryched, I shulde perhappes displease more in descrybyng the myserie of the one, then please other in expressynge the florysshynge state of the other, which by all reason is lyke dayly to increase."[65] Eden cited the auditor of the king of Spain's mint as a source for his information about the gold of the Indies and the silver of Peru, a great amount of which was brought to the Tower of London. He also surveyed the riches of the islands of the South Seas and the Moluccas. The Indies, which were still full of gold, had not rebelled successfully against Spanish rule, and the power of all rulers derived from God. As if having caught himself in a digression, Eden said that he would let Ferdinand be his captain and navigate back on course.[66]

One of the contradictions and ambivalences of Spain's lead in the New World was that it resulted in admiration and envy among its European rivals and led them to wish to emulate the Spanish when Spain did not want emulation because it did not desire to share its lands in the New World with any Christian power. In the last chapter, I provided examples of Spanish strategies against its rivals, especially surrounding the Cartier voyages, and later in this chapter I shall discuss the use of force against France in Florida. This Spanish propensity to exclusivity was still true when France and Spain were both under the Bourbons at the turn of the eighteenth century, and the Spanish did not want France in Louisiana. Eden made the trope of the example of Spain more explicit perhaps than any other person in England or France from Columbus's landfall to the Treaty of Utrecht: "The Spanyardes haue shewed a good exemple to all Chrystian nations to folowe."[67]

Like Hakluyt after him, Eden was interested in the land from Florida to Newfoundland (here called "Bacchalloas") as a land full of riches, with inhabitants ready for conversion, a place Sebastian Cabot had apparently visited. Eden also spoke of Nova Hispania and Mexico, reported that some writers connected this land with Asia, and lamented that many of its inhabitants were still "Idolatours." This pretext he used to reproach all Christendom, but particularly England, which was closer than Spain was to these lands to the northeast of Florida (only 25 days or fewer of sailing), so that his own nation had been remiss in helping the work of conversion of these people, which he made, as Columbus had made them, a *tabula rasa,* because they had not yet been exposed to false religion. Saint Paul would have gone to the New World to convert these people, so the English should follow this imagined example. Eden, playing on the themes of unity between Spain and England and the Spanish as an example to the English, did not consider the distinct possibility that the Spaniards thought the English heretics and did not want to share the work of development or conversion with a Catholic nation, let alone one with a Protestant majority. Just as Eden had seen some justice in Spain, the early provider of silver for Europe and beyond, now benefiting from the silver of the New World, so now he spoke about Pope

Gregory's likening of the English to angels and working to make their souls as perfect as their bodies through conversion, so that England could do as Gregory did to them in their work converting the Natives in the Americas. Perhaps through suggestion, Eden also worked in a little of the grail myth, saying that "Joseph of Arimathia," who had asked Pilate for the body of Christ and had buried it, was a missionary and had converted some of the English in this earlier time.

Throughout my study, in the example of Spain, we can observe various typologies, such as the one Eden was setting out here and the doubleness of the wild man (Briton) and the Native, which became prevalent in later English texts about the New World. According to Eden, the English should do unto other nations as had been done unto them: the converted should convert as they were the first to spread Christianity to the German tribes until the Franks themselves helped this cause. The Spaniards, too, converted barbarous nations in the New World and that subjection was a just means of conversion lest the patient die while the physicians argued over the cure. The will of God was in such work and since He wrought miracles in the time of Christ, then He would do the same in this era as it was required.[68] The Israelites needed the sword as well as miracles to get to the promised land. If they also defended their workmen with weapons when they repaired the walls of the "earthly Hierusalem" after their captivity in Babylon, then "howe muche more then ought the spirituall Israelites to vse all possible meanes to buylde vp the walles and temples of spirituall Hierusalem, whose fundation is Christe, wyllynge all the nations of the worlde to be buylded vppon the same."[69] Eden wanted the English to follow the example of Spain and become spiritual Israelites, fulfilling a typology, in this translator's preface, from one promised land to another. For Christian soldiers as for Prometheus and for physicians, "vehement remedies" were needed for "desperate diseases" as God turns evil to good.

The impatience Eden showed for his own country's lagging behind Spain sounds much like that found later in Hakluyt, Lescarbot, and others in England and France. In praising Spain, Eden revealed the deficiencies of his own country's contribution to colonization of the New World:

> although summe wyll obiecte that the desyre of golde was the chiefe cause that moued the Spanyardes and Portugales to searche the newe founde landes, trewly albeit we shulde admitte it to bee the chiefe cause, yet dooth it not folowe that it was the only cause, soasmuch as nothyng letteth but that a man may bee a warrier or a marchaunte, and also a Christian. Therefore what so euer owre chiefe intente bee, eyther to obteyne worldely fame or rychesse, (althoughe the zeale to encrease Christian religion ought chiefly to moue vs) I wolde to god we wolde fyrst attempte the matter.[70]

Eden preferred some movement toward English colonization and to seek blessings through the mixed motives of God and gold rather than a bystander's critique. Even if the barbarians of the New World were forced to converse with Christians, they would convert accidentally because neither they nor the Christians would seek conversion out and, in doing so, they would gain "ciuilitie and vertue."[71] These gentiles, not "already drowned in theyr confirmed erroure" like Jews and Turks, would be readily induced to "owre religion," a more problem-atic phrase than Eden admitted because others might wonder whether he was referring to the Church of England, to Catholicism, or to Christianity and something that the government of Philip and Mary later found a problem in relation to Eden himself: "But these simple gentiles lyuinge only after the lawe of nature, may well bee lykened to a smoothe and bare table vnpainted, or a white paper vnwritten, vpon the which yow may at the fyrste paynte or wryte what yow lyste, as yow can not vppon tables alredy paynted, vnlesse yow rase or blot owt the fyrst formes."[72] This passage resembled Columbus's view of the Natives as clean slates for religious conversion. The suspicion concerning Eden's religion is something that makes opaque some of the motivation of his rhetoric.

Eden's rhetoric seemed more concerned with action rather than divisions: "If we were therfore as desyrous to enlarge the fayth of Chryste as to seeke worldly gooddes, why do we deferre to aduenture that wherin we may doo bothe."[73] Rather than look for a new Saint Paul, Moses, or Philip the Apostle, the English must do as Isaiah said, to exhort neighbor, to bid brother to be of good cheer, to make God's temple lively, as Erasmus wrote in the first book of his *Ecclesiastes*. Eden said that Damanius a Goes reported in *De deploratione Lappianae gentis* that he first moved Erasmus to speak out, saying that Christ would judge Christian monarchs without favor, flattery, or pardon should they be guilty of heinous crimes. According to Eden, if secular powers would finance the neces-sities for those preaching the gospel to the "gentiles" in the New World, many would go on such a mission. He also appealed to rich men and the rulers of the world to use well the riches that God had given them. Alluding to Horace's satire on the greed of merchants for riches, Eden translated the Latin into Eng-lish and India into the West Indies.[74] As opposed to worldly fame, men should serve the cause of God. In a series of rhetorical questions (*erotema*), the transla-tor wondered how men could be so manly and adventurous in private ventures that were for the glory of the body and neglect the health of their souls and how could they in their covetousness neglect their poor neighbors and brethern at home, let alone finance voyages to the New World. This defense of the poor looked ahead to Hakluyt's in "The Discourse of Western Planting," a central text that we shall encounter in the following chapter. Eden claimed that the merchants of London, the noblemen and gentlemen and others who financed the voyages to new lands deserved "immortall fame." More specifically, Eden praised the search by Hugh Willoughby and Richard Chancellor to find a northeast passage to Tartary and Cathay. Eden commended the Greeks and Romans for making images of those who attempted great enterprises for the benefit of the humankind or the commonwealth in gold, silver, brass, marble, and ivory as examples to their successors.[75] In fact, Eden's preface was an exem-plum for England, a collection of heroic action and noble enterprise full of glory and fame. Even though he had spent so much space praising Spain and chastis-ing England, he ended with a climax that placed the accomplishment of Eng-land above that of Spain, the voyage of Columbus he had praised so much: "And surely if euer sence the begynnynge of the worlde any enterpryse haue deserued greate prayse as a thynge atchyued by men of heroicall vertue, doubtlesse there was neuer any more woorthy commendation and admiration then is that whiche owre nation haue attempted by the north seas to discouer the mightie and riche empire of Cathay."[76]

Besides wishful thinking, the basis of Eden's claim was a dream that such a voyage to Cathay would create an alliance of Cathay and Persia with the Christian princes of Europe against the great enemy, the Turk, just as in 1398, Tamburlaine, the emperor of the Tartars, had defeated the Ottoman emperor and taken him prisoner after slaughtering 20,000 of his men in battle. Here, the New World was elided, and Cathay, as it was for Columbus, was the real destiny. Once again, from our perspective, Eden's work looked backward to Iberian precedents and ahead to attitudes in England, which could be found in the popular theater of the day. It is not hard to see why, with such dreams still alive, Christopher Marlowe's *Tamburlaine* was so popular in the late 1580s. During the 1590s, "base Turk" was one of the favorite epithets in the spluttering verbal arsenal of Falstaff's ancient, Pistol, and the fear of the Turks, as well as the obsession with them, persisted, as they were at the gates of Vienna in 1683. It is no wonder, whatever the history of prejudice is here, that the military threat of the Ottoman empire often preoccupied many continental European states, like France, more than exploration of the New World did. Besides eastern riches, conquest is a theme of *Tamburlaine*. The Prologue to Part One speaks of "*Sythian* Tamburlaine/ *Threatning the world with high astounding tearms/ And scourging kingdoms with his conquering sword*" (lines 4–6).[77] Shakespeare's character, Pistol, who reviles Turks and Spaniards alike, echoes Marlowe's Tamburlaine.[78] When Pistol announces the death of Henry IV to Falstaff, he declares: "I speak the truth./ When Pistol lies, do this, and fig me like/ The bragging Spaniard."[79]

Eden was not alone among English writers in representing the threat of "Infidels." Some later English authors, as we have just seen, created characters who were not as charitable as Eden was toward the Spanish. Admiration for the models of Spanish writers about the New World marks Eden's text. After the three decades of Martyr and the papal bull, Eden wrote a brief note that informed his reader that the selection of Martyr and Oviedo was because they were the best writers, the first being the greatest philosophical writer of natural history and the second a historian whom others had likened to the ancients. He included translations of the dedications that both Martyr and Oviedo presented to Charles V. In Oviedo's "Epistle" to his *Summario,* Columbus's discovery was central, though the author likened his dedication to Charles to be like that of his model, Pliny, to the Roman emperor.[80] The Spanish influence on Eden did not stop in these two obvious and extensive resources: one of Eden's sources of information about America was Gómara's *Istoria de las Indias* (1552).[81] Eden had addressed his earlier work to Northumberland but seemed to have been forgiven after *Decades . . . ,* for he was afterward given a position in Philip's English treasury. Subsequently, however, Eden was relieved of his post on suspicion of heresy. How opportunistic he was in the dedications of his works is difficult to tell, but what is apparent is that despite this prefatory matter so ostensibly laudatory of Spain, Philip or his advisors did not trust Eden.[82]

While there was some hope in the 1550s that England and Spain would find mutual benefit, after the death of Mary, this vision, which Eden had set out with many of its aspects of ambivalence and contradiction, found less scope. During the 1560s, "heretics" from France, perhaps like those in England, like Eden himself, whose motives the Spanish suspected, challenged Spain in the New World. These Huguenots became positive examples, for English Protestants especially, of colonizers of the Americas, but soon their destruction at the hands of the Spanish in Florida provided, in France and England, a negative instance of Spanish cruelty. The Spanish actions in Florida became one of the chief strands of the Black Legend of Spain. Through translation, the English built up their own case against the Spanish. In what follows, we shall observe, nonetheless, that even at the height of the tensions, there was some admiration for the accomplishments and economic successes of Spain in the Americas. All the while texts moved through translation across borders in this representation of the New World.

III

The role of translation and the transmission and preservation of texts in representing the New World has many facets. Some important French texts of colonization, like the narrative of Cartier's third voyage, and Jean Ribault's account of Florida in 1562, which Thomas Hacket translated as *The Whole and True Discoverye of Terra Florida* in 1563, were lost or relied on transmission through the English. Suzanne Lussagnet, who was the first translator of Ribault's account in French (1958), said that the French original is not extant and may not have existed.[83]

The Protestant movements in France and England were close at this time. France had rivalries with the Iberian powers in the New World. In 1560, the Portuguese captured the French base but were not able to eliminate the French from Brazil until 1603, when they were in a political union with Spain.[84] Although it is not difficult to respond to the rhetoric concerning the French victims of the Spanish massacre in Florida, it is also essential to understand what motivated Spain. Over 40 years ago, Charles-André Julien called attention in France to the relative neglect among historians of these French narratives about Florida in the sixteenth century and said that this attempt at settlement was more than an adventure. Rather, in his view, this colonization was much misunderstood and was one of many pieces of Coligny's policy to ruin Spain by attacking it in the most vulnerable part of its American colonies and to unite a country torn by the Wars of Religion against a common enemy.[85]

One aspect of the controversy over French colonization centered on André Thevet. Part of Thevet's goal was to justify himself and his views on Brazil and other French failures in the colonization of the New World and to propose ways to future success. Although in his *Cosmographie universelle* (1575) Thevet would focus on the Spanish, the preliminary matter of *Les Singularitez de la France antarctique* (1557) ignored the example of Spain and revealed Thevet's own "neo-classical" intellectual project and the rhetorical moves in his representation of the New World. Like Oviedo's history in the 1520s, Thevet's was a historiography in search of official support even if it was not at this stage official history. By winning the favor of the king and his officers, each of these historians hoped to make his version the official version that would guide colonization and empire in his respective court, and prefatory materials were a good place to promote such ambitions and give advice. The promotion and critique of empire that existed in Spain was transmitted through translations in French and English. In France cosmographies, "collections" which were a mixture of natural history, redaction, and translation of classical and Spanish sources, history, and geography, were often used to promote French aspirations for trade and expansion in the world. In France and England histories and collections, from Thevet to Purchas, represented this ambivalence both in the prefatory matter and in the contradictory materials brought together. Writers like Eden, Thevet, and Hakluyt used the relation between European and Native to define their imperial and national identities. Thevet was a controversial figure: whereas Jean de Léry and François de Belleforest ridiculed his scholarship and character, Ronsard and Du Bellay esteemed his work.[86]

Although the next chapter will discuss Thevet's later views of French colonization, this section is calling attention to the desire he had for France to imitate the Spain's colonization of the New World and to learn from its books as a means of promoting empire. Between Thevet's *Singularitez* (1557) and *Cosmographie* (1575), the French tried and failed to establish permanent settlements in Florida, which the Spanish claimed for their own. The first French voyage under Ribault in 1562 failed partly because the French depended on the Natives, who came to resent them, rather than on farming; the second voyage under Laudonnière in 1564 failed because the settlers dreamed of riches, became involved in the wars of the Natives, traded guns to them and practiced piracy against the Spaniards in the Caribbean; the third under Ribault, which reinforced the settlers with laborers, artisans, and soldiers but which was primarily a military venture to attack Spanish commerce in the West Indies, failed because a storm drove Ribault's fleet off course as he was attacking Pedro Menéndez de Avilés, who had been sent to battle the French, later massacred 132 French at Fort Caroline, and who may have tricked Ribault into surrendering so he could kill him and his men.[87]

Menéndez seemed to have thought that he had saved the West Indies for the Spanish by preventing Ribault from joining forces with the Huguenot pirate, Jacques de Sores. Philip II approved of the massacre and used some of the prisoners on his galleys.[88] One of the Protestant nobles, Dominique de Gourgues, perhaps moved by the Huguenot pamphlets against Spain, raised volunteers and in 1568 took two Spanish forts in the New World and hanged his prisoners in a similar fashion to the way Menéndez had the Huguenots.[89] Gourgues raised the Natives against the Spanish, who wanted to free their leader and not because the French were liberating them (however the French might have thought so). As Julien suggests, the massacre of the Huguenots turned English opinion against the Spanish and helped to motivate the English seadogs and the intervention of England in America.[90] This piracy had a long history. French privateering intensified and led to the burning of Havana in 1555. The Peace of Cateau-Cambrésis in 1559 ended the Habsburg-Valois wars, but, as Ian K. Steele notes, it failed to bring peace to American waters even if Philip II had reasons to claim exclusive rights to America in the formal treaty.[91] The massacres in the 1560s were a continuation of this conflict between the French and Spanish, a struggle in which the English became involved.

On the fourth voyage, led by Jean Ribault, Nicolas Le Challeux, one of the survivors of the slaughter, acted as the chronicler.[92] Addressing a French official, probably Coligny, at the opening of *The Whole and True Discovery of Terra Florida* (1562), Ribault said that the admiral had long wished for the day when France could make new discoveries and find regions full of riches and commodities, which other countries (Portugal and Spain are implied though unnamed here) have done to the honor and merit of their princes and for the great profit of their state, provinces, and domains. In a refrain now familiar, Ribault followed this anatomy of riches with the ideal of God. The massacre of the French in Florida in 1565 evoked a strong reaction in France. The Spanish failure to conquer Florida seems to have created a vacuum for the French.[93]

Various editions of Le Challeux's text appeared in 1566, with and without the additional request to the king for redress. In the Dieppe version, which did not include "The Request," the title page of Nicolas Le Challeux's discourse on this event displayed outrage with the Spanish and solidarity among the French, for it in no way advertised the Protestant cause: *"Discourse of the history of Florida, containing the treason of the Spaniards, against the subjects of the King, in the year 1565. Written in truth by those who are left. A thing so lamentable to hear, that was premeditatedly and cruelly executed by the said Spaniards: Against the authority of our Sire, the King, to the loss and injury of all our kingdom."* [94] This appeal to emotion also represented the Spanish as contravening the authority of the king of France, a loss and wrong to all the kingdom. In an address to an old friend, Le Challeux said he had written down, rather than related orally, his account of Florida to his friend, who liked "the marvels of the Lord" and "the variable estate of kinds of men."[95] Le Challeux stated that his narrative would provide these marvels because God had delivered Le Challeux and his companions and deigned to let them see their country again and illustrated that a man whose highness is abased learns to feel God and his grandeur and to sense his own obedience and service.

This was the providential lesson of Le Challeux's book: we should not be carried away by our desires for those things God forbids. Should the artisan leave his shop and the father his wife, children, family, country, and goods for things false and strange, for shadows and blind fury? Men should attend to happiness, and, for Le Challeux, who wore his classicism more easily than did Thevet, lessons about the happy life derive from Aristotle, Horace, and Homer and have to do with Giges, Electra, and Odysseus. These authors and figures prompted questions about the dangers, hardships, and hard lessons of leaving home for a desired land or external good (in both senses of the word). In an illustrative passage, the

desire to understand Providence motivated Le Challeux to make sense of what
happened in Florida: God showed his ire ("courroux") in his judgment of the
men who should have been home with their families, for whom they should
have cared rather than sought adventure and comfort.[96] Le Challeux ended this
dedication with a prayer invoking the power and the glory of Christ. Not once
here, where rhetoric and polemic might demand it, did Le Challeux mention
the Spanish, let alone vilify them. In this providential view God must not have
been pleased with those who suffered in history: the victim became a victim-
izer, a possible traitor to family and country. This providential history created an
ambivalence in this writer, who took seriously the Calvinist belief in the
inscrutability of God's ways, trying to make sense, in this frame, of why God
punished some of them and spared others among them.

     Even if Le Challeux did not blame the Spanish for his misery in the epistle
to his friend, he felt compelled to tell his story, in which he could not avoid what
the title (perhaps the printer's work) advertised—the treason and cruelty of the
Spaniards. Nonetheless, Le Challeux presented his eight-line poem, written as
he returned hungry to his house in Dieppe, which did not mention Spain but
concentrated on the personal journey of the author. It began, "Who wants to
go to Florida" and ended its last line with the plaintive "I am dying of hunger,"
so that Florida led to pain and hunger.[97] The theme of God and the personal
journey continued.

     The opening of the body of the text gave the background of Jean Ribault's
voyage, emphasizing that the king, as well as princes and lords in his council, had
sent out Ribault with seven ships before troubles, tumults, and civil war rising
in the kingdom had prevented many men and ships from going to Florida,
"newly known and discovered by the French."[98] This claim for the French,
unless it was for the southern Carolinas or for the areas Verrazzano observed in
the 1520s, is doubtful. Ponce de León had dropped anchor south of St. Augustine, Florida in March 1513. The Spanish founded St. Augustine in 1565.[99] The
anxiety of being the first to occupy and possess the land continued into this
period, but so did the implicit awareness of heeding the Spanish, who insisted
on the legality of the division of the "unknown" world between Spain and Por-
tugual in the 1490s. The royal commission gave Ribault authority in the enterprise but "forbade him expressly to attempt an invasion of any other countries
or islands whatsoever, particularly of none which would be under the lordship
of the King of Spain" and ordered that he should take a direct route to
Florida.[100] The ghost of Spanish authority and the possibility of Spanish retalia-
tion haunted the voyage even in its commission. Le Challeux stressed the mixed
motives of the French settlers: some possessed the honest and laudable desire to
advance knowledge of the universe, whereas others had warlike hearts. He represented Florida's climate as being neither cold nor hot and its land as rich as
any on earth and in need of diligent and industrious men.

     There were English and Spanish dimensions of this voyage of the French to
Florida, which Le Challeux described as a land full of diverse plants and animals.
At this point in the text, Le Challeux left the telos of the journey—Florida—
and returned to the launching of the expedition. The French stopped on an

English island ("l'isle d'VVich"), where the English wanted to know about the French enterprise and offer them hospitality.[101] Le Challeux was being instrumental as he returned to the subject of Florida and the names the French would give to make claims in New France. On the coast of Florida, they found Natives with silver and a solitary Spaniard, who had escaped a shipwreck 20 years before. Whether this unnamed Spaniard had claimed the land for Spain, Le Challeux did not mention: had he been there before France discovered Florida? The Natives, whose claim to their own land was ignored, became sources of information. The French welcomed the Spaniard and asked him what he knew about the French in the area, and he responded, translating into Spanish or French (we are not told) what he had heard from the Natives—the French were 50 leagues north. When they found the French, the settlers rejoiced as they had not had heard from France and did not live like "savage peasants" ("païsans sauuages"), with whom, Le Challeux says proleptically, they had used force and violence.[102] He observed that the Native inhabitants seemed to him good and human enough ("assez humaine"), and while the "assez" did not place Le Challeux in Las Casas's camp, he did try, from a Francocentric point of view, to provide a balanced account of "ethnology" and natural history.[103]

Le Challeux represented the arrival of the Spanish on September 3 as a rupture of this narrative of French discovery and settlement. When the French asked why the Spaniards had come, they replied that they were enemies and that war had been declared. The Spaniards were full of ill will ("mauuais vouloir") and chased the French without success.[104] On September 10, the French took Native prisoners, despite their affection toward the French, and this created a situation in which one Native apparently plotted and collaborated with the Spanish.[105] The Spaniards had good espionage and learned that mainly the women, children, and sick were in the fort while the rest of the French settlers and soldiers were in ships on the river. Having traversed woods, strands, and rivers, conducted by the Native, they arrived, on 20 September, at the French fort, which they entered without resistance and where they executed "a terrible rage and fury that they had conceived against our nation" and "cut the throats of men, healthy and sick, women and small children, in such a way that it is not possible to think of a massacre that could be equal to this one in cruelty and barbarity."[106] Such was the rhetoric of the Wars of Religion and of the Black Legend.

Such scenes represented in French and in the English translations the first instances of this concerted representation of Spanish cruelty and barbarity. In the French and English vernacular, Las Casas came later. To my knowledge, this connection has been observed but not explored, that the Black Legend in France and England had much to do with the experiences that French Huguenots had with the Spanish in the New World.[107] In their vulgar or mother tongues, after the translation of Las Casas, the French and English later represented the Natives as victims of the Spanish.

Here, Le Challeux described Native treachery, as Bernal Díaz did, not Native innocence. How much the French and English were aware of Las Casas's *Brevissima relacion* (1552) in the Spanish original is hard to say, but with its translation into French in 1579 and English in 1583, it became widely disseminated to those who had access to the vernacular alone. After the massacre in Florida, Las Casas was made, though ten to fifteen years later, a tool of French, then English, then Dutch Protestant propaganda. In this Protestant representation the Spanish became cruel in Europe and in the New World, to other Europeans and to Natives alike. That in 1565 a Native would lead the Spanish into the French fort did not deter these later propagandists, as it would not stop Ralegh, in 1596, on his voyage to Guiana from representing the Spanish as cruel mistreaters of the Natives. Le Challeux's explanation that the Native was motivated by a natural human desire to avenge himself was probably much closer to the mark.[108]

Afterwards, at the fort, some of the French, like Laudonnière and Le Challeux, barely escaped with their lives. The narrative took up the personal strain with which it began. Le Challeux reminded the reader that he was old and gray and that only with the grace of God could his strength redouble and allow him to escape, so that he was himself a sign of Spanish cruelty to the old and weak. To save himself, he had to make his way toward the fort in order to rest. In that place, Le Challeux discovered "a horrible slaughter" ("vne horrible tuërie"), and, losing all hope of a French rally, "I resigned all my senses to the Lord and, commending myself to his mercy, grace and favour, I threw myself into the woods, for it seemed to me that I could not find greater cruelty amongst savage beasts than that of the enemy: that which I had seen spill over our people."[109] The Spanish were worse than animals, and in misery and anguish, pressed and enervated, Le Challeux made his testimony a testament of personal faith.

He said he could not find anything on earth to save him, so that God, with special grace and above all the opinions of men, delivered Le Challeux amid sighs, sobs, words of distress, and cries to the Lord.[110] God provided grace for him while his compatriots perished also crying for that grace. At this point of pressure in the text, Le Challeux broke into prayer to God, the lord of suffering, to show him the way of hope amid the depths of hell and the abyss of death, to end this miserable old age, plunged in a gulf of sorrow and bitterness, or at least to show mercy when he faced the cruelty of savage and furious beasts on one side and of the enemies of God and the French on the other ("de tes ennemis & les nostres d'autre").[111] As I later observe, Le Challeux was not an eyewitness to some of the events he described. In the prayer for divine help Le Challeux reiterated his comparison between beasts and Spaniards.

When he did discover his countrymen after a half-hour journey through the pathless woods, it was not simply a happy ending to a trial. One of them, learned in the Scriptures, spoke of the barbarity ("barbarie") they saw everywhere they turned and recommended that it was better to seek out the mercy ("miseri-corde") of the Spanish because they were men whose fury ("fureur") would abate to the extent that they would receive the French than to fall into the grasp ("gruelle") of savage beasts.[112] The art of persuasion, as Aristotle called rhetoric, occurs at three levels: it is part of a discourse or rhetoric of the time, the context of which we have been exploring; it is an intratextual attempt to persuade, made by one actor/rhetor over his audience within the narrative; it is the over-arching persuasive frame of the narrator/actor/author—Le Challeux. The first level was an emerging discourse of anti-Spanish sentiment, the second the learned speaker, conversant with the Bible; and the third Le Challeux, the "character" and member in the audience, who was also the narrator, who was in turn identified with the author.

The relation among the three levels became apparent in the effect of the speech of reconciliation with the Spanish. This speech won over most of the French company, notwithstanding Le Challeux's remonstration of the bloody cruelty of the enemy ("la cruauté encore toute sanglante des aduersaires") that was executed with such a fury ("fureur") that it could not be simply for a human cause or debate but because the French were of the reformed religion.[113] Le Challeux reported his typological method, how he cited examples from Scripture, including an appeal to the flight of the Israelites from Pharaoh, so that they would flee the tyrant. The rhetorical agon counted: six chose the proposition of Le Challeux's opponent. The unfortunate six descended to the fort, searching for grace from their enemy, but their folly, according to Le Challeux, the narrator/author, was that they had placed their faith in men rather than in the promises of God. When the six men went to the fort, the Spanish seized them, cut their throats, and massacred them as they had the others "and then dragged them to the bank of the river, where the others killed at the fort were in heaps: I do not wish here to be silent about an example of extreme cruelty."[114] Here literally was the example of Spanish cruelty: it involved a supplementation of the territorialism from the 1490s over the possession of the New World with religious strife between Catholic and Protestant. The Wars of Religion were translated to events in the New World and were represented in texts later translated in the parallel rhetorical battle of texts.

The description of the massacre continued just when it seemed over: this was the account of a series of disasters. Having seen that turning the French cannons on them was not working or intimidating anyone, the Spaniards sent someone with the authority of their commander, "Dom Pedro de Malueudo," to see on what conditions the French would leave their ships. The Spanish commander was Don Pedro de Menéndez. The French replied that they were not at war with Spain; that they had sailed six months before under the commandment of the king of France; that they were wronging no one; that they had obeyed his command not to go into or even approach any Spanish territory so as not to give Spain any offense; that the Spaniards could not therefore say that the French were to blame for the massacre they had wrought, "against all customs of war."[115] A rhetorical contest occurred between the French and the Spanish envoy. Whereas the French said that they had taken the ship to defend themselves, the Spaniard, justifying the actions of his compatriots, asserted that they were determined to defend themselves.[116] According to Le Challeux, the narrator (among other things), the Spanish wanted to dismember the bodies, and "plucking out the eyes of the dead, they stuck them on the ends of daggers, and then with cries, howls, and revelry, they threw them against our French people towards the water."[117]

Le Challeux's party, still on foot, proceeded in their long hard escape, where God led them, contending with a steep mountain and other adversity, including a deluge. As they waded through deep water and embraced each other, they cried out to God, accusing themselves of sin and recognizing his judgment of them, for mercy and for prevention of their deaths. Le Challeux described the river as being too dangerous to dare swimming across, and the French devised a way to cross it and, with the grace of God, did. After spending their night on the other side of the river, they walked and saw a group that they thought was the enemy but that turned out to be Captain Laudonnière and a group of about 26 French. They all made it to their ship, where they were fed bread and water and then recognized that the Lord had saved them, so that they spent the night telling about His marvels ("merveilles").[118] The next day, Jacques Ribault, captain of "la Perle," came aboard to confer on what to do to save the rest of the French and their vessels, but they decided to return to France in their two ships because they did not think they could do any better in the circumstances. On Thursday, September 25, they departed for France.

Nor did the suffering end there. After 500 leagues, a Spanish ship assailed and bombarded them, and another bloody skirmish ensued in which the French escaped, joyous and thanking God, because none of them died, except their cook.[119] After surviving this violent scene, Le Challeux said that the only threat to the French were the winds that tormented them and nearly threatened to throw them on the coast of Spain, a prospect they considered with great horror.[120] Cold, hunger, inadequate clothing, rotten bread, putrid water, and sickness all contributed to the misery of the crew in this perilous and lamentable voyage. When the survivors landed at La Rochelle, the people treated them humanely and graciously, an implicit comparison with the inhumane and ungracious Spanish. The first book ended, then, with a return to France, where God's grace—perhaps the protagonist of this narrative, along with Le Challeux—made the people gracious.

The second book, which is brief (eight pages), shifted the point of view by returning to Jean Ribault, who, with the elite of the French soldiers, sought out the Spanish for five days without any success. Ignorant of what had happened at the fort, Jean Ribault wanted to enter it, while a storm came up and destroyed the ships and their munitions, leaving all the French on land. There they met with hunger, thirst, and sickness. There was a reverse journey from sea to fort from Le Challeux's trek from fort to sea: once more, the river-crossing was the main obstacle and event. Le Challeux described Jean Ribault as speaking with accustomed grace and modesty as he led the French in prayers against the hardship. Ribault's speech repeated the pious rhetoric of the French Calvinists that recurred in these situations in Le Challeux's account. The French encountered the Spaniards, and the Spanish captain made signs and a promise of peace and treated Ribault humanely, although he separated him from his men, who were tied two by two:

> The delegates were received at first sight ["de prime face"] humanely enough. The captain of this Spanish company, called Vallemande, swore by the faith of a gentleman, knight and Christian, his good-will towards the French, and, likewise, that this was the way which, for all time, was practised in war, with which the victorious Spaniard contented himself, prin-

cipally with regard to the French. . . . [After] Captain Vallemande's speech, Captain Jean Ribaud [Le Challeux's spelling] first entered the boat with the others, up to the number of thirty, whom Vallemande received humanely enough, but the others who were of his [Ribault's] company were led far behind him and tied, two by two, hands behind the back.[121]

Le Challeux portrayed Ribault as a good man who simply had faith in Vallemande and represented the French and the Spanish, tied together two by two, making their way toward the fort. When Ribault and others saw this spectacle, they huddled together, changed color, and began to question having put faith in Vallemande, who continued to make excuses that they were tied for their safety. Le Challeux said that the scene of making the French march behind Vallemande and his company was like "a herd of beasts that one would chase to the slaughterhouse."[122] This contrast between the two captains, the one simple and good and the other dissembling, led to the next scene of the massacre of the innocents. The French trusted and were faithful and now paid with their lives. At the sound of fifes, tambourines, and trumpets, the Spaniards rushed upon "these poor French, who were bound and garotted," and with pick, halberd, and sword, "in half an hour they won the field and carried this glorious victory, killing valiantly those who had surrendered and those they had received into trust and safeguard."[123] Here then was a planned massacre against men who were bound and helpless, showing faith that the Spanish would safeguard them, but instead, the French found furious Spaniards.

Two more parts comprised Le Challeux's conclusion: the portrait of Jean Ribault's death and a summary of the narrator/author's views on the Spanish cruelty. From the general abuse the Spanish visited on the French, Le Challeux moved to the heroic portrait of the French leader, Jean Ribault:

> Now during this cruelty Captain Jean Ribaud made some remonstances to Vallemande to save his life. Mr. Ottigny threw himself at his feet, reminding him of his promise, but all that accomplished nothing, for when they turned their backs, he walked a few paces behind them and one of his executioners hit Captain Jean Ribaud from behind with a stroke of the dagger, so he fell to the earth and then very soon afterwards, he [the executioner] gave two or three strokes, so much so he took away his life.[124]

This death was the end of the narrative in Florida and the pretext of the drawing of the moral. The lesson and the genesis of the text, however, involved more horror. Le Challeux described the bad faith, cruelty, and barbarity of the Spanish: "they have cut the beard of a lieutenant of the King" and, "for a Trophy of their renown and victory, dismembered the body of this good and faithful servant of the King and made four quarters of his head and stuck it on four pikes and then planted them at the four corners of the fort."[125] The volume ended in a ritual dismemberment of a servant of the French king, a synecdoche for the entire French nation and not simply an appeal to members of the Reformed religion. This appeal and image recalled the address to the king at the beginning of the book: the implied message was that to dismember one of the servants of the king of France was to tear apart the king himself and to do that was to desecrate and break apart France itself. After the tribulations and the Spanish destruction of the French in Florida, Le Challeux put aside Ribault and the other martyrs and returned to where he left off at the end of Book One, which took up most of his narrative, the homecoming of the survivors.

The volume ended with Le Challeux's "Little Epistle" in verse, the author/narrator's ode to Dieppe on his arrival home. The poem was a homecoming, a love poem to the city he had so long desired in his absence, a celebration of a place that allowed for the glorification of God, where people could listen to God's word with sincerity and without frivolity, spoken by faithful ministers, not seducers, publicly preaching the Scriptures. It began "Thank God and the good king of France" and praised the king for his liberality toward the colonists.[126] God and the king framed the entire narrative. An implicit appeal to national unity, the king's protection and religious freedom represented the telos of the denouement. This was no call for revenge against Catholics but was framed in a narrative of nations, of Spain's oppression of France. If there were to be any revenge, it would be against Spain. The king was the just king of all the French and he was left with this outrage against his subjects and therefore himself.

Le Challeux's work is far less known than that of Las Casas but was a seminal text in the making of the Black Legend and in the relations of the French and English to the Spanish, so I have tried to quote from it at some length. As important as Las Casas was to the making and advancement of the Black Legend, he was not alone, and the rhetorical divide in this war of propaganda was not always religious. In fact, Las Casas would be summoned 13 years later in France and 20 years after in England to vilify the Spanish, but he was not the beginning of such a black legend in either country. The self-interest of the nations involved was always a factor. Sometimes the French and English texts were jarringly propagandistic as the countries officially and unoffically carried on a brisk trade with the apparent enemy: the Spanish.

In an edition of 1565 that is thought to have been printed in Paris, the printer added to the text a brief piece of seven pages, "Request to the King, made by the widows, children, orphans, relatives and friends of these subjects, who were cruelly massacred by the Spaniards, in France Antarctic, named Florida."[127] The rhetoric was one of supplication before the king. The opening sentence, which echoed the title page and the title that preceded the text of the request, got right to the point: "Sire, there is an infinity of poor and miserable persons, widows and orphans, all your subjects and vassals who present themselves at the feet of your Majesty, tears in eyes, with the entire obeisance and natural subjection that they owe you."[128] Besides an appeal to emotion, this opening also established the obedience of the supplicants and their supplication as natural, so that they were not subjects apart, a kind of Protestant splinter group but part of one kingdom and seeking a redress for the honor of all France. The author created a pitiful image of these victims holding in their hand before the king's excellence and grandeur "a pitiful discourse of their very just complaints and grievances."[129] If that were not enough, the author proceeded to the sad spectacle and visible portrait of their fathers, husbands, children, brothers, nephews, and cousins, up to 800 to 900 men, women and children, "massacred and torn to pieces in the land of Florida, by Capitain Petremclaude, and his Spanish soldiers."[130] This was a second and supplementary denunciatory climax in this edition, which did not denounce the Spanish explicitly on the title page. The epistle had begun with restraint: the request ended with excess. In a personification, the blood of the slaughtered innocents cried out to the king for vengeance: "And as much as the outrage of this act is odious enough and too villainous in itself, and that the blood of these poor subjects so traitorously spilt cries for vengeance before God."[131] There was nothing republican about this request for redress and restitution: the king was likened to a father and a master. His children and affectionate and faithful servants called out: "their complaints are not less worthy of commiseration and pity, that the cruelty of the Spaniard Petremclaude is contrary to all factions of the war and to all the laws of war and to all laws and ordinances that were ever received from God or from men."[132] The king was reminded that the colony in Florida was established under his authority and it was furiously invaded by five Spanish ships.[133]

As if the descriptions of Spanish cruelty had not been enough, this personal appeal to the king amplified them by representing another description of the massacre. In the fort that the French had built in the name of the king, the Spanish killed men, women, and children without mercy, "the bodies of little children run through, planted at the end of their pikes," killing Ribault and his company of 700 to 800 by breaking a promise, binding their arms and hands, "calling your subjects French buggers, lepers, thieves" in front of Ribault.[134] This passage then reiterated the account of Petremclaude's treachery and the stabbing of Ribault in the back, his decapitation, the shaving of his beard, the quartering of the head stuck on pikes in the midst of the French dead. One detail was new: the Spanish captain sent a letter to the king of Spain and enclosed in it the hair from Ribault's beard, a shameful act, delivered with bravado and without honor to the servants of the powerful king of France and therefore a personal insult to the king himself.[135]

This drama in the "Request" made this affront to Henri II's honor and the call for revenge quite explicit. That a Christian prince could condone such barbarous cruelty, performed with the rage and fury of tigers and lions, but in a show of friendship when the king of France was not at war with Spain, was unbelievable.[136] The Spanish did all this in a place that belonged to the king of France alone: Petremclaude was therefore a usurper. Henri II needed to avenge the death of Ribault, so the logic of the argument went, because through the letters patent of the commission, Ribault was, in that place, like the king himself.[137] The petition asked rhetorically whether such an indignity, which was an atrocity to the king because it was performed on his lieutenant, did not redouble, increase the dishonor, and extend the scandal if the murderers, violators of the public faith, were allowed to go unpunished and to be nourished in their malice and authority. The appeal continued by saying that such great cruelty broke all human and divine laws. An allusion to the classical past claimed that

the Carthaginians, African nations, and Romans would not break with their
faith. Petremclaude and those of his house, for their treachery and religious
hypocrisy, would suffer the judgment and vengeance of God.[138] In a personal
address asking Henri II to give them his charity and protection, the appeal, on
behalf of the petitioners, now ending the "Request" and the book, called out to
the king "to witness their innocence for all Christendom, and by this means you
will be loved and received by all nations, not only as King, but also as Father of
your people."[139] After the slaughter of the innocents, a true Christianity was
needed. The author appealed to the king to be a leader of a united Christianity
in his own country and in all nations. He could lead by redressing the wrongs
the people of the colony in Florida and their families have suffered. This rhetoric of the king as father was pervasive in French narratives of the New World,
something that occurred most notably in Lescarbot's work in the first two
decades of the seventeenth century.

In 1566, *A true and perfect description, of the last voyage or Nauigation, attempted
by Capitaine Iohn Rybaut, deputie and generall for the French men into Terra Florida,
this year past. 1565. Truelly sette forth by those that returned from thence, wherein are
contayned things as lamentable to heare as they haue bene cruelly executed* appeared in
London. The title of Thomas Hacket's translation of Le Challeux emphasized
the cruelty the French suffered without naming the Spanish perpetrators. In
keeping with my principle of discussing the influence of a text as it appeared,
Ribault's work, though that of a Frenchman, will be examined in the next chapter in terms of the English edition, probably a kind of transmission from a
ghostly French original. The speed of this translation showed how much interest in these events there was in England. As Jean Ribault's account exists only
in the English, which Hakluyt later published, and Laudonnière's *L'Histoire
notable de La Floride . . .* was published in Paris in 1586, Le Challeux's narrative
was the one that made an immediate impact in the French-speaking world.[140]
In 1566, this learned carpenter, who could quote Horace, Sophocles, Homer,
and Aristotle in his letter to his friend, was the only one to speak immediately
to the English of the massacre in Florida. Rather than repeat an analysis of Le
Challeux through Hacket's translation, I would like to set out a few examples of
what the English reader would encounter in the text.[141] Le Challeux closed his
epistle to his friend with a skepticism regarding the promises of riches made to
attract colonists and with a providential view of this historical event as punishment of the French and not as a revelation of Spanish cruelty:

Let them go to *Florida* who list, for my parte I would not wishe, that that
man, that is a housholder, should so leaue his occupation, for to seeke his
aduenture in a straunge countrey, & for a greater profite of gaine: what
faire promysse so euer is made of his enterprise. Also, we haue borne the
wrath and anger of God, as ye may see in this discourse of *Florida,* which
I do present vnto you, desiring you to receyue it as a token or pledge of
my good will and loue, the whiche this fiftene yeares hath held our
heartes, straightly lynked and joyned together by Jesus Christ our Lorde,

to whom alone appertayneth the rule, power & glory, for euer and euer. Amen.[142]

His prayer was penitential and followed Le Challeux's attempt to make sense of the terrible events in "The Epistle" and preceded his working out of the narrative of the massacre in the body of the text. An appeal to an old friend was a moving and personal way to make his point. Its simple rhetoric, despite its learning, presented a plain, natural, and sincere style, a rhetoric of no rhetoric. This providential view of history, in which God has punished his chosen people, while part of a biblical typology translated into historiography, was not unusual for this period, or any other period, for that matter, because after the defeat of the Armada, Philip II wondered why God had punished his most Catholic king, whose country was the champion of Catholicism in Europe and overseas.

Le Challeux's book then began with a prelapsarian plan to colonize Florida, the colonization of which was before the civil wars in France broke out, but it ended with the Spanish treachery toward the remaining French and Ribault, in which Vallemande broke his promise of clemency and literally stabbed him in the back, and quartered Ribault's body, sticking a piece at the four corners of the fort. Hacket added to the end of his English edition a moral about covetousness and a prayer that God keep England from "murther and bloudeshedde" that did not appear in the French original:

Here hasse thou (gentle Reader) seene the discourse of two sorts of people, wherein thou mayest iudge with indifferencie and see what couetousnesse causeth, being both desirous of gaine, and in specially the monstrous crueltie of the one part. But Historie suffiseth of it selfe, God is a righteous iudge which seeth the actes of all humaine kinde, and shall rewarde euery one according to their deserts. God keepe vs from murther and bloudshedde, and giue vs grace to feare him, and honour his holy name aright. Amen.[143]

Hacket was implying blame on those who went to the New World out of greed and, in the name of the impartiality he advised his reader to assume, blamed the Spaniards for their cruelty. The implication was that if in his letter to his friend Le Challeux blamed the French, God would also mete judgment out to Spain for its massacre of the French in Florida. Hacket left out Le Challeux's verse epistle that he addressed to Dieppe and the "Reqvest to the King" from, as the title says, the widows, orphans, parents, and friends of his subjects cruelly massacred by the Spaniards ("cruellement massacrez par les Espagnols") in Antarctic France or Florida.

Here, then, is a crucial instance of the many dimensions of the relations among the Spanish, French, and English. The events in Florida and the ways in which the French and English represented them were instrumental in developing a rhetoric of blame against the Spaniards. In this providential view, however, the French and the English did reserve some doubts about their own designs on the New World. The view that Spain was cruel began to enter the lexicon of French and English accounts of the Americas and, as we shall observe in subsequent chapters, intensified and was also used in describing Spanish power in Europe. A typology between the New World and the Old began to take hold. If Spaniards had behaved cruelly in the Americas, then they would do the same in Europe. The suffering of the French in Florida would give the English ground on which to use Las Casas's descriptions of Spanish cruelty against the Natives in the New World and to raise the alarm against Spain's actions in the Netherlands.

IV

The events in Florida moved Protestants in France and England to protest against the Spanish.[144] France's failure in Brazil led them to seek success in Florida. In *Les Singvlaritez* Thevet gave his account of his voyage to Brazil with Villegagnon in 1555, including his preference for the religion of the Natives, who recognized the eternal God, and the Protestants.[145] With a civil war on its hands, the government of Henri II, whatever Catherine de Medici and Coligny might have wanted, did not respond to the plea for revenge against the Spanish. Internal divisions were too deep to use a common enemy, like Spain, to unite the country. The English government was no better in its help. Apparently, the queen and Hawkins were playing both sides of the French and Spanish rivalry in order to give England an entry into the West Indian trade. They would learn over the next year, however, that Spain would not tolerate an English intrusion any more than a French incursion. Elizabeth I had, consciously or not, taken up François I's policy that discovery, conquest, and settlement means possession, although Henry VII had already taken the attitude that discovery meant title to lands in the New World. Later, her letter to Mendoza, the Spanish ambassador, would show that she was not interested in abiding strictly by the papal rules of empire.[146]

Spain, which was anxious over a union of French and English Protestants, or even of France and England, as enemies in the New World found that this massacre in Florida would prove to be the beginning of a black legend against the Spanish that would haunt the country on and off to the present. In Holland, France, and England Las Casas would be called on as a Spaniard to condemn the behavior of his own country in the New World. Whereas Portugal got off lightly with the destruction of the French settlement in Brazil, Spain would be taken to task for the massacre in Florida. While soon after the founding of Québec, France would not recognize officially Huguenot colonists in New France, it lost an important segment of its Protestant population to Switzerland, Germany, England, English America, and elsewhere. It was England and its colonies in North America that became the greatest beneficiaries of this population. Moreover, the English colonies in the Americas came to accept Catholics, as Maryland would show. Humphrey Gilbert would attempt to encourage Catholic participation in colonization during the 1580s. Only with the establishment of Maryland under Lord Baltimore did this contribution of Catholics occur. The

Wars of Religion in France brought Protestant Europe together, although each country also acted according to self-interest, so that Protestants developed the Black Legend of Spain from an occasional prejudice into a sustained weapon of propaganda.

The vision Richard Eden had expressed of Spain and England building an American empire together was something that would appear increasingly fantastic just over a decade afterwards. The events in Florida were to have rhetorical fallout in the years just ahead and far in the future. In this rhetorical and actual battle, no side could claim innocence and purity although both did. The next chapter will examine the anti-Spanish tracts of the 1560s and 1570s and the narratives leading up to the Armada (1567–88) while charting the increasing rivalry with Spain that both France and England experienced as they were attempting to secure permanent colonies.

CHAPTER 4

Facing the Greatness of Spain, 1567–1588

From the Reformation in 1517 to the Wars of Religion (1562–98), uncertainty and strife in Europe affected the expansion of France and England in the New World. What was to follow was even worse, especially in France, where a civil war fought on the pretext of religion, as Montaigne would later write, divided the country and prevented it from concentrating its efforts on western colonization. As France weakened, Spain grew in strength. As Spain's power increased, so did the dissenting voices within and without the country. The anxiety over Spanish material and imperial success, including the Christianization of the Natives, augmented in France and England.

During much of the sixteenth century, England had sought a foreign policy that would guarantee its own independence. This policy, as R. B. Wernham has observed, relied on three factors: the development of sea power to protect its coast; the neutralization of Scotland and Ireland; the balance between France and Spain, so that the one would defend England if the other attacked it.[1] Although Spain and England were divided by religion, the Spanish often sought good relations with England, sometimes as a balance against France. The *empresa de Inglaterra,* or the enterprise of England, had religious as well as economic and political dimensions, a Catholic power fighting with a Protestant country, but Philip II had strained relations with the papacy after the election of Sixtus V. Philip had not given unconditional support to putting Mary Stuart on the throne as he feared that the Guise and France would control her, resisted the excommunication of Elizabeth I, and refused to permit the excommunication of 1570 to be published in all his territories.[2]

Until the 1560s, France, an ally to Scotland, was the greatest threat to England, but Spain replaced France in that role. With the ascension of Elizabeth I, England made its final break with Rome, which rendered relations with France and Spain difficult and helped create more friendly relations with Reformed Scotland. Spain sent an army into the Netherlands in 1567 to crush the rebels and Protestantism. This action also damaged England's most lucrative overseas market, so that when the English sought alternative markets, they came up against Spanish might and interests. At the end of 1584, the secret treaty of Joinville meant that the Catholic League became a dependent ally of Spain and that France could not pursue her policy of balancing the power of Spain. The English feared the Spanish army, the finest anywhere, and, in August 1585 by the treaty of Nonsuch, Elizabeth I committed 7,000 troops to protect the Netherlands. These actions led to the clash between England and Spain in 1588.[3] The fear of Spain and the Catholic League in France had already helped to turn up the anti-Spanish and pro-Huguenot rhetoric in England, something we can observe from the translations of narratives concerning the Spanish massacre of the French Protestants in Florida from the 1560s to Hakluyt's "Western Discourse" in 1584 and beyond.

Having discussed the period from the deaths of Henry VIII and François I to the year of the first narrative of the Spanish massacre of the French colonists in Florida and examined the praise for Spain in England during the reign of Mary and the first important French description of Spanish cruelty in the New World, I will now analyze later trends in the relations among Spain, France, and England. More particularly, I wish to concentrate on the anti-Spanish tracts of the 1560s and 1570s to the narratives leading up to the Armada (1567–88) and the intensification of rivalry with Spain while France and England were attempting to expand and establish permanent settlements in the New World. The example of Spain now entered an intense phase.

Here, I will examine the development in France and England of anti-Spanish sentiment, much of which grew out of the conflict between Spain and the Huguenots in Florida. Even though the French and English continued to find positive models in Spanish America, their critique of Spain often became part of a mobilization of propaganda in the service of the national interests of the two countries and their desire for expansion and permanent colonies in the New World. The variety and range of French and English texts about the New World continued to increase and may have been a function of the very imitation of Spain that we have been examining. The more texts in France and England incorporated the varied and intricate texts of Spain concerning the New World, the more the French and English implied a deference or respect at one level for Spain and the more they were able to use this knowledge to challenge and displace Spanish power in the Americas.

By examining the representation of Spain in key texts from adventurers like John Hawkins and Dominique Gourges, cosmographers like Belleforest and Thevet, translations of Spanish writers like Gómara and Las Casas, Huguenot historians like Léry and Chauveton, and promoters of empire like Hakluyt the Younger, this chapter will demonstrate that the attitudes toward Spain in England and France were reaching a crisis and were becoming ever more intricate. The genres of exploration narrative, cosmography, translation, history, and government report were distinct but overlapped in some conventions and in content, so that while distinguishing them in separate parts, I will also admit their shared techniques and content. While the responses of these writers in these "genres," or kinds of writing, to Spain were still ambivalent and contradictory, the texts in the period from 1567 to 1600 were the most anti-Spanish in the period from 1492 to 1713 and provided the foundation for later and persistent outbreaks of negative representations of Spain.

I

Those who sailed to the New World continued to record their views of exploration and the new lands. Increasingly, the English mariners, who had been so reticent or who had left so few accounts in the first seven decades of voyages to the New World, began to produce texts about their experiences. The French, who, more like the Spanish, had recorded their observations during their voyages to the western Atlantic, continued the trend. These narratives of exploration and contact soon came to coexist, as we shall see in the next chapter, with accounts of settlement. Both the French and English were, in the seventeenth century, able to establish American-born authors, which would provide another dimension in the relations among the Spanish, French, and English empires both in Europe and in the Americas.

The narratives of the explorers included representations of these relations among the European imperial powers: Spain was still a powerful example that these practical French and English mariners contemplated. The captains and seamen wrote accounts of their experiences with the Spanish that were often framed in the language of romance and heroism but that frequently reflected what their own governments would tolerate or sanction unofficially. Economic self-interest and the balancing of power in European politics affected these apparently straightforward narratives. Through their written accounts, explorers and pirates (depending on whether the reports were from the point of view of Spain or not) like Hawkins and Gourges justified their actions, the one for breaking Spanish laws and the other for wreaking revenge on Spain. English and French narratives were instrumental, their ends often being political and economic, even as they protested motives of religion and liberty. These narratives reflected as much a battle for the seas as a conflict over land, for whatever nation controlled the oceans and the trade routes was much more able to impose its will over territory.[4] The battles on land and at sea occurred in Europe as well as in the New World. For instance, some important aspects of the relation between England and Continental powers were the English war with France, 1527–30, the civil war in France, the assassination of Henri III in 1589, the alliance between the Catholic League in France with Spain and the English alliance with Henri de Navarre, the role of Hawkins and Frobisher in the war against Spain, and the peace between France and Spain in 1598 (the treaty of Vervins) in which Spain withdrew from Calais and Brittany.[5]

The English thought they could balance Spain and France to gain entry into the slave trade or piracy in the West Indies, so that in 1567 John Hawkins made yet another slaving voyage, taking his cargo of 500 Africans from Sierra Leone to the Spanish Main. This time he found Spanish colonial officials more willing to put up a show of compliance with the king's law not to trade with foreigners. On his way home, Hawkins put into the harbor of San Juan de Ulúa to repair the *Jesus of Lubeck,* the queen's ship, and there the Spanish treasure fleet forced him to abandon that ship and, after severe losses, to escape in two small vessels.[6] Hawkins's account in 1569 was like Le Challeux's narrative about Florida, except that it had no prefatory matter. Both were about failure and martyrdom in the face of Spanish reprisal and cruelty. Using the topos of inexpressibility, Hawkins said that a man would have to have much more time to record "the lives and deaths of the martyrs."[7] The English had learned a similar lesson to the French: Spain would not tolerate piracy or trade that encroached on its monopoly in the New World.

That lesson was something the Huguenots would not accept, so that they concentrated on the Spanish cruelty. Other narratives, which supplemented or interpreted the events of Le Challeux's account for at least two decades, played on an emotional response to the Spanish destruction of the French because they were heretics and appealed to the French as a people regardless of religion to unite against Spain's threat to the honor of France in an act of revenge. In 1568, the *Histoire memorable de la reprinse de L'Isle de la Floride,* by Dominique de Gourgues or one of the members of his mission of revenge in Florida, appeared in France, another installment in the conflict between France and Spain in Florida. Spain did not want either France or England to follow its example and establish an American empire. The *Histoire memorable* began with a claim that the French under Henri II had discovered Florida, sent men and women to settle it and soldiers to guard them under the charge of captains Ribault and Laudonnière. The French had built a fort and cultivated the earth, but the Spanish were jealous of and sorry about this and did not want the French near the ships coming from Peru and the West Indies, so they murdered them.[8] This narrative alluded to Le Challeux's description of the inhuman cruelties ("inhumaines cruautéz") of the Spaniards who said that they wanted to exterminate the Lutherans.

The account tells the story of Gourgues, a Gascon gentleman, and how in April 1568 he set out to avenge this massacre. Gourgues had to convince the Natives that he was not Portuguese or Spanish, and the French sang psalms to prove it. The French assured the indigenes that they were there to free a Native king from the oppression of the Spaniards and to drive them from the French fort. In turn, the Native kings thanked the French king—the two sides exchanged hostages and gifts. The French were prepared for vengeance: this was clearly a well-planned military expedition.

In relation to French duty, the narrative was matter-of-fact, but the language used to describe the Spanish was negative and emotive. The French officer asked whether his men "did not have all the good will to do the duty of soldiers to avenge such inhumanity and cruelty."[9] They all answered yes and had faith that God would assist them in this affair, and the captain praised God to see such affection. In an act of revenge worthy of the Old Testament, Gourgues cut one party of Spaniards to pieces. The French took the two forts, "built by the Spaniards to hinder the invasion of the French and other nations."[10]

A Spaniard who was described as a spy and who claimed to have hanged six of the French was strangled on the spot. With their Native allies, the French burned and killed at the fort, where Petremclaude and Vallemande, villains of the

Le Challeux narrative, were commanders. The Native kings wanted to go to France, and the French left on May 3, 1568. Unlike Le Challeux's account, this one was sparse and brief in its description of the revenge. It did not dwell on the personal: the specific fates of Petremclaude and Vallemande were left unexpressed and no mention of the difference between Catholics and Protestants was explicitly made here. This was strictly a tale of French revenge for Spanish wrongs.

The English mounted their own kind of struggle against Spanish domination, but like the French, they found that Spain was not easy to displace or overtake. Discovering a sea route to Asia was one way the English thought they could challenge Spain. The dream of a northwest passage continued to motivate the English despite the display of Spanish sea power against French and English ships alike. Encouraged by the view of many European cartographers and scholars in a northwest passage, an opinion held by John Dee, the leading geographer in England at the time, Humphrey Gilbert was the first Elizabethan to take an active interest in reviving interest in discovering that route to Asia, which John Cabot had kindled. In 1566, along with Anthony Jenkinson, Gilbert petitioned the queen for the right to discover it and for a monopoly in the passage. Many of those who supported such a northwest venture—Gilbert, Martin Frobisher, Henry Sidney—were in Elizabeth's service in Ireland.[11] Ireland was, then, a type of *"Terra Florida."* Sir Thomas Smith distanced himself from Stukely's [Stukeley's] fraud in raising money for the Anglo-Huguenot attempt at a colony in Florida.[12] Like the Canary Islands for Spain, Ireland was a testing ground for expansion for England.

Humphrey Gilbert was an important figure in the renewed strategy of exploring a northwest passage as a route to China in order to challenge Spain. Composed in 1566 but printed in 1576, Gilbert's *Discourse of a Discoverie for a New Passage to Cataia* was an attempt to have the queen give him permission to sail in search of this passage and for a monopoly there, but Gilbert's efforts to that end were unsuccessful. When in 1572 he met Frobisher, a new scheme began when this sailor—taken with the learning of Gilbert and Michael Lok, a member of the Muscovy Company, which generally opposed the route to the northwest and preferred the one to the northeast—found favor with the earl of Warwick, who in turn was able to gain the approval of privy council for the plan. Gilbert revised *Discourse* considerably after his return from Ireland in 1570, but the work waited six years for publication.

George Gascoigne, the poet, provided "The Epistle to the Reader" as a promotional supplement to Gilbert's scientific cosmography that tried to attract adventurers and subscribers to the first Frobisher-Lok voyage partly by pursuing the common attack on idleness.[13] In a prefatory sonnet, Gascoigne began: "Men praise *Columbus* for the passing skil/ Which he declared, in *Cosmographie,*/ And nam'd him first (as yet we cal him stil)/ The 2. *Neptune,* dubbed by dignity."[14] Gascoigne's conceit was that in his book, Gilbert, the fifth Neptune after the third, Vespucci, and fourth, Magellan, had discovered something Columbus and those other famed explorers and the rest of the world had not.[15]

As usual the precedent of Spain was part of the English representation about their own part in the New World, but being conscious of the role of the Spanish, the English, like Gilbert, used sly means of qualifying, displacing, and circumventing Spanish origins to the discovery of these lands in the western Atlantic. Ancient Rome and Renaissance Italy were such means of evasion and paraphrasis, of casting doubt on Spain as the seminal country for exploration and possession of the New World. The question of first contact and the origins of discovery arose once again, and Gilbert amplified a mythological discovery of America, which might have been actual to the author, to be found at least as far back as Pliny. This origin would undermine the claim of Spain to America, but Gilbert went so far as to reveal the controversy of the modern "discovery" of the New World by attributing it to Vespucci, while admitting that some attributed this honor to Columbus, whose origins in Genoa were emphasized.[16] Gilbert himself thought a northwest passage would lead the English to 'ye East in much shorter time, than either the Spaniard or the Portingale doth,' and in arguing for a great ocean in the north between Asia and America, he called on Jacques Cartier, Verrazzano, and Sebastian Cabot as well as Portuguese and Spanish sources, including the report of Salvaterra, a Spaniard who said the Natives in America thought there was a passage and who offered to accompany Gilbert on the search for it.[17]

In the meantime, England was attempting to circumvent the Portuguese and Spanish monopoly on the New World. Elizabeth I was also pursuing a policy initiated under Henry VII but which François I had begun in earnest in France—discovery, conquest, and settlement means possession. Before Martin Frobisher's first voyage, the state papers included a document, a brief summa *avant la lettre* of Hakluyt's "Discourse," which I shall concentrate on in some detail later in this chapter, that set out an English colonial policy that sanctioned the discovery of lands that were unoccupied, the use of the commodities found there, and the spread of the Christian faith in that territory, all without offering "any offence of amitie."[18] This document suggested that the queen take up the lands toward the South Pole, which no other countries had possessed or subdued, so that providence had given the Spanish the west, the Portuguese the east, and the English the south and would allow England to bring "in grete tresure of gold, sylver and perle into this relme from those countries, as other Princes haue oute of the lyke regions."[19] The riches of Spanish America still danced before the eyes of the English.

A benefit of this enterprise would be to bring down the price of Spanish and Portuguese spices and commodities and to create a surplus in the English treasury. After dispelling fears over passage through the "zona torrida," an anxiety more persistent than might be expected, the author addressed a chief objection that might be raised against his proposal: "The perils of the Portugals or Spaniards violence that shall envie our passage. Our strengthe shalbe suche as we feare hit not, besides that we meane to kepe the Ocean and not to enter in or nere any their portes or places, kepte by their force."[20] This document recommended that the English try to avoid the Spanish power that they did not fear and that the government should not dread the depopulation of England, which could not provide for all its people, or the waste of ships and mariners, because the experience of France, Spain, and Portugal had shown that the trade with Newfoundland and the West Indies had increased the number of ships and skilled sailors.

Although the English set out in many directions to find its place in the colonial sun, including a series of northwest journeys under Frobisher and Humphrey Gilbert in the late 1570s and early 1580s, the principles stated here about how England could justify and safeguard its imperial policy related to a general theory and practice that those in the "American" party at court urged upon the queen. England must have its place among the European colonial powers. Answering the sixth objection that such colonization might offer injury or offend the friendship of other princes or countries, the author made claims that foreshadowed the carving up of Africa by Europeans during the nineteenth century. The French had their sphere, the Spanish theirs; Hawkins's voyages to Mexico created a legal precedent because the Spaniards did not inhabit and therefore did not possess the land; the same rule applied to Florida; the example of French settlement in Brazil and Florida negated the authority of the pope in these temporal affairs, even though the French acknowledged the papacy in spiritual matters, so that the Spanish and Portuguese alone respected the donation:

> The Ffrenche have their portion to the northwarde directlie contrarie to that which we seke.
>
> For the places alredie subdued and inhabited by the Spaniard or Portugall we seke no possession nor interest. But if occasion be free frendlie traffique with theim and their subiectes which is as lawfull as muche wythout iniurie as for the Quenes subiectes to traffiques as merchants in Portugall or Spain hit self.
>
> The passage by the same seas that they doe, offringe to take nothing from them that they haue or clayme to haue; it is not prohibited nor can be without iniurie or offense of amitie on their parte that shall forbyd hit.
>
> The voyages to Guynea and traffikinge in Mexico and in the verie places the Spaniards possession hathe in the president of Hawkyns voyage bene defended by her Majestie and counsell as frendlie and lawfull doenges; much more this which is but passinge in the open sea by theim to places that they nether hold nor knowe. Besyde that not onelie trafyke but also possession, plantinge of people and habitation hathe bene alredie iudged lawfull for other nations in suche places as the Spaniardes or Portugals haue not alredie added to their possession. As is proved by her Majesties most honorable and lawfull graunte to Thomas Stucle [Stukely] and his companie for terra Florida. Also the Frenche mens inhabitynge in Florida and Bresile, who albeit they acknowledge the Pope's authoritie in suche thinges as they grant to perteine to him, yet in this vniversall and naturall right of traffique and temporall dominion they haue not holden them bounde by his power; but do expounde his donation to the Spaniardes and the Portugals either as a matter not perteyninge to the Pope's authoritie, or at leste not byndinge any other persons princes or

nations but the Spaniards or Portugals onelie, who onelie submitted themselues, and were parties to the Pope's judgment in that behalf.[21]

The revisitation of origins to the right to settle the New World, which we
observed in detail in chapter 2, was something that the French and English
would not leave alone, perhaps because the Spanish and Portuguese insisted on
the legitimacy of the papal bulls of the 1490s. Even though the example of Spain
represented the primary one for the English, that relation depended on other
connections in the European context, most often with France. The French also
emulated but challenged Spain in the framework of the colonial ambitions of
other European countries, particularly England. Another example was Portugal,
which from 1580 to 1640 was united with Spain and thus had and did not have
a distinct imperial identity depending on the context. During the 1560s, the
French and the English almost seemed ready to join forces in Florida against
Spain. In the 1570s, this anonymous advisor, whose work we have been considering, was trying to have Elizabeth's government use Florida and the ambivalent
voyage of Hawkins, which wavered between slaving for the Spanish and pirat-
ing with the French as precedents to trading and settling in the New World.

Like Gilbert and the anonymous advisor, Frobisher challenged Spain in the
New World. His first expedition, which was to sail nowhere near the South
Pole, departed England on May 15, 1576, part of the search for a northwest passage preoccupied the English, French, Spanish, and Portuguese after John
Cabot's voyage in 1497. England was trying to reestablish itself in the northern
part of America, which it had been instrumental in calling attention to the rest
of Europe and whose example in this context the western European powers had
followed. Till now the English had been quite negligent in and about Newfoundland and had lost their advantage to other nations, especially France. In
October 1576, Frobisher returned to England thinking that he had found the
northwest passage, bringing with him an Inuit, and having discovered what he
thought was gold.

Whereas the first voyage had trouble attracting capital and subscribers (Lok
was the key supporter), the second voyage, under the aegis of the newly formed
Company of Cathay, included a £1,000 subscription of Elizabeth I and the use
of her ship. The goal of the voyage was gold. If Frobisher did not find gold, then
he was to proceed to Cathay, but without the queen's ship. The hope was not
for markets for English wool and merchandise but in John Parker's phrase, "an
arctic Peru."[22]

The second voyage set out on May 26, 1577 and Frobisher returned, as his
orders specified, with three ships full of ore from Baffin Island, reaching England
in September: the 200 tons of ore were perhaps "fool's gold" or iron pyrites.
The journey did have a chronicler in one of the participants, Dionyse Settle,
whose *True Reporte of the Laste Voyage into the West and Northwest Regions*
appeared the same year. Abraham Fleming's introductory poem praised heroic
Britain for its might, fame and goodness and, referring to Ulysses and Jason, suggested an inheritance in travel and empire.[23] Settle's "Epistle to the Christian
Reader" called the English to the conversion of the Natives and recommended

that England look for a northwest passage, which agreed with the English climate, rather than explore in areas already dominated by the Spanish, Portuguese, and French.[24] Settle was also doubtful about the possibility of gold and silver and became perhaps the first of many Englishmen to speak of the Native goods or desired goods as "trifles."[25] Nor did he see evidence of the passage.

In *A True Discourse* (1578), an account of the three voyages Frobisher made, George Beste addressed a dedication to Sir Christopher Hatton, a member of the privy council. Claiming that "the finding of the passage to Cataya" was "a matter in oure age above all other notable," Beste said he had applied himself to cosmography and the art of navigation in order to give a "true reporte" of the voyage and promised, as an antidote to untruths spread abroad and various "men's fantasies," to tell "the plain truth." This plain style was an underpinning of the rhetoric of sincerity. Beste then gave reasons why he, "an insufficient writer," addressed Hatton above all others—he had acted as a patron to the author and rewarded virtue, honor, and service to England.[26] Beste declared to Hatton that in this discourse Hatton could "behold the greate industrie of oure present age, and the invincible mindes of our Englishe nation, who have never lefte any worthy thing unattempted, nor anye parte almoste of the whole world unsearched."[27] The "almoste" was revealing, but the heroic "mind" of the English would overcome the great adversities and barriers of nature that Beste went on to enumerate. The anxiety of origination continued to afflict the English when they were under pressure to exceed the legacy of exploration and riches Spain and Portugal had established. Promotional literature and what might be called the literature of justification often fostered the following pattern: the more the English wanted a permanent settlement full of riches, the more they feared another failure and the more they had to devalue the example of Spain and Portugal. An analogous operation occurred in many French promotional and justificatory narratives of the New World. Beste promoted these journeys to the northwest and the expected wealth they would bring, greater than that of Spain and Portugal:

> if now the passage to CATAYA thereby be made open unto us (which only matter hytherto hath occupied the finest heades of the world, and promiseth us a more riches by a nearer way than eyther *Spaine* or *Portugale* possesseth) whereof the hope (by the good industrie and great attemptes of these men is greatly augmented) or if the golde ore in these new discoveries founde out, doe in goodnesse as in greate plenty aunswere expectation, and the successe do followe as good, as the proofe thereof hitherto made, is great, we may truely infer, that the Englishman in these our dayes, in his notable discoveries, to the Spaniard and the Portingale is nothing inferior: and for his hard adventures and valiant resolutions, greatly superior. For what hath the Spaniarde or Portingale done by the southeast and southwest, that the Englishman by the northeast and northweast hath not countervailed the same?[28]

Besides the string of conditionals Beste used, which created uncertainty in the statement that the English were the equals or superiors of the Spanish and Portuguese, the "gold" Frobisher's ship brought back to England was, like Cartier's diamonds and gold, not the real thing. The French and English were right: Canada was full of mineral wealth—even gold and diamonds—but it was not being mined and used in Native art and religion as it was in Mexico and Peru. This dream of comparable wealth would die hard among the French and English.

Interest in the Frobisher voyage, in gold and a northwest passage, was carried to the Continent: Settle was translated into French in 1578, Latin and German in 1580, and Italian in 1582. Translation was two-way between England and the Continent. It was the triumph of another Englishman, and not someone in the employ of Spain, that came to eclipse the contemporary hope of a northwest passage. Nonetheless, this realization was slow to happen. When in 1580 Francis Drake returned from his circumnavigation, it was apparent that England had another route to the East, and this one proven. Drake's ship was full of Spanish gold and returned home to a nation with factions for and against Spain. Only in Thomas Nicholas's translation of Augustín de Zárate's *Discovery and Conquest of the Provinces of Peru* in 1581 was there praise for Drake in a book immediately following the voyage. Nicholas saw Drake as an example for the English to rival Spain while showing the example of Pizarro as a dutiful servant of the crown and describing his reward, the mines at Potosí, at length. The specter of Spanish gold continued to haunt the English.[29] During this period, Gilbert and Hakluyt the Younger thought that North America would provide bases against Spain, a policy, as we saw in the last chapter, Coligny had tried during the 1560s. In facing the example of Spain, France and England turned to each other for instances of how to circumvent or oppose Spanish power.

Another example of the English imitation of France was in piracy and trade. During the 1550s, the English woolen trade had been declining in Antwerp, and during the 1560s, political and religious conflict made that trade even more difficult. As a result of the Revolt of the Netherlands, Spain moved its financial center from Antwerp to Genoa. Following the example of France, the English began to exchange cloth for goods directly with the eastern Mediterranean. By 1580, the English gained entry into a direct trade with Turkey. In that year, Richard Hakluyt the Younger, who had been influenced in the study of geography by his cousin, Richard Hakluyt the Elder, a lawyer, encouraged John Florio, the son of an Italian Protestant refugee who, like the younger Hakluyt, taught at Oxford, to publish a translation of Ramusio's 1556 Italian version of the first and second voyages of Jacques Cartier, probably in aid of the Gilbert expedition to the northwest.[30] In his "Preface" Florio claimed that Spanish success in its colonies was not based on wealth easily gained but on planting.[31]

At Elizabeth's court, a group favored expansion, which took three major forms: the American enterprise and the search for a northwest passage, Ireland, and the trade with Muscovy and the push for a northeast passage. In England at this time there was no great public doubting voice like Montaigne's to question the right of the country to embark on empire, but there were many doubters, whose concerns and opposition the promotional literature often addressed. As Nicholas Canny points out, individual cases, like Thomas Stukely's fraud for an Anglo-French settlement in Florida in 1563, could put off potential backers and colonists for Ireland and America, but other more practical objections occurred among the English, for instance, that, in Ireland, only financing from the crown could lead to successful colonies and that private profit had been placed before social and religious reform.[32] Canny makes an interesting connection between Richard Eden and Sir Thomas Smith, once Eden's tutor at Cambridge and a champion of Henry Sidney's promotion of colonies in Ireland. The Elizabethans often compared their colonization of Ireland with that of the *conquistadores*. Whereas Smith worried about Stukely's voyage to Florida as a negative example, he did not mind a comparison of this Irish venture with English colonies in the New World. Canny cites Essex, Leicester, and Davies as those who would probably know Eden's translation of Peter Martyr and who came to see the English in Ireland as following the harsh example of Spain in the New World.[33]

Westward expansion to Ireland and America were closely intertwined in the last half of the sixteenth century. At the center of this expansionism was Francis Walsingham, who, along with Humphrey Gilbert, Walter Ralegh, John Davis, Francis Drake, Martin Frobisher, John Dee, Richard Hakluyt Elder and Younger, and others, set out to make England a powerful empire with which Spain would have to reckon. Gilbert, Ralegh, and Davis were all related and their families lived in South Devon along the River Dart.[34] This "American" faction tended to be strongly Protestant and anti-Catholic, but as in Gilbert's case, this characterization needs modification. Gilbert, Hakluyt the Younger, and Ralegh best exemplified the ambivalent attitude this powerful coalition had toward Spain. The Spanish were to be emulated but overtaken. Of course the actual center of their promotional activities and rhetoric was the queen: the coalition had to get Elizabeth's attention and persuade her to support the colonization of North America.

Humphrey Gilbert, who was close to Elizabeth, also exemplified the American alternative and how it was connected to Irish and Continental politics and how it was presented as an alternative as the expansion of eastward trade to Muscovy. During the reign of Queen Mary, Gilbert served in the household of Princess Elizabeth. He became part of her court in 1558, and in 1562 Elizabeth made him captain in the army she sent to Le Havre under the earl of Warwick, which was to help the French Protestants against the Catholic League. The English force had to surrender in 1563, so that Gilbert returned home. In 1566 the queen and her privy council heard Gilbert argue against Anthony Jenkinson, who favored trade with Muscovy and a northeast passage, and for a northwest passage to Cathay. Gilbert would finance the expedition if awarded monopoly rights. In that same year, he wrote *A Discourse of a Discoverie for a new Passage to Cataia, Written by Sir Humfrey Gilbert, Knight* . . . which had to wait ten years for publication. Gilbert anticipated Hakluyt in his arguments for the establishment of English colonies in the New World to enhance trade and to decrease unemployment.

Gilbert spent the summer of 1566 in Ireland, and afterwards, he interested William Cecil, Elizabeth's advisor, in the project and presented a petition to the court asking for the vice-regal and territorial privileges similar to those Columbus had obtained in 1492.[35] Columbus was to be a model and precedent even as Gilbert planned to create a colony in territory that Spain claimed. When the Muscovy Company helped to block his plan, Gilbert returned to Ireland, where on and off for four years he fought and planned for English colonization in Ulster and Munster. In 1569 he ruthlessly crushed the Irish resistance in Munster, which led Henry Sidney, deputy of Ireland, to knight him in 1570.[36] Elected a burgess for Plymouth in the parliament of 1571, Gilbert held in 1572 a command in the queen's expedition to support the Dutch against the Spanish. During this time he wrote a proposal for a new academy in London that would train the sons of the nobility and gentry in mathematics, navigation, languages, law, and other pursuits.[37] Portugal and Spain had schools of navigation: England, too, should teach this subject seriously. This was an idea that Hakluyt the Younger later emphasized. Gilbert also developed plans for colonies, including the one to drive out the fishing fleets of Spain, Portugal, and France from the waters off Newfoundland and to plant a colony in the mouth of the St. Lawrence River on what is now called Anticosti Island.

The queen did not act on these plans, but on June 11, 1578, she granted Gilbert letters patent of such scope that in Samuel Eliot Morison's words, they "deserve the title of the first English colonial charter."[38] The letters patent of June 1578 allowed Gilbert "to discover, finde, searche out, and view such remote, heathen and barbarous lands, countreys and territories not actually possessed of any Christian prince or people."[39] This patent reflected the conventions of the time but also the care to tread softly among the Continental powers by stating that if Gilbert or his heirs or deputies should "robbe or spoile by Sea or by land" or do any injustice to any subjects of any Christian "kings, princes and states," or to Elizabeth's subjects, he or they would "make restitution and satisfaction of all such injuries done."[40] This legal ground was consistent with the attitudes of England in Henry VII's time and of France at least since François I: do and do not recognize the papal donation to Spain and Portugal. The recognition came in the notion of not inhabiting any place where there were other Europeans, and for the most part that would mean the Spanish and Portuguese in the New World, whereas the defiance derived from the intent and act to settle in lands Spain and Portugal claimed as their own but did not occupy. Gilbert was given vice-regal powers, such as those delegated to Columbus and, later, to Roberval in Canada. Besides being given military authority to seize vessels of those violating his possessions, Gilbert was instructed to give his colonists the rights and privileges of Englishmen as if they were born or living in England.

In 1578, besides Gilbert's efforts, a great deal of promotion occurred, some of the texts taking the form of translations and some of it the geographical work Hakluyt and John Dee performed. The Spanish ambassador could not find out where Gilbert was sailing. As it happened, the voyage never left European shores. Henry Knollys captured ships off the coast of France and Spain while Gilbert put in at Irish ports to revictual: while he was away, his sailors seized a Spanish ship at Dartmouth. To avoid greater friction with Spain, the privy council demanded the return of the ship and would not let Gilbert sail in 1579.

Gilbert had to raise money for another expedition, and he began to sell grants of land in the New World, basing one of them on the geography in Verrazzano's

"Letter," which Hakluyt the Younger had printed. These grants went to John Dee, Philip Sidney, and George Peckham and his son. Gilbert also wanted to raise funds from English Catholics, who were considered recusants and were fined £20 for each family per month, in exchange for a colony of their own with religious liberty, but the queen required that they pay their overdue fines before emigrating.

In the summer of 1582, the Spanish ambassador threatened these potential English Catholic settlers that if they were to settle anywhere near Florida they would meet the same fate the French Protestants did under Ribault. Mendoza said that some of the English Catholics used Cartier, the French Catholic and discoverer of New France, as an example of someone who had financed his own voyages. Mendoza wrote about Elizabeth's plans to settle Florida: "Through the clergy here I made known to the Catholics the purpose of the Queen and Council in admitting them to favour—and that these lands belonged to your Majesty, that you had garrisons and fortresses there, and that they would immediately have their throats cut as happened to the French who went with Juan Ribao [Jean Ribault], that further they were imperilling their consciences by engaging in an enterprise prejudicial to His Holiness."[41] In concluding his report to Philip II, Mendoza maintained that for Spain to reduce England, the Catholics must stay at home. They would be necessary instruments in the invasion that Spain was already planning.[42]

For Spain, religion did not seem as important as nationality in protecting its domains in America. The threat from Spain, which included papal displeasure, along with Elizabeth's penalties, seemed to have curtailed English Catholic interest in colonization in the New World. Thus, Gilbert had to work hard to finance this voyage. On November 2, 1582, he signed an agreement with the Merchant Adventurers of Southampton, which Gilbert hoped to make the supply town to the American colonies just as Seville was to the Spanish colonies.[43]

Gilbert's roommate at Christ Church, Oxford, Stephen Parmenius, a Hungarian, offered a poem as part of his request to be the chronicler on Gilbert's second and last voyage. In this embarkation poem in Latin, which was over 300 lines, America asked her sister, England, to rescue her from cruel Spaniards; recalled that Cabot sailed there just after Columbus; and begged Elizabeth I to extend her rule to the New World.[44] Parmenius declared: "recently the French/ And Spaniards steeped their hands in holy blood./ Such deeds do not become a Golden Age" (lines 107–9).[45] Gilbert was presented heroically: "His support of friends/ In war amazed the Belgians, his pursuit/ Of honest battle was recorded by/ Dishonest Spain, and warlike Ireland shakes/ Throughout her conquered shores in fear of his/ Victorious army" (lines 142–7). America addressed "independent England" with an ambivalence toward Spain, reviling its motives and actions in America but praising Columbus: "Are you not aware/ What times and what disasters I have seen/ After the Spaniards' endless appetite/ For gold had spurred them on to infiltrate/ My lands? (For certainly they were not moved/ By any moral zeal or holiness)."[46] The right of first discovery of Newfoundland was England's, "when spirited Cabot/ Approached these regions, following the wake/ Of great Columbus."[47] America, clearly a Native, complained about the

idolatry of Catholicism, so that the desire for an English rescue seemed to have
been based in part on her preference for Protestantism. This motif of England's
rescue of America or the Natives from Spain became a recurring theme in the
English literature of promotion.

On June 11, 1583, Gilbert sailed from Plymouth and, on August 5, took
possession of Newfoundland for England, something Cabot had done in 1497.
Edward Haie, whose account of the voyage was found in every edition of
Hakluyt's *Voyages,* described how in St. John's harbor the fishermen greeted
them in 20 ships from Spain and Portugal and in 16 from France and England;
how they all fired a salute of honor after Gilbert displayed his commission, sent
their longboats to tow the *Delight* free when it struck a rock, presented him
with turf and a twig to acknowledge they were now under English sovereignty. In turn, Gilbert laid out lots for shipowners, regardless of nationality, to
dress and dry their fish. The fishermen elected a new "admiral" every fortnight as a pretext for a feast.[48] Haie also dwelt on Columbus and Cabot, on
the English right to Florida, which the French had tried to usurp, and
attempted to set out two spheres of influence in the New World, the Spanish
south and the English north (Florida northward).[49] This scene is a reminder at
the commercial and unofficial level that the cosmopolitan nature of European
exploration of the New World, so evident before the Reformation, persisted
in the Newfoundland fishery. It is also a contrast to the massacre of the
Huguenots in Florida.

Gilbert's objective was Norumbega, and he decided to leave Newfoundland
despite dissension over the decision. The influence of the French, including their
Florentine and Portuguese pilots, drew Gilbert to this objective. 'Oranbega'
appeared on Girolamo da Verrazzano's map of his brother's voyage in 1524, a
mythical place, abundant and full of happy and peaceful inhabitants, that the
Europeans created. In 1545, Pierre Crignon wrote a discourse about Jean Par-
mentier, a sea captain from Dieppe and described Norumbega, which he said
had been discovered by Verrazzano 15 years before. In *La Cosmographie,* Jean
Alfonse, Roberval's pilot, enhanced Crignon's description of Norumbega, but
in his *Voyages avanureux* (1559), Alfonse attributed the discovery of the river
named after the *Cap de Norombègue* to the Portuguese, which went contrary to
expectations of chauvinism in these national rivalries in the New World, except
that it seems that he came from Portugal.[50] In this work on navigation, Alfonse
set out general observations about the New World, making, as Jean-Paul Duviols has observed, a similar point to one Las Casas used in his defense of the
Natives, for both followed Aristotle's view that it was illegal to reduce the indigenes to slavery because they were delicate: "The men of this land of Peru are
small, feeble and good. But the Spaniards mistreat them and make them their
slaves."[51] Gilbert and others in the "American" party at the English court could
find a mixture of anti-Spanish sentiment and descriptions of America that would
help to form, or at least confirm, attitudes in a challenge to Spain in North
America. The navigators were also capable of praising Spain, giving it grudging
respect, or representing it ambivalently. Jehan Mallart's rhymed "routier" of

1546–7, for instance, described the Portuguese and the Spanish as the discoverers of Norumbega.[52] Gilbert, like others of the "American party," owed a debt to earlier French explorers and texts about the northern parts of America.

While the loss of Gilbert and his ship was a setback to English colonial enterprises, the push for expansion continued in the country. The English captains were ready to take up where the French had left off: they would challenge Spain even as they tried to emulate it by establishing permanent colonies. Gilbert, like the Portuguese, Spanish, English, and French mariners before him, combined scientific and practical knowledge with political imperatives and dreams of riches. The accounts of captains and seamen shared this mixture with cosmographies and translations, some key examples of which will be examined next . The texts to be discussed also distinguish themselves, partly because, especially in the instances of the cosmographical works, they were not as often eyewitnesses of the events and places in the New World that they described.

II

Cosmographies and translations became increasingly important in the historiography of expansion after the destruction of the Huguenots in Florida. During these years, the question of religious difference tore France apart and left it unable to establish a coherent colonial policy. A terrible time of division and violence in the country surrounded the Massacre of Saint Bartholomew's Day at Paris in 1572. Even under these difficult internal circumstances, cosomographies like those of Belleforest and Thevet continued to look outward and to encourage French expansion. Although in his preface to Gilbert's *Discourse,* Gascoigne had struck on a truth that Columbus was in some regards interested in cosmography and although it might be said that Columbus was a cosmographer by virtue of his voyages and account, the use of "cosmography" and "cosmographer" here is restricted to those who, like Belleforest and Thevet, announced themselves in those terms.[53] Their use of Spain often appeared in the contexts of internal strife in France and French failures at colonization in the New World.

This discussion of Belleforest and Thevet will focus almost exclusively on the example of Spain, which is not always extensively represented in these texts but is done so in telling ways. In 1570, Belleforest's *L'Histoire Vniverselle dv Monde,* a cosmography reissued in 1572, appeared and described the history and geography of the four parts of the world.[54] In this epistle dedicatory Belleforest began with Seneca and used rhetorical questions to describe recent events in the Wars of Religion.[55] In the fourth part, "The New Lands," Belleforest, having granted that the Spanish had increased European knowledge of cosmography, made a claim for discovery that put the French before the Spanish in the northern lands. In his "Preface" to the fourth part of the world, which he sets out in "LIV. IIII. The New Lands," Belleforest admitted that the classical view of Ptolemy and Strabo, who did not have knowledge of these westward seas and lands, were wrong about the five zones of the earth and that Magellan's voyage gave an opposite understanding of the southern lands and the Antarctic pole.[56] One of his marginal notes proclaimed: *"Northern Lands Discovered by the French."*[57] Like the English, the French found their own precedents and glory in the New World while recognizing the accomplishment of Spain: the Spanish discovered Mexico and Peru, but Cartier was the first to claim Florida, Canada, "Baccaleos," and Labrador.[58] At the end of the fourth part, and the book itself, Belleforest acknowledged his debt to Spain and Portugal: he claimed that he could have represented more about the New World, drawing on "books and the Spanish and Portuguese who had roved all the Ocean and nearly all the corners of the earth," but the reader would have to be content for now with what the author had traced.[59]

Thevet's *Universal Cosmography* (1575), which derived from his experience with Villegagnon in Brazil, represented Spain in a positive light.[60] The Spaniards were the first to discover Peru and to see "the way of life of these poor barbarians and Savages, cruel through and through, and without civility, not more than beasts."[61] Thevet had more derogatory views of the Natives, which contrasted with his praise for explorers like Columbus, Magellan and Cartier. The Natives were "thieves, robbers, and without faith, or loyalty, that their God was imaginary."[62] The Spanish names in South America marked their presence during the French expedition there.[63] He gave the name Antarctic France to the region the French had explored in North America just as the Spanish had given their various names to their colonies.[64] Thevet also mentioned the myths of the Natives expecting the arrival of the Spanish in Mexico and Peru as being like those Natives who awaited the coming of the Portuguese and French.[65] Moreover, he discussed American diseases the Spanish may have brought back from the New World.[66] A community of European merchants, including the Spanish and French, traded with the Brazilian Natives.[67] Thevet admired Spain, so that he might have been complimenting the Spanish when he said that Christians put themselves in danger "with these Barbarian nations," except "the Spaniard and Portuguese, who know how to dissimulate and temporize with these Barbarians."[68] Portuguese slaves and rivalry with the Spanish appeared in Thevet's account.[69] He also discussed the cannibals, figures Columbus originally represented.[70] Thevet shared some of the same interests that his Spanish predecessors had in writing about the Americas.

It is sometimes too easy to stereotype Thevet as pro-Catholic and pro-Spanish, although he had these tendencies. In looking back to his time in Brazil, Thevet mentioned "my great friend and companion, Nicolas Barré, the memory of whom I revere" and who "was murdered by the Spanish, with other Frenchmen" in Florida about a dozen years after Thevet knew him in South America.[71] The time frame here is difficult because except for that of Le Challeux, most of the accounts of the conflict between Spain and France in Florida were delayed, most probably by the civil war in France. Consequently, the impact of this event recurred and, if anything, took on greater polemical significance during the 1570s and 1580s than during its occurrence in the 1560s.[72] Thevet was not, then, simply an admirer of, or apologist for, Spain in the New World.

It is also easy to dismiss Thevet as someone too given to the fantastic, but his "imaginary" was part of the geographical imagination that urged the French to the colonization of the New World.[73] Dreams and fictions were sometimes as important as reports and events in influencing the French and the English in their quest for America. In cosmography, even though Belleforest thought himself much more reliable and accurate than Thevet, it was difficult to separate myth from fact. Cosmographies, like translations, told as much about visions, illusions, and dreams that drew explorers to seek new lands and routes and to promote them to the court as well as authors to support the colonization of the New World.

Translations were a primary means for the French and the English of learning from the Spanish and therefore play a primary role in my discussion here. Although the work of Las Casas is the central example of a translated text in this chapter, and also of my study as a whole, many translations affected England and France in their rivalry with Spain. This *agon* also involved strife between the English and French, not to mention other conflicts in Europe, the New World, and elsewhere. The translation of empire relied heavily on the translation of study, narrative and technology.

These translations were not simple. For Protestants, Rome might be a good classical and republican source, but it was also the seat of the pope and therefore, in a commonplace metaphor among Calvinists, the Whore of Babylon, whose empire must be contained, opposed, and defeated. France and England had large populations of Catholics and Protestants, so that their responses to Spain and to Rome were complicated within and between religious groups. Those who became most obsessed with Spain were the English and French Protestants, so that many of the translations discussed here derive from the Protestant side. The war in the Netherlands involved Spain, France, and England and, like the conflicts in the New World, allowed factions among the French and English to focus on the role of Spain in Europe and America. The Revolt of the Netherlands provided a background to the typology of Spanish cruelty in the New World and in the Netherlands as most best exemplified in Cloppenburch's volume (including Miggrode's translation of Las Casas), *Le Miroir De la Tyrannie Espagnole Perpetree aux Indies Occidentales* (1620).[74] It is quite possible that Jacques de Miggrode, the translator of Las Casas, was Flemish. When I speak of French translations, I am, like André Saint-Lu, also referring to translations in French that would find a French audience even if their authors were not from France.[75] It is important, however, not to forget that these groups were using those who were Spaniards, like Las Casas, and others, like Benzoni, who worked in the Spanish colonies, as testimony of Spanish cruelty.

Before examining Hakluyt's contribution to the promotion of English colonization in North America and the challenge to Spanish domination in the Americas, it is important to shift to another development, which we can observe in Benzoni, Le Challeux, and others, that is a sustained anti-Spanish sentiment. During the 1570s and 1580s, the Black Legend of Spain took off in both France and England. The growing body of translations concerning the New World that the French and English produced, which was part of their growing production of texts generally about the New World, may have arisen from a growing sense that they should challenge Spanish hegemony in the western Atlantic. This sense may have had as much to do with the failure of France or England to establish permanent colonies in the New World as with an increasing confidence in and desire for them. The cause and effect of whether the texts helped to produce the momentum of France and England toward settlements that would persist or that momentum enabled the texts is difficult to say. Either way, the texts embodied the ambivalence of England and France in their challenge to Spain in the Americas, an *agon* that involved failures as well as successes. It is easy for us now, in retrospect, to ascribe to these French and English writers a much greater sense of certainty and confidence that they were on the verge of successful, permanent colonies, so that a look back becomes a look ahead. It is possible that some of this feeling of optimism existed in the 1570s and 1580s among the French and English, but too much of that kind of ascription would belie the very real inability of either country to contend with Spain and to establish any New France or New England in North America. The French and English translations still involved a learning from Spain's experience in the New World, but they became more and more weapons in a war of words.

Although these translations served as a means of gaining information about Spain and about the New World generally and as a weapon in a war of propaganda, they had more varied functions. The French and the English also translated each other's works, so that they were supports and rivals in their challenge to Spain. A year before the publication of Hawkins's narrative, Hacket, who was for, then against, and then for English colonization, published his third translation on the New World, his English version of Thevet's *Les Singularitez de la France Antarctique,* dedicated to Henry Sidney, lord deputy of Ireland and lord president of Wales, who was instrumental in the securing of the British Isles for England. Hacket praised those who would face dangers to increase the fame of their country. With this translation of Thevet's book, English readers, according to John Parker, had their first comprehensive view of the New World, a claim that may well have been true for a unilingual readership.[76] Eden's translations had been informative but had not covered the ground from the East Indies to Newfoundland. Thevet had left France with Villegagnon to establish a colony in Rio de Janeiro in 1555, when a religious conflict occurred among the French colonists and the subsequent reports of that venture, including Thevet's, were highly contested. Despite the controversy over Thevet, Martin Frobisher took Hacket's translation of Thevet with him eight years later, although he also had a recent edition of Mandeville's travels.[77]

From the mid-1550s, French and English translations were sending out mixed messages about the Natives through Spanish eyes. In a history of discourse in which, as in this case of the historiography of expansion, translation is so central, there is sometimes a lag between event or original textual argument, representation or record and its transmission into other languages. Latin was available to the elite, but most often the translation into Spanish and then into French and English or some variation on that process (Spanish to French, French to English) meant a greater and more popular dissemination than of the Latin original. Many Spanish authors decided to write in Spanish, and for some, especially among the captains, adventurers, and settlers, the vernacular was the only option, or what might be called the confident option. Some of the texts on Spain were not French or English translations but histories and narratives of exploration, encounter, and settlement that involved imitation of, allusion to, and commentary on Spain.[78]

The example of Spain was central in determining English attitudes to the New World and its inhabitants. In addition to Hakluyt, who translated or commissioned translations from the Spanish, other principal translators were Richard Eden, John Frampton, and Thomas Nicholas. Although the English adapted Spanish writings that glorified the Spanish conquest for their own purposes—providing propaganda to encourage potential investors and settlers—they often adopted Spanish representations of the New World and the Native.[79] The Spanish authors most translated into English, such as Peter Martyr, Oviedo, and López de Gómara, emphasized the glory of Spain in the face of Native American betrayal and barbarism even if they sometimes advocated conversion and condemned Spaniards for mistreating the Natives.[80]

Even though Las Casas thought important the work of his compatriots in the New World, he was not one to emphasize Spain's colonization of the New World and its treatment of the Natives as full of glory. Those Spanish authors who glorified Spain were the most often translated into English. Only one edition of Las Casas's *Brevissima relación* appeared in English (*The Spanish Colonie*, 1583). This translation was filtered through the French translation from which the Preface was taken. The Preface encouraged support for the Dutch revolt against Spain.[81] Much the same situation in the publication of translations of Spanish works concerning the New World occurred in France as in England. In French the translation of the anti-Indian work of Gómara, *La Historia* (1552), went through at least six printings of Part I between 1568 and 1580, and a minimum of six more printings of Parts I and II in the next 26 years (1584, 1587, 1601, 1605, 1606 [twice]) and one printing of Part II (the conquest of Mexico, 1588). Las Casas's pro-Native *Brevissima relación* (1552) was translated, often the first of the nine constituent tracts or the first and some selections from the remaining tracts, into French in various guises and under different titles: *Tyrannies et cruautez des Espagnols* (Paris, 1579; Paris, 1582; Rouen, 1630), *Histoire admirable des horribles insolences* (Geneva 1582), *Le miroir de la tyrannie espagnole* (Amsterdam, 1620), and, in the same place and time and with the same publisher, in a larger volume by Johannes Gypsius with the even more hyperbolically denunciatory title, *Le miroir de la cruelle & horrible tyrannie espagnole*.[82]

Two lags or gaps illustrate the complexity of the bibliography of translation as regards to internal and external opposition to modes of Spanish colonization of the New World. The first was the debate over the treatment of Natives in Spain and then the time lag between the Spanish text and the French and English translations. Although there were other defenders of the Indians, Las Casas's *Brevissima relación* became the chief textual vehicle in French, Dutch, and English for the Black Legend, which had ramifications into this century. The second was the temporal distance between the mission of the Huguenots in Brazil in 1556 and Jean de Léry's *Histoire d'vn voyage faict en la terre dv Bresil, avtrement dite*

Amerique (first edition 1578; second edition 1580). In that wide gap of time between the Brazilian colony and Léry's narrative lay Nicolas Le Challeux's account of the Spanish massacre of the French Protestants in Florida in 1565 and the Massacre of Saint Bartholomew's Day in 1572, not to mention the siege and famine of Sancerre that Léry survived. Le Challeux's narrative of 1566 was about disturbing events that supplemented those Léry described, which occurred about seven to eight years before but which Léry wrote about 12 years after Le Challeux did. To complicate matters, the account by Jean Ribault, the central figure (along with the author/narrator) in Le Challeux's work, had a complex textual history because the French original, which does not seem to have been published, is not extant and the English version had to wait for Richard Hakluyt the Younger to print it after the Spanish Armada. Moreover, Thomas Hacket's translation of Le Challeux appeared in 1566, the same year as the original. The textual responses to the events in Brazil and Florida in French and English were staggered over the years, and this response to events, as well as intervening events, complicated the representation of the example of Spain.

This historiography of expansion, which involves the production, dissemination, and reception of ideas about Spain, is not, as I said at the outset, strictly linear but is actually more like a double or multiple helix or some other metaphor that allows for a spiraling backwards and forwards of two or more strands to the genealogy of the representation of events themselves. These aspects of *mentalité* are at once retrospective and prospective. Thus, while we have heard briefly about Las Casas's defense of the Indians at Valladolid in the early 1550s and the French mission to Brazil in the mid 1550s, the translations or textual representations of these events occurred in such a fashion that the description of the massacre of 1565 in Florida appeared within the year whereas the French translation of Las Casas's text of 1552 and Léry's account of Brazil from 1556 to 1558 both came out in 1578. The events Léry described occurred after those Las Casas represented (from Columbus to the debate of 1551). Las Casas was translated into English in 1583: Léry first appeared in English in Purchas (1613–25).

Using this principle of textual priority as much as possible, I am, then, following up on the analysis of Le Challeux's account by examining the French and English translations of Francisco López de Gómara, *La Historia de las Indias y Conquista de México* (1552), which appeared in 1578, and Urbain Chauveton's edition of Benzoni's history (which included Le Challeux's account), and then I will proceed to the representations of Las Casas and Léry. Only in the next chapter will there be, in the discussion of Hakluyt as a collector of narratives of travel, exploration, and settlement about the New World, a third version of Ribault's experience in Florida. This recursive overlapping demonstrates the primary concern of interpretation in these accounts and histories of past events.

As their places of publication (Protestant centers) sometimes imply, these titles suggest that something of a split might have occurred between Catholics and Huguenots, though, as we shall see in the work of Lescarbot, a Catholic, anti-Spanish sentiment could run high in Catholic circles. Afterwards, the French titles seemed less sensational and virulent, while the rather bland English translation of the French version, *The Spanish Colonie* (1583), became in 1656 the more melodramatic and plaintive, *The Tears of the Indians*. Whereas the titles of the French translations of Las Casas were inflammatory, those of López de Gómara were not, and his work was issued more often. In English Las Casas appeared once and was not printed until 71 years later. The translation of Gómara's, *The Pleasant Historie of the Conquest of the Weast India,* which was only Part II (about Mexico) and yoked oxymoronically "Pleasant" and "Conquest," was printed in London in 1578 and 1596, hardly a runaway bestseller but at least appearing only 18 years apart. In French and English Gómara's work was apparently more popular than Las Casas's, though without print runs and other supplementary information, this hypothesis can be stated only provisionally. In the outrage over Spanish cruelty and the rhetoric of righteous and savage indignation Las Casas adopted and his French and English translators adapted, this ambivalence and balance in French and English attitudes toward Indians and Spaniards can be forgotten.[83] The French and English assimilated views that were both for and against "Indians," sometimes translating the other's rendition of the Spanish original.

In translating Spanish texts, the French and the English continued to choose sources that reflected a variety of points of view and not simply critiques of Spain's treatment of the Natives in the New World. Gómara certainly provided a different account of Spanish America from the version of Las Casas. The French translator of Gómara, Martin Fumée, saw a lesson or allegory in Spanish America that could teach France something about its own internal problems in Europe let alone its desire to colonize the western hemisphere. In the address, "To the Reader" (1578), he emphasized the Spanish civil war in the conquest of the Indies, something French histories lacked. Fumée's translation of Gómara (1578) began with a dedication to Monseigneur Le Mareschal de Montmorency in which Fumée said that he was offering his patron a discourse on the West Indies that he had translated as he waited for fortune to give him the sufficient occasion to do the Monseigneur a more agreeable service. After a sonnet, which emphasized the civil war and the secrets of nature represented in the book, the translator included his "Prologue of the Author," which stressed admiration for the marvels of the world and the desire to know, to find the wisdom of Solomon by realizing how difficult it was to discover divine truth in the nature humans inhabit. In short, God had made the world for humans and had given them a desire to know.[84]

Fumée wanted to fill a need in French to provide a proper history of the Indies, not the history of Hispaniola by the royal historiographer of Spain or Thevet's *Singularitez de la France Antarctique,* which recorded where Villegagnon had gone 30 years before and which was full of lies the mariners, not the author, forged in their accounts. In Thevet, "You see there fair accounts of Amazons, mistakes in the situation of places, and abuses, in the interpretation of many things, such as when he wishes to describe the division of the lands of the King of Spain and of the King of Portugal."[85] A Spanish source, through Fumée's French translation, would correct these errors, which were excused because Thevet was the first among the French to provide knowledge of the Indies. Oviedo and Thevet had emphasized their eyewitness accounts, and usually the anxiety over originality—who was there first?—motivated them as much as any of the Spanish, French, and English explorers and writers after Columbus. Various responses to Columbus were common: his successors praised him, supplemented him, claimed to have additional kinds of knowledge, undermined him as the discoverer of the New World, or tried to ignore him. Fumée's tactic was to say that it was difficult at first to gather the truth about something. The implication was that Fumée would get it right, but then he had the problem of using a Spanish text. He needed to praise it because the title page proclaimed that this was a faithful translation, but Fumée thought it necessary to deviate because, as his prologue demonstrated, he sometimes saw himself as an author who sought authority.

Spain sometimes served as a pretext, both as a text of provenance and as an excuse, to work out rivalries between authors and authorities within a country in setting out the course for expansion to the New World. Fumée's translation of Gómara would replace Thevet: "Observing therefore such a failure amongst our histories I think that the translation of this work would provide some profit to the public, not so much for the customs, religions and ways of doing things of the Indians who are included in this book as for the Geography of all the Indies described point by point by the Author as learnedly as it is possible."[86] Fumée appealed to a potential audience that would include cosmographers, historians, soldiers, and philosophers and, in ambiguous syntax, asked them to forgive the style of the author (because he apparently wanted to leave the text as it was because he would have had to change everything) and to support his translation above others in French and Latin, which were grossly done.

Sometimes the rhetoric of competition, as Fumée's relation with Thevet and other translators indicates, was a matter internal to a country. Who would gain readers and influence those who shape national policy on empire? Fumée then assured himself that the reader would not find his sweet and simple style bad. How faithful was this translation, perhaps no less so than many in the period? A distinction between translation and other kinds of imitation during the French Renaissance, which Valerie Worth makes, is germane to the question I am asking of Fumée and, more generally, to translation in this study: "a translation differs from other forms of imitation by maintaining its relationship with the source text for the duration of the translation. This does not of course prevent some translators from seeking a freer relationship with their model, but the continuity of the parallel between the two texts is the essential distinguishing feature."[87] Fumée called attention to his own relation as translator to the author. In a common trope during this time, Fumée asked the reader pardon for having to correct the translator's errors as he had pressing affairs (in this case, in Flanders).

Fumée continued to improve on his Spanish author, something that was consistent with views of translation at the time and of the ambivalent relation of France to Spain at the time. To make the book more readable, Fumée divided it into five parts. The first described Columbus, his enterprise, and Hispaniola ("l'isle Espagnole"); the second the geography of the mainland; the third the voyage of Magellan and differences between the Spanish and Portuguese colonies; the fourth geography and the civil war among the Spaniards in the conquest of Peru; the fifth geography once again. The translator did not change Gómara's chapter numbers, which were continuous, so that the reader could consult the original, but he admitted that in Paris he had not been able to find Gómara's volume that described Cortés's conquest of Mexico, a city more esteemed than Venice. Fumée promised to fulfill the desire of the reader in the second printing. The book helped the translator as he hoped it would the reader: "In reading it, it will serve you as an aid (as it has done for me in translating it) to push time with the shoulders during the next wars, which cruelly threaten to crush our France."[88] The example of Spain, of war and civil war in the New World, also had implications for the strife France found at home and in Europe. In his prefatory matter, Fumée did not make the Spanish into villains: there was a lesson in Gómara's book, but it is not the explicit denunciation of the Black Legend.

It would be too bald to say that personal motivations and emotions, whether of rivalry or jealousy or resentment, determined the representation of Spain in French and English texts about the Americas, and in these translations in particular. While these motives could affect the authors' rhetoric, more was at stake here, as can be observed in the case of Thomas Nicholas and his translation of Gómara. The heroic example of Cortés and his conquest also became available in England, for in 1578 Nicholas translated Part II of Gómara's *Historia General* (1552). In addition to translating accounts of its glorious history, this translator had hard personal experience with Spain. The second part of this popular work, which chronicled Spanish expansion in the New World to 1551, concentrated on the conquest of Mexico. In fact, Nicholas's free translation omitted over 230 pages of the original and, as Herbert Priestley has shown in his collation, most of the omissions involved natural descriptions and events, even those in which Cortés participated, remote from Mexico City.[89]

Nicholas's textual and rhetorical interests, like Le Challeux's, were born of experience and physical suffering. Having worked for the Levant Company in Palma, one of the Canary Islands, before the death of Queen Mary, Nicholas, along with his companion, Edward Kingsmill, ran into trouble in 1560, when the Spanish governor charged them with heresy. Having been accused of speaking against the mass, Nicholas was imprisoned and put in irons for almost two years.[90] On August 16, 1561, Nicholas asked the English ambassador to Spain to intercede for him with the inquisitor-general of Spain and the Spanish king. Although released for a brief time, he was imprisoned for another two years.[91] Nonetheless, in "The Epistle Dedicatory," dedicated to Sir Francis Walsingham, Nicholas bore no rancor toward Spain and did not relate his personal suffering at the hands of the Inquisition.

Nicholas's English translation of Gómara highlighted the heroism of Cortés, which was part of the *Pleasant Historie*. In the dedication to Sir Francis Walsingham, principal secretary to Elizabeth I, Nicholas appealed to the authority of his source: an ancient gentlemen who served under Cortés with whom the translator talked and who assured him of the "true and iust reporte of matter paste in effect" in Gómara's history.[92] It is important to remember the positive example that some Englishmen found in Spain's colonization of the New World. The shift or disjunction between Nicholas and Hakluyt, both addressing Walsingham and therefore the queen, in 1578 and 1584 respectively, was stark and represents a significant strand here and in my study.

Patrons, like Walsingham, often reflected the complex interests of England in Ireland, the Netherlands, and the New World.[93] The context is instructive here, for as Mitchell Leimon says, 1577 was the closest the English came to aiding the Netherlands against Spain before 1585; beginning in 1578, the Anjou match came to replace the Protestant policy of intervention in the Netherlands; Philip II had an interest in Ireland after the Munster Revolt in July 1579; Walsingham was ready to invest private funds in Don Antonio's attempt to recover the Azores from Spain.[94] In the midst of such a situation, to England, Nicholas held up Cortés and his cohorts as heroic examples of colonizers. For instance, he wrote: "And vvhere oure Captayne *Hernando Cortez,* of vvhose valiant actes this historie treateth, hathe deserued immortal fame, euen so doubtlesse I hope, that vvithin this happie Realme is novv liuing a Gentleman, vvhose zeale of trauayle and valiant beginnings dothe prognosticate greate, maruellous, and happie successe: for perfection of honor and profite is not gotten in one daye, not in one or tvvo voyages, as the true histories of the East and VVest Conquests by Spanyardes and Portingalles do testifye."[95] Beyond the model of Cortés, whose success was so sudden, lay the long way to the riches and honor of empire. England needed such a great man but also patience learned from reading the histories of the experiences Spain and Portugal had in colonization. How different would be the advice that Hakluyt gave to Walsingham in 1584, when anti-Spanish sentiment percolated through the "Discourse on Western Planting."

Translations could also treat of traumatic encounters with the power of Spain. One of the events that turned the rhetoric of Huguenots against Spain was the massacre of the French colonists in Florida in 1565. Las Casas was not the only source for the Black Legend. The title page of Urbain Chauveton's text of 1579, which included a translation of Benzoni, demonstrated that the Italians, as well as the Dutch, French, and English, fed this legend just as 15 years later Theodore de Bry's illustrations in Frankfurt would indicate the participation of artists and printers in Germany in anti-Spanish tracts.

Chauveton's title emphasized "the rude treatment that they [the Spanish] have shown to these peoples there [in the New World]" and that the book is "A little History of a Massacre committed by the Spaniards against the French in Florida."[96] The information on Benzoni, the massacre, and the Index were in small print, smaller with each of these topics, whereas the notice of the newness of the history of the New World was in largest capital type, then the information on the Italian and then on the name of the editor and apparent translator. The subtitle "Containing in sum that which the Spaniards did up to the present in the West Indies, & the rough treatment that they have done unto those poor peoples there. . . ." appeared in the largest size of regular type on the title page. The Spanish atrocities, declared but not with screaming emphasis, were presented with some heft: Chauveton added Nicolas Le Challeux's *Discours de l'histoire de la Floride.* (96 pages) and a request to Charles IX, "in the form of a complaint," on behalf of the widows, orphans, parents, and friends of those massacred in Florida for redress (8 pages) to 726 pages of Benzoni and over 20 pages of the translator's prefatory matter. On the title page before the second part of the book that reissued Le Challeux's *Discours,* Chauveton assured the reader of his own role as editor.[97] This second title page emphasized the massacre of 1565 and the barbarity of the Spanish and announced the redress the victims of the massacre in Florida sought. The headnote or title of the "The Request to the king," which used the phrase "cruelly massacred by the Spaniards" and equated Florida with "Antarctic France," echoed Le Challeux's title page of 1566.[98]

Like Le Challeux's work, which we discussed in the last chapter, this text focused on the Scriptures and godliness. The framing of a book in terms of the king or patron was common enough in this period. Urbain Chauveton, the editor, emphasized the glory of France and the translation of empire from Rome. He began with an address "To the most powerful and most Christian King of France, Henri, Third of this name." After due humility before Henri's greatness, including a comparison between the king and the sun and a couple of allusions to Scipio Africanus and Diocletian to convince the monarch that even great men can recreate through simple and humble pleasures (like the histories in the volume), Chauveton hoped that the king would read the work offered to him and that the writing would profit his men: they should learn from others to prize the name of Christian, which, if they abused it, would mean that the barbarians would condemn them in this world and at the Last Judgment.[99] The address, "To Christian Readers," interpreted the New World allegorically and typologically. Certainty of interpretation introduced the wonderful, strange, and terrible events that would appear in this volume, including Benzoni's history of the New World, Le Challeux's account of the massacre of the Huguenots, and the request of their widows, orphans, and families to the king for justice and restitution: the "Barbarians" of the West Indies are of Cham "who have succeeded to his curse (as Francisco Lopez Gómara believes)."[100]

The myth of origins of the Natives, which was based in the Bible but also had a classical dimension and recourse to a Spanish authority, were the first rhetorical moves in the Preface. The Lost Tribes of Israel, the Carthaginians, the Phoenicians, the Deluge, and the Tower of Babel all made their appearance in the first three pages of this discussion of Amerindian origins. American Natives were then said to be from the East Indies, which the Tartars originally inhabited, but were ultimately connected with European peasants. Chauveton returned once more to Gómara's view of the Natives as the successors to the curse of Cham.[101] The nude Natives were innocents and devil-worshipers who sacrificed humans as the French and Germans once did to their false gods until they learned that only one host and one blood—Christ's, once slain for their iniquities—could efface their sins.[102] This explanation led Chauveton to the fall of Adam, to original sin, and to how people refused to recognize and glorify God and how those who did not obey Christ were cursed and abandoned to the desires and passions of the heart. God would not have let the Europeans ("nous") discover these new lands at this time without good reason; He had presented the grandeur and variety of earthly riches ("richesses terrienes") in what the author had called "another World" as a new tableau to counter the one to which the Europeans ("nous") were accustomed; this living God and his holy Scriptures would transform these blind, naked "Savages," who inhabited the shade, would give them the light, reason, intelligence, civility, and policy of religion that the Europeans had.[103] The language of "otherness" began early in the European representation of Native Americans.[104] Here the mirror of otherness became a means of reminding Christians of their own blindness and sinfulness and urging them, through the Natives, to convert idols into a living God through obedience to Him and His Scriptures.

This godly argument served as a reminder to the Spanish and those who would conquer rather than convert the Natives: having abused the gift God gave them, the Spaniards had shocked rather than converted "these poor Barbarians" and "hunted them cruelly" in addition to giving them their vices, carrying disease to them, giving iron and bringing back gold, so that "Avarice and Idolatry" grew and abounded as it did in Europe and "whatever had been given for benediction had been converted to malediction and an instrument of ruin."[105] Gold, greed, and idols had spoiled the New World, and, ironically, Chauveton chronicled a conversion that had been perverted.

The providential view of history, with God as katascopos, or overviewer, led Chauveton to an eschatology in the New World. God yielded to gold in the Spanish conquest of the New World, but not without dangers for the conquerors, for the souls of these "ambitious Conquerors" were at risk because God could see all, and in his justice abuses would not go unpunished. Besides setting an example of cruelty, the Spanish showed the barbarity and hypocrisy of Christians, who spoke of God but worshiped gold as a god. Spain was spoiling the chances of conversion with a flouting of the Ten Commandments.[106]

By dwelling on the general term "Christian," Chauveton stressed this problem as one for all Europe and not simply Spain, however much it had done to set such a negative example. Christians should avoid disseminating this "blasphemy amongst these Nations" in the New World but should spread the Scriptures for the profit of these peoples.[107] This was a preface to a largely anti-Spanish world, or at least one of the cornerstones of the Black Legend, so a critique of Spain was to be expected, but it was also a lament for the division, strife, and false show among Christians. Even if this rhetoric were not sincere, a decision left to interpretation, it would still call attention to the internal contradictions among Christians in Benzoni's Milan or Chauveton's France as well as in the Spanish colonies. While criticizing Spain, then, Chauveton, inadvertently or not, was also providing a critique of Europe. This self-critical aspect of his work was part of the oppositional or alternative vein of the European tradition.

In the "Advertisement" Chauveton seemed to be claiming Le Challeux's work as his own even if he credited Benzoni for his part of the book.[108] The "Summary of the first book" stressed that Benzoni, who went to the West Indies, had written a history in Italian that represented the cruelty of the Spanish (how they hunted them for slaves) and asserted that some Spanish historian had taken away the honor of the discovery of the New World by Columbus.[109] The summary said that Benzoni described how the lands were found, how the Spanish abused such a singular gift from God, how they brought with them avarice, ambition, cruelty, war, and all their vices and very few virtues, and how there were in Hispaniola troubles, mutinies, uprisings, storms, and shipwrecks, "that is to say judgements of God on the head of those who have oppressed these poor people."[110] The French use of Las Casas and Benzoni was as a providential scourge of the Spanish colonists in the New World.

Natives had become a weapon against Spain. This summary then stressed Benzoni's discourse on the diverse views of the Natives on the American mainland. He wrote about "how the Spaniards made them believe that they were the children of God and had descended from heaven, but the others were not so loutish ("lourdauts") that they did not know well to judge the tree by its fruits. And how the King of Spain, from the report and persuasion of a few Monks, by Edict condemned these people of the Continent to perpetual servitude, if they did not want to convert, and has since revoked this Edict and given back liberty to the Indians by the advice of the Pope."[111] The ambivalence here is that Benzoni's argument showed the Spanish abuse of power but also the king's recognition of the mistake, reversing the enslavement of the Natives and giving them their liberty. In condensing the 387 pages of Benzoni's first book into 3 pages, the summary brought out the contradiction of Spain as tyrant and reformer. Another discrepancy was the revelation of the wrongs done to the Natives, whose "mortal enmity" the Spanish have gained, and the description of the superstitious nature of the inhabitants of Hispaniola.[112] The ethnological and the political discourses created a friction that brought out an ambivalence in which neither Spain nor the Natives could be entirely praised, although the summary of Benzoni's argument tended to sympathize with the Indians and criticize the Spaniards.

P. M.'s "Sonet," which follows the "Summary," was much more univocal in its condemnation of the Spanish in the New World. The poem described the arrival of the Spanish, who cruelly exploited the golden land of the New World and its peoples and then took their treasures:

> Of the new world & spacious abode,
>   The great treasures, the hidden riches
>   In the high mountains, & golden rivers:
>   All is briefly in this book included.
> The cruel fires of new world spirit,
>   The hard assaults, the wars ignited,
>   The regions of the Indies dispeopled
>   By the Spaniard, all is included here.
> How he dared to give himself to Fortune,
>   To take away from Ocean & Neptune:
>   How led by a desire to amass
> He placed under the yoke this strange people,
>   And exhausted the treasures of the earth,
> And now elsewhere he wants to go.[113]

The Spaniard of this poem found a spacious and bountiful land and exhausted it with cruelty and war, greed and slavery, so that he must now move on. All this the sonnet described in looking forward to a brief representation of the New World in the book.

The first book began Benzoni's memoir, in which within a few pages he was promised gold and in which the Natives fled the domination of the Christians.[114] This prefatory matter has helped to establish the role of French translations in the example of Spain, including a development of the Black Legend. While Benzoni's work and some of the translations we have just discussed are less well-known than the work of Las Casas, they are also significant contributions to representation of Spain in the New World. It is to Las Casas that we now turn.

A key translation in the establishment of the example of Spain in France and England was that of Bartolomé de Las Casas's *A Short Account of the Destruction of the Indies* (1542, pub. 1552). In a rhetorical exercise with legal and theological implications for colonization, the Spanish crown permitted the debate of 1551 between Las Casas and Juan Ginés de Sepúlveda over the treatment of the Amerindians.[115] It represented two ways of incorporating America into European history. Whereas Las Casas saw the contact as fulfilling Christian universal history in the conversion of the Indians, who were human and had souls to be saved, Sepúlveda advocated the growth of the Spanish monarchy and empire and denied the importance of the conversion of the Indians, who he thought were not completely human. In the history of Spanish colonization, Sepúlveda and Oviedo argued against the humanity of the American Indian, whereas Las Casas defended them. The synopsis of *A Short Account* said he spoke for Natives thus: "Prominent amid the aspects of this story which have caught the imagination are the massacres of innocent peoples, the atrocities committed against them and, among other horrific excesses, the ways in which towns, provinces, and the whole kingdoms have been entirely cleared of their native inhabitants."[116] This "discovery" of otherness was a matter of heroism and wonder, which evoked the traditions of natural history (Pliny), history (Herodotus), epic (Homer, Virgil), and travel literature (Marco Polo). But beside this tradition was Las Casas's outrage at genocide and his defense of the humanity of the Natives, which defied Sepúlveda's application of Aristotle's theory of natural slavery and which drew on a radical New Testament distrust of class and race that institutional Christianity has sometimes perverted. Here is opposition from within the "us" to stand up for "them," the tradition of the other from within.[117]

Miggrode's translation of Las Casas's *Brevissima relación,* which was printed in Antwerp (1579), then in Paris (1582), and finally in Lyon (1630), emphasized the tyranny and cruelty of the Spaniards in its title.[118] Miggrode began his address, "To the Reader," with a pronouncement like Fumée's, a kind of Augustinian postlapsarian epistemology in which divine knowledge is inscrutable on earth: "The judgements of God are abysses that are not in the power of men, nor of Angels, to penetrate."[119] Then he followed with the Spaniards, whose hell he described but did not name as such. In a frontal polemical attack he got to the point straightaway, appealing to the reader concerning the millions the Spanish had slaughtered "by all means that barbarism itself could imagine and forge on the anvil of cruelty": "they have destroyed a country three times larger than Christendom: the torments thought up by them, and the disloyalties are so great and so excessive that it would not be believable to posterity who has never been in the world a nation so barbarous and cruel as that one."[120] This hyperbolic attack led Miggrode to a confession: "I confess never to have liked that nation much in general because of their insupportable pride, however much that I give leave to praise and like excellent persons that there are amongst them. But God knows that hatred does not make me write these things, as even a Spanish national has written much more bitterly than I."[121] After dispensing with the Augustinian and Calvinist credo and trope of the inscrutability of God, Miggrode proceeded in his discourse to address the reader directly about the genealogy of Spanish barbarity and cruelty from the Goths through the Saracens to the Spaniards, all of whom had killed millions, especially the Spaniards who had massacred the inhabitants in the West Indies, an area three times as large as Christendom.[122]

As if the expression of these enormities were not enough, Miggrode represented them in terms of something beyond the utterable. Barbarity was limited by its imagination only; posterity would barely believe that such a barbarous and cruel nation existed, except for the witness of the sight and touch of Miggrode and his contemporaries. The bluntness of Miggrode's rhetoric created a kind of oxymoronic confessional attack. It was ambivalent because it moved in two directions; it was oxymoronic because it was conjoined and moved in two contradictory directions at once. There was even more subtlety to this apparently unsubtle bludgeoning of Spain. The personal attack, the worst kind of *ad hominem* abusive, was displaced on to the personality of the nation.

The stereotyping of national character took on personal traits, but Miggrode said he liked some excellent people among the Spaniards. The slippage occurred when he spoke of "the nation" but chose the plural "their pride" ("leur") instead of the singular "its" ("sa"), so that the Spanish nation was constructed as a collection of individuals. Miggrode confessed never to have liked this nation but spared some individuals who excelled the others, who were proud. This is a familiar form: I like the individuals but not the country. Miggrode, however, did not distinguish between the Spanish people and their government: he made the people, not the policy, barbarous and cruel. Pride was the worse sin for a Christian, something a postlapsarian doctrine especially emphasized, so that consciously or not, Miggrode attacked the Spanish nation and its people. He did so through a direct attack, then a retraction for the excellent among them, but a conflict occurred between the use of synecdoche (rhetoric) or the fallacy of composition (logic) to make the part represent the whole and the denial of that identity between Spanish people and the state. In a polemic, logical fallacies were masked in the emotive language of persuasion.

If the attack appeared hateful, Miggrode disclaimed hatred as a motivation because he was simply calling on a Spaniard, Las Casas, who showed even more asperity in his attack on Spain. Even though "God knows" was a figure of speech, it was also an appeal to that higher authority, the one whose judgments were abysses for men in Miggrode's opening sentence. Evidently, Miggrode had learned to read divine signs in a matter of a page. There is, of course, as Miggrode himself probably realized, a certain amount of disingenuousness involved in these shifts from person to nation and from heaven to earth and back again. The propaganda on both sides of the Wars of Religion was bitter and displayed figuratively and textually what literally and actually was a fight to the death.

Anyone who knew Las Casas's text would remember the chapter on Venezuela, in which Las Casas said of the Germans to whom Charles V had granted this vast territory, "In my opinion, the Venezuela expedition was incomparably more barbaric than any we have so far described."[123] Miggrode left this out of his translation of the text, fearing, perhaps, that the Germans might be taken for Protestants (whether they were or not), who could be more cruel than the Catholic Spaniards. This passage would qualify his objective argument and would hurt his cause amid the religious strife.[124] The example of Spain was as much about staying alive in Europe as it was about death in the New World.

Miggrode knew that he had to justify the presence of the address to the reader if he wanted simply to let Las Casas tell about Spanish cruelty. The address was there to awaken the provinces of the Netherlands from their sleep, so they could think on God's judgment and restrain themselves from their vices in order to consider who was their enemy for whom they had opened the door through their own quarrels, divisions, and partiality. Miggrode said that most men expected a just God to reward the good and punish the wicked, but God could also afflict the good, like Job, the prophets, the martyrs, and even Christ in order to mortify the flesh and to vivify the spirit of other men. He observed that still others assert that God did not let the wicked go long unpunished while others said the wicked had an advantage in a bad cause. But according to Miggrode, we see the contrary each day. The Turks' conquest of Christians, a pure tyranny and usurpation, was a punishment to Christians for sins and abuses in the service of God. Nonetheless, even Christians in doctrinal error were not as far from the truth than the Turks. They conquered Egypt, Africa, Spain, and Aquitaine all the way to the Loire, and had God not sustained Charles Martel, who pushed them back over the Pyrenees, all of Christendom would have fallen to these conquerors. The French were the heroes of Europe and turned back the invaders into Spain, which, he implied, was not as heroic and was stained by these events.[125]

The English translation of Las Casas, *The Spanish Colonie, Or Briefe Chronicle of the Acts and gestes of the Spaniards in the West Indies, called the newe World . . .* (1583), owed a debt to the French version of Miggrode. Translated by M. M. S., the English text was more than an indirect translation of Las Casas's *Brevissima relación.* The printer added a supplement of remedies that Las Casas recommended to the government of Spain and a summary of the debate between Juan Ginés de Sepúlveda and Las Casas at Vallodolid in 1550–51.[126] Whereas Sepúlveda, following Aristotle's doctrine of natural slavery, argued that the Spaniards could subjugate the Natives as slaves because they were of a lower order of nature, Las Casas opposed this view. In this opposition he related Spanish atrocities that the English and Dutch, enemies of Spain, as well as the French, seized on and used to help create the Black Legend of Spain.

In the Preface, M. M. S. spoke through Miggrode's French translation, so that although he was appealing to an English audience and was doing so in a translation that could never be exactly the same as the French version, itself a translation and therefore transmutation and interpretation of the Spanish original, he was imitating and reproducing his French source. In the prefatory address "*To the Reader,*" the English edition advertised Spain's atrocities from the opening words: "*Spanish cruelties and tyrannies, perpe*-trated in the West Indies, commonly termed *The newe found worlde.*"[127] After advertising Las Casas, the notice announced that the work was "faithfully translated by *Iames Aliggrodo,* to serue as a President and warning, to the xij. Prouinces of the lowe Countries."[128] The political struggle between the Dutch and the Spanish was mediated through its English allies via the French translation of Jacques de Miggrode. The English version of Miggrode's translation of Las Casas was then translated into Dutch and served as propaganda against Spain.[129] As this Englished "Las Casas" also translated Miggrode's preface, that is one place in this study where we can see explicitly the English view of Spain through French mediation: in what follows the translation will transmute the French text that was just discussed. The pan-European nature of textual, as well as actual, exploration of the New World differed from pre-Reformation Europe only in the religious conflict embodied and not in the transnational nature of the printing press.

The unidentified English translator, M. M. S., saw his work as prophetic warning: "*Happy is hee whome other mens harmes doe make to beware.*"[130] In the tradition of biblical prophecy this prophet began with "Gods iudgementes." Only "mans wisdome," and not the power of angels, was able to enter the depth of these judgments. By extension, the reader assumed this wisdom through the very act of address. With an immediate rhetoric of extremes, M. M. S., translating Miggrode and thereby authorizing and ventriloquizing him, set out the Spanish crimes that the French translation of Miggrode had already outlined.[131] The translator/author had the reader join him as a friend in his opposition to Spanish cruelty.

These translations, then, represented the different sides of Spain and did so in an apparently contradictory way. The heroic model of Cortés found in Gómara vied with the Spanish cruelty to the Natives described in Las Casas.[132] Nicholas, who seems to have suffered so much because of Spain, translated Gómara's account of the heroism of the Spanish conquest of Mexico, whereas Miggrode, who claimed to tell the truth so help him God, left out Las Casas's condemnation of the cruelty of the Germans probably because of the politics of the Netherlands and its neighbors as well as of Protestantism. An implied typology arose between the abuses of Spain in America and in the Netherlands. The so-called Black Legend was only one aspect of the intricate representation of Spain that this study is attempting to bring into focus.

Having examined the accounts by mariners, cosmographies, and translations, it is now important to turn to texts that called themselves histories. Three Huguenot histories, by Jean de Léry, Lancelot Voisin, sieur de La Popelinière, and Martin Basanier, will be the primary focus of the following discussion because they suggest, even as France was tearing itself apart over religion, that authors could still attack Spain. The motives were complex and could be as much about national as religious differences. It is also possible that these Huguenot historians viewed Spain and Portugal, but especially the Spanish, as threats to the desires of some French Protestants, in the face of religious tensions at home, for refuge in the New World, and not simply to the national interests of France there. The French wrote significant examples of histories of parts of the New World whether the author had been there, like Léry, or not, like La Popelinière. Léry's account of Brazil revisited the same occurrences Thevet described there. These controversial events that the French experienced in Brazil, like those in Florida, left an impression on the English and, during the French civil war, left a vacuum for England to fill in the New World. As we shall see later, Hakluyt the Younger came to draw on the French and to urge the English to take up their challenge in the New World.

IV

Histories, sometimes written by those who traveled to the New World, also contained important representations of the Spanish. These historical accounts often included a religious dimension that was controversial in an age of denominational strife. The Catholic and Protestant churches provided opposition to the greed and cruelty of conquest, although both sides of the religious conflict came to persecute the other, sometimes with the greatest cruelty. The Dutch and the French Protestants became victims of Spanish cruelty, a suffering that begot exempla, although many Dutch Catholics opposed Spanish rule in the Netherlands, particularly at the beginning, and some French Catholics criticized the Spanish for their treatment of the French colonists in the New World on the grounds of their being subjects of France and not of their Protestant religion.

Three histories, one by Léry that describes French colonization in Brazil during the 1550s, another by La Popelinière that is about France but that includes discussions of the New World, and still another by Basanier that brought together French writings about the events in Florida during the 1560s, provide strong examples of works that, while examining France in the New World, reveal the friction within France during its internal divisions. In this context I discuss Michel de Montaigne's views of Spain in his essays, which suggest a different perspective on his work in a distinct context based on the texts of these three historians. As France devoured itself, it could not so readily focus on Spain. Nonetheless, despite this stress, the matter of Spain remained. The French contribution to the Black Legend of Spain arose at the time of a terrible civil war. It was probably not lost on Léry that the cruelty of the French against the French was of a similar order to the Spaniards cruel treatment of the Natives in the New World that Las Casas described. Léry expanded his use of Las Casas in subsequent editions of his history. Variants of a typology between New World and Old World are something we will notice in the uses to which France, England, and the Netherlands put Las Casas. Spanish cruelty to "Amerindians" meant a similar cruelty to Europeans was possible and even likely.

Jean de Léry's *Histoire d'vn voyage faict en la terre dv Bresil, avtrement dite Amerique* (1578, revised 1580) was about his voyage to Brazil in 1556.[133] Its dedication was addressed to François de Coligny, the son of Gaspar de Coligny, the admiral of France, who had obtained royal support for Villegagnon's colony in Brazil and who, as the leader of Protestants in France, was killed in the Massacre of Saint Bartholomew's Day in 1572. The elder Coligny, having convinced Henri II that the trade in brazilwood was profitable and that it was important to challenge the monopoly of Spain and Portugal in the New World, was able to find the Huguenots a refuge there. Villegagnon supplemented Coligny's support for the Brazilian enterprise with that of the Cardinal de Lorraine, a member of the Guise family and the leader of the Catholic clergy in France.[134] Religion was a complex issue in this colonization as there were important Catholic and Protestant backers of French efforts at colonization in Brazil.

Léry's dedication began with the memory of François de Coligny's father.[135] In the memorial paean Léry called Gaspar de Coligny "the cause and the motive" of the mission in Brazil and, amplifying his rhetoric of praise, said that there had never been a "French and Christian Captain" who had spread the reign of Christ and his own sovereign so far.[136] To the critics who might object that the true religion and the French were no longer in Brazil, Léry replied that the gospel had been declared in America and had the affair been properly pursued, then a secure temporal and spiritual reign would have been founded. More specifically, he asserted that with this foundation "more than ten thousand persons of the French nation would be there and also in full and sure possession for our King as the Spaniards and Portuguese are in the name of theirs."[137] Even if Léry advocated religious reform, he did not place that above France and its king.

Spain and Portugal were rival nations that had been able to settle where the French should have stayed. Villegagnon was the first person Léry blamed, Thevet the second. Léry took these attacks personally, at least for Gaspar de Coligny, who claimed these lands for the French crown and for the proclamation of the gospel. From the beginning of the dedication, Léry made François a metonymy for his father, Gaspar. He now returned to this strategy by saying that the personal attacks on the father are really on the son, so that while Léry honored and praised the Coligny, *père et fils,* Thevet attacked François by attacking Gaspar. Generally, Thevet condemned and calumniated the cause for which Léry and his companions journeyed to America, when "in particular, speaking of the Admiralty of France in his *Cosmography,* he dared to rail against the good renown and repute, amongst all good people, of him who was the cause."[138] Thevet attacked Benzoni and "his pal Léry" for lack of proper knowledge and experience of the New World.[139] Just before this passage on the Isle of Cedars in Florida in *Grand Insulaire,* Thevet contested the Spanish claim to Florida. Having claimed that Verrazzano had discovered Florida, he concluded: "Therefore I hold that our French and even the English have much more right there than do the Spaniards, who however continually make war on those who cast anchor in Florida, where they have killed so many wrongfully and against their conscience, as also in the lands of Norumbeg and elsewhere. In short, they would make themselves masters of everything lying between the two poles."[140] Thevet's critique of Spain here was further evidence that it was too easy to call him "pro-Spanish." In the "Preface" Léry attacked Thevet at some length.[141] Léry criticized the French mariners' piracy against England, Spain, and Portugal while defending the claim of France in the New World against the hegemony of the Spanish and Portuguese.[142]

Spain made a few key appearances in Léry's text: he reported that the Spanish and Portuguese claimed to have been the first to discover Brazil and called the French usurpers.[143] In various places in his work Léry drew on Gómara's account of how the Natives in Peru thought the Spanish to be corrupt and rootless; how Pizarro attempted to use his horse to amaze and frighten Attabalipa, the king of Peru, who had not seen a horse; how the Spanish used writing to dominate the Natives (the invention of writing won Léry's praise, and it is clear the French, like the Spanish, were thought to be much luckier than the Natives, who lacked this art); how the Spaniards robbed the graves for gold and riches and scattered the bones.[144]

Over time, editions of Léry expanded, especially the section on cannibalism, which came to include the Spanish cruelty in the New World as Las Casas had described it. The material from Las Casas had soon grown so much that Léry created a new chapter for it.[145] Sensational cruelty, by the Spanish or the Natives, was obviously in demand and sold books, an aspect of the example of Spain that might be overlooked. Léry influenced Catholics and Protestants alike, so that some of his most important readers and successors could overlook the infighting of those involved in the Brazilian expedition and those committed to the ideological conflict being fought over religion in France at that time. Chauveton, De Bry, Montaigne, Purchas, Lescarbot, Claude d'Abbeville, Purchas, and others, as Janet Whatley documents, made use of Léry.[146]

One influence that was especially important textually was Léry on Montaigne's writing about the New World. Michel de Montaigne, born to a Catholic father and a Jewish mother who had converted to Protestantism, also criticized European abuses against the peoples they were subjecting. In his essay, "Des Cannibales" (1580), Montaigne used a classical context, including the Greek habit of calling all foreign countries barbarous and Plato's representation of Solon's account of Atlantis, to criticize French and European expansion and commerce in the New World, so that the simple equation, now made too often from neglect or ignorance, between classicism and the ills of colonization was too simple an assessment.[147] This essay, as David Quint argues, is as much about France as about the New World, and Quint does not seek to congratulate Montaigne for his freedom from prejudice.[148] This view supports my notion of typology between New World and Old.

As Montaigne is much discussed, I have decided to concentrate on him as developing in part from Las Casas and Léry, especially in terms of comments on Spain, an aspect that has been relatively neglected. Whereas in the essay on cannibals Montaigne had emphasized the French and Europeans in relation to the New World, in "Des Coches" ("Of Coaches") he represented the Spanish. He asked why the new lands could not have been conquered under the Greeks and

Romans to bring the peoples virtue rather than teaching them European avarice and "all sorts of inhumanity and cruelty and pattern of our customs."[149] Instead, in search of pearls and pepper, the Europeans had exterminated nations and millions of people, which Montaigne deemed "mechanical victories": Florio, Montaigne's translator in English, rendered the passage "Oh mechanicall victories, oh base conquest."[150] It is clear, however, that Montaigne meant to chastise the Spanish, the king of Castile, and the pope, who appeared in the usual Spanish ceremony of possession in which the Spaniards, searching for a mine, told the Natives that their king was "the greatest Prince in the inhabited earth, to whom the Pope, representing God on earth, had given the principality of all the Indies" and that they wanted the Natives to be tributaries that would yield up food, medicine, and gold, believe in one God, and acknowledge the truth of the Spanish religion.[151] The noble king of Mexico was subjected to Spanish cruelty and torture, which diminished Spain and not the victim.[152] Florio emphasized this contrast by applying the epithet "barbarous mindes" to the Spanish torturers.[153] These and other atrocities were a source of Spanish pride: "We have from themselves these narratives, for they not only confess but publish and extol them."[154] The Spaniards, according to Montaigne, exceeded the force necessary in conquest and had met with providential justice as they had fought one another in civil war and had had the seas swallow up some of their treasure.[155] Taken in context, then, Montaigne's comments on the Spaniards and their treatment of the Natives were not, as brilliant, elegant, and provocative as his work is, original or seminal. Beyond France, in England and elsewhere, in the works of well-known and lesser-known authors, representations of Spain in the New World shared similar content. A kind of mutual influence in colonization and intertextuality occurred, so that France and England helped to define each other in relation to Spain.

The French and English influenced each other in relation to colonization in the New World and in their representation of Spain. The civil wars in France made Huguenot exploration and settlement in the New World increasingly difficult. An important writer in this regard, although less renowned than Montaigne, was Lancelot Voisin, sieur de La Popelinière. In 1581, he published anonymously *L'Histoire de France . . . ,* which discussed events beginning in 1550, or, as he mentioned in the dedication "To the King," since the time of the king's father, François I to the present. As we shall see in the next chapter, this was the author whom Hakluyt would use in his prefatory matter to *Principal Navigations* (1589) in order to goad the English into a new navigation policy because he thought French scorn for the lag in English sailing and exploration would motivate queen, court, and country.

La Popelinière's dedication also included an offer of history as an example to the king and his councilors as well as a wish and a prayer for peace, an end to the "detestable effects of the bloody French mutinies."[156] Coming after "Lectori," a Latin poem on the civil war in France, full of classical references such as those to usual pairing of Venus and Mars but in concert with Christ, the "Advertissemens," written by "I. D. F. B. R. U. C. F. Escuier," discussed many topics, although it began in earnest with a comparison of the art of war ("l'art militaire") to letters and politics among ancients and moderns. During the Renaissance, the Baroque and the Enlightenment neoclassical revival became a way of reading political and imperial signs of the past in the present.[157] The "Advertissemens" developed a trope we have met before—that is, the implied or manifest truth of the author of this history as opposed to historians who have lied before: "That which is beyond ignorance, hatred, avarice and ambition: the principal occasion and most gracious pretext that historiographers of this time take to lie well and disguise the actions of men, with the assurance that the people will little know their imposture."[158] This anonymous author of *L'Histoire* attempted fairness and considered the valences of the various terms for Catholics and Protestants that each side of the religious strife used polemically, so that he employed these neutral names except when reporting the words of others in the controversy and civil war. This introduction or notice claimed that the author sought to use unprejudiced and natural language. The author did not put his name on the book because he wanted the recompense of honor rather than ambition and profit, although the author of the "Advertissemen" defended that name against false attribution and abuse.[159] The poem ended: "But you will be esteemed/ For effecting things/And for this polished writing/ Which learnedly you compose." The next prefatory matter was the "Ode" in French, which, amid more classical allusions, praised the author for his embodiment of Apollo and Mars, the truth of his history, his brave spirit, his ability to write learned and polished work while effecting things.[160]

The "Summary" of the first book of this history of France and its neighbors included as one of its marginal headings read: "Source of the hatreds and Wars between the French and Spanish."[161] This section explained the conflicts over Naples, Milan, Flanders, Burgundy, and other "rights." The main body of the text and indices were also revealing in the relations among France, England, and Spain. Four entries in the index to volume one should illustrate the sometimes negative attitude toward Spain: "The Spaniards proud and presumptuous with others," which described a battle in 1553; "The Spaniards cruel to the French," which recounted the war in Italy in 1557; "The Germans hate the Spaniard"; "The Spaniard hated by all," both of which described the war in the Netherlands in 1568.[162] The descriptions were brief "statements of fact" woven into detailed accounts of war but were not long and sensational as in Las Casas, Benzoni, and others. La Popelinière stated the charge of Spanish cruelty but not without emphasizing that this view was part of a campaign to turn popular feeling against Spain: "In many places there would be libelous forces, little treatises and defamatory posters of the life, lubricity, pilfering and cruelty of the Spaniards in Flanders to move the people to a revolt."[163] Another entry in that index is "the English hate the Spaniards," which referred to the reign of Philip and Mary during the 1550s.[164] At the end of the third book, one of the marginal headings noted: "Libels against the Spaniards in England."[165] While negotiations were going on over the marriage of Philip of Spain and Mary of England, some anti-Spanish sentiments surfaced in London: "During this assembly very stinging little Booklets were spread and scattered about London amongst which there was not any sufficient enough to move the populace to sedition against the Spaniards (to whom the English made a thousand annoyances) and to dissuade the Queen from the love of Philip."[166] The fourth book began with the marriage of Philip and Mary and included the divisions between the Spanish and the English even in 1558 when they were supposed to be united.[167] Moreover, the index highlighted what was a sub-theme of La Popelinière's history—that under Elizabeth England helped the Protestants in France and the Netherlands while Spain did the same for the Catholics.

The New World was also a concern of La Popelinière's *Histoire*. In book five he described Villegagnon's venture and the New World more generally, while in book ten he represented Ribault in Florida and in book 34 he referred to American themes. Villegagnon received no assistance from France, and after the Portuguese and their Native allies attacked his fort, he retreated to France. La Popelinière provided a context for this colony and for its demise. Villegagnon's enterprise was "badly conducted and badly executed," and he continued to attack the Reformers, "frustrated by his own fault of [achieving] an eternal renown similar to that which Christopher Columbus Genoese, Amerigo Vespucci Florentine, the Pizarros, Cortés, Albuquerque, Pedraluaret [Pedro Alvarez Cabral] and other Spanish and Portuguese Captains" received.[168] Instead, the refuge for those who would follow "the translation of faith" was a place where the viceroy, caught between court and Reformers, feared having his authority revoked and being punished as a heretic.[169] This passage was critical of Villegagnon's planning and leadership, and showed an ability in France for self-criticism. The translation of faith as well as the translation of empire was something, along with the tensions between Catholics and Protestants, La Popelinière emphasized. Villegagnon could not achieve the renown that the exemplars of Portugal and Spain in the New World had won. The author also tried to understand the motives for the Portuguese attack on the French and weighed into the controversy in France about the Brazilian colony in which Villegagnon, Thevet, Léry, and others were involved.

La Popelinière also discussed a recurrent concern among Europeans in the New World: the anxiety over origins and rivalry. He mentioned Cabral's voyage, which set out on April 9, 1500, but against this Portuguese claim to Brazil, he placed the French version. In France, mainly Normans and some Bretons maintained that they discovered Brazil and were the first to trade with the Natives. This claim rather surprisingly elicited the criticism of their compatriot, for they did not have the proof of public written documents, whereas the Portuguese had experience in "voyages and maritime discoveries superior to all nations" and in that province Cabral left "a cross blessed with all solemnities that the priests of his troop could practise."[170] La Popelinière preferred the original Portuguese name to the French name for Brazil. He then spoke about the greatest province in America, to the west of the mountains of Peru, which had gold and silver as well as commodities that Peru and the other provinces lacked. To complement this strange if not mythical geography, La Popelinière then introduced the Amazons, recalling the ransom King Atabalipa gave to Pizarro in the province of Cusco, something that Montaigne also discussed about the same time.

After all this praise of Spain and Portugal, partly at the expense of the French, La Popelinière distinguished between the Spanish and Portuguese in the New World and mentioned the resentment that Pope Alexander VI caused among the other European countries when he divided the "unknown" world between the Iberian powers. The Spanish had not listened to the advice of those like the Jesuits, who had counseled gentleness: "they have subdued their Indies but by force, deceit and strange cruelty" that is hardly believable and little by little they molest "the goods and freedom of the Savages."[171] La Popelinière seemed to have preferred a Portuguese model to the example of Spain: "The Portuguese have always had an altogether other goal in their discoveries than the Spaniard who has wished to make himself absolute Lord by force of all where he has set foot."[172] Although La Popelinière, a Huguenot, leaned toward a model from Catholic Portugal, he also had to define French colonization very much in terms of Spain. Spain was a positive challenge to French colonization. Elsewhere, La Popelinière wrote "The French above all were spurred by a desire to do like-wise in areas that had not been reached by them [Spaniards], for they did not esteem themselves less than they, neither in navigation, in feats of arms nor in any other calling. They persuaded themselves that they [the Spanish] had not discovered all, and that the world was large enough to reveal even stranger things than those already known."[173] The Portuguese were not interested in "putting the people into servitude" but in commerce "and in preventing the entrance in these countries of all other nations that could challenge its gain that was con-veyed by Pope Alexander who divided in two (always to the great discontent of the other Princes) the new lands discovered in the Orient and Occident between these two Princes, about whom I shall speak amply elsewhere."[174] Like the English, the French were sometimes obsessed with the papal division of the unknown world and the lost opportunity of employing Columbus, for both countries had traditions that Columbus had sought out their support. In his diary in 1536 Gaspar de Saulx lamented that France had turned Columbus down as did Montesquieu about 200 years later.[175] Whereas the Portuguese were tolerant and left the Natives alone, the Spanish were cruel and dominated the aboriginal inhabitants.

In North America the French appeared to adapt more the model of Portu-gal, building an economy based on trading posts for fish and furs, whereas within decades of first settlement, the English tended more toward the example of Spain insofar as they came to dominate the Natives and populate the country with their own countrymen and slaves. Both France and England, as part of their general ambivalent and contradictory representations of Spain, stressed Spanish cruelty in the New World.

At the very end of book ten, La Popelinière reiterated the complaints of other Christian nations against Spain and Portugal for prohibiting them from landing and trading rights in their discovered lands.[176] The second volume of the *His-toire* confirmed and supplemented these representations of Spain. For instance, in book 34, La Popelinière told of how the French Protestants resented the Spanish for helping French Catholics and for trying to extirpate Protestantism from France and how the Huguenots attacked as far away as Peru. He also called the French idiots for killing each other in a civil war—much to the great pleasure of foreigners—and questioned the right of Spain and Portugal to the lands Alexander VI gave them. One of the marginal notes revealed that the French, like the English, were anxious to claim priority in the discovery of the New World: "The French discovered the new Lands before the Spanish did, But our Princes did not recognize them and incited them to return there less than the King of Aragon and Castile did theirs."[177] In this description of the events of April 1573, La Popelinière also noted that the French Protestants displayed the flag of the red cross of England. This religious conflict, which involved England and Spain in the French civil war, affected events in Europe and America. In the 1580s and beyond, the bitterness over the conflict, which involved these and other neighboring states, found its way into the histories and the polemical wars between Catholics and Protestants.

The writing of "history," which the title of Léry's and La Poplinière's works emphasized, represented a New World that set out Spain, England, and France in America in a way that could not be reduced to simple categories of opposition. Martin Basanier's *Histoire notable de la Floride . . .* (1586), another example of a Huguenot history of French colonization, represented this intricate triangular relation and made Walter Ralegh a focus.

Martin Basanier, a gentleman and mathematician, included a dedication to Ralegh in his *Histoire . . . ,* which collected three chapters on the French expeditions in Florida of 1562 and of 1564–65, the work of Captain Goulaine de Laudonnière, and another chapter concerning the revenge of Dominique de Gourges, a Gascon captain, against the Spanish in Florida, written by Gourges. For French Protestants in the middle of the Wars of Religion, the events in Florida were still a controversy to keep alive. Basanier's "Epistle" used the common trope of the mirror of history. In representing the New World of Laudonnière and Gourges to Ralegh, Basanier drew out the moral and exemplary dimension of history and thereby kept within the Ciceronian notion of historical representation. In the body of Laudonnière's account of the events of 1564 in Florida, he addressed the temptations of avarice and ambition that led to sedition among the French. The mutineers wanted to go to Peru and the Indies to enrich themselves.[178] Laudonnière made an observation that revealed that some among the French were no better than certain Spaniards in their desire for riches: "This talk of riches sounded so good in the ears of my soldiers."[179] The greed of Spain here was reiterated as a negative example.

In their histories that relate to the New World, Léry, La Popelinière, and Basanier, like Montaigne in his *Essais,* all represented Spain in a complex fashion. Religious conflict is not as obvious in their work as the terrible divisions in France might lead us to expect. The Huguenots with a stake in the New World were, as we can see expressly in Basanier's address to Ralegh, closely connected to English Protestants involved in the exploration of the Americas. A good example of the debt of this group that benefited from the experience of the French Protestants in, as well as the knowledge concerning, the New World is Hakluyt the Younger, who spent crucial time in Paris in the early 1580s and brought back the benefit of what he learned to London. It is probably not an exaggeration to say that the Huguenots are the unsung begetters of English designs, from about 1580 to 1630, to establish permanent settlements on the eastern coast of North America.

V

At the heart of this English colonial design was the textual enterprise—the collecting, scholarship, translation, and editing—that Richard Hakluyt the Younger oversaw. A promoter of colonies, Hakluyt shared a number of ideas with Gilbert, and his work supported and promoted Gilbert's plan for a westward voyage. Hakluyt worked in France, where he learned from many sources. In the context of our discussions, the role of the Huguenots is of central importance. The most crucial text concerning the example of Spain that Hakluyt produced was "Discourse on Western Planting" (1584), but there are a few germane aspects of *Divers Voyages (1582)* that we should first touch on.

In the "Epistle Dedicatory" to Philip Sidney in *Divers Voyages*, Hakluyt included a list of geographers and travelers and an argument for the northwest passage. Some of the themes that would appear in "Discourse on Western Planting" occurred in the dedication in a much briefer form: the unjust punishment of people for petty crimes, the use of the New World as a place for England's excess population, the advocacy for the northwest passage, and the furthering of England's knowledge in geography and navigation, at this time deficient, through the endowment of a lectureship.[180] At the opening of the address to Sidney, Hakluyt expressed ambivalence to Spain and Portugal: they had come to possess the most temperate lands, but even though the English had missed this opportunity, the Portuguese were past their prime and "the nakednesse of the Spaniards" was apparent, so that the English could hope to share America with the Iberian powers. Hakluyt stressed the right of possession to North America owing to English discovery; the desire to use prisoners who had been jailed for petty crimes and others who constituted surplus population as colonists; the example of Greek and Carthaginian colonies; the appropriateness of colonizing North America as set out by John Barros, the chief cosmographer in Portugal; the confirmation of this opinion as well as evidence for the northwest passage by Sebastian Cabot, Verrazzano, Gómara, Cartier, Ribault, Drake, Mercator, Frobisher, and others.[181] In *Divers Voyages* Hakluyt had done much to contribute to knowledge of the New World through translation and his own writing and collecting, but he seemed to have thought that more should be done. He looked to the nobility for support: they needed to invest to build an empire. To develop the knowledge necessary for that task required investment and commitment, something England needed much more of to be successful in colonizing the New World.

This discussion will concentrate more on "Discourse" than on *Divers Voyages*, partly because it is less known and because it allows for an opportunity to examine a private document prepared for the government of England, in which Hakluyt could be more frank about Spain than he was in his published work.[182] In 1584, the Reverend Mr. Richard Hakluyt, chaplain and secretary to Sir Edward

Stafford at the English embassy in Paris, wrote his "Discourse on Western Planting," as it is now known. Paris, "a focus of anti-Spanish sentiment," was a substitute for a listening post at Madrid, where the English had no envoy: moreover, France was the first nation to challenge Spain in its American empire, and Spanish ships sometimes called into French ports.[183] The "Discourse," a state paper that remained in manuscript and was not published until 1877, when it appeared in Boston, was presented to Elizabeth I in October 1584. Sir Francis Walsingham, secretary of state, seemed to have employed Hakluyt as a support to Ralegh, who in the spring of 1584 had sent Philip Amadas and Richard Barlowe to look for a suitable site for a colony, both in giving advice and as a means of persuading the queen to back the venture.[184] Walsingham, as we have seen, was a central force in English expansion, so it is not surprising that Hakluyt, like Thomas Nicholas, worked within the secretary of state's network of patronage. Hakluyt was busy gathering information on rivals in North American colonization, especially on Spain. He knew the work of Peter Martyr, Gómara, Oviedo, Benzoni, La Popelinière (Lancelot Voisin), and others who wrote about Spanish colonization (and, in the last instance, French colonies) and seemed to have sought out pro-Dutch and anti-Spanish work.[185]

In Paris, Hakluyt may have met with Duplessis-Mornay (Philippe de Mornay, seigneur du Plessis-Marly), a Huguenot hostile to Spain, and a diplomat who, serving Henri de Navarre as his ambassador in London in 1577–78, knew Walsingham and Lady Stafford. On April 24, 1584, Mornay presented to the French king an unpublished work, "Discourse to Henri III. On the ways of diminishing the Spaniard," which was probably known to Hakluyt.[186] Duplessis-Mornay, reflecting the views of Henri de Navarre, asserted that Philip II was a tyrant who was undermining France, destroying the Netherlands and Europe; that the French should, along with England, blockade the English Channel from Spanish shipping; that France should attack the Spanish empire in the New World to seize it and to prevent the king of Spain from receiving the bullion that allowed him to tyrannize Europe. These anti-Spanish themes echoed similar positions in Drake and Coligny and foreshadowed those in Hakluyt. For Duplessis-Mornay, the French conquest would involve good treatment of the Natives, who should be enlisted against the Spanish conquerors who had exploited them.[187]

While Duplessis-Mornay was busy presenting his arguments against Spain to the king of France, Hakluyt was preparing a similar brief to the queen of England. Hakluyt's work was to gather as much knowledge of the New World as he could, from the Spanish but also from the French and others, in order to support Walsingham and Ralegh in the scheme for colonization of the New World, especially as a means of persuading the queen to back the venture and to become more and more involved in such colonies. In this way England would guard itself against the power of Spain. This rhetorical persuasion had much to do with the politics of power. In July 1584 Hakluyt returned to England to complete the "Discourse" and, on October 7, two days after it was presented to Elizabeth I, he returned to Paris.[188]

In the "Discourse" Hakluyt argued for the English colonization of North

America. To that end he concentrated on Spanish aggression in its colonies in the New World and envisioned the English American colonies as a curb to that abusive Spanish power. The Church of England was to help evangelize the Natives, who might also prove useful in the fight against Spain, whose Jesuits had had a head start in their mission. Hakluyt then argued for colonial expansion to North America as a means of addressing problems of trade arising out of the disruption of trade with the Netherlands and Spain (particularly in the cloth trade) and the civil war in France (even with its lulls as in 1584). North America was full of abundant resources to make England rich and keep masterless men at work.[189]

The "Discourse" was set up like a book, although it was not printed until modern times, perhaps being akin to briefs in government, literary manuscripts at court and to mediaeval manuscripts before Gütenberg. In this private government document, Hakluyt, in what is essentially a title, stated that the work was written in 1584 at the request of "Master Walter Rayley" and that the next leaf would contain the titles of the 21 chapters.[190] This beautifully copied and presented manuscript was meant for more than Ralegh's eyes: the queen was its ultimate audience. Even a sample of the titles, long in the fashion of the times, exemplifies the ambivalence or double action of English relations to the Spanish empire: it was to be envied, imitated, and displaced on the one hand; it was to be reviled, denounced, and replaced on the other.

Put together, the 21 titles were like the bare bones of a two-way argument. England needed Spanish trade and if it could not have it, it would have to push Spain aside and develop colonies for commodities, places to attack the Spanish West Indies, and stations on the way to Cipango and Cathay. The blows to English trade helped to inflame the rhetoric against Spain, which, to English eyes, did not seem to be hurting economically. The list was an advertisement for the project Ralegh and Walsingham backed.

Most of the chapter titles began with "That" as if they were part of an argument, if not a legal treatise or set of grievances, which often used an anaphoric formula. The first two titles culminated in "Elizabeth I." The Black Legend and the legal dispute over the Indies, demonstrated that while the anti-Spanish sentiment seemed to have been increasing in England, reflected in the attitudes of the "American" and Protestant party at court, the debate over the legal grounds of empire continued nearly a century after Columbus's landfall. Perhaps the papal bull of 1570, which excommunicated Elizabeth, was too fresh an insult to forget the legal origins of the Spanish empire in the New World. In addition, Spain insisted on this authority to try to bar other nations, like France and England, from direct trade with the its colonies. Issues of religion, trade, and politics were mixed throughout Hakluyt's text. I shall give a sample of Hakluyt's chapter titles as examples of his view of Spain:

> 2. That all other englishe Trades are growen beggerly or daungerous especially in all the kinge of Spayne his Domynions, where our men are dryven to flinge their Bibles and prayer Bookes into the sea, and

to forsweare and renownce their relligion and conscience and consequently theyr obedience to her Maiestie /. . .

5. That this [western] voyadge will be a great bridle to the Indies of the
kinge of Spaine and a meane that wee may arreste at our pleasure for
the space of tenne weekes or three monethes every yere, one or twoo
hundred saile of his subiectes shippes at the fysshinge in Newfounde
lande /

6. That the mischefe that the Indian Threasure wroughte in time of
Charles the late Emperour father to the Spanishe kinge, is to be had
in consideracion of the Queenes moste excellent Maiestie, leaste the
contynuall commynge of the like threasure from thence wee haue had
very dangerous experience /

7. What speciall meanes may bringe kinge Phillippe from his highe
Throne, and make him equall to the Princes his neighbours, where-
withall is shewed his weakenes in the west Indies /

8. That the lymites of the kinge of Spaines Domynions in the west
Indies be nothinge so large as ys generally ymagined and surmised,
neither those partes which he holdeth be of any suche forces as ys fal-
sly geuen oute by the poishe Clergye and others his fautors, to terrifie the Princes of the Relligion and to abuse and blynde them /. . .

11. That the Spaniardes haue executed moste outragious and more then
Turkishe cruelties in all the west Indies, whereby they are euery where
there, becomme moste odious vnto them, whoe woulde ioyne with
vs or any other moste willingly to shake of their moste intollerable
yoke, and haue begonne to doo it already in dyvers places where they
were Lordes heretofore /. . .

18. That the Queene of Englande title to all the west Indies, or at leaste
to as moche as is from Florida to the Circle articke, is more laufull and
righte then the Spniardes or any other Christian Princes /

19. An aunswer to the Bull of the Donacion of all the west Indies
graunted to the kinges of Spaine by Pope Alexander the vj^th whoe was
himselfe a Spaniarde borne /

Although in the titles and the chapters Hakluyt emphasized the enlargement of
the gospel in these new lands and the necessity of speedy colonization before
rivals could get there before the English, he displayed an overwhelming concern
with Spain. That rivalry, based on a desire for riches and land and an anxiety over
Spanish power and precedence in law, stood at the center of the "Discourse."

Even when other apparent topics occurred, arguments over English rights and the role of Spain in the New World ran throughout Hakluyt's "Discourse." The opening of the first chapter, which exhorted the queen to be a leader among princes of the Reformed religion in the enlargement of the gospel of Christ, got to the point. Like the French, the English had been eyeing the lands north of the Spanish settlements because they were unoccupied by Europeans and home to idolaters, like those "Stephen Gomes broughte from the coaste of Norumbega in the yere 1524 worshipped the Sonne, the Moone, and the starres, and vse other Idolatrie as it ys recorded in the historie of Gonsaluo de Ouiedo in Italian fol. 52. of th thirde volume of Ramusius."[191] In the quest for Norumbega the English followed the French, but Hakluyt also referred to the authority of Oviedo even in his plan to settle North America before the Spanish did and to beat the French to permanent settlement. Although Hakluyt wanted to spread the Reformed religion, he supplemented his view of evangelization by quoting Jacques Cartier, apparently a Catholic, on how the Natives were ready for the gospel. Hakluyt appealed to the title of Defender of the Faith, which the pope bestowed on Henry VIII in his fight with Luther (something Hakluyt did not mention but Elizabeth would obviously have known), as a means of supporting Elizabeth's claim to be a leader among Reformed princes who should perform a Christian mission in the New World. Surprisingly, the English, possibly more than the French, took the bulls of donation seriously and seized opportunities to discredit them, so that they feared papal authority and Spanish power while denying them.

This doublethink, which I have called the example of Spain, led Hakluyt to set out plans to supplant Spain by knowledge of the Spanish experience in the Americas. He recommended that the queen plant two secure colonies to provide safety to the clergy to avoid the fate of the Spanish friars in Florida whom the Natives massacred before Spain had established a settlement.[192] The double attitude toward Spain became explicit:

> Nowe yf they in their superstition by meanes of their plantinge in those partes haue don so great thinges in so shorte space, what may wee hope for in our true and syncere Relligion, proposinge vnto our selues in this action not filthie lucre nor vaine ostentation as they in deede did, but principally the gayninge of the soules of millons of those wretched people, the reducinge of them from darkenes to lighte, from falshoodde to truthe, from dombe Idolls to the lyvinge god, from the depe pitt of hell to the highest heavens.[193]

Here is praise and blame, the great things the Spanish have done in evangelization and their love of lucre and ostentation. The people of America have been crying out for help, and God will reward those who open up their coffers to further the godly enterprise in the Americas. Hakluyt used Queen Isabella as an example: she pawned her jewels "to furnishe oute Columbus for the firste discouery of the weste Indies."[194] After admitting the model of Isabella and the primacy of Columbus, Hakluyt seemed to catch himself because the "papists" claim to have converted millions of "Infidels" in the New World and when asked by them how many the Reformers had converted, Hakluyt, surveying the example of Protestant ministers and explorers (Villegagnon from Geneva to Brazil; Jean Ribault to Florida; Frobisher, Drake, and Fenton), had to answer: none.

Hakluyt then had to resort to the response that God has a time for all men and that the Catholics have taken the infidels from one error into another. English ministers would also benefit by leaving contention at home for the truth in the work on "reducinge the Savages to the chef principles of our faithe."[195] Hakluyt's plan would stop the mouths of Catholic adversaries, end contention among the English, and publish the gospel among the infidels.

The issue of God was also one of trade. Chapter two emphasized how in the king of Spain's dominions the English were driven to renounce their religion and, therefore, obdedience to their queen. The Spanish confiscated English goods in the Barbary trade and, if the English were blown on the Spanish coast, subjected the crew to the Inquisition. Of the king of Spain, Hakluyt said: "he beinge our mortall enemye, and his Empire of late beinge encreased so mightely, and our necessitie of oiles and of coulours for our clothinge trade beinge so greate, he may arreste almoste the one halfe of our navye, our traficque and recourse beinge so greate to his domynions."[196] Hakluyt showed that part of the English rhetorical belligerence was England's economic reliance on Spain amid uncertainty over the increase of Spanish power and of religious tension. He catalogued the dangers and woes of English trade in Turkey, France, Flanders, Denmark, Russia, and other places. Flanders, for instance, had floundered on 18 years of civil war that had ruined English trade there.

In returning to Spain, which is obviously the chief culprit in Hakluyt's analysis, he went into some detail describing the Spanish harassment of English ships, especially as regards to the policing of religion, which led to English merchants either dissembling conversion or converting, all the while keeping this secret: "The marchant in England commeth here devoutly to the communyon, and sendeth his sonne into Spaine to here masse."[197] This situation took Hakluyt in chapter 3 to North America, the lands in the New World the Spanish had not yet occupied, because it had all the commodities that these uncertain trading partners possessed. The "western discoverie" was an English declaration of independence in trade.

Hakluyt returned to the legal arguments that haunt the history of discourse over the European claims to the New World: we were there first and were the first civilized souls to occupy the land. He said that Sebastian Cabot's discovery gave England the rightful possession of lands in America from Florida to the lands at 67 degrees.[198] This original claim, however, also emphasized the lack of early English experience to follow up the work of the Cabots. If the English had, in European terms, discovered North America, they had not occupied it. Hakluyt could not provide English accounts of the land to bolster England's claim to the territory.

The Spanish and the French haunted this staking of North America. Later, Hakluyt could also call on English texts for evidence. Rather than being able to provide an eyewitness account of the lands between 30 and 34 degrees, he quoted from Jean Ribault's narrative, which then existed in French manuscript and an English edition but is now extant only in English, about the abundance of the country, the temperate climate, the gentleness of the people. The fate of Ribault colony was an unmentioned subtext. Hakluyt alluded to Nicolás Monardes, a Spaniard, whose work on the medicinal uses of plants in the West Indies (1569–74) relied on John Frampton's translation of most of the 1574 edition. Frampton combined the three parts of *La Historia medicinal,* under the title, *Ioyfull newes out of the newe founde worlde, wherein is declared the rare and singuler vertues of diuerse and sundrie hearbes . . . with their aplications, aswell for phisicke as chirurgerie* (1577). Monardes depended on the earlier French experience with the Natives in Florida who taught them about the medicinal properties of Sassafras. For the Spanish, as for the English, the French, who were most active in North America from 1525 to 1570, were a chief source of knowledge. Native knowledge lay behind all the early European efforts of survival and colonization in the New World.

For the areas northward, especially concerning Norumbega, Hakluyt depended on the accounts of the voyages of 1524 of Verrazzano, an Italian in the service of France, and Gomes, a Portuguese in the employ of Emperor Charles V, both of whom returned with Natives to France and Spain respectively. Hakluyt credited Gomes with the discovery of Norumbega and quoted Ramusio's Italian translation of 1556 of Oviedo's *Historia natural* (1526), presumably because the queen preferred or was more fluent in Italian or because Ramusio was a ready source (Hakluyt then quoted a captain of Dieppe about North America in his native Italian). In extolling the virtues of the land from Florida to Newfoundland, its temperate climate and its resources, Hakluyt also cited the recent experience of the French there, notably that of Étienne Bellinger (1583) and the marquis de la Roche (1584).[199] The accounts of Jacques Cartier and Vasques de Coronado also provided evidence of the abundance of North America: among the animal, plant, and mineral riches were silver and gold.

To supplement these examples in French and Spanish, Hakluyt quoted from George Peckham's *A true reporte of the late discoueries and possessyon taken in the righte of the Crowne of England of the Newfounde Landes: by that valiaunt and worthye Gentleman, Sir Humfrey Gilbert Knight* (1583) and from a letter Hakluyt received from his student roommate at Oxford, "one Stephanus Parmenius a learned hungarian borne in Buda," whom we met briefly before on Gilbert's expedition.[200] In his citation and quotation of these sources from Spain, France, and England, Hakluyt was interested in amplifying the effect of the masses of commodities to be found in England's desired land. For the moment, Hakluyt left God behind for gold.

Once again, it is noticeable how cosmopolitan Hakluyt was in his plans for English trade, glory, and expansion: he was too complex to settle for a chauvinistic yearning for wealth alone. His desire to promote North America for England never prevented him from also borrowing descriptions from narratives not written in English. To begin chapter 4, which concentrated on unemployment, he explicitly praised Spain and Portugal and offered them as a model of colonization:

> It is well worthe the obseruacion to see and consider what the like voy-
> adges of discouerye and plantinge in the easte and weste Indies hath
> wroughte in the kingdommes of Portingale and Spayne. Bothe which
> Realmes beinge of themselues poore & barren and hardly able to susteine
> their Inhabitauntes by their discoueries haue founde suche occasion of
> employmente, that these many yeres wee haue not herde scarcely of any
> pirate of those twoo nations: whereas wee and the frenche are most infa-
> mous for our outeragious, common and daily piracies.[201]

For more evidence on these lands, he went to a Portuguese origin, Corte Real's early voyage as presented in Ramusio, his chief source. France might have been piratical, but England was engendering pirates, loiterers, and vagabonds. This self-criticism in favor of the Iberian model (Spain had absorbed Portugal in 1580 and would govern it until 1640) had more than economic motives. Hakluyt's marginal notes presented starkly the political reasoning behind colonization: "Idle persons mutynous and desire alteration in the state" and "A remedy to all these inconveniences."[202]

Like loiterers and vagabonds, pirates in England were a concern to Hakluyt. The French and English committed piracy against each other, and the French long plundered in the Caribbean. English piracy in the West Indies came into its own with Francis Drake's plundering expeditions of 1570–73. The newfound lands would provide the epic catalogue of commodities he lists, rivaling Euro-pean resources, providing a substitute for sugar cane in Madeira, the "sowinge of woade" in the Azores, the making and gathering of salt in La Rochelle and Bay-onne, and so on. The idle should be employed in England "in makinge of a thousande triflinge thinges whiche wilbe very goodd marchandize for those Contries," evidence of which Hakluyt had found in earlier narratives, especially, it seems, that of Cartier.[203]

It must be said, however, that while this trifling with the Natives for the sake of full employment was hardly flattering, it is easy to make too much of it. As Thomas More showed with gold in Utopia, value is arbitrary. Gold was not a hard metal and so was useless in some applications. Hakluyt then described how in a cold country such as Canada, the Natives would want to buy cloth from England for warm clothes. Petty thieves could be sent as a labor force to the new colonies. Hakluyt did not propose enslaving or subjugating the Native populations as had occurred in the Portuguese and Spanish colonies of the New World. His proposals were much more humane than those in effect in England at the time. The French were already trading in the St. Lawrence but for furs and there is little evidence of France selling much cloth to the indige-nous population.[204]

In addition to Spain, Portugal, and France, the Netherlands were important in the typology between the Old World and the New and occupied a central role both in the preoccupations of the English state at this moment and in Hakluyt's "Discourse." The French and English translators of Las Casas had used and would use a typology between Spanish cruelty in the New World and in the Old. In the typological diptych, the victims in the Netherlands were like the Natives. For England, the Netherlands also meant the wool trade. Hakluyt also emphasized how the "flemishe nation" profited so much from English wool that when in 1550 Charles V had wanted to bring the "Spanishe Inquisition" to Antwerp and the Netherlands, he was dissuaded only when he was shown that the English wool merchants would then depart and Antwerp would lose over 20,000 jobs and almost 600,000 pounds sterling annually.[205] To Elizabeth I, Hakluyt proposed that with western planting, England would sell more cloth there than ever in the Netherlands, an opinion Robert Thorne provided for Dr. Lea, Henry VIII's ambassador to Spain. Thorne emphasized that this cloth trade would be more profitable than the trade of Spain and Portugal in the spice islands.[206] Here is another example of the typology of the Old and New Worlds: the events in Europe and the Americas were closely intertwined.

A primary reason Hakluyt gave for western planting was that a cloth trade there would employ the unemployed and underemployed in England in numbers at least as great as those engaged in the trade in Antwerp and would allow men to feed their families and have children, so that England would then rival France and Spain in population. It is only a matter of emphasis, as well as the usual question of space, that prevents me from exploring some of these connections even further. Another shift occurred in Hakluyt's argument, this time from the Old World to the New. The voyage Hakluyt proposed would allow England to arrest the Spanish in the Newfoundland fisheries.[207]

The fifth chapter continued this shift of emphasis to the New World by advising that the English set up three strong forts between Florida and Cape Breton in order to intercept the Spanish fleet in the West Indies: "for wee shoulde not onely often tymes indaunger his flete in the returne thereof, but also in fewe yeres put him in hazarde in loosinge some parte of Nova Hispania."[208] Even at the height of the Spanish empire, England should attempt to displace Spain in the New World.

In this attempt at displacement the English learned from the French. Using a strategy that foreshadowed Ralegh's in his account of Guiana, Hakluyt represented the Natives as allies against the Spanish while also calling on the example of France in resisting Spain:

> wee are moreouer to vnderstande that the Savages of Florida are the Spaniardes mortall enemyes and wilbe ready to ioyne with vs againste them, as they ioyned with Capitaine Gourgues a Gasgoigne, who beinge but a private man and goinge thither at his owne chardges by their aide wanne and rased the three small fortes which the Spaniardes about xx[ti] yeres agoe had planted in Florida after their traiterous slaughter of Iohn Ribault, which Gourgues slewe and hanged vpp diuers of them on the same trees whereon the yere before they had hanged the frenche.[209]

This gruesome tale of revenge had appeared in the anonymous pamphlet, *Histoire memorable de la reprinse de l'isle de la Floride* . . . (1568), which Urbain Chauveton added to his French translation of Benzoni.[210] From La Popelinière, Hakluyt gave more evidence of Native resistance to Spain and mentioned the Chichimici, who were in continual war against the Spanish, accounts of which he had read in Spanish histories and in the narrative by Miles Philips, who lived in that part of the New World for 14 years after John Hawkins had placed him and others on shore in 1568 after the battle of San Juan de Ulúa.

Part of the conflict with Spain involved strategies similar to those the Spanish used to destabilize England. The strife in Europe and America reflected each other: "Now if wee (beinge thereto prouoked by spanishe iniuries) woulde either ioyne with these Savages, or sende or giue them armour as the Spaniardes arme our Irishe Rebells, wee shoulde trouble the kinge of Spaine more in those partes, then he hath or can trouble vs in Ireland, and holde him at suche a Bay, as he was neuer yet helde at."[211] Hakluyt referred to Philips, whose narrative he printed in the 1589 edition of *Principal Navigations,* as further proof that the English could defy, rival, and displace the Spanish in the New World. If Philips was writing the truth "that one Negro which fledd from his cruell spanishe master is receaued and made Capitaine of multitudes of the Chichmici and daily dothe greuously afflicte them, and hath almoste enforced them to leave and abandon their silver mynes in those quarters, what dommage mighte diuers hundreds of englishe men doo them beinge growen once into familiaritie with that valiaunte nation"?[212] The alliance between European and Native as a weapon in conflicts between European nations was an idea that came into its own, especially in the seventeenth- and eighteenth-century wars between the English and the French. Hakluyt claimed that such an alliance to the north of New Spain was the greatest fear that the Spanish have. Captaine Muffet, an Englishman who had been a prisoner in Spain, told Hakluyt and others repeatedly the previous winter in France that the treasurer of the West Indies had said that such an alliance between Native and a European rival of Spain would be the best way to hinder his master and "that was the occasion why suche crueltie was vsed towardes Iohn Ribaulte and his Companie vpon his seekinge to settle there."[213] If the English do not want to come so close to Florida, they can build a fort near Cape Breton, where their fishermen already command those from other nations, so that the combined forces should be able to seize upon one or two hundred Spanish and Portuguese ships that fish in the Grand Banks for ten weeks to three months each year. Hakluyt, who overestimated English power in and about Newfoundland, used the example of French power in Flanders against the Spanish and Portuguese, which the English defended with some success in 1582.[214]

In Hakluyt's discourse the king of Spain was the figure of the greatest threat to England, someone who must be faced with brave words: "So shall wee be able to crye quittaunce with the King of Spaine if he shoulde goe aboute to make any generall arreste of our navye, or rather terrifie him from any suche enterpryse, when he shall bethincke himselfe that his navye in newfounde lande is no lesse in our daunger then ours is in his domynions wheresoeuer."[215] The end of the fifth chapter mixed plans to defy Spain, perhaps with Native support, with an implication that in this buildup to war each side blamed the other. Hakluyt wanted England to trade with Spain, but if it could not, he advised that it go fight the great power.

Amplification was the chief means Hakluyt used to persuade the queen, and he deployed this technique in his representations of the example of Spain. He piled example upon example of Spanish cruelty, aggression, and treachery. In this secret government document the author did as much as he could to build up a black legend of Spain. Through an anaphoric repetition of variants of "with this treasure dyd not the Emperour Charles" in chapter 6, Hakluyt employed rhetorical questions to remind Elizabeth I that with his West Indian treasury the Spanish monarch won the French possessions in Italy, took the pope prisoner and sacked Rome; made the French king prisoner and fought wars with France from 1540 to 1560; maintained cities in Italy against the pope; overthrew the duke of Cleves and seized Gelderland, Groningerland, and other dominions from him; and so on. Hakluyt also called on Peter Martyr's epistle dedicatory to Emperor Charles V to show that wealth leads to conquest and reminded Elizabeth of the ways the emperor's son, Philip II, had used his treasury to harm the princes of Europe. For Hakluyt, the Spanish West Indian treasury was behind Philip's seizure of Portugal; his attempts on the lives of Don Antonio, the claimant to the Portuguese throne, and William of Orange; his pensions to English rebels; his money given to seminaries in Rome; his forces sent into Ireland; his financing of Scotland to disturb the peace with England; his stirring up of troubles in France to renew the civil wars. The treasury could buy support for Spain and disruption and loss for its enemies.[216]

Hakluyt also foreshadowed the Whig argument that England (later Britain) represented freedom while Spain and other centralized Catholic monarchies, like France, were synonymous with tyranny. In chapter 7 Hakluyt said that Philip could be abased by attacking the West Indies, so that he now listed what would happen to the Spanish crown without the American treasury, whereas in the previous chapter he had dwelled on what had happened as a result of that wealth. Like the strongest walls falling without their foundations, "so this prince spoiled or intercepted for a while of his treasure, occasion by lacke of the same is geven that all his Territories in Europe oute of Spaine slide from him, and the moores enter into Spaine it self, and the people revolte in euery forrein territorie of his, and cutt the throates of the proude hatefull Spaniardes their gouernours."[217] Besides overestimating Spanish weakness, Hakluyt laced his analysis with a surprising amount of violence and hatred.

This emerging Black Legend of Spain told as much about those who represented the Spaniards as it did about the Spanish themselves. Hakluyt used English boasts even as he claimed that in England they should "not be abused with spanishe braggs."[218] Hakluyt's Philip II governed the New World by opinion and not might, just as the Romans had in Britain and the English had in France. Concerning the Spanish American colonies, perhaps neglecting the irony he had just raised about English history, Hakluyt sought the supporting evidence of Francis Drake, John Hawkins, and Miles Philips. Rhetorical incrementation, which became overkill, might have helped dissuade the queen from taking up Hakluyt's plan. He repeated assertions "That the Ilandes there abounde with people and nations that reiecte the proude and bluddy gouernemente of the Spaniarde, and that doo mortally hate the Spaniarde."[219] The revolt of the "moores," who were used as galley slaves, provided more evidence of the weakness of the Spaniards in the West Indies, and Hakluyt hoped to harnass this dissension, along with other revolts against Spanish authority, to establish an English stronghold in Panama, a scheme that supported Drakes's plans there.[220] Although Philip would be defeated in 1588, he was not going to lose his empire and become, as Hakluyt suggested in his overt Protestant analysis, like Aesop's bare crow, the laughing stock of Europe. The Hakluyt of the "Discourse," a secret state document, was more partial and anti-Spanish than the Hakluyt who appeared in his published work.[221]

In this amplification of Spanish weakness, especially in how thin its military power was in the New World, Hakluyt called on the testimony of the secretary to the Portuguese claimant, Don Antonio, who told him that Portugal had never had more than 12, 000 soldiers in its colonies in the East and West, to extrapolate that this was also the case for Spain. Hakluyt supplemented this usual complaint with Spanish contempt for and expulsion of the Italians from their colonies—resulting from the fear that they would reveal the weakness of the Spaniards there—and with Spanish exclusivity in the settlement of the American colonies. Depopulation from the wars in the Netherlands and tyranny plagued Philip's empire. Hakluyt kept harping on the Spanish American treasury, without which, he said, France alone could drive Philip out of all his dominions.[222] Hakluyt ended chapter eight with an appeal to the report of "an excellent frenche captaine" on the weakness of Spain and represented that report in the next chapter, which provided details on Natives, gold, fortifications, and other useful information and which focused on the theme of "Indians enymyes to the Spaniardes."[223]

In the midst of this "espionage" about Spain in the New World, Hakluyt reiterated *ad nauseam.*[224] This use of repetition to undermine Spain led up to chapter 11, which, as we shall observe, was the most deeply anti-Spanish part of the "Discourse." Before Shakespeare likened Pistol to a drum or empty vessel, Hakluyt used that metaphor to describe Spaniards and declared: "wee (vpon perrill of my life) shall make the Spaniarde ridiculous to all Europe, if with percinge eyes wee see into his contemptible weakenes in the west Indies, and with true stile painte hym oute ad vivum vnto the worlde in his fainte colours."[225] It was a good thing that Elizabeth did not find rhetorical overkill a treasonable offense even as Hakluyt called attention to his peril. He was bold enough to declare that his representation of Spain would expose its actual situation: weakness in the New World. What is curious here is that Elizabeth was presumably a highly sophisticated and multilingual writer and reader, so that the author of this discourse was taking a risk by using the long-standing rhetorical strategy of propaganda, now taken up by advertising, that if a claim is repeated enough, it will be believed. Perhaps his gamble was that in times of strife even the most wary readers can be swept away by repetitive appeals to emotion and irrationality. The queen, as usual, was not readily moved, so that Hakluyt, like Ralegh, Drake, and others at court, had to face her caution and ambivalence. In the service of his familiar theme of the weakness of Spain, Hakluyt ended the tenth chapter by playing on the enmity between the Portuguese and Spanish.

Chapter 11 represented the most extreme anti-Spanish rhetoric in the "Discourse" or anywhere in Hakluyt. The main argument of the chapter, both implicitly and explicitly, was that the Spanish had been so cruel to the Natives that these victims would rise up and join the English against Spain and that, should the Spaniards defeat the Netherlands and England, they would enact "Turkishe cruelties" on the Dutch and English.

> So many and so monstrous haue bene the Spanish cruelties, suche straunge slaughters and murders of those peaceable, lowly, milde, and gentle people together with the spoiles of Townes, provinces, and kingdomes which haue bene moste vngodly perpetrated in the west Indies, as also diuers others no lesse terrible matters, that to describe the leaste parte of them woulde require more then one chapiter especially where there are whole bookes extant in printe not onely of straungers but also even of their owne contrymen (as of Bartholmewe de las Casas a Bisshoppe in Nova Spania) yea suche and so passinge straunge and excedinge all humanitie and moderation haue they bene that the very rehersall of them drave diuers of the cruell Spanishe whiche had not bene in the west Indies into a kinde of extasye and maze, so that the sayenge of the poet mighte therein well be verified.[226]

After calling on Las Casas, a Spaniard to support anti-Spanish sentiment, Hakluyt used the topos of inexpressibility to say that the Spanish had massacred the Indians so often that he would mention but a few representative examples. He continued his description in extreme terms and referred once more to the revolt of the Indians against the Spanish. Hakluyt's representation of Las Casas as a Spanish bishop who witnessed the massacres and who dedicated his work to Philip, now king of Spain, was meant to support the view that the Spaniards were cruel and knew it. Their "straunge sortes of cruelties, neuer either seene or reade or hearde of the like" were similar to the slaughter of the innocents.[227]

The charges Hakluyt took from Las Casas, including those of depopulation and devastation of between 12 million men, women, and children over 40 years, were familiar as they appeared in earlier European sources, including the English and French versions of Las Casas that we saw earlier in the chapter. Hakluyt translated passages from Las Casas's description of Hispaniola, cruelties as yet unseen, unread, and unheard, which included the author's testimony, beside a marginal heading that highlighted his status of an eyewitness to the cruelty: "I haue seene all the aforesaide thinges and others infinite."[228] The section on Las Casas left off with the Spanish attacking the Indians with their dogs and making a pact to kill 100 Natives for every Spaniard they killed. To supplement this description of atrocities, Hakluyt turned to another authority, this time Johannes Matellus Sequanus, who was "a papiste and fauoured the spanishe superstition," and therefore not a Protestant propagandist like Hakluyt even if he would serve those ends in the "Discourse."[229] In this author's Latin, the queen could read about the Spanish cruelty and why the Natives and African slaves rebelled against the Spaniards. In keeping with Hakluyt's theme the passage from Sequanus began as follows: "But truly, in order that people may understand once and for all what drove the Indians to work up such frequent rebellions against the Spaniards and to incite revolts so persistently. . . ."[230] The coda began: "Thus the tyranny of the Spanish military in the Indies was so great that it drove not only the Indians but also the hearts of the Moorish slaves to rebellion."[231]

Hakluyt's strategy became ambivalent toward those who should help the English and repeated claims of Spanish weakness. The lands England should seize from Spain were "infested" by the very people whom Hakluyt was suggesting that the English join, the various Natives and Moors in revolt. Hakluyt thought that Philip was likely to die soon (in fact he lived to 1598), and his son was sickly and perhaps not a lawful heir (the son succeeded at his father's death and lived to 1621). For Hakluyt, the universal monarchy of Spain was like that of Alexander: it arose suddenly and would dissolve on the death of its ruler. Even though Hakluyt underestimated the Spanish and overestimated the crisis surrounding Philip's rule and succession, he asserted something that had some truth to it—that much of Europe was coming to fear the power of Spain—perhaps leading it to embrace the worst representations of Spain: "And to saye the truthe what nation I pray you of all Christendomme loveth the Spaniarde the scourge of the worlde but from the teethe forwarde and for advauntage."[232]

As if to make natural the anti-Spanish course he hoped Elizabeth would take, Hakluyt then catalogued the hatred other European nations had for the Spaniard. Hakluyt had left Christ Church, Oxford, in June 1583 to become, on Walsingham's recommendation, chaplain to the embassy in Paris, where he gathered diplomatic opinions, particularly in regard to Spain. The Italians, once "Lordes of the earthe in greate parte nowe broughte vnder his vile yoke," showed their dislike for the "satanicall arrogancie and insolences" of the Spanish and represented their soldiers as boasting and vain ravishers of virgins and wives. Charles V sacked Rome and took the pope and cardinals as prisoners, so that the Italians could not brook the Spaniardes in their hearts. The Venetians feared them as much as they did the Turks. They hated the Spaniards worse than scorpions because of the capture of François I in 1525, the massacre of the French colonists in Florida in 1565, the defeat of Philip Strozzi's fleet in the Azores in 1582, and the Spanish capture of Terceira in 1583. The Germans had sustained wrongs enough to make them mortal enemies. The Spaniards had committed "innumerable outrages in the netherlandes" and their "practises to supplant vs of England giue vs moste occasion to bethincke our selues how wee may abate and pull downe their highe myndes." As for the prince and the people of Portugal, they look for a convenient time to defect from Spanish rule. This was the language of the Black Legend: Spain is proud, cruel, and domineering.

Even if Spain did have designs on other places in Europe and overseas, it was not the only country with such ambitions. After all, that ambition for England was the gist of Hakluyt's advice to Elizabeth I. The Dutch, Portuguese, and

French had similar desires for power, wealth, and territory. As usual, Hakluyt was ignoring some evidence that countered his argument. The Guise in France, for instance, had close connections to Spain and, after Anjou's death, developed them.[233]

At the center of his report, Hakluyt placed a virulent attack on Spain. The Black Legend occupied the middle of this document that was not known to the public until it was published in Boston in 1877.[234] The reemergence of Hakluyt's manuscript occurred 21 years before the Spanish-American War of 1898, when, in the United States, Las Casas's text was reprinted. It would be interesting to see whether Hakluyt's "Discourse" played any significant role in the reemergence of or the ghost of the example of Spain during the events of 1898.

In chapter 12 Hakluyt returned to climate and fishing, the ease of the voyage to Newfoundland and Norumbega, which had no other coasts in the way, except Ireland, whose inhabitants needed to be drawn "little by little to more ciuilitie" and who would receive from the English the American commodities that the "Spanish now supply them in return for food."[235] The Spanish presence in Ireland had troubled and endangered England. Behind Hakluyt's proposal for trade with North America lay the larger issue of foreign trade and what he took to be English humiliation in not having legal access to Spanish markets owing to religious differences. By trading with North America, "wee shall not nede for feare of the Spanishe bloudy Inquisition to throwe our Bibles and prayer bookes overboorde into the sea before our arryvall at their portes, as these many yeres we haue don, and yet doe, nor take such horrible oathes as are exacted of our men by the spanishe searchers to suche dayly wilfull and highe offence of almightie god, as wee are driven to contynually in followynge our ordinary trafficque into the kinge of Spaines Domynions."[236] At one level, as in the time of Hawkins's slaving, there was a sense that England wanted to have a legal part of Spanish trade and felt spurned, shamed, and impotent not having attained that goal. For all of Hakluyt's rhetorical bluster, England's power had not yet been able to compete with Spain's in Europe or in the Americas. There was an element of envy and fear of domination, what might be called a strident vulnerability in the anti-Spanish rhetoric of the English.

As patriotic and as religious as Hakluyt could become, he still returned to issues of trade, using the testimonies of "Iohn Ribault, Iohn Verarsanus, Stephen Gomes, Vasques de Coronado, Iaques Cartier [,] Gasper Corterialis and others" to prove the existence of gold, silver, pearls, and other riches between 30 and 63 degrees.[237] The crown would be enriched according to the patent Henry VII gave to Cabot and his sons. Hakluyt based England's dream of riches on the use of the examples of the wealth Spain and Portugal had derived from their colonies. In the vision he set out in chapter 13, the English would exact customs on fish from the Spanish, Portuguese, and French, "our olde and aunciient enemyes," not to mention those on cloth from the Natives. At this time, however, the queen was seeking out France, which Hakluyt regarded an ancient enemy, as an ally.[238] Hakluyt was also concerned about developing shipbuilding and the navy in England and suggested that the English follow the Spanish and Portuguese experience of increasing the size of their ships. Newfoundland would supply the raw materials, and English shipwrights would not have to go abroad to countries like Denmark to find work.[239] Although Hakluyt had attacked Charles V earlier, he now praised him for instituting a lecture of navigation and having Spaniards take examinations before going to the West Indies, a model he recommended for England.

After such bitter attacks on Spain in chapter 11, it is surprising to find this archenemy being held up, along with Portugal, in chapter 14, as an important example of commercial success since "the first discouerie of their Indies."[240] For instance, Hakluyt said here: "For proofe hereof wee nede not to seeke any further then vnto our neighboures of Spaine and Portingale, whoe since the firste discouerie of their Indies have not onely mightely inlarged their domynions, marveilously inriched themselues, & their subiectes, but have also by iuste accompte trebled the nomber of their shipps masters and maryners, a matter of no small momente and importaunce."[241] Even though Hakluyt had represented the Natives as wanting English help to throw off Spanish rule, he suggested forts to "kepe the naturall people of the Contrye in obedience, and goodd order."[242]

God and gold, or at least religion and trade more generally, continued to make appearances side by side in Hakluyt's "Discourse." These were twin themes in Spanish narratives of the New World. In chapter 15 Hakluyt stated that after the advancement of the kingdom of Christ, "traficque" was the next reason for the western discovery. God guided this expansion so that England would sell cloth and other goods in return for commodities England now bought elsewhere.[243] The English should play one Native group against another. Hakluyt warned that the English should not let populous France build forts in and about Cape Breton, for if England did so, it would be like Juan de Grijalva, who had the opportunity to colonize Yucatan, allowing Cortés to do so afterwards. This example from the experience of Spain Hakluyt quoted from an Italian edition of Gómara.[244] Hakluyt used another illustration in the story of Francisco Vasquez de Coronado's cowardly behavior and missed opportunity as well as the cold reception Don Antonio de Mendoça gave him, which was similar to the one Grijalva had from his uncle. These exempla of individual rivals in Spanish America were used metonymically, allegorically, and symbolically for England and France.[245]

In speaking about Spain, Hakluyt also concerned himself with France, which had similar designs to those of England in the New World. Even as Hakluyt saw France as a rival for North America, he was not adverse to taking a good idea from it, so he praised Jean Ribault's speed and wisdom in planting and fortifying a colony, even with 30 inhabitants, in Florida. Hakluyt did not mention that the men deserted the settlement in 1562–63.[246]

For Hakluyt, England had more to worry about than France and Spain in the settlement of North America, as much as it had to consider these rivals there. In returning to the subject of the claim of England to these territories, Hakluyt harkened back some 87 years to Cabot's voyage to Newfoundland and how the wars with Scotland prevented Henry VII from developing colonies.[247] The implication was that after such procrastination, there was no time to lose. Rivals were busy with American plans and projects. Hakluyt catalogued the French effort at colonization and raised the possibility of Dutch colonization in America, which Abraham Ortelius, the cartographer, had told him in 1577 was delayed owing to the war in the Netherlands. The race was on for the St. Lawrence, which Hakluyt said was more suitable for the English than New Spain, but which was a place where the French had had a head start even though the English had published books about it before the French did. If the French succeeded there, then Catholics, "enemyes or doubtfull frendes," would surround England.[248] In regard to America, Hakluyt also feared the designs of English Catholics, who had attempted to associate with Gilbert the year before but who had apparently heeded threats from Spain and Rome. Hakluyt also admitted that the English could learn from French trading in the St. Lawrence and used Ramusio's description of Verrazzano to represent a neglected prophet of French colonization whose plans for colonists and exploration of the northwest passage went unfulfilled, an implied lesson for Elizabeth I in considering Hakluyt's request for English colonists for North America and an argument for finding the passage to Cathay. Hakluyt quoted Sebastian Cabot and Jacques Cartier, whose now-lost manuscript he had seen in the king's library in Paris, as authorities on the northwest passage as a spice route and called on numerous exempla, including those from Spanish and Portuguese sources.[249] One of the reasons Hakluyt gave for Philip II prohibiting Spanish exploration above the forty-fifth parallel is that Spain did not have enough people to possess the area and so the area was open for other nations.[250] Hakluyt, as David and Alison Quinn say, was the only source for this precise prohibition, although Charles V's New Laws of the Indies (1542–43) had required that conquests have official permission, and Philip II's *Recopilación* (1573, published 1585) gave qualified support to expansion.[251] Origins, precedents, and lost opportunities often haunted English and French works about the New World in the last decades of the sixteenth century and well beyond. They faced the example of Spain and would settle where the Spaniards had no settlements.[252]

As usual, the past was being used to justify future ambitions. Hakluyt employed a scattershot approach, so that perhaps one bit of evidence would, like one pellet among many, find its mark. Mythical origins, as well as legal arguments and the precedent of John Cabot, preoccupied Hakluyt in his analysis of England's relation to Spain in the New World. He devoted chapter 18 to establishing that the queen of England's title to the West Indies, or at least from Florida to the Arctic Circle, was more lawful than the king of Spain's or any other Christian prince's. It is remarkable how persistent this anxiety over origins, priority, and rightful claims was. The story of Madock, a Welsh prince, discovering America in 1170; Henry VII's acceptance of Columbus's offer by way of his brother, Bartholomew, before the king of Spain's (as Columbus was fleeing Portuguese double-dealing) as reported by Ferdinand Columbus; the priority of Sebastian Cabot's voyages to the New World or at least to the mainland (Hakluyt continued to confuse Sebastian for John as perhaps Sebastian had wanted it and used Oviedo and Peter Martyr as sources that establish 1498 as the year of Columbus's third journey); the voyage of Robert Thorne the Elder, and Hugh Eliot from Bristol in 1480 to the isle of Brazil (as reported by Robert

Thorne the Younger, in "A Declaration of the Indies" in 1527); Gómara's admission that Sebastian Cabot first discovered the West Indies from the fifty-eighth to the thirty-eighth parallel were all marshalled as evidence to support the English claim to the New World.

The origin of the Spanish claim to much of the Americas lay partly with papal authority. Hakluyt devoted chapter 19 to refuting the pope's right to have made the donation to Portugal and Spain in 1493. Along with chapter 11, this argument was the most extensive and the most anti-Spanish in the "Discourse." Hakluyt cited Christ and other biblical sources to say that the vicar of Christ, as Gómara called the pope, should follow their spiritual example and give up dividing the world. Hakluyt used Alexander VI's own words at the end of the bull against him: "To witt that god is the disposer and distributer of kingdommes and Empires, he woulde neuer have taken vpon him the deuidinge of them with his line of partition from one ende of the heavens to the other."[253] Hakluyt, as the Quinns note, borrowed a good deal of his material on the papacy from mainly Protestant works. While the Quinns do not think that this material is part of his personal polemics—and anyone familiar with Hakluyt's published work will find the bitterness of the anti-Catholic, anti-papal, and anti-Spanish rhetoric surprising and even off-putting, and so to that extent I agree with them—the Protestant polemics were also his by virtue of assimilation, allusion, and ventriloquy. Whereas on page 100 Hakluyt went on to allude to John Bale's *The Pagaent of Popes, Contayning the Lyves of all the Bishops of Rome* (1574), he did not mention Thomas Cooper's *Brutus fulmen* (1581), an attack on the pope for excommunicating Elizabeth I in 1570.[254] Interpreting the will of God became the line of demarcation between Hakluyt and Alexander VI. This difference was not surprising because the author of the "Discourse" was invoking the language of Protestant polemics.[255]

The pope, according to Hakluyt, "shoulde firste haue don as the prophetts dyd, that is he shoulde first haue gon himselfe and preached the worde of God to those Idolatrous kinges and their people, and then if they woulde not by any meanes haue repented he mighte haue pronounced the severe and heavie iudgemente of God againste them shewinge oute of the worde of God that one kingdome is translated from another for the sinnes of the Inhabitantes of the same, and that God in his iustice woulde surely bringe somme nation or other vpon them to take vengeaunce of their synnes and wickednes."[256] This passage combined the providental history of the Bible (especially the Old Testament) with the notion of *translatio imperii*. The pope would be, if he could live up to the prophets, God's messenger in the making of godly kingdoms and the suppression of idolatry. Clearly, in Hakluyt's view, the pope had no such virtue and authority. Such translations of empires were something the popes did from necessity or performed as rhetorical gestures and not with the power and justice of God:

> yea but the Popes can shewe goodd Recordes that they have deposed Emperors, y[t] they have translated Empires from one people to another, as that of the Easte vnto the Germaines, and that they have taken kingdommes from one nation and gauen them to another. In deede in somme

respectes they haue donne so: But how? They neuer gaue that which was
in their actuall possession yf by any meanes possible they mighte haue
kepte it themselues. It is an easie matter to cutt large thonges as wee say
of other mens hides, and to be liberall of other mens gooddes. Neither ys
it any marvaile thoughe (as Gomera saith) the Pope gaue all the west
Indies of his free grace to the kinge of Spaine, for they neuer coste him
penye.[257]

In a claim more notable for its polemical impact rather than its legal sophistica-
tion, Hakluyt argued that, in its claim to America, Spain had no right or precedent: just because a pope did or wrote something did not mean it was lawful.
The Spanish possession of the New World was, in Hakluyt's proof, unlawful.

From the general preamble to this chapter, Hakluyt proceeded to a six-part
analysis of the donation of 1493 itself. In examining these six aspects of Hakluyt's analysis, I will concentrate on those points that require more explanation.
The first and second elements of Hakluyt's analysis, while important, are more
self-explanatory and would involve going over ground we have already covered
in detail. First, Hakluyt assailed Alexander VI as a Spanish pope partial to Spain
in his appointment of cardinals and in his donation of the New World. Second,
he claimed that Spain lacked the resources that countries like England had to
explore the New World and did not have enough people to populate these vast
lands.

Third, Hakluyt argued that if Alexander VI had wanted to spread the Catholic
faith, he should not have restrained other Christian princes in that goal by the
threat of excommunication. Columbus had built a settlement based on the right
of discovery before the pope had granted the donation. Hakluyt, as was his
wont, blamed Alexander and imputed to him a motive for the donation—his
desire to defraud England and Portugal of their claim to Columbus and the benefits of his discovery. Having promised before not to tell the story from Gómara
about the child who derided the partition of the world that gave Spain the New
World, Hakluyt went ahead with it. It was an illustration of Hakluyt's theme that
God would not divide the world as Alexander did between Spain and Portugal.
In a familiar technique in the French and English use of Las Casas, Hakluyt
quoted "one of the Spaniardes owne Historiographers" against Spain and trans-
lates and interprets Gómara's story:

> As Fraunces de Melo, Diego Lopes of Sequeria and others camme to this
> assembly and passed the River by Quidiana a little Infant that kepte his
> mothers clothes which she had washt & honge abroade to drye, demaun-
> ded of them whither they were those that shoulde comme to devide the
> worlde with the Emperour? and as they aunswered yea, he tooke vp his
> shirte behinde and shewed them his buttocks, sayenge vnto them, drawe
> your Lyne throughe the middest of this place: This saieth the Author was
> published in contempte all abroade bothe in the Towne of Badayos & also
> in the assembly of these Committies. The Portingales were greately angrie
> therewithall, but the rest turned yt to a Iest and laughed yt oute, But what

wiseman seeth not that God by that childe laughed them to scorne and made them ridiculous and their partition in the eyes of the worlde and in their owne consciences, and caused the childe to reprove them, even as the dombe beaste speakinge with mans voyce, reproved the foolishness of Balam the prophett.[258]

Hakluyt seemed to have consulted Fumée's translation of Gómara (1569) because no other edition had these introductory remarks.[259] The French, like their neighbors, were familiar with this satirical story in Gómara that parodied the division of the world before Spain and Portugal. Hakluyt's version pointed a moral whereas the French version did not and was more explicitly anti-Spanish. This intertextuality demonstrated that sometimes an intricate series of translations and interpretations drew on themselves as well as on the Spanish original.

How effective was Hakluyt's tone? He tried to bring a moral seriousness to a comic incident amid long and sometimes wearing denunciations of Alexander VI and the Spaniards, something that might have been more appealing to Elizabeth I at a time of tension with Spain. If Hakluyt had been more ironical throughout, as More was in *Utopia* and Erasmus was in *Encomium Moriae,* then this child would have provided an instance of a fool in Christ, innocent to the all-too-experienced world. Perhaps the child still achieved that through the very contrast of his defiant irreverence with the solemn and bitter arguments that Hakluyt had placed before. The story might have made the bull of Spanish Alexander and his native country look ridiculous, but the danger was that Hakluyt's moralizing might have caused him to appear small and ludicrous. It is possible that Hakluyt explained a joke that is self-explanatory. The uncertain tone suggests one sign of the rawness of Hakluyt's *Discourse,* written in apparent haste in the face of pressing problems for England: trade, colonization, and the obstacle and threat of Spain. This tale illustrated the third point in his argument against Alexander's donation but also modified the dialectical structure with a telling anecdote, a story that upstaged Hakluyt's point and argument as much as the pope's commission to divide the world unknown to Europe between Portugal and Spain.

Fourth, Hakluyt analyzed the form and manner of the donation: once again, he used a story from a Spanish narrative to impugn the right of the Spanish to America. In his refutation of the pope's right to give the New World to Spain, he turned to Gómara for the case of Atahualpa, who responded with anger to Friar Vincent, one of Pizarro's men, who told him that he should become a Christian and obey the pope and the emperor, to whom the pope had donated his country.

Atabalipa beinge greately insensed replied that seeinge he was nowe free he woulde not becomme tributarye, nor thincke that there was any greater Lorde then himselfe, but that he was willinge to be the Emperours frende and to have his acquaintaunce, for that he muste needes be somme great Lorde that sente so many armies abroade into the worlde: He aunswered moreouer that he woulde not in any wise obey the Pope seinge he gaue away that which belonged to another, moche lesse that he woulde leave his kingdomme that came vnto him by inheritaunce to one which he had neuer seene in his life.[260]

Atahualpa and Hakluyt sounded alike. Hakluyt was selective in his use of Gómara, leaving out what the Italian and French translations (1564, 1569) both included, Friar Vincent's long explanation of the relations among God, the Trinity, Adam, Christ, Saint Peter, the pope, and the emperor, so to make the conflict seem more arbitrary and sudden. Whereas the Italian and French versions included Friar Vincent's warnings of dire consequences if Atahualpa did not do as he was asked and represented the Native ruler as saying that Christ was dead but the sun and moon never died, as asking him how he knew that the God of the Christians created the world and as throwing down the friar's breviary and Bible when he was not satisfied with the answer because he could not read the signs. Only then did Vincent run to Pizarro and cry for vengeance against the unbelievers. The Italian and the French versions were similar here. For instance, there was a chain of command from God through Christ as the redeemer of Adam's sins and as he who rose on the third day and left Peter and his successors as Christ's earthly representatives through the emperor, who was the universal monarch to whom the pope gave lands.[261]

In Hakluyt's analysis of the papal donation in this fourth point, he cut away the pretexts and represented the Spanish as irrational, cruel, and apparently unpredictable. Immediately following Atahualpa's refusal to cede his lands, Hakluyt gave Friar Vincent's reply:

And whereas Fryer Vincent beinge displeased at his replye was gladd to seeke any waye to wreake his anger vpon him, in somoche as when Atabalipa lett his portesse falle to the grounde, he was so testye, that he sett Pisar and his souldiers forwardes cryenge, vengeaunce Christians vengeaunce, giue the chardge vpon them, whereby many Indians withoute resistaunce or any stroke stricken on their partes were moste pitifully murdred and massacred, and Atabalipa himselfe taken, and afterwardes trecherously put to deathe: This Frier himself by gods iuste iudgement was afterwardes beaten to deathe with clubbes by the Inhabitantes of Puna as he fledd from Don Diego de Almagre, as Fraunces Lopes de Gomera precisely and of purpose noteth libro. 5. cap. 85. of his generall historie of the Indies, & besides him all the reste of the chefe that were the executioners of his rashe counsell and of the Popes donation camme to most wretched an vnfortunate endes as the aforesaide Author there setteth downe in twoo seuerall Chapiters of considerations as he calleth them.[262]

With a brevity that neglected the background, Hakluyt emphasized the rashness of the action. When Atahualpa threw the "portesse," or portable breviary, on the ground, a terrible violence broke out. Divine retribution and poetic justice illustrated for Hakluyt that this rashness and literal execution of the papal donation were wrong in the eyes of God. Hakluyt's use of the Spanish authority against Spain was incremental.

More Spanish authorities followed in his amplification of his fourth point. An irony occurred in Hakluyt's representation when he proceeded to contradict himself: after showing God's justice against those who executed the papal donation, he then said that one article of the bull was that the kings of Spain were supposed to send godly and sober men to instruct the inhabitants of the New World in the Catholic faith but have neglected that article by having "sent suche helhoundes and wolves thither as have not conuerted but almost quite subuerted them, and have rooted oute above fiftene millions of reasonable creatures as Bartholmewe de Casas the Bisshoppe of Chiapa in the west Indies a Spaniarde borne dothe write at large in a whole volume of that argumente."[263] In Hakluyt, as in many English and French narratives about the New World and a tradition that stretches back to Columbus, the Native was reasonable and unreasonable according to context. There was no fast rule for the shifts in this attribution of rationality, but here was a general practice: if Natives were allies or became Christians, they were reasonable; if they were enemies or refused subjection or Christianity, they were unreasonable. In the late seventeenth century and early eighteenth century, for instance, Pierre Boucher and John Lawson, whose work will be discussed in chapter 6, would represent a similar view. Hakluyt was writing in the wake of the English translation of Las Casas in 1583 and a number of translations in the vernaculars a few years before across Western Europe. The English and the French desire to be lords of the Natives was legitimate in their view, but the Spanish view that they were the only lords was not.

Whereas Las Casas was used in other European countries to illustrate Spanish cruelty, Oviedo, to whom Hakluyt now turned, was usually not. What made him an effective witness was that unlike Las Casas he was anything but a champion of the Indians. Having called attention to Oviedo's status as a Spanish historiographer and captain of the castle in Santa Domingo, Hakluyt then translated his denunciation of the destruction and ruin of the Natives.

For there hath Spaniardes comme into these contries saieth he, which havinge lefte their consciences and all feare of God and men behinde them, haue plaied the partes not of men but of dragons and infidells, and havinge no respecte of humanitie, haue bene the cause that many Indians that peradventure mighte haue bene conuerted and saved, are deade by diuers and sondrie kindes of deathes. And althoughe those people had not bene conuerted, yet if they had bene lett to live, they mighte have bene profitable to your Maiestie, and an aide vnto the Christians, and certaine partes of the Lande should not wholy have bene disinhabited, which by this occasion are altogether in a manner dispeopled. And they that haue bene the cause of suche destruction call this contrie thus dispeopled and wasted, the Contrie conquered and pacified. But I call it quoth Gonsaluo the contrie which is destroyed and ruyned.[264]

At this point, Hakluyt appeared to be translating freely from a passage that has not been located: he included Oviedo's censure of some of the Spanish as greedy but left out his negative views of the Natives. At the end of this passage, Hak-

luyt was familiar with Oviedo, using his first name, perhaps to imply a shared
view and the intimacy of minds. It is difficult to know, however, how freely
Hakluyt was playing with Oviedo's work while enlisting him to his cause. As it
was Hakluyt's usual practice to consult translations or the original or both,
depending what was at hand, it is possible that he had gone to an edition or a
translation that is no longer extant. Nor did Hakluyt mention the division
between the crown and the colonial owners of lands and mines in their attitudes
toward the Natives. Whereas all this conjuring and representation of anti-Spanish sentiment in Spanish sources might have convinced Elizabeth I of Spain's
abuses, it might also have reminded her of the debate and self-criticism among
the Spaniards. If the Spanish were so bad, why then were they so concerned
with debating the justice or injustice of their own actions in the New World?

To supplement Las Casas and Oviedo, Hakluyt referred to Girolamo Benzoni, although he forgot his first name, a Milanese who served Spain in the wars
against the American Indians for 14 years. Hakluyt actually went to the preface
to Urbain Chauveton's *Histoire nouvelle du Nouveau Monde* (1579), a translation
of Benzoni's *La Historia de Mondo Nuovo*, which had been published in Venice
in 1565. As we have met with Chauveton earlier in the chapter, there is no need
to go into detail here but simply to note that Hakluyt had displaced the experienced Benzoni, who was a severe critic of Spain and one of the contributors
to the Black Legend, for his translator, who published in Protestant Geneva.
French Protestant views of Spain were influential in Hakluyt's circle, and he
hoped that they could be marshalled in the arguments meant to sway the queen
into challenging Spain's virtual monopoly in the New World. In this Chauveton version, which Hakluyt had attributed to Benzoni and translated and quoted
to finish his fourth point, the Indians were logical without having studied logic
and saw that the Spanish, having spoiled their country, more furious than lions
and more dangerous than wild beasts, were cruel and devilish.[265] This was the
kind of view Montaigne's Natives often took. This kind of intertextuality helps
to demonstrate why a comparative view of representations of the example of
Spain is desirable.

Fifth, Hakluyt, trying a new interpretative strategy, examined Alexander VI's
intentions in the donation (although Hakluyt had given this pope a considerably
longer life than he had) and contrasted them to the actual exploration he permitted other monarchs in the Spanish sphere. If the pope had meant to excommunicate all those rulers and their subjects who set out to discover new lands
without permission of the king of Spain, then why did he not excommunicate
Henry VII, Henry VIII, and Queen Mary of England, François I, Henri II, and
Charles IX of France, Emanuel of Portugal, and the king of Denmark when they
were, at the times Hakluyt cited, Catholic monarchs? Hakluyt's catalogue of
explorers included Sebastian Cabot (whose claim as discoverer in Gómara he
reiterated), Verrazzano, Cartier, Roberval, Villegagnon, Ribault, Laudonnière, and
Corte Real. Hakluyt criticized the popes for cursing the other princes who had
used and would employ their people in the glory of God and lawful enrichment
of their subjects and turned the curse against any pope who would excommunicate any Christian prince for helping to convert the multitudes of heathens

and infidels in the West Indies, many of whom the Spaniards had yet to discover, let alone subdue or convert. The excommunication of Elizabeth I in 1570 was a subtext here. A feeling of exclusion in the New World through the donation and in the European community through the excommunication of Elizabeth seemed to underlie Hakluyt's defensiveness for and defense of his country. Elizabeth would have known that Philip II, as I have mentioned before, had tried to prevent her excommunication and had refused to publish it in his realms. Although Hakluyt's rhetoric is repetitive in the "Discourse," it is instructive how the ideas of the universal monarchy of Spain and the Spanish monopoly in the New World brought his emotions to the surface in a polemic.

Hakluyt may have intended the repetition to be incremental as part of a strategy of amplification, but it could also be read as the eruptions of a bitterness or defensiveness that blinded the author to an objective assessment of Spain:

To be shorte thoughe Pope Alexander the vj^th by his vnequall diuision hath so puffed vpp and inflamed with pride his moste ambitious and insatiable contrymen that they are growen to this highe conceite of themselues that they shall shortly attaine to be Lordes and onely seigniors of all the earthe, insomoche as Gonsaluo de Ouiedo sticketh not to write to Charles the Emperour sayenge, God hath geuen you those Indies accio che vostra maiesta sia uniuersale et vnico monarcha del mondo, to the intente that your maiestie shoulde be the vniuersall and onely monarch of the worlde: yet god that sitteth in heaven laugheth them and their partitions to scorne, and he will abase and bringe downe their proude lookes, and humble their faces to the duste, yea he will make them at his goodd time and pleasure to confesse that the earthe was not made for them onely, as he hath already shewed the Portingales, which not longe since takinge vpon them to devide the worlde with lynes, doo nowe beholde the line of gods iuste iudgmente drawen over themselues and their owne kingdomme and possessions.²⁶⁶

Hakluyt called once more on Oviedo, this time consulting an Italian version now apparently not extant, proclaiming Charles V lord of all the world. In his prophetic mode, Hakluyt was less favourable to Portugal, with which he had sympathized earlier in the *Discourse*. Philip II's invasion of Portugal in 1580 had erased the lines of demarcation of 1494 and 1527, where the undiscovered world was divided.²⁶⁷ Divine retribution against these proud Iberian countries, as if they were idolaters from the Old Testament, was Hakluyt's only solace.

Sixth, Hakluyt argued that the kings of Spain used the papal donation to blind the world with Rome because if they had really thought that they owed the title to Rome only, they would have been more grateful and shared the appointments of archbishops and bishops with the pope there instead of keeping that prerogative, an idea Hakluyt gleaned from Fumée's translation of Gómara. In pointing out this division between Spain and Rome, Hakluyt led up to the summation at the end of the "Discourse." To drive a wedge between Spanish and papal interests would leave some room for England to maneuver.

The last two chapters provided a coda to the book. Chapter 20 recapitulated and numbered the previous arguments. Hakluyt's fear that Spain would continue to flourish and plant throughout America and that without a colony in Norumbega or somewhere like it, which would provide commodities and employ the unemployed English youth, England would find its wool and cloth trade diminished and it would slip into beggary. Although Hakluyt scoffed at Oviedo's description of Charles V as the universal monarch and lord of the world, he had similar ambitions for Elizabeth I, whose navy would become lord of the seas and give her great power. Having such a colony, England would have many of the benefits, including

> the best and moste connynge shipwrightes of the worlde to be Lordes of all those Sees, and to spoile Phillipps Indian navye, and to deprive him of yerely passage of his Treasure into Europe, and consequently to abate the pride of Spaine and of the supporter of the greate Antechryste of Rome, and to pull him downe in equallitie to his neighbour princes, and consequently to cutt of the common mischefes that commes to all Europe by the peculiar aboundaunce of his Indian Treasure, and thus without difficultie.[268]

In the summation, Hakluyt brought the piracy and the anti-Spanish and anti-Catholic sentiments to the surface in its barest form. The French and later the English were pirates who had pillaged the Spanish treasure ships from the New World. The desire to be included in Christendom as converters of the Indians had faded and what remained was the radical Protestant rhetoric of Rome as the Antichrist (a favorite trope along with the Whore of Babylon). A sense of bringing Spain down to size—a leveling—made Hakluyt's program look small. As he puffed up England, he deflated Spain. In his course of empire, should there be a translation from Spain to England, England might make the same mistakes, presuming that its neighbors were not worthy to gather the crumbs from under its table.

Having criticized Spanish exclusivity in the New World, Hakluyt, admittedly implying no haven for Catholics, saw English America as a place of refuge for Protestants, perhaps following the example of the Huguenots colonies in the previous generation: "Wee shall by plantinge there inlarge the glory of the gospell and from England plante sincere relligion, and provide a safe and fine place to receave people from all partes of the worlde that are forced to flee for the truthe of gods worde."[269] Hakluyt wanted to increase the size and strength of ships and the number of skilled seamen, so the English navy and merchant ships would never be subject to arrest in any place and would provide for the defense of England. Norumbega would allow the English to have cheaper goods because of the circumvention of customs of other countries and would permit England to be independent in the production of goods it had to import from the French, Spanish, Portuguese, Flemish, Germans, and others.

After speaking of God and then asserting that frontier wars would train young English soldiers for conflicts in America and Europe, Hakluyt represented a utopian picture of England as the liberator against the Spanish tyrant, a trope that became part of English views of the roles of England and Spain in the New World.

> The Spaniardes gouerne in the Indies with all pride and tyranie, and like as when people of contrarie nature at the sea enter into Gallies, where men are tied as slaues, all yell and crye with one voice liberta, liberta, as desirous of libertie & freedomme, so no doubte whensoeuer the Queene of England, a prince of suche clemencie, shall seate vpon that firme of America, and shalbe reported throughoute all that tracte to vse the naturall people there with all humanitie, curtesie, and freedomme, they will yelde themselues to her gouernement and revolte cleane from the Spaniarde, and specially, when they shall vnderstande that she hathe a noble navie, and that she aboundeth with a people most valiaunte for theyr defence.[270]

The Natives understood a powerful navy, even in their defense. In writing about Guiana in 1596, Ralegh would apply this trope of English utopian liberation of the Natives from Spaniards worthy of the Black Legend. Hakluyt cited the revolt of the Symerons against the Spanish, the use of the soldiers trained in the wars in the Low Countries, Drake as an example of a valiant Englishman as means of this overturning the rule of Spain in America. As it did so often in the historiography of expansion, the talk shifted from God to gold: "and this broughte so aboute, her Maiestie and her subiectes may bothe enioye the treasure of the mynes of golde and silver," and other trade from the Indies. Hakluyt then set out the benefits for employment, one of his constant themes. In Hakluyt's representation Spain had been a block to trade and to the expansion that it had forced on England.

"Discourse" began and ended with religion, even if trade was a chief motif and motive in between. Still, Spain haunted Hakluyt's discourse of God and expansion. Chapter 21 listed provisions for the voyage: the book ended with things Hakluyt had forgotten and did not want to insert, thereby upsetting the order of his treatise. The first of these two subjects was the topic of preachers, and Hakluyt was a preacher. Bibles as well as books about discoveries and conquests of the East and West Indies would keep the minds of the voyagers off "worse cogitations" and common dangers and raise them to courage.[271] These discourses would affect the decisions the English took in their settlements. The examples of Spain and Portugal, despite Hakluyt's great criticism of the former, could not be escaped even in a polemic to unseat Spain in the New World:

> And because men are more apte to make themselues subiecte in obedience to prescribed lawes sette downe and signed by a prince, then to the changeable will of any Capitaine be he neuer so wise or temperate, neuer so free from desire of revenge, it is wisshed that it were learned oute what course bothe the Spaniardes and the Portingales tooke in their discoueries for gouernment, and that the same were deliuered to learned men that had perused moste of the lawes of thempire and of other princes Lawes, and that thereupon somme speciall orders fitt for voyadges and begynnynges

might vpon deliberation be sett downe & allowed by the Q<u>uenes</u> most
excellent maiestie and her wise counsell and faire ingrossed mighte in a
Table be sett before the eyes of suche as goe in the voyadge, that no man
poonished or executed may iustly complaine of manifest and open wronge
offred.[272]

Here is perhaps the central example in English colonization of what I call the
example of Spain, the ambivalence and contradictions in the representation of
Spanish colonization of the New World. In a secret document, at least one not
published for almost 300 years, Hakluyt ended with a model taken in part from
Spain. Before and after, he assailed Spain, but he could not deny how useful it
was, along with Portugal. After recommending taking on the voyage a physician,
surgeon, and apothecary (with honey for mead) and suggesting that merchants,
indebted and imprisoned through no fault of their own, should be considered as
colonists, he recommended that no Catholic should be allowed on these voyages
owing to their inclination to Spain, but that, instead, Protestant artisans, strong
and good with bow or gun, should be sent and all colonists should be registered.[273] Catholics or those with Spanish sympathies were not, according to the
Quinns, always prevented from taking part in subsequent voyages, and some of
the Irish Catholic colonists in 1585 and 1587 later helped the Spaniards.[274] The
controversy over Catholic colonists and their relation to Spain also surrounded
Gilbert's last voyage. Even if Hakluyt's proposal for English colonies in America
criticized the Spanish colonies for religious intolerance and lack of openness, he
would borrow ideas from them and then close the door on them and the English Catholics he presumed were their sympathizers.

Here I have concentrated on Hakluyt's "Discourse" because it centered on
Spain, is not one of his well-known works, and is not widely discussed. Moreover, I know of no detailed and extensive discussion of it in the histories of
expansion.[275] It is a rich and complex work that embodied at a crucial moment
English attitudes toward the example of Spain and that drew on and represented
the French, and especially Huguenot experience in Florida and in the New
World generally, as well as other Continental powers. Hakluyt's "Discourse" was
and is a crucial text in the various relations of the French and English uses of
the example of Spain, so that it occupies a place at the heart of my study.

Hakluyt's "Discourse on Western Planting" is a key text that helped to consolidate the work of earlier instructions as well as Gilbert's writing. It is part of
an effort by the "American party," which Walter Ralegh so notably represented,
to advance English colonial interests in the northern parts of America. This
remarkable document, meant for the private consumption of the queen and her
counselors, fell between the voyages of Frobisher and Gilbert on the one hand
and Ralegh's Roanoke and Chesapeake voyages on the other. The secretary of
state, Sir Francis Walsingham, as mentioned earlier, appears to have employed
Hakluyt as a means to support Ralegh.

Ralegh's example as a colonizer was known in France, particularly among the
Huguenots, whose leader Coligny was dead and who could find few leaders
interested in colonization during the French civil war. At this crucial moment,

English Protestants were pursuing settlement in "Florida" now that French Protestants had abandoned the project. The similarity in the two designs was colonization that would thwart Catholic Spain and develop a Protestant colony to the north of the Spanish holdings in America. In 1586 Basanier included a dedication to Ralegh in his *Histoire notable de la Floride,* which included accounts of the conflict between the French and Spanish in Florida. For Protestants in England and France, the Wars of Religion helped to keep before them those earlier events in Florida.

While Hakluyt's "Discourse" may have helped to prepare the way for Ralegh's ventures in North America, it would not be a prophecy of successful and permanent English colonies because English colonization over the next two decades was still halting and erratic. The fleet that set sail for Walter Ralegh's American colony on April 9, 1585 under the command of Sir Richard Grenville was established on Roanoke Island under the governorship of Ralph Lane. Being without proper provisions, the colonists returned with Drake to England before a supply ship, which Ralegh had sent, arrived. Finding the colonists gone, Grenville, who, like Drake, had visited the colony, left 15 colonists to retain possession of the territory for England. In 1587, Ralegh sent out a new group of settlers to Chesapeake Bay under the leadership of John White.[276] It was clear that Ralegh was now the leading force in England concerning the colonization of America. However, neither of his ventures succeeded. The Armada and the subsequent war with Spain slowed but did not stop Ralegh's push for permanent English settlements in the New World. Hakluyt would have more to say but did not live to witness strong and vital permanent colonies in what would come to be known as English America. The example of Spain was still a formidable challenge to England.

VI

The various kinds of writing, accounts by explorers, cosmographies, translations, histories, essays, and government documents and reports from Gourgues to Hakluyt suggest a complex idea of the English and French representation of the example of Spain during the critical years from the death of Jean Ribault in the mid-1560s to 1588. A key means of building up opposition or an alternative to Spain was through a growing body of writing. In the first 75 years after Columbus, neither the French nor the English could come close to rivaling the Spanish in writing about the New World. Even though they continued to rely on the Spanish for discourses of law, ethnology, history, and natural history into the eighteenth century, the French and English began to build up their own influential texts about the New World.

From the conflict in Florida between Spain and France to the defeat of the Armada, a shift was occurring in the role of Spain in the French and English representations of the New World. Increasingly taking advantage of the division within France, England learned from France and Spain in order to challenge Spanish dominance. Explorers like Gilbert and Frobisher, as well as editors and advisors like Hakluyt, looked at Spain partly through French mediation. As we can see in the relation between Hakluyt and Thevet, England could teach France as well as learn from it when it came to the matter of Spain.

Religion, while important, was not always the determining factor in representing Spain because, for instance, the Spanish threatened English Catholics that they would meet the same fate as Ribault if they joined the Gilbert expedition to North America and because La Popelinière, a Huguenot historian, thought that Catholic Portugal would provide a good example for France of how to colonize America. While translating and interpreting Spanish writers who were sympathetic to the Natives and those who were not, the French and English came to embody the same contradictions in their own views of the indigenous inhabitants of the New World. While Las Casas became a focal point in this translation of Spanish critique into anti-Spanish sentiment, the writings of Le Challeux, Benzoni, and Chauveton also contributed to the negative representations of Spain in France and England.

It is clear from English promotional literature that was always answering doubts at home about colonization and from remarks critical of France in Léry and La Popelinière that in England and France imperialism was not a unified and univocal enterprise. While the English and the French attempted to expand, they faced their own doubts as well as the threat of Spanish power. Their dreams of expansion and their early efforts in America were precarious and not at all a *fait accompli* or a manifest destiny. Both North Atlantic powers were on the verge of establishing permanent colonies, but it is only with hindsight that we can attach to these voyages and settlements the confidence of some instrumental or teleological triumph. The success of the English and French in the New World during the seventeenth century and beyond would bring at least as many problems with it as it would solve.

In this chapter I have focused on the development in France and England of anti-Spanish sentiment. The conflict between Spain and the Huguenots in Florida contributed strongly to this feeling. Whereas the French and English still found positive models in Spain's colonies in the New World, they criticized Spain in propaganda. Accounts in each of the two languages served the national interests of each country, which included advocacy of expansion and permanent colonies in the Americas The French and English texts about the New World grew in number and variety. The very imitation of Spain may have helped that efflorescence. As these texts in France and England incorporated the variety and complexity of texts of Spain concerning the New World, they showed both respect for and challenges to the example of Spain.

Having discussed the representation of Spain in principal works from adventurers and explorers, such as John Hawkins and Dominique Gourges, through cosmographers like Belleforest and Thevet, translations of Spanish writers like Gómara and Las Casas, and Huguenot historians like Léry and Chauveton, to promoters of empire, like Hakluyt the Younger, I have sought to show that the attitudes toward Spain in England and France were reaching a crisis in this period. In this discussion I have also tried to demonstrate that the genres of exploration narrative, cosmography, translation, history, and government report were distinct but overlapped in some conventions and in content and to acknowledge their shared content and techniques. Furthermore, I argued that while the responses of these writers in these genres, or kinds of writing, to Spain were still ambivalent and contradictory, the texts in the period from 1567 to 1600 were the most anti-Spanish in the period from 1492 to 1713. Moreover, I maintained that the texts in the last third of the sixteenth century provided the foundation for later and persistent outbreaks of negative representations of Spain. Hakluyt's "Discourse," although not alone, was held up as an important example of this negativity, but its intricacies, which included using Spain as a positive model, were also explored in some detail.

Having observed the role of the anti-Spanish tracts of the 1560s and 1570s and the narratives leading up to the Armada (1567–88) and having explored the intensifing rivalry that France and England had with Spain while trying to establish themselves in North America, we now move to an examination of the wake of these events, especially of the Armada. Hakluyt's "Discourse," a key text, was not part of print culture in this period; it was Hakluyt's next work that established his influence at the time and his reputation thereafter. In what follows I will undertake such an exploration from Richard Hakluyt's *Principall Navigations* (1589) to texts produced on the verge of the English Civil War (1642–49).

CHAPTER 5

The Making of Permanent Colonies, 1589–1642

In the making of French and English permanent settlements in New World, the ambivalent and contradictory representation of Spain in the New World was not a matter of religion only, as can be observed, for instance, in Walter Ralegh's work and in Marc Lescarbot's *L'Histoire de la Nouvelle France* (1609). Once France and England established permanent colonies in the New World and Spain began to decline in this period, the sustained intensity of anti-Spanish sentiment abated into periodic eruptions of the Black Legend of Spain. From the aftermath of the Armada to the founding of Montréal in New France, the example of Spain continued to change in complex and suggestive ways. Although Spanish power continued to be strong in the New World well beyond this period, it now faced the challenge Spain had long feared and had tried to prevent. France and England, no matter how tentative their exploration and the establishment of permanent settlements would be, were in this period of more than 40 years transforming themselves from explorers and pirates to settlers and neighbors. As worrisome as the English and French challenges on the sea and in exploration had been to Spain, the establishment of their colonies would begin the decline of Spanish supremacy in earnest.

The defeat of the Spanish Armada in 1588 was not the end of Spanish power. Between 1580 and 1640, the two great overseas empires of Portugal and Spain were united under the Spanish crown, so that to speak of the decline of Spain is to suggest a relative decline in a world power and not to confuse the anti-Spanish rhetoric of the rivals of Spain with its actual political and economic wealth and influence. Nonetheless, this discussion will address a period from the defeat of the Armada to the beginning of the English Civil War and the threshold of the reign of Louis XIV, when France became a dominant force in Europe until his death in 1715. The period is one that follows on the first great defeat of Spain to its collapse as the superpower in Europe. While this historiography of expansion centers on the ambivalent and contradictory rhetoric the French and English use to represent Spain, and particularly its empire in the New World, it also attempts, wherever appropriate, to place that discourse in the context of events.

Rhetoric is not the only actuality and can be counterfactual. Being able to establish permanent colonies so early in the New World, something the English and French could not or would not do, the Spanish had to have something going for them that the English and French did not. That is why the English and French representation of the Spanish and the New World could not simply be negative forerunners or examples of the Black Legend.

Nonetheless, I am not trying to play down the negatives views of Spain in both countries. An instance of anti-Spanish sentiment occurred in a French text, Antoine Arnauld's *Anti-Espagnol, avtrement Les Philippiques d'vn Demostenes françois touchant les menees & rvses de Philippe roy d'Espagne* (n.p. [Paris?], 1590), which was translated into English during the same year as *The Coppie of the Anti-Spaniard, Made at Paris, by a Frenchman* (London, 1590). In this brief work of thirty-two pages, Arnauld attacked the designs Philip II had on the French crown and referred to the Spanish destruction of the French in Florida. This is one example of Protestant anxiety in France about the succession, and in England about the conflict with Spain, despite the triumph over the Armada. During the 1590s, Arnauld's book was reprinted numerous times and was translated into several languages and published in Protestant centers like London, Leyden, The Hague, and Geneva. In *La Flevr de lys, qvi est vn discovrs d'vn François retenu dans Paris, sur les impietez et disgvuisements contenvs av manifeste d'Espagne* (n.p. [Paris?], 1593), Arnauld also spoke of Spanish cruelty and the depopulation of the Indies in the context of Spanish dynastic ambitions in France. One of the instances of ambivalence in England toward Spain was that in their conflict the English were not simply content with propaganda and continued to learn from the Spanish in translation such as Pedro de Medina, *The Arte of Navigation Translated out of the Spanish . . . by John Frampton* (London, 1595), a reprint of the first edition of 1581. This attention to navigation was one of the ideas that Gilbert and Hakluyt urged upon England.

Even at the height of the Armada and the subsequent war between Elizabeth and Philip, the English did not avoid the double action of imitation and displacement, of wondering after Spanish riches and reviling them. The French also noted the effects of Spanish wealth from the Indies on Spain's politics in Europe. In *Discovrs svr l'estat de France* (n.p. [Paris?], 1591), for instance, Michel Hurault alluded to the use of these treasures to support the duke of Mayenne.[1] Hakluyt used Spanish descriptions of the land and the indigenous inhabitants to give the English information to rival the colonies of Spain in the New World. The permanent colonies the Spanish had planted would serve as exempla for those the English wished to plant.

In attempting to establish colonies in the Americas, France also relied on the Spanish experience in the New World.[2] The founder of a permanent colony in New France, Samuel de Champlain, had sailed earlier for Spain in the West Indies. Often the French descriptions of Spain depended in part on whether the writer was Protestant or Catholic. Even among French Catholics like Champlain and Marc Lescarbot, the Spanish played different roles: Champlain did not discuss them much after his experience in the West Indies, whereas Lescarbot saw New France as a rival to New Spain. Although the English and French showed a different doubleness toward Spain, they both displayed an ambivalence toward the example of Spain.

Paradoxically, at the peak of Spanish power, the English and French established their first permanent colonies, at Jamestown in 1607 and at Québec in 1608. Sixteen years after the Armada, James I signed a peace treaty with Spain, so the balance of power among Spain, France, and England shifted once more. Henry VIII had been married to Catherine of Aragon and Mary had wedded Philip II. The French sought their own dynastic connections with Spain and had tried to block the marriage between Mary and Philip as they feared being surrounded by Spanish territories. Later the Bourbons, a French dynasty, would come to rule Spain, which caused England some anxiety. Crises and alliances modulated the rhetoric in the French and English representation of Spain. This discourse in France and England embodied anxiety, envy, fear, hatred, admiration, respect, hope, and celebration. In this crucial time, when France and England were only beginning to be serious rivals for empire, these countries needed to know about Spain's American empire more than they ever had, to use Spanish knowledge to undermine Spain.

For over three decades after the defeat of the Armada, Spain was still a great power, but it soon began to decline. How much contemporary rivals wished for this decline and how much they knew about it is hard to say. Between 1621 and 1641, the Spanish empire in the New World began to collapse.[3] Silver remittances from the Indies declined; Seville's Atlantic trade dwindled; after the peaceful era of Philip III, Spain became embroiled in wars fought in Europe and America during the 1620s and 1630s; Spain lost dominion over the seas. In an effort to reduce the Dutch trade in Spanish and Portuguese overseas possessions, which had so increased during the 12 year truce, Spain made an ill-fated decision to resume war with the United Provinces in 1621. The Dutch now turned their attention from Portuguese possessions in Africa and the Far East to Brazil. A joint force of Spaniards and Portuguese defeated the Dutch in Brazil, but the Dutch fell back: in the Caribbean in 1628 Piet Heyn captured the Spanish treasure fleet. Holland accomplished what France and the England had dreamed of in the sixteenth century. This great loss damaged the ability and the confidence of the merchants of Seville to invest in the American colonies. The Dutch gained a foothold in Brazil, which divided the Portuguese and the Spanish, who were both under the Spanish monarchy. In turn, the Spanish resented the Portuguese bankers who were involved in the Spainish–American trade from 1626-27. The great collapse of the power of Spain came in 1639–40. War with France was weakening Spain: the duke of Olivares's government intervened in the commercial life of Seville so often that by 1639 he had paralyzed Spanish trade with the West Indies. The Spanish navy lost the Battle of Downs in October 1639 and another in Brazilian waters in January 1640, the time of collapse.

No treasure fleet reached Spain that year—Spain was no longer the dominant sea power in the world. During the spring, the Catalans revolted; in August, the Spanish army was defeated in Flanders; in December, Portugal declared its independence. The Netherlands were becoming the great commercial power of Europe, and, having defeated the Portuguese and the Spanish, would later find themselves in conflicts with France and England. Still, despite the Spanish decline and collapse, which left the West Indies open to the Dutch, French, and English, anti-Spanish sentiment lingered and lingers still.[4]

None of this decline and collapse could the French and English have known about or surmised. In the last half of the sixteenth and the first quarter of the seventeenth century, France and England followed the example of Ramusio in producing collections of voyages in various forms, from André Thevet to Marc Lescarbot, from Richard Hakluyt the Younger to Samuel Purchas. These works shared a rhetoric of promotion: they urged the monarch, or encouraged courtiers to urge the monarch, to colonize and their fellow citizens to emigrate.[5] This French and English promotional literature also expressed the frustration of its authors, amid their imperial optimism, about the failed attempts to plant permanent settlements in the New World.

Here, my primary focus will be on important texts by Robert Payne, Hakluyt, Ralegh, Samuel de Champlain, Lescarbot, Robert Johnson, William Strachey, and Samuel Purchas, a mixture of collections about travel and eyewitness accounts of America. An interdependence of French and English accounts continued into the seventeenth century, not without its own rivalry and contention, and neither France nor England could ignore Spanish sources even as, or perhaps especially because these two countries were beginning to establish a permanent presence in the New World.[6] In Hakluyt, Lescarbot, and Purchas particularly, whose works were wholly or in part collections (even though Lescarbot called his work a history), translation was a significant aspect of their books. Lescarbot could criticize Spain in the New World but found Spanish sources to be indispensable. The views of colonization and of Natives current in England affected notions of "identity" and mediation between the English and aboriginal peoples they encountered. During the sixteenth century, English ideas about colonization, while deriving from classical and medieval concepts and from the involvement of England in Ireland, depended most heavily on continental sources. Even in the early seventeenth century, English promotional literature about America most often involved translations of continental authors, especially from Spain.

The example of Spain was central in determining English attitudes to the New World and its inhabitants. Hakluyt, who translated or commissioned translations from the Spanish, followed the example of other principal translators, such as Richard Eden, John Frampton, and Thomas Nicholas. Although the English adapted Spanish writings that glorified the Spanish conquest for their own purposes—providing propaganda to encourage potential investors and settlers—they often adopted Spanish representations of the New World and the Native.[7] The Spanish authors most translated into English, such as Peter Martyr, Oviedo, and López de Gómara, emphasized the glory of Spain in the face of Native American betrayal and barbarism even if they sometimes advocated conversion and condemned Spaniards for mistreating the Natives.[8] As we saw in the last chapter, only one edition of Las Casas's *Brief Relation of the Destruction of the Indies* appeared in English in 1583.[9] If anything, on the face of it, the imbalance was not in favor of the Black Legend of Spain but of the glorious deeds of the Spanish in the New World. In the period 1589 to 1642, the first great English collection of promotional literature was produced by Hakluyt, whose work led to a number of sequels by Purchas, and these texts provided information and interpretations that both reflected the increased interest in colonies in America and helped to produce that interest partly by trying to answer the doubts of those who wanted no part of empire and who thought that expansion was inimical to England itself.

Before turning again to Hakluyt, I would like to discuss an important text on Ireland by Robert Payne, published in 1589, the same year as Hakluyt's *Principall Navigations*. Just as the Canary Islands were the prelude and testing ground for Spanish colonization, so too was Ireland for the expansion of England to the New World. There was, for the English, a kind of typological relation between Ireland and Virginia. Following discussion will begin with this focus on Ireland and then widen its perspective to the more panoramic view in Hakluyt's great collection.

I

Spanish influence or presence in Ireland caused anxiety in England, especially in the Protestant circles at court, in what I have called the American party. The Armada was still fresh in mind, so that any comments concerning the Spanish in Robert Payne's *A Briefe Description of Ireland: Made in this yeare, 1589 . . .* would not have fallen on deaf ears.[10] There was, according to Payne, a double threat to England: Catholic Ireland and Catholic Spain:

> Some mistrust that the Spaniardes will enter the land, & that the Irish wil releeue them: no doubt there are some Traytors in Ireland, I would I could truely say there were none in England: but this I dare assure you the greater number, and al the better sort doe deadly hate the Spaniardes, & yet I thinke they beare them fayre weather, for that they are the popes champions, & a great part of the Irish (for want of good preaching & discipline) are greatly inclined to papistrie.[11]

Payne represented the contradictory response of the Irish to the Spaniards: a division existed between "the better sort" who "deadly hate" the Spanish and "the greater number" who sympathize with them. In this multitude, he saw a religious bond between Ireland and Spain that could threaten England. He reduced Catholicism among the many in Ireland, if only in a bracket, to a lack of "good preaching & discipline." This "great part of the Irish" consists of "the popes champions" and "are greatly inclined to papistrie." Class lines were perhaps as important in the attitude toward Spain in Ireland as religion was. Payne further complicated expectations in the representation of Spain and Ireland here:

he admitted there were traitors in England as well as in Ireland. He blurred the we/they and us/other divides that might be expected to be entrenched in such a text. This monological version did not exist in Payne's work.

Payne's ambivalent representation of the equivocal response of the Irish to the Spaniards was explicit about the typology between the New World and the Old. The events of the shipwrecked Spanish ships from the Armada haunted the text:

> But their intertainement this last yeare amongst the Irish (notwithstanding they brought the popes holy candles & pardons) sheweth how they affect Spanish gouernment. Most of the better sort of the Irish haue read of their monsterous cruelties in the west Indias, where they most tiranously haue murthered many millions moe of those simple creatures then now liueth in Ireland, even such as sought their fauours by offering vnto them al the [sic; should be "that"?] they had, neuer resisting nor offering them any harme. Wherfore I doubt not that the Irish are so foolish to entertain such proud guestes knowing their tyrannie, & hauing not so well deserued at their hands as those simple soules whom they so cruelly murdered.[12]

Once more, Payne distinguished between the literate classes and the illiterate populace. This "better sort" would have read about the Spanish cruelties in the West Indies and would realize that the Spaniards would be capable of similar atrocities in Ireland. This, as we have observed and will see later on, was a similar strategy to the one used in the typology of the New World and the Netherlands, especially in translations of Las Casas, which warned that the Spanish would be as cruel to the people of the Netherlands as they were to the American Indians. Payne attributed wisdom to this "better" class in Ireland amid a rhetoric that contrasted the Spanish tyrants to the "many millions" of "simple creatures" or "simple soules whom they so cruelly murdered." Besides the repetition of "simple" as a means of making the Natives into pastoral or perhaps pre-lapsarian inhabitants, Payne also described them as "creatures" and "soules," as created by God or spirits ready for heaven, their bodies strangely absent in the pain of the Spanish actions against them. Payne used polyptoton, or the repetition of words derived from the same root, to emphasize the negative image of the Spaniards: he chimed, also using a kind of chiasmic alliteration, "monsterous cruelties" with "cruelly murdered" some lines later. Similarly, Payne let variants, such as "tiranously" and "tyrannie," "murthered" and "murdered," reverberate through this passage to uncover the pretensions and barbarity of the Spanish tyrants, whom he called "proud guestes."

As such, the Spaniards, who are not at home in Ireland, could not rely on the Irish: "Neyther are the Spaniardes so vnwise to trust those Irish, who so lately imbrued their hands in their bloud, slaying them as doggs in such plentifull maner, that their garments went about the countrey to be sold, as good cheape as beastes skins."[13] Payne was driving a wedge between the Spanish and the Irish by representing Irish violence against these Spanish "tyrants." England would profit from this enmity and this scene of mutual terror and mistrust.

It comes as no surprise that Payne invoked Las Casas. He had already written about the Spanish having killed millions of Natives—a typological echo of the Massacre of the Innocents in the Bible—so that it is reasonable to expect that Las Casas's was the very book that he was using as evidence that the educated elite in Ireland would consult to understand the cruelty of the Spaniards as it had occurred in the Americas and as it might happen in Ireland. In addressing the reader, Payne "sold" Las Casas:

> If you haue not the sayd booke of the Spanishe cruelties, I pray you buy it, it is wel worth the reading, I haue forgot the title, but it is of a small volume in quarto: it is written by a learned Bishop of their owne countrey about forty yeares sithens[?] in the Castalian toonge, and dedicated to their king for reformation of those cruelties: afterwardes translated into English & diuers other languages, to make their monsterous tyrannie knowne to the worlde.[14]

Payne did not remember the name of Las Casas or the title of his work, but he called him "a learned Bishop of their owne countrey" who had dedicated the book to the king so he would reform "those cruelties." Whatever his purposes of invective and propaganda, Payne was cogent on the intentions Las Casas had had for his text and how England and other nations had used it to expose Spain, "to make their monsterous tyrannie knowne to the worlde." As we have seen and will see over and over, the rivals of Spain used Las Casas to whip his own country in a way that he himself would probably have found misguided and unfortunate.

This expatiation on Ireland and Spain also had a direct bearing on domestic affairs in England. The aftermath of Mary Queen of Scots and the Armada focused Payne's attention on English Catholics, something we observed in the discussion of Hakluyt's "Discourse on Western Planting." The English readers were supposed to pass on Las Casas to their Catholic neighbors as a warning of Spanish cruelty not unlike, if the analogical, anagogical, typological, and allegorical urges in Payne's text are kept in mind, the one he had issued to the Irish:

> When you haue read the same, commend it to our Catholickes that wil be saued by their workes, and yet will not giue God thankes at their meate, for that they will not once haue in their mouth the praier for our Queene, annexe to our vsual thanks giuing at meate. I pray God open the eies of their vpholders, and let them see what these men gape for, which is no doubt the ruine and ouerthrow of her highnesse, whome I pray God preserue. But none are so blind as they that will not se. The Catholikes are borne with for their conscience sake, yet from such consciences spring all the Traiterous practices agaynst her Maiestie.[15]

Another possible Spanish invasion of England might still have been in Payne's sights, but he was worried about further Catholic attempts on Elizabeth I's life. Payne had moved from two references to the pope to the queen, from Irish and

English traitors in a similitude, to English traitors alone. And these traitors, too, were Catholic. The implication was that they had listened to the pope—Rome had excommunicated Elizabeth in 1570—and not to the queen. They had put religion before nation. Still, there was a hope that if the Catholics read Las Casas, they would leave their blindness and see. Payne left off this topic, however, with the unpromising mock of Catholic "consciences," which caused "all the Traiterous practices agaynst her Maiestie." Payne was ambivalent about Catholics in Ireland and in England, although he was not as explicit and confident in his view that the "better sort" of English Catholic would resist the Spanish as he was of their Irish counterparts.

It is important to remember this precarious context in Ireland and England context in discussing Hakluyt's great public work on colonization. I concentrated on the "Discourse," which deserved particular attention, especially in its representation of the Spanish, sometimes in a deeply negative light. Here, Hakluyt's most famous work will receive less attention because it is so well-known and because my primary interest in this book is representations of Spain. For the purposes of this argument, "Discourse" plays a more important role than *The Principall Navigations of the English Nation* (1589). This decision is not intended to slight the significance of *The Principall Navigations* or to pretend that such a brief analysis is comprehensive. Rather, the following analysis of the public *Principall Navigations* is a supplement to my discussion of the private "Discourse" that concentrates almost exclusively on how both relate to the example of Spain. Once more, this study focuses most on prefatory or front matter because in these introductory pieces the authors often use the convention of speaking in their own voices. These parts of the texts throw into relief the rhetorical nature of the discourse. The art of persuasion is often at its most intense in these prefaces, introductions, and addresses to the readers.

Before proceeding to Hakluyt's "Preface" to the first edition of *The Principall Navigations,* it is better to begin at the beginning of his "Epistle Dedicatorie to Sir Francis Walsingham Knight," principal secretary to the Queen and a member of the Privy Council, in order to compare his appeal to a patron with those of Oviedo and Thevet, who provided models for Hakluyt. Hakluyt began with a story about his own life in order to remind Walsingham of his connections to the crown and to Walsingham himself. He evoked the memory of when he was "one of Her Majesties scholars at Westminster," and his visit to his cousin Richard Hakluyt the Elder, "a Gentleman of the Middle Temple, well knowen unto you."[16] In the elder Hakluyt's chamber, young Richard found books of cosmography and a universal map. His older cousin proceeded to give him a lesson on ancient and modern geography. After speaking on the specific bodies of water and land, Hakluyt the Elder brought the Younger to the Bible and directed him to Psalm 107, verses 23 and 24, "that they which go downe to the sea in ships, and occupy by the great waters, they see the works of the Lord, and his woonders in the deepe, &c."[17] The words of the prophet and his cousin convinced Hakluyt the Younger to "prosecute that knowledge and kinde of literature" at the university. At Christchurch, Oxford, he did just that. Richard Hakluyt the Elder wrote a tract encouraging colonization to Virginia for the glory of God, increasing "the force of the Christians," sales of woolen cloth, and a northwest passage to Asia (some of the 31 reasons he gives).[18]

Like Thevet, Hakluyt saw God in the great ocean, but he stressed the religious element even more as he began his dedication with a conversion experience. As with Oviedo's and Thevet's preliminary matter, Hakluyt's appealed to the authenticity of private experience and study.[19] Hakluyt explained that he read about discoveries in Greek, Latin, Italian, Spanish, Portuguese, French, and English. Like Oviedo and Thevet, Hakluyt also claimed a first: in his public lectures he "was the first, that produced and shewed both the olde imperfectly composed, and the new lately reformed Mappes, Globes, Spheares, and other instruments of this Art for demonstration in the common schooles, to the singular pleasure and generall contentment of my auditory."[20] Hakluyt's mode was narrative: his story involved a movement from study to observation in travel in a case of cause and effect. For instance, he wrote: "and by reason principally of my insight in this study, I grew familiarly acquainted with the chiefest Captaines at sea, the greatest Merchants, and the best Mariners of our nation: by which meanes having gotten somewhat more then common knowledge, I passed at length the narrow seas into France with sir Edward Stafford, her majesties carefull and discreet Ligier."[21]

It was the uncommon knowledge of Hakluyt that allowed him to serve his nation through the learning garnered from his travels. Five years in Paris Hakluyt spent with Edward Stafford "in his dangerous and chargeable residencie in her Highnes service."[22] Hakluyt appealed to what he heard in conversation and read in books—that is, "other nations miraculously extolled for their discoveries and notable enterprises by sea," but not the English, who, despite their enjoyment of peace, were "either ignominiously reported, or exceedingly condemned."[23] The author hoped to arouse English patriotism through praeexposito, a comparison of what has been done with what should have been done. The English should have made more discoveries, but have thus far squandered the opportunity.

Hakluyt used French texts to spur English interest in the New World. Like the analogies between the Old World and the New World in the first two dedicatory odes to Thevet's *Les Singularitez,* Hakluyt's comparison between other European nations and England was meant to show the shortcomings of his own country. Hakluyt called on La Popelinière's *L'Admiral de France* (1584), noting that it was "printed at Paris. Fol. 73. pag. 1, 2," and quoted him in French to shame the English. La Popelinière wondered why the Rhodians, an island people, were so good at navigation, and why the English did not surpass them. Hakluyt quoted La Popelinière's original: "les Anglois, qui ont d'esprit, de moyens, & valeur assez, pour s'aquerir un grand honneur parmi tous les Chrestians, ne se font plus valoir sur le' element qui leur est, & doit estre plus naturel qu'à autres peuples" ["the English, who have spirit, means and values enough to acquire a great honour amongst all Christians should place more value on this element than they do, which must be more natural for them than for other peoples"].[24] Hakluyt took these musings as an obloquy or detraction, as if the French were challenging the English.

France was another kind of challenge to England: it was divided from within but still found ways to concern Spanish authorities. The French were also powerful, although they had no coherent policy concerning the New World. The cardinal of Bourbon, one of the leaders of the Catholic League and an ally to Philip II, paid attention to Acadia, Maine, and Newfoundland rather than to areas vital to Spain, whereas Catherine de Medici confronted Spain in 1582 by attacking the Azores and taking control of the shipping lane between those islands and Brazil so that she could profit from the Portuguese empire, which was now a part of the Spanish empire.[25] France, then, harbored various factions, some friendly to Spain and others not. Hakluyt's interest in the Protestant La Popelinière had a certain strategic value: his patrons and he himself were advocates of Protestantism and the Huguenot experience in the New World was an object lesson to those English Protestants interested in colonization in the Americas.

In the dedication to a work devoted to translating accounts that were not in English and placing them beside those in English, Hakluyt chose to emphasize the foreignness of La Popelinière by quoting him in the original French. He did not domesticate the insult, but he may also have wanted to show his learning. Like Thevet, who emphasized his own hard work, Hakluyt made his labors epic: he was the only one to take up La Popelinière's challenge. As Pliny had complained about the malice of men in his time, so too did Hakluyt by quoting his predecessor in Latin. Thus, with an excitatio, an arousal of the audience by the invocation of La Popeliniere's alleged critique of the English nation, Hakluyt rushed into intellectual battle. Hakluyt's new scholarship would triumph in its vindication of England. Ironically, Hakluyt relied heavily on French texts and knowledge of the New World in order to bolster English ambitions there, but he seems to have felt the need to build up a rivalry with, and nurse a slight from, the French. There seems to have been some rhetorical aspect to this rousing of the English from their slumber from exploration, so that La Popelinière's challenge was really the call of a fellow Protestant for England, the leading Protestant power, to take up where the Huguenots left off. Hakluyt had learned a great deal about colonization in Paris and would make use of that knowledge to challenge himself and his own country.

At the end of the Epistle, Hakluyt turned to Walsingham, to whom he dedicated his book. Like Thevet, Hakluyt praised his audience, who was in the first instance his patron, to seek favor and thereby used comprobatio. For Hakluyt, Walsingham had sought the honor of the queen, the good reputation of the country and the advancement of navigation, so, the author implied, he too would answer the implicit criticism that La Popelinière leveled at the country. With Walsingham's help to fulfill Hakluyt's project, England would be the greatest seafaring nation in Europe. Walsingham had, as Hakluyt reported, encouraged the author's travels by letter and speech, so that Hakluyt saw himself "bound to make presentment of this worke to your selfe, as the fruits of your owne incouragements, & the manifestation both of my unfained service to my prince and country, and of my particular duty to your honour."[26] Hakluyt attempted to answer his patron's "expectation" partly by letting Doctor James look at the work and censure it "according to your [Walsingham's] order."[27] Official approval had cleared *Principall Navigations.* The author ended his "Epistle Dedicatorie" with a benedictio or blessing for his patron, who was the principal hearer while the reader overheard. In the background it was Elizabeth I for whom this work was ultimately made, a published sequel to "Discourse," which Hakluyt had presented her in 1584.

The "Preface" to the first edition also bore the title, "Richard Hakluyt to the favourable Reader."[28] Here was a direct address to the reader in which Hakluyt set out the method of his book and acknowledged those who helped in his endeavor. He had sought all testimonies relating to his topic and had recorded them word for word with the author or authority's name and the page number. If the work has not been translated, "I have first expressed it in the same termes wherein it is originally written, whether it were a Latine, Italian, Spanish or Portingall discourse, or whatever els, and thereunto in the next roome have annexed the signification and translation of the wordes in English."[29] It is clear that Hakluyt's project of building up England as a naval power and celebrating its glory through its great voyages and famous victories rested on a kind of collection, translation, and observation of other Europeans, ancient and modern. This nationalism had nothing to do with isolationism and everything to do with assimilating the experience of other nations into its own. Hakluyt appealed to his project of translation as a means of allowing "the paynefull and personall travellers" to "reape that good opinion and just commendation which they have deserved."[30] Furthermore, Hakluyt has "referred every voyage to his Author, which both in person hath performed, and in writing hath left the same" so "that every man might answere for himselfe, justifie his reports, and stand accountable for his owne doings."[31] Evidence and experience could be represented.

Hakluyt allowed the voyagers to speak for themselves, so they could be tested in what they said and gain any honor from what they had done and the events they had recorded. He would not ventriloquize them or take their glory unto himself: he would not be a rhetorical or editorial magpie but would let people speak for themselves. Hakluyt asserted: "for I am not ignorant of Ptolemies assertion, that Peregrination is historia, and not those wearie volumes bearing the titles of universall Cosmographie which some men that I could name have published as their owne, beyng in deed most untruly and unprofitablie ramassed and hurled together, is that which must bring us to the certayne and full discoverie of the world."[32] This trope of peregrination was one that Thevet borrowed from Ptolemy for his "Preface Aux Lectures" in *Les Singularitez,* but he did not seem to have convinced readers like Hakluyt. In Hakluyt's view these cosmographies were a miscellany of other people's views rather than the observations of voyagers.[33] This was the context for Hakluyt's allusion to Ptolemy "that Peregrination is historia" and his caustic remark about universal cosmography, which represented a crack at unnamed universal cosmographers, apparently like Thevet and Belleforest, who published their cosmographies in 1575. Hakluyt elided the question of editorial selection being more than just a collection on the topic, but on the other hand, he did bring together a vast array of materials and was cosmopolitan in the way he did it.

Hakluyt's project was, however, ambivalent about these foreign sources. He wanted to concentrate on the navigations of the English nation but found that "strangers" had cast more light on the voyages than had English historians, except for Bale, Foxe, and Eden.[34] In setting out further his method of selection, Hakluyt used a form of occupatio or telling something by pretending to leave it out. Although he was not going to describe English voyages to any part of Europe where English ships usually sailed, he did list briefly examples of English glory there. Having just listed the defeat of "that monstrous Spanish army," the Portuguese expedition, and two of Francis Drake's exploits, he did not concentrate on these victories closer to home but on the "discoverie of strange coasts."[35]

Even the English past had a built-in comparison that referred to a European or Continental dimension: Rome or Spain were never too far out of mind. Hakluyt enlisted England's classical past in the Roman Empire, as if the trope of *translatio imperii* were often implicit in the translation of classical texts into the vernacular. The western English navigations "came last of all to our knowledge and experience."[36] There followed the usual claim by different European nations of being the first to seek or arrive in America: in this instance a son of a prince of North Wales sailed west more than four hundred years before. Hakluyt told of Columbus "that renowned Genouoys to the most sage Prince of noble memorie King Henrie the 7. with his prompt and cheerefull acceptation thereof, and the occasion whereupon it became fruitlesse, and at that time of no great effect to this kingdome."[37] The author had to thread his way between representing the lost opportunities of English navigation and praise for the queen's ancestors and predecessors. Henry VII at least gave Cabot his letters patent "to discover & conquer in his name, and under his Banners unknowen Regions," and Hakluyt made much of Cabot being the first Christian to see the land from the Arctic circle to Florida.[38] Henry VIII's contribution seemed to have been glossed over, with three unnamed voyages and four intended for Asia. Even in talking about John Hawkins, it was difficult for Hakluyt to conceal that Mexico City in Nova Hispania and Hispaniola were marked in their very names as part of the Spanish empire, in which the English were, as they were in Portuguese Brazil, trading partners at best and pirates and interlopers at worst. Hakluyt was especially proud of six discourses by Englishmen on New Spain, "wherein are disclosed the cheefest secretes of the west India, which may in time turne to our no smal advantage."[39] Eyewitness reports became spying. Hakluyt celebrated the "enterprise" of Drake on Nombre de Dios, where he robbed the Spanish of their gold. The northwest passage, as sought by Frobisher and Davis, became a challenge to the English, and Hakluyt redoubled the challenge by calling it hopeful, probable, certain. He called attention to Humphrey Gilbert's reasons for believing in a passage, although, as in the case of John Oxnam, he admitted that the voyage was a failure.[40] Then Hakluyt continued in this vein with Ralegh's two colonies in Virginia, which had failed because of a lack of follow-up. He proceeded to "the two voyages made not long since to the Southwest, whereof I thinke the

Spanyard hath had some knowledge, and felt some blowes"—that is those of Edward Fenton and Robert Withrington.[41] For Hakluyt, the account of Thomas Candish's voyage into the south seas and circumnavigation supplemented and was more exact than that of Drake. The Candish account substituted for Drake's, which "(contrary to my expectation)" would allow another man to collect Drake's writings, and provided an excuse for the omission of Drake's first voyage in this volume.[42]

The last section of the "Preface" was acknowledgments. For the part of the book on the west, "besides myne owne extreeme travaile in the histories of the Spanyards," Hakluyt thanked Hawkins, Ralegh, and his own cousin and namesake. Hakluyt returned to study and observation as Oviedo and Thevet had: he listed the wonders of nature "and such other rare and strange curiosities, which wise men take great pleasure to reade of, but much more contentment to see."[43] What is curious is not Hakluyt's fascination with the strange but that he had not seen most of the distant lands of which he collected accounts. Nonetheless, he could speak of his great pleasure in reading, translating, editing: "herein I my selfe to my singuler delight have bene as it were ravished in beholding all the premisses gathered together with no small cost" in the cabinets of Richard Garthe and William Cope. It is as if the metonymy and synecdoche of relics and manuscripts could allow for vision and observation of the world, as if word and object became the world. These were officials of the government, the latter serving Lord Burleigh, the treasurer of England, whom Hakluyt called "the Seneca of our common wealth" in a Romanizing move worthy of Thevet turning the French monarchy into a republic.[44]

Another dimension of viewing was the map, and Hakluyt described the one "collected and reformed according to the newest, secretest, and latest discoveries, both Spanish, Portugall, and English."[45] In this advertisement, which promised knowledge that came from state secrets, Hakluyt even named the mapmaker and his patron. Like Oviedo and Thevet before him, Hakluyt hoped to spur his government into more effective policies in navigation and colonization in the New World. By building up pride in the nation, each historian wanted to see a translation of empire from the Romans to his country, even if metaphorically as an inspiration to further exploration. To this imperial theme was added the Christian dimension of the translation of faith. While being implicitly critical of his nation's lack in its policy in the New World, each historian wanted a favor from monarch and court, so that each had also to flatter and to seek patronage. As Hakluyt's use prefatory matter has suggested, he, like Oviedo and Thevet, desired an official or quasi-official role in molding and recording policy in America. Oviedo was a chronicler of empire, and Thevet and Hakluyt wished to assume a similar part. Unlike Oviedo, they had to promote an empire for their respective countries. Thevet and Hakluyt had great expectations for their respective countries in their navigation on the route to empire and used rhetorical means and motives in their texts that created intricate and ambivalent relations internally and to their reader, whether it was the patron addressed or the general reader. But Hakluyt was assuming a proleptic role in the 1580s that Thevet had been playing in the 1550s and Oviedo had occupied in the 1520s, though even by that time, Spain had established permanent colonies.[46] The example of

Spain for the French and the English involved textual influences and models that could be as oblique as the role of the historian/chronicler/geographer and not always as direct as allusion, citation, denunciation, and praise. Even in the shadow of the Armada, Hakluyt could look to the example of Spain, and to that of other European nations, even as he urged England to overtake Spain and all other European rivals.

Behind many travel narratives in the English Renaissance, such as Hakluyt's prose epic of the English nation (including Purchas's continuation of it), lay a whole network of Spanish, French, and English sources about mediation and the relation between Europeans and Natives. How different were the French and English practices from those of the Spanish when we look behind the rhetoric of the Black Legend? Until after 1590, English promotional literature did not take up the anti-Spanish and pro-Native stance of the Black Legend, so often associated with Las Casas. Later, in a work specifically on Virginia, Hakluyt continued his representation of the example of Spain.

In the Introduction to *Virginia Richly Valued* (London, 1609) Hakluyt assumed the Spanish view that the Natives were liars and dissemblers and suggested that if the inhabitants of America could not be converted, then English soldiers trained in the Netherlands against Spain should prepare the Natives for the hands of English preachers. In *Principall Navigations* Hakluyt did not pay much attention to the champion of the Indians—Las Casas. Whereas the first edition contained no mention of Las Casas, the second alluded directly to him only twice. Only in a work that remained unpublished until the late nineteenth century—the "Particular Discourse"—or what is also called "Discourse of Western Planting"—did Hakluyt show a clearly anti-Spanish and pro-Native stance. While seminal to the debate on promotional literature, Loren Pennington's view, while sound, needs to be qualified a little. Aspects of the Black Legend appeared before 1590 in "promotional" literature, or at least accounts of the New World used to gather knowledge of the New World. Whether Hakluyt's use of Las Casas was an accident of publishing history or whether this contrary position of Hakluyt as a proponent of the Black Legend was his private rather than his public view or whether there was a shift or tension in Hakluyt's thought is something that probably cannot be settled, but it was for others who sought to promote English colonization in the New World to emphasize the Black Legend.[47] In his own way Sir Walter Ralegh, like Sir Francis Walsingham, set out to affect attitudes at court toward the English prospects for colonies, and Hakluyt was someone both men called on to get the message out. Ralegh himself was, among many other things, an able poet, rhetorician, and historian who could also advance his own cause.

II

The career of Walter Ralegh shows the two-sidedness of English attitudes toward Spain but also provides an opportunity to study someone who was a colonizer, courtier, and historian and the texts he produced on the subject over a period of more than 25 years. Although Ralegh encouraged Hakluyt's "Discourse," he also wrote to persuade queen and country into supporting the American option. Nearly four decades after Las Casas's *Short Account* but only eight years after the English translation, in the aftermath of the defeat of the Spanish Armada, Ralegh, who lived as the enemy of Spain and died in 1618 as an alleged friend of Spain, represented the dark side of the propaganda of the Spaniards.

Ralegh's *A Report of the Trvth of the fight about the Isles of Açores, this last Sommer. Betwixt The Reuenge, one of her Maiesties Shippes, And an Armada of the King of Spaine* (1591) began with a denunciation of Spanish lies in the face of the author's truth:

Because the rumours are diuersly spred, as well in Englande as in the lowe countries and els where, of this late encounter between her maiesties ships and the Armada of *Spain;* and that the Spaniardes according to their vsu- all maner, fill the world with their vaine glorious vaunts, making great apparance of victories: when on the contrary, themselues are most com- monly & shamefully beaten and dishonoured; therby hoping to possesse the ignorant multitude by anticipating and forerunning false reports; It is agreeable with all good reason, for manifestation of the truth to ouercome falshood and vntruth.[48]

In the author's mind there was a typological connection between the Low Countries and the New World: Spain pillaged both. Ralegh told the ironic story of the burger of Antwerp who thought that the Spanish would spare him because he was a Catholic: they did but looted his house because his goods were all heretical.

With sarcasm, Ralegh called Spain "that holie and charitable nation."[49] Ralegh connected the Low Countries and the New World, where Spanish cru- elty should act as a negative example even to Flemish and English Catholics:

Neither haue they at any time as they protest inuaded the kingdomes of the *Indies* and *Peru,* and els where, but onely led thereunto, rather to reduce the people to Christianitie, then for either golde or emperie. When as in one onely Iland called *Hispaniola,* they haue wasted thirtie hundred thousand of the naturall people, besides manie millions els in other places of the *Indies:* a poore and harmelesse people created of God, and might haue beene won to his knowledge, as many of them were, and almost as manie as euer were perswaded thereunto. The Storie whereof is at large written by a Bishop of their owne nation cal-[led] *Bartolome de las Casas,* and translated into English and manie other languages, intituled *The Span- ish cruelties.*[50]

His Las Casas became a witness against Spanish aggression in Europe and the New World: the Dutch and English were, by implication, innocent victims like the Indians. The Natives were harmless; the Spanish were not. Other nations had manipulated a Spanish Catholic bishop's exposé of Spanish imperialism as a

means of denouncing the cruelty of Spain. The Spanish were "a nation of
rauinous straungers" who "more greedily thirst after English bloud, then after
the liues of anie other people of Europe" because of the many overthrows and
dishonors England had given Spain and thereby exposed its weakness to the
world. Spain would therefore try to enslave and subject all the English, including the Catholics and especially traitors, after they "bewitch" England from "the
obedience of our naturall prince."[51] Such traitors should not sell their country
to strangers and forsake obedience and faith contrary to nature and religion:
even heathen and irreligious nations would die for their country, prince, or
commonwealth. Ralegh concluded by appealing to God's defense of Elizabeth
I against enemies, traitors and invasions.[52] The Black Legend of Spanish cruelty
in the New World allowed the English to demonize the enemy, who had tried
to invade them, and their rival in American colonization.

Ralegh's *The Discouerie of the Large, Rich, and Bewtiful Empyre of Guiana*
(1596) tended toward the anti-Spanish and pro-Native position of the literature
of the Black Legend; although he argued that the Spanish conquest was an illegal act that killed 20 millions, his argument was also one of outconquesting the
Spaniards and finding even more gold.[53] It is apparent, then, that the English
representation of Natives was at least partly mediated through the relation
between England and Spain. Ralegh dedicated *Discoverie of Guiana* to Charles
Howard—the victorious admiral in the battle against the Spanish Armada—and
to Robert Cecil, and in it showed ambivalence toward Spain. It was a positive
and negative model. Ralegh was advising England how it could become rich
from gold in the New World as Spain had done and he was trying to demonstrate how the Natives would prefer to deal with the English owing to their distrust of the Spanish, who had been cruel toward them, a strategy the Huguenots
had used in their accounts of Florida.

In the "Epistle Dedicatorie," Ralegh spoke of his goal, "*that mighty, rich, and
beawtifull Empire of Guiana, and . . . that great and Golden City, which the Spanyards call El Dorado, and the naturalls Manoa.*"[54] Here, Ralegh sounded like
Columbus, although the latter mentioned God as much as gold (often in conjunction), while the English explorer was more often silent about the divine.[55]
Ralegh took his cue from Spanish legends as Columbus had been inspired by
the romantic tales of Marco Polo. The great reason England should be interested
in Guiana was that Ralegh claimed that it had more gold than the Indies or
Peru.[56] The Natives supported England's ambitions: "*All the most of the kings of
the borders are already become her Maiesties vassals; & seeme to desire nothing more then
her Maiesties protection, and the returne of the English nation.*"[57] In Ralegh's view
the Natives were awaiting their true Lord while others would throw off Spanish domination: Spain was so rich and had so many cities, it would not miss this
small area of America. He maintained that "*if it had not beene in respect of her highnes future honer & riches, I could haue laid hands and ransomed many of the kings &
Cassiqui of the Country, & have had a reasonable proportion of gold for their redemption.*"[58] Long-term rather than short-term profit was Ralegh's goal for England.
It seems, however, that even in light of his earlier attack on Spanish treatment of
the Indians, he would have been willing, at least rhetorically, to kidnap the local

chiefs and kings and gain riches. Instead, he led a life of poverty for the good and honor of his monarch. Ralegh did bring in God at the end: he delayed any action in this enterprise *"vntill I knew whether it pleased God to put a disposition in her princely and royall heart eyther to follow or foreslow the same."*[59] While Ralegh prayed for God's power to help his cause, he used the conventional topos of modesty to take responsibility for the errors in his book, which his dedicatees were asked to pardon.

The next layer of Ralegh's text was his address *"To the Reader,"* in which, in the first sentence, he got to the nub of his problem: an alderman of London and an officer of Her Majesty's mint had declared the gold worthless. Ralegh's address was a response to this "malicious slau-nder" by saying that some of his men kept marcasite, found in Trinedado and not in Guiana, even when he told them it was not gold. The minerals Ralegh saw in Guiana were *"El madre del oro* (as the Spanyards terme them) which is the mother of golde."[60] Ralegh testified to all those in London who made many trials of the gold ore and found it to be of high quality and once more refuted the unnamed alderman who had tried to make a scandal.[61] The theme here was always gold. He also maintained that the gold was from Guiana even if he did not bring more home: good gold was found in strong stone. The more than 100 persons in Ralegh's party could testify how impossible it was to navigate the rivers in Guiana from the beginning of June through the end of September.[62] A defensiveness also contributed to Ralegh's rhetorical motives in the text.

Self-defense was Ralegh's imperative: his only motivation in seeking gold was "to serve her majesty and my Country."[63] To defend himself, Ralegh brought back the image of Spanish menace and cruelty in order to stir feelings against his English detractors: "If the spanishe nation had beene of like beleefe to these detractors, we should litle haue feared or doubted their attempts, wherewith we now are daily threatned."[64] Spain's threat to England, which did not end with the defeat of the Armada, was used as a justification for Ralegh's plan to seize gold and land in the New World. One of Ralegh's lessons was that it pleased God that "the Spaniard, who seeking to deuour all nations, are themselues deuoured" even as "they seeke vnlawfull and vngodly rule and Empery."[65]

The trope of self-defense and the defensive position of the English is something to which Ralegh's double vision of, or typology between, Ireland and Spain vis-a-vis England contributed. After questioning the legitimacy of the actions of the Spanish empire, Ralegh spoke about those English and Irish Catholic traitors, like Morice Fitz John, who served Spain in the attempted invasion of England. The unnaturalness of these rebels in serving a foreign king was Ralegh's theme. He cited the example of the beheading of Morice's cousin, the earl of Desmond, the hanging of his other cousin, Sir John of Desmond, the hanging, drawing and quartering of still another cousin, Sir James Desmond, all of whom also supported Spain.[66] In Ralegh's interpretation Ireland was in Spain's pay against England.

Ralegh's narrative created implied structures of comparison—analogies, allegories, and explicit likenesses—that drew attention to Spain's aggression in the New World in order to make it legitimate for the Natives to seek the defense of

England, which itself was defending itself against Spain and those nations it would incite against the English. Ralegh implied the Spanish rape of these territories, saying that Charles the Fifth "had the Maydenhead of *Peru,* & the aboundant treasures of *Ataóalipa*" and how he and his successor had endangered kingdoms, so that, by the new king, "many vessels, treasures, and people are deuoured, & yet notwithstanding he beginneth againe like a storme to threaten shipwracke to vs all."[67] What enabled the king of Spain to threaten England and other nations was not any produce from Spain, Portugal, or any of his other provinces: "It is his Indian Golde that indaungereth and disturbeth all the nations of Europe, it purchaseth intelligence, creepeth into Councels, and setteth bound loyalty at libertie, in the greatest Monarchies of Europe."[68] The seeking of gold was not an activity in and of itself but a matter of national interest and security. Ralegh reasoned further that if the king of Spain could keep the English from his foreign enterprises and from impeaching his trade or could besiege England "in Britayne, Ireland, or else where" and would endanger "us" further, and therefore, Ralegh suggested implicitly, no one should stir up scandals concerning his enterprise in Guiana and the gold he claimed to have brought back.[69]

Rich princes could wage war more successfully because they did not impoverish and alienate their people. The moral was now pointed: "whatsoeuer kingdome shalbe inforced to defend it selfe, may be compared to a body dangerouslie diseased, which for a season may be preserued with vulgar medicines, but in a short time, and by little and little, the same must needs fall to the ground, and be dissolued."[70] Ralegh claimed that throughout his life, according to his small power and persuasion, he had attempted to achieve profit for England and to "be a lett & impeachment to the quiet course, & plentiful trades of the Spanish nation."[71] This portrayal of Spain in the New World was more peaceful and less sinister than some of Ralegh's representations of Spanish imperialism and by implication suggested his work as a kind of disturbance. Such a war could endanger and weaken the king of Spain as much as any prince in Europe because he relied on many nations for revenue and how weak they were "so farre seuered from mutuall succor."[72] Ralegh promised by Elizabeth's favor and good opinion of him and with his life that these provinces and the empire he had newly "discouered" should be enough to enable the queen and England to find more treasure than Spain and to achieve more than the author had declared or promised in his discourse. He appealed to the readers to accept as their reward this discourse that sought to profit and honor their monarch. Ralegh's gold would guard the realm.

The body of Ralegh's *The Discoverie of Gviana* developed the need to observe the Spanish model of colonization while using its own methods to subvert it. He began the text proper with a description of the route from England to the New World, natural phenomena, and the situational friendship and trade of the English with the Spanish and Indians, but it was clear that wherever he was, Ralegh had "*Guiana* (the *Magazin* of all rich mettels)" in mind.[73] One of the Native caciques came to speak with Captain Whiddon, who had met him the year before. The relations among English, Spanish and Native, no matter what war and rivalry had effected, were already mediated. Ralegh pretended to be on his way to supply English settlers in Virginia, but admitted to the reader his real purpose: to revenge the ambush of eight of Whiddon's men by the Natives and Spanish under the command of Don Antonio de Berreo and to learn more about Guiana from talking with Spaniards.[74] His mission is a little like Gourges's revenge of the Spaniard's execution of Ribault.

But Ralegh soon came to the subject of Spanish cruelty. A cacique gave Ralegh intelligence of Berreo, who mistreated the Natives, and Ralegh added his own eyewitness testimony of Spanish cruelty:

> For although he had giuen order through all the Iland that no *Indian* should come aborde to trade with me vpon paine of hanging and quartering, (hauing executed two of them for the same which I afterwardes founde) yet euery night there came some with most lamentable complaints of his cruelty, how he had deuided the Iland & giuen to euery soldier a part, that he made the ancient *Casiqui* which were Lords of the country to be their slaues, that he kept them in chains, & dropped their naked bodies with burning bacon, & such other torments, which I found afterwards to be true: for in the city after I entred the same, there were 5. of the Lords or litle kings (which they cal *Casiqui* in the west Indies) in one chaine almost dead of famine, and wasted with torments.[75]

Since the English, French, and Spanish had come among the Natives, they now called their leaders captains. Some of these Native captains Berreo had transplanted from other countries. Ralegh called together the captains that were enemies to Spain and, through the Indian interpreter he brought with him from home, portrayed Elizabeth I and England as liberators from Spanish tyranny, a ploy the Huguenots had used in Florida:

> I made them vnderstand that I was the seruant of a Queene, who was the great *Casique* of the north, and a virgin, and had more *Casiqui* vnder her then there were trees in their Iland: that she was an enemy to the *Castellani* in respect of their tyrannie and oppression, and that she deliuered all such nations about her, as were by them oppressed, and hauing freed all the coast of the northren world from their seruitude had sent me to free them also, and with al to defend the countrey of *Guiana* from their inuasion and conquest.[76]

Ralegh also said the Natives could have become idolatrous gazing on Elizabeth's picture, a hyperbole worthy of a courtier. If the queen could rid northern Europe of cruelty, she could do so in the New World, particularly in Guiana, the land of Ralegh's desire.[77] Against Spanish cruelty, an image built on the Black Legend, the English and Natives would unite. Ralegh was sure to represent the Natives paying homage to Elizabeth as "the great princesse or greatest commaunder."[78] He took Berreo prisoner and found out more about Guiana.

Ralegh's ambitions revealed his ambivalence to Spain. One of his regrets was that he did not have the opportunity to go to the city of Manoa or to take other

towns on the way. If he or someone else was given this chance, "he shall per-
forme more then euer was done in *Mexico* by *Cortez,* or in *Peru* by *Pacaro.*"⁷⁹
Clearly, the model was Spanish even if Ralegh wanted to exceed it. Ralegh's
words became his treasure, for some criticized him for not having brought home
more booty: "whatsoeuer Prince shall possesse it, that Prince shalbe Lorde of
more Gold, and of a more beautifull Empire, and of more Cities and people, then
eyther the king of Spayne, or the great Turke."⁸⁰ The gold that motivated the
Spanish, moved the English: part of Ralegh's motivation was promotional—he
wanted the English to build the greatest empire. Spain stood in its way; Spain
must be outperformed and devalued, if at first only in language. The English had
beaten Spain in Europe and now should take the fight to the New World.
Ralegh's text never made this claim so baldly, but its accumulated rhetorical
effects added up to such a strategy.

Once more in a French or English text about Spanish colonization, the Spanish were used as authorities to undermine their own imperial expansion. In
exhorting the English to build an empire, Ralegh referred to Spanish discourses
about the magnificent princes of Peru. He mentioned Pedro de Cieza and Francisco Lopez: their words seem to have affected Ralegh's actions, or desire for
action, as much as his writing.

Gold, as goal and theme, was never far away. According to Ralegh, Guiana
had more gold than Peru. His evidence was the word of the Spaniards he had
spoken to, they who called Manoa, the imperial city of Guiana, El Dorado.
These same Spaniards attested to the riches of this city: "it farre exceedeth any
of the world, at least of so much of the world as is knowen to the Spanish
nation."⁸¹ While undermining the Spanish, Ralegh relied on them. He quoted
at length in Spanish from chapter 120 of Lopez's history of the Indies, which
described the magnificent court of Guaynacapa, the emperor of Peru, whose
descendant was, in Ralegh's account, emperor of Guiana. His family had escaped
the Spaniards. Ralegh was implicitly building a coalition against Spain. So that
no one missed the description of gold and more gold in all shapes and sizes,
Ralegh translated the passage. He also furnished a translation from chapter 117
from Lopez that amplified the quantity of gold.

Prophecies of gold from the Spaniards themselves would spur on English
expansion to Guiana. Ralegh reported a prophecy that the Spanish general,
Berreo, related to him, as if to give it more credence. In the greatest Incan temple and other temples, a prophecy foresaw the loss of the empire to the Spaniards
and its restoration and deliverance by *Inglaterra* (England). The myth that Ralegh
was trying to propagate, especially by way of flattering Elizabeth, was that he put
her reputation before the sacking of towns and the hoarding of gold because this
strategy would support the desire of the Natives of Guiana for England to liberate them from Spanish cruelty. Elizabeth had sent Ralegh and his men for such
a purpose, and he was assured that the Natives would fight to the last person to
be rid of the Spaniards.⁸² This was Ralegh's hope. The good will of the Natives
would lead to gold.

Ralegh used repetition in his coda: "For whatsoeuer Prince shall possesse it,

shall bee greatest, and if the king of Spayne enioye it, he will become vnre-
sistable."[83] This is the kind of rhetoric that Gilbert and Hakluyt also employed,
so that the repeated tactics of the "American" party at court would have been
all too familiar to the queen. If Elizabeth were to act and take Guiana and
beyond, she would gain reputation and, as part of her secular cult of the Virgin
Queen, she would be the virginal queen of the Amazons, who would help her
to invade other empires. Here, the sexual roles were reversed. Ralegh had
described Guiana as a land that still had its maidenhead and needed to be
entered, but now the virgins were to invade other, presumably male-dominated,
countries.[84] Ralegh ended by appealing to God and Christ in royal imagery and
implicitly conflated Elizabeth with the Virgin Mary as the "Lady of Ladies." All
the men who would serve her in such an action would, with her grace and leave,
be kings. And all these military plans and invasions would be done in the name
of the "king of al kings."[85] In God Ralegh trusted, so the queen should trust
Ralegh. The climax was that this would be a holy war in which God and gold,
contrary to the Old Testament, were one.

Eighteen years later, over a decade after the death of Elizabeth I, Ralegh
found himself unpopular with James I but never gave up his dream of El Dorado
and the hope for redemption with his new sovereign, who had made peace with
Spain in 1604.[86] Ralegh's *History of the World* . . . (2 vols., London, 1614), like
Pierre d'Avity's work, often represented a providential history but also com-
pared the Romans negatively to the Spanish in the New World. Some of
Ralegh's friends tried directly and indirectly to rehabilitate his reputation with
James I.

One account praised Ralegh above all English travelers, every one of which
"hath had a noble ambition."[87] In *Nevves of S* *Walter Rauleigh. With a True
Description of Gviana* R. M., who completed his work on 17 November 1617
and sent it from Guiana to a mutual friend of Ralegh's and his in London,
claimed that from the relation that follows "you shall vnderstand that whatsoeuer hath beene done formerly by any of those already rehearsed, or by any
other Nation of Christendome, all their knowledges and experiences haue lib-
erally beene brought to his remembrance."[88] Ralegh, who was encyclopedic in
his knowledge of European exploration, became an example or icon to English
colonizers. R. M. reported that Sir Robert Dudley drew on his experience at
sea, and some letters he intercepted from the Spanish

gaue our Generall [Ralegh] a strong assurance, that yet there remained out
of the hands of all Kings and Princes in Christendome, in the South parts
of *America,* the very Magazine of all rich Metalls, and such an Empire as
whosoeuer shall haue the fortune to conquer it, shall so darken all the
actions either of *Cortez* or *Pescaro,* that nothing but pouerty will appeare
in their deeds, neyther *Mexico* nor *Peru* bee worthy to be compared with
it, and what Prince soeuer possesse it, shall bee Lord of more gold, of a
more beautifull Empire, and of more Citties and people then either the
King of Spaine or the great Turke.[89]

Ralegh would be more heroic than the great Spanish conquerors and with his greatness he performed his heroic actions in the name of James I.[90]

Like Cartier's and Roberval's kingdom of the Saguenay, Ralegh's El Dorado was an image of the desire for a golden world of gold. Ralegh could not give up his dream of an El Dorado greater than that the Spanish sought. The lure of gold, sometimes as much as a fetish or a dream from romance or the myth of a golden age as the ground of greed itself, did not respect boundaries. Neither the Pyrenees nor the English Channel could keep the pairing of God and gold from making its ambivalent and contradictory appearance in the expansion of England and France into the New World. In what follows, we shall focus more on the French representations of Spain, particularly in the first two decades of the seventeenth century, the time of Ralegh's demise and death.

III

The English and French representations of the New World, which included translation and editing, involved shifting emphases within the model of the imitation, displacement, and rejection of Spain. Classical and Christian paradigms, as well as concerns over trade, finance, and profit, provided a framework for French and English discussions of the New World. Using books and translations in concert with legal claims and trade, England, France, and the Netherlands began to challenge Spain in North America. In France, the Crown's interest in New France lapsed after the completion of the last voyage of Jacques Cartier in 1544, although the fishery and the fur trade continued to grow. By 1578, the French ports that profited from the fish and fur trade in New France asked for the protection of Henri III, who appointed Mesgouez de La Roche, a Breton noble, governor of the lands in the New World.[91] Although this commission achieved little, it did show a renewed royal interest in New France. In 1603, Pierre du Gua, sieur de Monts, was granted a monopoly in Acadia for ten years and his main goal was to find rich mineral deposits. In 1607 the French merchants who had opposed these monopolies in the New World, succeeded in challenging the exclusive rights of de Monts and others.[92]

It would be some time before the French would begin to eclipse the Spanish or the Portuguese in colonization, although Philip III, king of Spain and Portugal, faced difficulties in Europe. The Netherlands sought independence from Spain and were dominating European maritime trade while establishing overseas commercial posts. The Acadian settlement was abandoned the same year Jamestown was established. After the Armada, England could concentrate more on colonization. One of the key figures in the colonization of New France was Samuel de Champlain, who was an associate of de Monts. and who had experience in the Spanish West Indies before he founded Québec in 1608.

Champlain's, Lescarbot's and Pierre d'Avity's work embodied contradiction and ambivalence toward the Spanish in the New World but also complicated ideas of the French representation of the example of Spain. Like the English, the French demonstrated a marked ambivalence toward the Spanish empire. At the moment that France was on the verge of establishing permanent settlements in

North America, its colonizers and writers were learning from Spain as well as posing a serious threat to it. Three key figures should illustrate this ambivalence, which has analogous elements to the ambivalent and contradictory representations that Ralegh displayed in his texts. In this period, however, the French still seemed closer to the Spanish despite James I's policy of peace with Spain.

Champlain, who, according to Marcel Trudel, was quiet about his private life, might have converted from Protestantism to Catholicism, and crossed the Atlantic 21 times.[93] Apparently, Champlain served Spain before he set out to help France colonize Acadia and New France. Unlike Ralegh, who kept Spain before his reader, Champlain was less given to represent the example of the Spanish colonization of the New World. The chief work in which Champlain expressed his Spanish experience is *Brief Discovrs . . .* (1599–1601). Champlain went on a voyage for Spain, in whose service his uncle from Provence was engaged as pilot-general of sea forces.[94] Family concerns tempered national interests. While Champlain could praise the Spanish, he could also criticize them.[95] In one instance, Champlain reported that after one English attack on Margarita Island off the coast of Venezuela, 15 days later, some Indians were found taking refuge in the fortress, which they were also repairing. The Spanish general asked the Indians to file a report on the attack for the king of Spain and ordered them to go find those who had fled into the mountains so they could return home, "receiving such contentment to see the said general and to be delivered from the English, that they forgot their past losses."[96] Here the Natives were the eyewitnesses in the service of Spain against the English intruders, which was hardly the picture Ralegh represented of the nearby Guiana for Elizabeth I several years before.

Elsewhere Champlain described war and conflict between Spaniard and Native. The Spaniards were exploring the strait of Magellan and "had a war with these savages of the country, in which it is said that gold and silver mines are to be discovered."[97] After speaking about trees, plants, and animals, Champlain turned to a brief account of the Indians ["Indiens" here rather than the "sauuages" he often uses]: he described the moon-worship, which characterized most of the Natives "who are not under the domination of the Spanish." [98] In a ceremony the Indians asked the moon to allow them to conquer and eat the enemy: Champlain called the non-Christian Natives "these poor peoples, deprived of reason, whom I have portrayed here."[99]

If it were not for the attention of the king of Spain, the "Indians" under his domination "would be as barbarous in their belief as the others."[100] While showing pity and denouncing the cruelty of the Inquisition, Champlain saw the king of Spain as civilizing the Natives. Their resistance to Spanish cruelty at the beginning of the conquest led the king to grant them liberty on every *estancia,* or landed estate. Of the king of Spain, Champlain observed:

> At the beginning of his conquests, he had established the Inquisition amongst them, and made them slaves or put them to death in such great numbers, that the narrative of them alone arouses pity for them. This mal-treatment was the reason that these poor Indians, for the apprehension of

it, fled to the mountains like desperate people, and as many Spaniards as they caught, they ate; and for this reason the said Spaniards were compelled to remove the Inquisition, and give them their liberty of their person, giving them a rule of life milder and more tolerable, to bring them to the knowledge of God and belief in the holy Church: for if they had still wished to chastise them according to the rigour of the said Inquisition, they would have made them all die by fire.[101]

Champlain's enthusiasm for Mexico but his horror over the excesses of the Inquisition there may well be corroborated, as Joe Armstrong asserts, in the 37 illustrations in *Brief Narrative,* included in the copy at the John Carter Brown Library, inclusive of the one of the inquisitors burning victims in Mexico.[102] Champlain's attitude embodied some contradictions: although the Spanish were civilized, they were cruel, and although they were cruel, they could have been more so; even though the Natives forced them to give up the Inquisition, the Spanish could have exterminated all the Indians because they were incapable of maintaining Christian belief except under a vigilant domination. Champlain described the *estancia,* which he said were designed to keep the Natives in faith, while admitting that they did so partly from fear of being beaten.[103] The Indians in Champlain's description were melancholy, intelligent, docile in the face of abuse, and nomadic.[104]

While in many ways approving of the Spaniard's treatment of the Natives, Champlain could also give intelligence, for instance about the strategic river, Porto Bello, the heart of the gold and silver trade, and how Drake died after failing to take it.[105] Champlain was much more oblique than Ralegh was: he spoke of sailors, "even the English," smoking like the Natives, and he praised Florida, once the land the Huguenots desired with such disastrous results, as a beautiful and fertile land, which the King of Spain undervalued because it lacked gold and silver and where the Natives (Champlain oscillated between "sauuaiges" and "Indiens") made war on the Spaniards.[106]

On the way home, the Spanish expedition on which Champlain served on captured two English ships fitted out for war and took them to Seville. France, England, and Spain were inextricably connected in the New World. Champlain became involved with the second attempt at French colonization in North America by two friends of Henri IV. Aymar de Chastes, governor of Dieppe, who had been a great supporter of the king, made the first attempt. After de Chastes's death, the king and his admiral, Charles de Montmorency, issued commissions to Pierre de Gua [or Guast], sieur de Monts, and governor of Pons, on December 18, 1603. The commission emphasized God and trade as well as the experience of de Monts and his company in the region. Champlain was de Monts's pilot and geographer.[107]

More than Champlain, however, Marc Lescarbot became the chronicler of Acadia and was more apt to comment on Spain. Lescarbot, lawyer, poet, humanist, lived in the Port-Royal colony from July 1606 to the next summer when the expiration of de Monts's licence meant the return of the entire colony to France. He was a Catholic but maintained friendships with Protestants.[108]

Although there was a strong tendency for anti-Spanish sentiment to be Protestant, there were Catholic examples of the Black Legend. One of the functions of my discussion of Lescarbot is to provide an illustration of this modification of the stereotype of what constitutes the Black Legend. Anthony Pagden has made a similar point: "Most of what was said about Spain during the Eighty-Years War was inevitably harnessed to the war effort. Spanish atrocities in general, and the sack of Antwerp in 1576 in particular, led to the creation, at Flemish and English hands, of the so-called Black Legend. The Spanish image in Protestant Europe (and it must be said, in many areas of Catholic Europe as well) as proud, cruel, and overbearing was in large part based on Dutch, and later English, propaganda."[109] As W. L. Grant noted early in the century, "How lightly his Catholicism sat upon Lescarbot may be judged from the fact that his frequent quotations from the Bible are from the Geneva version of Olivetan, revised by Calvin."[110]

Lescarbot's text also presents difficulties and challenges to the interpreter. Late in the study, when I was advised and decided to substitute English translations for the original languages, I determined, whenever possible, to consult accessible translations such as Grant's translation of Lescarbot, but to work with original texts and translate them because of my emphasis on close reading. The various editions of Lescarbot, for instance, vary and cannot be reflected in a standard collated edition like Grant's, which presents the edition of 1618. In Lescarbot's case the differences among his prefaces are quite striking. Grant observes of Book I, chapter 1, differences that make it difficult to use Grant's translation for my present comparative purposes: "This chapter differs almost wholly from the introduction to the editions of 1609 and 1611. In particular, a number of attacks on Spain are softened or omitted, probably as being out of place in a book dedicated to the youthful husband of Anne of Austria."[111] In France, as in England, the political winds blew across the leaves at the printers' shops. Lescarbot's history of New France was popular in England as well as in France because it appeared in two English translations by Pierre Erondelle in 1609 and, subsequently, by Samuel Purchas.[112]

The original French versions of Lescarbot's text best illustrate the example of Spain in France. Lescarbot concentrated on French discoveries in the New World. In the prefatory matter of the first edition of 1609, he addressed Henri IV about New France, provided the queen with the memory of Verrazano and the view that God had blessed the "conquests" of the kings of France to be zealots of his name ("zelateurs de son nom") for "the conversion of these poor peoples, who easily receive the Evangelical doctrine," and represented a vision to the dauphin of "the conquest of the Occident, and the establishment of New France (where an effort by arms has not yet been made)," which "is easy to execute" and of a large number of the French sailing the Atlantic "for the exaltation of the name of God, of the King, of your grandeur, and of all France."[113] Lescarbot then presented a paean to France, expatiating on the greatness of his country, so that the Orient and south equate "Christian" with "French."[114] France was the mother in this address. Lescarbot emphasized the Roman connection with France, first with Julius Caesar civilizing Gaul and second with the

French saving the popes from persecution.[115] Lescarbot was defensive about the relation of Spain to France: "The Spaniard shows himself more zealous than us, and has carried off the palm of navigation that was ours. But why envy him that which he has so well acquired? He has been cruel. This is what has soiled his glory, what otherwise would be worthy of immortality."[116] Besides cruelty, another element of the Black Legend appeared here: greed. France as a mother would produce "the Children of the West," who would settle New France: "Even if they do not find there the treasures of Atabalippa [Atahualpa] and others, which have lured them to the West Indies, they will, however, not be poor, for this province will be worthy to be called your daughter."[117]

Like Hakluyt, Lescarbot envisaged discontents and unemployed tradesmen going to the colonies rather than being lost to foreign lands, but unlike his English predecessor he emphasized the arts and, perhaps following the model of Spain, spoke about "men of courage" settling in the New World.[118] H. P. Biggar called Lescarbot, "the French Hakluyt," although Lescarbot was probably more elegant and put more of himself in the text as he was an eyewitness in New France and Hakluyt never voyaged to America.[119] Frank Lestringant asserts that Lescarbot imitated La Popelinière and puts him in the legal and historical contexts of Chauveton, Hakluyt, and Jean Bodin. Like Lestringant, I think that Lescarbot's history goes farther than Hakluyt's in establishing a new form, what Lestringant calls "the digressive narrative of the failures of France in the New World."[120] Lestringant also points out Lescarbot's debt, in the third book, to Acosta and Lafitau, and whereas Lescarbot mostly borrowed from Léry (ten chapters), he did defend Thevet's imaginative Brazil as a means of inciting others to support and transform the colony (which drew so much sarcasm in Belleforest).[121] Lescarbot, like a number of the French chroniclers of the New World I am discussing, is relatively unknown outside a small group of specialists. He deserves to be much better known. In a recent history of Canada, for instance, he is barely mentioned, except as the first playwright in the country.[122]

What distinguishes Lescarbot from Hakluyt is that he used the language of Christian republicanism and of a French preoccupation, which probably reached its greatest intensity under Louis XIV: "la gloire."[123] This glory involved honor, courage, civilization, and evangelization in a way that only France could produce. Paradoxically, Spain caused France to be defensive, but, in Lescarbot's rendition, the French should reclaim their past glory and go into the New World as the Spanish had but in a manner that was inimitable. Lescarbot's French settler was not a pagan looking down on New France as Tacitus had on Germany, but someone concerned with the honor of God.[124] Like so many of the early French and English promoters of colonies, Lescarbot had to address the problem of the precarious private funding of these outposts of empire and answered objections in a rhetorical and logical tradition that went back to Aquinas and beyond.

Lescarbot drew on the prophets and answered the objections: New France had no pleasure and beautiful castles ("beaux chateaux").[125] In this vision of French expansion, he met the objections of the timid afraid of pirates and, more importantly, of the "scrupulous men who put into doubt if one could justly occupy the lands in New France and to strip the inhabitants of them."[126] These objections began early in Spain about the right to possess the lands of the Natives in the New World. Debates over the rights of property and the legitimacy of empire, as Anthony Pagden has argued, "began in 1512, almost as soon as a Spanish monarch first attempted to take formal possession of American soil, and continued, in one mode or another, until the end of the eighteenth century and the effective end of the Empire itself. The extent and the intensity of the struggles over the rights of Spaniards in America are, perhaps, unequalled in the history of European colonization."[127] Lescarbot answered this objection over legitimacy and right with the parable of the talent in the Scriptures, in which the man who did not turn it to good account had it taken away, so that the Natives should lose their "first title of possession," if they did not use it wisely and obey God, to Christians who had been obedient.[128] This was a kind of typological Christian interpretation in which Lescarbot prophesied the union between France of the East and France of the West.[129]

In establishing this new French empire he heeded the example of Spain but had also to distinguish the expansion of France in the New World from that precedent: "I would not, however, exterminate these peoples here, just as the Spaniard has done to those in the Indies, taking as the pretext the commandments once given to Joshua, Gideon, Saul, and others, fighting for the people of God."[130] Instead, he argued for using Christ's example of peace against the Natives, who were defenseless and did not resist the conquerors. Lescarbot expressed this idea in the following way: "For we are in the law of grace, the law of meekness, of pity, and of mercy, in which our Saviour has said: 'Learn of me that I am mild, and humble of heart.' Item, 'Come to me all of you who labour and are laden, and I will comfort you.' And then, 'these poor Indian peoples were without defence in the presence of those who ruined them, and did not resist like the peoples whom the holy Scripture mentions.'"[131] The 1612 and 1618 editions added the following sentence: "And moreover, if it were meant that the conquered people be ruined, it would be in vain that the same Saviour said to his Apostles: 'Go into all the world and preach the Gospel to every creature'."[132]

Lescarbot's history would help to translate a French imperial imagery and vocabulary. In his dedication to King Louis XIII in the edition of 1612, Lescarbot said that two principal things motivated kings to make conquests: zeal of the glory of God and their own glory and grandeur. Whereas the edition of 1612 spoke of "gloire et grandeur," that of 1618 left out the "grandeur."[133] He reminded the king that his predecessors were invited to extend their domination overseas but had been content with the discovery, rather than the settlement, of the country. In the edition of 1612, Lescarbot stated that he did not know how the enemy of France triumphed, but in the 1618 edition he asserted that settling for French discovery, and not settlement, occurred because of the plots, artifice and practices of the enemies of the French crown.[134]

In a refrain now long familiar in France and England, Lescarbot set out the example of Spain as a goad to colonization: "Many men still alive can give witness to the violence, injuries, and outrages that the Portuguese and Spanish have done to our good and faithful subjects in Brazil in 1558, and in Florida ten years after. And yet these lands were a just conquest of our Kings Henri II and Charles IX, not being, before the coming of the French here, occupied by any Christian Prince."[135] In this case the 1612 and 1618 editions varied in their descriptions of Spain. This last version emphasized the contempt in which the French name was held, a rhetorical strategy—shaming the reader to whip up patriotism—that Hakluyt had used to promote English colonization in North America:

> Meanwhile the Spaniard, once feeble, by our nonchalance has rendered himself puissant in the Orient and in the Occident, without our having had this honourable ambition, not to precede him but to second him; not to second him, but to avenge the injuries done by him to our French, who under the patronage of our Kings, have wanted to have part of the heritage of these new and immense lands that God has presented men on this side [of the Atlantic] since about six score years.[136]

Like Hakluyt, Lescarbot was concerned with origins, with the shame of the precedence of Spain in the New World and the late arrival of his own country.

Pierre d'Avity, sieur de Montmartin, like Hakluyt and Lescarbot, collected information about the New World, but, unlike his countryman, he was more interested in Catholicism as a key factor in colonial policy and relations with Spain. The writers in France could frequently be more generous toward Spain than the English were. Often, but not always, this generosity stemmed from a shared Catholicism. While assuming an ideology of a united Catholicism, d'Avity concentrated most on geographical information and described America in his *Les Estats, empires et principavtez dv monde . . .* (1613). He provided an inventory of the world, and in his description of Spain he listed its vast possessions in the New World, from California and Florida in the North to Peru and beyond in the south, something he did not do in his chapters on France and England.[137] The sheer bulk in d'Avity devoted to the description of the Spanish empire attested to its preeminence.

Two years later an English edition of d'Avity appeared in London, but Edward Grimstone, its translator, sometimes made changes that indicated different and supplementary attitudes to Spain, a carrying-over or "translation" that was part of the larger project of ideological editing in France and England during this period. Grimstone's two-page "The Translator to the Reader" recommended d'Avity's book as advice for travelers. While claiming that he did not need to write a preface because d'Avity had done so, Grimstone said that, most importantly, the English version was not "a meere translation" but differed from the author in places where Grimstone had more experience, where there were omissions, and in religious matters.[138]

In d'Avity's scheme the New World received almost as much space as France, which itself received a third as much again as England, Scotland, and Ireland together were allotted.[139] The opening sentence of the section, "Le Nouueau

Monde," showed that the king of Spain had all that he wanted in the New World because no one could be found there to contradict him.[140] D'Avity noted that the depopulation of the Natives in Peru occurred because of disease and civil war among the Spaniards, who moved the "Indians" from place to place far from their country and worked them excessively.[141] Grimstone's translation was more explicit about Spanish cruelty. One of the causes of the million and a half Native dead, a figure that author and translator both used, Grimstone gave as "the cruelties and disorders of the Spaniards in the beginning, not onely murthering them most cruelly but also toiling the people infinitely, transporting them from one place vnto another, far from their country aire, which was the death of many."[142] D'Avity did not speak of Spanish cruelty explicitly when he spoke of the same cause of Native depopulation. He also presented colonization positively: after Columbus "many people, full of boldness, and of singular valour, as much from Italy, Spain, England as from Portugal and France, were employed in this pursuit."[143]

These multicultural or pan-European aspects of the early exploration and settlement of the New World, which were discussed in chapter 2, seemed obvious to an early modern writer like d'Avity but became occluded in the chauvinism of later European nationalisms in France and Britain that involved the construction of exclusive identities as part of the building of the ideology of empires. In official ideologies these later empires of the nineteenth and early twentieth centuries were presented as the culmination of the European imperial enterprise since antiquity. Only with recent recognition of multiculturalism and post-colonialism has the minority skepticism of alternative critique and opposition from within become more widespread. In d'Avity it is a matter of recognizing the pan-European nature of expansion and not necessarily using that realization as an unraveling of singular imperial identity at the center. That would be to read d'Avity in terms of a history his culture had not yet experienced, but it is a way of setting out what intervenes between d'Avity and present-day readers and so has a bearing on the interpretation of d'Avity's text. In this multinational context he mentioned the discoveries of Jacques Cartier, Gaspar Corte Real, and Sebastian Cabot.

Despite crediting Columbus generally, d'Avity claimed that the most northern reaches of America were discovered long before Columbus by fishermen from Friesland, a claim later confirmed by a Venetian in the service of the king of Friesland in 1390.[144] D'Avity caught himself in representing the contributions of other Europeans and returned to the places where the Spanish possessed the land, a strategy that praised Spain but not as a universal monarchy or the inheritor of the New World, especially as he suggested, in a section including the ever-sensitive Florida, boundaries by listing the neighboring French and English colonies.[145] Amid his description of the customs, religion, government, riches, natural resources, natural history, and other aspects of the various colonies, d'Avity stated that Mexico, which has a printer, mint, and university, was, according to Acosta, the most agreeable and fertile province in the New World.[146] French and English texts of this period continued to seek the authority of Spanish authors. The colonies of France and England in North America, which d'Avity had just mentioned, were still precarious and would not have such cultural institutions for a few decades. The silver mine found in 1545 at Potosí in Peru, whose wealth d'Avity chronicled, had no rivals in French or English America.[147] Part of his description consisted of Native resistance to the Spanish.[148] The cruel and barbarous cannibals, described in Columbus, also made an appearance in d'Avity.[149] D'Avity also talked about other barbarous nations under Spanish rule in contrast to Christianity and in terms of missionary work.[150]

His section that provided a general discourse on the New World began with the declaration: "The states that the king of Spain possesses in the New World are so large and so strong that they need not fear enemies who would attack them."[151] D'Avity then said that the Spanish occupied the best places in the provinces and could therefore dominate those who would fight against them. He described how the English, especially Drake in 1586, had attacked the Spanish colonies but with the result of giving the Spanish ideas about ensuring the safety of their possessions, so that he concluded that just as nature seemed to have made Italy to dominate the Mediterranean, so too did Spain appear to be made to command the Ocean Sea.[152] Moreover, the Spanish could suffer through all kinds of climates and countries.[153] D'Avity also lauded them for their work of conversion, bringing the eternal word of Christ to the New World.[154] In this version Cortés became as much an agent of God as of the emperor.[155]

In such a context, it was not surprising to find the bull of Alexander VI presented in a favorable light. This division of the world was an originary or primal act that French and English interpretations of the New World revisited from the 1490s to the period following the Treaty of Utrecht. Alexander divided the undiscovered lands between Spain and Portugal, prohibiting other nations from entering into this sphere, and obliged the Iberian nations to "a work so beautiful and so generous of the best kind that could be."[156] D'Avity emphasized the courage the Spanish demonstrated in spreading Christianity and claimed that there was no place where it had made such progress as in the New World.[157] He accepted the negative accounts of the Natives, an aspect of many early Spanish accounts from Columbus onward—the Indians practised sodomy, idolatry, and cannibalism—but he balanced this with the cruelty of certain Spanish soldiers away from their prince and with Charles V's attempt during the 1540s to remedy the abuses and to protect the indigenous population.[158] Although Grimstone, d'Avity's English translator, referred to the good and conscientious nature of Charles V and those men of conscience who wrote him and who came to court to allow the emperor and the Council of the Indies to understand the mistreatment of the Natives, he dwelt on Spanish cruelty much more than d'Avity did. Grimstone used the word "cruelty" in his amplification of this passage in d'Avity: "the countrie was in a manner vnpeopled by the barbarous and butcherly crueltie of the Spaniards."[159] While I have left many of the comparisons between d'Avity and Grimstone to the notes and later in this discussion, where there are close textual comparisons, I thought that one example here would help to suggest how this English translation was more critical of Catholicism, the papacy, and Spain than the French original.

The Natives were a diverse group that had potential for conversion and could not simply be dismissed as "barbarians," a term that d'Avity thought applied to the Romans and Greeks, owing to their different ways of living and their views of reason, but not to other nations and for which he provided a taxonomy based on degrees of brutality in reason and religion, way of life (especially food), nudity, habitation, and government.[160] *Translatio imperii* was also an idea that could be qualified or opposed, so that by itself it was not a sufficient factor in motivating European expansion.

Throughout this study, we have also observed that while religious difference was not a sufficient condition to predict whether a writer was for or against Spain, it was often a contributing factor. Whereas Lescarbot represented those moderate or skeptical Catholics and Protestants who were appalled at the civil war and some of whom preferred "nationalism" to religious division, d'Avity saw America in religious terms:

> Even if at the beginning of the enterprise of the New World one could doubt and dispute whether it were permissible or not to assume the government and superiority there, today it can be no subject of dispute, owing to the danger of the Mohametans and English, because it is certain that the Mohametans would make themselves masters of the Philippines and the English, of America, if the Spanish did not resist them.[161]

Although the rhetoric was not explicitly anti-Protestant, in this warning the Spanish seemed to be the champions of Catholicism against the English Protestant and the Muslim threats. Religion modified national characteristics in the rhetoric of the representation of Spain: one Frenchman's Spain as a providential leader was not the Spain that destroyed the Huguenots' colonies.

D'Avity's typology of conversion of the Natives was very different from Le Challeux's. Admitting difficulties in the conversion of the Indians in the New World, d'Avity outlined some remedies the Spanish themselves undertook to repair the defects of the first conversion of the Natives, citing, above all, the positive example of Vasco de Quiroga, first bishop of Mechouacán, who, in addition to abolishing polygamy, idolatry, and superstition, showed charity toward the poor.[162] Catholics in Europe, including those in France, could learn from the strengths and weaknesses of the bold enterprise that Spain undertook in the conversion of the inhabitants of America. After this discussion of religion and conversion, d'Avity saw no contradiction in setting out the revenues of the king of Spain in his American colonies.[163] For d'Avity, truth in history was Christian providence, which profited the soul while filling the treasury.

The question of religion continued to divide France at home and in its colonies, sometimes in strange ways. Gabriel Sagard, a contemporary historian of New France, recorded that for Port Royal, where some of the settlers were Catholic and some Protestant, sieur de Monts, the leader of the colony, had provided a Huguenot minister and a Catholic priest, both of whom squabbled and came to blows until scurvy claimed them and the men buried them in one grave to see whether they could in death rest in peace as they could not when alive.[164]

Such an event could not have occurred in the exclusively Catholic colonies of Spanish America. De Monts and Champlain were the founders of New France, which was in 1627 to become for Catholics only or for those who wished to convert to Catholicism. Philip P. Boucher complicates this point and assumptions concerning the emigration of Huguenots, saying that their failures in the sixteenth century and the fight at home helped to dissuade them from emigrating. After the Peace of Alais in 1629, which took away the political privileges of the Huguenots, Richelieu's adversarial policy toward them changed and he protected them, whereas the Cardinal was no longer on good terms with the "ultra-Catholics" because they were allies with Spain, a country Richelieu was wary of and a part of the Habsburg lands that surrounded France.[165]

The religious missionary work in the New World interested the French clergy, but was something the French Protestants could no longer approach officially. In this respect, Cardinal Richelieu made French America more like Spanish America. As the French did not seem to emigrate in large numbers, Cardinal Richelieu also encouraged the Flemish and Dutch to emigrate as long as they were Catholics or converted to Catholicism. In building the power and glory of a centralized monarchy, he did not like the privileges, especially control of fortresses like La Rochelle, that the Edict of Nantes had granted to Protestants in 1598.

In May 1628, before La Rochelle, which had been subdued after a long siege, a charter was signed creating *La Compaignie des 100 Associés,* a provision of which specified that the company people New France with Catholics only. Another article of the new charter declared that converted Natives would be considered French subjects and could settle in France with full rights. This new company was to replace *La Compaignie de Caen,* whose directors were Huguenots and who were suspected of planning to make Canada Protestant in order to secede from France and to ally itself with the Netherlands and England. Like the Dutch, the French first commissioned companies to trade its colonies in 1602, but the French companies, 75 of which were chartered from 1599 to 1789, were undercapitalized. The Levantine trade was still too profitable to attract much financing for New France.[166] The Jesuits and Capucins had concentrated on bringing back French Protestants to Catholicism, but they began to look overseas.[167] As W. J Eccles says, "In America they [these orders] had the example of the Spanish and Portuguese to challenge them."[168]

IV

In North America during the seventeenth century, the English became the biggest challengers to the French, but England, and especially in its southern colonies, like Virginia, could not ignore the presence of Spain. Before proceeding to some key English texts about the New World, I will revisit briefly Edward Grimstone's translation of Pierre d'Avity. This return to Grimstone should be one more instance in a series of examples throughout the study that suggests the differences between the French and English in regard to Spain in America. While they shared much, their responses had many distinct aspects. In both countries, as we have seen and will observe, the example of Spain, while having holding power, shifted with the times.

As a mediator between French and English representations of the example of Spain, Grimstone provides a good transition between d'Avity and contemporaries like William Strachey and Robert Johnson. While I have been calling attention to similarities between the French and English uses of the example of Spain, I want also to show some of the nuances and distinctions between them. Grimstone differed most from d'Avity in matters of religion. To a discussion of cannibalism and communion in d'Avity, Grimstone added the marginal gloss: "This hath some resemblance to the opinion of the Papists touching the Eucharist."[169] Grimstone likened the distribution of the pieces of the bodies of captives sacrificed to Idols to the Catholic view of communion. He implied a kind of barbarity and idolatry in the notion of transubstantiation. Grimstone left in d'Avity's providential view of Cortés, who "preuailed in his enterprise, and subdued the realme of Mexico, both to Iesus Christ and to the Emperor, whose captaine he was."[170] In the English translation Grimstone raised the familiar complaint: "But *Alexander* had no more authoritie to dispose of the New world, nor to giue vnto them the kingdomes which had neither beene discouered nor conquered, than his successors haue had sence to arrogate vnto themselues power to depose lawfull kings and princes from their crowne and estates."[171] Here the English version of d'Avity was more critical of the papacy and Spain than was the original. Even though, as we have seen, Grimstone referred to the conscientious nature of Charles V and those people of conscience who called attention to the mistreatment of the Natives, he concentrated on Spanish cruelty considerably more than d'Avity did. Moreover, Grimstone introduced the term "cruelty" when amplifying d'Avity.[172] The English were ambivalent about how Spain treated the Natives and the relation between the "Moors" and the Spanish and Europeans. This Spanish experience seemed to affect their way of regarding the American Natives. Grimstone left out d'Avity's passage asserting that the Mohametans would take the Philipines and the English, America if the Spanish did not resist them. Here is one final and telling instance of the divergence between French and English interpretations of the instance of Spain.[173]

A few years before Grimstone's translation, William Strachey could write dedicatory verse that declared:

Till of most noble, you become diuine
And imitate your maker in his will,
To haue his [God's] truth in blackest nations shine.
VVhat had you beene, had not your Ancestors
Begunne to you, that make their nobles good?
And where white Christians turn in maners Mores
You wash Mores white with sacred Christan bloud.[174]

Racial and religious anxiety may here define Englishness as much as Spanishness in the works of writers in Spain. On page 27, item 44 in his section, "The Summarie of the Marshall Lawes," he stated: "Whosoeuer shall giue offence to the Indians in that nature, which truly examined, shall found to haue beene cause of breach of their league, and friendship, which with so great trauile, desire, and cir-

cumspection, we haue or shall at any time obtaine from them without commission so to doe, from him that hath authoritie for the same, shall be punished with
death." There were similar items in this section that listed punishments of crimes
by the English against the indigenous population. Apparently the crimes attributed to the Natives, like sodomy, were not confined to the Natives alone. Strachey's whole code testified to an attempt to control behavior and punish
crime.[175] One interesting article was item 29: "No man or woman, (vpon paine
of death) shall runne away from the Colonie, to Powhathan, or any other sauage
Weroance else whatsoeuer."[176] Whether this article represented a fear of escaping an exclusive English justice or a resistance to the phenomenon of the
"White Indian" is hard to say.[177] Strachey shows anxiety over the boundaries
between being English and being Native: it was not only the Spaniards who
worried about the blurring of the border between civility and barbarism. Even
in promotional texts, writers in England and France as well as Spain display, wit-
tingly or not, ambivalence toward the American Indian.

Here, I have, for the moment, decided to concentrate more on Robert Johnson than on his better-known contemporary, William Strachey, whose *The Historie of Travell into Virginia Britannia* (1612) expressed a similar view on the papal
donation to Spain and to which we shall return.[178] This objection to the origins
of the Spanish claim to the New World was, as my study has shown and will
continue to demonstrate, a commonplace in French and especially English narratives of the New World. The rest of my discussion here will examine principally the promotional work of Robert Johnson, John Smith, Samuel Purchas,
and Thomas Scott, the first the author of promotional tracts; the second a governor, promoter and historian of Virginia; the third a collector and editor, literal
heir to Hakluyt, and someone who never traveled to America; and the fourth a
Protestant propagandist of the 1620s who was bent on creating opposition to the
royal marriage between Spain and England. Their work demonstrated the differences and divisions within English views of Spain, but none could think
about the establishment of a permanent settlement in Virginia without considering Spanish America.

In *Nova Britannia* (1609), which was a promotional tract about Virginia,
Robert Johnson had much to say about the Spanish. This work was dedicated
to Thomas Smith, a member of the king's council for Virginia, treasurer of the
colony, governor of the Moscovy and East India companies, all of which Johnson noted in his address to Smith.[179] Johnson proclaimed the fame of the English in their exploration of Virginia and reiterated the kind of assertion that
possession was the key to claiming this region of America, something, as we have
observed, that François I and Elizabeth I maintained in facing Spain in the New
World. In fact, Johnson invoked the memory of Elizabeth in building his case
for an English Virginia or a New Britain there:

> There are diuers monuments already publisht in Print to the world, man-
> ifesting and shewing, that the coastes and parts of *Virginia* haue beene long
> since discouered, peopled & possessed by many English, both men, women
> and children, the naturall subiects of our late Queene *Elizabeth,* of famous

memorie, conducted and left there at sundry times, And that the same footing and possession, is there yet kept and possessed, by the same English, or by their seede and of=fspring, without any interruption or inuasion, either of the Sauages (the natiues of the countrie) or any other Prince or people (for ought we heare or know) to this day, which argueth sufficiently to vs (and it is true) that ouer those English and Indian people, no Christian King or Prince (other then *Iames* our Soueraigne Lord and King) ought to haue rule or Dominion, nor can, by possession, conquest or inheritance, truely claime or make iust Title, to those Territories, or to any part thereof: Except it be (as we heare of late) that a challenge is laide to all, by vertue of a donation from *Alexander* the first Pope of *Rome,* wherein (they say) is giuen al the West *Indies,* including *Florida & Virginia,* withal America, and whatsoeuer Islands adiacent.[180]

Johnson appealed to books and maps as a record of the English claim to Virginia: the appeal to earlier assertions of a state was made to constitute a proper claim. He effaced "any interruption or inuasion" as the English themselves might be said to have invaded the lands of the Natives. Nonetheless—as seen in previous English works, including Hakluyt's "Discourse"—the specter of Alexander's papal donation in the 1490s still had the power to haunt those who in England who would promote colonization in the northern reaches of America. Within a page, Johnson had moved from an appeal to follow him in investing his money and "endeavours" in the colony to a recollection of all the works in print that showed that Virginia had been "long since discouered, peopled & possessed by many English."[181] Men, women, and children who settled Virginia in the time of Elizabeth I had enjoyed the land without interruption or invasion from Natives or other Europeans, so that, in keeping up this fiction, Johnson concluded that James I alone possessed this land.

The worry about possession soon came into focus, for once again, an English author addressed the claims of Spain and Portugal: "Except it be (as wee heare of late) that a challenge is laide to all, by vertue of a donation from *Alexander* the sixt Pope of *Rome,* wherein (they say) is giuen al the West *Indies,* including *Florida & Virginia,* with al *America,* and whatsoeuer Ilands adiacent."[182] Johnson protested too much. He asked what this donation was to the English, but if it were nothing, he would not spend time on it at such a key place in his text. In his defense of the English possession against Spanish claims, Johnson ridiculed the donation of Constantine of the western Roman empire to Rome, wondering, in his appeal to "truth," how a temporal prince could give that empire to a pope and how a pope could donate the West Indies to a temporal prince.[183] Here was a reversed typology through these donations, a satire on this legal typology or precedent.

The purpose of Johnson's ridicule appeared to be twofold—to express anxiety over the power of Spain in the New World and to satirize Spain as a defensive mechanism in the face of such force. He likened the donation of Alexander to the legalistic and tyrannical manœuvres of the flatterers of Cambyses, king of Persia, who justified the king's incestuous marriage with his own daughter by finding a law that said that the kings of Persia could do what they wished. In likening the pope to King Cambyses, who committed incest with his daughter, doing whatever he wanted, Johnson was sarcastic about those who assume that there is also a law that "the Pope may doe what he list, let them that list obey him, for beleeue not in him."[184] Johnson called the papal donations "legendarie fables."[185]

Johnson was not alone in this countering of papal authority to divide the New World between Spain and Portugal with myths of "British" precedence. When Virginia was being established, its promoters relied on the myth of Madoc, the Welshman, who discovered America in 1170, England's claim to North America through John Cabot's voyage (given at various dates), and opposition to Alexander VI's donation. After dispensing with Madoc and Cabot (who was said to have sailed in 1495), one tract dismissed the donation pithily: "As for the donation of *Alexander* the sixt; it is but a reciprocal clawing, when Emperors create their seruants Bishops vniversall, and shauelings create their Lords, Emperors generall."[186] This immoderate rhetoric, which Johnson and this anonymous pamphleteer shared, suggests an aggressive defensiveness before a powerful enemy, but the contradiction lay in the fact that Spain and England were at peace at the time. That peace was obviously ambivalent and difficult for those who would have England expand into the Americas. Against this incestuous law underpinning the claims of Spain to the New World, Johnson represented the "honest enterprize and lawfull purpose" of the English in Virginia.[187] He also set out the support of James I for "our old Colony."[188] This ancient colony was a fiction: although the English had been trying to establish a colony on the southeastern coast of North America for over 25 years, they were just beginning to create something permanent and the colony was still precarious. This fragility was one of the reasons for Johnson's promotional tract.

In the dedication and in the opening pages of *Nova Britannia* the missionary work of God was represented as the main motivation for Virginia. The other reason was expansion and to find supplies to preserve and defend the small number of friends and countrymen already living in the colony, "least for want of more supplies wee become a scorne to the world, subiecting our former aduentures to apparant spoyle and hazard, and our people (as a prey) to be sackt and puld out of possession, as were the French (to their infamie) cut of *Noua Francia,* not many yeares agoe."[189] Another revisited theme was the incident in the 1560s when Spain purged Florida of the French, something we examined in the last chapter. Here, Johnson was concerned with the reputation of England and used French colonization as a negative example. The implied text was that England could now plant a Protestant colony in the region where the Huguenots failed. Possession was not so easily forgotten. Johnson praised Elizabeth I and restated her policy, which seemed to have been similar to Henry VII's unstated strategy in the New World and to François I's position for French colonization: "to plant and settle English Colonies, in places not already possessed and inhabited by Subiects of other Christian princes."[190]

The presence of Spain was not so easy to erase. The "savage people, which haue no Christian, nor ciuill vse of any thing," were those in the previous paragraph to be converted to see the "true light": they were now portrayed as a danger that the courageous English had been overcoming, and therefore these brave colonizers were worthy of support.[191] Englishness was something honorable as Johnson praised the English involved in "our honest enterprise"—"the further planting and succouring our old Colony."[192] England was building up its claim and its colonies through persons and purse "tending to aduance and spread the kingdome of God, and the knowledge of his truth, among so many Millions of men and women, sauage and blinde."[193] Johnson urged the country to supply the colony.[194]

The ghost of Spain and its ruin of the French colonies in Florida in the 1560s haunted the English texts of expansion. It is hard to overestimate the importance of the knowledge, experience, and failure of the French colonial enterprise in the Americas in the birth of the English permanent colonies. The French were, in tandem with the Spanish who drove them out, key to defining how important English texts portrayed England's enterprise in North America.

Ambivalence between blaming and praising England, as well as Spain, informed Johnson's rhetoric. Sometimes this ambivalent attitude found mediation between representations of France and, in this period, particularly the Huguenots. Johnson, too, spurred on gentlemen.[195] The argument Johnson made here is that England must supply the colony "for preservation and defence" and to avoid the experience of the French in Florida.[196] The Huguenots continued to haunt English writing about North America: Le Challeux and others seem to have spoken more to the English to the French, who were more interested in Catholic colonies at this time. Increasingly, France seemed to be leaving England room to maneuvre in the areas south of Acadia.

The Natives could not possess the land owing to the principle of *terra nullius,* because by definition, following the example of the Portuguese in Africa and Spain the New World, these pagans could not inhabit a territory, but then Johnson turned around and applied an aspect of this "law" to dispossess the Spanish in America. Johnson built up his case through accumulated repetition. He repeated his attacks on papal and Spanish authority. For instance, his variations on a theme involved a likening of the pope to King Cambyses, who committed incest with his daughter and did whatever he wished.[197] Johnson was not shy about using incremental repetition: he reiterated the legendary and fabulous nature of the papal donations.[198]

Resources and fertile land, not always gold, were significant prospects from the beginning of European accounts of the New World. Representing these riches was still important to Johnson, who portrayed the lands that would make up his New Britain as "huge and spacious countries," a fourth part of the world, and "the greatest and wealthiest part of all the rest."[199] Although not named, Spain remained an obstacle to the subduing of the Natives:

> the Subiects onely of one Prince Christian, which but within the memorie of man began first to creepe vpon the face of those Territories, and now by meanes of their broken remnants setled heere and there, doe therefore imagine the world to be theirs, shouldring out all other nations, accompt-

ing themselues kings and commanders, not onely in townes and places
where they haue planted, but ouer all other parts of *America,* which con-
taine sundry vast and barbarous Regions, many of which (to this day) they
neuer knew, nor did euer setle foote therein; which notwithstanding, if it
were yielded them as due: yet their strength and meanes farre inferior to
their aspires, will neuer stretch to compass or replenish the hundreth part
thereof, and this wee proued true not many yeeres agoe, our prince and
theirs being then at open hostilitie, their best and chiefest residences were
scattered with so poore and slender troupes, that with handfulls of men (at
sundry times) wee ran through all, surprizing and sacking their strongest
forts and townes in those parts, and might long since, with ease, following
and seconding our forces, haue set them to their stint.[200]

Dreams of English or British wealth, at least in Johnson's title, found a block or
nemesis in Spain, which had wealth and possessions enough. Johnson challenged
the Spanish notion that they were lords of the New World not just because the
papal donation had been misguided but because they lacked the possession and
the military strength to make such a claim. Instead, the English needed courage
to raise a challenge to Spain in the Americas:

But seeing we so passed by their dwellings, that in seating our selues, wee
sought not to vnsettle them, but by Gods mercy after many stormes, were
brought to the Coast of another countrie, farre distant and remote from
their habitations: why should any frowne or enuie at it, or if they do; why
should wee (neglecting so faire an opportunitie) faint or feare to enlarge
our selues, where is our force and auncient vigour? Doeth our late reputation sleepe in the dust? No, no, let not the world deceiue it selfe, we still
remaine the same, and vpon iust occasion giuen, we shall quickly shew it
too.[201]

Johnson then noted how the English had exposed the weakness of the Spanish in the New World and had shown the gap between their aspiration to dominate it and their actual means of controlling it. Even though he had argued for
the justice of England's claim in America and maintained that it should not be
envied because it was far from where Spain dwelt, he appealed to the military
strength of England, which was lately shown to this unnamed rival but which
clearly alluded to the defeat of the Spanish Armada. Johnson had the delicate
task of whipping up the glory of Elizabeth's reign to raise money for, and attract
people to, Virginia, while not securing the support of James I, who had chosen
peace with Spain.

The question of rightful possession and of origins continued in Johnson's
text, so that he could not resist for long the temptation of naming Spain. Before
describing "this earthly Paradise," Johnson claimed "that the first discouery and
actuall possession taken thereof, was in the raigne, and by the subiects of *Henry*
the seuenth of England, at which time did *Spaine* also discouer; and by that right
of discouery, doeth retaine and hold their *Noua Hispania,* and all other limmits

vpon that coast."[202] Johnson was trying to establish spheres of influence, North America for the English based on Cabot's discovery and New Spain based on the voyages of Columbus and other Spanish captains. To shore up the argument for English possession of Virginia, Johnson added the most recent to the most ancient claim, so that the possession that Elizabeth I and Walter Ralegh, "(then a Gentleman of worth)," enacted in the 1580s became further proof of the right of England to the territory.[203] In the process of making claims for English possession, Johnson revealed that John White's colony, under the aegis of Walter Ralegh, was abandoned by those who preferred to pillage off the coast of Spain than supply the 100 colonists.[204]

The weakness and dissension of the English came to light even in its rivalry with Spain. Johnson lamented this corruption and said that the colony would have been a strong addition to the English crown had it been given a proper beginning. Amid this mixture of self-criticism and patriotism, he represented the story of Columbus, another recurring motif in the example of Spain.[205] Like a wistful gash or memory of regret or a path of glory not taken, Johnson returned to this recurring motif—Columbus—in the English narratives of the time. This originary anguish could also take the form of self-criticism as well as envy of the Spanish boldness and honor in being the first Europeans to the New World:

> When *Christopher Columbus* (the first bewrayer of this new world) was to make his proffer where he liked best, he chose *Henry* the seuenth of *England,* as in those dayes the most worthy and best furnished for Nauigations, of all the Kings in Christendome; offering to inuest his Maiestie with the most pretious and richest vaines of the whole earth, neuer knowen before, as he did also the like, to the Kings of *Portugale* and *Spaine,* who (as the story saith) for his poore apparell and simple lookes, and for the noueltie of his proposition, was of most men accounted a vayne foole, and vtterly reiected: saue that the *Spanish* better conceiuing then some others, beganne to entertaine and make vse of his skill, which within these hundred yeares, hath brought forth those apparant fruits to the world as cannot be hidde. Their Territories enlarged, their Nauigations increased, their subiects enriched, and their superfluity of coyne ouerspreading al parts of the world, procures their Crowne to flourish, and highly commendeth the wisedome of *Spaine;* whose quicke apprehension and speedy addresse, preuented all other Princes: albeit (as you know) their greatnes of mind arising together with their money and meanes, hath turmoiled all Christendome thse fourtie yeares and more.[206]

Although Johnson praised Henry VII and England, he embodied the regret and mythology over the lost opportunity with Columbus, who in this version was such a visionary that he seemed to have foreseen the rich deposits of gold and silver his successors later came across. Columbus, not Cabot, who was not named, became the first discoverer and possessor of the New World. The wisdom of Spain above England and Portugal in making use of Columbus's talents and taking advantage of his enterprise of the Indies had, in Johnson's view, enabled the Spanish to prosper and, with this great economy whose currency dominated the world, to create turmoil in Christendom the past four decades. Johnson stated the case starkly: Henry VII's mistake and "the most pretious and richest vaines of the whole earth," which the New World furnished for Spain, have been cause for regret in England.

Spain and Columbus provoked ambivalent rhetoric in England, something that manifested itself in Johnson, his predecessors, and contemporaries. Even if Columbus was mocked, he soon found an audience with Spain, which represented reluctant praise for the rival of England and implied criticism for Johnson's native country.[207] This praise for Spain recurred in England from Richard Eden onward. It balanced anti-Spanish sentiment and provided a reminder of the ambivalent responses to Spain throughout the period. The intricate mixture of contradiction and ambivalence occurred with a similar nexus of attitudes toward English efforts at colonization. Spain was to be admired for its transformation of the world, but such great change also caused some resentment and self-doubt among the English. The constant revisiting of the origins of rights to the New World and of the mythical, factual, and legal interpretations of the papal bulls, Columbus's discovery, and Cabot's voyages decades before and after Johnson supports an argument for intricacy in the English attitude to the example of Spain.

Pressing the point of English error even further, Johnson said:

And this I but mention, to note the blind diffidence of our *English* natures, which laugh to scorne the name of *Virginia,* and all other new proiects, be they neuer so probable, and will not beleeue till we see the effects; as also to shew how capable men ought to be, in things of great importance, auisedly to take the first occasions. We reade of *Haniball,* who chasing home the *Romanes* to the gates of *Rome,* and neglecting then to scale the walles, could neuer after with all his strength and policies come neere the like aduantage.[208]

The precariousness of English colonization in the northern part of the Americas was something Johnson emphasized here. He also remarked on the realism and skepticism of the English: they laughed at their own efforts in Virginia and had to see results before they took a risk. This anti-triumphalism was not *translatio imperii* here but an identification of the Spaniards with the Romans and the English with Hannibal. Johnson, like many of his compatriots, was critical of his own nation. This was the attitude that Hakluyt had worked against, the kind of puzzlement that the English had caused La Popelinière, a response to which Hakluyt felt he had had to respond.

Johnson and the English found themselves in a similar position to the Spanish, whose clergy, like Las Casas, had questioned the treatment of the Natives and whose jurists, like Vitoria, had called into doubt the legitimacy of the Spanish and European claim to possession of the New World.[209] In the face of past failures in this English colony and the doubt in England about Virginia, Johnson used Spain as a positive example of how the English should be bold in coloniz-

ing Virginia and held up Hannibal as a negative illustration of someone who hes-
itated at the wrong time. He then began to discuss the "good land" of Virginia
to promote it.[210] Johnson described Virginia's natural bounty and commodities
and raised the topics of "God and the publike good."[211]

The doubt and opposition in England was built into Johnson's argument
when he faced the two major objections to the colonization of Virginia: "For
the first (if I forget not my selfe) how it may tend to aduance the kingdome of
God, by reducing sauage people from their blind superstition to the light of religion, when some obiect, we seeke nothing lesse then the cause of God, being
led on by our owne priuate ends, and secondly how we can warrant a supplan-
tation of those *Indians,* or an inuasion into their right and possessions."[212] Once
the English had to face the possibility of a permanent settlement, they had to
address the same doubts and cast about for the same rationalizations as the Spanish had decades before. Johnson addressed the first objection by saying that "as
many actions both good and bad in themselues, and in their successe, haue
beene performed with bad intents, so in this case, howsoeuer our naughtines of
minde may sway very much" and then stated that it would be better "to recti-
fie our harts, and ground our meditations before we begin."[213] To the second
objection, the English, being wary of greed hiding behind pretense, intruded
into Native possessions to bring them Christ and a better material life and not
to supplant them, and that they would make this interpretation public. Johnson
made a problematic use of the invasion of Ireland by "Don John Daquila," who
acted under the publicly proclaimed pretense of freeing it from tyranny and
bringing it the true Catholic religion. Thus Johnson justified what he overtly
calls "our Inuasion."[214] Consciously or not, he had called into question the sincerity or pretense of his "open" proclamation and "publike interpretation" of
the English intentions toward the Natives, even though he had warned against
such subterfuge.[215]

At this stage, I want to examine this moment in Johnson's text in more detail.
Rather than to supplant the Natives, the English came to make them more civil:

> And as for supplanting the Sauages, we haue no such intent: Our intrusion
> into their possessions shall tend to their great good, and no way to their
> hurt, vnlesse as vnbridled beastes, they procure it to themselues: Wee pur-
> pose to proclaime and make it knowne to them all, by some publike inter-
> pretation, that our comming thither is to plant our selues in their
> Countrie: yet not to supplant and roote them out, but to bring them from
> their base condition to a farre better.[216]

The Natives, if they behave like animals, would bring upon themselves harm
from the English. In Johnson's construction the indigenes had to accept the
intrusion of the English or that would be unreasonable and uncivil, beastly in
fact, so that they would get whatever hurt the English offer them. England
offered "great good" so the Natives would improve their "base condition" by
far. Civility and material improvement were the goods the English had to offer.
According to Johnson, the Natives will believe in Christ and God and, the Eng-

lish "promise to defend them against all publike and priuate enemies."[217] England would act as a protector to the Natives in the New World, something that Ralegh had argued in his narrative on Guiana but more directly in relation to the Spanish presence there.

The typology between Ireland and the New World, which we have encountered before, arose again in Johnson. Unlike Ralegh, where Spain and England contended in the New World, in Johnson the two rivals sought conquest in Ireland as well as in the Americas:

> Wee can remember since *Don John Daquila* with his forces, inuading *Ireland,* a noble ciuill kingdome, where al (except a few runnagates) were setled in the truth of Religion, and liued by wholsome lawes, vnder the milde gouerment of Christian Kings and Princes, long before his grandsires cradle: yet hee thought it no robberie to proclaime and publish to the world, that his comming thither was to none other end, but to free the Nation from their bondage and tyrannous subiection, and to bring the blind soules to Catholike Religion: a plausible pretence, the least end of his thought.
>
> But if this were coyned in those dayes by the Minters themselues, to passe for currant through the world: howsoeuer base it was indeede, we hope they will be as fauourable to our case, and giue as free passage and alowance to our Inuasion, much more currant, and so farre different.[218]

Robert Johnson promised to defend the Natives against enemies, perhaps including the Spanish, then made an analogy between a Spaniard, Don John Daquila in Ireland and the English in Virginia, except Daquila was invading a Christian country and the English were not. Johnson argued that the English invasion was therefore more legitimate than the Spanish intrusion even though the structure of the analogy related the Spaniards and the English in their narrative of liberation. This trope of the liberating invasion is no stranger in our time. It does not matter whether the Natives of the land wore clothing or were naked, were Christian or not, for the invader sought to uphold "civilization" or to "civilize" as a means of gaining control and influence.

The English, in Johnson's representation, were able to inhabit Native lands with impunity. There is a religious dimension to this possession: if, "in this last age of the world," the Natives resisted conversion,

> or shall maligne or disturbe our plantation, our chattell, or whatsoeuer belonging to vs, they shall be held and reputed, recusant, withstanding their owne good: and shall bee dealt with as enemies of the Commonwealth of their country: wherby, how much good wee shall performe to those that be good, and how little iniurie to any, will easily appeare, by comparing our present happinesse with our former auncient miseries, wherein wee had continued brutish poore and naked *Brittans* to this *day,* if *Iulius Cæsar* with his *Romaine* Legions, (or some other) had not laid the ground to make vs tame and ciuill.[219]

In resistance, according to Johnson, Natives became recusants who would suffer the fate of enemies. In Johnson's interpretation here, the Natives should be thankful to the English for making them civil just as the English, who would have "continued brutish poore and naked *Brittans* to this day" without Julius Caesar and his legions, who brought civility with them, were grateful.[220] Once more, the typology between British wild man and Native is used to justify the invasion and "civilization" of the New World. In Thomas Harriot's *A Briefe and True Report of the New Found Land of Virginia* (1590), an appendix of engravings of ancient Britons appeared to show how the past inhabitants of Britain had been as "sauage" as the indigenous peoples in Virginia.[221]

The relation of classical mythology, religion, and conquest became intertwined in Johnson's text. King David and Hercules provided models for righteous conquest. To subdue and conquest was the glory of King David.[222] Classical, as well as biblical, heroes were seen as models for conquest:

> Honorable I graunt is iust Conquest by sword, and *Hercules* is fained to haue had all his felicitie, in subduing and rooting out the Tyrants of the world, but vnfainedly it is most honorable indeede, to subdue the tyrannie of the roaring Lion, that devoures those poore soules in their ignorance and leads them to hell for want of light, when our Dominions shalbe enlarged, and the subiects multiplied of a people so bought and ransomed, not by stormes of raging cruelties (as *West India* was conuerted) with rapiers point and Musket shot, murdering so many Millions of naked *Indians,* as their stories doe relate, but by faire and louing meanes suting of our *English* Natures, like the gentle voice the Lord used to appear to *Elias*.[223]

This English conquest of the New World, as Johnson saw it, did not debase the example of Hercules, clearing the world of tyranny with his sword, but it appealed more to a gentler model, being in this similitude like the voice of God to Elias, not the rapiers and muskets the Spanish used in subduing the West Indies, a representation of the Spanish conquest that Johnson said he was taking from Spain's own stories. Although Johnson did not refer to Las Casas directly, he appeared to be evoking the most famous Spanish chronicler of the atrocities of Spain in the conquest of the West Indies, what Johnson described here as the "murdering of so many Millions of naked *Indians*." This gentle revelation, this presence of God, was to be the way of the English in the New World: here was the authority Johnson was trying to establish for them. The context for the voice of God that Johnson alluded to here depended on Yahweh, a God who punishes the heathen and rewards those who convert to his faith and follow his servant, Elias or Elijah (see 1 Kings). The gentle whisper of God's voice, full of power and glory, was also an instrument of retribution: the heathen could die through God's direct power as well as through the swords that King David and Hercules, or the Spaniards in the Indies, did yield. In the Americas, the gentleness of the English, more of the Word than the sword, might well have been as potentially violent as the weapons of the Spanish. Elijah also had typological significance as Matthew and Mark recorded that the crowd interpreted Christ's crying out in agony on the cross as an appeal to Elias or Elijah (see Matthew 27:47–9, Mark 15:35–6). Elijah was sometimes seen as a type of Christ in the Old Testament, converting those to the one and true God. Elijah ascended into heaven in a chariot of fire: Christ later ascended to heaven and, risen, sanctified the crowd at Pentecost with fire. Both Elijah and Christ preserved a small band of the faithful in a hostile world. Elijah, then, was and is and ambivalent figure of righteous war and peace, so that the example of Spain in conversion of the New World and that of England there, which Johnson projected, might not be as different as Johnson intimated. There was a blurring of the Old and New Testaments here in this typology, so that the law and the spirit, violence and peace were hard to separate.

The figure of Daniel supplemented Johnson's appeal to Elias or Elijah in Johnson's framework for the English conquest and conversion of the Natives in Virginia: "The prophet *Daniell* doth assure, that for this conquest, of *turning many vnto righteousnesse,* he shall shine as the starres for euer and euer."[224] Johnson was echoing the twelfth and last chapter of the Book of Daniel in a vision in the end times in which the man with a multitudinous voice and clothed in linen proclaims that the wise and the righteous shall be delivered in a kind of apotheosis. Wise, patient and holy, Daniel is promised his inheritance: he will understand whereas the wicked will not. Daniel, a prophet of the Exile, had already dreamed of the future of great empires and the coming of the kingdom of the Messiah (Daniel 5:7–12). It is as if Johnson were making this kind of prophecy for the English as wise and holy inheritors of the New World. In his rhetorical and prophetic rousing of his compatriots, Johnson also appealed to Moses, Solomon, Christ, Caleb, Joshua, Alexander, and others.[225]

Besides this religious aspect of the westward expansion or the American enterprise, the material and demographic dimensions persisted in Johnson's work. In addition to the desire to relieve "our men already planted," Johnson, like Hakluyt, repeated the themes of commodities such as wood, iron, copper, silk worms, and mulberry trees.[226] To promote colonies in the Americas, he held up the riches of other English enterprises—he praised the East Indies for bringing wealth to English merchants—but, like Hakluyt of the "Discourse," he feared that Continental powers were getting the better of England, whose inhabitants were idle: "yet our want of industrie be such, that Netherlanders which haue not a sticke of wood growing, nor any land for sowing, should surpasse and go beyond vs in continuall plenty of coyn and shipping."[227] The argument that colonies prevented over-population, which was current at the time in writers like Gilbert and Hakluyt, also occurred in Johnson: the English could learn from the Goths and Vandals that excess population abroad prevented "vice and villany" at home.[228]

Nonetheless, religion and classical mythology, whether representing glory or honor, were never far from the framework of Johnson's text. The honor of a king depended on the number of subjects, so that for James I to enlarge his kingdoms would, like the conquests of David for Israel, bring glory to him and his country. Hercules's conquests of tyrants were also summoned as evidence of the justice of Johnson's vision of a conquering England. The implication was that the Natives had tyrannical regimes that deserved to be conquered. Johnson was singing a paean to conquest, the very thing for which some of his countrymen had criticized Spain.[229] It is as if he caught himself because he then thought it necessary to distinguish between English and Spanish conquests. The English would ransom the souls of the multitude of Natives under their rule in this visionary future "by faire and louing meanes suting to our *English* Natures."[230] This passage was reminiscent of Ralegh's use of Las Casas and similar to the French insistence that they would convert the Natives and not exterminate them as the Spaniards had. God was made to prefer English conquests to those of the Spanish. King James would profit spiritually and materially from providence: Johnson expatiated on the commodities that would flow from Virginia and on the importance of navigation—themes Humphrey Gilbert and Richard Hakluyt the Younger had developed during the early 1580s.[231]

There were, for Johnson, many threats to the English home and in the colonies. His concerns, as we have seen, were not too different from earlier writer from the 1560s onward, such as Gilbert and Hakluyt the Younger. Like the Goths and Vandals, the English should expand to allow its multitudes scope rather than to have them pester and infect themselves "with vice and villany," but Johnson, using an extreme rhetoric, did not mean the "unsound members" like those with vile minds (often the bad sort from cities), Catholics ("Papists, professed or Recusant") and "euill affected magistrates."[232] In addition to being against any "Papists" in the colonies, he feared that England was not making proper use of its shipping and its sailors: "you know how many good shippes are daily solde, and made away to forreine nations: how manie men for want of imployment, betake themselues to *Tunis, Spaine* and *Florence*," so that Virginia would provide for the unemployed and stop the flow of men looking for employment outside England.[233] Johnson resurrected other arguments that go back to Gilbert and Hakluyt that "the *Indians* brought to our Ciuilitie" would provide a large market for English clothes.[234] Besides needing what Johnson considered to be "our best sort of Citizens," Virginia required money.[235] The final issue was land and rents, which led to the lost opportunity that Virginia offered. The English should have backed Columbus:

> Our forefathers not looking out in time, lost the prime and fairest proffer, of the greatest wealth in the world, and we taxe their omission for it, yet now it falles out, that wee their children are tryed in the like, there being yet an excellent portion left, and by diuine prouidence offered to our choice, which seeing we haue armes to embrace, let it not be accounted hereafter, *As a prize in the hands of fooles, that had no hearts to vse it*.[236]

Johnson reiterated the wistful tale of England's lost opportunity with Columbus, which served as a wondering trope in the discourse of the English in America. The figure of Columbus, then, haunted the Virginian enterprise. Johnson came full circle to the Spanish origins of the European settlement in the New World and how the English had made a mistake and now had to take what the Spanish did not occupy. Johnson warned the English not to make the mistake the Romans did, leaving the goddess Victoria to languish after conquests, and he admonished against miscreants, advocated the conversion of the Natives, and celebrated the valiance of English and Scottish captains in Palestine.[237]

> But what is this to vs: they are blind indeede that stumble here, it is much like that great Donation of *Constantine* whereby the Pope himselfe doth hold and claime, the Citie of *Rome* and all the Westerne Empire, a thing that so crosseth all Histories of truth, and sound Antiquitie, that by the apt resemblance of those two Donations, the whole West Empire, from a temporall Prince to the Pope, and the whole West Indies, from the pope to a temporal Prince, I doe verily gesse they be neere of kinne, they are so like each other, the one an olde tale vaine and fabulous, the other a new toye most idle and ridiculous.[238]

Johnson emphasized a reversed typology expressed through these donations, a satire on this legal typology or precedent. He questioned this translation of empire from Roman emperor to the pope in Rome and from the pope to the king of Spain, a shift from the temporal to the ecclesiastical and then a reversal of that movement, so that the "donations" had come full circle and had nothing but what they started out with—temporal authority. That temporal power and authority was, Johnson implied, a move from an "olde tale vaine and fabulous" to "a newe toye vaine and ridiculous" because that authority was not English or held no sway over England. The donations involved, for Johnson, an ancient fiction and a new gewgaw: here is his typology of the absurd.

This attack on the donations was one of the means that Johnson used to clear the way for the claims of English forebears to the land in Virginia. Another was the examples of classical antecedents, a kind of rival interpretation of the heroic nature of conquest to that of the Spaniards, who also drew on Greco-Roman models:

> if we sitte still and let slip occasions, we shall gather rust, and doe vnfeather our owne wings, committing the folly of the wise Romanes heerein, that in time of their glory, flowing with the Conquestes and spoiles of the world, and hauing gotten the Goddesse *Victoria* to *Rome,* they clipt her wings, and set her vp among their Gods, that shee might take her flight no more, as shee had formerly done from the *Grœtians,* and others, and so effeminating their valor with idlenesse and security, it brought confusion and ruine to their state.[239]

Here is a competition in the interpretations of, and between the inheritors of, the Roman Empire, different translations of empire. Manly valor and conquest is a model that Johnson was holding up to the English. He also shifted to the crusades, for he asserted that had the English and Scottish captains, who had sought "to reconquer *Palestina* from the *Turkes* and *Sarazen*," known about the lands the author discusses in the Northwest, then there would not be a job for the British Isles to do in Virginia.[240] This is a kind of negative typology of crusade.

An incipient Britishness, which connected the Scots and the English (implicitly through King James), seems to be part of Johnson's project. In this myth of England as a sleeping state waiting to arise, Johnson appears to have been implying that religious dissension, with a patina of Catholic allusion, had kept Europe from realizing its potential trade with the East:

> How strange a thing is this that al the States of *Europe* haue beene a sleepe
> so long, that for an hundred yeares and more, the wealth and riches of the
> *East* and *West* should runne no other current but into one coffer, so long,
> till the running ouer, spread it selfe abundantly, among a factious crew of
> new created Friers, and that to no more speciall end, then with instigating
> bloody plottes to pierce the heart of a Christian State and true religion.[241]

Nor could Johnson, having spoken of Turkey, leave off without an apparent swipe at Spain. The context of this passage made it a little hazy as Johnson moved into a vague prophecy and a historical example to rouse his nation. He used examples of Scotland and England working together as a means of flattering James VI of Scotland who had also become James I of England. Whether these are Spanish and Catholic plots Johnson did not say explicitly, but it is likely, from what we have seen in Johnson and in earlier English writers like Hakluyt, that the riches in one coffer—that of Spain—and its resulting political and economic domination of Europe referred to Spanish domination of Europe through its trade in the Americas and the East. In an attempt to mythologize the union of Scotland and England at least symbolically under James, Johnson used the topos of inexpressibility to intimate a great mythological origin to this Britannic power : Johnson would tell of "great wonders that shoulde bee wrought by *Scots* and *English,* before the comming of *Christ*" but he has almost forgotten and can't call it to mind.[242] A search for more prestigious origins to Spain and other rivals continued to inform English representations of their efforts at colonization in the New World. The papal donations, honor in conquest, the crusades and current European relations all implicitly and explicitly led Johnson to build up his idea of Britannia as a nation and as a colonizer at the expense of its rival: Spain.

The English conquest of the New World should involve mercy on the Natives, unlike the Spanish destruction that Johnson had described earlier in his text. In this place in the appropriately entitled, *Nova Britannia, Parts 1 and 2,* Johnson showed compassion for the indigenous population whereas elsewhere in this work he justified English threats and violence against them: "And for the poore Indians what shall I say, but God that hath many waies shewed mercie to you, make you shew mercie to them and theirs."[243] Johnson yoked wisdom, gentleness, and mercy in this part of his text as a positive example of conquest: "Take their children and traine them vp with gentlenesse, teach them our English tongue, and the principles of religion; winne the elder sort by wisedome and discretion, make them equal with your English in case of protection of wealth and habitation, doing iustice on such as shall doe them wrong."²⁴⁴ He was advocating a form of equality between English and Native on the terms of the English. While limited, this argument is laudatory and, in its own way, not too different from that which Las Casas had made in Spanish America. If all roads led Johnson to English glory, so that he did not admit here any affinities with like-minded Spaniards, then he was also able to praise.

Ambivalence and contradiction were key aspects of Johnson's portrayal of Spain and of England itself. The two nations were entwined in English representations of the New World. The English writers often defined England and themselves through their attitudes toward Spain:

> And so I come to you that be the Aduenturers here in England: with which I will conclude, it is not much aboue an hundred yeeres agoe, that these Aduentures for discoueries were first vndertaken by the Southerne parts of Christendome, but especially so seconded and followed by the Spanish nation both to the East and West Indies, that *Mendoza* (their countriman) in his treatise of Warre, extolleth King *Philip* and the Spanish nation aboue the skies, for seeking in such sort to inlarge their bounds by sea and land, seeming (as it were) with a secret scorne to set out the basenesse of our English and other nations in this, that they neuer intend any such attempts, but with a king of sluggish contentment, doe account it their happinesse to keepe that poore little which they possesse. Indeed wee must acknowledge it, with praise to God, that when some of [in the margin 'Ireland' appears here] theirs had cast an euill eye vpon our possessions, it was our happinesse to preuent their longing, and to send them emptie home. But for that other part of inlarging their bounds, in truth their praise is duly giuen, and well deserued: and it may iustly serue to stirre vs vp by all our means to put off such reprochfull censures; and seeing when time did offer it, our nation lost the first opportunity of hauing all, yet now to make good that common speech, that English men are best at imitation, and doe soone excell their teachers.²⁴⁵

The contention over Ireland led Johnson to censure Spain, but its bold initiatives in the New World seem to have elicited admiration from him. In fact, he blamed the English for not having taken up what was implicitly Columbus's plan to sail into the western Atlantic and subsequent voyages there. Johnson censured those in England who would censure Spain with this example of what might be called the wound of Columbus. Still, Johnson snatched victory from the jaws of defeat and turned lost opportunity into present advantage: in his view, the English were the best at imitation and so would imitate the example of Spain only to exceed their Spanish teachers.

Johnson also demonstrated his ambivalence by criticizing English relations with contemporary Italy and Rome and by complaining about "English Italionate trauellers" but appealing to an example from classical Rome as a model—

Scipio who defended Rome against Hannibal (even though Johnson had elsewhere praised Hannibal as a good example).[246] Exemplarity, even after Johnson had spent his time defining it in terms of ancient Rome and of Spain, would be English. England's leaders in the New World will be an "example to posteritie, in being the first props and pillars of the work, the records of time shall publish your praise; not stained with lies as the Legends of Saints, but as those renowned deedes of your noble ancestors, truly set out in our English stories."[247] The remembrance of gestures and deeds of noble ancestors had a long tradition in English historiography and included narrative works by Hall and Holinshed and chronicle plays like the anonymous *The Famous Victories of Henry V* in the 1580s and Shakespeare's English histories in the 1590s. Here were some of "our English stories." Johnson took up this Native tradition: after all, Heminges and Condell, who brought out Shakespeare's First Folio in 1623 classified history plays only those that were about the English (not the British or Scottish past). Johnson was a little softer on making these distinctions. In Johnson, there is also a sense that the Catholic is to be shed as he specifically mentions the "lies" in "the legends of the saints." Like Hakluyt in *Principall Navigations,* Johnson defined Englishness paradoxically through Continental sources. The so-called English identity, even as it was being made British, was founded on other languages: through the translation of study, English writers like Hakluyt and Johnson, for all their claims, were establishing a translation of empire. It comes as no surprise, then, that Johnson ended his work on a typologically new Britain, set out in its Latin form in the title, with a call to honor King and country.

The English representation of Spain and the New World was a kind of oxymoronic and paradoxical meeting of opposites. It was an imitation that contended with as much as it borrowed from the source. Johnson's *The New Life of Virginea* (1612) also used the ideas of *translatio imperii* and the example of Spain.[248] The Spanish might have been wrong to covet English possessions in 1588 and paid for it, but they were to be admired for their overseas expansion. In what is a representative passage for my study as a whole, Johnson expressed his mixed feelings toward the example of Spain.[249]

Johnson thought that the English should emulate Spain in the New World: he reiterated a recurring trope in the English discourse of America—the lost opportunity to be there first. This rhetoric of regret—that Henry VII, and not Ferdinand and Isabella, should have commissioned Columbus—erupted in these texts but, as in Johnson, also provided a cautionary tale for this generation of Englishmen to seize the day and colonize the New World and so not to cheat their heirs as their ancestors cheated them. At the very least, Cabot's lead should have been followed up in England. Such wistfulness could be implicit and explicit in English writing. Praise and blame were mixed in this passage. As we have seen, the French, too, wanted to re-create the origins of the discovery and division of the New World. The only hope for Johnson, as we have observed before, was that the English were such great imitators that they would excel their Spanish teachers.

Robert Johnson had anti-Catholic moments as he also criticized those Englishmen who traveled to Spain and Rome for reasons of religion and to hatch plots at home. He appealed to Scipio who faced Hannibal and stopped the Roman flight and suggested books of the deeds of noble English ancestors rather than the lies in the legends of saints: both models would lead to the honor of the king and the good of England.[250] Despite the emphasis on English heroism for promotion of the colonies in the New World, Johnson could tell of Native generosity in the survival of the early settlement of Virginia in the story of Captain Newport and Powhatan:

> Their barbarous king *Powhatan* entertained them louingly, and admitted them a large countrie to inhabit, the poore Sauages brought them such reliefe as they had; our owne people wrote letters home in praise of the countrie, and labored their friends to come hither, they began to fortifie where they saw conuenient, they built a Church and many houses together, which they named *James Towne.*[251]

The "poore Sauages" saved the colony and its Englishness, so that the Natives, like the Spaniards, helped to provide examples for the English and to define Englishness itself. The precariousness of the English efforts at colonization in Virginia can be seen in the balance of allusions in Johnson's text, for instance, the shipwreck of the *Sea Venture* in 1609, which is often regarded as an event that influenced Shakespeare's *The Tempest,* and the description of Henry V before Agincourt.[252] In another appeal to Englishness, Johnson said of the English colonists: "let them liue as free English men."[253] The precedence or importance of Spain in the New World was, however, something that Johnson and the English writers of his period could not ignore for long.

Another key figure in English representations of the New World, especially regarding the example of Spain, was William Strachey, whose *The Historie of Travell into Virginia Britannia* (1612) is an important text for this study.[254] These English texts sometimes reflect the wider institutional connections their authors possessed whether with universities or with poetry circles and the theater. The level of language and authorial contacts could be very high indeed. Strachey became a catalyst for such relations.

The promotion of English colonization in Virginia appears to have had literary associations. Thomas Campion, who here addressed an epigram to Strachey, had literary aspirations, having composed a sonnet in commendation of Ben Jonson's *Sejanus.* Campion was also connected to the theater in London, for he was a shareholder in the acting company, the Children of the Queen's Revels, which in 1606 had taken over the Blackfriar's Theatre from Shakespeare's associate, Richard Burbage. John Marston was also a shareholder and Ben Jonson wrote for this company.[255] In a deposition Strachey testified that he usually attended Blackfriars, "sometymes once, twyce, and thrice in a weeke," which suggests that he knew the theater company, including Shakespeare, who later used Strachey as a source for *The Tempest.*[256] Samuel Purchas published the Strachey letter to a certain "noble lady" that Shakespeare is thought to have used as a source for *The Tempest.*[257] Strachey based his narrative on 11 months on

Bermuda after the shipwreck of the *Sea Venture*. Strachey's account, *True Reportory*, was not published perhaps because it took a hard view of Virginia and Jamestown, and the Virginia Company did not want that kind of negative publicity.[258] On December 14, 1610, Richard Martin, secretary to the Virginia Company of London, wrote to Strachey asking him to provide a report of the colony, so that the officials of the company were, in the view of Louis B. Wright and Virginia Freund, too realistic to believe their own propaganda.[259] Strachey's unvarnished view and the Virginia Company's defensiveness suggest the fragility and precariousness of the English colonies in the Americas, like the instability of the French colonies there, something that a retrospective view from our vantage and projected teleologically can obscure.

The dedication to Strachey's *For the Colony in Virginea Britannia. Lawes Diuine, Moral and Martiall, & c.* (London 1612), which, while dwelling in Blackfriars, Strachey dedicated to the officers and members of the Virginia Company, declared: "I haue both in the Bermudas, and since in Virginea beene a sufferer and an eie witnesse, and the full storie of both in due time shall consecrate vnto your viewes, as vnto whom by right it appertaineth."[260] Strachey seems to have borrowed from earlier English translations, redactions, and translations of key Spanish works about the New World: Richard Eden's *The Decades of the New Worlde* (1555), Richard Willes's expansion and simplification of Eden, *The Historie of Trauale in the West and East Indies* (1577), Acosta's *The natural and morall historie of the East and West Indies* (1604); and Hakluyt's *Voyages*.[261] Strachey appears to have found no favor with any of the three potential patrons: there is some speculation that Northumberland, the addressee of the dedication was a Catholic because he was imprisoned in 1606 in the wake of the Gunpowder Plot; a second manuscript went to Sir Allen Apsley, purveyor of the Navy; and a third copy to Francis Bacon.[262] If Northumberland were a Catholic, then Strachey's address to him would be further evidence of one of the elements of the argument of this book, that the example of Spain in England, as in France, was not a simple matter of religious divisions, in which Protestants from other countries picked up on and fed the Black Legend of Spain with a fierce rhetoric. Moreover, the promotion of the fledgling colonies in the New World was not a guarantee of success in France or England. Strachey, for instance, apparently died without property or money, his career in adventure, literature, and diplomacy having yielded no lasting material rewards.[263]

It is, then, as I have suggested, tempting in retrospect to make the colonial effort a more concerted, sure, and successful enterprise for the individuals involved and for England itself. Strachey's position resembled other English writers on colonization in the New World, for he justified England's rights in the northern parts of the Americas based on the Cabot voyages, refused Spain's claim to the New World beyond the line of demarcation with Portugal, and asserted that the establishment and expansion of colonies, rather than being unjust to the Natives, would benefit them because they would be converted from a heathen state to Christian salvation while learning the advantages of trade with the English.[264] Strachey, like the other authors, while sharing attitudes and patterns of rhetoric with his contemporaries, also expressed his representation of the New World in a distinct way.

Continuing my practice in this study, I want to turn to the text itself to consider the ambivalence and contradiction in the representation of the example of Spain. Strachey's *The Historie of Travell into Virginia Britania* (1612) began with an epigraph chosen from the last twenty lines of the first epistle from the second book of Horace's *Epistles:*

> But I, rather than these conversations
> That creep close to the ground, would compose an epic
> Of the earth, of the rivers and the forts
> High in the mountains, and of barbarous kingdoms.[265]

The context for these lines, which Strachey may have assumed his readers would know and which he did not mention, was the end of Horace's epistle to Augustus. The very next lines, which he did not note, might be translated as "A world whose wars you have ended." This great Roman emperor had brought peace to the world, and by implication his English counterpart would do the same, subduing the barbarous realms such as those in the New World. It comes as no surprise that in the "Dedication to the Earl of Northumberland" that Strachey still had this part of Horace's *Epistles* on his mind, so that the image of Janus that Horace used—the gates shut in times of peace—now transposed from Augustus to Northumberland.

This was high typological praise founded in the context of the movement from *pax* to peace—from one empire to another, the poetic and rhetorical echoes of textual history. Strachey's own literary translation was part of this translation of empire:

> Wild as they are, accept them, so were we,
> To make them ciuill, will our honour bee,
> And if good workes be the effectes of mindes
> That like good Angells be, let our designes
> As we are Angli, make vs Angells too
> No better work can Church or statesman doe.[266]

The English were angels come with honor to make the wild Natives civil. This verse encapsulated the typology of the Natives being like European wild men, as were the ancient British before the Roman conquest, and the English now acting as inheritors of empire and civility would do the same for the Natives that the Romans had done for them—bring them within the *civis*. Strachey placed this verse under the Latin heading for church and state.

What Strachey argued for in "A Premonition to the Reader" was the English claim to "this part of America."[267] This part began in a very defensive way against the critics of English colonization in northern stretches of the New World:

> The many Mouthes of Ignorance, and Sclaunder, which are ever too apt
> to let fall the Venome of their worst and most depraving Envyes, vpon the
> best and most sacred workes, and so not affrayed to blast both this Enter-

prize, and the divoutest Labourers therein, wrings from me the necessity
of this imperfect defence, whome yet I haue observed more in Clamour
(me thought) then at any tyme in force, to cry out still vpon yt, calling it
an *vnnationall, and vnlawfull vndertaking.*[268]

Strachey's image of the many mouths of Ignorance and Slander resembled
Shakespeare's Induction to *2 Henry IV,* Rumor, who is painted full of tongues,
and many other medieval and early modern portraits of Rumor that reiterate
Virgil's account, in Book 4, lines 181–83 of the *Aeneid,* of Fama as a monster
that ears, eyes, and tongues cover. This commonplace both discounted and
admitted the critics of English colonization in the Americas: they were full of
ignorant slander but they were powerful enough that their existence needed to
be addressed and they required ridicule. Like the voices of Natives in European
narratives about the New World, the words of opposition from within or alternative critique in England are something of which we catch a glimpse. The critics seemed to be saying at the English expansion to North America was against
nation, nature, and the law. It is no wonder that Strachey and his fellow "promoters" of the colonies would harp on the translation of empire and the legal
underpinnings of the colonization.

Religion was one of the justifications that recurred in these narratives. For
Strachey, the aim was "to endeavour the conversion of the natiues, to the knowl-
edg and worshippe of the true God, and the world's-Redeemer Christ Iesus."[269]
He returned to the critics who had been against the authority of church and
state—the themes of Strachey's argument. These critics, "out of Ignorance,"

quarrell, and traduce the Proceedings of a whole State, and to which the
royall Auctoritie by Letters made Pattents, both in her Maiesties tyme (of
famous memory,) and now likewise, hath bene 5. tymes concurrant? May
yt be supposed any one but luke-warme in christian Charity, would be
parcell guilty herein? or make yt questionable, whether should be
attempted a worke of this Piety, vpon a barbarous Nation?[270]

Strachey aligned these critics of empire with the "barbarous Nation" of the
Natives and made them opponents of the king and Christian charity and piety
by invoking Elizabeth I "(of famous memory)" and her legal authority. In
returning to the image of Janus, Strachey showed that the Christian context was
never far from the classical antecedents and examples. The translation of tradition was itself Janus-faced.

In the *translatio imperii* that Strachey described, England found rivals in Spain
and Portugal for the Roman mantle. Religion had a Roman twist in Strachey's
scheme:

the growndes of Goodnes, are not layd so weake in well weighed Coun-
sells, that the calmour of a Centurion or twooe, can disturb *Numa-Pompilius* kneeling at the Aulter; let them giue yt up in rumour, or more subtilly
cry out that our Enemyes at *Siuil,* or *Lishbourne,* at *Dominicus, Meuis,* or at

the *Hauana,* are vp in Armes for vs, we can yet goe on in the Iustifiablenes
of our Cause, making only *Pompilius* answere, *And we doe sacrifice;* will yt
please the Reader to favour me a little?[271]

Numa-Pompilius was a legendary king of Rome who was supposed to have been
responsible for many religious practices of Rome.[272] English piety was founded
here on an example from Roman piety: one origin underwrote another. The
critics, like the occasional centurions, had their rumor, but in the face of enemies
like Spain, the English (and Strachey used "our" and "we" to bond with the
reader in a greater Englishness) should look to the example of the now-familiar
(the form is even so) Pompilius. Then proper sacrifices for empire would be
made and the projected teleology of England would follow the grandeur of the
progress of Rome. Yet, in all this talk of swearing and sacrifice, of "the Iustifiablenes of our Cause," the ghost of Spain and Columbus haunted the scene.
Besides a reference to enemies in Seville, there was a reference to "Meuis," or
Nevis, an island in the West Indies that Columbus had "discovered."[273]

The nagging legal issues of priority and title in the New World, which we
have observed in previous English writers, also recurred in Strachey. Spain and
Columbus and the papal interpretation of their "discoveries" represented a central part of this discourse of legality. According to Strachey, the mere ignorant
and the mere opposite

> saie, how the vndertaking cannot be lawfull, why? because the *King of
> Spayne* hath a primer Interest into the Country; next yt canot be honest
> in yt self, why? because iniurious to the Naturalls, and which connected
> togither, yt must then necessarily follow (say they) that yt can be no other
> than a Trauayle of flat Impiety, and displeasing before god: indeed no
> meane obiections, to stumble shallowe home-witts, who whilst they look
> lazely, and broadly on, are presented with vgly face; but if by a more per-
> spective direction, we will examyne howe these perticularityes may lye
> togither, we shall fynd another Modell, and an Aire of that dignity and
> Truith which aspires to a cleane contrary Comlynes.[274]

Strachey contended that there was another model than the views of English critics of empire who asserted that the king of Spain had a prior claim, that colonization was harmful to the Natives ("Naturalls") and that such expansion was
an act of impiety. This model, rather than being the product of such shallow wit,
was true and comely. In this satirical use of *argumentum ad hominem,* Strachey
sought to destroy ideas opposed to those that underwrote Virginia by reducing
the debate to personal attack, even of a nameless and general personification.

In the passage that followed immediately, Strachey focused his attack on the
right of the king of Spain to the New World and the pope's role in lending
authority to that legal position:

> For the *King of Spayne;* he hath no more Title, nor coulour of Title, to this
> place, (which we by our Industry and expences haue only made ours (as

for the *Popes Donatiue* of all *America* vnto him, that is sufficiently elleswhere answered, in a Discourse allready published by a most worthy Vndertaker) then hath any Christian Prince, (or then we or any other Prynce, maye haue to his *Mexico,* and *Peru,* or any dominions ells, of any free State, or Kingdome:) how neere soever the *West-Indies,* and *Florida,* may ioyne therevnto, and lye vnder the same portion of Heauen; with as great bravery, may we lay Clayme to all the Islandes, which the *Seignory* of *Venice* now holdes in the *Leuant Seas,* because *Ciprus* was once ours, by the Conquest of *Richard cœur de Lion,* and confynes with theirs, then which what more infirme, and ridiculous pretence could be framed? and yet is the king of *Spaines* argument to our Interest in *Virginia,* iust in this Mood and figure.[275]

Strachey dismissed the papal donation and Spain's claim to Virginia, saying that it was not necessary to spell this out as one of his own predecessors had already presented such an argument and asserting that if the king of Spain could make this case, then others could do the same for making incursions into Mexico, Peru, and other of his dominions, and by the same logic, England, based on its earlier possession of Cyprus, could make the ridiculous claim that this island belonged to it and not to Venice. Once again, Strachey attempted to reduce the arguments of those who would oppose the English colonization of Virginia, whether within England or without, to absurdity. Spain's domination of all the New World was, at least rhetorically, a laughing matter.

Strachey set out a sphere of influence argument based on a position that François I and Elizabeth I had taken years before, something I have discussed in earlier chapters. The English had left the Spanish alone on the North American continent, so Spain should leave England alone there:

No Prynce may lay clayme to any more amongst these new discoveryes (and so yt was heretofore, a iust distinction being therefore kept, between the king of *Castile* and *Portugall:*) then, what his People haue discouered, tooke actuall possession of, and passed over to his right; and noe otherwise from *Columbus,* doth the king of Spayne hold his strength, and dominions to this day, in his *golden Indies;* and no otherwise from *Soto,* his *Adelantado;* Concerning our neighbour *Florida;* and so we allow him, (without any one Inche of Intrusion:) both his Longitude, and Latitude, in this new world, we keeping from *Cape Florida,* Norward, to Cape *Briton;* the landes, countries and territories of this parte of *America,* which we call ours, and by the name of *Virginia,* or *Noua Britania,* being carefully layd out, of purpose, (to avoyd offence,) into certayne bowndes, and Regions.[276]

This kind of doctrine of *terra nullius* and the notion that possession occurs through occupying and using the land persisted for hundreds of years. Peaceful coexistence was the rhetorical aim of Strachey, whose colony of Virginia, was much more like the Huguenot colony that the Spanish had destroyed almost fifty years before than like the well-established Spanish settlements in the Americas to which the Virginia Company aspired. Although Ralegh, Hawkins, Drake, and others had harassed Spain in the New World, Strachey asserted elsewhere that the English did not come "neere any Land, in his [the king of Spain's] possession," something that may have been true in a narrow sense: Spain also knew the Chesapeake and had apparently given places Spanish names there.[277]

Having made an argument for peaceful coexistence and mutual respect of title through possession, Strachey then proceeded to undo it. He could not, like some other English and French writers, resist the urge to assert for the mother country, claims to "discovery" before Columbus:

> But what now, (concerning this point, for the more cleering of yt, to such who stumble thereat) yf we should say, that our right to the *West-Indies* themselues, (since they will needes awaken vs with pretence of Tytle) is as firme, proper, and far more ancyent then the Spaniards, and before the royall spiritted Lady *Isabella Princesse of Castile,* layd her Iewells to pawne, to *Lewis of St Angelo, the King her husbands secretarye* to forward the designe, and to prevent our *Kinge Henrye the 7th* (who was both offred, and accepted *Columbus* offer and entred into Capitulations with his brother *Bartholomewe* about them, *Anno 1489?* sure we should not want some pregnant Likelyhoodes, and those not only by our simple discoveryes, but by our planting, and Inhabiting them with the People of our owne Nation 400.yeares before Columbus had notice of them by the *Biscan pilot;* who, when he dwelt in the Islands of *Madera,* arrived with a Weather-beaten Caravell, and dying in his howse bequeathed (as they say) to *Columbus,* his Card of the discription of such new Landes as he had found: true yt is the first Shipps that *Columbus* carryed thither were but in *Anno* 1492. which is now sice 120. yeares, when let any man be but pleased to look into the learned and industryous Antiquities of Mr. *Camden.*[278]

The repetition was such here—we have witnessed it in earlier English writers on the New World—that the wistful tale about how Henry VII was about to make an agreement with Columbus only to lose out to the Spanish crown had become all too familiar. Here Strachey's rhetoric was stronger and more negative toward the Spanish than in similar descriptions among his contemporaries: Queen Isabella "prevented" the wise and accommodating Henry VII by pawning her jewels to send Columbus westward. In some earlier accounts, we have observed more blame being assigned to Henry VII and to their English ancestors for missing such an opportunity. Strachey then went on to talk about the claim of Madoc, the prince of North Wales sailing to the West Indies in 1170.

Despite this patriotic search for origins to underpin a new "British" empire, or at least to make room for a fledgling English colony in Virginia, Strachey could not avoid references to earlier Spanish feats and texts. For instance, he alluded to Francisco López de Gómara, who wrote *Historia general de las Indias* (1552–53) and whose translation by T. N., *The Pleasant Historie of the Conquest of the Weast India, now called new Spayne* (1578), I discussed in chapter 4.[279] Here Strachey attempted to undermine Spain with a prior "British" claim and

Columbus with Medoc while at the same time trying to argue for an accommodation between Spain and England—the north of America to the English and the south to the Spanish. There was, regarding Strachey's representation of Spain in the New World, a swaying back and forth between assertion and conciliation. He could not let go of prior English claims and repeated his argument with some variation:

> But this is materiall, and punctuall to our Hypothesis: *King Henry 7th* gaue his Letters Patents Anno 1495. vnto *Iohn Cabot,* a *Venetian,* (identized his subiect, and dwelling within *Black-friers*) and to his 3. sonnes, who discovered for the king, the north partes of *America,* to *Meta-incognita;* and annexed to the Crowne of England, all that great Tract of Land, stretching from the cape of *Florida,* vnto those partes Mayne and Islands, which we call the *New found Land,* some of which were not before knowne to *Columbus* nor afterwardes to *Nicuesa, Colmenaris,* nor *Vasquez Nunnez,* nor any of the *Castilians;* the draught of which Voyage, is yet to be seene in his Maiesties pryvie Gallery, in his Pallaice at *Westminster:* but the Tumults (say they who wrought of those tymes) then, and preparations for Warrs in *Scotland,* tooke away the seconding of that Enterprize, yet no whit tooke away (I hope) our Tytle, more then the king of Spayne may loos his, to those parts covered wit the same Heavens, which he neither fortefies nor planteth to this day.[280]

Caboto, or Cabot, became the means of making a claim based on discovery to what is now North America. One of the versions of Strachey's text underscored this claim according to the "discovery" in the reign of Henry VII and the nomenclature of maps in the era of Elizabeth I. In the British Museum manuscript, a marginal note appears beside Cabot's name in this passage: "John Cabot dicouers from Florida nor-ward to Meta Incognita, set out by King Henry the Seauenth."[281] Meta Incognita, as R. H. Major noted in the first Hakluyt Society edition, was "An indefinite name subsequently given to the north part of America by Queen Elizabeth upon the return of Frobisher from his second voyage, "as a marke and bound hitherto utterly unknowen."[282] In Strachey's text the king of Spain benefited from England's war with Scotland that distracted Henry VII from Columbus's enterprise.

Strachey could not leave the matter of Columbus alone, but what is most curious is that while having made an argument for the priority of Cabot on the American continent, he yielded the southern part of the continent to Columbus, who, as far as we know, never set foot on the mainland.

> So as, we may conclude then at least, that as *Christopher Columbus,* discovered the Islands, and Continent of the *West Indies* for *Spayne: Iohn,* and *Sebastian Cabot,* made discovery no lesse of the rest from *Florida* nor-ward, to the behoofe of *England,* being supported by the regall Aucthority, and sett forth at the Charge, and Expence of *King Henry the 7th;* and we hope th[at] they will leaue vnto vs, the same waie, and propriety, both to goe

vnto our owne, and hold yt by, as we giue them and if they will does soe (and all Lawes of Nations will assist vs herein) how vniust, and parciall shall that Subiect be, "etc. disloyal to king" as well may such a Traytor lay the Crowne of his Maiestie vpon the *Spaniardes* head.[283]

This is taking the spheres-of-influence argument—Spain in the south and England in the north—to contradictory lengths. Once again the double movement of assertion and conciliation occupied Strachey's account.

This ambivalence and contradiction between asserting England's right and admitting Spain's also occurred between parts of Strachey's text and not simply within paragraphs and brief passages. After the emphasis on Columbus, whose greatness had made Spain great, Strachey turned to Elizabeth I. Columbus could not have been subject to criticism because he was about to make an agreement (or had made one in some versions of the narrative) with Henry VII, and Elizabeth was the granddaughter of that wise king. Strachey was easier on Henry VII than were some of the English writers about the New World, although they were careful not to be too directly critical of that king. The heroic memory of Elizabeth and her explorers now became, for Strachey, a way of shoring up the Virginian enterprise:

> Her Maiestie of famous memory, so well vnderstood her princely right herin, (derived downe from her heroyick Grand-father to her self) as she graunted many large Pattents, and gratious Commissions, to divers gentle-men of birth, and quality; to inhabite those partes, and to keepe her Tytle quick, and panting still therein.[284]

Habitation meant possession, and that is why Elizabeth, whose heroism Strachey identified with that of her grandfather in this passage, commissioned great explorers to colonize the northern part of the American continent. Strachey combined the legal with the romance of exploration to praise Elizabeth as well as Gilbert, Ralegh, Grenville, Lane, and others. The contradictory message that Strachey was sending out involved a double standard: he talked about Drake sacking St. Domingo, Carthagena, and St. Augustine but warned that the Spanish had better not do the same.[285]

English representations of Spain in the New World became triangulated with representations of French relations with Spain in the Americas. Strachey warned Spain, and his English readers about Spain, through what might be called the lesson of Florida:

> and to avowe vnto the world, that if the Spaniard shall attempt vs at any time with ill measure, offring either to make surreption of our Shipps by the way thither, or to break into our Planations with acts of hostility (as most despightfully did Pedro Melendes, their Admirall, into the French-Colonie 44. yeares synce in *Noua Francia* who rased their fort, and hung vp the common Soldiers (Laudonnier the Generall, being straungely escaped) and wrought ver them disdeignefull Inscriptions in Spanish,

importing, *I doe not this as vnto Frenchmen, but as vnto Lutherans,* which Spanish crueltie was yet in the wynding vp, as bloudily revenged agayne, by Dominique de Gourgnes of Burdeux, who not long after arryving there, trussed vp the self-same Spaniards, vpon the boughes of the same Trees wherein they hung the french, with these wordes, *I doe not this as vnto Spaniards: But as vnto Tirants, and Murderers:*) now we are set downe here, how vniustly they shall proceed herein, and how much they shall lay themselues and their faythes open to the construction of all the nations, and peradventure to our Reuenge, which cannot strike weakly, which strikes with the sword of Iustice, in all quarrells the good successe of the same ever depending vpon the Innocency of the cause.[286]

Religious difference within Christianity, which became important after the Reformation in Europe, as I have argued, was not a sufficient means of describing how the authors of French and English texts about the New World represented Spain and its colonies. This incident supports my assertion. In 1565, Pedro Menéndez de Avilés destroyed the French Huguenot colony that René de Laudonière, under the command of Jean Ribault, established the previous year at Fort Caroline on the St. John's River in Florida: in 1568, Dominique de Gourges, a French soldier and sea captain, avenged the killing of the Huguenot colonists. Strachey showed a kind of typology of Florida, the Spanish commander insisting that the killing, which Strachey characterized as "cruelty," resulted because the victims were Lutherans and not Frenchmen, but Gourges, himself a Catholic, insisted that his victims died because they were tyrants and murderers and not because they were Spanish. The French response, as Strachey framed it, suggested a shift from religious motives in the initial killing that the Spaniards had perpetrated to revenge that the French enacted over the injustice that cruelty had caused. The French in Strachey's account, as in Le Challeux's earlier narrative, were innocents slaughtered: the English reader would not miss the biblical echoes. Strachey made an implicit typological identification between the tyrants of the Bible and the Spaniards on the one hand, and the innocents, like Christ, with the French on the other. This implied blame suggested the motives and blows of tyranny, which Christ himself had faced as the French had: the Spaniards were as Herod and Pilate. In establishing colonies in North America, the English should, as Strachey set out in the climax of his work, resist Spanish cruelty by learning about the woeful example of the French in Florida.

Without earlier Spanish writers about the New World, it would have been hard for those, like Strachey, to frame their narratives. Predecessors from Spain also haunted some of Johnson's and Strachey's contemporaries who were promoting Virginia: T. A.'s dedication to John Smith's *A Map of Virginia* (1612) is such an instance.[287] For now, the Spanish were spared the role of villain. Having often criticized the Spanish treatment of the Natives during the conquest of the New World, the English now found themselves in conflict with the inhabitants of America and in constructing narratives in which Natives desired to surrender their sovereignty to England. "The Proceedings of the English Colonie in Virginia . . . " by William Symonds, which was appended to Smith's work in one volume, portrayed the Natives and the Dutch as treacherous in their dealings with the English. The Dutch were said to have supported Powhatan, a chief, in the betrayal and attempted murder of John Smith.[288]

Smith made an ambiguous remark about "M. *Hakluyt*" (the ambiguity came from the syntax and punctuation), but he also continued to criticize Spain: "His Maiesty of *Spaine* permits none to passe the Popes order for the East and West *Indies,* but by his permission on, or at their perils. If all the world be so iustly theirs, it is no iniustice for *England* to make as much vse of her own shores as strangers do. . . ."[289] In the last paragraph of this work, a key passage for illustrating the shift from conquest to settlement, precious metals to staples, Smith, who elsewhere would imitate the heroic model of Cortés, exhorted his reader to read his *Description,* and whatever defects might be found there, the author claimed that he

> hath throwne my self with my mite into the Treasury of my Countries good, not doubting but God will stir vp some noble spirits to consider and examine if worthy *Collumbus* could giue the *Spaniards* any such certainties for his designe, when Queene *Isabel* of *Spaine* set him foorth with fifteene saile. And though I can promise no Mines of gold, yet the warlike *Hollanders* let vs imitate, but not hate, whose wealth and strength are good testimonies of their treasure gotten by fishing. Therefore (honorable and worthy Countrymen) let not the meanesse of the word *Fish* distaste you, for it will afford as good gold as the mines of *Guiana* or *Tumbatu,* with lesse hazard and charge, and more certaintie and facilitie; and so I humbly rest.[290]

Smith simultaneously used the example of Spain for inspiration for the bold vision and royal support of the Columbian enterprise and of colonization and discarded the Spanish model of precious metals for the Dutch instance, where wealth had been made from fishing.

Smith's *A Description of New England* (1616) had several dedications, and in the first, to Prince Charles, Smith spoke of changing "Barbarous names" for English ones, so in this practice the English were no different from the Spanish.[291] The styling of Smith as admiral imitated Columbus's title. The title of the book went on to mention "*the accidents that befell him among the French men of warre.*" Part of Smith's book consisted of the examination of his steward, Daniel Baker, who reported on English and French pirates, including the French attacks on Spanish ships.[292] Smith said that the Spanish would not abide French trade in the West Indies.[293]

The prefatory poems sang the praises of Smith, Virginia, and expansion. In a poem in which the initial letters of the lines spell IOHN SMITHE, N. Smith addressed his friend and cousin and declared a theme similar to Robert Johnson's call for an expanding England: "*S*'ith thou, the man, deseruing of these Ages,/ *M*uch paine hast ta'en for this our Kingdoms good,/ *I*n Climes vnknowne, Mongst *Turks* and Saluages,/ *T*inlarge our bounds."[294] George

Wither raised Spain more explicitly: "And the spatious *West* / Being still more with *English* blood possest,/ The Proud *Iberians* shall not rule those Seas,/ To checke our ships from sayling where they please;/ Nor future times make any forraine power/ Become so great to force a bound to *Our*."[295] In the body of Smith's *Description* the French appeared on the first page and on the second he situated New England between New France in the south and Virginia and New Spain in the north. An impetus to writing the book were questions Smith was habitually asked about the spaciousness of these lands and "how they can bee thus long vnknown, or not possessed by the *Spaniard*."[296] The theme of the vastness of America led Smith to say how much people erred who thought that all those who travelled to Virginia knew it, "Or that the *Spaniards* know one halfe quarter of those Territories they possesse; . . . It is strange with what small power hee hath raigned in the *East Indies;* and few will vnderstand the truth of his strength in *America:* where he hauing so much to keepe with such a pampered force, they neede not greatly feare his furie, in the *Bermudas, Virginia, New France,* or *New England*."[297] With the memory of the French demise in Florida and the previous conflicts between Spain and England in the West Indies still circulating, Smith may have been hoping that he was right, trying to appease potential investors and emigrants or reporting one Spanish blind spot—the inability to expand northward rapidly enough to keep the French and English out of North America. He praised Henry Hudson's discovery in the north, "the greatest discouerie of any I know of, where he vnfortunately died."[298] While showing grudging admiration for the Spanish, making a strength from a weakness, Smith used a superlative to transform an "English" failure—Hudson's—to eclipse the accomplishment of Spain in America. In this passage, however, Spain and England supplemented each other. The Portuguese success in Africa was another example that Smith called upon in this passage.[299] To be a colonizer one must have at least the following qualities: "Art, Iudgement, Courage, Honesty, Constancy, Dilligence and Industrie."[300] A few pages later, he set out the laudable example of the "poore Hollanders" who had made themselves rich through trade and hard work.[301] Men should not be misemployed and misplaced in such colonization, which brought this admiral back to the original one—Columbus. Smith saw himself and future English colonizers as following the model of Spain. Smith wrote:

> *Columbus, Cortez, Pitzara, Soto, Magellanes,* and the rest serued more then a prentiship to learne how to begin their most memorable attempts in the *West Indies:* which to the wonder of all ages succesfully they effected, when many hundreds of others farre aboue them in the worlds opinion, beeing instructed but by relation, came to shame and confusion in actions of small moment, who doubtlesse in other matters, were both wise, discreet, generous, and couragious. I say not this to detract any thing from their incomparable merits, but to answer those questionlesse questions that keep vs back from imitating the worthinesse of their braue spirits that advaunced themselues from poore Souldiers to great Captaines, their pos-

terity to great Lords, their King to be one of the greatest Potentates on earth, and the fruites of their labours, his greatest glory, power and renowne.[302]

Columbus made another appearance as a bold visionary.[303] Smith called attention to the notion of imitation. The class mobility, skill as soldiers and captains, and the memory of their great glory as servants to the king of Spain all presented Smith with a personal and national model. America would allow scope to men of merit and daring. As great as Hudson might have been, these Spaniards led by the example of their fame and success.

The example of Cortés was part of the exempla in another tract on Virginia, which, after praising the soil, climate, government, godly and good people, asked: "Why should the successe (by the rules of morall iudgement) be despaired? Why should not the rich haruest of our hopes be seasonably expected? I dare say, that the resolution of *Caesar* in Fraunce, the designes of *Alexander* in Greece, the discoueries of *Hernando Cortes* in the West, and of *Emanuel* of Portugale in the East, were not vpon so firme grounds of state and possibility."[304] This was another of the promotional works of the Council of Virginia. The mixture of classical and Iberian examples of empire were common in the English narratives of the New World at this time.

The Pilgrims and Puritans were not as apt to follow this example as the Virginians, but even Plymouth would have its strangers and soldiers like Miles Standish and Stephen Hopkins. As late as 1630, however, John White used the example of Spain to justify English colonies in New England:

> As for the enlargement of Trade; which drew on the *Spanish* and *Dutch* Colonies in the East *Indies,* or securing of conquered Countries, which occasioned many Colonies of the *Romanes* in *Italy* and other lands, they may bee so farre warranted, as the grounds of the Conquests, or Trades were warrantable; (if they were caried without injury or wrong to the natives) seeing naturall commerce betweene nations, and Conquests upon just warres, have beene alwayes approved by the Lawes of God and man.[305]

The title alone—*The Planter's Plea. Or the Grounds of Plantations Examined, and Vsuall Objections Answered. Together with a Manifestation of the Causes Mooving Such as Have Lately Undertaken a Plantation in New-England: for the Satisfaction of Those That Question the Lawfulnesse of the Action*—showed the defensiveness of colonizers about the legality and justice of imperial expansion and settling among the Natives. Even the Puritans used the example of Rome, of *translatio imperii,* to justify their settlements. White employed the now-familiar argument of overpopulation and unemployment to justify English colonization in New England.[306] He also said that "before our breach with *Spaine*" England sent out 40 or 50 fishing ships to New England each year.[307] Some of the fish from New England went to Spain.[308] Although at the beginning of his work White sought out the precedent of Spanish settlement to justify his own colony, at the end he could not avoid an attack on its Catholicism: "Why may not wee conceive that

God may prevaile upon the hearts of his servants, to set them on as effectually to seeke the inlargement of his kingdome; as a blind zeale fomented by the art and subtilitie of Satan may thrust on Priests and Iesuites, and their partisans, to engage their persons and estates for advancing of the Devils Kingdome?"[309] In the midst of a discussion of land grants, White attacked the "Popish partie" at the end of his book.[310] Thomas Morton could be quite satirical in his assessment of the settlers in Plymouth and New England. At one point, Morton likened the separatists to Don Quixote tilting against the windmill as they tried to ostracize Morton's host, "the supposed Monster (this seaven headed hydra, as they termed him)."[311] Morton adapted the device from a recent Spanish novel to satirize the excesses of intolerance in New England.

Even though Smith was describing the commodities of New England that made it ripe for colonization, he did so in the context of troubles with the French and his praise for Columbus and Spain. After the heading, "The blisse of Spaine," which was indented in the left margin, Smith praised the Spanish:

> Who seeth not what is the greatest good of the *Spanyard,* but these new conclusions, in searching those vnknowne parts of this vnknowne world? By which meanes hee diues euen into the verie secrets of all his Neighbours, and the most part of the world: and when the *Portugale* and *Spanyard* had found the *East* and *West Indies;* how many did condemn themselues, that did not accept of that honest offer of Noble *Columbus?* who, vpon our neglect, brought them to it, perswading our selues the world had no such places as they had found: and yet euer since wee finde, they still (from time to time) haue found new Lands, new Nations, and trades, and still daily dooe finde both in *Asia, Africa, Terra incognita,* and *America.*[312]

Not since Eden was there such a critique of English colonization in view of the accomplishment of Spain. Smith did stress the many times the English had censured themselves for not taking up Columbus's offer, but seldom did an Englishman show such high regard for Spain. Smith's ambivalence was often directed toward the English failures in colonization. He was not impressed by the way the English persuaded themselves that the world was not as Spain had discovered and mapped it. There was no sense, Smith implied, in denying the present positive example of Spanish exploration. Rather, it was better to emulate the success of the Spaniards.

Like Gilbert and Hakluyt, Smith saw full employment through overseas expansion and trade, but unlike them, he was unabashed in offering Spain as his model for this economic triumph.[313] Smith thought that England was better able to spare people for emigration than Spain was. If Spain had not sent out thousands of people of all kinds, they would have caused trouble for their neighbors "or haue eaten the pride of *Spaine* it selfe."[314] He chastised the English for dullness and challenged them to give up "the titles and honours of their predecessors," the shows and shadows, idleness, and vice, for "honor, by heroycall deeds of action, iudgement, pietie, and vertue" in the New World.[315] This appeal

to the honor of classical epics and medieval and early modern romances—a
courage exemplified in Cortés—would be available to men who followed Smith
to America.

The one reservation Smith expressed about Spain was its Catholicism, but he
used that qualm as a way of goading England to follow the Spanish in missionary work: "Religion, aboue all things, should moue vs (especially the Clergie) if
wee were religious, to shewe our faith by our workes; in conuerting those poore
saluages, to the knowledge of God, seeing what paines the *Spanyards* take to
bring them to their adulterated faith."[316] In "Discourse" Hakluyt had hoped for
such a religious mission, but he was less sardonic about his countrymen than
Smith was and less tolerant of Catholics.[317] Smith exhorted his countrymen to
leave idleness and to work hard, so that they would achieve much in America
for their king, their nation and themselves rather than serve Portugal, Spain,
Holland, France, and Turkey because these countries were more enterprising.[318]
This rhetoric of blame, insult, and challenge to encourage investment and emigrants was a precarious strategy.

Having provided the heroic model of Spain as something to follow, Smith
now looked for other ways to attract support. He wanted to account for failure
and hardship and regular citizens as being part of successful colonization: "All
the *Romanes* were not *Scipioes:* nor all the *Geneweses, Columbuses:* nor all *Spanyards, Corteses:* had they diued no deeper in the secrets of their discoueries, then
wee, or stopped at such doubts and poore accidentall chances; they had neuer
beene remembered as they are."[319] Daring to know and persist would make the
English colonies succeed: giving into their surface failures would only ensure
their failure. But Smith returned to heroic action as a means of ending his book.
The greatest princes were known in histories for "planting of countries, and
ciuilizing barbarous and inhumane Nations, to ciuilitie and humanitie."[320] Part
of Smith's challenge to his English readers was that they should win the esteem
of Portugal and Spain: "Lastly, the *Portugales,* and *Spanyards:* whose euerliuing
actions, before our eyes will testifie with them our idlenesse, and ingratitude to
all posterities, and the neglect of our duties in our pietie and religion we owe
our God, our King, and Countrie; and of want of charity to those poore saluages, whose Countrie wee challenge, vse and possesse."[321] This lack of pastoral
mission and heroic actions would prevent the English from being included in
the glory of the memory of history. Good actions would lead to honor, which was
the ambition of the English, whose "honourable memorie" would be preserved
should they imitate the virtues of their predecessors in order to be their worthy
successors.[322] Smith set out this course in a context in which detractors were
doubting and criticizing Virginia. If there was a little defensiveness to his rhetoric,
the circumstances in Virginia, much more protracted than those that faced Cortés,
were precarious and required as much promotional work as possible.

Samuel Purchas, who, unlike Smith, almost certainly did not model himself
on Cortés, translated or reworked translations of Spanish works in Hakluyt's
papers but did not do so in chronological order.[323] Purchas included "A Note
touching the Dutch" in his prefatory matter, where he declared:

Some perhaps will blame me for relating some Truths, specially the Dutch Zelots, in that I have related such abuses of some of that Nation in the East Indes and Greenland to the English there, as if I sought like an unseasonable and uncharitable Tale-bearer to raise discord betwixt Neighbours. I answere that no Nation is in this World so pure, but hath both officious members, and some bad members also as Diseases thereof; which to impute to the whole, were as if a man should kill himselfe a felon in his Thumbe. . . . [324]

The same logic, which Purchas also applied to England, could be applied to Spain as well. Purchas's editions grew: the prefatory matter of the 1613 edition emphasized almost exclusively the religious dimension of English colonization. He began with Antonio de Herrera's description of the West Indies (1601), noting that Hakluyt's unpublished translation was so literal it was sometimes obscure and senseless and said that he had corrected and polished after consulting Latin, Spanish, and French originals of the work and had not contracted, which Purchas often did, because he considered it important in setting out Spanish-Indian affairs and settlements. Hakluyt's translation was preserved, though it represented a selection of Herrera's eight decades. Purchas presented the dedication of Herrera, the king of Spain's chief chronicler of the Indies and his chronicler of Castile, to the president of the royal and supreme council of the Indies, a preface that celebrated the role of the chronicler and the president as fostering the recording of the deeds of the Spaniards in the Indies worthy of memory.

The example of Spain was disputed not simply along national lines but also according to what kind of historiography was best. Herrera defended the traditional role of the chronicler as someone who recorded noble deeds, who acted as the memory for the famous victories of the great. The Spanish conquest of the New World was renowned in even barbarous nations, so that "your Lordship shall be praysed eternally, and thanked of all that are interested in it."[325] Purchas's marginal note did not quarrel with this Ciceronian view of history as an example of perpetual memory of moral deeds, but declared, "*Ramusio uncharitable taxed: for he doth blame the folly of Spanish Authors*" who are more apt to record the name of Spaniards in the Indies who have done nothing but take part in rebellions rather than a description of the natural history "*in the Indies: for which hee there commends Oviedo.*"[326] Whether Cicero or Pliny was the right authority was a question that crossed the borders of Spain, Italy, England, and France, where Ramusio was also influential. Purchas did represent this natural history in his collection as he included selections by Acosta and Oviedo. From Acosta, the English reader would learn about the riches of the silver mines at Potosí, the quicksilver mines, and the abundance of pearls.[327]

Using different historiographical methods, Purchas collected a variety of representations by Spanish historians. In Gómara, Purchas's reprint of Thomas Nicholas's translation of 1578, readers would find the story of the conquest led by Cortés.[328] Although Purchas was encyclopedic and reflected pro-Spanish and

anti-Spanish sentiments in his vast collection, he did not shy away from
indulging in Protestant ideological verbal attacks against the Catholic church
and from making some use of Las Casas. In the context of continued anxiety
over the myth of origins and the papal authority behind the Spanish empire,
Purchas first referred to Las Casas. The compiler presented a commentary on the
papal donation of 1493, which gave Spain the New World, which he reprinted
and which, he noted, Gómara and Richard Eden had included in their work.
Purchas called on divine Providence, Seneca, and Cicero (history as the only life
of memory) as he began his attack on the bull and the papacy that issued it. By
choosing the name Alexander, Rodericus Borgia, a Spaniard, sent out the wrong
signals and embodied the wrong kind of translation of empire, becoming with
his bull like Alexander the Great, a pirate. Purchas then proceeded to identify
the corruption of Alexander VI with the corrupt nature of the papacy, calling
him at one point in the fashion of an *ad hominem* abusive attack, "the Monster
of men" or "an incarnate Devill."[329] This Alexander, as Purchas claimed in his
Ciceronian gloss of the etymology of "conversion," would convert the world to
Christianity by sweeping the world of men, turning the converted into the children of hell as the Indians testified.[330] The rhetorical strategy here was to attack
the papacy and the pope who gave Spain authority to colonize the New World
and so to attack Spain indirectly. Purchas made that clear:

> I question not the Right of the Spanish Crowne in those parts: Quis me
> constituit judicem? It is the fault I find in this great Ardelio. The Castilian
> Industry I honour (as appeares in the former Relations) their right may,
> for that which is actually in their Possession, without this Bull, plead Dis-
> coverie even before this was written, the Sword, Prescription, subjection
> of the Inhabitants, long and quiet Possession; which, howsoever the Case
> was at first (wherewith I meddle not) must now, after so long Succession,
> be acknowledged Just. I quarrell the Pope only, and the Clayme of that
> See, herein truly Catholike, or Universall, challenging in the Devils
> Stile. . . .[331]

And that style is baroque. This Protestant allegory spun clause after qualifying
clause (using parentheses as additional qualifications) as Latin illustrated English
claims in English in an insubordinate, that was heretical, subordination in grammar but not in theological terms.

After pages of learned polemics and invective, bolstered with biblical typology and legal argument, Purchas quoted Vitoria, "a Spanish divine," to prove
that the pope had no authority in temporal matters and that the donation of
1493 was void. Vitoria's proofs supported Purchas's following propositions:
"That the Pope is not Lord of the World, That the Temporall Power depends not
of him. . . ." The passage continued:

> That it is not subject to his Temporall Power, and that he hath nothing to
> doe ordinarily to judge of Princes Cases, Titles, Jurisdictions, nor hath any
> Power meerely Temporall; That the Temporall Power doth not depend of

the Spirituall. And in his Relections of the Indians he sayth, That it doth not appeare to him, that the Christian Faith hath so beene preached to them, that they are bound sub novo peccato to beleeve it, having had no probable perswasion, as Miracles and examples of Religious life, but the contrairie.[332]

By attacking the origins of Spanish authority, Purchas hoped to give more room to English colonization. Possession, as François I and Elizabeth I had argued and so many of their advisors, promoters, and colonizers had also held, was based on discovery, conquest, and settlement and not on a papal bull. For more than two centuries, through their books, decrees, and pronouncements, France and England spoke to themselves, to Spain, and to Europe, trying to have the Spanish admit that there was no basis to the papal donations of the 1490s. Much of this rhetoric was to clear the way for trade and settlement to the benefit and even the advantage of England and France, over Spain. Purchas asserted "that had not the pietie and pittie of some eye-witnesses excited the Royall Provision of the Catholike Kings in this case (which over so wide Seas and spacious Lands they could not discerne) even Hell it selfe had beene loosed on Earth, under the pretext of Heaven, and the Prince of Darknesse had effected his blackest and cruellest Designes, in habite of an Angell of Light."[333] This eschatology led Purchas from Vitoria's legal pronouncements to Las Casas's moral indignation.

From Las Casas, amid this ornate style, Purchas in an address to the reader seized on the image of the Spanish having their dogs hunt and devour the Natives.[334] Purchas followed a well-established tradition in France and England of having Spaniards testify against their nation in a hypothetical case about the right of Spain to its monopoly and a judgment of its empire: "After so many other Spanish Discourses and Discoveries, I have added for a Spanish farewell this of Bartholomew de las Casas a zealous Dominican Frier, after made Bishop of Chiapa, touching the excesses committed by some Spaniards in the Continent and Ilands of America."[335] Purchas did not miss this occasion to point out the irony that "the godly zeale of converting soules to Jesus Christ from the power of Ethnike darknesse, was hindered by a worse darknesse, which was hindered by a worse darknesse in those who proclaimed themselves children of Light, and had the name and Sacraments of Christians."[336] Although he was careful to use "some" and not "all" Spaniards, as he had in the case of the Dutch, Purchas still used this abuse of the Spanish mission in the New World to say that the Spanish had not fulfilled the role the pope had given them in his bull. Nonetheless, Purchas complicated the representation further because he then turned to this view that Las Casas, the emperor, and other Spaniards deserved praise for the reform of the laws and that "evill manners" produced "good Lawes"; Purchas said that he had recorded evil acts by Spaniards, Portuguese, Dutch, and English in their quarrels among one another.[337] He also stated that he found virtue in Catholics.

Finding Las Casas's rhetoric extreme, full of "fiery tearmes, . . . blackest Inke, and most Hyperbolicall Phrases," Purchas "left out many many invectives and bitter Epithetes of this Author, abridging him after my wont, and lopping of such superfluities, which rather were the fruit of his zeale, then the flowre of his History."[338] Having deleted a third of Las Casas's text, Purchas seemed to have criticized the Spaniards for wrongly executing the Natives on exaggerated charges of man-eating, sodomy, and idolatry but then, in his baroque style, muddied the issue or turned it on its head with a conceit: he said that the Spaniards' injustice was "most just in regard of God, which knoweth how to punish sinne by sinne, by Sinners."[339] Purchas mentioned that he was using the English edition of 1583, "when as peace was yet betwixt England and Spaine," and he included a summary of the debate between Las Casas and Sepúlveda in 1551, in which, in the marginal notes, Purchas discredited Sepúlveda's appeal to the papal bull and amplified Las Casas's description of millions of Native dead through condensing and listing the huge numbers for many places.[340] Purchas clearly took sides: "Sepúlveda coloureth his Treatise" under the pretense of the titles of the kings of Castile and Leon to "universall sovereigntie of this Indian world."[341] Moreover, Purchas also described the French piracy, discoveries, the right of England, not France, to North America (mistakenly attributed to Sebastian Cabot) and the demise of the French in Florida.

Purchas, like John Smith, was not a one-dimensional figure and not simply a Protestant zealot or an editor who promoted dominating or cheating the Natives: he professed to go beyond stereotypes and to have achieved objectivity, and this claim, while exaggerated, had some truth to it.[342] The very qualification of Purchas's allusive, periphrastic, and baroque style embodied a content that was deferred, ambivalent, and self-opposing.

Some writers, like Thomas Scott, were far more direct and one-sided in their depiction of Spain than Purchas was. Anti-Spanish sentiment in England persisted and coincided with the Pilgrims' voyage to the New World as well as the publication of *Purchas His Pilgrims*. One of the best instances of this negative use of the example of Spain was the work of the prolific Scott during the 1620s. I am referring to a few of Scott's texts only. His anti-Spanish and anti-Catholic propaganda included *An Experimentall Discoverie of Spanish Practises or the Counsell of a Well-Wishing Souldier* ([London], 1623); *A Second Part of Spanish Practises. Or, a Relation of More Plots* [attributed to Scott, but the attribution is contested]; *Certaine Reasons and Arguments of Policie, Why the King of England Should Enter into Warre with the Spaniard* ([London], 1624); *England's Joy, for Suppressing the Papists, and Banishing the Priests and Jesuites* ([London?], 1624). His *Vox Popvli* (1620), an apparent translation of an unnamed Spanish source, was a dialogue that represented a meeting the king of Spain called upon the return of Gondomar, his ambassador to England. Gondamar represented the resistance of his king and country to English expansion: "As for the West Indian voyages, I withstand them in earnst because they begin to inhabit there and to fortifie themselves; and may in tyme there perhaps raise an other England to withstand our new Spaine in America, as this old England opposeth our present State, and cloudes the glorious extent therof in Europe."[343] In *The Second Part of Vox Popvli* (1624) Scott continued to demonize Gondomar.[344]

As in the days of the marriage between Mary and Philip, a match between England and Spain intensified anti-Spanish feelings in England, only this time the rhetoric was even more virulent because the propaganda surrounding Spain in the New World and the Netherlands, often using and abusing Las Casas as a source, created a framework and a vocabulary undeveloped during the 1550s. The very end of the book included Thomas Scott's letter to parliament in which he talked about "Spanish abuses" and attempted to rouse "our Brittaine so famous of ould, for her triumphes and many victories over other nations" not "to care a strawe for the vaine and windy threats of proude Spain."[345] Scott's *The Spaniards Perpetvall Designes to an Vniversall Monarchie. Translated According to the French* included an argument against the Treaty of Marriage and the French fear of being surrounded by Spanish possessions.[346] On the opening page of *Sir VValter Ravvleigh's Ghost,* (1626) Scott presented Gondomar as an archenemy to England and a fox. On page 2, Scott characterized England as a jewel Spain had long set its heart on for its universal monarchy.[347] The ghost of Ralegh appeared to Gondomar.[348] Ralegh's sword might, had Gondomar not taken off its edge with his subtleties, "neere made a new conquest of the West Indies."[349] Scott's representation also called attention to Spanish ambition: for instance, Ralegh warned Britain of this universal monarchy and protected Charles I from Gondomar before he vanished to King James from Spain, which is also called cruel.[350] This lexicon and structure of discourse allowed for writers like Thomas Scott to vent their spleen in the service of the Protestant cause.

Other texts concerned themselves with Spain. While there is not space to discuss all these texts in detail as we have with key works, I would like to call attention to a few. Francis Bacon's *Considerations Touching a Warre with Spaine,* in *Certaine Micellany Works . . .* (London, 1629), discussed English exploits against Spain in the Caribbean (it was translated into French in 1634 and Italian in 1641). James Wadsworth's *The Present Estate of Spayne, or a True Relation of Some Remarkable Things Touching the Court and Government of Spayne* (London, 1630) mentioned offices in Spanish America and who held them. John White's *The Planters Plea . . .* (London, 1630), which I have mentioned earlier in this chapter, advocated a plantation in New England. Thomas Nash's *Quaternio, or A Fourefold Way to a Happie Life* (London, 1633) referred to tobacco, Columbus, and the northwest passage. In *A Petition of W. C. Exhibited to the High Court of Parliament Now Assembled, for the Propagating of the Gospel in America, and the West Indies* ([London], 1641), William Castell created a work that reflected the growing tensions over the Christianization of the Natives between Protestants and Catholics. The issue of religion was still unresolved in English colonization, but these conflicts were vital on the Continent and in the Americas.

V

Although it is necessary to focus on the New World in this study, I cannot avoid discussing Spanish involvement in the Netherlands when it affected the English and French use of the example of Spain in America. Many of the translations about Spain appeared in the Netherlands during its revolt against Spain from 1565 to 1608, so that this was yet another way that the rebellion affected the relation of the French and English with the Spanish. Nonetheless there is no better example of this typology between the actions of Spain in the New World and in the Netherlands than the translations of Las Casas that I will now discuss.

This typology developed as the Revolt of the Netherlands became more bitter, so that some background might serve as a reminder of this view of Spain as a cruel and unjust power in America and Europe. In 1576, the year after Philip II declared the Spanish treasury bankrupt, and after 22 months without pay, his soldiers mutinied and sacked Antwerp, killing 7,000 people. This was a turning point in the succession of Holland and Zeeland. In stereotyping the Spaniards, the propagandists and pamphleteers were not so balanced as Sir Roger Williams, who noted that the atrocities at Waterlant and Rotterdam happened under the command of Walloon noblemen; he also served the Spaniards.[351] They also neglected the tortures that Lumey de la Marck, leader of the Sea Beggars, personally undertook or the terror his followers visited on their own people. In 1573, about 14.5 percent of the royal army in the Netherlands was Spanish and about 56 percent was made up of Netherlanders.[352] American silver could not pay for the Spanish wars in Europe. The Spaniards might have been leaders in the reign of terror, but they did not act alone: bitter religious and ethnic division began to manifest itself in this revolt and civil war.

George Gascoigne, who later wrote a preface to Humphrey Gilbert's *Discourse,* was present at the sack of Antwerp, a city with strong ties to the English woolen trade, and recorded the atrocities committed by an entirely Spanish party of soldiers. His pamphlet was later made into a brief play, which even returned the duke of Alba to the scene to take part in the pillage. Gascoigne represented the European dimension of the Black Legend: "It is then to be understoode that the sacking & spoyle of ANTWERPE hath been (by all lykelyhoode) longe pretended by the Spanyerds' and he speaks about "theyr mallicious and cruelle intente."[353] Gascoigne was ambivalent, caught between Spanish victory and Spanish cruelty : "Apittifull massacre though God gaue victory to the Spanyerdes. And surely, as their vallyaunce was to be much commended, so yet I can much discommende their barbarous cruelty, in many respectes."[354] Gascoigne made the cruelty of Spain a lesson to the honor of England: "Let vs also learne to detest the horrible crueltics of the Spanyerdes in all executions of warlike stratagemes, least the dishonour of such beastly deedes, might bedymme the honour wherewith Englishe Souldiours haue alwayes bene endowed in theyr victories."[355] The assassination of William the Silent, prince of Orange, and the leader of the rebels in the Netherlands, brought England closer to the conflict with Spain. All the while this war in the Netherlands took place on the northern borders of France.

One of the drains on the power of Spain, then, was the so-called Dutch Revolt, the uprising of the Netherlands against the Spanish from about 1565 onward, about the time of the Spanish destruction of the Huguenots in Florida. The duke of Alva became a means of attacking Philip II and was a centerpiece of the Black Legend of Spain in the Netherlands: "he put to death or drove away innumerable other nobles and excellent citizens so as to be able to confiscate their goods; he lodged common Spanish soldiers in the houses of the other inhabitants and these molested them, their wives and children and damaged their property."[356] The political treatises of France and the Netherlands influenced each other, often sharing a Protestant perspective, especially the view that kings reign from God but by the people and that the representatives of the people have the right to resist a prince who had broken the law of nature and the terms of the contract for his appointment. This view can be found in Junius Brutus, *Vindicae contra tyrannos* (1579), which Martin van Gelderen maintains was a pseudonym for one of the leading Huguenot thinkers, Philippe Duplessis-Mornay.[357]

On July 22, 1581, the States General of the United Netherlands passed an edict declaring that the king of Spain had forfeited sovereignty of the Netherlands, where he had had his investiture in 1549. The edict, which reviewed past wrongs almost over the previous two decades, blamed the Council of Spain for misleading the king because its members envied the wealth of the Netherlands and were excluded from office there unlike in Naples, Sicily, Milan, and the Indies and wanted their sovereign to conquer the Low Countries and rule absolutely over them with no regard to their ancient liberties. This document also cited a letter from the Spanish ambassador in France to the duchess of Parma in 1566 that said that the Council had been seeking to revoke those privileges and to have the Netherlands "tyrannically governed by Spaniards like the Indies and newly conquered countries."[358] The duke of Anjou was to replace the king of Spain as sovereign of the Low Countries.

This policy, formulated by William of Orange, was not popular, for in some parts of the country France was more resented than Spain, and Anjou made it difficult to implement as he tried to take Antwerp and other towns in January 1583.[359] In this 80–year struggle with Spain, the Dutch themselves influenced England. In 1585, Queen Elizabeth reluctantly came to the aid of the Netherlands.[360] Ironically, the Spanish Netherlands eventually became a buffer that the Dutch wished to maintain against an expansionist France. Despite its trade deals with Spain after 1661, Holland was reluctant to ally itself militarily with Spain until the alliance against France in 1672.[361]

France and England worked out their relations to Spain partly through the Netherlands. Las Casas was translated to consolidate a typology between the cruelty of Spain in the New World and in the Netherlands. The shift in the balance of power in Europe and in its colonies affected the views of Spain among the English, French, and Dutch. During the 1620s and 1630s, Protestants writing in French represented the Black Legend while the French Recollets and Jesuits often sought out the example of Spanish missions in the New World and elsewhere.

Las Casas was reprinted in French in 1620 and 1630, the first appearing in Amsterdam without any prefatory matter, including the author's, and the second in Rouen, which reproduced almost all the material from the Miggrode editions of the 1580s, except the "Extract of the Privilege."[362] The year the English Pilgrims were sailing from Holland, a French edition of Las Casas appeared there, relying largely on copper plates to tell a pictorial story of torture and cruelty, on the title page and throughout the text. The publisher, Jean Everhardts Cloppenburch, presented a typology of Spanish cruelty. He included two title pages set up with in identical ways with the same pictures. The first, which introduced the first part of the book, was on the Low Countries and the second, about halfway through the volume, was about the New World and preceded Las Casas's account. Only the writing in the center of each title page differed, although the second echoed the first. The pictures surrounded the title. Pictures of torture and cruelty to men, women, and children were about Philip, who presided top and center above the title; his vassals, Don John (to the king's left and to the reader's right) and the duke of Alva (on the other side), faced the title: the Spanish cruelty in the Netherlands was parallel to that in the New World. The reader traveled back from Spanish atrocities in Europe to those that had occurred earlier in the New World. As Christians read the Old Testament through the New, they were asked to see the Old World through the New: this is the central typology we have been discussing. The first title page introduced this visual propaganda of scenes of Spanish brutality, again typologically arranged to show that Spain was the universal tyrant and ill-treated the Dutch as it had the Natives.[363]

In the address to the reader in the first part, Cloppenburch said that the Spanish had perpetrated war and tyranny in the Low Countries under the pretext of a change in religion, calling the inhabitants heretics and Lutherans, disobedient to the king of Spain, and saying that a hundred years before they had done the same in the Indies, claiming that the people there were pagans, idolaters, dishonest and unreasonable people, invokers of devils. The king of Spain had tried to revoke the privileges and liberty of the Netherlands, and while the Protestants there attempted to negotiate, the king used force against them. The duke of Alba ruined everything by tyranny and war, and all those who were not totally Catholic ("totalement Catholiques"), Cloppenburch asserted, were considered heretics and were burned, drowned, strangled, killed in prison.[364] After giving a list of tyrants who served the Habsburgs (Spanish and Austrian) in the Netherlands, he shifted to the New World. Cloppenburch, who wanted "to make known to the inhabitants of the world the cruelty of the Spaniards," said that the second part of the book touched on "the cruelties committed in the West Indies, and principally in the islands at the beginning of the entrance of the Spaniards" and asserted that the Spanish mishandled "innocent and benign peoples."[365] He gave these events in the New World a providential and typological reading. God had tested the people of the Low Countries with this tyranny and cruelty in order to deliver them with grace from the Spaniards.

Cloppenburch then introduced Las Casas as a holy Catholic bishop: "he wrote this book with a great Zeal, like a Christian, to prevent cruelty and tyranny, committed by the Spanish in the West Indies."[366] Las Casas, the author noted, addressed his work to the Emperor Charles and his son Philip to stop the cruelty. The emperor issued ordinances for the better treatment of the Natives, but the tyrants remained and scornfully continued the massacres in search of the gold and silver with which they vexed the world. The connection between parts one and two, the Netherlands and the Indies, was that the kings of Spain had not learned the lesson Las Casas was trying to teach them. Cloppenburch ended his address with a plea: "I beg of you Reader to read it, & re-read it, so that you can flee Tyranny & take up arms against such Tyrants, wanting to tyrannize everywhere: In closing I commend you to the grace of God, asking him to give you salvation and happiness."[367] The call to arms for liberty was also a call in the name of the grace of God that would deliver them. In some of the engravings of Spanish cruelty in the Netherlands, the inhabitants were naked, like the Natives in the second part of the book (which comes after, but in it Las Casas described an earlier time than the Revolt of the Netherlands). The images, which are often striking, supplemented the appeal to emotion.

A few more editions of Las Casas appeared in the period before 1713. The Rouen version of 1630, as mentioned, reproduced Miggrode's translation, demonstrating some demand for anti-Spanish tracts in France even after the Wars of Religion.[368] Like the edition of 1630, that of 1642 (also published in Rouen) featured Las Casas on the title page, but it was a different translation and presented its own brief preface. The editor began the "Preface to the Reader," which faces the "Approbation" that gave the permission of the Catholic church and the "Permission" that granted the king of France's approval, with an attack on Spain: "FRIEND READER, Perhaps in reading this Book and seeing the inhuman cruelties practised by the Spaniards (who call themselves good Christians and Catholics) you will call into question the truth of this History, attributing it to a fabulous invention and to the imposture of some Spirit passionate against this Nation. To which I respond that you must not in any way doubt it and so receive this narrative as very certain and true."[369] Like Cloppenburch, the editor addressed the reader with the familiar "tu." He gave three reasons for the narrative being true. First, he established the credentials of an honest, virtuous religious Las Casas of great reputation, who spent 40 years in the West Indies administering to and converting the Indians and whom the king of Spain made a bishop in New Spain; Las Casas represented with Christian compassion the cruel and inhumane treatment of the poor Indians ("pauures Indiens") to Prince Philip, later the king, that occurred in these conquests.[370] Notwithstanding the Inquisition, he published his history in 1542 (actually in 1552) and presented it to the king, who had all the copies seized, fearing that his subjects' actions in the New World would appear to everyone. God, according to the editor, permitted a few copies to escape the king's grasp. He noted how the book was translated and appeared throughout Western Europe: "The Dutch at once translated the Book into their language word for word, and in the French language. The Venetians also put it into Italian, and it spread through Italy to Spain in one volume."[371] Second, the Dominican order so esteemed Las Casas that it wrote a biography of him. The editor took this estimation and publication as a sign that the contents of Las Casas's work were still true, so that the Spanish were still the same, "& that by their inhumanity, cruelty, evil life, they have rendered the name *Christian* so odious that the Indians believe that to be Christian was to be a murderous Tyrant, wanton thief, cruel homicide, violator of women, burner of houses, & c."[372] Third, to confirm the cruelty of the Spanish, the editor recommended Benzoni's *L'Histoire du nouueau monde,* translated from the Italian into the French, for the author lived for 14 years in the New World when Las Casas was alive. The editor claimed that all the writers who write about the West Indies, except for those historians who flattered and made pale ("pallié") this truth to blind the world to the advantage of the Spaniards, mentioned their cruelty. No one had been able to contradict Las Casas.

The editor then referred to a history of the preachers in the Province of Chiappa as substantiating evidence and also gave three reasons why the Spanish were tyrants in the West Indies. First, they wanted to be masters of that country and to people it as they wished; second, they desired gold and silver; third (and here the editor provided a national stereotype that was part of the Black Legend), this nation was "haughty and proud ("superbe") and where it has superiority it is cruel; and the most cruel amongst them esteems himself the most valiant, and glory in it," and so on.[373] As so often occurred in prefatory matter, the raison d'être for the book rose to the surface—Spain was the enemy of France:

> friend Reader, if you are a good Frenchman, take this warning; that if the Spaniard had the power over you, that he had usurped over the poor Indians, you would not be treated any more gently and that this little book serves as an example to you. I hope that the reading of it, will give boldness to the most timid and move the most bold to conquer souls for God, riches for their country and an immortal glory for their virtue. Serve faithfully therefore your most-Christian and most-Just King and pray to God that he will give you the grace to gain the victory over his cruel enemies.[374]

The example of Spain in the New World was a negative exemplum of what Spain might do in France. This was another typological use of Las Casas to deploy America as a warning in Europe: the Dutch, French, and English all used this strategy. Nonetheless, these nations also saw each other as rivals and, if anything, during the seventeenth century this rivalry intensified and sometimes eclipsed, or at least qualified, the anti-Spanish feelings in these countries.

During the 1630s and 1640s, religious concerns heightened once again in the colonization of the New World. After the English and French were establishing permanent colonies in North America and were trying to maintain them and to encourage their growth, England and France became rivals and focused their attention on each other as well as on the power of Spain. An example of the French preoccupation with the English in North America can be observed in Gabriel Sagard's *History of Canada . . .* (1636). Sagard, a Recollet who traveled among the Huron or Ouendat, concentrated on conversion, but in his history from 1615 to the fall of Québec to the English in 1629, he could not avoid the English presence, whereas the Spanish were not a force in Canada.[375]

Sagard remonstrated against those who would not help the mission in Canada and some merchants who worked against the design of the Recollets to convert the Natives and make them sedentary while peopling the country.[376] He said that America was named after Vespucci but reminded his reader that the honor was due to Columbus, who had discovered the New World five years before. Conversion became a central goal of New France in its first decades, which was one of the pretexts, as well as the occupation of the land, France used from the early sixteenth century to challenge the right of Portugal and Spain to the New World. A similar split occurred among the French that happened among the Spanish, when the landowners opposed the clergy.

This anti-Spanish sentiment was not universal: the French missionaries to

America kept the example of their Spanish counterparts before them.[377] Another example that raised expectations among the French were the riches of Peru. Sagard described Peru as perhaps having the richest deposit of gold and silver in the world as a means of talking about the Spanish possession of that country and the ransom king Atabaliba offered the Spaniards. This description might seem out of place in a history of Canada, but the reason for its presence becomes readily apparent. The anxiety Sagard anticipated in his readers was the inadequacy of New France beside the Spanish colonies.[378] The success of Spanish Recollets, real and imagined, in conversion in America and the Far East became a model that the French among the Hurons in Canada sought to imitate. Sagard thought in 1632 that even the most successful Jesuit missions in New France, like the one in Ouendake or Huronia, was "very far away from the ten of million souls that our confrères have baptised . . . in the East and West Indies."[379]

The 1630s would see the work of Jesuit missionaries among the Hurons, like Jean de Brébeuf and Gabriel Lalemont, a Huguenot convert, who in the late 1640s would die at the hands of the Iroquois.[380] The cruelty was not always Spanish but could be Native. The complication is that such cruelty led to martyrdom in the view of the Catholic Church, which involved an imitation of Christ. Another example of a discussion of the cruelty and barbarity of cannibalism occurred in the work of Claude d'Abbeville, someone, in Lestringant's view, whom Léry influenced.[381] Like the Recollets, the Jesuits often looked to the success of Spanish Jesuits for inspiration: Igatius Loyola, the founder of the Society of Jesus, was a Spaniard. From Huronia, Paul Le Jeune could write in 1637 about the success of turning the Paraquais from cruel cannibals to gentle lambs of God and of the good results of Portuguese conversions of the American Indians.[382] Catholic religious orders, like Protestant sects, complicated loyalties to language and nation in a period during which regions and national boundaries were in flux.

The complication of the boundaries between Catholicism and Protestantism also occurred in English America among the Jesuits. The relations between the Spanish and other nations in the New World were problematic but not always in predictable ways. For instance, Andrew White and his fellow Jesuits, following a tradition begun by the founder of the Society of Jesus, wrote a series of reports about the colony in Maryland. Even though the Jesuits were sent out with Rome's permission, they encountered the possibility of Spanish resistance: "Reflection on Divine Providence mitigated the cruel treatment of men; for we understood that a Spanish fleet was lying at the isle of Bonavista for the purpose of prohibiting all foreigners from trading in salt. Moreover, if we had proceeded on our appointed voyage we should have fallen into the snare, and become prey to them."[383] White commended John Smith's discovery and description of the lands, so that religious differences did not always matter.[384] The English Jesuits gave the sacraments to a dying Frenchman, restoring him "to the catholic church, he prepared him, by virtue of the sacraments, for dying happily."[385] The example of the spiritual discipline of Loyola found its way into an English colony: "By spiritual exercises we have formed several of the principal men to piety, a fruit not to be repented of."[386] This mission was going on at the same time (from the 1630s onward) as that of the Jesuits in New France. The danger in Maryland in 1656 came from other Englishmen, who killed three Catholic captives.[387] This kind of troubling of religious waters is something we shall continue to observe.

There was also, as we have seen, an anxiety in France and England of losing people to Holland and Spain because of their flourishing economies, so that national borders were not as fixed and patriotism not as deep as the ruling elites would have desired. Thousands of French artisans and merchants had crossed into Spain after the expulsion of the Moriscos in 1610.[388] The Flemish and Swiss were French and then French-speaking as such a distinction became possible. The Pilgrims lived in Holland, and those who feared assimilation left for America, but those who did not stayed. The national feeling and anti-Spanish sentiment, only part of the example of Spain, while there and important, were not fixed entities, but rather were qualified by religion, region, language, and commerce.

VI

Despite the use of Las Casas in French and English texts to build anti-Spanish feelings in a critical period of colonization for France and England, ambivalence and contradiction toward Spain remained. In spite of their differences in religion or national interests, Hakluyt, Ralegh, Champlain, Lescarbot, d'Avity, Johnson, Strachey, Smith, Purchas and others expressed such an ambiguity. Even the French translations of Las Casas continued to use an admirable Spaniard to criticize Spain. Whereas French and English writers concerned with the New World could not ignore Spain, they had to take into account the ways in which France and England contended with each other and with the growing influence and power of Holland.

During the late 1580s and the 1590s, writers such as Payne, Hakluyt, and Ralegh embodied the complex attitudes of English writers to Spain and the New World. Payne's *A Briefe Description of Ireland* asserted that there existed a double threat to England: Catholic Ireland and Catholic Spain. For Payne, there was a contradictory response of the Irish to the Spaniards—the "better" few who hated the Spanish and the multitude who sympathized with the Spaniards. Payne described the Spanish having killed millions of Natives, which echoed typologically the Massacre of the Innocents in the Bible, something we can also see later in Strachey. Las Casas became an example for Payne of someone the educated elite in Ireland would consult to understand the cruelty of the Spaniards. In this regard, the Spanish abuses in the Americas prefigured possible violence by the Spaniards in Ireland. Payne's discussion of Ireland and Spain also concerned domestic affairs in England: the aftermath of the death of Mary Queen of Scots and the defeat of the Armada helped Payne to concentrate on English Catholics, something Hakluyt did in "Discourse on Western Planting." Religion was an important factor in how English authors represented Spain but it was not the only one or always the primary determinant. In *The Principall Navigations,* Hakluyt called on La Popelinière's *L'Admiral de France* (1584) to challenge his English readers to make England into a sea power and colonizer. In the last decades of the sixteenth century and the first decades of the seventeenth century, important English promoters of empire used French texts, especially by Huguenots, to build an empire in the Americas to rival the Spanish American colonies. Ralegh and Hakluyt were closely connected. In *A Report of the Trvth of the fight about the Isles of Açores* . . . Ralegh saw Spanish pillage as a typological connection between the Low Countries and the New World. The tendency in Ralegh's *The Discouerie of the Large, Rich, and Bewtiful Empyre of Guiana* was toward the anti-Spanish and pro-Native position of the literature of the Black Legend. Even though Ralegh maintained that the Spanish conquest was an illegal act that killed 20 millions, he argued for England to outconquest the Spaniards and to discover even more gold.

In the opening decades of the seventeenth century, the French still seemed closer to the Spanish than the English were despite James I's peace with Spain. The texts of Champlain, Lescarbot, and d'Avity, three key figures in the French colonization of the northern part of America, exemplified this doubleness, which shares ambivalent and contradictory aspects with those in Ralegh's work. The French representations of the example of Spain, like the English ones, displayed ambivalent attitudes toward Spanish colonies in the western Atlantic. When France was on the brink of establishing permanent settlements in the northern hemisphere of the New World, its colonizers and writers were both learning from Spain and threatening to displace its claims. *Brief Discovrs* . . . is the principal text in which Champlain expressed his Spanish experience. Whereas Champlain denounced the cruelty of the Inquisition, he thought that the king of Spain was civilizing the Natives. Although Champlain was also in Acadia, he was less apt than Marc Lescarbot, the chronicler of Acadia, to comment on Spain. Like Hakluyt, Lescarbot saw discontents and unemployed tradesmen settling the colonies rather than moving to other countries. What most differentiates Lescarbot from Hakluyt is that he employed the language of Christian republicanism and the French preoccupation—"la gloire" or glory. In establishing these French colonies, Lescarbot attended to the example of Spain but had also to distinguish France's relations to the Natives in the New World from Spain's treatment of them by suggesting Christ's example of peace in the treatment of the indigenes. In France and England both, the Spanish destruction of the Huguenots in Florida during the 1560s was something much repeated in narratives about the New World. In Lescarbot, and even in Purchas, we saw that religion was not a simple line of division between the French and the English on the one hand and the Spanish on the other. Lescarbot was defensive about the relation of Spain to France: he represented Spanish cruelty and greed, aspects of the Black Legend. France as a mother would produce New France: a worthy daughter even if she did not supply the treasures of Atabalippa. In *Les Estats, empires et principavtez dv monde* . . . , Pierre d'Avity, like Hakluyt and Lescarbot, collected information about the Americas. Unlike Lescarbot, d'Avity was more interested in Catholicism as a major aspect of colonization and relations with Spain. Having drawn on an ideology of a united Catholicism, d'Avity focused most on geographical information and described America. The long description of the Spanish empire attested to its preeminence in d'Avity's view.

As a mediator between French and English representations of the example of Spain, Edward Grimstone provided a good transition between d'Avity and contemporaries like William Strachey and Robert Johnson. Unlike d'Avity, Grimstone questioned Catholicism, Alexander VI's donations and the view of Spain as the savior of America from the English and the Philippines from the Muslims. In *For the Colony in Virginea Britannia* Strachey showed anxiety over the boundaries between being English and being Native, so that it was not only the Spaniards who fretted over the blurring of the border between barbarism and civility. Texts about the New World in English and French, like those in Spanish, suggest an ambivalence toward the American Indian. The friction between Spain and England over Ireland led Johnson to censure Spain, but the initiatives by Spain in the Americas appear to have elicited admiration from him. Having blamed the English for not having taken up what is implicitly Columbus's plan to sail into the western Atlantic, Johnson censured with this example—what might be called the wound of Columbus, those in England who would fault Spain. Johnson still claimed that the English were the best at imitation and so would imitate the example of Spain only to exceed their Spanish mentors. There were, for Johnson, many threats to the English home and in the colonies. His concerns, as we have seen, were not too different from those of earlier writers from the 1560s onward, such as Gilbert and Hakluyt the Younger. John Smith was more positive about the example of Spain than Strachey was. In Smith, who wanted to establish England in North America, we found an imitation of Spanish models. Smith emphasized the many times the English had criticized themselves for not taking up Columbus's offer, but he himself held Spain in high regard. Most often, Smith was ambivalent toward the English failures in colonization: it was better to emulate the success of the Spaniards. Purchas did not, as Smith did, follow a heroic model. Instead, Purchas translated or reworked translations of Spanish works in Hakluyt's papers: he collected texts by a variety of Spanish historians using different historiographical methods

This period was a fulcrum: it looked backward and forward. The texts drew on Spanish precedents and did so positively and negatively, but they also looked ahead to a displacement of Spain. In this chapter I have tried to break up further stereotypes and misconceptions about the French and English representations of Spain, which have been too often left to the unremitting negativity of the Black Legend. In the period after 1642, England and France not only rivaled Spain but succeeded it, so that by the first decade of the eighteenth century, Europe was literally fighting a war over the Bourbon succession in Spain. Whereas Richelieu had worried about the encirclement of France by the Habsburgs, the potential union of the thrones of France and Spain created great anxiety in England and other countries that the French, as the Spanish had when they acquired Portugal, would dominate Europe and the New World.

CHAPTER 6

Rivaling and Succeeding Spain, 1643–1713

In 1643 England was embroiled in a civil war that would only six years later make it a "republic" while France was beginning what would be a long and, in its own iconography and rhetoric, glorious reign under the sun king. For France, European hegemony had long been more important than gaining a foothold in North America. Even during the reign of Louis XIV, who came to be the most powerful monarch in Europe, this subordination of the interest of France in America to that in Europe continued. France's chief rival in Europe was Spain, but after the decline of Spanish power and the advent of a Bourbon on the Spanish throne, the Dutch and English were becoming the main rivals, both commercially and militarily.[1] Whereas the power of Spain was declining in Europe, it remained strong in America and Asia, something that the French and especially the English underestimated during this period.

After the Glorious Revolution of 1688, France found that its ambitions in Europe and America met with a more sustained English opposition.[2] The establishment of Louisiana in 1699 allowed for a strategic colony in a conflict with Spain or England in America, although Louis XIV became allies with Spain, when his grandson, Philip V, assumed the Spanish throne. Louisiana, which Pierre Le Moyne d'Iberville established, could be a support to a Bourbon Spain or a place from which France could attack Spain should the Austrian Habsburgs gain the succession. France acquitted the *asiento*, the privilege to trade slaves in the Spanish colonies, in 1701, and in St. Domingue the colonists used Spanish currency.[3] With the abdication of James II and the rule of William of Orange, England would not abide a Catholic monarch. It would oppose France and Spain on several occasions in the 25 years from the Glorious Revolution to the Peace of Utrecht.

The French and English colonies were fragile and experienced internal conflicts, which, like those in Spanish America, were many. They often centered on problems of religious, economic, and political control. The law was frequently used to challenge an opponent. Just as the English challenged the right of Spain to the New World, so too did factions within England and its colonies question one another's rights. One tract tried to question the legality of Lord Baltimore's establishment of Maryland. It claimed "by the Arbitrariness of his own will, he appoints Laws for us, and sets up Popish Officers over us" and called the rule of Lord Baltimore "a Popish Antichristian Government."[4] This religious division occurred very early in Virginia and later in New England. During the morning or evening, the captain of the guard or one of his principal officers was supposed to read out a long prayer. The prayer, which concluded Strachey's work, was inspired by Calvinism, proclaiming the settlers to be among the Elect, and saying: "O Lord we pray thee fortifie vs against this temptation: let *Samballet,* & *Tobias,* Papists & players, & such other *Amontis* & *Horonits* the scum & dregs of the earth, let them mocke such as helpe to build vp the wals of Jerusalem, and they that be filthy still, & let such swine still wallow in their mire, but let not yᵉ rod of the wicked fal vpon the lot of the righteous."[5] An appeal to "Christ Jesus our glorious Mediator for vs all," this prayer ended Strachey's book with a call for the blessing of England, and for its salvation from "Popery, . . . heathenisme, . . . Atheisme."[6] This internal ambivalence and contradiction, and not just the ambivalent and conflicting policies of France and England toward their colonies, should also show that French and English America were not simply following the example of Spain or were chronically obsessed with the Spanish colonies. In the period of permanent settlement, New France and the English colonies had a life of their own.

Some of the changes in New England during this period should suggest that despite the confident anti-Spanish rhetoric in England that Thomas Gage and others provided, the colonies in America struggled. In January 1649 Charles I was executed. Until the Restoration in 1660, prominent New Englanders often thought they could give advice to Cromwell or his son, something that was exemplified in a work like John Eliot's *The Christian Commonwealth* (ca. 1651, published 1660). In this cluster of colonies, some were also later worried about the conflicts with the Natives, especially with Metacomet (1676–77).[7] One major figure in the internal divisions of New England was Increase Mather. In 1677, in writing about these wars, Mather was able to sum up the division in colonization that set Las Casas against Spanish colonizers and that created such anxiety in Eden, Hakluyt, Lescarbot, and others—the worldly goal of trade and the aim of conversion: "from the *History* of these *Troubles,* that whereas there have been two sorts of men designing settlement in this part of *America,* some that came hither on the account of Trade, and worldly Interests, by whom the Indians have been scandalized, others that came whither on a Religious and conscientious account, having in their Eye, the Conversion of the *Heathen* unto Christ."[8] The royal government in England began in 1678 to set in motion reforms for New England in order to make it more tolerant. Obviously, the colony was subject to internal pressures among Protestant sects in addition to those relating to foreign powers, Catholics, and witches. King William's War, the American part of the War of the League of Augsburg (1689–1697), involved a conflict with the French and their Indian allies. As French power and its colonial presence grew during the seventeenth century, the Black Legend of Spain, although not forgotten, had to coexist increasingly with a fear of the ambitions of France in Europe and America. The exemplum of Spain came to be only one consideration in England and the colonies in America.

To discuss French and English representations of Spain and its colonies in the New World in these changing circumstances, I will concentrate on a variety of important texts, such as those by Thomas Gage, Melchisédech Thévenot, Louis Hennepin, Las Casas (in translation), and John Harris, and will provide some contexts for their representations. The popularity of most of these authors might attest more to their shared views with their audiences in England and France than to an accurate representation of the Spanish colonies. As in previous chapters, different kinds of writing served the purposes of representing Spain in the New World, from a confessional conversion narrative and travel account in Gage, through translations of one of the key figures in my study—Las Casas—through collections by Thévenot, Harris, and Stevens, as heirs to Hakluyt, Lescarbot and Purchas, to an eyewitness account by Hennepin. As the great transformation in the example of Spain occurred from about 1565 to the early part of the seventeenth century, I will attempt here to avoid unnecessary repetition and to suggest the range of material produced by either France or England rather than be comprehensive. There is not space to perform close readings of all the texts that deserve attention, but I have tried to select the most germane works. I have chosen some of the texts, like those by Thévenot and Harris, that are not well known but deserve to be.

The following discussion is arranged by kinds of writing—conversion narratives, travel accounts, translations, collections, promotional literature, plays, poems, and other types—and concentrates on texts that should receive more attention than they have. During the English Civil War, Thomas Gage produced a work, at once confession, autobiography, conversion narrative, travel narrative, and other genres, that would become popular, would catch the attention of Oliver Cromwell and would be used in his "Western Design" and Edward Williams's, *Virginia: More Especially the South Part . . .* (1650), a "Puritan" narrative, to parliament. A revival of Las Casas was also part of this republican propaganda against Spain when, in 1656, John Phillips's translation of Las Casas, *The Tears of the Indians . . .* , presented Spanish cruelty in an allegory for Cromwell's era. French religious writing about the New World was also indebted to Spanish influences while showing ambivalence over Spain in the New World, especially in its treatment of Natives. In France, collections also helped to promote colonies in the New World. Between 1632 and 1672, the Jesuits published their annual relations. In chapter 5 we observed that accounts of America in French in the sixteenth century had been mainly Protestant; in the seventeenth century they were largely Catholic. Ambivalence in the example of Spain occurred in religious accounts in French, such as in the work of Louis Hennepin and the translation of Las Casas in 1698. Lahontan, however, criticized previous relations about the New World because their authors were missionaries with motives that colored their work. Some important English representations of the New World were literary: Dryden and Dennis provide good illustrations of that preoccupation during the Restoration and after the Glorious Revolution. Whereas in writing about the Americas Dennis focused more on the French, Dryden concentrated on the Spaniards. Collectors and editors in France and in England from 1663 to 1713, such as Thévenot, Harris, and Stevens, also showed similar contradictory and ambivalent attitudes toward Spain. Promotional authors who were not collectors, like R. B., John Oldmixon and John Lawson, also had much to say about Spain in the New World.

Surprisingly, as France and England came to rival Spain and then to succeed it in this period, some of those same concerns about origins, precedence, right, greed, and conversion and Spain's role in them all in the New World persisted. Even in 1713, the English and French were talking about some of the same topics concerning Spain as they did in the 1490s and the sixteenth century, despite the changes in the balance of power. Here, I will demonstrate this unexpected continuity while discussing a period of change in the European empires in America. The priority of the Spanish, in writing as much as in conquest, provided a body of acts and texts that the French and English were drawn to interpret, to measure themselves against, to imitate, and to distinguish themselves from increasingly.[9]

I

The supporters of the commonwealth or republic in England were not any kinder to Spain than were their royalist opponents. In the middle of the English Civil War, Thomas Gage produced a work that would become popular, catching the attention of Oliver Cromwell and being used in his "Western Design," the attempt to attack and supplant Spain in the West Indies.[10] Gage's work became more instrumental politically than most of the French and English narratives of the New World we have discussed.

In "The Epistle Dedicatory" to *The English-American his Travail by Sea and Land: Or a New Survey of the West Indias* . . . (1648), addressed to Sir Thomas Fairfax, the captain-general of the parliamentary army, Gage began by telling how Divine Providence made him an exile from his native England partly because he was a Roman Catholic, had studied in foreign universities, and had entered monastic orders. Gage offered a brief story of his time in New Spain and of how Fairfax rescued him and others like him in Kent, where he was now a preacher. This providential plan had made Gage do something of benefit to his country, so that, claiming that nothing had been written about this area of the New World for a hundred years, he wanted, as opposed to presenting a collection, to offer "mine own observations," which differed as much from what was written before on the topic "as the picture of a person grown to mans estate, from that which was taken of him when he was but a Childe; or the last hand of the Painter, to the first or rough draught of the picture."[11] This language of artistic representation extended to Fairfax, whose "high protection," or political and religious representation as God's instrument, sheltered Gage's person and his work, which to others seemed "acceptable" but which was, in Gage's deferential rhetoric, "lame and imperfect."[12] As we have observed throughout, the writer or representer, French or English, often needed a powerful patron to ensure the public and material existence of the book or pamphlet. In the epistles dedicatory, reception and politics defined some of their rhetorical moves of praise and blame. Here, God had led Fairfax to settle peace on England and reduce Ireland, and He would guide him to just and honorable designs in America. Providential design led to land for England. In his address to Fairfax, Gage defined a role for himself in what would become known as Cromwell's "Western Design": "To your Excellency therefore I offer a New-World, to be the subject of your future pains, valour, and piety, beseeching your acceptance of this plain but faithfull relation of mine, wherein your Excellency, and by you the English Nation shall see what wealth and honor they have lost by one of their narrow hearted Princes, who living in peace and abounding in riches, did notwithstanding reject the offer of being first discoverer of America."[13] By yoking his own representation of the New World with the place itself, Gage represented his book as a means to America. Even as late as 1648, the English view of Spain in America resonated with a discussion of origins and lost opportunities. A year before Charles I was to lose his head, another king was being blamed for his greed and abuse of his people: Henry VII. Gage rehashed the lost opportunity of Columbus discovering America for England.

Shifting his strategy, Gage now said that England did not come to America so far behind the Spanish and that, in fact, English settlements in the Caribbean had been so successful and their inhabitants so inured to the climate that these plantations should serve as bases in order to conquer cities and territories on the American continent. In attacking the Spanish, something advocated in the reign of Elizabeth I, Gage proposed Holland as a model: "Our Neighbors the Hollanders may be our example in this case; who whilst we have been driving a private Trade from Port to Port, of which we are likely now to be deprived, have conquered so much Land in the East and West-Indies, that it may be said of them, as of the Spaniards, That the Sunn never sets upon their Dominions."[14] Gage raised the recurrent objection to the seizure of Spanish colonies in the New World that the French and English had largely balked at since the 1490s— that the Spanish were entitled to these lands and to take them would be unlawful and against all conscience—as an opportunity to play down the significance of the papal bull of 1493. To that objection against conquering Spanish possessions, Gage answered "that (the popes donation excepted) I know no title that he [the Spaniard] hath but force, which by the same title, and by a greater force may be repelled."[15] The papal donation had now slid into a subordinate clause in this doctrine of "might is right."

Gage then suggested that the title of first discovery was of "little reason" because a Spanish ship sailing off the coast of "India" should have no title to that country just as an Indian or English ship should have like title to Spain by sailing off its coast. This attempt to make the Spanish colonies sound unoccupied harkened back to the 1580s when Drake, Ralegh, Hakluyt the Younger, and others, as Francois I had before them, attempted to say that wherever the Spanish had not settled was fair game for other European nations. In Hakluyt's "Discourse" and Ralegh's narrative about Guiana, the authors represented the hope that the Natives would welcome or invite the English to fight the Spaniards.

Gage continued this desire but did so with a twist—he admitted Native sovereignty: "No question but the just right or title to those Countries appertains to
the Natives themselves; who, if they shall willingly and freely invite the English
to their protection, what title soever they have in them, no doubt but that they
may legally transferr it or communicate it to others."[16] Gage assumed that the
Natives would want English protection, something far from certain. Continuing
in the rhetorical mode of a debate, he raised more possible objections to answer
them. To say that the inhumane practice of sacrificing humans, "so many reasonable Creatures to their wicked Idols," gave the Spanish warrant to possess
Native lands was a position Gage refuted: "The same argument may by much
better reason be inforced against the Spaniards themselves, who had sacrificed so
many millions of Indians to the Idol of their barbarous cruelty, that many populous Islands and large Territorities upon the main Continent, are thereby at this
day utterly uninhabited, as Bartholomeo de las Casas, the Spanish Bishop of
Guaxaca in New-Spain, hath by his Writings in Print sufficiently testified."[17]
The Black Legend was baldly stated here. After saying the Natives had title to
their land, Gage suggested that as God had given "the sons of Men" the world
to inhabit and so many lands were uninhabited either by Indian or Spaniard,
"why should my Country-men the English be debarred from making use of
that, which God from all beginning no question did ordain for the benefit of
mankinde?"[18] *Terra nullius* had returned in the company of the directive of "Go
forth and multiply" in Genesis: God had become a guarantor of what was lawful between nations. Gage had come full circle, beginning with providence and
ending there. He then left off his arguments and offered his services to Fairfax
and to England.

In his poem, "To the Reader," Thomas Chaloner used the occasion of the
"worthy work" of "his most worthy friend" Thomas Gage to interpret the book
and the context of books in English about the New World. In his praise for
Gage, Chaloner persuaded the reader to the merits of the book, partly by reit-
erating what had just appeared in "The Epistle Dedicatory":

> READER, behold presented to thine eye,
> What us Columbus off'red long agoe,
> Of the New-World a new discoverie,
> Which here our Author doth so clearly show;
> That he the state which of these Parts would know,
> Need not hereafter search the plenteous store
> Of Hackluit, Purchas and Ramusio,
> Or learn'd Acosta's writings to look o're;
> Or what Herera hath told us before,
> Which merit not the credit due from hence,
> Those being but reck'nings of another score,
> But these the fruits of self-experience.[19]

Chaloner repeated the lost opportunity of Columbus sailing for England and the
claim that Gage's work was new, not just another collection of narratives of the

New World. Since Columbus and in the work of writers like Oviedo the authors of these accounts had emphasized their status as eyewitnesses. Gage and Chaloner made that claim for the author of *The English-American*.[20] Appealing to classical authority, Chaloner concluded: "So what they were, not what they are, they sing,/ And shew their reading, not their travailing."[21] This appeal to experience was not new because Acosta, described as a learned but worn authority, laughed when he sailed through the torrid zone and found that Aristotle had been wrong. The experience and observations of Gage faced the received opinions of tradition, not just the famous collections but newly-written books on the Levant, which appealed to Greece and Troy, to authorities such as Thucydides, Strabo, Homer, Plutarch, Polybius, and others.[22]

Chaloner assured the reader that Gage told only about what he saw in his own time and that he was in the line of Hawkins, Drake, and Ralegh, who, unlike others since, wrote about what they had seen.

And yet it must be acknowledg'd be for true,
Since worthy Hawkins, the famous Drake
Did first present unto the English view
This New-found-world, for great Eliza's sake;
Renowned Rawleigh twice did undertake
With labours great, and dangers not a few,
A true discovery of these Parts to make,
And thereof writ both what he saw and knew.[23]

If eyewitness reports were the only true relations, then how could the English find out about the Spanish colonies in the New World? Chaloner had thought of this objection and had framed Gage's account in the language of danger, secrecy, and miracle.

But how these truths reveal'd to us should bee,
When none but Spaniards to those Parts may go;
Which was establish'd by severe Decree,
Lest Forain people should their secrets know;
This Order yet to be neglected so,
As that our Author had permission free,
Whose Nation too they count their greatest foe,
Seemeth almost a miracle to me.[24]

The theme of Spanish exclusivity recurred in the context of a kind of interpretation of divine revelation through Gage to England. Chaloner made Gage's 12 years in New Spain an exercise in the patience of exile, never mentioning that the author was a Catholic monk in Spain's service but suggesting instead that he was already gathering information for his book and was planning to reveal it in England.

As Chaloner represented this miracle, he changed Gage's "Relations" into a guiding star of the future and explicitly linked it typologically to the star that guided the wise men at the birth of Christ. The English wise men would look

on the New World after the bloody Civil War, in which the English were fighting each other when once they performed their "Martiall dance" and "trode
measures through the Realm of France" and fought holy wars under Richard
I.[25] In this prophecy the English ships would unmoor from Severn, Trent, and
Thames and sail once more like chariots to the sun, sail the ocean and transplant
the English to the Western shore. Of these ships, Chaloner said:

> And in their hollow bottoms you convay
> To Lands inrich'd with gold, with pearls and gems,
> But above all, where many thousands stay
> Of wronged Indians, whom you shall set free
> From Spanish yoke, and Romes Idolatry.[26]

God led to gold, and the English would free the Indians from the yoke of Spain
and Rome, a major motif of Hakluyt's "Discourse," which looked ahead to the
Whig notion of England as bringing liberty to the world.[27] To these lines
Chaloner added the disclaimer that ended his poem: "All this and more by you
shall sure be done,/Yet I no Prophet, nor no Prophet's sonne."[28]

Gage described Catholic missions to America and Asia. He set out his principle that proximity in religion bred hatred, especially when wealth and ambition lay behind those near differences. Thus the religious orders of Rome, being
so close, hated each other the more just as "a Papist hates a Protestant worse then
he doth a Jew, and a Formalist hates a Puritan worse then he doth a Papist."[29]
The Jesuits tried to squeeze out the friars in the eastern and western colonies by
offering to be self-sufficient, thereby relieving the king of Spain of the expense
of supporting the other religious but, according to Gage, with the ulterior
motive of relieving the various Natives of their wealth and with the result of
trading more than any other merchants. The tenor of Gage's mission, where he
set up this context of Catholic deception in the New World before offering his
own eyewitness account, was epitomized in the climactic end to chapter 2: "O
that this my discovery made to *England* of those dissembling and false Preists,
would make us wise to know and discover under the ashes of their pretended
Religion, the fire of strife and contention which they kindle in Kingdomes, and
to rake up that covetousnesse, which we may easily find in them; tending to the
ruine of many fair estates, and to the temporall and spirituall danger of this our
flourishing Kingdome!"[30] Here was another kind of discovery in a representation of discovery, a recognition that what appears to the eye is not actual but a
show. In revealing the nature of the dissembling work of conversion in the Spanish colonies, Gage also warned England of Catholic attempts to convert its people and did so implicitly and explicitly.[31]

Like Hakluyt in the "Discourse," Gage liked to emphasize division in the
Spanish empire. He said that the difference between native-born Spaniard and
the Spanish born in the colonies, or Criollos, was greater than the opposition
between the Spanish and French or the Spanish and the Dutch: "This hatred is
so great, and I dare say, nothing might bee more advantagious then this, to any
other Nation that would conquer *America*."[32] This rhetoric of hatred was some-

thing that continued from Hakluyt to Gage, from those who would advise those at the center of power, Walsingham, Ralegh, and Elizabeth I in the first instance and Fairfax and Cromwell in the second. Like Hakluyt and Ralegh, Gage brought out the liberation narrative. His version described how the Criollos, now joined with the Natives, would combine with any other nation (read England) in rebellion against Spain should they be allowed to maintain their religion. Gage had even heard Criollos make this claim in regard to a preference for Dutch rule. In his anti-Catholic and anti-Spanish account, Gage, once a friar in New Spain, made an implied plea for religious toleration as a means of conquering Spanish America. This hatred between Criollo and native-born Spaniard occurred because the Spanish feared that the colonists would throw off Spanish commerce and government and because the Criollos in turn resented that the Spanish-born occupied the highest posts in church and government.[33] As in Hakluyt's "Discourse," rebellion in Spanish America simmered and erupted and needed English leadership to make it successful.

Gage's work was also a personal journey which ended with conversion to the true Protestant faith. This book influenced Cromwell in his Western design, so that the parts leading up to the journey itself constituted a preface of Gage's motives and a personal religious account that must have helped to move Cromwell to action against Spain or to represent similar views to the ones he held. Gage's autobiographical approach to the America as a representation of the relations between Protestantism and Catholicism, England and Spain was another genre of narrative of the New World. On the way home, he faced many dangers and he was able to represent these in ways that affirmed his trouble with Spain and Catholicism and his identification with England. In chapter 21, he said: "The greatest feare that I perceived possessed the *Spaniards* in this Voyage, was about the Island of *Providence*, . . . from whence they feared lest some *English* Ships should come out against them with great strength. They cursed the *English* in it, and called the Island, the den of theeves and Pirates, wishing that their King of *Spain* would take some course with it; or else, that it would prove very prejudiciall to the *Spaniards*." The Spanish also feared the Dutch.[34] Gage became close with English prisoners whom the Spaniards abused, especially after an act of English piracy. In Spain Gage changed his clothes and made much of it allegorically: "And thus being now clothed after a new fashion and ready to lead a new life; being now changed from an *American* into the fashion of an *English* man, the tenth day after my abode in *San Lucar*, I bad adieu to *Spain* and all *Spanish* fashions, factions, and carriages . . . "[35] His clothes had hidden the inner truth of a man in spiritual turmoil who was in the process of conversion. At home in England, he wavered inwardly between Protestantism and Catholicism, between duty to his family and to himself and country. One concern was his share of his father's will: having a living was never far from Gage's mind from the beginning to the end of his book. He had lost the English tongue and had to regain it: his Spanish was a protection in some instances and a liability in others. Caught in the subterfuge among Jesuits, Catholics, Anglicans, Puritans, cardinals, archbishops, and others, Gage traveled to the Continent to find his brother (and perhaps his patrimony) and the true religion within him. His family was well established, and through them and his position in the church Gage had access to the highest church officials in England, Rome and elsewhere.[36]

The experience of the mission, which took up most of the book, made Gage reconsider Catholicism. Many fascinating byways inhabit Gage's text, and this is especially true as it approached its apparently receding conclusion, but one passage in particular clarified the recognition toward which Gage had been moving his narrative:

> Whereby I perceived that *England* was comming neere to *Rome,* and that my design of professing and following the truth in *England* blasted, and that in vain I had come from *America* for satisfaction of my conscience in *England.* I was more troubled now then ever; and desired to try all wayes, if I could bee better satisfied concerning the Popish Religion in *Rome, Naples* or *Venice* (whither I went) then I had been in *America* and among the *Spaniards.* But I found such exorbitances and scandalls in the lives of some Cardinals of *Rome,* whilst I was there, especially in *Don Antonio Barbarini,* and Cardinal *Burgesi,* who at midnight was taken by the *Corchetes* or Officers of justice in uncivill wayes, and came off from them with money, that I perceived the Religion was but as I had found it in *America,* a wide and open doore to loosnesse and policy, and the like in *Naples* and *Venice,* which made mee even hate what before I had professed for Religion, and resolve, that if I could not live in *England,* and there injoy my Conscience, that I would live in *France,* for a while, untill I had well learned that tongue, and then associate my selfe unto the best reformed Protestant Church.[37]

He was also interested in reaffirming his English identity. When he heard that within the year that Rome would appoint an English cardinal, Gage declared the reason he wished to convert: the Catholic church in America and in Rome were open to "loosenesse and policy." Ironically, America became an experience that did not increase Gage's missionary zeal but was a means of convincing him that the Spain he had lived in and the Catholic church which it championed were corrupt and needed to be abandoned.

The Continent, especially Rome, confirmed that view, though his final test was whether a picture of the lady of Loretto would blush and sweat for him in a miracle that would reveal his sin of doubt of the true Catholic faith. She did neither, and Gage set off to London to choose England and Protestantism over his family, which tried to bribe and threaten him further while he provided information under oath against Jesuits, priests, and friars. He preached his conversion sermon in St. Paul's as a public act to convince the doubting multitude of his sincerity and he became a preacher under the protection of parliament, which gave him a benefice, an act that caused some envy.

Gage feared being accused of the religious hypocrisy he criticized.[38] He ended his book, which he saw as a "small volume against Popish superstition," with a representation of himself as a preacher of the "godly Reformation," whom providence had used "as a *Ioseph* to discover the treasures of *Egypt,* or as

spies to search into the land of *Canaan,* even the God of all Nations" to whose
power, glory, and majesty Gage and all believers prayed ever more. To the body
of the book, Gage appended nearly eight pages of rules for learning Poconchi,
a native language in Honduras.[39]

Gage's work was translated into French and served, perhaps unexpectedly, the
interests of Colbert, who saw Spain as a rival to France. More predictably, a later
translation seemed to justify the Protestant position. Huës ô Neil's "Epistre"
emphasized Gage's influence on Cromwell, how he presented new and important information on the Spanish colonies in America and how Gage dwelt on
"the weakness of the Spaniards in these countries there, and the designs that
could form there against them."[40] Spain and Holland were allied against France
in the Dutch War (1672–78), and this is one reason Colbert sponsored the translation of Gage, which was supposed to reveal Spanish secrets about its American
colonies.[41] About two decades before, Cardinal Mazarin had focused on the war
with Spain, and to gain Cromwell's support, he gave him free run of the
Atlantic.[42] France's war with Spain ended in 1658.

Another French edition was published in 1720.[43] In that volume, the dedication was to "Monseigneur de Witsen," ambassador of the Estates General to
Britain. The "Preface" spoke about "an infinity of Histories that the Spanish
have given us of their first Conquests in America" but added that their politics
prevented them from publishing accounts that their "vanity" made them publish at the beginning of their "discovery," so that "it was almost a miracle that
we could see what they were hiding from us with so much care since more than
a century of peaceful possession" through "rigorous Laws that they made concerning the Indies, testifying how far their jealousy went, so that they forbade
access to Foreigners under pain of death."[44] In 1720 the translator was still talking about the riches of New Spain, the annual flotilla with "an immense profit,"
and the exclusion of foreigners from Peru, and asserted that was why Thomas
Gage's relation was still valuable. After providing his route and his life, the translator ended with a comment about the wisdom Colbert had in having Gage
translated because otherwise the French would not have been able to have
obtained this knowledge of the Spanish colonies, including the secrets Spain
guarded.[45]

Another example of a narrative of the New World in the Puritan tradition,
and much less known, is Edward Williams's, *Virginia: More Especially the South
Part . . .* (1650), which he dedicated to parliament: it will illustrate briefly the
push for expansion that Gage and others promoted in England. The parliamentary victory required "a vertue no lesse exalted than the acquisition and tenure
of conquests, made good in the eyes of Christendome by vindicating the English Honour upon the British Ocean with a Puissant Navy, a formidable subject
of amazement to the Forraine Enemies of your *Sion,* by a strong winged prose-
cution of the Irish Assassinates, a spacious lettred example to teach English Mutineers what they may expect by the red sentence of justice upon Irish Rebells."[46]
For Williams, the *translatio imperii* from Rome to England was not from Augustus to the king of England, but from the Roman senate to parliament.[47]

Despite his republicanism, Williams gave many of the same reasons Hakluyt did for the colonization of Virginia: it would disburden the nation of its poor and malcontents, develop trade and provide commodities beneficial to England and Europe, and give opportunities to the industrious.[48] Williams was still concerned to stake the English claim in America based on John Cabot's discovery and "*the voluntary submission of the Natives to the English obedience of all that Continent from* Cape Florida *Northward.*"[49] Conquests and punishment in Ireland and abroad would maintain the peace and authority at home. Now Spain was one of several rivals whom the English resented for their behavior in the colonies: "*And by this meanes the Hollander, Spanyard, and Portuguall, (who by the supine negligence of this nation; and its Merchant Adventurers) do with insufferable insolence Lord over us in both the Indies.*"[50] Williams, who had an imperial vision in which "The English name shall keepe company with the Sunne," described a scene in which the nations of the East would throw off their "slavery" with adoration and honor of England, who would give them liberty from the oppression "of those illustrious horseleeches their princes" and thereby come under the sacred English shadow.[51] In this vision of expanding liberty from the English center, England would rule the persons and art of those countries, who would give up cattle and horses "for nothing, for European trifles."[52] This motif of liberation was a republican version of Ralegh's representation of the Natives of Guiana waiting for Elizabeth to liberate them from Spanish tyranny. Williams then proceeded to speak about the practicalities of invasion and was worried about the reaction of Spain. When the Spanish learn about the plan, as inevitably they would, they "will roule all stones under Heaven to dispossesse or prepossesse, and indeed the danger his Peru, Chili and Philipines, by such seating, may lie obnoxious to, will adde spurres to his inclination to prevent us, which till wee bee in a condition to resist, may be effected with our absolute ruine."[53] At the same time, while planning an invasion of Spanish territory, he referred to the authority of Fernando Soto.[54] If Spanish power had declined in Europe, it was still something to fear and respect in America and Asia. Williams hoped to find the South Sea, which might provide a buffer between Virginia and "the jealous Spanyard" who had unjustly claimed "Florida, which is indisputably English."[55] Florida remained a disputed area. Although the French had abandoned it, the Spanish would not do so until the early nineteenth century.

Williams and his contemporaries represented Spain in various contexts, sometimes in relation to France, sometimes not, and at other times the very fragility of the English colonies in America made for a kind of isolated self-examination. Still, writers saw in commodities like tobacco and silk a utopian future for Virginia. In Williams's theory of the South Sea and other waterways, Williams also cited Cartier.[56] The example of Spain, including some English jealousy, can be observed in phrases like "why may not the Cloves perfume Virginia with as aromatick redolency as the Philipine Garden."[57] The table of contents declared that on page 41 if an Indian plants the vine, it "will cement him to the English to the disadvantage of the Spaniard."[58]

Another contemporary, John Hammond, blamed early failures in Virginia on diet and not on the climate as the English were now healthy there.[59] Tobacco had become Virginia's gold and silver, according to Samuel Hartlib: tobacco is "now their money, and that with which all Commerce is driven, and payments made in."[60] Hartlib also hoped to promote the silkworm in Virginia, as if to bring Chinese products to the New World, so that England could be more self-sufficient. Writers defined Virginia in connection to Spain and in terms of its own internal anxieties and hopes.

Virginia continued to have problems under the English republic, and soon the Caribbean would create obstacles for the English who had designs on the Spanish colonies there.[61] On April 19, 1654, peace with Holland was proclaimed, and soon after, the Western Design against Spanish America was begun. At this time, Cromwell was said to have identified the English with classical Rome and created fears that he wanted to be emperor, while others, like John Cotton, saw a typology between the expulsion of the Spanish from America and the drying up of the Euphrates in Revelation.[62] In 1654 Thomas Gage, who became chaplain to the expedition to the West Indies, wrote a government report on the proposed attack, and the next year his work, *The English American his Travail by Sea and Land* (1648), was reprinted under another title, and in 1655 Roger Williams wrote to John Winthrop about the expedition and connected Cotton's interpretation with the Protector's "strong thoughts of Hispaniola and Cuba."[63] This drive for expansion under the republic did not have a happy ending: the Western Design was largely a failure, an embarrassment, and a defeat for Cromwell and England. Spain was not a straw man in a propagandist's pamphlet, so that the discourse of Gage and the expansionist party in England came up against the wall of actuality.[64] Another important figure in the Western Design was James Harrington, a Machiavellian critic who suffered through the collapse of the English republic's western expansion and who produced *The Common-wealth of Oceana* (London, 1656). My argument, by definition, is more interested in Gage, who paid extensive attention to Spain and who was instrumental in moving Cromwell into attacking the West Indies. After this humiliation, which caused Cromwell self-doubt, England was soon at war with Spain, and in his *Declaration . . . Setting Forth . . . the Justice of Their Cause Against Spain* in October 1656, Cromwell did what a long line of English rulers, historians, collectors, and writers had done: he attacked the right of Spain to the New World.

A revival of Las Casas was also part of this republican propaganda against Spain. In 1656 John Phillips began his dedication of his translation of Las Casas, *The Tears of the Indians . . . ,* whose extended title appealed even more to the victims of Spanish cruelty and to the emotions of the English reader, to the Lord Protector in dramatic fashion: "May it please your Highness, I Have here laid prostrate before the Throne of Your Justice, above Twenty Millions of the Souls of the slaughter'd Indians; whose forc'd departure from their Bodies, Cruelty it self compassionates."[65] Phillips represented Cromwell as the arm of God's revenge, the advancer of his glory, so that God would recompense the Protector, crowning him with fame as he did his "holy Warriour" David, inspiring him with the prowess of Joshua, the zeal of Jehu, and giving him such divine virtues "that there is no man, who opposes not himself against Heaven, but doth extol Your just Anger against the Bloudy and Popish Nation of the Spaniards, whose Superstitions have exceeded those of *Canaan,* and whose Abominations have excell'd those of *Ahab,* who spilt the Blood of the innocent *Naboth,* to obtain his Vineyard."[66] Against the facts, Phillips celebrated Cromwell's victory over the Spanish, and he asserted that his "zeal to Heaven, the loud Cry of so many bloudy Massacres, far surpassing the Popish Cruelties in Ireland, the Honour of my Country," as well as his affection to Cromwell's service, had caused Phillips "to publish this Relation of the *Spanish Cruelties,*" confident that God, "who hath put this Great Designe" in to the Protector's hands, would bless the book.[67]

Phillips supplemented this dedication with an address "To all true English-men," which began with a statement of the just cause of England and an appeal to the prophet Jeremiah, so that, in Phillips's gloss, "we" (the English) should weep over the innocent blood of the Indians just as Las Casas had done, "by rea-son of the cruel Slaughters and Butcheries of the Jesuitical Spaniards, perpetrated upon so many Millions of poor innocent Heathens, who having onely the light of Nature, not knowing their Saviour Jesus Christ, were sacrificed to the Poli-tick Interest and Avarice of the wicked Spaniards."[68] As if this hyperbolic and extreme language of self-justification were not enough, Phillips then compared the horrors of Catholic actions in Ireland with those in the New World and found the American atrocities much worse: "The blood of *Ireland,* spilt by the same Faction, in comparison of these Massacres, was but a Drop in the Ocean."[69] Blood and more blood, the Spanish hounds eating innocent children, the Spaniards as "Death" itself, invaders and murders, as "Pestilence" to the "poor Indians" were some of the appeals to emotion that Philips employed.[70] In a direct address full of breathless rhetorical flourishes in which clause built on clause and that arrogated to itself Las Casas's personal experience, Phillips spoke apocalyptically that had the readers been "Eye-witnesses of the transcending Massacres here related" or had witnessed the depopulation of that "pleasant Country," "drown'd in a Deluge of Bloud," the "poor innocent Heathens" torn by "the devilish Cruelties of those that called themselves Christians" and taken from these habitations, "where God had planted them, to labour in "Torment-ing Captivity," much worse than that of Algier or the Turkish galleys, then human tears could hardly be enough, for "these are Enormities to make the Angels mourn and bewail the loss of so many departed souls, as might have been converted and redeemed to their eternal Mansions."[71] The movement of the rhetoric was toward this climax near the end of a series of climaxes, building on the innocence of Indian blood as a Christ-like sacrifice that could not be one because they had not known Christ (like the innocents Herod slaughtered) by those who professed to be Christians but were not (being Spanish Catholics and so enemies on two accounts), and did not have, as did Cromwell and the Eng-lish, God on their side. Phillips then compared the slaughtered Indians to the early Christians who suffered through ten persecutions, the "Cruelties of the Heathen Emperours," but the Spaniards, the new persecutors, were professors of Christianity, the religion of love and charity but the purveyors of "Barbarism," now worse than the Turks and Sythians, and whom "Wickedness had so far transform'd them into Devills, they were resolved to deface the image of God, so innocently conversing among them."[72] One of Phillip's main rhetorical ploys was literally to demonize the Spanish. Phillips proceeded to rouse his countrymen, whose birthright from God was to be a magistrate among the nations, to be "his Great Instrument to revenge the Blood of the that innocent People," more of the Old Testament cry for vengeance that Phillips had used in his dedication to Cromwell than the religion of love, Christ's sermon on the mount, that he had just employed rhetorically against the cruel Spaniards.[73]

The appeal to war against the Spanish became even blunter and more hateful than before in perhaps the most blatant and condensed representation of the Black Legend: he roused his countrymen to fight "against your Old and Constant Enemies, the **SPANIARDS**, a Proud, Deceitful, Cruel, and Treacherous Nation, whose chiefest Aim hath been the Conquest of this Land, and to enslave the People of this Nation."[74] Queen Elizabeth came in for criticism because she was not warlike enough with the Spaniards, but the Englishman did not have to look for "ancient Examples," possessed of recent ones near to him and in the West Indies, so that the Protector had become the champion of the innocent Indians.[75] Phillips proposed that the English should not fear "the Vaunts of the Spanish Monarch" and his empire built on the weakness of "Blood and Tyrannie" but "chase him from his Indian Treasures" and help improve "the General Peace of *Europe,* whereby we should be strengthened against the Common Enemy of Christianitie."[76] In this language of warmongering and ideological aspersion, Phillips continued to demonize the Spanish "enemy": "For doubtless it hath been the Satanical Scope of this tyrant, To set all the European Princes at Variance, and to keep them busie at home, that they might not have leasure to bend their Forces against his Golden Regions."[77] As in Columbus, God could not be separated from gold. Once again, we find the Spanish claim to the New World scorned and challenged, the proclamation of the better English claim through Cabot (here again we find the mistaken attribution of Sebastian Cabot) and Henry VII and the lament of the neglect of the English kings for not doing more about settling in America, only now with a republican twist, for that they might " be almost guilty of the Bloud shed in those parts, through their neglect."[78] Phillips promised to bring out a treatise on this English right to the West-Indies and he celebrated that divine providence would move his countrymen under the "Supreme Magistrate" to embrace opportunities to avenge "the cruelties and barbarous Massacres of the Spaniards."[79]

Another translation came out after the Glorious Revolution: *POPERY Truly Display'd in Bloody Colours: Or, a Faithful NARRATIVE of the Horrid and Unexampled Massacres, Butcheries, and all manner of Cruelties, that Hell and Malice could invent, committed by the Popish Spanish Party on the Inhabitants of* West-India . . . (London, 1689). I have approximated the typography of this screaming title, which emphasized the horrors of "popery" in wake of a Protestant revolution in England. The title page also stressed that Las Casas had been translated into Latin, High Dutch, Low Dutch, and French *"and now Taught to speak Modern English."* The same old charges of the Black Legend appeared here: the header on pages 76 to 79 read *"The Cruelty of the Spaniards Committed in America."* Las Casas's *Brevíssima relación* was translated again during the build-up to the War of the Spanish Succession, and the anonymous translator stressed Las Casas as representing liberty of conscience and the natural right of humankind to liberty and property against the inquisition, oppression, and tyranny of his Spain against the Natives.[80] This book was translated from the French version of J. B. Morvan de Belle-Garde, *La découverte des Indes Occidentales, par les Espanols* (Paris, 1697), which was reprinted with "Relation curieuse des voyages du Sieur de Montauban . . . " in Amsterdam in 1698.[81] The intertextuality of French and English editions of Las Casas is an intricate maze that, as we have seen, sometimes has branches in other countries like the Netherlands.

The use and abuse of Las Casas for propaganda would last well beyond the end of the seventeenth century.[82] This employment of Las Casas in propaganda and polemics also involved self-serving national expansion and religious partisanship. Rhetoric can be counterfactual, so that the massacre of the Pequots in New England in 1636–37 would force the English at home, if not those among the Puritans in New England, to make the comparison Thomas Scanlan sees between English and Spanish brutality in the New World when reading texts like John Underhill's *Newess from America . . . Containing a true Relation of their War-like Proceedings These Two Years Last Past* (London, 1638), even if that comparison was ultimately scuttled in favor of rationalization and denial.[83] Underhill used David's war as an excuse for bloodshed (that God punished sins against God and humans with a vengeance that spared no person): "sometimes the Scripture declareth women and children must perish with their parents; sometime the case alters; but we will not dispute it now. We had sufficient light from the word of God for our proceedings."[84] The inner light justified a slaughter that, committed by the Spanish or described by Las Casas, would have raised condemnation in these same English.

Even in the rhetoric, the English had a much harder time distinguishing themselves from the Spanish and were much more ambivalent toward them (they did imitate them as well). Between Gage and Phillips, the anti-Catholic, anti-Spanish rhetoric reached possibly its highest pitch in England, perhaps even surpassing the intensity of the French representations of Spain in the Wars of Religion. This centrality of the example of Spain generally persisted in diverse forms and for complex religious, economic, and political motives.

II

French religious writing in and about the New World was also indebted to Spanish influences even as, in some instances, the writers resisted Spain or felt ambivalent about its colonization, particularly in its treatment of the Natives. In France, collections also helped to promote colonies in the New World, and between 1632 and 1672, the Jesuits published their annual relations, partly in order to promote their mission to the Natives to patrons from the upper class. A Huguenot convert, Paul Le Jeune, was the Jesuit superior at Québec during the 1630s, but although the French Jesuits, as we saw in the last chapter, were well aware of the example of the Spanish Jesuits, they did not, in their relations, dwell directly on Spain.[85] The Society of Jesus did have as its founder a Spaniard, who set out his own example in the way of letters as reports from the field. Apparently, from the first years of the existence of the Society of Jesus (founded in 1540 through a bull by Paul III), Ignatius Loyola, the founder of the Jesuits, encouraged his companions dispersed in Italy to write him regularly, so that he set a precedent for the whole notion of relations.[86] Occasionally, the Jesuits in New France found themselves commenting on more temporal and political matters. Francisco Bressani, an Italian, wrote a relation from New France in 1653 that discussed the lands between the forty-fourth and forty-seventh degrees of latitude and declared, in a brief history of the relations between the French and the English and other Europeans, that although some had supposed that the Spanish had discovered and named Canada, the French had taken possession in 1504. The English captured Québec in 1629 and the English escorted the French priests back to Europe, but after the peace was made, Bressani said, only the Jesuits returned to the mission in New France.[87] In the missions of French priests to the New World, whose accounts include those by Sagard, Le Jeune, Hennepin, and others, there was a double movement of French colonial thought on policy and the transnational nature of religious orders or sects.

Whereas accounts of America in French in the sixteenth century had been overwhelmingly Protestant, in the seventeenth century they were Catholic. The French aspect of the mission to New France was part of Christianization, the post-Tridentine or Counter-Reformation attempt to spread spiritual discipline through lay culture in France and overseas, and civilization, the effort to civilize the marginal parts of French society and Natives abroad. While at a general level the French Jesuits followed the example of their Spanish counterparts, they did not take full advantage of the insights of the Spaniards about Native culture precisely because, as Peter Goddard has argued, they sought, as part of a program of the Catholic élite, to suppress traditional life and beliefs within France and overseas ("outre-mer") and saw the Natives as a *tabula rasa,* attributing to them characteristics they had used to describe the lower classes and marginal peoples of France.[88] The French Jesuits, I would suggest, were taking a view that was more akin to that of Columbus, who thought the Natives had no religion or at least were clean slates for conversion. On the other hand, the French Franciscans, who from 1612 to 1614 were part of the colony of Maragnan in the Amazon delta that usurped what was called Maranhoa, seemed to have had a closer connection with Franciscans in Iberian colonies.[89]

Sometimes the French priests, such as the Dominican and so-called "Herodotus of the Indies," Jean Baptiste Du Tertre, could take a sympathetic view of Natives and try to disabuse people in France of misconceptions. In *Histoire générale des isles de S. Christophe . . .* (1654), he declared of the Natives, who are portrayed "more as monsters than as reasonable men," that "in truth our Savages are Savages only in name" and have "true virtues"; in fact, "the Savages of these islands are the most content, the most happy, the least vicious, the most sociable, the least misshapen and the least tormented of maladies of all the nations of the world."[90] Du Tertre, who could be Columbus here, had also spoken of glory ("gloire") in his "Epistle,"[91] another Spanish preoccupation in the New World; in his address "To the Reader," he promised "to give an entire knowledge of all the good ("bien") encountered there [in America] without any exaggeration and of all the bad ("mal") without any disguise ("déguisement"), which is something rare enough in most Authors, which have written about America until now"[92]—an assertion that became a familiar topos in New World narratives from the Spanish onward; he also recorded the way the French watched the English colony flourish with a large population while the French settlement diminished.[93]

The influences on Catholicism in France came from Italy, from the Council of Trent—which attempted to restore Christianity to its essence, in which individuals integrated rules of living into their lives in a context that restored to society discipline and the authority of the Church—and from Spain, with whom the Catholic League had maintained close ties. Through translations, particularly after the marriage of Louis XIII and Anne of Austria, who favored Castilian, the spiritual works of Spaniards—which emphasized internal renewal, particularly the spiritual exercises of Ignatius Loyola, who set out a model of how to be a missionary as a man who worked on himself in order to work on others—became influential in France.[94]

The French had their own history of conquest that they failed to raise when criticizing Spain for being conquerors. In France as well as Spain, there was a tradition of conquest despite what the French would later deny, although they do not seem to have used it extensively in Brazil, the Caribbean, or New France. It is sometimes forgotten that the Norman nobles, who were still settling the Caribbean islands during the seventeenth century and hoped to be lords and to supplement their income through plunder, had a long tradition of piracy and conquest, from before the Norman conquest of England to that of Sicily and the Canary Islands (which they then yielded to Spain), something we observed in chapter 2.[95] A literature of piracy or buccaneering in the Caribbean grew up in the 1680s.[96] The "Epistle," signed by De Frontignieres, declared that he had something new to teach about the example of Spain: "For example you will learn there [in his *Histoire*] many curious particulars, unknown until now, regarding the King of Spain. You will see there in what manner he governs the Indies, the Dignities, whether Temporal or Ecclesiastical in which he is endowed, the revenues to which he has a title; so that these Kingdoms of New Spain are worth more to him than all those of Old."[97] De Frontignieres then talked about the triumph of the French under "LOUIS LE GRAND," so that through imitation the example of Spain and French triumphalism coexisted ambivalently.[98] To glory, the "Preface" added that it was nearly "impossible to know well the grandeur of their adventurers' ("aventuriers") enterprises."[99] It declared "he [the author] makes seen the treatment they [the adventurers] give the Spanish when they take them and that which they receive from the same Spaniards when they are taken."[100] Old habits die hard.

In the seventeenth century, France often shifted its policy on religion in the New World, sometimes resembling Spain's religious politics and sometimes not. Religious directives also had racial and economic dimensions. In order to encourage the growth of the white population in the islands, like Martinique, during the 1660s, Colbert advocated the toleration of Jews and Huguenots, a divergence from the Catholic only policy that Spain had followed and that France had considered when Richelieu assumed power in the 1620s, but he repealed this tolerance and the liberal conditions for African slaves, Huguenots, and Jews in the "Code noir" (1685), which was instituted under his son, Seignelay.[101] Article I gave the Jews, "the declared enemies of the name of Christian," three months to leave the islands.[102] Huguenots and galley slaves were forcibly transported to the French colonies in the Caribbean during the 1680s.[103] Slavery, which occurred in the French and English colonies that relied on tobacco, sugar, and cotton, is one of the most shameful examples of how the French and English, as much as the Spanish, were lords and conquerors, ruining lives and working others to death for their own gain. Once again, to paraphrase Lipsius, the conquerors were conquered. Once more, the "liberalization" or movement to a progressive and enlightened empire did not develop evenly.

Even when England used a rhetoric of triumphalism in the face of the fear of a new universal monarchy that joined Spain and France under the Bourbons, there was an uncertainty and some unexpected anxieties and differences that the English and their rivals experienced. The translations of Spanish works, and the fascination with the Spanish origins of European settlement in the New World and with their conquests, even while that attraction was denied, continued into the eighteenth century but did not always seem to have the same urgency. Las Casas, however, was still used for political ends, as we observed with the role of the English translation of 1656 in Cromwell's Western Design. It is also possible that Comte de Pagan's *Relation* (1655), a translation of Spanish texts on the Amazon, was, as Philip Boucher has suggested, part of French plans for an assault on the Spanish colonies in South America, a kind of French counterpart to the Western Design.[104] In the "Epistle Dedicatory" of the English translation of 1661, the translator, William Hamilton, explained to Charles II that the work was first addressed to "Cardinal *Mazarine,* in order to have set his Majesty of *France* on conquest of the great Kingdome of the *Amazone* to himself."[105] Hamilton exhorted the king to seek out this land unpossessed by the Portuguese and Spanish, "For it is possest by the barbarous Natives only."[106] A similar narrative of liberation arose here: "And the Natives not only in their forlorn condition, but by singular junctures of providence, call for the Christian religion from us, while others cease from that duty."[107] As Spain, Portugal, and France had not pursued this design, England should, and Hamilton quoted Pagan, whose noble background he provided to prove how easy this "design" would be and reminded the king of his own family's service to the royal family; Hamilton even sought reparations for his lost estates from "the troubles of the times."[108] This was a balder proposal than Ralegh's advice to Elizabeth I concerning Guiana. Even as the French and English moved on to commerce from conquest, with a fair bit of backsliding or side-stepping, and their colonies grew in strength, they could not ignore the example of Spain.

As late as 1744, Pierre Charlevoix, a Jesuit and thus another part of the representation of the New World (although Le Jeune had made recommendations on military action), claimed that the French, unlike the Spanish, had no conquerors like Cortés and Pizarro on the stage of the New World, a statement that was true if measured by his term *"éclat"* but inaccurate if the would-be conquerors, pirates, and lords of the French (and often Norman) in the Caribbean were taken into consideration.[109] The term, *"éclat"* can mean a burst of noise, the glitter of a gem, or brilliance, all appropriate for the conquerors whether Charlevoix intended all these meanings. In the "Advertisement" Charlevoix said that some people thought that he should have included the Spanish conquerors, like Cortés and Pizarro, as part of his description of San Domingo, so that "the History of Saint Domingue would have been that of nearly all the Spanish Empire in the new World."[110] Long after the first few decades of contact between European and Native, Spain maintained an influential and originary role in writing about the Americas.

Positive and negative attitudes toward Spain coexisted in France from the six-teenth century through the eighteenth century. An ambivalent attitude toward Spain occurred in France in matters of religion because some objected to the means of converting the Natives and cruelty toward them. Part of the suspicion of the Spanish among the French might have been derived from Jacques de Miggrode's translation of Las Casas in 1578, which Lescarbot, who questioned the godliness and zeal of the Spaniards, made popular (Lescarbot even inflated the number of Native dead that Las Casas had given), but as we have seen, the *légend noire* was not the only view in France, so that the Thevet of *Singularitez* thought that God had rewarded the Spanish with America for taking Granada.[111] Two instances—the work of Louis Hennepin and the translation of Las Casas in 1698—should illustrate the ambivalence in the use and example of Spain in religious accounts in French.

The French and the Natives did not always get along and they sometimes regarded the aboriginals in a much harsher way than did the Spanish missionaries. In his *Description of Louisiana . . .* (1683), Louis Hennepin, a Recollet father, wrote a record of the La Salle expedition, which he dedicated to Louis XIV, as the title page advertised and as the subsequent dedication made plain.[112] Hennepin said that he would never have dared to offer the king a relation of the new discovery, which La Salle, the Governor of Fort Frontenac, Hennepin, and his companions made southwest of New France, if it had not been made under order and if the author had not had the glory of obeying such a glorious monarch in "the conversion of the Infidels."[113] Nothing could keep Hennepin from such a long, hard, and dangerous voyage and from representing it: "I even dare say to YOUR MAJESTY, that the bloody death of one of my Recollet Companions, massacred by these Barbarians, a captivity of eight months where I saw myself cruelly exposed, could not enfeeble my courage, making in me always a mildness in the middle of my pains of working for a God that I wanted to make known to, and worshipped by, these peoples and for a King for whom Glory and virtues were without bounds."[114] Louis XIV and his minister, Seignelay, were both receptive to La Salle's proposal for a second expedition because they hoped his expedition would help provide a base for an attack on Mexico and help them gain control over Spain's silver mines or trade.[115] The second expedition of 1684 was recounted in Henri Joutel's *Journal Historique du dernier voyage que feu M. de la Sale fit* (Paris, 1713), which also sought to refute

Hennepin.[116] This account recalled the deaths of Jean de Brébeuf and his fellow missionaries at the hands of the Iroquois in New France during the 1640s.

The more utopian view of the Natives, which occurred at first contact with Columbus and which happened in Las Casas and then in Rousseau, deserted Hennepin as he reported his torture and enslavement. He sounded more like Oviedo and Sepúlveda on the Natives: the specter of barbarism, which had a classical inheritance, never quite went away. In many European representations of the Natives, even this late and much later, it was hard for the Natives to be human, a mixture of many positive and negative qualities. They were barbarous and cruel or saintly and noble. Although the French had used Las Casas as a means of criticizing Spanish cruelty against the Natives, Hennepin forgot the Spanish here and concentrated on the cruel barbarity of the aboriginals. This constituted a contradiction in the French view of the Natives and in their relation with their Spanish antecedents. In the "Discourse" Hakluyt had complained about the universal monarchy of Spain under Charles V and the growing power under his son, Philip II, while hoping that Elizabeth I would grow in power and glory. Under Louis XIV, the languages of universalism and glory were as great and pervasive as under the monarchs at the height of the Spanish empire. In the process of rivaling Spain, England and France were succeeding it.

Even in grammar there was a translation of empire. Whereas Julius Caesar in his account of the wars in Gaul referred to himself in the third person, Hennepin addressed Louis XIV in the second person plural and in the third person singular.

It is constant, SIRE, that no sooner that we have been able to win them over and gain their friendship, the account that we have given them of a part of the heroic virtues of YOUR Most-Christian MAJESTY, of his surprising actions in his Conquests, of the felicity and the love of his Subjects, moved them to receive more easily the principles of the truths of the Gospel and to revere the Cross that we have engraved on the trees above your arms, for a mark of continual protection that you give to the Christian Religion and to make them remember again the principles that we have happily taught them.[117]

The Natives were to be tamed and won over as friends in part with an account of the heroic virtues of the French king. From the beginning, as with Gonneville and Cartier, the French had used the cross as a sign of religious teaching and territorial possession.[118] The religious preceded the secular power in the visual imagery and the rhetoric of the inscriptions and the accounts representing the planting or inscribing of the crosses. Teaching the Natives Christianity was central to French representations of the New World. As the ultimate compliment, La Salle, Hennepin, and their companions had named the new territory "Louisiana" after their king, a land larger than Europe that they could have called "the Delights of America," just as Verrazzano had named the land he saw "Francesca" after François I and Ralegh had named "Virginia" after his virgin queen.[119] This land, which was capable of forming a great empire, was henceforth known by the name of Louis and might thereby pretend to the honor of his protection and hope for the advantage to be part of, or belong to, him.[120] In keeping with this providential view of history, Hennepin continued to court Louis's favor, praising him in terms of the sun and glory and putting this praise in the mouths of the Natives. This passage is reminiscent of some of the flattery Ralegh had put in the mouths of the Natives of Guiana, the people who lauded and magnified the queen of England and the monarch who would deliver them from the tyranny of Spain; Hennepin wrote: "It seems, SIRE, that God has destined you to be the Master, by the happy account that he has of your glorious Name of Sun, that they call in their language Louis, and to which, as a sign of their respect and of their adoration, before they smoke, they present their pipe with these words: *Tchendiouba Loüis;* that is to say, smoke Sun."[121] This representation, which sounded as though Versailles had come to the Mississippi, led to the question: were these the same barbarous Natives whom Hennepin had just described? If so, was the name of Louis enough to pacify them? If they remained as they had been, had Hennepin complimented his king by having these barbarians pay homage to Louis? This apparently contradictory rendition of the Indians continued as Hennepin said that at all moments they kept the name of "Louis" in their mouths and did nothing that did not pay homage to the sun, under the name of Louis. This was a circular rhetoric in which the name of the king began and ended all thought, word, and deed for the French and the Natives, even though there had been serious conflict between them.

Dissent from this providential view, not that different from Oviedo's paean to Charles V as the universal monarch and lord of the world or Hakluyt's image of Elizabeth as the champion of Protestants, was something that Hennepin could not tolerate. His praise or flattery of Louis XIV extended to the king as leader of the true Catholic faith in America and Europe.

> After that, SIRE, no one will doubt that this is a mystery hidden by providence, who has reserved to your care and to your piety the glory to carry the light of Faith to these blind people and to pull them from the shadows where they would always have lived if YOUR MAJESTY, still more applied to the Service of God and to Religion than to the Government of States, had not honoured us with these pious Employments, while It [glory] works with success for the destruction of Heresy.[122]

God worked through Louis who would lift the shadows from the blind Natives and destroy the Protestants: the implication was that both these groups represented darkness and ignorance. Hennepin prayed that happiness would accompany Louis's holy enterprises, and he assured the king that these constituted the prayers and wishes of all the Recollets of France and Hennepin in particular, "who wishes only to have the honour to continue to YOUR MAJESTY the services that I swore to him as early as the Campaigns in Holland, where I had the honour to follow his sacred person in the capacity of Missionary."[123] The Spanish had once tried to subdue Holland, and the French now made the attempt. Philippe Quinault wrote an epic and Charles Perrault an ode to the newly converted in 1686 to honor the persuasive powers of the magnanimous king, Louis XIV, who often had an aggressive policy against Protestants.[124] The champion of Catholicism was shifting from Spain to France—France would succeed Spain and then, under Napoleon, subdue it. Hennepin left off with his greatest passion to adore his God and serve his king and give him signs of zeal and the deepest respect. For this Recollet missionary, the discovery of Louisiana was a pretext to address Louis himself, the absolute monarch of the absolute God.

Other related works took up these concerns: Louis Hennepin's *Nouveau voyage d'un pais plus grand que l'Europe* (London, 1698), dedicated to William III of England, and Antonio de Solís's *Histoire de la conquête du Mexique,* translated by S. de Broë (Paris, 1691), which was about the riches of Mexico (one of Iberville's and La Salle's goals) and was one of many French translations of Spanish works about the New World during the 1680s and 1690s. The "Preface" to Solís's text justified the translation: the Spanish received "The History of the Conquest of Mexico" with approbation, the action of Cortés, a hero, "and if this example makes us see of what importance is the choice of a Historian, for the glory of a Prince and a great Man, it teaches us elsewhere in what way to judge their conduct."[125] The translator observed Cortés's flaws and in places differed with Solís, who used the "excellent models" of Tacitus and Sallust, but thought the conqueror a hero nonetheless, for he still spoke of "the glory of Cortés."[126] The translator declared that "The goal of the Spanish in these expeditions, was not glory alone; they also sought gold. . . . This dangerous passion [avidity] pushed them to commit horrible cruelties, for which even the Authors of their own Nation reproached them. Cortés was not exempt from that."[127] Moreover, the translator praised him for introducing the Catholic faith into Mexico. Envy attacked this general who was "at the highest point of his glory, loved like a father, and respected like a Sovereign by the Spaniards and the Mexicans."[128] Then the translator complained that the rulers and government of Spain did not use Columbus and Cortés well.[129] Lust for Spanish gold was persistent among the French. The Spanish, unlike the English, who were making slave raids into Native territory in the southeast, were friendly toward the French and, from Pensacola, which was founded in 1698 to put off French colonization of the Gulf Coast, helped the French who had problems such as starvation. The relations between the French and the Spanish on this coast were ambivalent.

The contradictory attitude toward the Natives in Hennepin's account—they were barbarous but honored and paid homage to Louis—had related contradictions in Solís's narrative and coexisted with anti-Indian rhetoric and the continued influence of Las Casas in France 120 years after the first translation appeared. In another French edition of Las Casas, *Relations of the Voyages and the Discoveries that the Spaniards Made in the West Indies . . . ,* published in Amsterdam in 1698, Pralard, a bookseller, addressed his "Epistle" to the Count of Toulouse, the grand admiral of France. He praised the West Indies as the being something worthy of the count's attention, where he would see a description of the most beautiful, rich, fertile, happy country in the world, where God had gathered for pleasure a great deal of gold, silver, pearls, and emeralds as well as people who hardly make wars, ready to acquiesce, it seemed to Europeans. The editor said that perhaps the count would go to these regions and personally conduct the king's navy and seek glory. The "Advertisement," which followed, spoke of Columbus and Vespucci, Cortés, Pizzaro, and others and of the various parts of America. The note stated that it would be hard to believe all the cruelties the Spanish had wrought in the New World except that they were reported by the Spanish themselves, and Las Casas was mentioned as a prime example of someone who had tried to have the Council of the Indies stop this destruction.[130] In this translation, the editor noted at the end of the "Advertisement": "In some places the things that appeared too cruel and that could have caused pain for delicate persons were softened."[131] This was a new twist, a suggestion that left something even more terrible to the imagination. The next section was an address, "The Bookseller of Holland to the Readers," in which the editor/bookseller said that he was renewing an old book and that it was 70 years since it had appeared in Holland, that in France the populace should heed that this book spoke against persecution of the Indians, and that the French continued to persecute the Protestants.[132] Las Casas wrote about converting by good example and not by violence: Las Casas's views of the New World once more became a typological parable for the Old. Protestants especially but not exclusively would not let his example die, so that it continued to qualify the religious model of Spain in the Americas.

The French published other important eyewitness accounts during this period: although they could be written by secular writers, the debate over religion was central. One account appealed, for instance, to the experience of the Frenchman born in America, Pierre Boucher. In the "Epistle" to his *History . . . of New France* (1664), Pierre Boucher addressed Colbert because "God having given you a particular love of this country, also without a doubt it will increase, when you will have been more amply informed of the bounty and the beauty of all our countries."[133] Boucher was a go-between who used his rhetoric and natural history to make greater Colbert's great love for New France. He said that those who knew Colbert thought that the only thing that moved his spirit was the glory of the king and the interests of France. Boucher believed that his narrative would contribute something to the inclinations that Colbert already had, "to make flourish our New France and to make it a new World."[134] In the "Foreword," Boucher mentioned that he was saying nothing that could not be found in the Jesuit relations or in Champlain's accounts but stressed that their descriptions were not in a brief single volume and emphasized the spiritual work of the bishops (like those in the primitive church, something that would have made the Hakluyt of chapter 11 of the "Discourse" happy, at least in theory), priests, and Jesuits and the virtue of the colony. He actually uninvited "the wicked."[135] Early in the first chapter, Boucher returned to the block to French exploration and expansion into the interior, the Iroquois.[136] Geography affected rhetoric. Boucher, living between Québec and Montréal on the St. Lawrence River, was not concerned with the Spanish, whereas La Salle and others in Louisiana and in the region of the Mississippi generally had to be.[137] In discussing New France, he paused to give the English colonies to the south as an example worthy of imitation, its buildings, large number of settlers bearing arms, its abundance of merchandise, its postal service—and Boucher's challenge is "what can be done there, can be done here."[138] In representing the New World, both the English and French, especially because of the proximity of their colonies, could be as interested in each other's efforts as in those of Spain.

Another significant account was the self-defense of Baron Lahontan for his work in the New World and how that was received in France. Lahontan concentrated on the theme of the struggle of French colonies to survive in America and the English as an example. The long title of Baron Lahontan's *New Voyages* . . . (1703) advertised the volume's description of the nature, commerce, customs, religion, and warfare of the Natives. One of the subtitles declared: "*L'intérêt des François & des Anglois dans le Commerce qu'ils font avec ces Nations; l'advantage que l'Angleterre peut retirer dans ce Païs, étant en Guerre avec la France.*" The French and the English were at war, but even in peace, France increasingly saw England and Holland as its principal rivals. Lahontan's epistle dedicatory was to Frederick IV of Denmark in which he paid homage to the king and his family while denying that the author was guilty of any of the charges leveled against him.[139] Like Lafitau, Lahontan took up the old hypothesis of cannibalism.[140] Lahontan's book, published in the Netherlands, involved criticism of France, representations of the Natives and assessment of the English in America. The opening of the preface, which referred to the author in the third person, seemed to be by, or to have met with the approval of, Lahontan, who, unlike Boucher, criticized previous relations about the New World because "The Authors were Missionaries that is to say people engaged by their profession to persuade the World that their pain, which is elsewhere laudable, is not altogether unfruitful."[141] As in England, in France, there was no consensus about the New World, its inhabitants, and the most effective way of representing it.

Both Boucher's and Lahontan's accounts revealed that the French in North America were now often more concerned about the English than the Spanish, a sign that the balance of power was shifting and that concerns about the closest threats often won out over distant theoretical problems. Promotion in Boucher and self-promotion in Lahontan continued a long tradition in writing about the New World, first in Spain and later in France and England. The various aspects of French writing about the New World—having to do with religion, exploration, ethnology, and politics—suggest the tentativeness of generalizations about this or any "national" writing. Some authors were visitors to the New World, while a few, like Boucher, were born and lived there. One fairly constant topic in these variegated texts was the Natives. These accounts in French faced, occluded, displaced, and vacillated over the example of Spain. The French Jesuits, as we observed in the last chapter and touched on here, knew about the example of the Spanish Jesuits but did not in their relations focus on Spain. Perhaps much of this influence was assumed and left unsaid: both Spanish and French Jesuits set out to convert the Natives by learning their culture and language. As this study concentrates on texts and pays close attention to their rhetoric and language more generally, it has not focused so much on implied models or exemplarity as it might have otherwise. Hennepin's work, which involved a contradictory attitude toward the Natives as barbarous peoples who honored and paid homage to Louis, possessed similar contradictions to those found in Solís's narrative. For 120 years after the first translation of Las Casas appeared in French, his influence persisted but in tandem with a textual practice that embodied an anti-Indian rhetoric. This coexistence of extremes, and various attitudes blended between them, could be found in the same texts. In England at this time, in drama and poetry, ambivalence and contradiction in the presentation of Spain and of the Natives in the New World occurred in the work of leading figures, such as John Dryden and John Dennis, who faced Spain and the New World in more explicit but not necessarily more suggestive ways than William Shakespeare and John Milton did.

III

The literary efforts of the English by writers like John Milton, John Dryden, and John Dennis, and the ambivalence of the first, the romance of the second, and the triumphalism of the third, can only be touched upon here. Here I am concentrating more on collections, which made a more direct contribution to the historiography of expansion, although the literary and dramatic productions were also significant. The theme of Spain remained important in English literary representations of the Americas. John Milton, Renaissance poet, Latin secretary to Cromwell, and Restoration recluse, was a link between the Commonwealth and the Restoration.[142] Even though *Paradise Lost* contained references to Columbus and the New World, this kind of allegory is often tricky: to say that Milton had contradictory roles, someone who was part of Cromwell's government and a poet of liberty, would be, in my view, a more suggestive approach.[143] Is the rebellion against empire in *Paradise Lost* a desire for liberty in the safe retrospective putative space of fiction, or was it always part of Milton's ambivalence over empire? This is a difficult question to answer. A related and more commonly discussed case is allegorical readings of Shakespeare's *The Tempest* (1610).[144] John Dryden and John Dennis represented continental rivals more directly than Milton and Shakespeare did in these texts.

The fascination with Spain was still very much a part of English representations of the New World, including its arts, such as drama and poetry. Dryden and Dennis provide good illustrations of that preoccupation during the Restoration and after the Glorious Revolution. Dryden's *The Indian Emperour* (1667) was a fantastic drama about, and sometimes a comic and romantic rendition of, the Spanish conquest of Mexico, as if the threat of Spain were no longer serious or based in the world of economics and politics. After the usurping queen of Mexico, Zempoalla, had killed herself (her son Acacis, has also done the same) and Amexia, the lawful queen, and Montezuma had drawn a moral of the tragedy, Montezuma spoke the epilogue to *The Indian Queen, written by Sir Robert*

Howard and John Dryden, reducing the Spanish conquerors to a joke in which they were preferable to London wits: "Our naked Indians then, when Wits appear,/ Wou'd as soon chuse to have the Spaniards here."[145] This Restoration tragedy was a romance in which the Spanish conquest, rather than bringing with it the hard consequences of empire, became a pretext for love gone wrong. The Spanish were absorbed into the urbanity of London society, forged into a joke about wit by Montezuma, no longer the captive king who met with a harsh end at the hands of the Spaniards but a mediator of taste between playwright and audience. In "The Epistle Dedicatory" to the Princess Anne in *The Indian Emperour, or, the Conquest of Mexico by the Spaniards* (1667), Dryden, declaring his freedom as a poet to deviate from history, pursued metaphors of English grace, Spanish violence, and Indian simplicity: "Under your Patronage *Montezuma* hoped he was more safe than in his Native Indies: and therefore came to throw himself at your Graces feet; paying that homage to your Beauty, which he refus'd to the violence of his Conquerours. He begged only that when he would relate his sufferings, you would consider him as an *Indian Prince,* and not expect any other Eloquence from his simplicity."[146] The play ended with Guyomar lamenting the death of his father, Montezuma, and wishing freedom from the Spanish. The liberation from Spanish tyranny was a fantasy found in Hakluyt's "Discourse" and Ralegh's *Discovery of Guiana.* Dryden's Natives loved freedom but were not eloquent like Europeans.

Holland and Spain remained in Dryden's representations of British triumph. Dryden's *Conquest of Granada by the Spaniards* (1672) was dedicated to "His Royal Highness the Duke," just as "*Virgil* inscribed his *Æneids* to *Augustus Caesar.*"[147] Although this play was about the victory of the Spanish, the dedicatee, the duke, defeated the Spaniards and forced Dunkirk to surrender. Dryden called him a Conqueror.[148] He also condemned the Dutch for rebelling against their lawful sovereign, for neglecting English charity in that cause and for becoming swelled up with their preeminence in trade, so that when they "dar'd to dispute the Soveraignty of the Seas," three nations wanted the duke to revenge these wrongs.[149] Just as the French found the English to be rivals in the New World, the English were disturbed by Dutch success in the Americas and in colonization and world trade. The Spanish were not necessarily the primary focus anymore, but they were surprisingly important in English representations of the New World even as Spain declined. In "The Preface" to *Don Sebastian, King of Portugal* (1690) John Dryden represented another aspect of the tyranny of Spain, its absorption of Portugal from 1580 to 1640.[150]

As it was becoming "Britain," "England" was sensing the possibility of its becoming the supreme empire in the world, and leading up to and during the War of Spanish Succession, France became the great threat to European peace and English or British interests largely because it looked as though the House of Bourbon would absorb Spain. In 1704 John Dennis published a poem with the revealing title, *Britannia Triumphans: or the Empire Sav'd and Europe Deliver'd. By the Success of her Majesty's Forces under the Wise and Heroick Conduct of his Grace the Duke of Marlborough* (London, 1704). The title page also included, as classicism and *translatio imperii* might demand, a quotation from Virgil: "*Ab Jove Prin-*

cipium Musae." Dennis's work suggested the dawn of Britain as a great imperial power seeking itself as the balance of power in Europe. His dedication equally supported this national self-image: "To Her Most Sacred Majesty/ **ANNE**, / Queen of *Great Britain, France* and *Ireland*./ The True Defender of the Protestant Faith;/ The Great Supporter of the Liberties of *Europe;*/ The Illustrious Maintainer of the Honour of the *English* Nation; and,/ The Victorious Asserter of the Empire of the Ocean," . . . The only word that almost rivaled the size of type in the queen's name was "Poem," which appeared near the bottom of the page and was lined up with "Anne," which dominated the top of the page if not the entire dedicatory page. This Britannic England now defended the Protestant faith (not the original Catholic one that gave Henry VIII his title, Defender of the Faith), stood for liberty in Europe (something still maintained in the Second World War) and now would rule the waves. After praising the peace "that flies to *Anna*'s sacred Breast" for refuge and that from there will influence the world, Dennis scorned the heart of the new tyrant and rival, which was now France and not Spain: "But the *French* Tyrant's Breast had never Peace,/ There endless Strife, there dire Ambition reigns,/ He what he never had can ne'er bestow. / Peace without Freedom is an empty Name, But he calls miserable Bondage Peace,/ As Plunder, Murder, Rape he Empire calls."[151]

Like his contemporary, John Harris, Dennis represented France as a rival and showed the reversals in the English views of Holland and Spain. Although England was the new great empire of the title page and of the dedication, Dennis could not forget the Holy Roman Empire as the heir to Rome. The poem declaimed: "*Germania,* raise thy tuneful Voice on high,/ This is the Nation preordain'd by Fate/ To save thee Daughter of Imperial *Rome,*/ Just sinking in the vast Abyss of Time."[152] The new empire would save the old: even though both were heirs to Rome, England was fated to be the savior of the Roman tradition. Dennis now commented on history, more specifically on this strange shift in alliances and enemies: "Oh *Austria, Austria,* had thy *Philip* known/ That time e'en then was harnessing the Years,/ When this brave People, Object of his Rage/ And of his Hate, should prove thy Noblest Friends,/ Should rescue both thy bright Imperial Crowns,/ Deliver *Germany,* recover *Spain*."[153] In a twist, it was Spain who hated the English, "such a generous Race," so that had Philip known the future, "He great *Eliza* would have courted then/ For Friendship, as *Maria* for Desire."[154] In Dennis's mythology the league that had just been victorious was *ab ovo* then and Philip, like Leopold or Charles, "With great *Britannia*'s awful Queen had joyn'd/ To establish Right and Peace, and from the Proud/ And strong Oppressor vindicate Mankind."[155] Here was a revisionary political typology in which Elizabeth and Anne were both the friends of Spain and the defenders of Europe against French tyranny. The language of scapegoating in England was now directed at France as it had long been applied to Spain and, in the heat of commercial rivalry and conflict, to Holland.

These English literary representations showed an ambivalent representation of Spain in the New World while forging an English and a "British" identity. In this period the work of Dryden and Dennis suggests that whereas Spain remained important in these representations, France and Holland, who were now great rivals in Europe and beyond, helped to define the anxieties of English writers over the life of their nation and the power of their empire. The translation of empire, as Dennis represented it, produced a line from Rome to Britain. Dryden's Spain was the stuff of romance, a cruel and feudal power that had wronged the noble savage. Whereas Dennis focused more on the French than on the Spanish, Dryden, reducing the Spaniards to comic ridicule, still framed them in a romantic and heroic world of honor and glory. The collectors and editors of the time in France and in England displayed similar contradictions and ambivalence in their attitudes toward Spain.

IV

The great age of collections of narratives in French and English about the New World occurred from about 1580 to 1630, but some interesting collections continued with Melchisédech Thévenot, John Harris, and John Stevens from 1663 to 1711. Throughout this study, we have seen how, through translation, France and England exchanged ideas about Spain, and rather than focus on the literary uses of Spain, I will concentrate here on collections and their work of translation because they were more self-consciously part of the historiography of expansion than were the plays of Dryden and the poems of Dennis. One of Cartier's voyages had to be re-translated from the English version in Hakluyt because the French original was lost. Sometimes the views of Spain traveled between the two countries by comments and analysis of works in the other language that the author had read but had not translated. Hakluyt's *Principall Navigations* made much of La Popelinière's comments on English navigation and colonization. This discussion will focus on collections primarily but will also examine related authors who were not collectors, like R. B., John Oldmixon, and John Lawson (collected in Stevens), all of whom had much to say about Spain in the New World. These authors were continuing the promotional work of someone like Hakluyt the Younger.

In 1663 Melchisédech Thévenot's *Relation de divers voyages cvrievx . . .* provided French translations of Hakluyt, Purchas and others. In the dedication to the king, Thévenot said that Louis XIV's glory had filled Europe and that his subjects were ready to carry it beyond the ocean. The "Epistle" also set out examples from Portuguese maps, letters from Dutch and English generals and presidents of companies revealing their mistakes, and secrets about countries the Dutch had tried to keep hidden while asserting the "natural right" of France to furnish settlers enough to people the New World.

> These Relations will make them see that the other Peoples of Europe who have undertaken the peopling of some part of these vast lands, have exhausted themselves in executing this design. Only France alone can afford it, only she alone can send enough people to plant Faith there and to maintain the Colonies that they cultivate. It seems that the possession of it belongs to them by this natural law and that it had been reserved for her in the time of Your reign, under which there is no exaltation that she cannot promise.[156]

Thévenot exalted the glory of his king, who gave the law to the other princes of Europe and who was distinguished from other conquerors by the number and grandeur of his victories. Louis XIV would order discoveries of distant lands and increase knowledge in medicine, arts, silk-making, artillery, and printing. All this would bring the admiration of all men for Louis, as men admired the gods of antiquity. This collection was an example of Thévenot's zeal and faithfulness in his service to the king. The "Note" began with the justification of the collection: "I UNDERTAKE to give to France the English Voyages of Hakluyt and of Purchas, which for a long time she has wished to have in her Language."[157] Thévenot supplemented Hakluyt and Purchas with material that had not seen the light of day, especially works about Asia by Asians. Thévenot mentioned that through trade and navigation Portugal had spread all over the world and that the United Provinces, covering a small territory, had moved beyond fishing to possess the East Indies and the richest trade of the seas and to be recognized as equals with their former sovereigns. The Netherlands used French labor and had many French inhabitants.[158] He attested to the accuracy and the choice of the best sources and sought to save from oblivion the memorable actions and voyages of the French.

Navigation and trade in the past two centuries had played a role in all the great revolutions. The neighbors of France had been elevated through these two means: "That way Spain found itself in a state of a dispute of magnitude with France."[159] Although Thévenot praised the Spanish, Portuguese, and Netherlanders for achieving so much through trade and navigation, he set out their problems of exhausting men and resources, not reaping all the profits, and using foreigners. Of Spain, he said: "But the Spaniards exhausted themselves of soldiers to arm those rich Fleet and to provide the Place of their numerous Establishments; and perhaps the gold and silver of Peru and of Mexico did not enrich them in proportion to how this draining-off of men enfeebled them."[160] Thévenot presented the negative side of empire: the Spanish had lost more in manpower than they had gained in riches. The problems of the expansion of Spain, Portugal, and the United Provinces, although a warning, did not prevent Thévenot from calling on his country to follow these examples: "I imagined that the examples of these Conquests and the riches of our Neighbours derive from them could one day excite those of our Nation to undertake the same thing and to navigate in those distant Seas, under the Colours of France and that the reading of Voyages would excite them to do the same and would also serve to instruct them in the conduct needed there."[161] Thévenot also made a shipwrecked Basque the first European to land in America, an inspiration to Columbus, whose enterprise cost Spain so little and whose discovery so profited the Spanish kings.

Reading narratives of the new lands had helped the navigators and companies of Portugal, the United Provinces, Spain, and England. It was obvious that Thévenot was also following the example of England: "and I remarked in many of the English voyages that the reading of Hakluyt had often got their Navigators and their whole Fleets out of scrapes."[162] Perhaps Thévenot's work would perform the same function in France, whose glory and interest he wished to serve. He would provide the best foreign examples to help the French in navigation, commerce, and the establishment of colonies. Thévenot suggested that it was not division in France that put a damper on the success of Villegagnon, Ribault, and others in establishing colonies: "I shall try to disabuse them of this opinion, for they will see in the Relations of the Establishment of all the colonies of the others, and principally the English, the Hollanders, the Spanish and the Portuguese, who will be in a volume apart, of a fair size, what happened at the beginning of their enterprises, the revolts and the divisions of the Pizzaros and the Almagres in Peru and the Cortes and the Narvaes in Mexico."[163] This topos of plenitude through allusion, the brief expression that was a substitute for the narratives themselves that would not be included in the collection, helped to create the impression that the negative examples of the colonization by other nations should inspire France to persevere on its own and to enjoy the positive results that its neighbors now reaped in their overseas possessions. France should learn from England, which did not allow the first disgrace and ruin in Virginia to prevent it from establishing a colony.

Thévenot saw other advantages to reading about voyages; for example, it mitigated against condemning out of hand anything that was not done according to one's country and improved knowledge of history, geography, natural history, navigation, and commerce. He reiterated his imitation of Hakluyt and Purchas.[164] In setting out the structure of the collection, Thévenot showed that he was using material from after Purchas's death. The "Note" of the second volume said that, as mentioned in the note to the first volume, the collection was meant to instruct the Frenchman: "I believe that the History of Commerce and of Navigation of the other Peoples of Europe will serve him to conduct better similar enterprises."[165] Even in the 1660s, the use of the example of Spain and other countries could be instructive for France: Thévenot represented the negative and positive aspects of the example of Spain.

John Harris's collection more resembled Thévenot's than the promotional work of R. B., whom the British Library identifies as Nathaniel Crouch. Before we get to Harris, it is important to show that how the English—or, for that matter, the French—represented the example of Spain did not develop in an entirely linear way. There were tendencies and trends that refracted the change that was going on in the actuality and experience of colonization, but there was a haunting or recurrence of old attitudes and tropes that led to a kind of multiple concurrence in these representations. R. B.'s work is a good way of illustrating this double action of recurrence and concurrence.

In *The English Empire in America* . . . (1685), R. B. returned more to origins and was reminiscent of earlier English texts that emulated the Spanish drive for God and gold in the New World. According to R. B., the English laureate sang of the New World: "Nay in this Bounteous, and this Blessed Land,/The Golden Ore lies mixt with Common Sand."[166] Despite the title, he preferred the term "New World," to "America," "*this Land of Wonders,*" whose discovery he attributed to Columbus.[167] This attribution of Spanish origin did not prevent R. B. from bringing up the previous claim of Madoc ap Owen Gwyneth of Wales, the view that Welsh words could be found among the Mexicans and the pilot who knew of America and who left his papers to Columbus. R. B. did view these stories as "uncertainties" and turned his attention to "the real discovery thereof by *Columbus,* which is thus related by *Gomara* and *Mariana,* two Spanish writers."[168] The ambivalence to Columbus was mild but intricate, resembling the topos of inexpressibility that mentions something by claiming not to say it.

As judicious and fair as R. B. was, he did some damage to the reputation of Spaniards. Concerning the mythic pilot story, which was found elsewhere, R. B. reported on the other representations of the pilot:

> the time, place, Countrey, and name of this Pilot is uncertain, and therefore other Authors affirm it to be a fable or *Spanish* contrivance, as envying that an *Italian* and Forreigner should have the glory of being the first discoverer of the Indies, and the more judicious *Spaniards* account it a Tale, and give a more probable Relation thereof, and of the cause which moved *Columbus* to this mighty undertaking, and not the Pilots Papers or reports.[169]

While showing the judiciousness of the best Spanish authors on the subject of Columbus, R. B. also demonstrated the dissension from within. The envy might be a little displaced as the English were so often uncomfortable with the priority of Columbus and the antecedent of Spain. In fact, R. B. revisited the story of how Columbus, through his brother Bartolomé (here "*Bartholomew*") did not agree to terms with Henry VII: in this version, which is the stuff of romance and actual experience in marine travel and commerce in the Middle Ages and early modern Europe, pirates seized Bartolomé on his way to England and he had to fend for himself by making sea cards before he could approach Henry VII, by which time it was too late because Columbus had hastened his suit beforehand in Spain.[170] This is the great lost chance of England, perhaps as much mythology as fact, but a story the English seldom got tired of telling. After all, R. B. was recounting the story almost 200 years after. The swings in tone themselves highlighted the ambivalence concerning Columbus and Spain in this text.

All was forgiven in a short space: Columbus became a hero in a romance or travel narrative. R. B.'s style was more literary here: a story lay within the larger narrative. It was a heroic tale of Columbus taking possession of the New World:

> With Tears of Joy, the late mutinous Mariners behold the desired Land, and that Yesterday were ready to destroy, now as far distracted with contrary passions, imbrace and almost adore their dear *Columbus,* for so happily bringing them to this Land of Promise; On shore they go, and felling a Tree, make a Cross thereof, which they there erected, and took possession of this New World, in the name of the Catholick King; . . .[171]

This was a seminal moment in the possession of the New World: the English were absent here and, like the sailors who had wanted to mutiny against Columbus, came to celebrate him. R. B. made Columbus heroic and gave an emotional, if not a sentimental, view of the turning point. He came to praise

Columbus even as he had reported objections against him here and earlier. Legal and religious possession followed the outpouring of joy. The English, once a Catholic nation in Columbus's day, were, as were the French in the 1680s, in the process of making a national religion: while the French opted for Catholicism in 1685, the English chose Protestantism in 1688. The glory of the Catholic king in this passage would have had certain resonances for many English readers, and they might not necessarily have added to a feeling of Columbus's glory.

Spanish kindness mixed with cruelty in R. B.'s account of Columbus's first encounters with the Natives. He reported that the Spanish were so kind to a woman that the Natives came to the ships and thought

> the Spaniards to be some Divine Nation sent from Heaven; Though they thought them Canibals or Man-eaters, and such indeed they afterward proved in some sense, not leaving in some few years after their arrival above two hundred *Indians,* alive, of four Millions that before inhabited these Countries.[172]

R. B. began gently, as did the Spanish in his description, but then showed a reversal: the Natives thought the Spanish to be cannibals and they did end up devouring their hosts. What appeared to be a pastoral version of the Spanish turned into an indictment of them. Columbus's glory found qualification. In R. B.'s account Native oracles predicted that strangers would come to destroy the images of their gods. Rather than godliness, R. B. implied, the Spanish sought gold: "Nothing more pleased the *Spaniards* than the Gold, which the innocent Inhabitants exchanged with them for Bells, Glassess, Points, and other Trifles."[173] Here was the gold and God complex of the Black Legend of Spain, which we have seen repeatedly in this study. The stories of Cortés, Pizarro, and others haunted the English and gave them a chance to dream of riches or to denounce the Spanish for moral depravity, or both at once.

R. B.'s Spanish were grasping gods. Whereas Columbus used his knowledge to predict the lunar eclipse and so appeared as a god to the Natives, Cortés concentrated on gold, exchanging trifles for it. To the Governor, Cortés declared: "I and my Companions are troubled with a Disease at the Heart to which Gold is the only Soveraign Remedy, and therefore we desire him [Montezuma] to furnish us with the greatest quantity he can possible of that Mettal."[174] In the midst of these images of Spanish gold-hunger and cannibalism, R. B. expressed that the Spanish distaste for Native human sacrifice. One envoy bragged that Montezuma "Sacrificed some years Fifty Thousand Men to his Gods."[175] R. B. juxtaposed this enormity beside the deeds of a Spanish captain who massacred nobles and their youths while Cortés was away fighting other Spaniards sent by Velasquez to stop or interrupt Cortés's campaign against Mexico. In R. B.'s account the Natives sought revenge on the cruel Spaniards after long endurance of wrongs: "The *Indians* beholding this unheard of cruelty and injustice, having long endured with patience, the imprisonment of their King, who had charged them to be quiet, now fly all to arms, and falling upon the *Spaniards* wounded many, and pursued others, . . ."[176] The Spaniards lost their treasure and the

Natives sacrificed 40 Spanish prisoners, but R. B. noted that 100, 000 Mexicans died (not including those taken by plague) as opposed to 50 Spaniards and six horses. The contrast was stark.

R. B. emphasized the classical notion of heroes as exemplars in his description of two great explorers, both Italian and neither sailing for England. While giving Columbus his due, he qualified that attention by focusing also on Vespucci:

> Neither ought *Americus Vespusius,* a *Florentine,* to be forgotten, who was Second to *Columbus* in the glory of the grand and successful enterprize of discovering the *New World,* who at the charge of *Emanuel* King of *Porttugal,* undertook the business; He had been one of *Columbus* his Companions in the first expedition, and consequently did now but trace the way that *Columbus* had before shewed him, yet had he this happiness and Honour above his Predecessor, to give his name unto the discovered Country; the whole continent of the *New World* being ever since from him generally called *America.*[177]

The example of Spain, known through Columbus, was able to guide Portugal in the New World, but it was its captain who, in R. B.'s account, gave the new lands in the Western Atlantic their name. Vespucci learned from the master Columbus but stole some of his glory. The English and the French would try to do some of the same.

Pizzaro, another example of a Spanish predecessor in the New World, played a more ambivalent role in R. B.'s work than Columbus did. His desire for gold and riches was a primary theme. As in Ralegh and earlier English texts, R. B.'s narrative represented the tyranny of the Spaniards over the Natives. Pizarro and his party got to "*Puna,* where they were well received of the governor, till by abusing their Wives, they provoked the *Indians* to take Arms, but were soon defeated, and thereby their Riches became a prey to the prevailing *Spaniards.*"[178] The sexual and financial greed of the Spanish against the innocents was another angle of the abuses that Las Casas had set out. In R. B.'s version of events, Pizarro speaks about himself as "*an Ambassador from the Pope and Emperor,* who were Lords of the World."[179] R. B. showed a religious foundation to the Spanish conquest.

In developing this episode in the conflict between Native and Spaniard, R. B. developed a specific scene that encapsulated the tension between the sides. Vincent, a Dominican friar, warned King Atabaliba about Christ, who ascended into heaven,

> *leaving for his Vicar on Earth St. Peter and his Successors, which we call Popes, one of whom hath now given the most Puissant King of Spain Emperor of the Romans, the Monarchy of the World. Obey the Pope therefore worthy Prince, and receive the faith of Christ, which if you will believe to be most Holy, and your own most false, you shall do well, but know, that if you do the contrary, we will make War upon you, and destroy and break your Idols to pieces; Let me then advise you to leave off your false worship, and thereby prevent all those mischiefs.*[180]

Atabaliba did not accept this view: R. B. caused him to waste no time in contradicting the friar's assertion and thereby contrasted the Spanish and Native positions:

> *Atabaliba* seemed to wonder at the Preaching of this Frier, and replied, *That he was a free Prince, and would become Tributary to none, neither did he acknowledg any greater Lord than himself; As for the Emperour he could be well content to be in friendship with so great a Monarch, and to be acquainted with him, but for the Pope, he would not obey him, who gave away what was none of his own, and took a Kingdom from him whom he had never seen; As for Religion he liked well his own, neither would nor ought he to question the Truth therof, it being so ancient and approved, especially since Christ died, which never happened to the Sun and Moon whom he worshipped. And how do you know, said he, that the God of the Christians created the World?*[181]

This is a kind of implied criticism, as if the Native king were speaking for English critics of Spanish and Catholic cruelty in the Americas, a kind of ventriloquy that Montaigne used in his critique of France when the Natives, who had come to Europe, expressed doubts about the French social order. Atabaliba was on his home ground when he questioned the arrogance of the invading Spaniards. This is an example of an implied typology of Old World and New World with the Natives as voices of wisdom, reason, and liberty against European inequality, superstition, and callousness.

The conflict between Atabaliba and the Spanish friar did not end there. Not content with the friar's response, Atabaliba threw the Bible that the friar had given him on the ground, which caused the friar to call out: "He hath cast the Gospels on the Ground, Revenge it O Christians upon these Infidel Dogs, and since they will not accept our friendship nor our Law, let us utterly destroy them."[182] Pizarro then routed the Indians without losing a person and gained great riches from the captive king, whom he chained, and the Spanish decided to kill Atabaliba anyway.[183] This call to arms was hardly in the tradition of the alternative critique or oppositional criticism of the Dominicans, which made these religious quite different in R. B. than in Las Casas. Under the guidance of their leader, Pedro de Córdoba, the Dominicans, as Las Casas had reported in chapters 3 to 5 in Book III of his *History of the Indies,* had, after they had arrived in Hispaniola in 1510, started in private to be critical of the Spanish treatment of the Natives. Las Casas described the first public denunciation of Spanish cruelty to the Natives and of their enslavement of them: Father Antón Montesino's sermons in December 1511, which showed a split from the ruling land-owning and governing elite of the colony. Las Casas himself had been inspired by seeing Columbus in Seville and was first a landowner in the West Indies and became a Dominican friar a couple of decades or so later. R. B.'s scene was not as obvious as the abuses of the Requirement, which the Spanish read to the Natives in an incomprehensible language before the massacre, but it was part of the Black Legend. The *Requerimento,* which compelled Natives to be obedient to the Spanish crown, might have been indebted to the *jihad* of the Moors on the Iberian peninsula because both were fights based on legal foundations.[184] These contexts were not ones that R. B. provided for his readers. Ambivalence—Columbus the glorious and good example and Pizarro the cruel conqueror—were two sides of the example of Spain in the New World as portrayed by R. B. The representations of the Dominicans are split and contradictory between Las Casas's work and R. B.'s.

In R. B.'s account Atabaliba became a tragic figure. The Spanish ignored his reasonable objections and his plea for life. Of the Atabaliba's death at the hands of the Spanish, R. B. said:

> Notwithstanding those so reasonable Remonstrances, they consulted whether they should burn him alive, and at last Condemned him so that cruel death, but by the Intreaty of some, that Sentence was mitigated, and he was ordered to be strangled by four *Negros,* whom *Pizarro* kept for that purpose, which one night was accordingly performed; the King understanding he was to dye, spake thus to his Murderers, *Why do you kill me? Did not you promise to set me at liberty, if I would give you Gold? I procured it for you, yea, more than you required, yet if it be your pleasure that I must be killed, send me your King of Spain, that I may clear myself of what you falsly object against me;* but the Executioners stopt his Breath before he could proceed further, yet did not vengeance suffer these Ingrateful Villains to escape.[185]

Poetic justice emerged as a device in R. B.'s account of this incident between the Dominican friar and the Native king. Some kind of providence punished the Spanish, whom R. B. labels as murderers, who showed so little respect for the wise and reasonable king that they had what appears to have been four of their African slaves stifle him to death. The struggle was not meant to be fair, one to one, hand to hand. Besides calling the Spaniards "Murderers," R. B. spoke about the "cruel death" they inflicted on the unfortunate king. There is little doubt as to the side with which the readers were supposed to sympathize. R. B. relished the curse the Spaniards brought on themselves through this cruelty. Here is the list of internecine violence:

> *Almagro* was Executed by order of Pizarro, and young Almagro slew *Pizarro,* who was likewise put to death by *de Castro* [.] *John Pizarro* was slaughtered by the *Indians, Martin* and *Francis,* two other of his Brethren were likewise killed; *Ferdinand* was imprisoned in *Spain,* and his end unknown; *Gonzales* was put to death by *Gasca,* and the Civil Wars among themselves utterly destroyed the rest of these Treacherous *Spaniards.*[186]

In this fall into civil strife, justice—providential and poetic—is done. R. B. spared no effort in pointing out the treachery and greed of Pizarro and his fellow Spaniards. Perhaps not enough for R. B., Atabaliba's death was avenged. The hero was now the Indian "prince" just as it was in Dryden where Montezuma is a heroic exemplar before Spanish cruelty. Jean-Jacques Rousseau's "noble savage" was invented long before Rousseau (we see him in Columbus). Here, R.

B. and his fellow English writers were using this noble figure, an example of heroism that was worthy of the ancients, as a means of criticizing the Spanish in the New World.

In R. B.'s text there were other examples of Native resistance to Spanish cruelty. A lord who had fled the Spaniards to Cuba from the Continent "to avoid either death or perpetual Captivity" assembled the principal Indians because he heard the Spaniards were coming.[187] The lord's speech was typological in the sense that it involved a double Native and English critique of the Spanish, a criticism deriving from the Native leader and R. B., author of a book whose title contained the words "English empire":

> *Countrymen and Friends, you are not ignorant of the rumour that the Spaniards are arrived amongst us, neither need I tell you how barbarously they have used the Inhabitants of Hispaniola, you know it by too certain Intelligence, nor can we hope to find them more merciful than they did; But my dear Countrymen, do you know their Errand? if not, I will tell you the cause of their coming, they worship some covetous and insatiate God, and to content their greedy Deity, they require all our Gold and Silver from us, for this they endeavour continually to murther and enslave us. See here this little chest of Gold, and therein behold the God of the Spaniards, therefore if you think fit, let us dance and sing before this their God, perhaps we may hereby appease his rage, and he will then command his worshippers to let us alone.*[188]

This satirical speech that R. B. gave to this Native lord was worthy of Montaigne. This Native lord reversed the usual terms of barbarity and its implied opposite—civility—by claiming that the Spaniards have acted "barbarously." The God-and-gold nexus was a motivation for Cartier and Ralegh as much as for Cortés and Pizarro. R. B.'s Native lord has conflated God and capitalized Gold as one and the same, so that the Spaniards really worship gold as their divinity and will enslave and kill the Natives for this deity. In a kind of mock prayer of appeasement, the Natives sang and danced before this God, now reduced to a chest of gold.

R. B. continued this satirical scene with an unrelenting critique of the Spanish by and through this Native lord:

> To this mention they all assented and danced round the Box till they were thoroughly wearied, when this Lord thus proceeded, *If we should keep this God till he be taken from us, we shall be certainly slain, I therefore think it expedient for us to cast him into the River;* whose Counsel being followed, the Chest was thrown into the River.[189]

In an act of self-preservation the Natives get rid of the chest of gold because the Spaniards will sacrifice them for it. Unfortunately, for the Natives, nothing could spare them from Spanish cruelty, for, as R. B. reported it:

> When the *Spaniards* first landed in this Island, this Nobleman having sufficient experience of their cruelty, avoided them as much as possible,

still flying and defending himself by the force of Arms upon all occasions;
at length being taken, for no other reason, but endeavouring to preserve
his Life from his Enemies, he was by the *Spaniards* burnt alive; being tied
to a Stake, a *Franciscan* Monk began to discourse him of God, and the articles of his religion, telling him that the small time allowed him by the Exe-
cutioner, was sufficient to make his Salvation sure, if he did heartily believe
in the true Faith; having a while considered his words, he asked the Monk,
whether the Door of Heaven was open to the *Spaniards,* who answering
yea, then, said he, *Let me go to Hell, that I may not come where they are.*[190]

The Native nobleman, having experienced Spanish "cruelty," tried to avoid the
Spaniards in order to preserve his people, but in a brief exchange with a Franciscan monk, R. B. caused him to wish to be in hell rather than in heaven with
the Spaniards. Here is the heroic image of a Native lord being brave and defiant in the face of torture, at the prospect of being burnt at the stake. There is, in
R. B.'s account, an implied anticlerical or anti-Catholic position. The monk,
like the Spanish soldiers, looked bad in this narrative and their negative characteristics confirm, through contrast, the positive attributes of the Native lord.

After this other example of a story within his larger narrative, R. B. continued immediately with a more general statement about the Spanish possession of
this territory:

In this Island the *Spaniards* got above a Million of Gold, and vast sums
more in the other spacious Provinces of this *New World,* the greatest part
whereof came into their Possession in a few years, and which they enjoy
to this very day.[191]

In the end the Spanish, cruel or not, greedy or not, possessed this island in the
account of the Native lord burnt at the stake and came, in like fashion, to call
the New World their own—at great profit. R. B.'s tabulation of the riches was
ambivalent because by listing its yield at millions, he was appealing, inadvertently
or not, to the greed in his English readers as well as their moral outrage at Spanish aggression against the Natives. In building this English empire, profit was also
a consideration. This ambivalence and contradiction in R. B.'s text became
more apparent as it proceeded. R. B. claimed that he had given "a sufficient
account of the Fortunate Aquisitions of the *Spaniard.*"[192] The figure of Sebastian Cabot—sometimes mixed up with his father, John, as in earlier accounts—
was presented as an example of lost opportunity for the English. The ghost of
Columbus, with which R. B. began, now haunted the end of R. B.'s ambitions
for his own country: England. According to R. B., Sebastian Cabot had set out
on a voyage Columbus had proposed, had gone to Spain and helped in Brazil,
and had come back to England in 1549.[193] Most of all, R. B. returned to the
scene of the crime—the missed opportunity that England had given up in the
time of Henry VII and Columbus owing to their distraction of England with a
war against Scotland: Sebastian Cabot's (it was actually John Cabot's) design of

sailing to the western Atlantic (here it seemed as though this proposal had colonization much in mind). In R. B.'s words, "this design was wholly laid aside to the great prejudice of the *English* Nation, who in all probability might have made themselves Quarter-masters, at least with the *Spaniards,* in the wealthiest Parts and provinces of *America,* if the business had been well followed." The regret almost 200 years later is palpable. The wistful loss of wealth—even just after a story that was a condemnation of Spanish greed and cruelty toward the Natives—suggests that R. B., like many of his English predecessors and peers, was conflicted about the example of Spain. Would the English have performed similar acts of cruelty and greed had Columbus sailed for England instead of Spain? This question arises from a reading of R. B.'s text and other English accounts of the New World, especially those that dwell on the missed opportunity with Columbus, but it is not a query he and the others would probably have welcomed. Having represented the Native resistance to Spain in the New World, R. B. also gave the European view of profits and dominion over the lands that had belonged to those aboriginal peoples.

Whereas R. B. attempted to represent the Native point of view in Spanish America, John Harris was, in the tradition of Hakluyt of *Principall Navigations,* more interested in compiling British and European texts that contained their attitudes toward America and its inhabitants. Harris, like R. B., did address Columbus and the subsequent rights of Spain to the New World. The precedent of the example of Spain and how that affected English claims in America persisted even as the idea of "Britain" and a "British empire" was being forged anew. As a new British nation was being made politically, the old questions about Spain, with their ambivalent and contradictory aspects, haunted writers in English.

In 1705, Harris, a Fellow of the Royal Society, continued the polyglot and pan-European collection of travel and exploration narratives we have observed most notably in Thevet and Belleforest in French and in Hakluyt and Purchas in English. Unlike Gage, Harris obviously saw the benefit of the collection as a means of representing lands in which the English had an interest. The title of Harris's two-volume folio, which most resembled an inventory, announced the tradition within which he was working (proclaiming its debt to Hakluyt, Ramusio and others), stressed that the volumes included original papers, such as *"the Pope's Bull, to Dispose of the West-Indies to the King of Spain"* and emphasized that the histories and other allied works related to the four parts of the world, especially America.[194] Once the English entered into collections in the last quarter of the sixteenth century, they continued the tradition, though without the same distinction of Hakluyt and Purchas, beyond the Treaty of Utrecht. Just as Thévenot had borrowed from Hakluyt and Purchas, so too had Harris used Thévenot.[195] Even if during this period English anxieties about rivalry in the New World shifted in part from Spain to Holland and France, the Spanish origins to colonization of the New World and worry about Catholicism remained in England into the eighteenth century.

A relatively new chauvinism and confidence about the preeminence of England (about to become Great Britain in 1707) was characteristic of Harris's prefatory matter. In the "Epistle Dedicatory," in which he addressed the queen, Harris, making a claim that reflected in certainty and tone chauvinism and providentialism, declared:

> The Discoveries that have been successively made of the Religions, Manners, Customs, Politicks, and Natural Products of all Parts of the World, will *here* give your Majesty an *agreeable* and *useful* Entertainment: And, I'm sure, it will add to Your Satisfaction to see, that they have been chiefly made by those of Your *Own Nation*. It hath been thought by some a laudable Reason for sending our Gentlemen Abroad, that they may the better learn to value their Native Country. And this I dare say, That when either a Man hath actually travell'd the whole World over himself, or carefully consider'd the Accounts which those give us that have done so, he will be abundantly convinced, that Our own Religion, Government and Constitution is, in the Main, much preferable to any he shall meet with Abroad; And especially under the happy Influence of Your Majesty's Reign, whom Providence seems graciously to haue design'd to make us Great and Happy, even whether we will or no.[196]

Here was a triumphalism based on the Protestant victory in the Glorious Revolution of 1688, successful wars with rivals, and the decline of Spain. There was no sense in Harris, as there was in Hakluyt, that the queen should read the collection in order to catch up with and emulate Spain. Confidence in providential manifest destiny for England and empire against the country's would also serve as great contrasts between Harris and Hakluyt. The myth was born, here and elsewhere, that England ruled out of duty and against its will, something, in more extreme Protestant terms, Phillips had represented to Cromwell in 1656.

Queen Anne, as Harris characterized her, is good to all her subjects, and her wisdom and judgment disappoints the designs of the enemies of her government while her "steady Affection for the Establish'd Church damps all the Hopes of *Faction* and *Fanaticism*."[197] The queen's compliance with the laws and constitution of England and her study of the happiness of her people above her own "frustrates and blasts all the barbarous Contrivances of those, who would enslave Us to Arbitrary Power, *French* and *Popish* Tyranny."[198] We have seen how John Dennis would, a couple of years later, mythologize Queen Anne. In Harris's dedicatory scene the queen's sacred person and excellent government were what the English fought for: this was the narrative of liberty. The Whig version of British and British imperial history was evident here, a view that would dominate well into this century.[199] Queen Anne and her government made her "Armies conquer Empires Abroad." Harris invoked providence by speaking of the poetic justice of her virtues' "just reward" and by representing Anne as "the Glorious Instrument of Settling Peace and Liberty of *Europe* on a safe and lasting Foundation." England now became the defender of liberty and the assurance of the peace in Europe. This statement of the present state of affairs and evocation of prophecy were based in contemporary events: "The mighty Success Your just Arms have obtain'd already, against the Common Enemy, doth fairly foretell *This*. And as I doubt not but This is the Universal Prayer of all *true English* Men." No one prayed more zealously and more earnestly to this end than did Harris, who ended his dedication with this declaration.

The "Preface," which was an address to the reader, announced that the first volume owed much to Hakluyt and Purchas and began in 1626, the year in which Purchas ended his collection, while volume 2 was entirely new. Harris said that he used Sir Thomas Herbert's *Travels* as a means of correcting Purchas. In his Introduction, Harris included scientific material from fellow members of the Royal Society, such as Robert Boyle's experiments with the magnet.[200] In chapter 2 Harris included a copy of the papal bull in Latin and in English translation, and, in a marginal note, mentioned that Lopez de Gómara and Richard Eden had also reproduced this bull. This return to the origins of European exploration and settlement of the New World contradicted or at least offered a contrast to the situation Harris set up in the Epistle. If Anne was the choice of providence to bring universal peace to Europe and to be the imperial power, how times must have changed since Columbus or Hakluyt, when the Spanish monarchs were given that role. Harris observed, "What Interest the *Spaniards* had in the New World, 'tis certain the *Portugueze* might have had before them, had they been so wise as to have embrac'd *Columbus*'s Offers. But having rejected them as vain and ridiculous, and thereby neglected a very favourable Opportunity of advancing the Interests of their Nation: Now seeing the *Spaniards* so well seated there, where they might have been themselves, they began to grow very angry at them."[201] The author then explained the differences between Spain and Portugal and how they both worked "to preserve the ancient Peace between those two Crowns," through the treaties in 1493–94 following on the papal bull, which left both of them to proceed with their individual discoveries unencumbered. Even in a book on the triumph of England, the Spanish and Portuguese accord and discoveries were remembered. The origins, although suppressed and not emphasized in the scheme of the volumes, were there, near the beginning of the first book, as a reminder. The first chapter was comprised of the discoveries made under Henry and Alphonsus, kings of Portugal, and the second chapter began with Columbus. Some of the concerns of Hakluyt's "Discourse" in England's claim and right to America persisted 121 years later.

It is not a surprise that in the War of the Spanish Succession or Queen Anne's War, British writers would be concerned with Spain's role in Europe and America. Like Harris, John Oldmixon cast his sight on the Spanish: in *The British Empire in America . . .* (1708) Oldmixon recalled the Romans, Columbus, and the Dutch, which suggested the continued importance of trope of *translatio imperii*, the preoccupation with Spain and the origins of European settlement in the Americas, and the developing rivalry with the Netherlands. For Oldmixon, the war with Spain and the contention with the Spanish in the West Indies proved the importance of American colonies to the Spanish and British:

There are some Persons who pretend the *Spaniards* have ruin'd themselves, by exhausting their Country, for the sake of their *American* Acquisitions. To which may be answer'd, their banishing the Convert-Moors, the *Jews,* and the setting up of the Inquisition, with the Tyranny of their Government, have more exhausted *Spain* than all their Settlements in the *West-Indies.* Had moderate Counsels prevail'd, there would have been no Scarcity of Men in the Kingdom, and their Pride and Sloth have impoverish'd them much more than their Want of Hands. Besides, grant that every Nation best understand their true Interest, do not the *Spaniards* Politicks even now justify our Assertion, That the *West-India* Colonies are highly advantagious to their Mother Countries? What do they fight for at this time? Why do they suffer themselves to be torn to Pieces on all sides? What is this Dispute for? Would they give up the *West Indies* to the right Owner, K. *Charles* III. Matters would soon be accommodated; and without doing it, this war can never be well ended.

We hope the Reader is by this time satisfy'd, that our *American* Plantations are an Advantage, and a very great one, to the Kingdom; and the Arguments brought from Antiquity will be of no use to the Enemies of the Colonies.[202]

The weakening of Spain had to be shown to have had internal causes related to mismanagement of its own country in Europe rather than its exhaustion through a misguided colonial policy. Oldmixon wanted to demonstrate how American colonies invigorated the mother country rather than depleted it. While wishing to displace Spain, he had to tread delicately because the relation between the two countries was symbiotic insofar as Spain could be used as a negative precedent for those who would oppose the promotion of England's American colonies and its ambitions in the West Indies.

Spain had to be shown to be weak so it could be displaced but not weak for reasons that would doom Britain in the same way. Oldmixon also railed against the appeal to antiquity in anticolonial arguments but made use of the example of Romans colonies in his own argument for colonization of the Americas, and he called on Aristotle, who, he said, referred to a land that was America.[203] In taking into account other rivalries long after Columbus, Oldmixon spoke of the panoply of rivals: Spanish, Portuguese, Dutch, Danish, and French America. He also saw the Spanish West Indies in terms of French and British power: Britain could damage the French and Spanish from Jamaica.[204] War against Spaniards was a central theme in Oldmixon: he proposed a British expedition against "the common Enemy, *French* and *Spaniards.*"[205] Cromwell's Western Design would have payoffs for the English/British empire.

Oldmixon set up a rhetoric of displacement while attempting to find grounds that were not contradictory because if he condemned Spain for reasons that those opposed to expansion into Americas used in England, then his promotion in Britain of the American enterprise might have foundered. This worry about losing population and weakening Britain continued well into the eighteenth century and was never quite quelled. Oldmixon attempted to avoid contradictions but could not always sidestep the examples of the ancients and the Spaniards that he said his opponents were using.

Like Harris and Oldmixon, John Stevens mixed the preoccupation with Spanish colonization with later rivals that might have kept Britain from being heir to Spain in empire. In 1711, Stevens's *A New Collection of Voyages and Travels,* appeared, and the first text in the collection was *The Discovery and Conquest of the Molucco and Philippine Islands . . . ,* first printed in 1708, by "Bartholomew Leonardo de Argensola, . . . a Learned Clergyman," and whose title promised less than it delivered in the Spanish manner and not more as was the English habit.[206] Stevens represented Argensola as an eyewitness who told about the conquest of the "Molucco Islands" under Philip III. He had a high opinion of Argensola, who also included a description of China, the Dutch voyages, the undertakings of Francis Drake, and other English "Adventurers" and who "Embelishes the whole with such variety of pleasing Incidents, that few Books of Travels afford so much Profitable Entertainment, with such good Authority."[207] The goal of entertaining in addition to instructing motivated the collectors and authors of travel books, now giving them even more of a self-conscious literary, if not Horatian, bent.

In praising Argensola as a rare author in Spain and therefore even more so in England, Stevens continued his preference for the Spanish and offered this rarity as a reason why this valuable and scarce author had not been translated into English till now, when, Stevens implied, they would be as fortunate as the Spanish. Novelty was still important. In another rhetorical move Stevens said he did not want to "prepossess the Reader, who is left to make his own Judgment, and therefore a long Preface is designedly avoided, that he may the sooner enter upon so Useful and Diverting a Work."[208] Nonetheless, immediately after making this statement, Stevens sought to preempt injudicious readers, those who were anti-Spanish and anti-Catholic, and in doing so revealed the tension between the work of a translator in early-eighteenth-century England (often having less latitude and demanding more accuracy than his Elizabethan counterpart) and the prejudices at work in a Protestant country, especially in the wake of the Glorious Revolution of 1688, in which Protestant William replaced Catholic James. In this context Stevens addressed the reader:

> It is not improper, nevertheless, to Advise the Reader not to take notice of some Reflections in Point of Religion, and in other Cases, considering the Book was Writ by a *Spaniard,* and that it was not proper to Omit, or Alter any thing, where a Fair, and Entire Translation is promised. Besides, That these are very few, and inconsiderable, and consequently not worth observing, as indeed the generality of Judicious Readers will be sufficiently satisfy'd, and this Caution is given for their Sake, whom perhaps Passion, or overmuch Zeal may move to condem a Work on such an Occasion, when they can find no other matter to Carp at.[209]

In ending this Preface, Stevens made a claim for balance and good judgment, which he asserted with the phrase "the generality of Judicious Readers" after his initial disclaimer of attempting to affect the reader. This attitude was a long way from Hakluyt's "Discourse" and Gage's *The English-American.* . . .

The text by this Spanish author, Argensola, embodied attitudes that were contrary to those of the Protestants who had just over two decades before gained control over the constitutional and political life of Britain. As for anti-English and anti-Protestant attitudes, a good instance is Argensola's description of Elizabeth I's execution of Mary Queen of Scots "for some Politick Reasons, or Fictions" and her help to the Flemmings obstinacy and "Disobedience to the Church" as a means of "flattering herself with the Hopes of a New Monarchy" that would be built on "*Spain*, the Robbing of which had already made an Addition to her power." [210] Stevens was asking his reader to overlook national interpretations and rivalries in order to enjoy and learn from this Spanish work. The view of Philip was, as to be expected, quite distinct from the English representations I have discussed throughout, and this difference is refreshing: "King *Philip*, whose great Soul ever entertain'd both Forebearance, and Counsel, resolv'd to cut off the Heads of this *Hydra* at the Neck they all sprung from. He gather'd, for the Conquest of *England*, the mightiest Fleet that has been on the Ocean in our Days."[211] This version of Elizabethan politics included a view of Scotland and the Netherlands, the latter as a country England had designs on, and represented England as provoking Spain into rightful action. Argensola later described the English, when at peace, as helping the Spanish in the Far East against the Dutch.[212] His account had some balance and, as is the case with most the narratives we have examined, the representation of the other country often had to do with how friendly its relations were with the author's country at the time of the event described and of writing.

The other works that Stevens collected also testified to an openness to other points of view concerning America: for instance, the Preface to John Lawson's *A New Account of Carolina* said that the French outstripped the English in representing America because, unlike the French, the English sent out, on the whole, "Persons of the meaner Sort" who were "uncapable of giving any reasonable Account of what they met withal in those remote Parts."[213] For Lawson, the rivalry was with France and not Spain, which he did not mention in the Preface. The reasons for French superiority were their numerous clergy and missionaries who were obedient to their superiors; they always sent gentlemen with the clergy and obliged them to keep a strict journal so they could report to their governor, fathers, friends, and relations, "For their Monarch being a very good Judge of Mens Deserts, does not often let Money or Interest make Men of Parts give Place to others of less Worth."[214] Lawson was concerned with class matters and wanted to be identified as a gentleman who kept a journal and used the example of France to reaffirm that status and to suggest, as a benefit to Britain, that it followed that model. The French king's system of obedience and preferment, according to Lawson, "breeds an Honourable Emulation amongst them, to outdo one another, even in Fatigues, and Dangers; whereby they gain a good Correspondence with the *Indians*, and acquaint themselves with their Speech and Customs; and so make considerable Discoveries in a short time. Witness, their Journals from *Canada*, to the *Missisipi*, and its several Branches, where they have effected great Matters, in a few Years."[215] Verisimilitude in representation now accompanied first discovery as a justification of the authors of narratives of the New World. Lawson described a country as pleasant as any in Europe, "the Discovery of which being never yet made publick, I have, in the following Sheets, given you a faithful Account thereof, wherein I have laid down every thing with Impartiality, and Truth, which is indeed, the Duty of every *Author,* and preferable to a smooth Stile, accompany'd with Falsities and Hyperboles."[216] Having mentioned the good relations that the French had with the Natives, Lawson now represented them as coveting "a Christian Neighbourhood, for the Advantage of Trade" and enjoying "all the Comforts of Life, free from Care and Want." Rather than amuse his readers further with "the encomium of *Carolina,*" he referred them to his journal and the natural history which was exact and well-ordered.

Lawson's "Introduction" began with his intention, during the celebration of the Grand Jubilee at Rome in 1700, "when People flock'd from all Parts of the Christian World" to witness it, to travel.[217] In the next sentence Lawson showed the instability of what identity the empire was taking because in it he referred to both Britain and the English. After 1707, the year of the Act of Union, I refer to the British Empire rather than to England, but the authors were in the process of making the switch and illustrate our difficulty, as well as theirs, in coming to terms with this shift. There he met a man who convinced him to go to Carolina: Lawson described the journey over, including a stopover in New York, where "A good Part of the inhabitants are *Dutch,* in whose Hands this Colony once was."[218] A large part of the prosperity of the English/British colony of New York was owing to Holland and to the Dutch inhabitants of the city. After a fortnight in New York, Lawson's ship left for Charlestown in the Carolinas, a plantation in "*English America*" most advantageous to the crown of "*Great Britain*" after Virginia and Maryland only. Lawson also mentioned the contribution of citizens of Charlestown from other nations, especially Huguenots from France, who had become rich in trade with Europe and the West Indies. He also noted the "Liberty" of worship in Charleston and said that this freedom from oppression, an example and prolepsis, was the intent of the Lords Proprietors (whom he addressed in the dedication) for Carolina, so that the inhabitants of the southern colony "should be as free from Oppression, as any in the Universe; which doubtless they will, if their own Differences amongst themselves do not occasion the contrary."[219]

This example of tolerance did not extend to wars with France and Spain. The genteel and prosperous inhabitants of this rich and grand colony on the frontier, which had a well-disciplined militia whose infantry and cavalry "prove such troublesome Neighbours to the *Spaniards,* that they once laid their Town of St. *Augustine* in Ashes, and drove away their Cattle; besides many Encounters and Engagements, in which they have defeated them, too tedious to relate here."[220] The French attack under admiral Mouville is one of loss and disgrace, and these English colonists of Carolina "are absolute Masters over the *Indians.*"[221] If anyone in their circle of trade killed an Englishman, he was punished by death, but Lawson seemed to see, unless he was distinguishing between crime and resistance, no contradiction in claiming that the English "have an entire Friendship with the neighbouring *Indians* of several Nations, which are a very warlike People, ever faithful to the *English,* and have prov'd themselves brave and true on all Occasions; and are a great Help and Strength to this Colony."[222]

The decline of Spain was relative. It still had a vast empire and its presence still concerned the English, who continued to foster anti-Spanish attitudes in themselves and their Native allies. According to Lawson,

> The Chief of the savage Nations have heretofore groan'd under the *Spanish* Yoke, and having experienc'd their Cruelty, are become such mortal Enemies to that People, that they never give a *Spaniard* Quarter; but generally, when they take any Prisoners, (if the *English* be not near to prevent it) sculp them, that is, to take their Hair and Skin of their Heads, which they often flea away, whilst the Wretch is alive. Notwithstanding the *English* have us'd all their Endeavours, yet they could never bring them to leave this Barbarity to the *Spaniards;* who, as they alledge, use to murder them and their Relations, and make Slaves of them to build their Forts and Towns."[223]

Here Lawson questioned whether the English had control over the Natives or the will to prevent the scalping of the Spaniards, whose cruelty Lawson asserted and the Natives were, in his rhetoric, allowed only to allege. In Lawson's representation the Natives faithful to the English were helpful but were warlike and barbaric. He ended his introduction with a praise of the inhabitants and commodities and, after speaking of merchants and slaves, he called attention to his authority, to his eight years there.[224] That the African slaves might feel toward the English as the Natives did toward the Spanish seems never to have occurred to Lawson. Some of this liberational rhetoric—the English will act as protectors and civilizers of the Natives—is, as we have seen in earlier chapters, something found in Hakluyt, Ralegh, and other English writers over a century before.

The next prefatory matter Stevens presented was his own dedication, addressed again to Edmund Poley, to the translation, *The Seventeen Years Travels of Peter de Cieza through the Mighty Kingdom of Peru . . . ,* printed before in 1709.[225] In this dedication Stevens began with the conventions of addressing a patron but ended up by appealing to an Iberian figure, even if only in passing as a negative example, coupled with Sir John Mandeville, a legendary English author. Stevens said he would not go on about the usefulness of such a work but did anyway, listing the benefits to gentlemen, merchants, and others, not to mention patrons. Stevens praised Poley as a worthy patron (others had "ill-gotten Wealth") but insisted that, as fortunate as he was in his patronage, the author would not stoop to flattery. The apotheosis of the praise of the modest but great patron, framed periphrasically from beginning to end, concluded the dedication. In the Preface, which dealt with tastes in reading, Stevens faced a generalized, if not allegorized, and certainly abstract series of vices and habits that made less tasteful readers, as opposed to the "Wiser and better Sort," seek out a different kind of collection or travel narrative. Then he became more specific: "There are some Gusts so deprav'd, that, to come to what we have in Hand, they are more taken with *Sr. John Mandevil, Fenan Mendez Pinto,* and such like Romantick Writers of their own Dreams, than with those, who giving sincere Relations of their Travels, could not furnish them with so much matter of Surprize, and Admiration."[226] Stevens wished to present his reader with the usual appeals to eyewitness reports, realism, and the world. This was a different kind of Spanish narrative of the New World that he was presenting to the reader and not the stuff of romance.

Like Lahontan, Stevens pleaded for his truth but not without self-interest. Stevens said that some gentlemen of taste vouch for de Cieza, as do "all the best Spanish writers, who have treated of that Part of *America,* . . . Even Garcilasso de la Vega, tho' born and bred in *Peru,* and so well acquainted with it, being his Native Country, in his History of that Kingdom makes often Use of him, as a most Authentick Voucher."[227] Plain style and sincerity (Lahontan's standards as well) were something, along with exactness, that Stevens attributed to de Cieza in the last sentence of the Preface. Stevens portrayed de Cieza as a man of arms, trained in conquest and discovery, who reluctantly came forward as the chronicler of this new country, in order to provide "true Knowledge" of it, when no other author of greater merit appeared. De Cieza wrote "of the almost incredible Actions, and Sufferings of the *Spaniards,* his Country-Men; and of the manner how it pleas'd God, after those Immense Regions had lain so long unknown to the rest of the World, to lay them open to *Europeans.*" Stevens spoke as a European Christian when he represented this providential plan and not as an Englishman or a Protestant. De Cieza's narrative itself began with Columbus, the first discovery of the West Indies, the hardship of the Spaniards in Peru amid "many barbarous Nations," how Charles V had strictly ordered that Spaniards treat the Natives as brethern and fellow subjects and how some in authority contravened those laws and cruelly abused and oppressed the Indians until they "took up Arms in their own Defence."[228] De Cieza was somewhat defensive about Spanish cruelty and torture and, while admitting these practices had occurred, said "that all the *Spaniards* were not guilty of this misusing the Indians" and in fact some were generous to them.[229] After giving some examples of Spanish kindness, de Cieza stated that the king protected the Natives so that they were now equals with the Spaniards. If the Black Legend was too extreme in its rhetoric, the White Legend of Spain, a kind of counter-reformation of the county's reputation, also had its excesses. De Cieza provided a balance but, as a corrective, might have been exaggerating the status and well-being of the indigenous peoples in Peru.

In Stevens's Preface to the second volume he said that the design of this collection was to entertain the public with "valuable Travels" that have not yet appeared in English. While the value of instruction was still admitted, this admission of the motive of entertainment, something that was an unspoken or largely suppressed aspect, represented a shift in the public rhetoric of collections and narratives about the New World.[230] Stevens concentrated here on travels to Ethiopia, the best account of which was "*Francis Alvarez* his History of this Empire." Although Stevens had praise for Purchas, whose work, he told us, "is grown scarce," he noted that Alvarez appeared in that collection in abridgment only. Stevens offered accounts of Ethopia by Jesuits, "who were all Learned and Able Men," and who were Portuguese and French. In passing he mentioned the land of Prester John. The second volume also included accounts of Morocco, India, and Madagascar but nothing specifically of America. Once again, Stevens was looking for novelty and quality and not the ideological divisions that had divided Europe politically and religiously. In this aim he was attempting to make travel an entertainment and not simply a means to political action and imperial expansion.

In creating empires that were to be built on a "national" self-interest and identity, as shifting as that was, editors of collections and writers, such as Melchisédech Thévenot, R. B., John Harris, John Oldmixon, and John Stevens, drew on examples and narratives from Spain to help to build their come-lately American colonies. While these editors and authors were not generally of the magnitude of Hakluyt, Ralegh, Champlain, Lescarbot, and Purchas, who worked at the critical moment when France and England were establishing permanent colonies in the New World, they were involved in representing the new power that their own countries exercised in the New World as potent and worthy rivals to Spain in the western Atlantic. The French and English continued to collect narratives about the New World and admitted their mutual influence even as they were becoming the chief rivals for empire in North America, the Caribbean, and the world beyond.

V

As the Counter-Reformation grew in strength and England became a Protestant republic and France banned Huguenots from its colonies, the religious divisions intensified in French and English representations of the example of Spain. Gage and Phillips engaged in an anti-Spanish propaganda that was at least as intense as that created by the Huguenots in the wake of the Spanish massacre of the French in Florida. The work of the Recollets, Jesuits, and Franciscans in New France, the Caribbean, and Louisiana revealed the tensions between the "nationalism" in France and the patriotism over expansion and evangelization and the use of Spanish models and of Spanish spirituality and institutions as well as transnational Catholic institutions. Although the example of Spain was an important concern for France and England, they came to see each other as key rivals and thought about following the other's example, so that writers like Sagard, Boucher, and Lahontan could view the English colonies as the biggest threat and best example to New France whereas Harris could recommend the French way of colonizing America to his English readers. The collectors, Thévenot, Harris, and Stevens, admitted a common ground and influence between the French and English collections, but they also claimed a unique imperial mission for France and England. Rivalries between England and Holland still flared up, as expressed by Dryden, but increasingly an English and then a British triumpalism was beginning to take hold. The great surprise is that the example of Spain persisted so long, and it was an idea, both as a precedent and as something to displace, that endured well beyond the period of this study.

While France and England came to rival Spain and then to succeed it in this period, some of those same concerns about origins, precedence, right, greed, and conversion and Spain's role in them all in the New World continued. Perhaps as Spain was still powerful in the Americas even as its power waned in Europe, writers in France and England had to continue to pay close attention to those Spanish colonies in the western Atlantic and the empire they helped to comprise. In spite of these shifts in the balance of power, the English and French were talking—in the late seventeenth and early eighteenth century—about Spain as they had in the 1490s and the century afterwards. This unexpected continuity occurred in a period of change in the European empires in the New World. Spain had priority and precedence in writing as much as in conquest: Spanish explorers, priests, and officials created acts and texts that the French and English interpreted, emulated, and displaced. In measuring themselves against these Spanish precursors and rivals, these English and French writers, themselves serving posts in the church, the government, and commercial and courtly ventures, sought to imitate and to distinguish themselves from the Spaniards in a balancing act that was not over even at the end of the War of the Spanish Succession in 1713, when Spain was no longer the great power in Europe and France and England would dispute that role for over a century.

CHAPTER 7

Concluding Remarks

This has been a study in the historiography of expansion, of how England and France used the example of Spain in their exploration and settlement of the New World, from 1492 to 1713. Rather than repeat the "conclusions" reached in the earlier chapters, I wish to end with a few suggestive remarks. Although the Black Legend was important in the representation of Spain in France and England, it was only part of the story. French Catholics like Marc Lescarbot were capable of resenting Spain's power, success, and presumption. It was not until the revocation of the Edict of Nantes in 1685 and the Glorious Revolution of 1688 that France and England went their separate Catholic and Protestant ways, and it was not until the Bourbons occupied both the French and the Spanish thrones before Spain and France could, at least while Louis XIV lived, put their differences aside. In Louisiana, however, the Spanish did not want the French there even if their king, Philip V, was the grandson of Louis XIV. National self-interest often cut across the lines of religion.

In discussing the polemical conflicts surrounding the Spanish colonization of the New World, particularly from about 1566 to 1626, the "history of prejudice" is another description of one of the principal concerns of this study—that is, the negative aspect of the example of Spain. None the less, the intricacy of the textual representations, both internally and in relation to other texts (what I have called the "context"), also implied positive views of Spain, which, together with the negative elements, created ambivalence or contradiction, something that prevented a straightforward and unqualified generalization about the relations among the Spanish, English, and French in their image and colonization of the New World.

It was quite apparent that by the end of the sixteenth and the beginning of the seventeenth century the Spanish, English, and French, not to mention the Dutch and the Portuguese, all contended in trade and war in the New World. By the eighteenth century the rivalries continued and the English still seemed to rejoice in having Spain as an enemy, so that the War of Jenkins's Ear (1739–48) was like old times.

How much of the ground for British and French identities in mid- and late-eighteenth-century North America was set by the example of Spain, especially the relation of the French and British to the American Indian as set against the earlier experience of Spain in this kind of cultural encounter and definition? The answer is multifold, but one of its aspects is this—the example of Spain was and is more germane than most English- and French-speaking writers have recognized or would recognize.

When the *philosophes* and British Whig political thinkers like David Hume later came to portray Spain as the sick old man of Europe, reactionary and to be superseded, this attitude reflected real shifts away from a Spanish model, but it also suggested a secret admiration of—or at least a grappling with—the Spanish discovery as the moment of modernity. Moreover, the trauma of the encounter and conflict with and devastation of the Amerindians could not be chased from the progressive and revolutionary minds that would proclaim that time as a feudal and futile past. In the Enlightenment the disdain for the Spanish conquest was built on a hidden foundation of ambivalence and contradiction. The example of Spain persisted and persists.

NOTES

Chapter 1

1. See Anthony Pagden, *Lords of all the World: Ideologies of Empire in Spain, Britain and France c. 1500–c. 1800* (New Haven, 1995), 3. John Elliott's Radcliffe Lectures at University of Warwick, "Worlds Apart: British and Spanish Colonial America," May 3–12, 1994, still seem to have maintained a bi-polar structure, although the first lecture, which I attended, did present a larger comparative framework. The lectures were as follows: "Conquest and Settlement" (May 3), "Colonists and Colonized" (May 5), "Cities, Space and Hierarchy" (May 10), "Colonial States and Imperial States" (12 May). James Axtell has made some important bilateral or general comparisons. See James Axtell, *The Invasion Within: The Contest of Cultures in Colonial North America* (Oxford, 1985) and *Beyond 1492: Encounters in Colonial North America* (New York, 1992). Patricia Seed has produced a comparative study on the ceremonial aspects of European claims in the Americas. See her *Ceremonies of Possession in Europe's Conquest of the New World, 1492–1640* (Cambridge, 1995). An important study from France is Jean-Paul Duviols, *L'Amérique espagnole vue et rêvée. Les livres de voyages de Christophe Colomb à Bougainville* (no place. [Paris?], 1985). What distinguishes my comparative history is its emphasis on how England and France used the example of Spain in establishing and maintaining their American colonies.
2. See Aristotle, *Rhetoric*, trans. John H. Freese (London, 1947), 1355a4.
3. For the foundational role of Aristotle, see, for instance, Christian Mouchel, *Cicéron et Sénèque dans la rhétorique de la Renaissance* (Marburg, 1990), 26–7.
4. See Amélie Oksenberg Rorty, "Preface," *Essays on Aristotle's* Rhetoric, ed. A. O. Rorty (Berkeley, 1996), ix-xi.
5. On these types of rhetoric and on persuasion, see A. O. Rorty, "Structuring Rhetoric" and Christopher Carey, "Rhetorical Means of Persuasion" in ibid., 1–33 and 399–415 respectively. Carey's discussion of *pathos* is especially suggestive. For a useful analysis of Ciceronian and technical aspects of rhetoric and of the education of English colonizers, see Andrew Fitzmaurice, "Classical Rhetoric and the Literature of Discovery 1570–1630" (unpublished Ph.D. dissertation, University of Cambridge, 1995), especially chaps. 1, 2, 4. My study is much more thematic than Fitzmaurice's: my discussion will analyze how England and France represented the example of Spain in the New World and how such representation involved contradiction and ambivalence. In this study I have placed my earlier rhetorical reading in this new context. For instance, having left out most of the analysis of Oviedo and some on Thevet and Hakluyt, I have divided my work on Thevet and Hakluyt, refocused it as part of this larger argument, thereby putting it in new contexts in the chapters that follow. For an earlier version, see Jonathan Hart, "Strategies of Promotion: Some Prefatory Matter of Oviedo, Thevet and Hakluyt," *Imagining Culture: Essays in Early Modern History and Literature*, ed. Jonathan Hart (New York, 1996), 73–94, 201–2.
6. Charles Gibson, "Introduction," *The Black Legend of Spain: Anti-Spanish Attitudes in the Old World and the New*, ed. Charles Gibson (New York, 1971), 5, see 3–27.

7. Julián Juderías, *La Leyenda Negra* (Madrid, 1914); his study, which by the mid-1950s had been reprinted 13 times, led to a number of books and articles on the topic, such as Rómulo D. Carbia, *Historia de la Leyenda Negra Hispano-Americana* (Buenos Aires, 1943), Manuel Cardenal, "La Leyenda Negra," *Diccionario de Historia de España* (2 vols., Madrid, 1952), II, 231, Ignacio Escobar López, *La Leyenda Blanca* (Madrid 1953).

8. In *La Leyenda Negra: Estudios Sobra sus Orígenes* (Göteburg 1960), Sverker Arnoldsson provides a good summary of the secondary work as well as the origins of the Black Legend. He says that Carbia clearly demonstrates what a tool Las Casas's *Short Account of the Destruction of the Indies* played in Dutch propaganda before William of Orange's apologia (8), that López thinks that the Black Legend and its variants in the Americas stem from hatred toward Catholic Spain and comprise part of the Anti-Catholic Legend ["la Leyenda anticatólica"] (8), that Cardenal presents the most precise explication of the Black Legend Arnoldsson knows. Having provided a useful summary of Cardenal's view (8), Arnoldsson traces anti-Spanish models in Italy and Germany that he thinks influenced the Black Legend in the Netherlands before the duke of Alba entered the Low Countries in 1567. (Alba and the Jesuits are also elements of the Black Legend). He traces Spanish writing contra an Italian propaganda against Spain (a "Black Legend") as early as 13 years before William of Orange's apologia (10). Arnoldsson quotes Gonzalo Jiménez de Quesada's observation in *El Antijovio* (1567), which says that above all peoples, the Italians are particularly hateful toward Spain (ed. Rafael Torres Quintero (Bogotá 1952), 27). Given the pan-European nature of the exploration and the influence of the Reformation on the Netherlands, Arnoldsson's thesis has some merit.

9. Jaime de Ojeda, *Spain and Spanish America: The Past and the Future* (Providence 1996), 11–12, 16–20. Another recent study is Miguel Molina Martinez, *La leyenda negra* (Madrid, 1991), which also presents a case book of important earlier articles on the topic by Keen, Hanke, Juderias, Carbia, Gibson, and others as well as primary texts; see 151–282.

10. Two other discussions of the Black Legend, which John Elliott drew to my attention, are Carbia's *Historia*, which discusses the legend in the American context, and Pierre Chaunu, "La Légende Noire Antihispanique," *Revue de Psychologie des Peuples* (Caen, 1964), 188–223. In *Anglo-Spanish Rivalry in North America* (Athens, GA, 1971), J. Leitch Wright, Jr. studies "Spain's response to English intrusions into North America" (xi). He does not emphasize ambivalence. Duviols (1985) includes in his discussion of Spanish America some significant work on the Black Legend. See also Anthony Pagden, "Introduction" to Bartolomé de Las Casas, *A Short Account of the Destruction of the Indies*, trans. Nigel Griffin (Harmondsworth, 1992), xiii. My own discussion, which concentrates on Ralegh and Champlain and which represents an earlier and more extensive version of the close readings that appear in chapter 5, may be found in "The Black Legend: English and French Representations of Spanish Cruelty in the New World," *Comparative Literature Today: Theories and Practice/ La Littérature comparée d'aujourd'hui. Théories et réalisations*, ed. M. V. Dimić et al. (Paris, forthcoming). The emphasis in my study is not simply on the Black Legend, because while it is an important part of the French and English uses of Spain, it is not the sole view in France and England. My argument should help to serve as a corrective by providing balance in the representation of Spain in the New World.

11. Pagden, "Introduction," *Short Account*, xiii–xiv.

12. Lewis Hanke, *Bartolomé de Las Casas: An Interpretation of his Life and Writings* (The Hague, 1951), 1, 43–4, 55.

13. David Ramsey, *The History of the American Revolution* (2 vols., Philadelphia, 1789), I, 2, cited in Anthony Pagden, *Lords of all the World: Ideologies of Empire in Spain, Britain and France c. 1500–c.1800* (New Haven, 1995), 64. Pagden's chapter, "Conquest and Settlement," which concentrates most on the eighteenth century, provides additional evidence for this shift from conquest to trade and agriculture as models for English and French colonies in the New World. It also gives a subtle extended discussion of legal issues surrounding the changes in these empires. Ibid., 63–102.

14. Ramsey, *History*, I, 1.

15. Ibid.

16. Ibid., 2.

17. David Armitage maintains that in *Paradise Lost* Milton presents a critique of colonial schemes in hell, where Satan and his followers covet empire: "By implication, conquest and imperial enterprise are characteristics of fallen creatures, whether they are Spanish or English, Catholic or Protestant"; Armitage, "The British Empire and the Civic Tradition 1656–1742" (unpublished

Ph.D. dissertation, University of Cambridge, 1992), 113. For a general discussion, see David Armitage, "The Cromwellian Protectorate and the Languages of Empire," *The Historical Journal* 35 (1992), 531–55.

18. Pagden, *Lords,* 67, 93. See also Marcel Trudel, *The Beginnings of New France,* trans. Patricia Claxton (Toronto, 1973), 48–50, and W. J. Eccles, "Sovereignty Association, 1500–1783," *Essays on New France* (Toronto, 1987), 159.

19. Of these three expeditions, Boucher says: "The intentions of these expeditions was to imitate the Spanish pattern of exploration, conquest, and exploitation of land and aborigines. The search for golden cities and dense populations of aboriginal serfs galvanized the energies of these would-be conquistadors." Philip P. Boucher, *Les Nouvelles Frances: France in America, 1500–1815: An Imperial Perspective* (Providence, 1989), 5, see 12.

20. Philippe Duplessis-Mornay, "Discours au roy Henri III sur les moyens de diminuer l'Espagnol" (1584) in *Mémoire et correspondence* (12 vols., Paris, 1824–5), II, 590. He advocated an attack on Spain and a settling of the isthmus of Darien. For a discussion of Duplessis-Mornay in the context of "Protestant geopolitics," see Frank Lestringant, *Le Huguenot et le sauvage* (Paris, 1990), 123–4, see 119–26; for his relation to the ill-fated Scottish "Darien Venture" of 1698–99, which had some of the same goals, see Armitage, "The British," 132, see 124–59. Armitage also discusses works that further prove my point about the persistence of earlier ways of representing Spain; see William Paterson, "Proposal for Settling on the Isthmus of Darien, Releasing the nations from the Tyranny of Spain . . . " (B.L. Add. MS 12437), January 1, 1701/2, [appears under the title, "Memoir Upon Expeditions against Spanish America"] in Paterson, *The Life and Writings of William Paterson, Founder of the Bank of England,* ed. Saxe Bannister (3 vols., London, 1859), I, 140–1, cited in Armitage, "The British," 133; Charles Davenant, *An Essay upon Universal Monarchy* (1701) in *Essays upon I. The Ballance of Power. II. The Right of Making War, Peace, and Alliances. III. Universal Monarchy* (London, 1701), cited in ibid., 142. Armitage and Pagden also speak about Andrew Fletcher's and David Hume's view of Spain and universal monarchy; see ibid., 141–6; Pagden, *Lords,* 63, 70, 118–20. As Louis XIV sought to assert the right of his grandson, Philip of Anjou, over the claim of the Austrian Habsburgs to the Spanish throne (the Parlement registered Philip as successor to the French throne in February 1701), the threat of universal monarchy, which helped to set off the War of Spanish Succession, returned, a fear that Spain under Emperor Charles V and even Philip II had engendered in France and England.

21. See Richard Hakluyt, "Discourse of Western Planting," ed. David B. Quinn and Alison M. Quinn (London, 1993).

22. For *translatio imperii,* see Ernst Breisach, *Historiography: Ancient, Medieval & Modern* (Chicago, 1983), 13, 23, 29–30, 46–51, 162–3, 172–9 and Jonathan Hart, "Translating and Resisting Empire: Cultural Appropriation and Post-colonial Studies," *Borrowed Power; Essays in Cultural Appropriation,* ed. Bruce Ziff and Pratima Rao (New Brunswick, NJ, 1997), 137–68.

23. On his first voyage Columbus had divided the Natives into good and bad, depending on how pliable they seemed and how pro-Spanish they were. He subdivided the bad Natives into Amazons and Cannibals. Peter Hulme, *Colonial Encounters: Europe and the Native Caribbean 1492–1797* (1986; London, 1992); Jonathan Hart, "Images of the Native in Renaissance Encounter Narratives," *ARIEL* 25 (1994), 55–76.

24. Edward Said's *Orientalism* (New York, 1978) and Anthony Pagden's *The Fall of Natural Man: The American Indian and the Origins of Comparative Ethnography* (Cambridge, 1982, rev. ed. 1986), discuss the Greeks' understanding of barbarians as a means of explaining the European views of another culture. See Edward W. Said, *Culture and Imperialism* (1993; London, 1994), xxviii, and Pagden, *The Fall of Natural Man,* 14–26.

25. John Florio, "To the Curteous Reader," *Montaigne's Essays: John Florio's Translation,* ed. J. I. M. Stewart (2 vols., London, 1921), I, xxi. The quotations are from the first edition of 1603. Florio also defends Montaigne's "discourses" and "Essayes" against possible critics and satirists; ibid., xxvi.

26. Ibid.

27. See Peter Burke, *Montaigne* (Oxford, 1981), 46. Todorov discusses Montaigne in terms of views of the other, especially in terms of the "barbarian"; see Tzvetan Todorov, "L'Etre et l'Autre: Montaigne," *Montaigne: Essays in Reading,* ed. Gérard Defaux (New Haven, 1983), 118–19, see 113–44. For a discussion of Montaigne's discussion of cannibals in relation to his own political and historical preoccupations, see David Quint, "A Reconsideration of Montaigne's *Des canni-*

bales" in *America in European Consciousness, 1493–1750,* ed. Karen Ordahl Kupperman (Chapel Hill, 1995), 166–91.

28. Ibid. For a useful discussion of Florio, especially of Cicero's influence and his ideology of translation and for an account of theories of translation in the English Renaissance, see Warren
Boutcher, "Florio's Montaigne: Translation and Pragmatic Humanism in the Sixteenth Century"
(unpublished Ph.D. dissertation, University of Cambridge, 1991), Introduction, ch. 1, 2. One of
the practical topics in debating exercises that Boutcher mentions is whether the English were
stronger than the Spanish; ibid., viii.

29. For a discussion of this notion, see Terence Cave, *The Cornucopian Text* (Oxford, 1979) and Irene
Worth, *Practising Translation in Renaissance France: The Example of Étienne Dolet* (Oxford, 1988),
1–11.

30. In discussing Cicero's *De oratore,* Alain Michel and Boutcher employ *translatio* in the wider sense
I am using it here, the carrying of skills and knowledge from foreign texts into practical and public life. In my view, this carrying over, or translation, was not always direct and involved a whole
new body of texts that were now in the national literature (in this study in French and English).
They were slowly assimilated into the national traditions. See Alain Michel, *Rhétorique et philoso-
phie chez Cicéron: essai sur les fondements philosophiques de l'art de persuader* (Paris, 1960), 68 and
Boutcher, "Florio's Montaigne," 20.

31. The Europeans experienced what Anthony Pagden has called the problem of recognition.
Europeans of each age brought with them a set of expectations. Many of the fantastic natural
phenomena, like fauna and satyrs, pygmies, cannibals, and Amazons, that the Europeans expected
to see in America during the late fifteenth and early sixteenth century came from popular oral
tradition and from travel writers and scientists from Pliny to John de Mandeville. The spectre
of a new barbarian raised itself repeatedly in the colonial world. Pagden, *The Fall of Natural
Man,* 10.

Chapter 2

1. Daniel J. Boorstin uses an appropriate phrase, "the geography of the imagination." This is the
title given to Part IV of Daniel Boorstin, *The Discoverers* (1983; New York, 1985), 82–113. My
discussion of the medieval background owes something to Boorstin's account; ibid., 124–38,
162–4. See Felipe Fernández-Armesto, *Before Columbus: Exploration and Colonisation from the
Mediterranean to the Atlantic 1229–1402* (Philadelphia, 1987); Edward Burman, *The World Before
Columbus 1100–1492* (London, 1989).

2. For Polo, see *Cathay and the Way Thither, Being a Collection of Medieval Notices of China,* ed. and
trans. Henry Yule, rev. and expanded by H. Cordier (4 vols., London, 1913) and Boorstin, *The
Discoverers,* 133–8.

3. See Frances Gardiner Davenport, *European Treaties bearing on the History of the United States and
its Dependencies to 1648* (4 vols. Washington, D.C., 1917), I, 1, 9–10.

4. Davenport, *European Treaties,* 1, 10–12, 34. For the treaty of 1479 and its ratification, see ibid.,
36–41 (trans. 42–8).

5. *Fontes rerum canariarum,* ix, 15, 33, cited in Fernández-Armesto, *Before Columbus,* 180–81. See also
Fernández-Armesto's discussion on these pages.

6. See Fernández-Armesto, *Before Columbus,* 248, 250–1. Columbus's desire for gold in the service
of God was textual and practical, for such dreams were also fed in his reading of Polo. *The Four
Voyages of Columbus,* trans. and ed. Cecil Jane (2 vols., London, 1930, 1933; rpt. New York, 1988),
2 vols. in 1 vol., I, 11 n .3; II, 3 n. 4, 5. See also Jane's Introduction, II, lvii. Marcel Trudel, "New
France, 1524–1713," *Dictionary of Canadian Biography,* gen. ed. George W. Brown, vol. 1,
1000–1700 (Toronto and Québec, 1966), I, 26; see also 27–37. Fernández-Armesto, *Before
Columbus,* 5–6, 218. His book concentrates mainly on the expansion of Portugal, Genoa and
Castile.

7. See, for example, Anthony Grafton with April Shelford and Nancy Siraisi, *New Worlds, Ancient
Texts: The Power of Tradition and the Shock of Discovery* (Cambridge, MA, 1992), 13–54.

8. See Raymonde Litalien, *Les Explorateurs de l'Amérique du Nord 1492–1795* (Sillery, 1993), 52. In
the Préface to this volume, 7–9, Étienne Taillemite makes a similar point.

9. See Fernández-Armesto, *Before Columbus.* For a discussion of diplomats in this period, see Burman, *The World,* 64–86.

10. Pierre d'Ailly, *Imago Mundi,* in James A. Williamson, *The Voyages of the Cabots and the Discovery of North America under Henry VII and Henry VIII* (London, 1929), 10–11; see 11 n.1. Anthony Grafton assumes Columbus read d'Ailly: see Figure 1.7, Grafton with Shelford and Siraisi, *New Worlds,* 27. Anthony Pagden discusses Columbus's attitude to gold and the way in which he shrank the globe as a way of bringing the New World closer to the Old World, a kind of paradigm or example of the European attempt of reducing distance by substitution as a means of coping with the newness of experiencing the "New" World. See Pagden, "*Ius et Factum:* Text and Experience in the Writings of Bartolomé de Las Casas," *New World Encounters,* ed. Stephen Greenblatt (Berkeley, 1993), 85–6.

11. Like Spain, England and France used Italian captains and finance for exploration in the New World.

12. See Jonathan Hart, *Theater and World: The Problematics of Shakespeare's History* (Boston, 1992), esp. 105–08.

13. Tzvetan Todorov speaks about Montezuma's divided mind but also represents the differences among Spaniards. He sees similarities between Montezuma and Columbus (they gather information about things but fail in their communication with men) and differences between Columbus and Cortés; see Todorov, *The Conquest of America,* trans. Richard Howard (1984; New York, 1992), 57, 75.

14. William D. Phillips, Jr., and Carla Rahn Phillips, *The Worlds of Christopher Columbus* (Cambridge, 1992), 110–24.

15. Montaigne was also skeptical about European expansion and superiority. For his debt to Erasmus, see Frank Lestringant, *Le Cannibale: Grandeur et décadence* (Paris, 1994), 165, 168, 182.

16. The bull *Romanus pontifex,* January 8, 1455, in Davenport, *European Treaties,* 21.

17. All the bulls and treaties mentioned here, as well as other documents, can be found in ibid, 77–8. Quotations of over seven lines in the notes will be indented.

18. This is Green's legal view in L. C. Green and Olive P. Dickason, *The Law of Nations nd the New World* (Edmonton, 1989), 7. This book provides a good discussion of the bulls and of the legal aspects of the colonization of the Americas; see esp. 4–6.

19. Original ms. (Latin) of William of Worcester's *Itinerarium* is at Corpus Christi College, Cambridge; printed in James Naismith, *Itineraria Symonis Simeonis et Willelmi de Worcestre* (Cambridge, 1778), 267, in James A. Williamson, *The Voyages of the Cabots and the Discovery of North America under Henry VII and Henry VIII* (London, 1929), 18–19. On the role of Bristol, see Patrick McGrath, "Bristol and America," 1480–1631 in *The Westward Enterprise: English Activities in Ireland, the Atlantic, and America 1480–1650,* eds. K. R. Andrews, N. P. Canny and P. E. H. Hair (Detroit, 1979), 81–102.

20. The Petition of John Cabot and his Sons, March 5, 1496 in H. P. Biggar, *The Precursors of Jacques Cartier 1497–1534* (Ottawa, 1911), 6. On Cabot and his successors, see, for example, Lucien Campeau, "Les Cabot et l'Amérique," *Revue d'Histoire de l'Amérique Française* 14 (1960), 317–52, and John L. Allen, "From Cabot to Cartier: The Early Exploration of Eastern North America, 1497–1543," *Annals of the Association of American Geographers* 82 (1992), 500–21.

21. The First Letters Patent Granted to John Cabot and his Sons, London, March 5, 1496 in Biggar, *Precursors,* 7 (translation 9).

22. The Second Letters Patent Granted to John Cabot, February 3, 1498 in ibid., 22–4.

23. Dispatch of Ferdinand and Isabella to Gonzales de Puebla, their ambassador to England, March 28, 1496 in ibid., 10–11 (translation 11).

24. During Philip's reign, English writers often identified Spain with gold and silver. For instance, Jeffrey Knapp says that in *Midas* (1589), the playwright John Lyly identified Philip II and Midas, who hoped that he would become "monarch of the world" owing to his golden touch (I.i.116–17); see Jeffrey Knapp, *An Empire Nowhere: England. America, and Literature from Utopia to The Tempest* (Berkeley, 1992), 80. For a discussion of trade and overseas expansion, see Kenneth Andrews, *Trade, Plunder and Settlement: Maritime Enterprise and the Genesis of the British Empire, 1480–1630* (Cambridge, 1984).

25. Lorenzo Pasqualigo to his Brothers at Venice, August 23, 1497 in Biggar, *Precursors,* 13 (translation 14).; the translation of this letter is also found in Williamson, *Voyages,* 29.

26. Whereas Biggar thinks the dispatch was the first from Raimondo di Soncino to the duke of Milan, Williamson provided convincing evidence that if the date is correct, it would have to be from someone else because the ambassador was still at Dover on August 24. Dispatch to the duke of Milan, August 24, 1497 in Biggar, *Precursors,* 15 (translation 15–16), translation also in

Williamson, *Voyages,* 29–30; and in *Calendar of State Papers, Milan,* vol. 1, ed. Allen B. Hinds (London, 1912), no. 535.

27. Raimondo de Soncino to the duke of Milan, December 18, 1497 in Biggar, *Precursors,* 17 (translation 19). A less grandiose translation appears in Hinds and Williamson: "Having observed that the sovereigns first of Portugal and then of Spain had occupied unknown islands, he decided to make a similar acquisition for his Majesty," in *Calendar* ed. A. B. Hinds, I, no 552; for reproduction of the English translation in Hinds, see Williamson, *Voyages,* 30–2.

28. Raimondo di Soncino to the duke of Milan, December 18, 1497 in *Precursors,* 17 (translation 21); for another translation, see "De Socino in *Calendar,* ed. Hinds, I, no 552; and in Williamson, *Voyages,* 30–2. Cabot claimed the New World with a banner of St. Mark (Venice) and another for England. On this point, see Knapp, *Empire,* 28.

29. See, for instance, *The Italians and the Creation of America,* ed. Samuel J. Hough (Providence, 1980). For the contribution of the Genoese to trade and colonization before Columbus, see Fernández-Armesto, *Before Columbus,* 96–120.

30. See Burckhardt's *The Civilization of the Renaissance in Italy* (New York, 1992), 172.

31. Pedro Ayala to the Spanish sovereigns, July 25, 1498 in Biggar, *Precursors,* 27 (translation 28). The words in italics are in cipher in the original; also in translation in Williamson, *Voyages,* 39.

32. Ayala in Biggar, *Precursors,* 27 (translation 28); translation also in Williamson, *Voyages,* 39.

33. See Luca Codignola, "The Holy See and the Conversion of the Indians," *America in European Consciousness, 1493–1750,* ed. Karen Ordahl Kupperman (Chapel Hill, 1995), 199.

34. Ayala in Biggar, *Precursors,* 27 (translation 28).

35. Ibid.

36. Ibid., 27–8 (translation 28–9).

37. For a detailed discussion of the Cabots and the Portuguese, see H. P. Biggar, *Voyages of the Cabots and of the Corte-Reals* (Paris, 1903) and also Williamson, *Voyages,* 119f., esp. 200–3. For treatments of the Cabots, see Henry Harrisse, *Jean et Sébastien Cabot* (Paris, 1882) and John T. Juricek, "John Cabot's First Voyage, 1497," *Smithsonian Journal of History* 2 (1967), 1–22. See also Allen, "From Cabot," 500–21.

38. Williamson, *Voyages,* 204. For a study of the Corte Reals, including documents, see Henry Harrisse, *Les Cort-Real et leurs voyages au nouveau-monde . . .* (Paris, 1883).

39. Grant of Pension to Sebastian Cabot, Public Record office, Exchquer, K. R. Memoranda Roll 20 Hen. VII in Williamson, *Voyages,* 70; on Cabot and the northwest passage, see Williamson, *Voyages,* 223–43.

40. For instance, the Cabots appeared in the contemporary chronicle of Robert Fabyan (paraphrased in Stow and Hakluyt), Peter Martyr's *De Orbe Novo Decades* (1516), Marcantonio Contrari's report on Sebastian Cabot to the Venetian senate (1536), inscriptions about the Cabot discoveries in Spanish and Latin on the back of the world map of 1544 (now called the Paris map), the Venetian Giovanni Battista Ramusio's *Navigationi et Viaggi* (1550), Francisco López de Gómara's *La historia general de las Indias* (1552), Richard Eden's *Decades,* an English translation of Peter Martyr (1555), André Thevet's *Les Singularitez de la France Antartique, autrement nommé Amérique* (1558), the Portuguese Antonio Galvano's *Tratado* (1563), the Huguenot Jean Ribault's *Discovery of Terra Florida* (1563), Humphrey Gilbert's *Discourse* (early 1560s, pub. 1576), Richard Willes's *History of Travel in the East and West Indies* (1577), George Beste's *A True Discourse of the Late Voyages of Discoverie . . .* (1578), his book on Frobisher, Urbain Chauveton, *Histoire Nouvelle du Nouvelle Monde* (1579), John Stow's *Chronicles* (1580), and Richard Hakluyt's *Divers Voyages* (1582), to name a few. For an assessment of the information about Sebastian Cabot in these sources, see Williamson, *Voyages,* 225–43.

41. On the English, French, and Portuguese fisheries in Newfoundland, see K. G. Davies, *The North Atlantic World in the Seventeenth Century* (Minneapolis, 1974), 12–17.

42. The tax regards "das pescarias da Terra Nova" (96) (the fisheries of New foundland). Letter from the king of Portugal in regard to the tithe on Newfoundland codfish in Biggar, *The Precursors,* 96–7 (translation 97–8).

43. Ibid., 13.

44. See Selma Barkham, "The Basques: Filling a Gap in Our History between Jacques Cartier and Champlain," *Canadian Geographical Journal* 96 (1978), 8–19.

45. Ramusio, *Navigationi et Viaggi* (Venetia, 1550), III, 423 verso, cited in Biggar, Introduction, *The Precursors,* xxii. See also Charles-André Julien, *Histoire de l'expansion et de la colonization françaises,* (Paris, 1948), I, 336; Carl Ortwin Sauer, *Sixteenth-Century North America: The Land and the Peo-*

ple as Seen by Europeans (Berkeley, 1971), 51–2; Eugène Guénin, *Ango et ses pilotes, d'après des documents inédits, tirés de archives de France, Portugal et d'Espagne* (Paris, 1901). See also Litalien, *Les explorateurs,* 53. For another account of Essomericq, see Frank Lestringant, *Le Huguenot et le sauvage: L'Amérique et la controverse coloniale, en France, au temps des Guerres de Réligion (1555–1589)* (Paris, 1990), 29.

46. Warrant of Queen Joanna to John de Agramonte Covering an Agreement with King Ferdinand for a Voyage to Newfoundland, 8, October 29, 1511 in Biggar, *The Precursors,* 102–7; translation 107–11. See also Letters Patent from Queen Joanna confirming the appointment of Agramonte as captain of the expedition, October 29 (?), 1511 in ibid., 111–12.

47. Warrant, in ibid., 102–3; the translation reads "the secret of Newfoundland," "(except that two of the pilots may be Bretons or belong to some other nation which has been there)," "our son," "the Most Serene King of Portugal" in ibid., 107.

48. Warrant in ibid., 103–5.

49. King Ferdinand's letter to Sebastian Cabot, September 13, 1512 in ibid., 115 (translation 116).

50. Biggar includes a number of French documents pertaining to the Newfoundland fishery—a pardon to the mate of a Newfoundland fishing vessel, January 1513, in ibid., 116–18; an agreement between the monks of the Abbey of Beauport and the inhabitants of the Island of Bréhat, which mentions Newfoundland cod, December 14–17, 1514 in ibid., 118–23; documents concerning vessels going from Bayonne to Newfoundland, vessel of February 18, 1520 in ibid., 124, and a vessel for March 6, 1521 in the same volume in ibid., 125–6. For discussions of the fisheries, see Charles de la Morandière, *Histoire de la pêche française de la morue* (Paris, 1962) and Harold Innis, *The Cod Fisheries: The History of an International Economy,* rev. ed. (Toronto, 1954, rpt. 1978).

51. Letter from Vice-Admiral Fitzwilliam to Cardinal Wolsey, August 21, 1522, and another from Fitzwillam to Henry VIII in Biggar, *The Precursors,* 142–3.

52. "An answer made to serten of the kinges counsell as consernyng the kinges shippes to be occupyed," Records of the Drapers' Company of London, vol. VII (1514–50), 167–70, 175–6 in ibid., 134–42; see 136–7.

53. Confirmation of the letters patent to Fagundes, March 13, and May 22, 1521 in ibid., 127–9; translation 129–31.

54. Agreement with Gomez for the discovery of a northwest passage, in ibid., 145–7 (translation 147–50).

55. See Jacques Cartier, *Voyages au Canada avec les relations des voyages en Amérique de Gonneville, Verranzano et Roberval,* ed. Charles-André Julien, René Herval, and Théodore Beauchesne (Paris, 1981), 40. This includes a modern-spelling version of Gonneville. See Charles-André Julien's Introduction to this volume, which is reprinted from his *Les Français en Amérique dans la première moitié du XVIe siècle* (Paris, 1946), 10. The original source of knowledge about the New World here was Portugal, and, in this account at least, the French voyage does not seem to have much official backing.

56. See Jean-Paul Duviols, *Voyageurs français en Amérique (colonies espagnoles et portugaises)* (Paris, 1978), 3–4.

57. Charles-André Julien, "Introduction," *Les Français en Amérique pendant la première moitié du XVIe siècle,* ed. Charles-André Julien, René Herval, and Théodore Beauchesne (Paris, 1946), 1–4, see also 5–22. See E. Cleirac, *Us et coutumes de la mer . . .* (Bordeaux, 1647), 151, cited in Julien, *Les Français* (1946), 4 and Charles Demarquets, *Mémoires chronologiques pour servir à l'histoire de Dieppe et à celle des navigations françaises . . .* (2 vols., Paris, 1785), I, 91–98, cited in ibid., 1.

58. Julien cites many French historians who agree with the claim that he makes: "The *Authentic Relation* of Gonneville represents the oldest testimony of the contact of the French with a territory and the American indigenes"; ibid., 5; my translation. For Michel de Certeau's interest in this topic from Gonneville onward, a project he never completed, see his "Travel Narratives of the French to Brazil: Sixteenth to Eighteenth Centuries," *New World Encounters,* ed. Stephen Greenblatt (Berkeley, 1993), 323–8.

59. Binot Paulmier de Gonneville, *Relation authentique . . .* in *Les Français* (1946), ed. Julien et al., 36.

60. On Díaz and the role of writing for Cortés and his associates, see J. H. Elliott, "Cortés, Veláquez and Charles V," Hernán Cortés, *Letters from Mexico,* trans. Anthony Pagden (1971; New Haven, 1986), xvi.

61. See René Laudonnière, *Histoire notable de la Floride située es Indes Occidentales* (Paris, 1586) in *Les Français en Amérique pendant la duxième moitié su XVIe siècle* (Paris, 1958), 38, cited in Patricia Seed, *Ceremonies of Possession in Europe's Conquest of the New World, 1492–1640* (Cambridge,

1995), 56. Seed discusses Gonneville and this French ploy of a conquest by love in such cere-monies of planting a cross, pillar or royal standard; ibid., 56–63.

62. Gonneville, 37. See n. 7 on that page.
63. Ibid., 37. The editors gloss this Latin inscription at ibid., 37–8; my translation.
64. Ibid., 38.
65. Gonneville is not alone in misreading the signs. For a discussion of how Verrazzano and Cartier misread the Natives' religious beliefs, see Stephen Greenblatt, *Marvelous Possessions: The Wonder of the New World* (Chicago, 1991), 102–4.
66. Gonneville, *Relation,* 39.
67. Gonneville, *Relation,* 44, see 40–3. The editors have calculated the number of men lost ; ibid., 44.
68. Ibid., 44–5. See Julien, "Introduction," *Les Français* (1946), 5.
69. See Gonneville, *Relation,* 25.
70. P. Fauchille, *Traité de Droit International Public* (Paris, 1925), I, part 2, 687, cited in Green and Dickason, 7. For similar references to François I on Adam's will, see Lyle N. McAlister, *Spain and Portugal in the New World 1492–1700* (Minneapolis, 1984), 199, and Anthony Pagden, *Lords of All the World: Ideologies of Empire in Spain, Britain and France c. 1500–c. 1800* (New Haven, 1995), 47.
71. Litalien, *Les explorateurs,* 53.
72. See Lawrence C. Wroth, *The Voyages of Giovanni da Verrazzano 1524–1528* (New Haven, 1970), 58–9.
73. René Herval's French translation, *Giovanni da Verrazzano et les Dieppois à la Recherche du Cathay (1524–1528)* (Rouen and Caen, 1933), was based on Alessandro Bacchiani's Italian text (1909 edition) and was republished in *Les Français,* ed. Julien et al., in 1946. For a detailed account of the versions of the text, see Wroth, *Voyages,* 93–5.
74. The Italian original and the English translation in Wroth, *Voyages,* 125, 135 respectively (English trans. by Susan Tarrow); for the French translation, see *Les Français* (1946), ed. Julien et al., 58–9.
75. Verrazzano seems to have been educated in the humanist tradition, although he did not choose to write in Latin, so that his mastery of style and rhetoric makes the question of tone more intri-cate. The Italian and English in Wroth, *Voyages,* 127–8 and 138 respectively; the French in *Les Français* (1946), ed. Julien et al., 64–5.
76. Wroth, *Voyages,* 138. On the early French exploration of North America, see Camillo Menchini, "Il Canada di Jacques Cartier e di Giovanni da Verrazzano," *Veltro* 29 (1985), 115–25.
77. Wroth, *Voyages,* 130 (Italian), 140–1 (English); *Les Français* (1946), ed. Julien et al., 70 (French).
78. Wroth, *Voyages,* 141.
79. The influences are difficult to trace as there appears to have been various texts that discussed this theme. See Thomas More, *The Complete Works of St. Thomas More,* ed. Edward Surtz and J. H. Hexter (4 vols., New Haven, 1965), IV.
80. More, Book II, 150–9, 428.
81. See Todorov, *Conquest,* 194–5.
82. See chapter 5 for the second part of this circulation of ideas.
83. Ibid.
84. Ibid., 131–2 (Italian); 142–3 (English); *Les Français* (1946), ed. Julien et al., 72–6 (French).
85. Wroth, *Voyages,* 29.
86. Sauer, *Sixteenth,* 52; see Wroth, *Voyages,* 71–3. Concerning Verrazzano's death, Julien says that Ver-razzano was said to have been eaten with six of his companions in the Antilles. See Julien, "Intro-duction," *Les Français* (1946), I, 10. There is no evidence of Verrazzano's birth; until recently, he was assumed to have been born in Florence, but now an hypothesis has the birth occurring in Lyons in a Florentine family. See Wroth, 6–8.
87. Sauer, *Sixteenth,* 52–4, 61; Litalien, *Les explorateurs,* 54–9. For documents, see Jacques Habert, *Vie et Voyages de Jean de Verrazane* (Ottawa, 1964).
88. *Erasmus Epistolae,* II, 333, 70, quoted in Roland Bainton, *Erasmus of Christendom* (New York, 1969), 104. Sverker Arnoldsson, as I mentioned in the Introduction, has done detailed work on anti-Spanish sentiments in sixteenth-century Italy and Germany; see his *La Leyenda Negra: Estu-dios Sobra sus Orígenes* (Göteburg, 1960).
89. John Parker, *Books to Build and Empire: A Bibliographical History of English Overseas Interests to 1620* (Amsterdam, 1965), 21–3. For *Of the new landes . . . ,* see *The First Three English Books on America [?1511]-1555 A.D. . . . ,* ed. Edward Arber (Westminster, 1895), xxiii-xxxvi.

90. W. P. D. Wightman, *Science in a Renaissance Society* (London, 1972), 101–02. On the knowledge of theoretical science and of practical navigation of Columbus, Vespucci and others, see ibid., 65–75.

91. See More, *The Complete Works,* IV.

92. More, Book II, 218–19; Amerigo Vespucci, *Quatuor Americi Vespucij nauigatones* (St. Dié, 1507), vol. 1, sig.c8, rpt. *The Cosmographiae Introductio of Martin Waldseemüller in Facsimile, Followed by the Four Voyages of Amerigo Vespucci, with Their Translation into English,* ed. C. G. Herbermann and trans. Mario E. Cosenza (New York, 1907).

93. For a reading of *Utopia* that discusses the new mobility of capital in the "prehistory" of capitalism and drawing on Marxism, see Richard Halpern, *The Poetics of Primitive Accumulation: English Renaissance Culture and the Genealogy of Capital* (Ithaca, 1991), ch. 4, 136–75. A detailed reading that provides useful background information can be found in George M. Logan, *The Meaning of More's "Utopia"* (Princeton, 1983).

94. John Rastell, *A new interlude . . . of the iiii elements* (n.p., n.d.), fol. Ci verso, quoted in Parker, 24–5. See Parker's discussion on those pages. See also M. E. Borish, "Source and Intention of *The Four Elements,*" *Studies in Philology* 35 (1938), 149–63. For Rastell's *Interlude of Four Elements,* see David B. Quinn, *New American World: A Documentary History of North America to 1612* (5 vols., New York, 1979), I. Rastell advocates exploration of the West and the establishment of colonies there. On Rastell, see R. W. Chambers, *Thomas More* (London, 1935), 141–3, J. H. Hexter, "Introduction, Part I," *The Complete Works of St. Thomas More,* ed. Edward Surtz and J.H. Hexter (4 vols., New Haven, 1965), IV, xxxi and Knapp, *Empire,* 44–6. Knapp concentrates on Rastell's contribution—even in a poem on colonization—to the myth of Brutus of Troy as the founder of Britain.

95. Parker, *Books,* 25–6.

96. Ibid. See also F. A. Kirkpatrick, "The First Recorded English Voyage to the West Indies," *The English Historical Review* 20 (1905), 115–24.

97. Martyr's *Opera: Legatio babylonica, Oceani decas, poetata epigrammatica* had been printed in 1511 in Seville.

98. Pietro Martire d'Anghiera [Peter Martyr], *De orbe nouo decades* (Alcalá de Henares, 1516), ai verso. P. M. d'Anghiera, *Extrait ov recveil des ileseles nouuelleme[n]t touuees en la grande mer Oceane ou temps du roy Despaigne Ferna[n]d & Elizabeth sa femme, faict premierement en latin par Pierre Martyr de Millan, & depuis* (Paris, 1532). For the 1524 volume, see P. M. d'Anghiera, *De rebus, et insulis noviter repertis* and Hernando Cortés, *Praeclara . . . de nova maris Oceani. Hyspania narratio* (Nuremburg, 1524). P. Savorgnanus translated Cortés's *Carta de relacion* (Seville 1522). This is just a small example of the bibliographical intricacies of translation and transmission of the Spanish writings about the New World. It illustrates where the history of the book meets the history of ideas. Martyr's address to "Clarissimo Principi Rolo Regi Catholico," which begins "Servavit Divina Providentia," is not included in the French translation of 1532.

99. P. M. d'Anghiera, *Extraict,* aii.

100. Ibid., aii; my translations here and below.

101. Ibid., aii recto.–aii verso

102. Ibid., aii verso

103. Ibid., aiii recto; see aii verso

104. Ibid., 1. On the discovery, see 2 recto.

105. Ibid., 114 verso–115 recto. Sebastian Cabot seems to have taken credit for his father's discovery. The text referred to "lisle britannique," which is "vulgarly called England."

106. Charles-André Julien, *Les Voyages de découvertes et les premiers établissements* (Paris, 1948), 115–17, 135–8; David B. Quinn and Alison M. Quinn, "Commentary" in Richard Hakluyt, *Discourse of Western Planting,* ed. D. B. and A. M. Quinn (London, 1993), 187. In *Les Français* Julien outlines Le Veneur's principal part in the Cartier expedition and the family connections and friendships behind this; see Julien, "Introduction," *Les Français* (1946), I, 11. Some of this material he says he owes to the groundbreaking work in Baron de La Chapelle, "Jean Le Veneur et le Canada," *Nova Francia* 6 (1931), 341–3.

107. Ibid. For a recent discussion of Cartier, gold, and El Dorado, see Jean-Pierre Sanchez, "Le Royaume de Saguenay: un Eldorado Septentrional?" *Saguenayensia* 30 (1988), 15–32.

108. On Cartier, see François-Marc Gagnon, *Jacques Cartier et la découverte du Nouveau Monde* (Québec, 1984). Patricia Seed asserts that the French had ceremonies of possession that involved a "conquest by love." René Laudonnière thought that the Spanish had recognized one territory in the New World as being French because they saw signs and the French coat

of arms that Verrazzano had supposedly left; see Laudonnière, *Histoire notable de la Floride . . .* (Paris, 1586), 38 and Seed, *Ceremonies,* 56. Seed also mentions that Gonneville and Cartier had used tricks to take possession from the Natives because they could not gain consent for their actions. See ibid., 57.

109. Julien, *Les Français* (1946), I, 11–12, see 13–18. I am indebted to Julien here and below for the basic outline of Cartier's voyages. On the geography of the voyages of Cartier and his predecessors, see Allen, "From Cabot," 500–21.

110. Julien, *Les Français* (1946), I, 13.

111. "To this great enterprise the King officially assigned the elevated purpose of propagating Christianity; for, ever since the Pope's division of new lands between Portugal and Spain, the role of missionary was the only justification France could use for her actions without affronting the Holy See. This was an obvious diplomatic façade, since the first baptism by the French in North America did not take place until 1610." M. Trudel, "Section One: Introduction to the New World" in *Canada: Unity in Diversity,* ed. Paul G. Cornell et al. (Toronto, 1967), 9.

112. Julien, *Les Français* (1946), I, 14.

113. See Keller et al., *Creation of Rights of Sovereignty,* 23–5, cited in Olive Dickason, "Concepts of Sovereignty at the Time of First Contacts" in Green and Dickason, *The Law,* 221, 287.

114. Tim Rowse, *After Mabo: Interpreting Native Indienous Traditions* (Melbourne, 1993), 8, 21.

115. "Copia de lo que el embaxador de França scrivé á Su Magestad á los XXVII de diziembre 1540" in H. P. Biggar, *A Collection of Documents Relating to Jacques Cartier and The Sieur de Roberval* (Ottawa, 1930), 169–71.

116. The commission allowed Roberval to claim "countries that are not held, occupied, possessed and dominated or being held under the subjection and dominion of any princes or potentates, our allies and confederates, and likewise of our most-dear and loved friends the emperor and the King of Portugal"; "Roberval's Commission," January 15, 1540/1, in Biggar, *Collection,* 180; my translation.

117. For instance, see "Rapport d'vn espion espagnol sur les armaments de Jacques Cartier" [Saint-Malo, avril 1541] in Biggar, *Collection,* 275–9.

118. "[El Emperador] al Cardenal de Toledo" in Biggar, *Collection,* 283–4 (translation, ibid).

119. "[El Emperador]" in Biggar, *Collection,* 286–7 (translation, ibid).

120. "Memorandum of the Councils of State and of the Indies," before June 26, 1541, in Biggar, *Collection,* 320. The translation is from Biggar; the original reads: "ques es la tierra que pretenden que descubrieron los Bretones muchos dias ha"; ibid., 320.

121. Ibid., 320–1.

122. Ibid. The translation is at ibid., 321.

123. Ibid., 321–4.

124. "Traslado de la carta que el Cardenal de Sevilla escrivió á Sa mano" in Biggar, *Collection,* 325–6; see Biggar, "Introduction," xxx–xxxii. Biggar's translation at ibid., 325–6.

125. Biggar, *Collection,* 403–5; see Biggar, "Introduction," ibid., xxxi–xxxii.

126. For recent works on Cartier, which discuss relations with the Natives, interpretation, and the nature of exploration, see *Le Monde de Jacques Cartier: L'aventure au XVIᵉ Siècle,* ed. Fernand Braudel (Montréal, 1984); François-Marc Gagnon and Denise Petel, *Hommes effarables et bestes sauvages: Images du Nouveau-Monde d'après les voyages de Jacques Cartier* (Montréal, 1986); Marie-Christine Gomez-Graud, "Le Proces d'une relation coupable. De quelques interpretations des récits de Jacques Cartier," *Études Françaises* 22 (1986), 63–71.

127. Biggar, "Introduction," *Collection,* xxxiv.

128. Quoted from the *Correspondence Politique de MM. de Castillon et de Marillac Ambassadeurs de France en Angleterre (1537–42),* ed. Jean Kaulek (Paris, 1885), 390 in Biggar, *Collection,* 441; my translation. See Biggar, "Introduction," *Collection,* xxxiv.

129. "Paget to King Henry VIII" in Biggar, *Collection,* 444.

130. Biggar, "Introduction," *Collection,* xxxv.

131. Julien, *Les Français* (1946), I, 14–15.

132. "English Report on the French Expedition," in Biggar, *Collection,* 188. See also Biggar's note 1 on 188.

133. Julien, *Les Français* (1946), I, 17–18.

134. Biggar, *Voyages,* 85 note 3, cited in Julien, *Les Français,* I, note 3.

135. On the provenance and history of the texts of Gonneville, Verrazzano, and Cartier, see La Chapelle, 18–22.

136. "Deuxième voyage de Jacques Cartier" 1535–6 in Julien, *Les Français* (1946), I, 1, 117–18; my translation. I have consulted the original editions of Cartier in Houghton Library, but given their relative scarcity and the availability of the Julien edition, I have chosen to cite from this original or old spelling edition of 1946.
137. "Troisième Voyage de Jacques Cartier," 1541, and "Voyage de Roberval au Canada," 1542–3, both translated into modern French from Hakluyt's translation; *Les Français* (1946), ed. Julien, I, 193–6, 206–7. See Lestringant, "The Philosopher's Breviary: Jean de Léry in the Enlightenment" in *New World Encounters*, ed. Stephen Greenblatt (Berkeley, 1993), 127.
138. See Lestringant, "The Philosopher's Breviary: Jean de Léry in the Enlightenment," 127.
139. Rastell's son sailed to America in 1536; on the use of allegory by father and son, see Knapp, *Empire*, 45. On the failures of the voyages of John Rastell and later of Humphrey Gilbert, see Mary C. Fuller, *Voyages in Print: English Travel to America, 1576–1624* (Cambridge, 1995), 32.
140. Parker, *Books*, 27.
141. Ibid., 28–30.
142. Ibid.
143. Ibid. Lestringant notes that Thorne is one of the list of English and French explorers of North America to appear in a list in Hakluyt's *Divers Voyages* (1582); see Lestringant, *Le Huguenot*, 214.
144. More generally, James Axtell has chronicled the phenomenon of the "White Indian"; see Axtell, "The White Indian," *The Invasion Within: The Contest of Cultures in Colonial North America* (New York, 1985), 302–28. Nicholas Canny and Peter Hulme have noted that some English abandoned their colonies for assimilation among the Natives, especially before 1622; see Canny, "The Permissive Frontier: the Problem of Social Control in English Settlements in Ireland and Virginia 1550–1650" in *The Westward Enterprise*, ed. K. R. Andrews, N. P. Canny, and P. E. H. Hair (Liverpool, 1978), 17–44; Hulme, *Colonial Encounters: Europe and the Native Caribbean, 1492–1697* (1986; London, 1992), 143. Jeffrey Knapp picks up on that theme of fragilty and failure and includes a reminder that is easily forgotten: the most famous English voyagers (Drake, Cavendish, Frobisher, Hawkins) had all perished at sea; see Knapp, *Empire*, 63. Henry Hudson, Humphrey Gilbert, and others also died during their voyages, something apparently much less common among the Spanish and the French.
145. Parker, *Books*, 28–30.
146. Ibid.
147. Biggar, *Collection*, xviii.
148. Ibid., xviii–xix, xxii, xxxvii, 476.
149. Jean Cauvin (a native of Picardy and later known as Calvinus or Calvin) became a Protestant in about 1533, and he soon left for Basel because his life was in danger in France. In 1541, Calvin translated the second edition of his *Institutes* into French. Calvin consented to the trial and execution, though not to the mode of death—burning alive—of the Spanish religious radical, Michael Sevetus, who sought refuge in Geneva in 1553. See Peter Gay and R. K. Webb, *Modern Europe* (New York, 1973), 152. Other refugees had better fortune in Geneva, which provided refuge for Protestant Europe. French and English Calvinists were instrumental in exploring and settling the New World.
150. For a discussion of this tension between an anti-Rome and anti-Spain policy, see Julian Lock, "'How Many Tercios Has the Pope?' The Spanish War and the Sublimation of Elizabethan Anti-Popery," *The Historical Journal* (1996): 197–214.
151. Public Record Office [PRO] State Papers Ireland (Elizabeth), SP 63/88/29, Grey to Elizabeth, Nov. 12, 1580, quoted in Lock, "How," 198.

Chapter 3

1. Charles Weiss, *Papiers d'état du Cardinal de Granville* (Paris, 1872), iii, 296, quoted in H. P. Biggar, "Introduction," *A Collection of Documents Relating to Jacques Cartier and The Sieur de Roberval* (Ottawa, 1930), xxxvii.
2. Frances Gardiner Davenport, *European Treaties bearing on the History of the United States and its Dependencies to 1648* (4 vols., Washington, D.C., 1917), I, 205–7; for the unratified article on the West Indies concerning the right for France to trade there, see the treaty concluded between France and Spain at Crépy-en-Laonnois, September 18, 1544 in ibid., 208–9. On Cartier's third voyage, the war with Spain, and the fate of Donnacona and other Natives trans

ported back to France, see Ramsey Cook's introduction to H. P. Biggar's translation of Cartier (with some emendations to come closer to Cartier's diction; for instance, "savage" for "Indian"); Cook, "Donnacona Discovers Europe: Rereading Jacques Cartier's *Voyages*" in *The Voyages of Jacques Cartier* (1993; Toronto, 1995), xxxix-xl; on the translation, see his "Preface," vi-vii. For a recent edition, see Jacques Cartier, *Jacques Cartier Relations,* ed. Michel Bideaux (Montréal, 1986). Bideaux is clear on the textual problems and question of authorship (the Italian text of the first voyage and the English version of the third); see Bideaux, 9–72.

3. Davenport, *European Treaties,* 206. Some of the failure has to do with unsuccessful claims and with convincing the Natives of French possession. The question of French and European contact with Native Americans, which Ramsey Cook highlights in his introduction (see note 2 above), has produced some important scholarship, including controversies over the legality of the French claim. See Cornelius Jaenen, *Friend and Foe: Aspects of French-American Cultural Contact in the Sixteenth and Seventeenth Centuries* (Toronto, 1973); Bruce Trigger, *The Children of Aataentsic: A History of the Huron People to 1660* (2 vols., Montreal, 1976), I, 177–208; Brian Slattery, "French Claims in North America, 1500–54," *Canadian Historical Review* 59 (1978), 139–69; Michael T. Ryan, "Assimilating New Worlds in the Sixteenth and Seventeenth Centuries," *Comparative Studies in Society and History* 23 (1981), 525–6; *Le Monde de Jacques Cartier,* ed. Fernand Braudel (Montréal, 1984), especially John Dickenson, "Les Précurseurs de Jacques Cartier," 127–48; Michel Mollat, *Les Explorateurs du XIIIᵉ au XVIᵉ siècles: Premiers regards sur des mondes nouveaux* (Paris, 1984), 184–5; Olive Dickason, "The Brazilian Connection: A Look at the Origins of French Techniques for Trading with Amerindians," *Revue française d'outre-mer* 71 (1985), 129–46; François-Marc Gagnon and Denise Petel, *Hommes effarables et bestes sauvaiges* (Montréal, 1986), 90–115; James Axtell, *After Columbus* (New York, 1988), 144–81; Jody Green, "New Historicism and Its New World Discoveries," *Yale Journal of Criticism* 4 (1991), 182; Bruce Trigger, "Early Native North American Responses to European Contact: Romantic versus Rationalistic Interpretations," *Journal of American History* 77 (1991), 1195–1215.

4. Another aspect of the French response to the New World is the work of André Thevet, who claimed to be Cartier's friend and whose self-promotion and advocacy for French expansion I have discussed elsewhere and so have relegated my analysis to the notes in this chapter. See Jonathan Hart, "Strategies of Promotion: Some Prefatory Matter of Oviedo, Thevet and Hakluyt," *Imagining Culture: Essays in Early Modern History and Literature,* ed. J. Hart (New York, 1996), 73–94.

5. Samuel Eliot Morison, *The European Discovery of America: The Northern Voyages A.D. 500–1600* (New York, 1971), ix.

6. As Arthur Ray says, "In the 1560s and 1570s more than a thousand whaling men were summering—and sometimes wintering—there [on the strait of Belle Isle in eastern Canada] every year"; see Ray, "When Two Worlds Met," *The Illustrated History of Canada,* ed. Craig Brown (1987; Toronto, 1991), 21.

7. On the relation between gender and the land in the colonization of the Americas, see, for instance, Annette Kolodny, *The Lay of the Land: Metaphor as Experience and History in American Life and Letters* (Chapel Hill, 1975), 3–25; Louis Montrose, "The Work of Gender in the Discourse of Discovery" in *New World Encounters,* ed. Stephen Greenblatt (Berkeley, 1993), 177–217; Jonathan Hart, "Images of the Native in Renaissance Encounter Narratives," *ARIEL* 25 (1994): 55–76; Richard C. Trexler, *Sex and Conquest: Gendered Violence, Political Order, and the European Conquest of the Americas* (Ithaca, NY, 1995).

8. In the notes to the Introduction, I listed some of the earlier studies of Las Casas and the Black Legend as well as some of the recent ones. Here I shall refer to some of the criticism of the past 25 years or so. John Elliott's discussion provides a useful overview of the background of "the Protestant grand design" behind the Black Legend; see his *The Old World and the New 1492–1650* (1970; Cambridge, 1992), 92; see also 48–50, 92–96. More recently, Elliott discussed Las Casas in his "Final Reflections: The Old World and the New Revisited" in *America in European Consciousness, 1493–1750,* ed. Karen Ordahl Kupperman (Chapel Hill, 1995), 392, 398. An analysis of Las Casas and the uses of anti-Spanish sentiment in Thomas Gage (which includes a French translation of 1699) occurs in Salvador Bueno, "Al Lector" in Thomas Gage, *Viages en la Nueva España* (Havana, 1980), 9–15. In chapter 6, I discuss Gage. For a discussion of the relation between Las Casas and Jean de Léry, particularly how Léry incorporated the horrors of the Spanish conquests of the New World into the edition of 1599 of *L'Histoire d'un voyage,* see Janet Whatley's "Editions and Reception of Léry" in Jean de Léry, *History of a Voyage to the Land of*

Brazil, trans. Janet Whatley (Berkeley, 1990), 220. Peter Burke places Las Casas in the context of images of the New World and the history of historical writing, including the related work of Girolamo Benzoni; see Burke, "America and the Rewriting of World History" in *America in European Consciousness,* 33, 36, 39, 46. For other important discussions of the Black Legend, see Charles Gibson, "Introduction," *The Black Legend of Spain: Anti-Spanish Attitudes in the Old World and the New,* ed. Charles Gibson (New York, 1971), 3–27; Anthony Pagden, *Spanish Imperialism and the Political Imagination: Studies in European and Spanish-American Social and Political Theory 1513–1830* (New Haven, 1990), 4, 32 and his Introduction to Bartolomé de Las Casas, *A Short Account of the Destruction of the Indies,* trans. Nigel Griffin (Harmondsworth, 1992), xiii. See also Inga Clendinnen, "'Fierce and Unnatural Cruelty': Cortés and the Conquest of Mexico," *Representations* 33 (1991), 65–100.

9. See, for instance, *America's War for Humanity Related in Story and Picture, Embracing a Complete History of Cuba's Struggle for Liberty, and the Glorious Heroism of America's Soldiers and Sailors,* ed. John J. Ingalls (New York, 1898), 13–20, in Gibson, *The Black Legend,* 173–8. There is a vast body of scholarship on the Black Legend. A recent study on the Black Legend includes a useful overview of the primary documents, like the works of Las Casas, Benzoni, Chauveton, and de Bry, and also secondary materials, such as translations of articles by Lewis Hanke and Benjamin Keen into Spanish; see Miguel Molina Martinez, *La leyenda negra* (Madrid 1991). See Keen, "The Black Legend Revisited: Assumptions and Realities," *Hispanic American Historical Review* 49 (1969), 703–19; Hanke, "A Modest Proposal for a Moratorium on Grand Generalizations: Some Thoughts on the Black Legend," *Hispanic American Historical Review* 51 (1971), 112–27. On Las Casas, see Marcel Bataillon, *Etudes sur Bartolomé de las Casas* (Paris, 1965). He discusses Montaigne's use of sources from New Spain, such as Gómara and Benzoni, and looks at Urbain Chauveton, who will be a key figure in chapter 4 of my study.

10. André Thevet, "Le Grande Insulaire," and his *Les singularitez de la France Antarctique* (Paris, 1558) in translation in *New American World: A Documentary History of North America to 1612,* ed. David B. Quinn (5 vols., New York, 1979), I, 219. On this conference at St. Malo, a meeting that cannot be proven, see Frank Lestringant, *Le Huguenot et le sauvage: L'Amérique et la controverse coloniale, en France, au temps des Guerres de Réligion (1555–1589)* (Paris, 1990), 213.

11. Jehan Sheyfue to the Queen Dowager, June 24, 1550, Vienna State Archives, Charles V, E 17 in *Calendar of State Papers, Spanish, 1550–52,* ed. R. Tyler (London, 1914), 115; in translation in Quinn, *New American World,* 219.

12. Jehan Sheyfue, *circa* January 1551 in ibid., 219.

13. Sheyfue to Charles V from London, March 7, 1553 in ibid., 219–20. Sheyfue to the Bishop of Arras, April 10, 1553 in ibid., 220. Sheyfue to Charles V from London, May 11, 1553 in ibid., 220.

14. On the abdication of Charles V and the transition to Philip II in the Netherlands and for the English intervention, see Charles Wilson, *Queen Elizabeth and the Revolt in the Netherlands* (London, 1970), ix–xiv and 1–20 respectively. Wilson also discusses the French hatred of the English (16) and the possible alliance of France with the rebels in the Netherlands (32).

15. MM de Comières and de Thoulouse, Simon Renard, and Jehan Sheyfue, Four Ambassadors in England to Charles V, 4 September 1553 in ibid., 220.

16. For a brief discussion of Ascham, see John Parker, *Books to Build and Empire: A Bibliographical History of English Overseas Interests to 1620* (Amsterdam, 1965), 30–1. There were certainly other French works on the New World besides those by Eden's famous contemporaries Thevet and Belleforest. See, for example, Jean Macer's *Indicarum historiarum linri III* (Paris, 1555), which appeared in French as *Les Trois livres de l'Histoire des Indes . . .* (Paris 1555) and Guillaume Le Testu, *Cosmographie vniverselle selon les nauigateurs tant anciens que modernes . . .* (Paris, 1556). Le Testu, a mariner and cartographer, was with Villegagnon and Thevet in Brazil and died with Drake at Nombre de Dios in Panama. See Jean-Paul Duviols, *L'Amérique espagnole vue et rêvée. Les livres de voyages de Christophe Colomb à Bougainville* (Paris, 1985), 357.

17. For discussions of this rivalry and the reign of Mary, see E. H. Harbison, *Rival Ambassadors at the Court of Queen Mary* (Princeton, 1940), S. T. Bindoff, *Tutor England* (1950; Harmondsworth, 1975), 165–82, and Joan Marie Thomas, "Before the Black Legend: Sources of Anti-Spanish Sentiment in England, 1553–1558" (unpublished Ph.D. dissertation, University of Illinois at Urbana-Champaign, 1984).

18. See Bindoff, *Tudor England,* 165–82 and Thomas, "Before."

19. See Thomas, "Before," 5, 13, 17–60.

20. For Renard's comment on the barbarity of England, see *Calendar of Letters, Dispatches and State Papers Relating to the Negotiations between England and Spain, 1553,* 425, 444, quoted in trans. in ibid., 50; and for Charles V's drafting of the *entente*, see *Calendar . . . 1553,* 386–7, cited in ibid. 52; for Philip's displeasure with the supplementary articles and his plans to ignore them, see *Calendar . . . January-July 1554,* 4–7, cited in ibid., 53.

21. See Thomas, "Before," 17–60.

22. See J. H. Elliott, *The Old World and the New 1492–1650* (1970; London, 1992), 91–2.

23. Richard Eden, *A treatyse of the newe India, with other new founde landes and Ilandes, as well eastwarde as westwarde, as they are knowen and found in these our dayes, after the descripcion of Sebastian Munster in his boke of universall Cosmographie: wherein the diligent reader my see the good successe and rewarde of noble and honeste enterpryses, by the which not only worldly ryches are obtayned, but also God is glorified, and the Christian fayth enlarged. Translated out of Latin into Englishe. By Rycharde Eden* (London, 1553), rpt. in Richard Eden, *The First Three English Books on America [?1511–1555 A.D., Being Chiefly Translations, Compilations, & c., by Richard Eden . . . ,* ed. Edward Arber (Westminster, 1895), 5.

24. Eden, *A treatyse,* 5. See Franklin T. McCann, *English Discovery of America to 1585* (1951; New York, 1969), 112–13. McCann presents some close reading. For an extensive discussion of Eden in context, see Parker, *Books,* 36–53.

25. Eden, *A treatyse,* 5–6.

26. Ibid., 11, see 8–10.

27. For brief comments on Eden's "pathbreaking" study, see Jeffrey Knapp, *An Empire Nowhere: England, America, and Literature from* Utopia *to* The Tempest (Berkeley, 1992), 18, see 19–20.

28. See the title page of *The Decades . . .* a Readex Microprint facsimile (n.p. 1966) of Richard Eden, *The Decades of the newe worlde of west India . . .* (London, 1555).

29. Eden, *The Decades,* [a.3. recto]; pagination on one page, the rest is extrapolated and appears in brackets.

30. See McCann, *English,* 116–17.

31. Eden, *The Decades,* [a.1. recto]; my translation from the Latin. This honorific address or salutation on the first page used the typography of an inverted pyramid or triangle, which had the unfortunate effect of literally enlarging Philip and diminishing Mary, although Eden listed Mary's possessions first and wished for their perpetual happiness.

32. Eden described this entry in Latin; ibid., [a.1. recto–a.1. verso].

33. The phrase is "in mundo theatro"; ibid., [a.2. recto]; my translation.

34. The phrase is "quibis hæc vestra India plena est"; ibid., [a.3. recto]; my translation.

35. "Virtus non exercita (inquit Seneca ad Neronem) paruam laudem meretur." Eden, *The Decades,* b.i.; my paraphrase in the text.

36. Ibid., b.i. verso.

37. Eden, *The Decades,* a,i, recto.

38. This Ciceronian view was something Philip Sidney would mock in *An Apology for Poetry* (ca. 1580, pub. 1595), where he left history, that study of particulars, in third place as he tried to reverse Aristotle's ranking of philosophy over poetry as the most universal subject. Philip Sidney, "An Apology for Poetry," in D. J. Enright and Ernst de Chickera, *English Critical Texts: 16th to 20th Century* (London, 1962), 13–21; Aristotle, "On the Art of Poetry" in T. S. Dorsch, ed. *Classical Literary Criticism* (1965; Harmondsworth, 1975), 43–4.

39. Eden, *The Decades,* a,i, recto.

40. For a discussion of this point, see Jonathan Hart, *Theater and World: The Problematics of Shakespeare's History* (Boston, 1992), 268–9.

41. Eden, *The Decades,* a,i, recto-verso. The theme of writing making others immortal is also common among the poets: Ovid, *Amores,* I, XV, 3142, Petrarch, *Rime sparse,* 104, Shakespeare, Sonnets 54 and 55. See William Shakespeare, *The Sonnets,* ed. G. Blakemore Evans (Cambridge, 1996), 59–60, 162–4.

42. Eden, *The Decades,* a,i, verso.

43. Ibid., a,i, verso-a,ii, recto.

44. See his *France in America* (1972; Vancouver, 1973), 7; see 8. Like Marcel Trudel's scholarship, Eccles's work in the field of French America is seminal. See also W. J. Eccles, *Canada Under Louis IV, 1663–1701* (Toronto, 1964).

45. Eden, *The Decades,* 171–2.

46. For a similar point, see Parker, *Books,* 45.

47. Eden, *The Decades,* a,ii, recto–a,ii, verso.

48. Ibid., a,ii, verso.

49. On barbarity, cannibalism, and civility as ideas used in European expansion in the New World, see Anthony Pagden, *The Fall of Natural Man: The American Indian and the Origins of Comparative Ethnology* (1982; Cambridge, 1986), 15–26, 80–7. For the representation of Natives as cannibals and Amazons, see Duviols, *L'Amérique espagnole,* 101–16. Peter Hume, *Colonial Encounters: Europe and the Native Caribbean 1492–1797* (1986; London, 1992). As elsewhere I have discussed Columbus's representation of the Natives, I have chosen not to duplicate the discussion here; see Hart, "Images," 55–76.

50. The phrase is James Froude's; see his "England's Forgotten Worthies" (1852) in *Short Studies on Great Subjects* (1867; London, 1888), I, 446. For a brief discussion of Froude's views of Hakluyt, see Knapp, 1, 3 and Mary C. Fuller, *Voyages in Print: English Travel to America, 1576–1624* (Cambridge, 1995), 14, 159–62.

51. Eden, *The Decades,* a,ii, verso.

52. Ibid., a,iii, recto.

53. Ibid., a,iii, recto.

54. Ibid., a,iii, verso.

55. Ibid.

56. Ibid.

57. Ibid., a,iv, recto; see a,iv, recto–b,i, recto.

58. Ibid., a,iv, recto–b,i, recto.

59. Ibid., b,i, verso.

60. Ibid., b,ii, recto.

61. Ibid. This is the kind of plea to his country John of Gaunt would make on his death bed in Shakespeare's *Richard II* (1595); II.i.5–67, *The Riverside Shakespeare,* ed. G. Blakemore Evans with J. J. M. Tobin (Boston, 1997).

62. See Hart, *Theater,* 268–9; also 43–4, 103–4, 114–15.

63. Eden, *The Decades,* b,ii, verso.

64. Ibid., b,ii, verso–b,iii, verso. For a discussion of Eden and other English and French writers about the New World, see Myron P. Gilmore, "The New World in French and English Historians of the Sixteenth Century" in *First Images of America: The Impact of the New World on the Old,* ed. Fredi Chiapelli et al. (2 vols., Berkeley, 1976), II, 519, see 520–27.

65. Eden, *The Decades,* b,iii, verso–b,iv, recto.

66. Ibid., b,iv, recto–b,iv, verso.

67. Eden, *Decades,* c,i, recto.

68. Ibid., c,i, recto–c,ii, verso.

69. Ibid., c,ii, verso–c,iii, recto.

70. Ibid., c,iii, recto.

71. Ibid., c,iii, recto–c,iii, verso.

72. Ibid., c,iii, verso.

73. Ibid., d,i, verso–d,ii, verso.

74. See ibid.

75. Ibid.

76. Ibid., d,iii, recto.

77. Christopher Marlowe, *The Works of Christopher Marlowe,* ed. C. F. Tucker Brooke (1910; Oxford, 1946).

78. *2 Henry IV,* II.iv.163–7: All Shakespearean citations and quotations from *The Riverside Shakespeare.*

79. *2 Henry IV,* V.iii.117–19; see *Henry V,* III.vi.59–60.

80. Ibid., verso. d.iii, verso–d,iv, verso, 173 verso–176 recto. For a close reading of the preface to Oviedo's *Sumario,* see Hart, "Strategies," 74–8.

81. McCann, *English,* 120. See Parker, *Books,* 44.

82. Ibid.

83. See *Les Français en Amérique pendant la deuxième moitié du XVIᵉ Siècle: Les Français en Floride,* ed. Charles-André Julien (2 vols, Paris, 1958), II, 1–2. For the connection between Elizabeth and the French Protestant cause in Florida, see Woodbury Lowery, "Jean Ribaut and Queen Elizabeth," *American Historical Review* 9 (1904), 456–9 and Parker, *Books,* 57–8. Frank Lestringant has helped to answer Julien's call for more work on the Huguenots; see Lestringant, *Le Huguenot.*

84. W. J. Eccles, *France in America* (1972;Vancouver, 1973), 9.
85. Julien, "Introduction," *Les Français* (1958), II, v, see vi–viii.
86. See *André Thevet's North America: A Sixteenth-Century View*, ed. Roger Schlesinger and Arthur P. Stabler (Kingston and Montreal, 1986), xxxiii, xxxix; Jean Céard, *La Nature et les prodiges: L'insolite au XVIe siècle, en France.* (Geneva, 1977), 283; Frank Lestringant, "L'Avenir des terres nouvelles," *La Renaissance et le Nouveau Monde.*, ed. Alain Parent et al. (Quebec, 1984), 50–1. See also his *L'Atelier du Cosmographe ou l'image du monde à la Renaissance* (Paris, 1991).
87. Cornelius Jaenen has a series of important articles on the French view of America and especially Amerindians; see his "Conceptual Frameworks for French Views of America and Amerindians" *French Colonial Studies* 2 (1978), 1–22; "French Attitudes Towards Native Society" in *Old Trails and New Directions*, ed. Carol Judd and Arthur Ray (Toronto, 1980), 59–72; "France's America and Amerindians: Image and Reality," *History of European Ideas* 6 (1985), 405–20.
88. Julien, "Introduction," *Les Français* (1958), II, v, see vi–viii. On Spain and France in Florida, see Sauer, *Sixteenth*, 189–227.
89. On Gouges, see Lestringant, *Le Huguenot*, 156–64, 174–5.
90. Julien, *Les Français* (1958), II, viii.
91. See Steele, *Warpaths: Invasions of North America* (New York, 1994), 11–12.
92. For a discussion of Le Challeux, see Lestringant, *Le Huguenot*, 113–15, 152–5.
93. See Steele, *Warpaths*, 7–20. On the French failure in Florida, including dissension among the French, and their piracy, as well as a balanced account of the conflict between Spain and France in this region, see ibid., 25–8. Apparently the Spanish expedition to Florida, 1565–68, cost the king one-fifth of the military budget for his empire; ibid., 27. For other discussions of this conflict, which, along with the war in the Netherlands, fed the Black Legend; see Eugene Lyon, *The Enterprise of Florida: Pedro Menéndez de Avilés and the Spanish Conquest of 1565–1568* (Gainsville, FL, 1976) and Paul E. Hoffman, *The Spanish Crown and the Defense of the Caribbean, 1565–1585: Precedent, Patrimonialism, and Royal Parsimony* (Baton Rouge, 1980), 218–28.
94. My translation. Le Challeux's original reads: *Discours de l'histoire de la Floride, contenant la trahison des Espagnols, contre les subiets du Roy, en l'an mil cinq cens soixante cinq. Redigé au vray par ceux qui en sont restez, Chose autant lamentable à oüir, qu'elle a esté produitoirement & cruellement executee par les dits Espagnols: Contre l'autorité su Roy nostre Sire, à la perte & dommage de tout ce Royaume.* (Dieppe, 1566). This is the edition I am using (in Houghton Library, Harvard), except I am drawing on one of the two editions that do not specify a place of publication and that scholars think were printed in Paris. Another edition appeared in Lyons during the same year. The translation of the title and Le Challeux's text are mine here and below.
95. Ibid., 3; my translation. Little is written on Le Challeux; see Lestringant, *Huguenot*, 105. Urbain Chauveton used Le Challeux's text against Spanish Catholics; see Chauveton's *Brief Discours et histoire d'vn voyage de qvelqves François en Floride . . .* (Paris, 1579). In the next chapter I discuss Chauveton. On bibliographical information on Le Challeux's account, see Jean-Paul Duviols, *L'Amérique*, 363–4.
96. Le Challeux, *Discours*, 6–7.
97. The phrases are "Qui veut aller à la Floride" and "je meurs de faim."
98. Le Challeux, *Discours*, 9.
99. See Steele, *Warpaths*, 7, 23–36.
100. Le Challeux, *Discours*, 10.
101. Ibid., 14.
102. Ibid., 17.
103. Ibid., 18.
104. Ibid., 23.
105. Ibid., 25.
106. Ibid., 26–7.
107. I discovered that I was not alone in making this connection, that in France this idea had been suggested although not amplified to the extent it requires, particularly concerning the role of Le Challeux's text. For suggestive remarks on Le Challeux, the Huguenots, and the Black Legend, see Duviols, *L'Amérique*, 183–4 and Lestringant, *Le Huguenot*, 104–6.
108. Le Challeux, *Discours*, 25.
109. Ibid., 28.
110. Ibid.

111. Ibid., 29.
112. Ibid., 30.
113. Ibid., 30–1.
114. Ibid., 32.
115. The phrase is "contre tout vsage de guerre." Ibid., 33.
116. Ibid., 34.
117. Ibid.
118. Ibid.
119. Ibid., 42.
120. Ibid., 43.
121. My translation; I have broken up some of Le Challeux's long sentences with refractory syntax. Ibid., 48–9.
122. Ibid., 50.
123. In this passage Le Challeux calls the Spanish "ces furieux Espagnols." Ibid., 50–1.
124. Ibid., 51.
125. I am interpreting "picque" here as pike, but it might be a pick or pickaxe. In this edition in Houghton Library, 52 is misnumbered as 54, which I have emended.
126. Ibid., [g3 verso]; my translation.
127. "Reqveste av Roy, faite par les femmes vefues, enfans orphelins, parens & amis de ses subiects, qui onte esté cruellement massacrez par les Espagnols, en la France Antarctique, nommée la Floride," which differed from the title page only in that it uses "massacrez" for "tuez" and does not announce that the request is made "en forme de complainte," *Discovrs et Histoire de ce qui est advenv en la Floride, en lan mille cinq cents soixante cinq: Redigé au vraye par ceux qui s'en sont retirez. Ensemble La Requeste presentee au Roy en forme de complainte, par les femmes vefues, & enfans orphelins, parens & amis de ses suiects, qui ont esté tuez en ladite Floride* (n.p. [Paris?], 1566) in *Deuxième Voyage du Dieppois Jean Ribaut à la Floride en 1565: Relation de N. Le Challeux: Précédée d'une notice Historique et bibliographique par Gabriel Gravier* (Rouen, 1872), 49, cf. the title page of the original, on which Nicolas Le Challeux's name does not appear.
128. Le Challeux, *Discovrs* (Paris?, 1566) in ibid., 49.
129. Ibid.
130. Ibid. One edition uses "Petremclaude" (Gravier) and the other "Petremelande" (Julien). Le Challeux, or the author of the "Reqvueste," is referring to Pedro Menéndez.
131. Ibid., 49–50. The sentence fragment is Le Challeux's.
132. Ibid., 50.
133. The phrase is "esté furieusement invahis par cinq nauires Espagnols." Ibid., 50.
134. Ibid, 51–2.
135. Ibid.
136. Le Challeux's phrase is "vn faict de cruauté si barbare." Ibid., 52.
137. The original is "comme vostre personne mesme." Ibid., 53, see also 52.
138. Ibid., 53–4. In the Gravier edition, the phrase is "Petremclaude & ceux de sa maison" (54), whereas in the Julien edition it is "Petremelande ey ceux de sa nation" (237). The second of these phrases makes the condemnation of Spain even clearer.
139. Ibid.
140. Parker thinks that Le Challeux's work is anticolonial and shows that Hacket printed Ribault's pro-Florida work only to reverse his support; Parker, *Books,* 57–9. Perhaps, Hacket was reflecting shifts in opinion in England generally or at court, or he might also have had a profit motive.
141. See the Miggrode and M. M. S. versions of Las Casas in the next chapter.
142. Nicolas Le Challeux, "The Epistle," *A true and perfect description,* A. iv. verso. I am using the British Library copy of Hacket's translation and have consulted original French versions in the Houghton at Harvard as well as Gravier's edition of 1872 and the one in *Les Français* (1958), ed. Julien, II, 201–38. Gravier and Julien both include the verse epistle and the "Reqveste."
143. Le Challeux, *A true and perfect description* [E.iv. verso].
144. On the pretensions of claims among the European powers, including those made by Spain and France in Florida, see ibid, 22–3. On Geneva and America, see Frank Lestringant, *Le Huguenot,* ch. 3, 83–132.
145. For a discussion of Thevet regarding this voyage, see Gilmore, "New World," 520–1 and Lestringant, *Le Huguenot,* 13–14.

146. William Camden, *Annales Rerum Angliae* (1717), II, 259–60 in Green and Dickason, *The Law*, 11.

Chapter 4

1. R. B. Wernham, *After the Armada: Elizabethan England and the Struggle for Western Europe 1588–1595* (Oxford, 1984), vii.
2. See Carlos Gómez-Centurión Jiménez, "The New Crusade: Ideology and Religion in the Anglo-Spanish Conflict" in *England, Spain and the Gran Armada 1585–1604: Essays from the Anglo-Spanish Conferences London and Madrid 1988* (Edinburgh, 1991), 264–7.
3. Wernham, *After the Armada,* vii–ix.
4. See, for instance, David B. Quinn and A. N. Ryan, *England's Sea Empire, 1550–1642* (London, 1983).
5. Quinn and Ryan, 232–4, 75, 78, 112–19, 122.
6. John Parker, *Books to Build and Empire: A Bibliographical History of English Overseas Interests to 1620* (Amsterdam, 1965), 61. See James A. Williamson, *Hawkins of Plymouth* (London, 1949), 132–46.
7. John Hawkins, *A True Declaration of the Troublesome Voyadge . . . to the Parties of Guynea and the West Indies* (London, 1569), b7 verso.
8. Dominique de Gourgues, *Histoire memorable de la reprinse de L'Isle de la Floride* (1568) in *Les Français en Amérique pendant la deuxième moitié du XVIᵉ Siècle: Les Français en Floride,* ed. Charles-André Julien (2 vols., Paris, 1958), II, 241–2; the whole discourse was short and appeared at pages 241–51; my translation here and below. The narrative was often in the third person, but I have referred to Gourgues as the author more from convention than proof.
9. Gourgues, *Histoire memorable,* 246 here and above; see 243–5.
10. Ibid., 248, see 247.
11. Parker, *Books,* 65–6. See Nicholas Canny's work on the English in Ireland, *The Elizabethan Conquest of Ireland: A Pattern Established 1565–76* (Hassocks, Sussex, 1976); "The Permissive Frontier: Social Control in English Settlements in Ireland and Virginia, 1550–1650" in *The Westward Enterprise: English Activities in Ireland, the Atlantic, and America 1480–1650,* ed. K. R. Andrews, N. P. Canny, and P. E. H. Hair (Liverpool, 1978), 17–44; "Identity Formation in Ireland: The Emergence of the Anglo-Irish" in *Colonial Identity in the Atlantic World, 1500–1800,* ed. Nicholas Canny and Anthony Pagden (Princeton, 1987), 159–212; *Kingdom and Colony: Ireland in the Atlantic World 1560–1800* (Baltimore, 1988).
12. See ibid. and also Canny, *Elizabethan Conquest,* 54, 133–4. For another discussion of the connection between Ireland and the New World, see David B. Quinn, *Ireland and America: Their Early Associations, 1500–1640* (Liverpool, 1991). Quinn discusses the Irish and Spanish America; ibid., 11–16.
13. Humphrey Gilbert, *Discourse of a Discoverie for a New Passage to Cataia* (London, 1576), j ii recto-j ii verso.
14. George Gasgoigne, "A Prophetical Sonnet of the Same George Gascoine, Vpon the Commendable Trauaile Disclosed in this Worke," in Gilbert, qqq.i. Lescarbot later used this imagery of Neptune in his pageant in New France.
15 Ibid.
16. Gilbert, B.ii recto.
17. Ibid., B iii-verso-B iiii recto, D ii recto, F iii recto.
18. Anon., "A Discovery of Lands Beyond the Equinoctial" in *The Three Voyages of Martin Frobisher,* ed. Richard Collinson (London, 1867), 4. Whereas Hakluyt would look to North America, this advisor and promoter of colonization was apparently thinking about the southern end of South America.
19. Ibid., 5.
20. Ibid., 6.
21. Ibid., 7.
22. J. Parker, *Books,* 70, see 69.
23. Abraham Fleming, " . . . Capteine Forbisher" in Dionyse Settle, *True Reporte of the Laste Voyage into the West and Northwest Regions* (London, 1577), A i verso.

24. Dionyse Settle, *True Reporte,* Aiiii recto. See J. Parker, *Books,* 70–1. See also Louis B. Wright, *Religion and Empire* (Chapel Hill, NC, 1943).

25. Settle, *True Reporte,* Ci verso-Cii recto; see Biiii verso.

26. George Beste, "The Epistle Dedicatory" to "A True Discourse of the Late Voyages of Discoverie for Finding of a Passage to Cathaya, by the North-weast, under the Conduct of *Martin Frobisher* General . . . " in *Three Voyages,* 17–18.

27. Ibid., 19.

28. Ibid.

29. J. Parker, *Books,* 72, 104–8. John Parker observes that it is curious that no book is extant describing Drake's pre-eminent Elizabethan voyage (107). See Augustín de Zárate, *Discovery and Conquest of the Provinces of Peru* (London, 1581) j 4 verso. In an account printed almost 50 years later, Drake's chaplain, Francis Fletcher, described the Spanish as thinking they do favors in whipping and torturing the Natives. See Francis Fletcher, *The World Encompassed by Sir Francis Drake* (London, 1628), 104.

30. J. Parker, *Books,* 102–3, 105. For good accounts of the war in the Low Countries, see Pieter Geyl, *The Revolt of the Netherlands, 1555–1609* (London, 1958); Charles Wilson, *Queen Elizabeth and the Revolt of the Netherlands* (London, 1970); Geoffrey Parker, *The Dutch Revolt* (Harmondsworth, 1979); Jonathan I. Israel, *The Dutch Republic and the Hispanic World 1606–1661* (Oxford, 1982); Hugh Dunthorne, "The Dutch Revolt in English Political Culture 1585–1660," *From Revolt to Riches: Culture and History of the Low Countries 1500–1700,* ed. Theo Hermans and Reiner Salverda (London, 1993), 235–47.

31. Jacques Cartier, *A Shorte and Briefe narration of the Two Navigations and Discoveries to the Northwest Partes called New France* (London, 1580), B ii recto.

32. Canny, *Kingdom,* 1–6.

33. Ibid., 85, 133–4.

34. Samuel Eliot Morison, *The European Discovery of America: The Northern Voyages A.D. 500–1600* (New York, 1971), 561.

35. Morison, *European,* 563–5.

36. See Canny, *The Elizabethan Conquest,* 66–7, 72.

37. Morison, *European,* 565–6.

38. Ibid., 566.

39. "June 11, 1578. Patent granted to Sir Humphrey Gilbert by Elizabeth I" in *New American World: A Documentary History of North America to 1612,* ed. David B. Quinn (5 vols., New York, 1979), III, 186.

40. Ibid., 188–9.

41. July 11, 1582. Documentos inéditos para la historia de España, XCII (1888), 396–7 in D. B. Quinn, ed. *New American World,* 246.

42. For the correspondence of Don Bernardino de Mendoza, the Spanish ambassador to England, concerning Gilbert's expedition of 1578–9, see *New American World,* ed. D. B. Quinn, 193–4.

43. On the underfinancing of the voyage and the queen's reluctance to allow Gilbert to sail because he was not "of good happ by sea," see Morison, *European,* 567–72 and *Voyages and Colonising Enterprises of Sir Humphrey Gilbert,* ed. David. B. Quinn, Hakluyt Society, 2nd. ser. vols. 83, 84 (London? 1940). The group from Southampton put up £500, Walsingham £500, and Ralegh £2000 and a ship.

44. Morison, *European,* 580–1.

45. For the poem, *De Navigatione illustris & magnanimi equitis aurati Humfredi Gilberti ad deducendam in Novum Orbem Coloniam suscepta* (London, 1582) and translation in *The New Found Land of Stephen Parmenius,* ed. David B. Quinn and Neil M. Cheshire (Toronto, 1972), 80–105. The lineation is from the English translation, which is 423 lines as opposed to the 317 lines of the Latin original.

46. Parmenius, "De Navigatione," lines 320–5.

47. Ibid., lines 395–7. The poet praised the exploits of Willoughby, Jenkinson, Frobisher, and Drake; see lines 357–82.

48. Morison, *European,* 574–5.

49. See "A Report of the Voyage and Successe Thereof, Attempted in the Yeere of Our Lord, 1583. by Sir Humphrey Gilbert . . . " in Richard Hakluyt, *The Principall Navigations Voiages and Discoveries of the English Nation . . .* (London, 1589), facsimile, ed. David Beers Quinn and Raleigh Ashlin Skelton (Cambridge, 1965), 680–1.

50. Jean Alfonse, "*La Cosmographie* . . . (1545?), ed. Georges Musset (Paris, 1904) and *Les Voyages avantureux du capitaine Ian Alfonse Sainctongeois* (Poitiers, 1559). This work was reprinted in Rouen in 1578 and La Rochelle in 1590.

51. Alfonse, *Les Voyages,* quoted in Jean-Paul Duviols, *L' Amérique espagnole vue et rêvée. Les livres de voyages de Christophe Colomb à Bougainville* ([Paris], 1985), 183 n.23; my translation. For Duviols's view, see ibid.

52. Jehan Mallart, *Premier Livre de la description de tous les portz de mer de lunivers* (Paris, 1546–47?). For a discussion of the text and its interpretation, see Lestringant, *Le Huguenot,* 223.

53. See note 14 above in this chapter.

54. In the "Epistle" he addresses the "tres-illvstre, et tres-vertvevse Dame Madame Clavde de Tvraine Dame de Tournon, & Contesse de Roussillon" with great praise for her bravery and exemplary behavior. François de Belle-forest Comingeois's *L'Histoire Vniverselle dv Monde . . .* (Paris 1570), ij. Hereafter referred to as Belleforest.

55. Ibid.

56. Ibid., 246 recto.

57. Ibid., 247 recto.

58. Ibid., 247 recto—247 verso.

59. Ibid., 317 verso.

60. On Belleforest and Thevet, see Olive P. Dickason, "Thevet and Belleforest: Two Sixteenth-Century Frenchmen and New World Colonialism," *Proceedings of the Annual Meeting of the French Colonial Society* 16 (1992), 1–11.

61. Thevet uses the phrase "cruels jusques au bout"; André Thevet, *La Cosmographie Vniverselle D'André Thevet Cosmographe dv Roy . . . Tome Second* (Paris, 1575) in *Les Français en Amérique pendant la deuxième moitié du XVIᵉ Siècle: Le Brésil et les Brésiliens,* ed. Charles-André Julien, with notes by Suzanne Lussagnet (2 vols., Paris, 1953), II, 29.

62. Ibid., II, 29.

63. See ibid., II, 218.

64. Ibid., II, 31. On French views of the Natives, including those of Thevet, see Olive P. Dickason, *The Myth of the Savage and the Beginnings of French Colonialism in the Americas* (Edmonton, 1984).

65. Thevet, *La Cosmographie* in *Les Français* (1953), ed. Julien, II, 82.

66. Ibid., II, 142.

67. Ibid., II, 221.

68. Ibid., II, 251.

69. Ibid., II, 263.

70. Ibid., II, 271.

71. Ibid., II, 304. See Nicolas Barré, *Copie de quelques lettres sur la nauigation dv Cheualier de Ville-gaignon es terres de l'Amérique . . .* (Paris 1556). For a brief discussion of Barré, see *André Thevet's North America: A Sixteenth-Century View,* ed. Roger Schlesinger and Arthur P. Stabler (Kingston and Montreal, 1986), 153, 157, 162.

72. For a discussion of French Florida, see Frank Lestringant, "Les Séquelles Littéraires de la Floride française: Laudonnière, Hakluyt, Thevet, Chauveton," *Bibliothèque d'Humanisme et Renaissance* 44 (1982): 7–36. A wider context for the French in Florida may be found in Arthur P. Stabler, "En Marge des récits de voyage: André Thevet, Hakluyt, Roberval, Jean Alfonse et Jacques Cartier," *Etudes Canadiennes/Canadian Studies* 17 (1984), 69–72.

73. As I discussed Thevet's reputation in chapter 3, I have not done so here.

74. See *Le Miroir De la Tyrannie Espagnole Perpetree aux Indies Occidentales . . .* (Amsterdam, 1620).

75. For this view and for a discussion of French translation of Las Casas, see André Saint-Lu, *Las Casas Indigeniste: études sur la vie et l'œuvre du défenseur des Indiens* (Paris, 1982), 161, see 159–70. For examples of English and French texts that represent the Netherlands, see, in English translation, William of Orange's *Declaration & Publication of the Prince of Orange. Contayning the cause of his necessary defense against the Duke of Alva (20 July, 1568)* (London, n. d.) and *A Supplication to the Kings Maiestie of Spayne, made by the Prince of Orange* (London, 1573) and also A. L. E. Verheyden, *Le Conseil de Troubles: Liste des condamnes, 1567–1573* (Brussels, 1961), cited in William S. Maltby, *The Black Legend in England* (Durham, NC, 1971), 48.

76. André Thevet, *The new founde worlde, or Antarctike* (London, 1568), *iii recto. See also J. Parker, *Books,* 60–1 for a discussion of Hacket and for his mention of Frobisher, which I use below. Frank Lestringant's epithet for Thevet is "L'hispanophile Thevet"; see Lestringant, *Le Huguenot,* 270. On Henry Sidney and the colonization of Ireland, see Nicholas Canny, *The Elizabethan*

Conquest, 46–75, 90–115; Karl S. Bottigheimer, "Kingdom and Colony: Ireland in the Western Enterprise 1536–1660" in *The Western Enterprise,* eds. K. R. Andrews, N. P. Canny, and P. E. H. Hair (Liverpool, 1978), 49–50; and Brendan Bradshaw, "Native Reaction to the Westward Enterprise: A Case-Study in Gaelic Ideology" in ibid., 67–9.

77. Sir John Mandeville, *The voiage and travayle, of Syr John Maundevile knight, . . .* (London, 1568), cited in Parker, *Books,* 62. For Eden's influence on English colonizers interested in Ireland and the New World, see Canny, *The Elizabethan Conquest,* 85, 133–4.

78. For details of the lag, see J. Parker, *Books;* Saint-Lu, *Las Casas;* and *European Americana . . . .*

79. Loren E. Pennington, "The Amerindian in Promotional Literature, 1575–1625" in *The Western Enterprise,* eds. K. R. Andrews, N. P. Canny and P. E. H. Hair (Liverpool, 1978), 179.

80. Ibid., 179–80.

81. M. M. S., *Spanish colonie,* sigs q2 recto–qq recto .

82. For a sound bibliographical account of early French editions of Las Casas, see Saint-Lu, *Las Casas,* 159–70.

83. See *European Americana: A Chronological Guide to Works Printed in Europe Relating to the Americas, 1493–1776,* vols. 1–2, 4–5, ed. John Alden with Dennis C. Landis (New York, 1980). I have also consulted volume 3, which is still unpublished at John Carter Brown Library.

84. Francisco López de Gómara, *Histoire Generalle des Indes Occidentales et Terres Nevves, qui iusques à present ont estre descouuertes. Traduite en françois par M. Fumee Sieur de Marly le Chatel.* (Paris, 1578), ãiv verso; see also ãiv recto. For the sonnet, see ãiii and for the "Prologue of the Author," see ãiii verso.

85. Ibid., ãiv verso; see also aiv recto; my translation.

86. Ibid., ãiv verso- ãv recto.

87. See Worth, *Practising Translation in Renaissance France: The Example of Étienne Dolet* (Oxford, 1988), 3. See also G. P. Norton, *The Ideology and Language of Translation in Renaissance France and their Humanist Antecedents* (Geneva, 1984).

88. Gómara, *Histoire Generalle,* ãiv verso- ãv recto. Ibid., ãvi verso; my translation. He would be like Diogenes who took refuge in a barrel while watching the Corinthians at war.

89. Herbert Ingram Priestley, "Introduction" in *The Conquest of the Weast India (1578) by Francisco López de Gómara.* Facsimile of the copy in the New York Public Library of *The Pleasant Historie of the Conquest of the VVeast India, now called new Spayne, Atchiued by the vvorthy Prince Hernando Cortes Marque of the valley of Huaxacac, most delectable to Reade: Translated out of the Spanishe tongue, by T. N.* (London, 1578), iii–xxi, esp. xvii.

90. *Dictionary of National Biography,* XL, 432–3 (1894), cited in Priestley, "Introduction," xvii-xviii.

91. *Calendar of State Papers,* 1560, 313 and for 1561–2, 256, quoted in ibid., xviii.

92. Thomas Nicholas, "The Epistle Dedicatory," *The Pleasant Historie of the Conquest of the VVeast India, now called new Spayne, Atchieued by the vvorthy Prince Hernando Cortes Marques of the valley of Huaxacac, most delectable to Reade: Translated out of the Spanish tongue,* by T. N. (London, 1578), a.aij.

93. For an examination of Walsingham's patronage in Ireland (1574–80), his embassy to the Netherlands in 1578 (with the backing of Leicester and Hatton at court), and his promulgation of the marriage between Elizabeth I and the duke of Anjou (1579–81), see Mitchell MacDonald Leimon, "Sir Francis Walsingham and the Anjou Marriage Plan, 1574–1581" (unpublished Ph.D. dissertation, University of Cambridge, 1989), esp. ch. 3, 5, 6, 8.

94. Ibid., 28, 34, 185, 216.

95. Nicholas, *Pleasant Historie.,* aiv recto.

96. *Histoire Novvelle dv Novveav Monde, Contenant en somme ce que les Hespagnols ont fait iusqu'à present aux Indes Occidentales, & le rude traitement qu'ils ont fait à ces poures peuples-la. Extraite de l'italien de M. Hierosme Benzoni Milanois, qui ha voyagé XIIII ans en ce pays-la: & enrichie de plusieurs Discours & choses dignes de memoire. Par M. Vrbain Chavveton. Ensemble, Vne petite Histoire d'vn Massacre commis par les Hespagnols sur quelques François en la Floride. Auec un Indice des choses plus remarkable* (Geneva 1579); my translation here and below.

97. The original reads: "Par ci devant redige au vray par ceux qui s'en retirerent: & maintenant reueuë & augmentee de nouueau, par M. Vrbain Chavveton." On Chauveton and Gómara, see Lestringant, *Le Huguenot,* 119–21.

98. The original reads: "cruellement massacrez par les Hespagnols." Ibid., 97 [sig.]G.G.j. *Brief Discours* and *Requeste au roy* were numbered together and continuously after Benzoni's work, which was first published in Italian in 1565. For a discussion of Chauveton, see Benjamin Keen, "The Vision of America in the Writings of Urbain Chauveton" in *First Images of America: The Impact of the New World on the Old,* ed. Fredi Chiapelli *et al.* (2 vols., Berkeley, 1976), I, 107–20.

99. Urbain Chauveton, *Histoire Novvelle dv Novveav Monde,* i verso.
100. Chauveton, "Preface," ibid., i .
101. Ibid., ii verso-iii.
102. Chauveton used the second person plural ("nous")—which I report in the third person plural but try occasionally to mark in my analysis—as a means of creating a rhetorical bond with the French reader.
103. Ibid., iii verso-iv.
104. For the application of a theory of alterity to the meeting of Natives and the Spanish, see Tzvetan Todorov, *The Conquest of America* (1984; New York, 1992), 3, 42–44, 100–1, 248–9.
105. The original phrase is "les ont mastinez cruellement" which might also imply an abuse with dogs. The Spaniards did use dogs as weapons in the New World. "Preface," iiij verso-iiij recto.
106. Ibid., iiij verso-v recto.
107. Ibid., v recto.
108. Here I was tempted to leave the original French word, "Avertissement," which can mean preface or advertisement in its original sense and one that is still used in bibliography. As there is already a "Preface," I have selected the first term.
109. "Sommaire," no pagination [1st page recto]. Benzoni's Italian original appeared in 1565.
110. Ibid., [1st page verso].
111. Ibid., [1st page verso-2nd page recto].
112. Ibid., [2nd page recto].
113. "Sonet," ibid., no pagination; my translation.
114. Ibid., 4, 8.
115. On Sepúlveda's argument for the inferiority of the American Indian, see Anthony Pagden, *The Fall of Natural Man: The American Indian and the Origins of Comparative Ethnography* (1982; Cambridge, 1986), 109–18. Pagden provides an incisive comparison of Oviedo with José de Acosta: while the one included fantastic accounts of the "unnatural" Indian practices as well as a collection of ethnographic observation without much analysis, the other classified, explained, and included the first systematic attempt to differentiate between the different groups of Natives (151–2). For the belated English translation of Acosta, see *The Natvrall and Morall Historie of the* East and West *Indies . . . ,* trans. Edward Grimstone (London, 1604). The author's advertisement to the reader said that Acosta's book described the wonders of nature and not the acts, adventures, and conquests of the Spaniards in the New World.
116. Bartolomé de Las Casas, *A Short Account of the Destruction of the Indies,* ed. and trans. Nigel Griffin and introduction by Anthony Pagden (Harmondsworth, 1992), 3. In the "Introduction" Anthony Pagden sets out the background and terms of the debate; see xxviii-xxx. On Las Casas and alternative discourse and the representation of history, see Stephanie Merrim, "The Counter-Discourse of Bartolomé de Las Casas," in *Early Images of the Americas: Transfer and Invention,* ed. Jerry M. Williams and Robert E. Lewis (Tuscon, 1993), 149–62 and Santa Arias, "Empowerment Through the Writing of History: Bartolomé de Las Casas's Representation of the Other(s)," in *Early Images,* 163–179.
117. For an informative survey of European attitudes toward Natives, see David B. Quinn, "European Technology and Preconceptions" in *The Discovery of North America* (London, 1971), 13–18; on alterity or otherness, see Todorov, *The Conquest,* 42–4, 100–1, 185–6, 195–200, and, more generally, his *La réflexion française sur la diversité humaine* (Paris, 1989); Michel de Certeau, "Montaigne's 'Of Cannibals':The Savage 'I'" in *Heterologies: Discourse on the Other,* trans. Brian Massumi (Minneapolis, 1986), 79; Stephen Greenblatt, *Marvelous Possessions: The Wonder of the New World* (Chicago, 1991), 135–6; Jonathan Hart, "Mediation in the Exchange between Europeans and Native Americans in the Early Modern Period," *Canadian Review of Comparative Literature: Revue Canadienne de Littérature Comparée* 22 (1995), 321–2.
118. Bartolomé de Las Casas, *Tyrannies et crvavtez des Espagnols, perpetrees és Indes Occidentales, qu'on dit le nouueau monde: brieuement descrites en langue Castillane, par l'Euesque Don Frere Bartelemy de las Casas ou Casavs, Espagnol de l'ordre Sainct Dominique, fidelement traduites par Iaques de Miggrode* (Paris, 1582); my translation here and below. The "Privilege" granted Guillaume Julien, a printer at the University of Paris, the sole right to this French edition of Miggrode's translation, addressing explicitly Julien's fears that others were about to profit from his labor. It seems that Las Casas was a hot property at this time. In Geneva in the same year G. Cartier brought out the same translation under the equally sensational title, *Histoire admirable des horribles insolences, cruautez, & tyrannies exercees par les Espagnols es Indes Occidentales . . .* For an

argument that Miggrode was Flemish but chose French because of its literary quality and its ability to reach a large audience in Europe, see Saint-Lu, *Las Casas*, 161.

119. Ibid., *ii recto.
120. Ibid., *ii-*ii verso.
121. Ibid.
122. Ibid.
123. Las Casas, *A Short Account*, 96.
124. See Saint-Lu, *Las Casas*, 162–3.
125. Las Casas, *Tyrannies*, *ii-*ii verso.
126. M. M. S., Foreword. The identity of the translator does not seem to be known. On the translations and text, see Nigel Griffin, "A Note on Editions and on this Translation" in Las Casas, *A Short Account*, xlii-xliii.
127. M. M. S., q 2 recto.
128. Ibid., q 2 recto.
129. Ibid., Foreword.
130. Ibid., q 2 recto.
131. Ibid., q 2 recto- q 2 verso. I have tried to include reminders of this homology between M. M. S. and Miggrode. As I have discussed this English translation of Las Casas elsewhere, I shall not go into great detail here. See Jonathan Hart, "The Black Legend: English and French Representations of Spanish Cruelty in the New World," *Comparative Literature Now Theories and Practice/ La Littérature comparée à l'heure actuelle Théories et réalisations*, ed. S Tötösy, M. V. Dimić , and I. Sywenky (Paris, 1999), 375–87. In this essay I did not discuss the French translation on which it hinges and which is a foundational text for the English version.
132. For a lucid assessment of Cortés, see J. H. Elliott, "Cortés, Velázquez and Charles V" in Hernán Cortés, *Letters from Mexico*, trans. and ed. Anthony Pagden (1971; New Haven, 1986), xi-xxxvii.
133. Owing to the Wars of Religion, this book was not published until 1578. As is common practice, the edition I am using here is the corrected and augmented 1580 edition, which, in the matter I treat does not differ, except in the corrections, from the 1578 edition. There is no augmentation. Jean de Léry, *Histoire d'vn voyage faict en la terre dv Bresil, avtrement dite Amerique* . . . (Geneva, 1580). For the difficult circumstances of the writing and publication of this text, see Paul Gaffarel, "Préface de l'éditeur" in Jean de Léry, *Histoire d'un voyage faict en la terre du Brésil, nouvelle édition avec une introduction & des notes par Paul Gaffarel* (Paris, 1880), I, vi-xii and note 58 in this chapter. On pages vii and viii, Gaffarel cites an unidentified but poignant contemporary account of the mutual cruelty of the Protestants and Catholics in Midi. Léry, whose parents were reformers in Burgundy, became one of Calvin's missionaries to the New World in the colony of Durand de Villegagnon, one of Calvin's fellow students at University of Paris. See Gaffarel, "Préface de l'éditeur," i-v; Lestringant, *Le Huguenot*, 79–119; Greenblatt, *Marvelous*, 14–22.
134. See Janet Whatley, "Introduction," Jean de Léry, *History of a Voyage to the Land of Brazil*, trans. and introduction by Janet Whatley (Berkeley, 1990), xx.
135. Léry, *Histoire* (Geneva, 1580), Aij recto. Unless otherwise indicated, the translation is mine: I sometimes refer to Whatley's notes to her fine translation. I use the original editions in the notes and use my own translation because of my emphasis on close reading and the language.
136. Ibid., Aij.
137. Ibid., Aij verso.
138. Ibid., Aiij recto. On Thevet, see Whatley, xx-xxi; on Thevet's relation to and view of Léry, see Schlesinger and Stabler, ed., *André Thevet's*, xxiii-iv, xxxiii, 161.
139. Ibid., 161.
140. Ibid., 160.
141. See Léry, *Histoire*, ed. P. Gaffarel, 11–37.
142. Ibid.
143. Ibid., 9.
144. Ibid., 103, 120, 133–4.
145. Ibid., 220. Léry obviously appealed to Catholics and Protestants. Whatley says in one place that with the edition of 1599 Léry made a new chapter for the material from Las Casas (220) and in another that this occurred in the edition of 1611 (246 n14). For related topics, see Janet Whatley, "Savage Hierarchies: French Catholic Observers of the New World," *Sixteenth Century Journal* 17 (1986), 319–30; "*Une révérence réciproque:* Huguenot Writing on the New

World," *University of Toronto Quarterly* 57 (1987/88), 270–82; "Impression and Initiation: Jean de Léry's Brazil Voyage," *Modern Language Studies* 19 (1989), 15–25.

146. See Whatley, "Editions and Reception of Léry," in Léry, *History,* 221.
147. Michel de Montaigne, *Essais de Michel Seignevr de Montaigne* (Paris, 1588); rpt. as *Les Essais de Montaigne: reproduuction typographique de l'exemplaire annoté par l'auteur et conservé à la Bibliothèque de Bordeaux avec un avertisssement et une notice par M. Ernest Courbet* (4 vols., Paris, 1906), I, 167.
148. In Quint's words, "'Des cannibales'turns out to be at least equally about his own France and that the terms with which it discusses the Brazilian natives are deeply rooted in his own historical and political preoccupations." See Quint, "A Reconsideration of Montaigne's *Des cannibales,*" in *America in European Consciousness, 1493–1750,* ed. Karen Ordahl Kupperman (Chapel Hill, 1995), 168, see 166–91
149. Montaigne, *Essais,* III, 399–400; my translation here and below.
150. See Michel de Montaigne, *Montaigne's Essays: John Florio's Translation,* ed. J. I. M. Stewart. (2 vols., London, 1921), II, 314.
151. Montaigne, *Essais,* III, 399.
152. Ibid., 401.
153. Montaigne, *Montaigne's Essays,* II, 317.
154. Montaigne, *Essais,* III, 401.
155. Ibid., 401–2.
156. Lancelot Voisin, sieur de La Popelinière, "Av Roy," *L'Histoire de France* . . . (n.p. [La Rochelle], 1581), I, a. & b. ij recto."
157. "Lectori" in La Popelinière, I, a. & b. ij verso; "Advertissemens Necessaires, esquels outre plusieurs auis les desseins de l'Auteur, sont au vray representez par I. D. F. B. R. U. C. F." in La Popelinière, I, a. & b. iij verso–a. & b. iiij verso.
158. "Advertissemens," I, a. & b. iiiij recto; my translation here and below. On the author's anonymity and reputation, see I, a. & b. iiiij verso– a. & b. iiiiij verso.
159. Ibid., I, a. & b. iiiij verso–iiiiiij verso.
160. "Ode," ibid., I, a. & b. iiiiiij recto.
161. Ibid., I, 3 recto.
162. Ibid., I, CC iij verso and CC recto; see I, 55 recto (Spanish pride); I, 74 verso (Spanish cruelty); I, book 14, 52 recto and verso (Spanish dishonor). The pagination begins at 1 after the tenth book.
163. Ibid., I, book 14, 52 recto. On La Popelinière, see Lestringant, *Le Huguenot,* 156–8, 226–34, 258–61.
164. La Popelinière, *Histoire,* I, CC recto.
165. Ibid., I, 71 verso.
166. Ibid.
167. Ibid., I, 101 verso.
168. Ibid., I, 122 recto.
169. Ibid. The phrase is "la Traditiue de la foy."
170. Ibid., I, 122 recto–122 verso. For a different version of Cabral's possession, see Patricia Seed, *Ceremonies of Possession in Europe's Conquest of the New World, 1492–1640* (Cambridge, 1995), 103–4.
171. La Popelinière, *Histoire,* I, 122 verso–123 recto.
172. Ibid.
173. La Popelinière, *Les Trois Mondes* (Paris, 1582), book 2, 26 verso, translated and quoted in Dickason, *The Myth,* 125. For her perceptive discussion of La Popelinière, see Dickason, *The Myth,* 125–6, 147–9, 154.
174. La Popelinière, *Histoire,* I, 122 verso–123 recto.
175. See De Saulx, in *Collection complète des mémoires relatif à l'histoire de la France* (52 vols., Paris, 1819–26), XXIII, 241 and Montesquieu, *Œuvres* (7 vols., Amsterdam, 1785), II, 321 in Dickason, *The Myth,* 126.
176. La Popelinière, *Histoire,* I, 385 verso.
177. Ibid.,, II, 151 recto, see 150 verso.
178. Martin Basanier's *Histoire notable de la Floride* . . . (Paris, 1586).
179. Laudonnière in Basanier, ed., *Histoire notable,* 64 recto. For another account of this mutiny and other events on this expedition to Florida, see Jacques Le Moyne, *Brevis narratio eorum quae in Florida Americae provincia Gallis acciderunt, secunda in illam Navigatione, duce Renato de Laudonniere*

classis Praefecto, ed. Théodore de Bry (Frankfurt-am-Main, 1591), 10–13. For a discussion of the relation among Basanier, Hakluyt, and Ralegh, see Lestringant, *Le Huguenot,* 163, 170–1.

180. Richard Hakluyt, *Divers Voyages Touching the Discoverie of America, and the Islands Adjacent unto the Same . . .* (London, 1582). For a brief analysis, see J. Parker, *Books,* 109–11.

181 Hakluyt, *Divers Voyages,* ¶ recto.

182. What follows is a shortened version of my analysis of "Discourse." For a brief discussion of Hakluyt's "Discourse," especially how it relates to labor, see Mary C. Fuller, *Voyages in Print: English Travel to America, 1576–1624* (Cambridge, 1995), 27–9.

183. The phrase is Jack Beeching's; see his "Introduction" in Richard Hakluyt, *Voyages and Discoveries: The Principal Navigations Voyages, Traffiques and Discoveries of the English Nation,* ed. Jack Beeching (1972; Harmondsworth, 1985), 18. For Beeching's comments on "Discourse," see ibid., 16–18. Lestringant leaves out a discussion of "Discourse" in his section on Hakluyt in Paris, which might be because Hakluyt's role in the disappearance of French manuscripts could be of more interest to the French reader than a secret document to the English crown; see Lestringant, *Le Huguenot,* 213–18. Both aspects of Hakluyt's work in Paris were, however, complementary and should be seen together. David Armitage discusses Hakluyt in terms of the relation between his humanism and ideology; see Armitage, "The New World and British Historical Thought From Richard Hakluyt to William Robertson" in *America in European Consciousness, 1493–1750,* ed. Karen Ordahl Kupperman (Chapel Hill, 1995), 52–9.

184. For an informative examination of the context of this state paper (one that informs my account), see David B. Quinn and Alison M. Quinn, "Introduction," Richard Hakluyt, *Discourse of Western Planting* (London, 1993), xv-xxxi, esp. xv.

185. For a reconstruction of Hakluyt's reading, particularly of works pertaining to Spanish colonies in the New World, see ibid., xviii-xx.

186. The Quinns seem certain that Hakluyt knew this work; ibid., xvii. See Philippe Duplessis-Mornay, "Discours au roy Henri III, sur les moyens de diminuer l'Espagnol' in *Mémoire et correspondence,* ed. Auguis et La Fontenelle de Vaudoré (Paris, 1824–25), II, 580–93. For a discussion of Duplessis-Mornay, see Lestringant, *Le Huguenot,* 119–26.

187. Quinn and Quinn, "Introduction," *Discourse,* xx-xxi.

188. Ibid., xxi.

189. The Quinns provide a good summary of the *Discourse;* ibid., xxii—xxx.

190. Hakluyt, *Discourse,* 2. All letters deleted in abbreviations in this and other primary documents in the study are underlined.

191. Hakluyt, "Discourse," 8. Stephen Gomes is Estevão Gomes, who is also called Estevan Gomez in Spanish.

192. In the chronicles the Portuguese, Hakluyt says, vaunted more about their colleges and bishoprics that administered to the Natives than about any other feat. He listed the sixteenth bishoprics and two hundred houses of religion in the Spanish colonies established in the past 50 years.

193. Hakluyt, "Discourse," 11.

194. Hakluyt, "Discourse," 11.

195. Hakluyt, "Discourse," 11.

196. Hakluyt, "Discourse," 12. For a text about the persecution of Protestants in Spain, see Reginalus Gonsalvius Montanus, *A discovery and playne declaration of sundry subtill proactises of the Holy Inquisition of Spayne* (London?, 1569). David Quinn thinks that Hakluyt was probably aware of this work, which also includes a description of the taking of an English ship. See Quinn's Commentary to the "Discourse," 135.

197. Hakluyt, "Discourse," 15.

198. John Cabot actually made this "discovery" of Newfoundland, but, for some time, his son displaced his rightful claim to that first.

199. Hakluyt speaks of his friend "Stephen Bellinger"; see "Discourse," 20.

200. Hakluyt, "Discourse," 24.

201. Ibid., 28.

202. Ibid., 28. For a brief discussion of piracy, see the Quinns' "Commentary," 143.

203. Hakluyt, *Discourse,* 28.

204. Hakluyt, *Discourse,* 28–9. On the penal laws and French fur trade, see the Quinns' "Commentary," 144, especially notes to lines 636 and 665–78.

205. Hakluyt, *Discourse,* 31–2.

206. Ibid.
207. Ibid.
208. Ibid., 35
209. Ibid., 35. I have changed the Quinns' transcription from "this owne chardges" to "his owne chardges" because in Hakluyt's hand the word appears to be "his" to my eye and makes more sense as such.
210. See *Histoire memorable de la reprinse de l'isle de la Floride, faicte par les François sous . . . Capitaine Gourges* (n.p. 1568) and Lancelot Voisin, Sieur de Popelinière, *Les trois mondes . . .* (Paris, 1582). See the Quinns' "Commentary," 146. On Philips below, see 147. In *Les trois mondes . . .* (1582) Lancelot Voisin, Sieur de Popelinière, someone to whose work Hakluyt returned in *Principall Navigations* (1589) as a means of defining England against France and Spain, published Gourgues's own story.
211. "Discourse," 35.
212. "Discourse," 35–6.
213. "Discourse," 36.
214. See the Quinns' note, 147 and David Beers Quinn, *North America from First Discovery to Early Settlements: The Norse Voyages to 1612* (New York, 1977).
215. "Discourse," 36
216. "Discourse," 39–40.
217. "Discourse," 40
218. "Discourse," 40.
219. "Discourse," 43.
220. "Discourse," 43; see 44 for below and the Quinns's "Commentary," 149–50.
221. This is one reason that I have not followed Steele and other fine histories of printing in their exclusion of manuscript works. Hakluyt's "Discourse" was influential because Walsingham and Ralegh encouraged its production, and presumably the queen read it. It had the effect of a policy paper and was probably more influential at court than most of the published works about the New World and touching on the Spanish influence there.
222. Ibid., 52.
223. "Discourse," 48. Hakluyt does not identify the French captain.
224. "Discourse," 52. See the Quinns's "Commentary," 162. The lines from Virgil's *Aeneid,* II, 6–7, are in my translation. As I have mentioned, this use of Las Casas's *Breuissima relacion de la destruycion de las Indias* (Seville 1552) for anti-Spanish propaganda occurred in various languages. The first translation was in Dutch, *Seer cort verhael vande destrucie van d'Indien . . . uyte spaensche ouergeset* (Antwerp, 1579). See also the Quinns's "Commentary," 162 and John Alden and Dennis C. Landis, eds., *European Americana, Volume I: 1493–1600* (New York, 1980), 69.
225. "Discourse," 52.
226. Ibid., 52.
227. Hakluyt, *Discourse,* 55.
228. Ibid., 56.
229. Ibid., 59. Sequanus was Jean Matal, born in Burgundy but an inhabitant of Cologne, who edited the *Historiae Hieronymi Osorii, Lusitani, Silvensis in Algarbiis episcopi. De rebus Emmanuelis, regis Lusitaniae invictissimi virtute et auspicio* (Cologne 1574) and whose epistle dedicatory became a treatise on Spanish America in its own right. Hakluyt used the 1581 edition. See the Quinns' "Commentary," 132, 163.
230. Translation by Neil M. Cheshire in the Quinns "Commentary," 163–4; original Latin, Hakluyt, *Discourse,* 59.
231. Ibid., 164. There is some controversy over whether such slaves were actually Moors or Africans.
232. Hakluyt, *Discourse,* 60.
233. See the Quinns' "Introduction," xv and their "Commentary," 165.
234. See the Quinns' "Introduction," xv. Hakluyt, *Discourse,* 64.
235. Ibid.
236. Ibid.
237. Ibid.
238. Ibid., 67; see the Quinns' "Commentary," 168.
239. Hakluyt, *Discourse,* 67–8. For a more discussion of the English context, see David W. Waters, *The Art of Navigation in England in Elizabethan and Early Stuart Times* (London, 1958).
240. Hakluyt, *Discourse,* 71.

241. Ibid.
242. Ibid., 72.
243. Ibid.
244. The Italian editions appeared in 1556 and 1564. See the Quinns' "Commentary," 172 for a discussion of the editions.
245. See Hakluyt, *Discourse*, 74–5.
246. Ibid., 75; see "Commentary," 173.
247. Hakluyt, as the Quinns note, had published the record of the patent of 1496 to John Cabot and sons but continued, perhaps owing to the influence of Peter Martyr and Ramusio, to attribute John's voyage to Sebastian (he also placed it in 1498 instead of 1497 and thus the possible mistake of 86 years unless this part of the *Discourse* was written in 1583). Ibid.
248. Hakluyt, *Discourse*, 76.
249. Ibid., 79. For more on Gilbert and Catholic colonists, see David B. Quinn, *England and the Discovery of America, 1481–1620* (London, 1974), 370–81 and also "Commentary," 174.
250. Hakluyt, *Discourse*, 82–7.
251. See the Quinns' "Commentary," 178.
252. Hakluyt, *Discourse*, 88–96.
253. Ibid., 96.
254. See the Quinns' "Commentary," 183–4 .
255. Hakluyt, *Discourse*, 99–100. The *Discourse* was first published in 1877, and the Quinns' edition of 1993 (Hakluyt Society) is the only recent one. It is a beautiful and well-edited volume that includes a facsimile of the scribal manuscript facing a transcription and a useful "Commentary." The 1877 edition, while a good work of scholarship and obviously groundbreaking in bringing the work to publication, does not.
256. Ibid.
257. Hakluyt, *Discourse*, 100.
258. Hakluyt, *Discourse*, 107, see 100–106.
259. Fumée writes, "Auant que finir ce Chapitre ia reciteray pour resiouir le Lecteur, ce qui aduint sur ce faict aux Portugallois," which Hakluyt translated as "before I finishe this Chapiter (saieth he) I will recite to recreate the Reader that which happened vpon this partition to the Portingales," which precedes the passage quoted above. Francisco Lopez de Gómera, *Histoire generalle des Indes Occidentales & terres Neuues . . . Traduite . . . par M. Fumée, sieur de Marly le Chastel* (Paris, 1569), 117, quoted in Quinns, "Commentary," 185; Hakluyt, *Discourse*, 107. The Quinns say that there were also 1568, 1577, 1578 and 1580 editions of Fumée's French translation.
260. Hakluyt, *Discourse*, 108.
261. Francisco Lopez de Gómara, *Historia delle nuoue Indie Occidentali . . . Tradotta . . . per Augustino di Craualiz,* 3 pts (Venice, 1564), f. 159 recto-159 verso, in Quinn s, "Commentary," 185. *Histoire*, ed. Fumée, ff.132 verso-133 verso in ibid., 186.
262. "Discourse," 108.
263. Ibid., 108.
264. Hakluyt, *Discourse,* 108. The Quinns point out that the passage Hakluyt said he was translating from Oviedo has not yet been found. They quote a passage from Oviedo that is analogous but not that close and that reflects Oviedo's condemnation of the greedy mine owners and the lazy, vicious, mendacious, and inconstant Indians; the Quinns' "Commentary," 186.
265. Hakuyt, *Discourse,* 111. For the passage from Chauveton's Preface, *Histoire,* 23, see the Quinns' "Commentary," 186–7. This was the kind of view Montaigne's Natives often took.
266. Hakluyt, *Discourse,* 112, see 111.
267. On the Italian version, as well as Hakluyt's use of Fumée below, see the Quinns' "Commentary," 187.
268. Hakluyt, *Discourse,* 116, see 115.
269. Ibid., 119, see 116.
270. Ibid., 119.
271. Ibid., 127; see 120–26.
272. Ibid., 127.
273. Ibid., 127–8.
274. Ibid., 195.
275. While my book was at the publisher's, I was informed that another study by Andrew Hadfield

had also discussed Hakluyt in an important way, but, unfortunately, I was unable to consult this study in time to take into account. I did want, however, to make the reader aware of this source.

276. John Parker, *Books,* 121.

Chapter 5

1. There are various discussions of rhetoric in the field. Andrew Fitzmaurice asserts the differences in the use of rhetoric by the English and Spanish (the one is promotional and the other Aristotelian and Thomist, although Fitzmaurice admits to Hakluyt and others using Aristotle and Aquinas); see Fitzmaurice, "Classical Rhetoric and the Literature of Discovery 1570–1630" (unpublished Ph.D. dissertation, University of Cambridge, 1995), 73, 133–5, 171–9, 189. Elsewhere, I have argued for Thevet's and Hakluyt's imitation, rhetorical and otherwise, of Oviedo; see Jonathan Hart, "Strategies of Promotion in Oviedo and Thevet and Hakluyt," *Imagining Culture: Essays in Early Modern History and Literature,* ed. Jonathan Hart (New York, 1996), 73–92.

2. On relations between France and Spain, what Philip II called "the principal thing" in 1589, see J. H. Elliott, *Europe Divided 1559–1598* (1968; Glasgow, 1974), 339–50 and for Spain's crisis in the 1590s, see J. H. Elliott, *Imperial Spain 1469–1716* (1963; Harmondsworth, 1990), 285–300.

3. In the brief discussion of the collapse that follows, I am indebted to the following sources: Huguette and Pierre Chanu, *Séville et l'Atlantique, 1504–1650* (8 vols., Paris, 1955–9), VIII, ii.ii, ii, cinquième partie, and J. H. Elliott, *The Old World and the New 1492–1650* (1970; Cambridge, 1992), 97–104.

4. See Rómulo D. Carbia, *Historia de la Leyenda Negra Hispanoamericana* (Madrid, 1944), which discusses the legend in the American context and Pierre Chaunu, "La Légende Noire Antihispanique," *Revue de Psychologie des Peuples* (Caen, 1964), 188–223, which J. H. Elliott drew to my attention.

5. For a discussion of the promotional rhetoric of Oviedo (1526), Thevet (1558), and Hakluyt (1589, 1598, 1600), see Hart, "Strategies," 73–92. The section of Thevet's *Singularitez* in chapter 2 and on Hakluyt's *Principal Navigations* in this chapter derives from, but is not the same as, the analysis in the above essay. A different emphasis occurs in this essay, which discusses how Oviedo sets the example for Thevet and Hakluyt by seeking to be the royal chronicler of the New World for his country and to affect national policy. While Thevet and Hakluyt attempt similar roles officially and unofficially, thereby following the example of Spain, so that they share a rhetoric of promotion, they differ in their geographic and historiographical methods. While the essay examines the implicit or implied similarities of Thevet and Hakluyt with Oviedo, chapter 5 and this chapter analyze more explicit uses of the Spanish example in these French and English writers and place their work in more intertextual and rhetorical contexts.

6. On this rivalry, see Lestringant's account of Hakluyt's use or acquisition of Thevet's French manuscripts (Laudonnière and others) during his mission in Paris from 1583 to 1588; Frank Lestringant, *Le Huguenot et le Sauvage* (Paris, 1990), 213–18. Lestringant observes that in *Divers Voyages* (1582) Hakluyt mentioned Thevet with approval and Hacket translated *Singularitez* in 1568, whereas in France and Germany, those with knowledge of the sea and travel had condemned Thevet for a long time: Hakluyt's stay in France would have made him aware of the critiques of Thevet. This cosmographer, in La Popelinière's view, was given to fantasy, a mythical geography rather than a geography of the imagination. He wrote that those who knew the particulars of the world would not believe "how much Belleforest and Thevet have prejudiced the youth and, consequently, the State. Interpreting so badly, and often all against the good, infinite passages: corrupting and falsifying the materials"; Lancelot Voisin de La Popelinière, *L'Histoire des histoires. Avec l'idée de l'histoire accomplie . . .* (Paris 1599), 457–8; my translation. Thevet's *Le Grand Insulaire . . . ,* which is in manuscript at la Bibliothèque Nationale and appears in part in English translation in *André Thevet in North America,* ed. Schlesinger and Stabler, discussed the commodities found in Canada in contrast with the silver of Potosí and denounced the "marvellous gulf of avarice and ambition" that Spain opposed to France and England; see Thevet's *Le Grand Insulaire* I, folio 150 verso, quoted in Lestringant, *Le Huguenot,* 218; my translation. Despite Hakluyt's newfound differences with Thevet, he shared this anti-Spanish sentiment, which Thevet seemed to developed more in his later work.

7. Loren E. Pennington, "The Amerindian in Promotional Literature, 1575–1625" in *The Western Enterprise,* eds. K. R. Andrews, N. P. Canny, and P. E. H. Hair (Liverpool, 1978), 175–94, 179.

8. Ibid., 179–80.

9. This translation was filtered through the French translation from which the Preface is taken. The Preface encouraged support for the Dutch revolt against Spain; see Bartolomé de Las Casas, *The Spanish Colonie, or Briefe Chronicle of the Acts and Gestes of the Spaniardes in the West Indies,* trans. M. M. S. (London, 1583), q2 recto-qq recto.

10. Robert Payne, *A Briefe Description of Ireland: Made in this yeare, 1589* . . . (London, 1589). I have checked copies at Houghton Library, Harvard; the University Library, Cambridge; and the British Library against the copy in the Bodleian at Oxford Shelfmark: Mal. 551. See *The English Experience,* 548, for a modern reprint. My thanks to Nicholas Canny for reminding me of the importance of the Spanish in Payne.

11. Ibid., A3 recto-A4 verso.

12. Ibid., A4 verso.

13. Ibid.

14. Ibid., A4 recto-A4 verso.

15. Ibid., A4 recto.

16. Hakluyt, *Principal Navigations* . . . in *Voyages* (1907; London, 1967), I, 1.

17. Ibid.

18. See Hakluyt, the Elder, "Inducements to the Liking of the Voyage Intended towards Virginia . . ." (1585) in *The Original Writings & Correspondence of the Two Richard Hakluyts,* ed. E. G. R. Taylor (2 vols., London, 1935), II, 327–38. This volume also includes Hakluyt the Younger's "Discourse."

19. Hart, "Strategies," 73–92.

20. Hakluyt, *Principal Navigations* (1967), 2.

21. Ibid., 2.

22. Ibid.

23. Ibid.

24. Ibid; my translation.

25. See Lestringant, *Le Huguenot,* 216.

26. Hakluyt, *Principal Navigations* (1967), 5.

27. Ibid.

28. Ibid., 6.

29. Ibid.

30. Ibid.

31. Ibid.

32. Ibid.

33. See Roger Schlesinger and Arthur P. Stabler, "Introduction," *André Thevet's North America: A Sixteenth-Century View,* ed. Roger Schlesinger and Arthur P. Stabler (Kingston, 1986), xxiii. Hakluyt is described in various terms. For Wayne Franklin, he is someone who appears incidentally, as a collector of narratives and a recipient of letters; Franklin, *Discoverers, Explorers, Settlers: The Diligent Writers of Early America* (Chicago, 1979). 135–36, 160–65. Karen Kupperman discusses the Hakluyts as agents for Francis Walsingham and notes their desire for educational reforms at Oxford and Cambridge (moving from a medieval curriculum to one including mathematics and geography); Karen Ordahl Kupperman, *Settling with the Indians: The Meeting of English and Indian Cultures in America, 1580–1640* (Totowa, NJ, 1980), 9; she also notes the international nature of Hakluyt the Younger's material (ibid., 23, 150); how Hakluyt recommended the robbing of Amerindian graves to achieve riches (ibid., 125). Stephen Greenblatt mentions Hakluyt twice, once in observing the paradox that the patriotic Hakluyt includes international material and then in connection with Mandeville; Stephen Greenblatt, *Marvelous Possessions: The Wonder of the New World* (Chicago, 1991), 8–9, 30–1.

34. Ibid., 6–7. On English nationalism and writing in this period, including the work of Hakluyt, see Richard Helgerson, *Forms of Nationhood: The Elizabethan Writing of England* (Chicago, 1992). He emphasizes the experience of the voyages before the written account of them (ibid., 151), a point Philip Edwards also makes in his *Last Voyages: Cavendish, Hudson, Ralegh* (Oxford, 1988), 7. For an extended discussion of Hakluyt's *Principal Navigations,* which includes an examination of the success of Hakluyt's writings in promotion as opposed to failure in that regard but the fame of John Smith's works, see Mary C. Fuller, *Voyages in Print: English Travel to America, 1576–1624* (Cambridge, 1995), 141–74.

35. Hakluyt, *Principal* (1967), 7.
36. Ibid., 9.
37. Ibid.
38. Ibid. On Hakluyt in the context of taking possession, see Patricia Seed, *Ceremonies of Possession in Europe's Conquest of the New World, 1492–1640* (Cambridge, 1995), 26–7.
39. Hakluyt, *Principal* (1967), 10.
40. For a perceptive discussion of Gilbert in relation to his contemporaries, like Eden and especially Hakluyt, and for his use of literary devices and defensive maneuvres, see Fuller, *Voyages,* 20–42. On Edward Haie's criticism of Gilbert, see Edwards, *Last Voyages,* 285. For a discussion of Gilbert and Hakluyt, which implies a connection between the two (although here the evidence is taken from the second edition (1598) of *Principall Navigations*) as they use scarcity of resources as a reason for expansion, see Jeffrey Knapp, *An Empire Nowhere: England, America, and Literature from Utopia to* The Tempest (Berkeley, 1992), 74–5.
41. Hakluyt, *Principall* (1967), 10.
42. Ibid., 11.
43. Ibid., 12.
44. Ibid.
45. Ibid.
46. See Hart, "Strategies."
47. Pennington, "The Amerindian," 180–83.
48. Walter Ralegh, *A Report of the Trvth of the fight about the Isles of Açores, this last Sommer. Betwixt The Reuenge, one of her Maiesties Shippes, And an Armada of the King of Spaine* (London, 1591), A 3 recto.
49. Ibid., D recto.
50. Ibid. D recto-D verso. The title was actually *The Spanish Colonie.*
51. Ibid., D verso.
52. Ibid., D 2 verso.
53. Walter Ralegh, *The Discouerie of the Large, Rich, and Bewtiful Empyre of Guiana, with a Relation of the Great and Golden Citie of Manoa (which the Spanyards call El Dorado* . . . . (London, 1596), q 2, 76–9.
54. Ibid., A 3 verso.
55. For a discussion of Ralegh in Guiana, especially how he personalized his schemes of colonization even though he did not participate in most, see Fuller, *Voyages,* 55–84 and in an earlier form as "Ralegh's Fugitive Gold: Reference and Deferral in *The Discovery of Guiana*" in New World Encounters, ed. Stephen Greenblatt (Berkeley, 1993), 218–40. Fuller's earlier version begins with the second section of the later version and so emphasizes gold more directly.
56. Ralegh, *Discouerie,* A 4 recto.
57. Ibid.
58. Ibid., q verso.
59. Ibid.
60. Ibid., q 2 recto.
61. Ibid., q 2 verso.
62. Ibid., q 3 recto.
63. Ibid., q 3 verso.
64. Ibid.
65. Ibid., C 3 recto.
66. Ibid., C 3 recto-C 4 verso. On English colonization in Ireland, see Nicholas Canny, *Kingdom and Colony: Ireland in the Atlantic World 1560–1800* (Baltimore, 1988), ch. 1; and for the relation of Ireland to America, see David B. Quinn, *Ireland and America: Their Early Associations, 1500–1640* (Liverpool, 1991).
67. Ibid., q 3 verso.
68. Ibid.
69. Ibid.
70. Ibid., q 4.
71. Ibid.
72. Ibid.
73. Ibid., 3.
74. Ibid., 4–5.

75. Ibid., 5–6.
76. Ibid., 7.
77. On Ralegh and sexual desire in Guiana, see Louis Montrose, "The Work of Gender in the Discourse of Discovery" in *New World Encounters,* ed. Stephen Greenblatt (Berkeley, 1993), 177–217. For a more general discussion of Ralegh, see Pierre Lefranc, *Sir Walter Ralegh Ecrivain: l'œuvres et les idées* (Paris, 1968) and Stephen Greenblatt, *Sir Walter Ralegh: The Renaissance Man and His Roles* (New Haven, 1973).
78. Ralegh, *Discouerie,* 7.
79. Ibid., 9.
80. Ibid.
81. Ibid., 10.
82. Ibid., 79.
83. Ibid., 100–01.
84. Ibid., 101, see 96.
85. Ibid., 101.
86. Ibid. I, A recto and verso; II, 367.
87. See R. M., *Nevves of Sʳ Walter Rauleigh. With a True Description of Gviana* (London, 1618) in *Tracts and Other Papers, Origin, Settlement, and Progress of the Colonies in North America, from the Discovery of the Country to the Year 1776,* collected by Peter Force (4 vols., Washington, 1836–46), III, 11. Each tract has its own pagination, so that the volume does not use consecutive pagination. The author's initials appear on the last page (28) and not on the title page.
88. Ibid., 11.
89. Ibid., 12.
90. Ibid.
91. For an account of Acadia, see Marcel Trudel, *Histoire de la Nouvelle-France,* vol. 1, *Les vaines tentatives, 1524–1603* (Montréal, 1963). My discussion of New France is indebted to W. J. Eccles, *France in America* (1972;Vancouver, 1973), 12–15. Concerning internal divisions in Spain, see John Lynch, *Spain Under the Hapsburgs* (2 vols., Oxford, 1969), II, 1–13.
92. Marcel Trudel, *Histoire de la Nouvelle-France,* vol. 2, *Le Comptoir, 1604–1627* (Montréal, 1966), 9–15. See Eccles, *France,* 14–15.
93. For a general account of Acadia from its origins to the present, see Père Anselme Chiasson, "Acadia," *The Canadian Encyclopedia,* second edition (Edmonton, 1988), 5–10. For biographical information on Champlain and Lescarbot, see Marcel Trudel, "Champlain, Samuel de", 186–99 and René Baudry, "Lescarbot, Marc," 469–71, in *Dictionary of Canadian Biography,* gen. ed. George W. Brown, vol. 1, 1000–1700 (Toronto and Québec, 1966).
94. *Brief Discovrs Des Choses Plvs Remqvables Qve Sammvel Champlain De Brovage A Reconneues Aux Indes Occidentalles . . .* (1599–1601) in Samuel de Champlain, *Works,* ed H. P. Biggar (6 vols., Toronto, 1922–36), I, 4. This is a bilingual edition. My translation here and below. The translations in Biggar are good, but in places I have sometimes differed in matters of diction. I am assuming that the work is by Champlain (the traditional editorial view), whereas this assumption is not universally held. Champlain's uncle's position and Champlain's early experiences appeared to have provided a situation where he could have taken the journey and written the account. Joe C. W. Armstrong also considers this text to be by Champlain; see Armstrong, *Champlain* (Toronto, 1987), 23–35. H. P. Biggar includes it in his edition.
95. Champlain, *Brief Discovrs,* 15.
96. Ibid., 19.
97. Ibid., 61.
98. Ibid., 61–2.
99. Ibid., 63.
100. Ibid., 63.
101. Ibid., 63–4.
102. See Armstrong, *Champlain,* 33. Lestringant provides a perceptive and sweeping analysis of cannibalism, but he does not mention Champlain's comments; Frank Lestringant, *Le Cannibale: Grandeur et décadence* (Paris, 1994). For more on cannibalism, see William Arens, *The Man-Eating Myth: Anthropology and Anthrophagy* (New York, 1979).
103. Champlain, *Brief Discovrs,* 64–5.
104. Ibid., 65–6.
105. Ibid., 68.

106. Ibid., 78–9. Little appears to have been written in English about the French and tobacco, but for a recent discussion of the English and tobacco, see Knapp, "Divine Tobacco," *An Empire,* 134–74; Knapp also mentions the Spanish trade in tobacco but not the French interest in it ; ibid., 134–5.

107. See *Commissions Dv Roy et [?] de Monseigneur 'lAdmiral, au sieur de Monts, pour l'habitation és terres de Lacadie Canada, et autres endroits en la nouvelle France. Ensemble les defensees preieres & secondes à toutes autres, de trafiquer auec les Sauuages desdites terres. Auec la verification en la Cour de Parlement à Paris* (Paris, 1605). Facsimile from the copy in Lennox Library, Bar Harbor, Maine n.p., 1915.

108. All of the editions of Lescarbot's *Histoire de la Nouvelle France* (1609, 1611–12, 1617–18) included an appendix consisting of a short collection of poems, *Les Muses de la Nouvelle France.* The last two editions involved a reshaping and a completion of the account of New France until the date of composition. See Pagden, *Spanish Imperialism and the Political Imagination, Studies in European and Spanish-American Social and Political Theory 1513–1830* (New Haven, 1990), 4.

109. See Pagden, *Spanish Imperialism and the Political Imagination, Studies in European and Spanish-American Social and Political Theory 1513–1830* (New Haven, 1990), 4.

110. Grant, I, xx. On Lescarbot, see Biggar, "Introduction: Marc Lescarbot" in *History of New France,* ix-xv.

111. Grant, "Translator's Preface" in Lescarbot, *The History,* I, 33.

112. It is a shame that no copy of the contemporary biography of Lescarbot by the poet Guillaume Colletet has been found. See Baudry, "Lescarbot," 469–71. W. L. Grant, the translator of Lescarbot, writes of him: "Lescarbot, like Herodotus, whom he so much resembles, should be read in the original"; see Grant, "Translator's Preface," in Marc Lescarbot, *The History of New France,* trans. W. L. Grant and introduction by H. P. Biggar (3 vols., Toronto, 1907) I, vii.

113. Marc Lescarbot, *Histoire de la Novvelle-France . . .* (Paris 1609), ã ij recto, ã iij recto and verso, ã iiij recto; my translations here and below.

114. Lescarbot, *Histoire* (1609), b ij verso.

115. Ibid. b ij verso-bij recto.

116. Ibid., b iij recto-b iij verso.

117. Ibid., b iiij recto.

118. Ibid.

119. See H. P. Biggar, "The French Hakluyt: Marc Lescarbot of Vervins," *American Historical Review* 6 (1901), 671–92.

120. Lestringant, *Le Huguenot et le Sauvage* (Paris, 1990), 267; my translation.

121. Ibid., 266–70.

122. See Christopher Moore, "Colonization and Conflict: New France and its Rivals (1600–1760)" in *The Illustrated History of Canada,* ed. Craig Brown (1987; Toronto, 1991), 158, 169.

123. Lescarbot, *Histoire* (1609), b iv verso. In his address to Pierre Jeannin in the 1612 edition, Lescarbot used this language of republicanism; see Marc Lescarbot, *Histoire de la Novvelle-France . . .* (Paris 1612), jx.

124. Lescarbot, *Histoire* (1609), b iiij verso.

125. Ibid., b ij verso; b iiij verso-c recto.

126. Ibid., c verso.

127. Pagden, *Spanish Imperialism,* 5. In a wide-ranging discussion of the possession in the context of theology and law, Pagden discusses the "School of Salamanca." He analyzes the work of the Dominican Francisco de Vitoria (ca. 1492–1546), who was trained at Paris; see Ibid., 18–22; Pagden, *The Fall of Natural Man: The American Indian and the Origins of Comparative Ethnology* (1982; Cambridge, 1986), 60–80. In *Fall* Pagden notes that Vitoria questioned the justice of the Spanish conquests in the period 1526–9; ibid., 65. A few months before the completion of this book, I attended a talk in which Pagden discussed this subject in the context of Vitoria's fellow jurists, his student Domingo de Soto, and Fernando Vásquez de Menchaca; Pagden, "Shadows of an Unquiet Sleep," John Carter Brown Library, Providence, March 4, 1997.

128. Lescarbot, *Histoire* (1609), c verso.

129. Ibid., b iij verso.

130. Ibid.

131. See ibid., e ij.

132. Lescarbot, *Histoire* (Paris 1612), xvij and his *Histoire de la Novvelle-France . . .* (Paris 1618), 21. For the biblical reference, see Matthew II, 28–9.

133. Lescarbot, *Histoire* (1612), iij and *Histoire* (1618), 3.

134. Lescarbot, *Histoire* (1612), jv and his *Histoire* (1618), 4.

135. See Lescarbot, *Histoire* (1612), jv.

136. See Lescarbot, *Histoire* (1618), 4. For another translation, see Lescarbot, *History,* 3–4.

137. Pierre d'Avity, sieur de Montmartin, described America in his *Les Estats, empires et principavtez dv monde . . .* (Paris, 1613), 133–4.

138. In 1615 Edward Grimstone translated D'Avity (he used "Avity" whereas modern historians seem to use 'd'Avity') and dedicated it to the Earl of Suffolk, who had provided the translator protection in France, the Netherlands, and Spain. Pierre d'Avity, "The Epistle Dedicatorie" in *The Estates, Empires, & Principallities of the World . . . ,* trans. Edward Grimstone (London, 1615), n.p. [2pp.]. As a result of these differences, I include my own translations and in key places compare d'Avity's original with Grimstone's translation. Grimeston and Grimestone are variants of his name.

139. D'Avity, *Les Estats.* British Isles (1–42); France (131); Spain and its possessions (132–333), and its colonies in the New World (257–333). I am using d'Avity's headings, which included Ireland under the rubric of "Grande-Bretagne." Portugal is placed under the Spanish possessions.

140. Ibid., 258. Here I paraphrase d'Avity: 'L'Avtre partie des Estats du Roy d'Espagne consiste au Nouueau Monde, où il a tout ce qu'il veut, pource qu'il n'y trouue personne qui luy contrarie."

141. Ibid., 263–4; d'Avity, *Les Estats,* 263.

142. D'Avity, *The Estates,* 222, see 221.

143. Ibid., 265.

144. Ibid., 266.

145. Ibid., 267.

146. Ibid., 271.

147. Ibid., 286.

148. Ibid., 292–4.

149. Ibid., 297; see 300, 318.

150. See ibid., 301–25. On Columbus and cannibals, see Lestringant, *Le Cannibal,* 43–7.

151. D'Avity, *Les Estats,* 297. Grimstone translated the sentence as follows: "The Estates of the king of Spain at the New world are so great and powerful, as they need not to feare any enemie"; Pierre d'Avity, *The Estates,* trans. E. Grimstone, 250. I have provided my own translations because Grimstone, as he claimed, did not follow the text in places.

152. D'Avity, *Les Estats,* 298. D'Avity's phrase is "commander à la Mer Oceane." Surprisingly, Grimstone leaves in his text this claim about Italian and Spanish dominance, a kind of translation of empire from the Old World to the New World. D'Avity, *The Estates,* 250.

153. D'Avity, *Les Estats,* 298.

154. Ibid., 312–13. D'Avity spoke of the "Verbe eternel" and of the opportunity the Spanish had had in spreading their state and the kingdom of God ("& et le Royaume de Dieu"). Grimstone differed most from d'Avity in matters of religion. To a discussion of cannibalism and communion in d'Avity ("*Comme le Diable auoi t contrefait quelques sacrements de l'Eglise*"), an earlier section (*Les Estats,* 306–9), Grimstone added the marginal gloss: "This hath some resemblance to the opinion of the Papists touching the Eucharist"; D'Avity, *The Estates,* 257. Grimstone likened the distribution of the pieces of the bodies of captives sacrificed to idols to the Catholic view of communion. He implied a kind of barbarity and idolatry in the notion of transubstantiation.

155. D'Avity, *Les Estats,* 313. See ibid., 315, 317 for a amplification of this idea. There the Spanish invasion of Peru was presented in similar providential terms. Grimstone left in this providential view of Cortés, who "preuailed in his enterprise, and subdued the realme of Mexico, both to Iesus Christ and to the Emperor, whose captaine he was." D'Avity, *The Estates,* 262.

156. D'Avity, *Les Estats,* 316. In the English translation Grimstone added: "But *Alexander* had no more authoritie to dispose of the New world, nor to giue vnto them the kingdomes which had neither beene discouered nor conquered, than his successors haue had sence to arrogate vnto themselues power to depose lawfull kings and princes from their crowne and estates." D'Avity, *The Estates,* 263–4. Here the English version of d'Avity was more critical of the papacy and Spain.

157. D'Avity, *Les Estats,* 316. His claim, which I am paraphrasing, was that "Il n'y eut iamais pays où l'Euangile fist de plus grands progrez, qu'au Nouueau Monde, veu que les peuples entiers s'y conuertissoient."

158. Ibid, 317–18; ibid, 16. Whether this article represented a fear of escaping an exclusive English justice or a resistance to the phenomenon of the "White Indian" is hard to say. See James Axtell, *The Invasion from Within: The Contest of Cultures in Colonial North America* (Oxford, 1985), 302.

159. D'Avity, *The Estates,* 264.

160. D'Avity, *Les Estats,* 318–22. See d'Avity, *The Estates,* 266–9. For a discussion of d'Avity's degrees of brutality, see Olive P. Dickason, *The Myth of the Savage and the Beginnings of French Colonialism in the Americas* (Edmonton, 1984), 65–70. She says that contemporaries would probably have found perplexing d'Avity's omission of sexual disorder, cannibalism, dirtiness, and cruelty from his list of degrees of brutality.

161. D'Avity, *Les Estats,* 322. D'Avity's syntax and diction here are difficult if not awkward, so I have taken some liberties in the translation to render the two sentences in a clear and coordinated sentence. Grimstone left out this passage, so that he kept his promise, in the prefatory matter, to make changes to d'Avity's text. This is one example of the divergence between French and English interpretations of the example of Spain.

162. Ibid., 324–5. Pagden discusses Quiroga in *The Fall,* 35. The place is also known as Michoacán.

163. Ibid., 326–33. Nor did Grimstone see a contradiction. D'Avity, *The Estates,* 272–83. Grimstone's list did not end with the revenues of the Crown of Portugal as d'Avity's did.

164. Sagard, quoted in W. J. Eccles, *The Ordeal of New France* (Toronto, 1967), 21–2.

165. Boucher, *Les Nouvelles Frances: France in America, 1500–1815: An Imperial Perspective* (Providence, 1989), 24–7.

166. For background on these companies and Richelieu's colonial policy, which has informed my discussion here and below, see Mathé Allain, "French Colonial Policy in America and the Establishment of the Louisiana Colony," (unpublished Ph.D. dissertation, The University of Southwestern Louisiana, 1984), 17–31. On the number of companies with royal charters, see Emile Salone, *La Colonisation de la Nouvelle-France: Étude sur les origines de la nation canadienne française* (Paris, n.d.), 18. See also Marcel Trudel, *The Beginnings of New France, 1524–1622* (Toronto, 1973), 171.

167. On religious policy in New France and on the status of French Protestants, see J. Saintoyant, "Des Politiques religieuses et indigènes des diverses colonisations européenes avant le XIXᵉ siècle," *Revue d'Histoire des Colonies Françaises* 23 (1935), 235–304 and Cornelius Jaenen, "The Persistence of Protestant Presence in New France," *Proceedings of the Second Meeting of the Western Society for French History* (1974), 29–40, cited in Allain, "French Colonial," 27.

168. W. J. Eccles, *France in America* (1972; Vancouver, 1973), 24.

169. D'Avity, *The Estates,* 257. In the main text here I have purposely repeated some of the material in my notes to this section so that the reader will be able to make some close comparisons between D'Avity's text and Grimstone's translation and will also be able to glean a brief but integrated interpretation in my main argument.

170. D'Avity, *The Estates,* 262.

171. D'Avity, *The Estates,* 263–4.

172. D'Avity, *The Estates,* 264.

173. See note 159.

174. See William Strachey, "To the Right Honorable, the Lords of the Councell of Virginea," in William Strachey, *For the Colony in Virginea Britannia. Lavves Diuine, Morall and Martiall, & c.* (London, 1612), n.p.

175. See Strachey, *For the Colony,* 20, 32. For a general treatment of relations between the English and the Natives, see Karen Kupperman, *Settling.*

176. Strachey, 16.

177. See notes 157 and 158.

178. William Strachey, *The Historie of Travell into Virginia Britannia* (London, 1612), 9.

179. See Robert Johnson, *Nova Britannia, Offring Most Excellent Fruites by Planting in Virginia* (London, 1609), A 3 recto. In *European Americana . . .* vol. 2, the editors note that for Johnson's *Nova Britannia* there are two settings of the type (in which the sheets have been indiscriminately gathered) and three states of the title page. Although I have consulted a number of copies in various libraries, I have decided to quote from the Princeton copy.

180. Ibid., A4 recto.

181. Ibid., A 4 recto-A 4 verso.

182. Ibid., A 4 verso.

183. Ibid., A4 verso.

184. Ibid., B recto
185. Ibid.
186. See Anon., *A Trve Declaration of the Estate of the Colonie in Virginia, with a Confutation of Such Scandalous Reports as haue Tended to Disgrace of So Worthy an Enterprise* (London, 1610), in *Tracts,* ed. Force, III, 8.
187. Johnson, *Nova Britannia,* B recto.
188. Ibid.
189. Ibid.
190. Ibid., B verso. English narratives of the New World, however, show a recurrent ambivalence toward Henry VII, often pointing out his lost opportunity with Columbus. See, for instance, Anon., *A Trve Declaration,* in *Tracts,* ed. Force, III, 24: "*Henry* the seuenth by too-much ouerwarines, lost the riches of the golden Indies."
191. Johnson, *Nova Britannia,* B verso, see B recto.
192. Ibid., B recto.
193. Ibid.
194. Ibid.
195. Ibid.
196. Ibid.
197. Ibid.
198. Ibid.
199. Ibid., B verso
200. Ibid., B verso and B 2 recto.
201. Ibid., B2 recto.
202. Ibid., B 2 recto and B 2 verso.
203. Ibid., B 2 verso.
204. Ibid., B 2 verso and B 3 recto.
205. Ibid., B 3 recto.
206. Ibid., B3 recto and B3 verso.
207. Ibid., B 3 recto and B 3 verso.
208. Ibid., B3 verso.
209. Todorov denies Vitoria's reputation as a defender of the rights of the Natives because of the negative effects of his contribution to international law. See Tzvetan Todorov, *The Conquest of America* (1985; New York, 1992), 150. For a contrary view, which emphasizes Vitoria's challenge to Spanish claims to the Indies, the apparent contradictions in Vitoria's thought, and his emphasis on education and environment as determining the mind of humans, including Natives, see Pagden, *Fall,* esp. 32–3, 64–104. On the study of "otherness" as it relates to the encounter between Europeans and Natives, see J. H. Elliott, "Final Reflections: The Old World and the New Revisited," *America in European Consciousness, 1493–1750,* ed. Karen Ordahl Kupperman (Chapel Hill, 1995), 398–9.
210. Johnson, *Nova Britannia,* B 3 verso.
211. Ibid., B4 recto-verso and C recto.
212. Ibid., B 3 verso- C recto.
213. Ibid., C recto.
214. Ibid., C recto- C verso.
215. Ibid., C verso.
216. Ibid., C recto-verso.
217. Ibid., C verso.
218. Ibid.
219. Ibid., C 2 recto.
220. Ibid.
221. Thomas Harriot's *A Briefe and True Report of the New Found Land of Virginia* (1590), E recto. For an interesting discussion of Harriot, Philippe Galle and others in this context, see Stephen Orgel, "Introduction," William Shakespeare, *The Tempest,* ed. Stephen Orgel (Oxford 1987, rpt. 1994), 34–5.
222. Johnson, *Nova Britannia,* C2 recto-verso.
223. Ibid., C2 recto-verso.
224. Ibid., C2 verso
225. Ibid., C2 verso-C3 recto.

226. Ibid, C2 verso, see C3 verso–C4 verso.
227. Ibid., C4 verso; D recto for the quotation.
228. Ibid., D recto.
229. Ibid.
230. Ibid., C 2 verso.
231. Ibid., C 2 verso– D recto.
232. Ibid., D verso–D 3 recto.
233. Ibid., D 3 recto.
234. Ibid., D 3 verso.
235. Ibid., D 3 verso–E verso.
236. Ibid., E2 recto–E2 verso.
237. Ibid., E 2 verso.
238. Ibid., E2 recto. For Johnson's discussion of money and planters, divisions of lands, see E1 recto–verso, 2 recto–verso
239. Ibid., E2 Verso.
240. Ibid., E2 verso and E3 recto.
241. Ibid., E3 recto.
242. Ibid., E3 recto
243. Ibid., E4 recto.
244. Ibid., E4 verso.
245. Ibid., F1 verso–F2 recto.
246. Ibid., F4 verso, G recto, G4 recto.
247. Ibid.
248. Robert Johnson, *The New Life of Virginea: Declaring the Former Successe and Present Estate of that Plantation, Being the Second Part of* Noua Britannia (London, 1612) in *Tracts,* ed. Force, I, 19. I have also consulted the copy in Houghton Library, Harvard, and where indicated will refer to this edition in the discussion that follows in the main text. Once again, Johnson dedicated his work to Thomas Smith. For brief discussions of Johnson, both of which relate to Providence, work, and resources, see Knapp, *Empire,* 231 and Fuller, *Voyages,* 86–7.
249. Ibid.
250. Ibid., 21–4.
251. R[obert] J[ohnson], *The New Life of Virginea: Declaring The Former Svcesse and Present estate of that plantation, being the second part of* Noua Britannia. London 1612, B3 verso. Houghton copy.
252. Ibid., B4 verso–C recto, D4 verso.
253. Ibid., E2 verso.
254. William Strachey, *The Historie of Travell into Virginia Britania* (1612), Hakluyt Society Second Series CIII, ed. Louis B. Wright and Virginia Freund (London, 1953). See the Introduction by Louis B. Wright and Virginia Freund, xiii–xxxii. One manuscript is in the British Museum as Sloane MS 1622 (presented to Francis Bacon in 1618) (Ist Hak. Soc ed.); another is the Percy manuscript at Princeton University in the family of the earl of Northumberland until 1928 (ed. Wright and Freund); still another ms. in the Bodleian Library as Ashmole MS 1758 (presented to Sir Allen Apsley, purveyor to the King's Navy). All three manuscripts are substantially the same, in a professional scribe's hand, but showing alterations in Strachey's own hand. The Princeton manuscript is, according to Wright and Freund, the most carefully prepared; it also includes John Smith's map of Virginia (1612) and 27 engravings from Theodor DeBry's 1590 edition of Thomas Harriot's *A briefe and true report of the new found land of Virginia,* engravings from the original DeBry and colored by hand with written descriptions, sometimes slightly different from those in Harriot, descriptions and various alterations and corrections seem to be in Strachey's hand;. The engravings are well-known but are not in the 2nd Hakluyt Society edition. (xii–xiv).
255. Ibid., xviii–xix.
256. Ibid., xix.
257. Ibid., xxi. See also Leslie Hotson, *I, William Shakespeare* (New York, 1938), 225–6.
258. Wright and Freund, xxiii, see xxii–xxiv
259. Ibid., xxv.
260. Quoted in ibid., xxvi.
261. S. G. Culliford as well as Wright and Freund discuss these and other sources. See S. G. Culliford, "William Strachey, 1572–1621," Ph.D. dissertation, University of London, 1950 in

Wright and Freund, xxvii. They think that Strachey borrowed in the following ways: chapter 2, book 2 (as the British Museum copy is divided) condenses material on Bartholomew Gosnold's voyage from John Brereton, *A Briefe and true Relation of the Discouverie of the North part of Virginia* (1602); for about half of chapter 7, book 2, Strachey condensed James Rosier's *A true Relation of the most prosperous Voyage made this present yeere 1605 by Captaine George Waymouth, in the Discovery* [xxviii] *of the land of Virginiea* (16050; 1/3 of bk 1, Strachey paraphrased, adapted, and condensed material from John Smith's *A Map of Virginia: With a Description of the Countrey, The Commodities, People, Government and Religion* (1612). Other works from which Strachey seems to have borrowed ideas are: William Symonds, *Virginia. A Sermon preached at Whitechapel in the presence of the adventurers and planters for Virginia. 25 April, 1609;* Thomas Cogan, *The Haven of Health* (1589); Johan Boemus Albanus, *The maners, Lawes, and customs of all Nations* (1611); George Percy, *Discourse of the Plantation of the Southern Colonie in Virginia by the English* (1606), first printed by Purchas in 1625, and Strachey saw it in manuscript; James Davies, *The relation of a Voyage unto New England,* which Strachey saw in manuscript, first published in 1880; Saint Augustine, *De Concensu Evangelicarum.* See Wright and Freund, xxvii–xxviii.

262. Ibid., xxviii and xxix.
263. Ibid., xxx.
264. Ibid., xxxi.
265. My translation. The original, in William Strachey, *The Historie of Travell into Virginia Britania* (1612), reads:
    —Nec sermones ego mallem
    Repentes per humum, quam res componere gestas,
    Terrarumque situs, et flumina dicere, et arces
    Montibus impositas, et barbara regna.

    Hor: EP:lib.2.Ep.1.

266. Ibid., 6.
267. Ibid., 7.
268. Ibid.
269. Ibid., 7–8.
270. Ibid., 8.
271. Ibid.
272. Ibid., 8n1.
273. Ibid., 8n2. On the Virginia Company's campaign to refute criticism of the colonial enterprise, see Louis B. Wright, *Religion and Empire: The Alliance between Piety and Commerce in English Expansion, 1558–1625* (Chapel Hill, N. C., 1943), 84–114.
274. Strachey, *The Historie of Travell into Virginia Britania,* 9.
275. Ibid., 9. This "Vndertaker" might be Hakluyt as Wright and Freund say, or, as the first Hakluyt Society editor R. H. Major suggests, the allusion may be to Hieronymous Benzo, who questions, in *Novae novi Orbis Historiae,* the pope's right to dispose of the New World. It is hard to know precisely as this reference is vague.
276. Strachey, *The Historie of Travell into Virginia Britania,* 9–10. In note 1 (page 10) the editors gloss *Adelantado* as following: "Hernando de Soto, who had taken part in the conquest of Peru, reached Tampa Bay in 1539 for his exploration of Florida and the lands beyond. He had received the title of 'Adelantado of the Lands of Florida' from Charles V."
277. Ibid., 10. In fact, as the second edition of the Hakluyt Society notes: "The marginal note of the British Museum's manuscript mentions that the Spanish maps call a bay within Chesapeake Bay 'Santa Maria'."
278. Strachey, *The Historie of Travell into Virginia Britania,* 10–11. Two editorial glosses on page 11 are helpful. The first concerning Henry VII in the quotation above notes that in the margin of the British Museum manuscript the following words appear: "Vide Hackluite's discoveries, Lib.1." and the second, about Camden, says that Strachey was really following a passage in Hakluyt that was attributed to Camden.
279. Ibid., 12.
280. Ibid., 12–13. The document is, as the editors note, supposed to have perished when that gallery burned in the time of William III.
281. Ibid., 1.2
282. Ibid.

283. Ibid, 13. The word after "giue" is barely legible, and I have construed it as "them."
284. Ibid., 14.
285. Ibid., 15.
286. Ibid., 15–16.
287. T. A., "To the Hand" in John Smith, *A Map of Virginia with a Description of the Covntrey, the Commodities, People, Government and Religion . . .* (Oxford, 1612), ★ 2.
288. William Symonds, "The Proceedings of the English Colonie in Virginia . . . " in John Smith, *A Map of Virginia with a Description of the Covntrey, the Commodities, People, Government and Religion . . .* (Oxford, 1612), 63–81. Symonds's tract comprised part two of the book. On a later crisis in the relation with the Natives, see Alden T. Vaughan, "'Expulsion of the Savages': English policy and the Virginia Massacre of 1622," *William and Mary Quarterly* 35 (1978), 57–84.
289. John Smith, *New Englands Trials. . . ,* second edition (London 1622) in *Tracts,* ed. Force II, 21, see 19. The first edition was 1620.
290. Ibid., II, 23.
291. John Smith, *A Description of New England: or the Observations and Discoueries of Captain Iohn Smith (Admirall of that Country) in the North of America . . .* (London, 1616), n.p.
292. See Ibid., 28–30.
293. Ibid., 32.
294. "To my Worthy friend and Cousen, Capitaine Iohn Smith," in Smith, *A Description,* n.p.
295. "To his friend Cap: Smith vpon his description of New England," Smith, *A Description,* n.p. Although to my knowledge no one has discussed at any length John Smith's view of Spain, some important work has been done on Smith. On Smith and Pocahontas, see Peter Hulme, *Colonial Encounters: Europe and the Native Caribbean 1492–1797* (1986; London, 1992), 149–52 and J. A. Leo Lemay, *Did Pocahontas Save Captain John Smith?* (Athens, GA, 1992); Margaret Holmes Williamson, "Pocahontas and Captain John Smith: Examining a Historical Myth," *History and Anthropology* 5 (1992), 365–402. Jeffrey Knapp mentions Smith's admiration for the Dutch because they had few natural resources yet used their industry to prosper; Knapp, *Empire,* 327 n61. Another view of Smith's attitude to gold and resources are found in James David Taylor, "'Base Commoditie': Natural Resource and Natural History in Smith's *The Generall Historie,*" *Environmental History Review* 17 (1993), 73–89. For a discussion of Smith's *Generall Historie,* see Fuller, *Voyages,* 116–39. For general assessment of Smith, see Karen Ordahl Kupperman, "'Brasse without but golde within':The Writings of Captain John Smith," *Virginia Calvacade* 38 (1988), 66–75 and *Virginia Calvacade* 38 (1989), 134–43 and her introduction to John Smith, *Captain John Smith: A Select Edition of His Writings,* ed. Karen Ordahl Kupperman (Chapel Hill, 1988) and the introduction to Philip L. Barbour's edition, *The Complete Works of Captain John Smith* (Chapel Hill, 1986). Kupperman notes briefly that Cortés and Smith both compared themselves to Julius Caesar; see Kupperman, "Introduction: The Changing Definition of America," in *America in European Consciousness 1493–1750,* ed. Karen Ordahl Kupperman (Chapel Hill, 1995), 15–16.
296. Smith, *A Description,* 3. Karen Kupperman says that Smith thought God had prevented the Spanish from the successful settlement of North America; Kupperman, "Introduction," *Smith: A Select Edition,* 19.
297. Smith, *Description,* 3–4.
298. Ibid., 6.
299. See ibid. Hudson sailed for the English (1607, 1608, 1610-11) and for the Dutch (1609).
300. Ibid., 7.
301. See ibid., 11.
302. Ibid., 7.
303. See ibid., 20.
304. See Anon., *A Trve Declaration* in *Tracts,* ed. Force, III, 21.
305. See White, *The Planter's Plea. Or the Grounds of Plantations Examined, and Vsuall Objections Answered. Together with a Manifestation of the Causes Mooving Such as Have Lately Undertaken a Plantation in New-England: for the Satisfaction of Those That Question the Lawfulnesse of the Action* (London, 1630) in *Tracts,* ed. Force, II, 5–6.
306. Ibid. 9–10.
307. Ibid., 13.
308. Ibid., 39.

309. Ibid., 45.
310. Ibid., 47.
311. See Morton, *The New English Canaan; or, New Canaan. Containing an Abstract of New England* (London, 1632) in *Tracts,* ed. Force, II, 95.
312. Smith, *A Description,* 43.
313. Ibid.
314. Ibid., 44.
315. Ibid.
316. Ibid.
317. See the discussion of *Discourse* in chapter 4.
318. Smith, *A Description,* 34-5.
319. Ibid., 59.
320. Ibid., 60.
321. Ibid., 60-1.
322. Ibid.
323. Samuel Purchas, *Hakluytus Posthumous or Purchas His Pilgrimes Contayning a History of the World in Sea Voyages and Lande Travells by Englishmen and others,* (20 vols., Glasgow, 1906), XIV, 427–8. This edition, which consists of 20 volumes, is a reprint of the 1625 edition. I have also consulted the 1613, 1614, 1617 and 1626 editions. See also Purchas, *Hakluytus,* I, xxiv-xxvii for discussion of the editions. The "Publisher's Note" asserts that the last edition (1626) to be a distinct work and not volume five of the "Pilgrimes" as it is often considered.
324. Purchas, I, xlix.
325. Antonio de Herrera, "The Fifthe Booke," *A Description of the West Indies,* in Purchas, *Hakluytus,* XIV, 429.
326. Ibid.
327. José Acosta, in Purchas, *Hakluytus,* XV, 79, 90, 100. For a discussion of the economics of empire, see Kenneth Andrews, *Trade, Plunder and Settlement: Maritime Enterprise and the Genesis of the British Empire, 1480–1630* (Cambridge, 1984).
328. Gómara, in Purchas, *Hakluytus,* XV, 437, 505–18.
329. Purchas, II, 45, see 33, 43, 58. Purchas calls his analysis "Animadversions on the Bull."
330. Purchas, II, 46–7.
331. Ibid., II, 47.
332. Ibid., II, 57.
333. Purchas, *Hakluytus,* II, 58. On Vitoria, see Pagden, *Fall* and Dickason, *Myth,* 130–1.
334. Purchas, *Hakluytus,* II, 59.
335. Ibid., XVIII, 80.
336. Ibid.
337. Ibid., XVIII, 81–2.
338. Ibid.
339. Ibid., XVIII, 82.
340. Ibid, XVIII, 82, 177, 180.
341. Ibid., XVIII, 176; see 181 for the list of Purchas's description below.
342. For Smith and Purchas as advocates of trifles in the trade with Native Americans, see Knapp, *Empire,* 2–3.
343. [Thomas Scott], *Vox Popvli or Newes from Spayne, translated according to the Spanish coppie. Which may serve to forewarn both England and the United Provinces how farre to trust to Spanish pretences* ([London?] 1620), B 4 recto.
344. [Thomas Scott], *The Second Part of Vox Popvli, or Gondomar Appearing in the Likenes of Matchiauell in a A Spanish Parliament, Wherein Are Discouered His Treacherous & Subtile Practises to the Ruine as Well of England as the Netherlandes. Faithfully Translated out of the Spanish Coppie by a Well-willer to England and Holland* ([London], 1624).
345. Ibid., 59–60. See Scott's *Sir VValter Ravvleigh's Ghost, Or Englands Forewarner. Discouering a Secret Consultation, Newly Holden in the Court of Spaine, together, With His Tormenting of Count de Gondomar, and His Strange Affrightment, Confession and Publique Recantation: Laying Open Many Treacheries Intended for the Subuersion of* England (Vtrecht, 1626). For Spanish ambition, see ibid., 30; ibid., 38–41.
346. See [Thomas Scott], *The Spaniards Perpetvall Designes to an Vniversall Monarchie. Translated According to the French* ([London], 1624, ** verso; ** 2 verso- ** 3 recto.

347. Ibid., 2.
348. Ibid., 100.
349. Ibid., see also 25–6.
350. Ibid., 30, 38–41.
351. See Williams, *The Actions in the Low Countries,* ed. D. W. Davies (Ithaca, 1964), 112–13; first published in London in 1618.
352. For the numbers of soldiers, which I have converted into percentages, see L. van der Essen, "Croisade contre les hérétique ou guerre contre des rebelles: La psychologie des soldats et des officiers espagnols de l'armée de Flandres au XVIe siècle," *Revue d'histoire ecclesiastique* 51 (1956), 43, cited in Maltby, *Black Legend,* 50; see Maltby, 51. On the turning point, see Pieter Geyl, *The Revolt of the Netherlands, 1555–1609* (London, 1958), 127–43.
353. See Gascoigne, *The Spoyle of Antwerpe* . . . (London, 1576), A iii verso- A iiii recto.
354. Ibid., B vii verso.
355. Ibid., C vii verso. I am using the Bodleian copy. See also Gasgoigne, *A Larum for London or the Siedge of Antwerpe* . . . (London 1602). See Maltby, *Black Legend,* 51–3.
356. "Edict of the States General of the United Netherlands . . . , 26 July 1581," *Texts Concerning the Revolt of the Netherlands,* ed. E. H. Kossman and A. F. Mellink (Cambridge, 1974), 221
357. Martin van Gelderen, *The Political Thought of the Dutch Revolt 1555–1590* (Cambridge, 1992), 3, 270–1.
358. "Edict of the States General," 220, see 216–28. K. W. Swart, *William the Silent and the Revolt in the Netherlands* (London, 1978), 34–6.
359. K. W. Swart, *William the Silent and the Revolt in the Netherlands* (London, 1978), 34–6.
360. See Hugh Dunthorne, "The Dutch Revolt in English Political Culture 1585–1660," *From Revolt to Riches: Culture and History of the Low Countries 1500–1700,* ed. Theo Hermans and Reiner Salverda (London, 1993), 235–47.
361. See Jonathan I. Israel, *The Dutch Republic and the Hispanic World 1606–1661* (Oxford, 1982), xiv, 1–3, 374, 437–41.
362. *Le Miroir De la Tyrannie Espagnole Perpetree aux Indies Occidentales. On verra icy la cruaute plus que inhumaine, commisse par les Espagnols, aussi la description de ces terres, peuples, et leur nature. Mise en lumiere par un Evesque Bartholome de las Casas, de l'Order de S. Dominic. Nouvellement refaicte, avec les Figurs en cuyvre* (Amsterdam, 1620). I have consulted the various original editions. The publishers' name appears in various forms to the one I have given in the text. Two such forms are Jan Evertsoon Cloppenburg and Jan Evertz Cloppenburg.
363. *Le Miroir De la Cruelle, & horrible Tyrannie Espagnole perpetree au Pays Bas, par le Tyran Duc de Albe, & aultres Commandeurs de par le Roy Philipe le deuxiesme.*
364. The "To the Reader, Greetings" is two unnumbered sheets or four pages. I am summarizing its contents and am translating it here. The phrase I have noted in French, partly as a matter of style, is on the second page of the address to the reader, or the first sheet verso.
365. "Av Lecteur," second unnumbered page verso and the third recto; my translation here and below.
366. Ibid., third page recto.
367. Ibid., third page verso.
368. The title is *Tyrannies et Crvuatez des Espagnols Commises es Indes Occidentales, Qu'on dit le Nouueau Monde* . . . (Rouen, 1630). For a discussion of French translations of Las Casas, see André Saint-Lu, *Las Casas Indigeniste: études sur la vie et l'œuvre du défenseur des Indiens* (Paris, 1982), 159–70.
369. "Preface Av Lectevr," *Tyrannies et Crvuatez des Espagnols Commises es Indes Occidentales, Qu'on dit le Nouueau Monde* . . . (Rouen 1642), ã 2 recto.
370. "Preface," ã 2 verso.
371. "Preface," ã 3 recto.
372. "Preface," ã 3 recto–ã 3 verso.
373. "Preface," ã 4 recto, see ã 4 verso.
374. "Preface," ã 4 verso. The familiar "tu" is used here, perhaps to create a more intimate bond between writer and reader as Frenchmen united against the Spanish threat.
375. Gabriel Sagard, "Av Lecteur," *Histoire dv Canada et voyages qve les freres mineurs Recollets y ont faicts pour la conuersion des Infidelles* . . . (Paris, 1636).
376. Ibid, 16–19.

377. Ibid, 627.
378. Ibid, 787.
379. Gabriel Sagard, *Le Grand Voyage du Pays des Hurons,* ed. Réal Ouellet and Jack Warwick (Montréal, 1990), quoted and translated in Luca Codignola, "The Holy See and the Conversion of the Indians in French and British North America, 1486–1760" in America in European Consciousness, 1493–1750, ed. Karen Ordahl Kupperman (Chapel Hill, 1993), 215. On Sagard's view of the Natives, see Dickason, *Myth,* 78–9.
380. On the torture of the Jesuits, Jean de Brébeuf, and Gabriel Lalemant, and the acts of anthropaphagy by the Iroquois in that instance, see Lestringant, *Le Cannibale,* 218–23.
381. See ibid., 208–11 and Claude d'Abbeville, *Histoire de la mission des Peres Capucins en l'Isle de Maragnan et terres circonvoysines* (Paris, 1614), 294–6 and Yves d'Evreux, *Suitte de l'Histoire des choses memorables advenues en Maragnan es annees 1613 et 1614* (Paris, 1615). D'Evreux was d'Abbeville's successor. More generally, see Charles Arpine, *Histoire generale de l'origine mineurs de S. François* . . . (Paris, 1631), which looked at the Recollets from 1486 to 1606, and Philippe de Bethune, comte de Selles et de Charost, *Le Conseiller d'estat* . . . (Paris?, 1632), which in chapter 15, examined the Christianization of peoples of Brazil, Mexico, and Peru.
382. Paul Le Jeune, "Le Jeune's Relation, 1637" (Rouen, 1638) in *The Jesuit Relations and Allied Documents,* ed Reuben Gold Thwaites (73 vols., Cleveland, 1898), XII, 221.
383. Andrew White, "A Relation of the Colony of the Lord Baron of Baltimore, in Maryland, Near Virginia; A Narrative of the Voyage to Maryland by Father Andrew White; and Sundry Reports, from Fathers Andrew White, John Altham, John Brock, and Other Jesuit Fathers of the Colony, to the Superior General at Rome," from the manuscript in the archives of the Jesuits' College in Rome, trans. N. C. Brooks in *Tracts,* ed Force IV, 15, see 11.
384. See ibid., 3.
385. Ibid., 27.
386. Ibid., 28.
387. Ibid., 44.
388. Boucher, *Les Nouvelles,* 27.

Chapter 6

1. One example of many may be found in Anon., *A Perfect Description of Virginia* . . . (London, 1649) in *Tracts and Other Papers, Origin, Settlement, and Progress of the Colonies in North America, from the Discovery of the Country to the Year 1776,* collected by Peter Force (4 vols., Washington, 1836–46), II. Each tract is numbered separately from one onward, so that the volumes do not have continuous pagination. *A Perfect Description* says "the *Hollanders* have stolen into a River called *Hudsons* river in the limits also of *Virginia*" and "Thus are the English nosed in all places, and out-traded by the *Dutch*"; ibid., II, 9. This view of Holland as a new example for England to emulate and envy occurred early in the seventeenth century. See, for instance, Anon., *A Trve Declaration of the Estate of the Colonie in Virginia, with a Confutation of Such Scandalous Reports as haue Tended to Disgrace of So Worthy an Enterprise* (London, 1610), in *Tracts,* ed. Force, III, 25: "What created the rich and free states of Holland, but their winged Nauy?"
2. For contemporary accounts of the Glorious Revolution in New England, see Nathaniel Byfield, *An Account of the Late Revolution in New-England* . . . (London 1689); Anon., *A Brief Relation of the State of New England from the Beginning of the Plantation to the Present Year, 1689* . . . (London, 1689); and Edward Rawson and Samuel Sewell, *The Revolution in New-England Justified* ... (Boston, 1691), in *Tracts,* Force, IV, 1–13, 1–17, and 1–59 respectively. The major conflicts in this period were the War of the League of Augsburg (1689–97) and the War of the Spanish Succession (1702–13), which were known in English America as King William's War and Queen Anne's War.
3. See Philip P. Boucher, *Les Nouvelles Frances: France in America, 1500–1815: An Imperial Perspective* (Providence, 1989), 62–3.
4. See Anon., *Virginia and Maryland, Or, the Lord Baltamore's Printed Case, Uncased and Answered. Shewing the Illegality of his Patent and Usurpation of Royal Jurisdiction and Dominion There* . . . (London, 1655) in *Tract,* ed. Force, II, 30–1.
5. William Strachey, *For the Colony in Virginea Britannia. Lavves Diuine, Morall and Martiall, & c.* (London, 1612), 67. The prayer occupied over five pages of small print, 63–8.

6. Ibid., 68.

7. For a discussion of the changes in New England, including King Philip's war, the Glorious Revolution, the Quebec expedition, and other related topics, see Stephen Carl Arch, "Mastering History: Puritan Historians in Colonial America" (unpublished Ph.D. dissertation, University of
Virginia, 1989), 171, 181–9, 261–71, 306, 321, 353. I am indebted to Arch in this paragraph. On
identity in New England, see Sacvan Bercovitch, *The Puritan Origins of the American Self* (New
Haven, 1975). Concerning conversion, see Patricia Caldwell, *The Puritan Conversion Narrative*
(Cambridge, 1983). See also David S. Lovejoy, *The Glorious Revolution in America* (New York,
1972).

8. Increase Mather, *A Relation of the Troubles which have hapned in New-England, By Reason of the
Indians there* (Boston, 1677), 75, quoted in Arch, "Mastering History," 229–30. On Increase
Mather, see Michael G. Hall, *The Last American Puritan: The Life of Increase Mather 1639–1723*
(Middletown CT, 1988). For the role of merchants, see Bernard Bailyn, *The New England Mer-
chants in the Seventeenth Century* (Cambridge MA, 1955).

9. David Brading thinks that the debate between Sepúlveda and Las Casas was unparalleled in European imperial history, but David Armitage points to John Milton, James Harrington, Andrew
Fletcher, and David Hume as evidence of an intellectual movement—the "civic tradition"—
opposed to European imperialism; see David Brading, *The First America: The Spanish Monarchy,
Creole Patriots, and the Liberal State 1492–1867* (Cambridge, 1991), 1, and David R. Armitage,
"The British Empire and the Civic Tradition 1656–1742" (unpublished Ph.D. dissertation, Cambridge University 1992), 3–4. Armitage's point is well taken. Nonetheless, whatever one might
decide on this question, regardless of considerations of Quattrocento Italian civic humanism, the
classical republicanism of mid-seventeenth-century England or the Whiggism after the Glorious
Revolution, or of a tradition derived from Aristotle's *polis* or Cicero's *civis* as an opposition to
the Spanish feudalism or universal monarchy, it is undeniable that the Spanish came first and that
the French and British had to react against them as well as imitate them; see ibid., 5–6. The Spanish, as Armitage admits, could also use the language of the classical republics; ibid., 15. Armitage
has some interesting comments on Machiavelli's assessment of the defeat of Venice in 1509 and
its loss of an empire aimed at the Roman model of universal monarchy; see ibid., 7. The British
were most responsible in the Americas for passing the civic tradition from metropolis to colonies;
ibid. 16.

10. For a useful study, including translation and background such as Cromwell's "Western Design,"
especially in Hakluyt, Purchas, Gage, Stevens, and others, see Colin Steele, *English Interpreters of
the Iberian New World From Purchas to Stevens: A Bibliographical Study, 1603–1726* (Oxford,
1975); and for a helpful annotated bibliography, including a good account of the versions of Las
Casas, see A. F. Allison, *English Translations from the Spanish and Portuguese to the Year 1700: An
Annotated Catalogue of the Extant Printed Versions (excluding Dramatic Adaptations)* (London, 1974).

11. Thomas Gage, *The English-American his Travail by Sea and Land: Or a New Survey of the West
Indias . . .* (London, 1648), A 3 verso, see A 3 recto.

12. Ibid., 2.

13. Ibid., A 3 verso.

14. Ibid., A 4 recto.

15. Ibid.

16. Ibid.

17. Ibid., A 4 recto–A 4 verso.

18. Ibid., A 4 verso.

19. Chaloner, "To the Reader" in ibid., A 5 recto.

20. Ibid. On Oviedo in relation to Las Casas and Léry, see Anthony Pagden, *European Encounters with
the New World: From Renaissance to Romanticism* (New Haven, 1993), 56–68. See also Jonathan
Hart, "Strategies of Promotion: Some Prefatory Matter of Oviedo, Thevet and Hakluyt," *Imagining Culture: Essays in Early Modern History and Literature,* ed. J. Hart (New York, 1996), 73–8.

21. Chaloner, "To the Reader" in Gage, *The English-American,* A 5 recto.

22. José de Acosta, quoted in Anthony Grafton with April Shelford and Nancy Siraisi, *New Worlds,
Ancient Texts: The Power of Tradition and the Shock of Discovery* (Cambridge, MA, 1992), 1.

23. Chaloner, "To the Reader" in Gage, *The English-American,* A 5 verso.

24. Ibid., A5 verso.

25. Ibid., A 6 recto.

26. Ibid.
27. For background, see Armitage, "The British Empire," 24–53, his first chapter entitled, "Liberty and Empire: The Whig History of the New World."
28. Chaloner, "To the Reader" in Gage, *The English-American,* A 6 verso.
29. Gage, *The English-American,* 4.
30. Ibid., 7, see 6.
31. See ibid., 9.
32. Ibid.
33. Ibid., 10–11.
34. Gage, 199. See Karen Ordahl Kupperman, *Providence Island, 1630–41: The Other Puritan Colony* (Cambridge, 1993).
35. Gage, *The English-American,* 204.
36. Ibid., 209, see 205–8.
37. Ibid., 209.
38. Ibid., 212.
39. Ibid.
40. See Thomas Gage, *Nouvelle Relation des Indes Occidentales, contenant les voyages de Thomas Gage . . .* (Paris 1676), ã iij recto; my translation here and below; see ã iij verso.
41. Philip Boucher, *Les Nouvelles,* 54.
42. See ibid., 31.
43. See Thomas Gage, *Nouvelle Relation des Indes Occidentales, contenant les voyages de Thomas Gage . . .* (Amsterdam, 1720); my translation here and below.
44. Ibid., ã iij recto.
45. Ibid., ãviij recto.
46. Edward Williams, "To the Supreme Authority of this Nation, the Parliament of England," *Virginia: More Especially the South Part . . .* (London, 1650) in *Tracts,* ed. Force, III, 3.
47. Ibid., 4. On the relation between Ireland and America, see Nicholas Canny, *Kingdom and Colony: Ireland in the Atlantic World 1560–1800* (Baltimore, 1988), ch. 1. In an interesting study, Thomas J. Scanlan argues that the English colonial experience in both Ireland and America determined the identity of English Protestants, that Hakluyt's descriptions of the atrocities the Spaniards committed in the New World influenced English colonists to convert Native populations and not to exterminate them, that the example of the English devastation of Ireland was also a negative example to New England, expressed in the much misunderstood work by Edmund Spenser, *A View of the Present State of Ireland* (a critique of being a Protestant colonist rather than the received view that it is a reactionary work); see Thomas J. Scanlan, "Conversion, Suppression, or Limited Partnership: Problems in the Protestant Colonial Ethic" (unpublished Ph.D. dissertation, Duke University, 1992), ch. 2. Scanlan's reading of Spenser is presented as a corrective, and in so far as it does that, it is useful, but it probably goes too far in "redeeming" Spenser.
48. For a discussion of Hakluyt and his English context as well as "England's belated entry into the race with Spain, Portugal, and France for the conquest and settlement in the New World," see Armitage, "The British Empire," 34, see 33–42. Some of the originary myths of who got to America first persisted well into the eighteenth century (and perhaps beyond). As late as 1739, anti-Spanish propaganda was still using Madoc, whom I discussed earlier, as a means of claiming British priority in the New World. See Anon., *The British Sailor's Discovery* (London, 1739), 12–14, 17; reprinted in *Old England for Ever, Or, Spanish Cruelty Display'd* (London, 1740), 26–9, 35, cited in Armitage, "The British Empire," 40.
49. Williams, *Virginia,* 7. He also praises "*the most incomparable* Ralegh" who preferred south Virginia to north Virginia or New England.
50. Ibid., 9.
51. Ibid., 42.
52. Ibid., 43. For a study that focuses throughout on this notion of "trifles" and "trifling," see Jeffrey Knapp, *An Empire Nowhere* (Berkeley, 1992).
53. Williams, *Virginia,* 43.
54. Ibid., 44.
55. Ibid., 45. Hartlib hoped to promote the silkworm in Virginia, as if to bring Chinese products to the New World, so that England could be more self-sufficient.
56. Ibid., 45.

57. Ibid.
58. Ibid., 57.
59. See John Hammond, *Leah and Rachel, or, the Two Fruitfull Sisters Virginia, and Mary-land . . . VVith a Removall of such Imputations as are Scandously Cast on those Countries* . . . . (London, 1656) in *Tracts,* ed. Force, III, 10.
60. See Samuel Hartlib, *The Reformed Virginian Silk-Worm* . . . (London, 1655) in ibid., III, 14.
61. On Virginia's problems, temporal and spiritual (and of its neighbor Maryland), see Anon., *Virginia and Maryland.—Or, the Lord Baltamore's Prited Case, Uncased and Answered.—Shewing, the Illegality of his Patent* . . . (London, 1655); Hammond, *Leah and Rachel,* (London, 1656); R. G., *Virginia's Cure: or an Advisive Narrative concerning Virginia. Discovering the True Ground of the Churches Unhappiness, and the only true Remedy* . . . (London, 1662); "A List of Those That Have Been Executed for the Late Rebellion in Virginia, by Sir William Berkeley, Governor of the Colony . . . " in *Tracts,* ed. Force, II, 1–48; III, 1–32 and 1–20; I, 1–4.
62. Armitage, "The British Empire," 61–2; see Karen Ordahl Kupperman, "Errand to the Indies: Puritan Colonization from Providence Island through the Western Design," *William and Mary Quarterly* 44 (1988), 70–99.
63. Roger Williams to John Winthrop February 15, 1654/5 in *The Correspondence of Roger Williams,* ed. Glenn W. LaFantasie (2 vols., Providence, 1988), II, 248, quoted in Armitage, "The British Empire," 63. In Gage's terms the true Rome was attacking the Romish Babylon. Apparently, Cromwell found it hard to assimilate the defeat of the English in a providential framework just as Philip II had with the defeat of the Armada. Roger Williams reported this retrospectively; see Williams to John Leverett, October 11, 1675 in *The Correspondence of Roger Williams,* quoted in ibid., 66–7.
64. For a fine discussion of Harrington that argues that *Oceana* was not a utopia and was "a blueprint, not a fantasy," see Armitage, "The British Empire," 17, 80–91 .
65. Bartolomé de Las Casas, *The Tears of the* INDIANS: *BEING An Historical and True Account of the Cruel Massacres and Slaughters of above Twenty Millions of innocent People; Committed by the Spaniards in the Islands of* Hispaniola, Cuba, Jamaica, *& c. As also, in the Continent of* Mexic, Peru, *and Other Places of the West-Indies, to the Total Destruction of those Countries. Written in Spanish by* Casaus, *and Eye-witess of those Things; and Made English by J. P.* (London, 1656), A 3 recto-A 3 verso. Some of the pages of the prefatory matter are numbered and some are not, and their numbers are extrapolated from the numbered pages. Another translation came out after the Glorious Revolution: POPERY *Truly Display'd in Bloody Colours: Or, a Faithful* NARRATIVE *of the Horrid and Unexampled Massacres, Butcheries, and all manner of Cruelties, that Hell and Malice could invent, committed by the Popish* Spanish *Party on the Inhabitants of* West-India . . . (London, 1689).
66. Las Casas, *The Tears,* A 3 verso-A 4 verso.
67. Ibid., A 4 verso-A 6 recto.
68. Ibid., a recto-a verso.
69. Ibid., a 2 recto. On England in Ireland and America, see Nicholas Canny, "The Ideology of English Colonization: From Ireland to America," *William and Mary Quarterly* 30 (1973), 575–98 and his *Kingdom,* ch. 1.
70. Las Casas, *The Tears,* a 2 recto-a 2 verso.
71. Ibid., a 2 verso-b 2 recto. In "To all true English-men," English "Enormities" in Ireland were, by implication, represented as the avenging sword of justice.
72. Ibid., b 2 verso-b 3 recto.
73. Ibid., b 3 recto-b 3 verso.
74. Ibid., b 3 verso-b 4 recto. I have approximated the typography to illustrate another strategy of revilement.
75. Ibid., b 4 recto-c 1 recto.
76. Ibid., c 1 recto-c 2 recto.
77. Ibid., c 2 recto.
78. Ibid., b 2 recto-b 2 verso.
79. Ibid., b 2 verso-b 3 verso.
80. See Anonymous, "Preface" in Bartolomé de Las Casas, *An Account of the First Voyages and Discoveries Made by the Spaniards in America* (London, 1699), no pagination.
81. See André Saint-Lu, *Las Casas Indigeniste: études sur la vie et l'œuvre du défenseur des Indiens* (Paris, 1982), 168–9. Allison speculates that the reason for this English version of Las Casas (1699) might "have had some connection with the Spanish opposition to the Darien Expedition of

1698–1700"; Allison, *English Translations,* 42. On the 1699 English version and general information on the French and English translations of Las Casas, see Steele, *English Interpreters,* 107–8, 175–6.

82. This anonymous Preface to the 1699 edition of Las Casas, Thomas Scanlan observes, echoes of John Locke's *Two Treatises of government,* published the year before; see Scanlan, "Conversion," 14–17. More generally, Scanlan's reading of the English appropriation of Las Casas examines an important topic but seems to take at face value that the Protestants learned from Las Casas's exposé without qualifying that understanding enough with their uses of Las Casas in propaganda and polemics in self-serving national expansion and religious partisanship.

83. Ibid., 13. Scanlan's reading is suggestive. His claim, "The English could only safely reprint Las Casas' text if they felt certain that their own colonial project bore absolutely no resemblance to that of the Spanish," illustrates my point; ibid., 4. Scanlan emphasizes one part only when he observes that "eventually the Spanish became for the English emblematic figures against whom they could define their own colonial enterprise as uniquely English and Protestant"; ibid. 5. Moreover, Scanlan neglects the vast secondary literature on Las Casas and on the Black Legend; see ibid., ch. 1.

84. Ibid., 40.

85. Boucher, *Les Nouvelles,* 28. On Le Jeune, see Peter A. Goddard, "Christianization and Civilization in Seventeenth-Century French Colonial Thought" (unpublished D. Phil. dissertation, Oxford University, 1990), 57–119; Rémi Ferland, "Procédés de rhétorique et fonction conative dans les Relations du Père Paul LeJeune" (unpublished Ph.D. dissertation, Université Laval, 1991); Yvon Le Bras, *L'Amérindien dans les* Relations *du Père Paul Le Jeune* and Pierre Dostie, *Le Lecteur suborné dans cinq textes missionaires de la Nouvelle-France,* 2 vols. in 1 vol. (Sainte-Foy, 1994); Dostie begins at 159. Ferland, who is interested in rhetoric and discourse analysis, examines Le Jeune's work in terms of one of Roman Jakobson's six inalienable factors of communication— "la fonction 'conative'"—or the orientation toward addressee to modify his comportment or opinion, the purest form of which occurs in the imperative or vocative; ibid., 4. Le Bras and Dostie both explore the Amerindian as other in Le Jeune and various French missionaries like Gabriel Sagard and Louis Hennepin. Neither of these authors touches on the example of Spain or any other topics concerning Spain.

86. Léon Pouliot, *Étude sur les* Relations *des jésuites de la Nouvelle-France (1632–72)* (Montréal, 1940), 3, cited in Le Bras, *L'Amérindien,* 15; see Ferland, "Procédés," 6.

87. Francisco Bressani, *Breve Relatione d'alcvne missioni de' PP. della Compagnia di Giesù nella Nuova Francia* (Macerata, 1653) in *The Jesuit Relations and Allied Documents,* ed. Reuban Gold Thwaites (73 vols., Cleveland, 1896–1901), XXXVIII, 227–8. Bressani was also a mapmaker; see Olive Dickason, *The Myth of the Savage and the Beginnings of the French Colonialism in the Americas* (Edmonton, 1984), 110.

88. Goddard, "Christianization," i–v, 25–56. Goddard, whose terms I am using here, doubts the view that the French Jesuits were the connection between José de Acosta at the turn of the seventeenth century and Joseph-François Lafitau in the 1720s because he does not see these missionaries from France as embodying comparative ethnology and ethical relativism; ibid., iii. For a discussion of Lafitau, see Anthony Pagden, *The Fall of Natural Man* (1982; Cambridge, 1986), a section he adds to the revised edition. For a recent discussion of the relation between Jesuits and Natives, see Maxime Haubert, *La vie quotidienne au Paraguay sous les Jésuites* (Paris, 1967); Alain Beaulieu, *Convertir les Fils de Caïn—Jésuites et Amérindiens en Nouvelle-France, 1632–1642* (Québec, 1990). For relations between the French and the Amerindians, see, for instance, Cornelius J. Jaenen, *Friend and Foe: Aspects of French-Amerindian Cultural Contact in the Sixteenth and Seventeenth Centuries* (New York, 1976); Dickason, *The Myth;* John W. Grant, *Moon of Wintertime: Missionaries and the Indians of Canada in Encounter since 1534* (Toronto, 1984); Denys Delâge, *Le pays renversé. Amérindiens et Européens en Amérique du nord-est 1600–1664* (Montréal, 1985); Bruce Trigger, *Natives and New comers. Canada's "Heroic Age" Reconsidered* (Montréal, 1985). See, for instance, the work of the Dominican and so-called "Herodotus of the Indies," Jean Baptiste Du Tertre, *Histoire générale des isles de S. Christophe . . .* (Paris, 1654), 396–8. On Du Tertre, see Boucher, *Les Nouvelles,* 29, and Dickason, *The Myth,* 82. Another account of glory can be found in Hébert de Rocomont, *La Gloire de Louis le Grand dans les missions étrangères* (Paris, 1688). Jean Baptiste Labat, a Dominican like Du Tertre, wrote *Nouveau voyage aux Isles de l'Amérique . . .* (Paris, 1724), which was a natural history but also represented conflicts with the English.

89. Goddard, "Christianization," viii, 183–212.
90. Jean Baptiste Du Tertre, *Histoire générale des isles de S. Christophe* . . . 396–8.
91. Ibid., ã ij verso.
92. Ibid., ã ij verso.
93. Ibid., 24.
94. Dominique Deslandres, "Le modèle français d'intégration socio-religieuse, 1660–1650. Missions intérieurs et premières missions Canadiennes" (unpublished Ph.D. dissertation, Université de Montréal, 1990), 247, 255–6.
95. On settlement of the Caribbean by Norman and Breton nobles, see Philip Boucher, *Les Nouvelles,* 37. The French population of Canada later referred to Wolfe's victory over Montcalm at Québec in 1759, which ultimately led to France ceding Canada to Britain, as "La Conquête" or the Conquest. The British population in Canada was often later puzzled by this term, and perhaps this misunderstanding indicates something of the difficulties of the political relations between the two groups.
96. See Alexandre Exquemelin's [Oexmelin] *Histoire des avanturiers* (3 vols., Paris, 1686).
97. Ibid., ã ij verso- ã iij recto; my translations here and below.
98. Ibid., ã iij recto.
99. Ibid., n.p. [page 2 verso of the Preface].
100. ibid., ê iiij recto.
101. Philip Boucher, *Les Nouvelles,* 49–51.
102. *Loix et constitutions des colonies françoises,* ed. Médéric Louis Elie Moreau de Saint-Méry (Paris, 1784–90), (March 1685), 415, reproduced in ibid., 51; my translation.
103. Boucher, 53.
104. Blaise François de Pagan, Comte de Merveilles, *Relation historique et géographique* (Paris, 1655); see also Philip Boucher, *Les Nouvelles,* 37.
105. Blaise François de Pagan, *An Historical & Geographical Description of the Great Country & River of the Amazones in America* . . . , trans. William Hamilton (London, 1661), A 3 recto.
106. Ibid., A 3 verso.
107. Ibid.
108. Ibid., A 3 verso-A 4 verso.
109. Pierre François-Xavier Charlevoix, *Histoire et description générale de la Nouvelle-France avec le journal historique d'un voyage fait par ordre du Roi dans L'Amérique Septentrionale* (3 vols., Paris, 1744), I, 2, quoted in Boucher, 86.
110. Charlevoix, I, iii–iv. On Charlevoix, see Bruce Trigger, "The Historian's Indian: Native-Americans in Canadian Historical Writing from Charlevoix to the Present," *Canadian Historical Review* 67 (1986), 315–42.
111. Ibid., 16–24.
112. Louis Hennepin, *Description de la Louisiane, nouvellement decouverte au Sud'Oüest de la Nouvelle France, par ordre du roy. Auec la carte du pays: les mœurs & la maniere de vivre des sauvages. Dedie'e a sa Majeste* . . . (Paris, 1683); my translation here and below. Besides mentioning that Hennepin was a Recollet missionary, the title page listed him as a "Notaire Apostolique." I am using the 1688 edition at Houghton Library, which is a reprint, page for page, of the edition of 1683. Philip Boucher calls much of Hennepin's work "unreliable because he did not accompany La Salle to the mouth of the Mississippi"; Boucher, *Les Nouvelles,* 59, 64–6.
113. Hennepin, "Epistre," ã ii verso, see ã ii recto.
114. Hennepin, ã ii verso- ã ii j recto.
115. See Philip Boucher, *Les Nouvelles,* 59.
116. On Hennepin, in a study that concentrates on the representations made to the reader and on the way the Native is represented, see Dostie, *Le Lecteur,* 183–94, 213, 219. Dostie discusses Sagard, Le Jeune, and other French missionaries in New France; ibid., 161–70.
117. Hennepin, ã iij recto- ã iij verso.
118. Patricia Seed discusses this ceremony at some length; see Patricia Seed, *Ceremonies of Possession in Europe's Conquest of the New World, 1492–1640* (Cambridge, 1995), 56–63.
119. Hennepin, ã ii j verso-ã iv recto.
120. Ibid., ã iv recto.
121. Ibid., ã iv recto-ã iv verso.
122. Ibid., ã iv verso-ã v recto.
123. Hennepin, ã v recto-ã v verso.

124. See Peter Burke, *The Fabrication of Louis XIV* (New Haven, 1992), 102–4, 132. For a discussion of religion in Louis XIV's imperial policies, see Natasha Jovita Ali, "Concept of Empire: The Role of Religion and Orthodoxy in French Imperial Thought during the Late Reign of Louis XIV" (unpublished M.A. thesis, Queen's University, Canada, 1994). Ali argues that Louis's ideas of religion and religious orthodoxy influenced New France and the French West Indies and were not simply cover-ups for economic expansion and political glory.

125. Antonio de Solís's *Histoire de la conquête du Mexique,* translated by S. de Broë (Paris, 1691), ê recto and ê verso.

126. Ibid., ê verso-ê ij recto.

127. Ibid., ê ij recto.

128. Ibid., ê ij recto.

129. Ibid., î recto.

130. Bartolomé de Las Casas, *Relations des Voyages et des Decouvertes que les Espagnols on fait dans les Indes Occidentales . . . ,* (Amsterdam, 1698), no pagination.

131. Ibid., ★ 3 recto-★3 verso.

132. Ibid., 4 pages unnumbered.

133. Pierre Boucher, "Epistre," *Histoire veritable et natvrelle des moevrs et prodvctions dv pays de la Novvelle France, vvlgairement dite le Canada* (Paris, 1664), ãii recto and verso; my translation.

134. Pierre Boucher, "Epistre," ibid., ãii verso; see ãii recto.

135. Boucher, "Avant-Propos," unnumbered [9–10].

136. Ibid., 5.

137. Ibid.

138. Ibid., 144. The page is misnumbered as 344 in the copy at Houghton Library, Harvard.

139. Louis-Armand de Lom d'Arce, le Baron de Lahontan, "Epistre," *Nouveaux Voyages de M͏ͬ Le Baron de Lahontan, dans l'Amerique Septentrionale . . .* 2 vols. (La Haye, 1703), vol. 1, ★ 2 recto—★ 3 verso. I am assuming that Lahontan wrote the Preface but have no definitive proof that this is the case. I refer to the author of the Preface in the impersonal form rather than referring to him as Lahontan. For Lahontan's writing as well as knowledge of Amerindian languages and culture, see Barbara Elisabeth Knauff, "Multilingualism in French Late Seventeenth- and Eighteenth-Century Imaginary Voyages" (unpublished Ph.D. dissertation, Yale University, 1995), 116–201.

140. See Lestringant, *Le Cannibal,* 280

141. Lahontan, "Preface," ★ 4 recto-★ 4 verso.

142. In David Armitage's allegorical reading, in which he takes the content of what the narrator and the characters say as reflections of Milton's personal views, Milton is a poet against empire; see Armitage "The British," ch. 3.

143. See John Milton, *Paradise Lost* (London, 1667), IX, 1115–18 for a reference to Columbus.

144. On the importance and dangers of reading it allegorically, see Jonathan Hart, "Redeeming *The Tempest:* Romance and Politics," *Cahiers Élisabéthains* 49 (1996), 23–38.

145. Sir Robert Howard, *Four New Plays . . .* (London, 1665), 175, see 170–4.

146. John Dryden, "The Epistle Dedicatory," *The Indian Emperour, or, the Conquest of Mexico by the Spaniards* (London, 1667), A 3 recto, see A 3 verso.

147. John Dryden, *Conquest of Granada by the Spaniards : In Two Parts* (London, 1672), ★ 2 recto.

148. Ibid, [★ 3 recto].

149. Ibid., [★3 verso].

150. John Dryden, "The Preface," *Don Sebastian, King of Portugal: A Tragedy Acted at the Theatre Royal* (London, 1690), a verso.

151. John Dennis, *Britannia Triumphans: or the Empire Sav'd and Europe Deliver'd. By the Success of her Majesty's Forces under the Wise and Heroick Conduct of his Grace the Duke of Marlborough* (London, 1704), 14.

152. Ibid., 17.

153. Ibid., 18.

154. Ibid., 19.

155. Ibid.

156. Melchisédech Thévenot, "Avis, Sur le dessein, & sur l'ordre de ce Recueil," *Relation de divers voyages cvrievx, qvi n'ont point este' pvbliees; ou qui ont este' tradvites d'Haclvyt; de Purchas, & d'autres voyageurs Anglois, Hollandois, Portugais, Allemands, Espagnols; et qvelqves Persans, Arabes, et avtres avteurs Orientaux . . .* (Paris, 1663) I, ã ij verso; my translation here and below; see ã ij recto-ã

iij recto. This edition appears in two parts or volumes bound as one. I have used I and II to indicate the parts that correspond to volumes in the 1664–66 edition.

157. Ibid, I, ã ij recto. I am using both the 1663 edition at the John Carter Brown Library and the 1664–66 edition of this rare book (2 vols., Paris, 1664–66), at Houghton Library. Volume 1 is dated 1664 and volume 2, 1666.

158. For some background to the New World in French and English historiography, see Myron P. Gilmore, "The New World in the French and English Historians of the Sixteenth-Century" in *First Images of America,* ed. Fredi Chiapelli, ed. (2 vols., Berkeley, 1976), II, 519–27 and Amy Glassner Gordon, "Confronting Cultures: The Effect of the Discoveries on Sixteenth-Century French Thought," *Terrae Incognitae* 8 (1976), 45–56.

159. Thévenot, I, ã ij recto.

160. Ibid. "Establissemens" can also mean trading posts as well as establishments.

161. Thévenot, "Avis," *Relation de divers voyages,* I, ã ij verso.

162. Ibid.

163. Ibid. I have retained Thévenot's spelling of proper names here.

164. The phrase reads "ie les imiteray dans ce Receuil." Thévenot, "Avis," I, ã iij recto.

165. Thévenot, "Advis svr l'order des pieces de la seconde partie," II, O ij recto.

166. R. B., *The English Empire in America: Or a Prospect of His Majesties Dominions in the* West-Indies . . . (London 1685), A2. I am actually using the edition of 1698 as I was informed at the British Library that the rare edition of 1685 was missing, perhaps for a very long time.

167. Ibid., A2 recto-1.

168. Ibid., 3.

169. Ibid.

170. Ibid., 4.

171. Ibid., 5–6.

172. Ibid., 6.

173. Ibid., 6–7.

174. Ibid., 9, see 7–8.

175. Ibid., 10, see 8–9.

176. Ibid., 14, see 15–16.

177. Ibid.,

178. Ibid., 19, see 18.

179. Ibid.

180. Ibid., 20–1.

181. Ibid., 21.

182. Ibid.

183. Ibid., 21–2.

184. See Patricia Seed, *Ceremonies of Possession* (Cambridge, 1995), 72f.

185. R. B., *English Empire,* 23.

186. Ibid.

187. Ibid., 25–6.

188. Ibid., 26.

189. Ibid.

190. Ibid.

191. Ibid., 26–7.

192. Ibid., 27.

193. Ibid., 27–8.

194. John Harris, *Navigantium atque Itinerantium Bibliotheca: or, a Compleat Collection of Voyages and Travels: Consisting of above Four Hundred of the most Authentick Writers; Beginning with Hackluit, Purchass, & c. in English; Ramusio in Italian; Thevenot, &c in French; De Bry, and Grynæi Novus Orbis in Latin; the Dutch East-India Company in Dutch: And Continued, with Others of Note, that have Publish'd Histories, Voyages, Travels, or Discoveries, in the English, Latin, French, Italian, Spanish, Portuguese, German, or Dutch Tongues* . . . (London, 1705).

195. Harris devoted several chapters in the second volume to Thévenot's travels in the Middle East; see ibid., Book II, chapters, ix–xi.

196. Harris, "The Epistle Dedicatory," ibid., 1; neither the "Epistle" nor the Address "To the Reader" is paginated; each is two pages. There will therefore be no additional notes to page

numbers in these two brief prefatory pieces. Unlike Gage, Harris was presenting a collection and obviously did not see the need for criticism.

197. Ibid.
198. Ibid.
199. On the Whig history of the New World, see Armitage, "The British," 24–54.
200. Harris," Introduction," *Navigantium,* lxii-lxiii. The bull, which I discuss below, appears on pages 6 to 8.
201. Harris, *Navigantium,* 8.
202. John Oldmixon, *The British Empire in America* . . . (London 1708), xxxv.
203. Ibid., xxxv-xxxvii.
204. John Oldmixon, *The British Empire in America* . . . (London 1714), xxv-xxvi.
205. Ibid., xxx ii.
206. John Stevens, "Preface" to Bartholomew Leonardo de Argensola, *The Discovery and Conquest of the Molucco and Philippine Islands* . . . , (London, 1708) in John Stevens, *A New Collection of Voyages and Travels, Into several Parts of the World, none of them euer before Printed in English* . . . (2 vols., London, 1711), I, recto. The Preface was one page, recto and verso, and was not numbered. This book appeared with a dedication to the Honourable Edmund Poley of Badley in the County of Suffolk, Esq., an indication in part that the patrons of these collections were still influential but not necessarily as powerful as the Elizabethan patrons. The dedication was an understated praise that questions the flattery of this genre while using the unexpressed and the implied because the patron or dedicatee was so well known. Stevens was anxious to keep his all his prefatory matter brief.
207. Stevens, "Preface" to Argensola, "Molucco," ibid., verso.
208. Ibid.
209. Ibid.
210. Ibid., 113–14.
211. Ibid., 114.
212. Ibid., 232.
213. John Lawson, "Preface," *A New Account of Carolina* (London, 1709) in Stevens, *A New Collection,* I, A4 recto.
214. Ibid.
215. Ibid., I, A4 recto and verso.
216. Ibid., I, A4 verso here and below.
217. Lawson, "Introduction" in Stevens, *A New Collection,* I, 1.
218. Ibid., I, 2.
219. Ibid., 3 .
220. Ibid., 3–4.
221. Ibid., 4 .
222. Ibid.
223. Ibid.
224. Ibid., 5, see 54. Stevens, "Dedication," ibid., 1, unnumbered. The phrase here quoted is from the third unnumbered page of the dedication, which followed Lawson's account.
225. *The Seventeen Years Travels of Peter de Cieza through the Mighty Kingdom of Peru* . . . (London, 1709) in Stevens, *A New Collection,* 2 vols. (London, 1711), I.
226. Ibid. Stevens, first page of the unnumbered "Preface," which follows the "Dedication" I just discussed.
227. Ibid., the verso of the one-page preface here and below.
228. De Cieza in Stevens, *A New Collection,* I, 2, see 1.
229. Ibid., I, 2, see 3 for the discussion below.
230. Stevens, "Preface," *A New Collection* II, A2 recto. The discussion below is of this brief preface, which consists of two pages, A2 recto and verso.

INDEX